We Men Who Feel Most German

We Men Who Feel Most German

A Cultural Study of the Pan-German League, 1886–1914

Roger Chickering

Boston
GEORGE ALLEN & UNWIN
London   Sydney

George Allen & Unwin (Publishers) Ltd,
40 Museum Street, London WC1A 1LU, UK

George Allen & Unwin (Publishers) Ltd,
Park Lane, Hemel Hempstead, Herts HP2 4TE, UK

Allen & Unwin, Inc.,
9 Winchester Terrace, Winchester, Mass. 01890, USA

George Allen & Unwin Australia Pty Ltd,
8 Napier Street, North Sydney, NSW 2060, Australia

First published in 1984

British Library Cataloguing in Publication Data

Chickering, Roger
 We men who feel most German: a cultural study of the Pan-German League, 1886–1914.
1. Pan-German League – History
I. Title
3 20.5'4'0943   DD119
ISBN 0-04-943030-0

Library of Congress Cataloging in Publication Data applied for

Set in 10 on 11 point Times by Herts Typesetting Services Ltd, Hertford
and printed in Great Britain by Mackays of Chatham

Contents

Preface   *page* ix

List of Abbreviations   xiii

1   The Pan-German League as a Historical Problem   1

'True Germans who show the world the real Prussian soul'   2
'Representatives of the most reactionary wing of the ruling class'   9
'The Empire's modern opinion-managers'   12
Plan of the Study   15

2   Patriotic Societies in Bismarckian Germany   23

The Incubation of Patriotic Societies in Imperial Germany   24
Patriotic Societies of the First Generation   29

3   The Formation and Early Development of the Pan-German League, 1886–1902   44

The General German League, 1886–93   44
The Pan–German League: Consolidation, Expansion, and Competition, 1894–9   53
The Development of a National Opposition, 1899–1902   62

4   Ideology   74

The Program   75
Outposts amidst the Flood   81
Order, Culture, and Authority   86
Bismarck and Hamlet   93

5   Social Foundations of Ideology   102

The Pan-German League: a Social Profile   102
Custodians of Culture and Authority   108

6   Ideology and Psychology   122

A World of Enemies   122
Toward a Social Psychology of Radical Nationalism   125

7   A Favorable Climate   *page* 133

The Pan-German League in the East and South   138
Regional Strongholds   142
Gaudeamus igitur   145

8   Social Experience in a 'German-National Public
    Realm'   152

Spontaneity and Structure in the Local Chapters   152
Sociability and Patriotism   161
Private Virtue and the German-National Public Realm   167
The Public Obligations of Patriotism   172

9   The Scope of the German-National Public Realm   183

The Pan-German League and Other Patriotic Societies   185
Patriotic Societies and Other Voluntary Associations   198
The German-National Public Realm and the Structure of
Party Politics   202

10 In the Wilderness   213

The Growing Rift with the Government   213
The Financial Consequences of Opposition: the Business of
Patriotism   223
The Ideological Consequences of Opposition: the Embrace
of Racist Antisemitism   230

11 The Fronde   253

Prelude: the Crisis in the German Navy League   253
Morocco   261
The German Defense League   266
Consolidation of the Right   267
Va banque   282

Conclusion   299

Statistical Appendix   306

Bibliography   331

Index   357

Preface

My interest in patriotic societies in Imperial Germany grew out of work I did several years ago on the German peace movement during the same epoch. I found then that the peace movement in Imperial Germany consisted of a small group of well-meaning men and women, who hoped for patriotic reasons – because they were convinced that their country would benefit – to eliminate war by means of an effective international organization. I also concluded that these German pacifists found virtually no support for their ideas in their own country. My confidence in concluding that the influence of the German pacifists was so minimal was reinforced by a lot of evidence that most of their contemporaries viewed them as harmless eccentrics.

I was fascinated, however, by evidence that some Germans regarded the peace movement in an entirely different light, as part of an international conspiracy whose goal was to undermine Germany's ability to defend itself. One document I found summed up well the tone and thrust of this indictment:

> Since the German Defense League began its activity two years ago, the peace movement in Germany has devoted itself with special zeal to spreading ideas dangerous to national security, in an attempt to emasculate the spirit of the German people. The clear recognition that the peace movement, were it fully to succeed, would bring about the internal degeneration of the German people has prompted the German Defense League dutifully to take up with all its resources the struggle against this movement, which proceeds in many instances under the cover of deceptive guises.

Because their assessment of the peace movement differed so radically from my own, I became curious about these men and about the patriotic societies, such as the German Defense League, in which they seemed to congregate. I spent the year 1976–7 in East and West Germany collecting materials on about a dozen patriotic organizations, in the expectation that I would write a book about their history in the Imperial era – the sources of their dynamism and appeal, and their impact on German society and politics. Upon my return from Europe, I looked more closely at the mountain of documents, newsletters, and journals which I had brought back. It then impressed me that the project I was planning would occupy most of the rest of my professional life. This was a commitment I was not willing to make, so I began to consider ways to make the project more manageable. I had long been interested in the Pan-German League, which was the most active and radical of all the major patriotic societies (and the most alarmed critic of the peace movement). I calculated that writing the history of this organization would necessarily involve me more than peripherally (although now with a more specific focus) in the history of other patriotic organizations in Imperial Germany, so that I would not have to abandon completely my original ideas about the scope of the study. The fact that numerous studies of the Pan-German League already existed did not deter me, for I hoped to answer new questions about the organization.

The discrepancy between the Pan-Germans' perception of the peace movement and that of most of their contemporaries (and my own) suggested the possibility of using psychological theories to study the League. I accordingly immersed myself in the literature, where I discovered models that conformed exactly to the conspiratorial thinking and exaggerated apprehensions which governed the Pan-Germans' view of the peace movement and the rest of the world. Most of these models were psychoanalytical, however. They offered me little or no help in explaining the roots of this kind of thinking, for the evidence I possessed about the Pan-Germans simply would not permit generalizations about the intra-psychic etiology of paranoid modes of thought.

I then read more broadly into social psychology and cultural anthropology. I began to ponder the symbolic dimensions of what the Pan-Germans were saying and doing. I discovered symbolic patterns in their activities and the recurrence of several suggestive images and metaphors in their language. Using this symbolism as a guide, I began to think about what activity in the Pan-German League might have signified to the men who joined the organization. Approaching the League from this direction finally suggested some basic social concerns that might have made radical nationalism appealing to these men.

It is a truism, but it bears repeating, that studies like this do not appear without a great deal of help. This one would never have appeared without a grant from the Fulbright Commission, which made possible my odyssey through German archives and libraries in 1976–7. The study would be appearing years hence but for the generous financial assistance of the John Simon Guggenheim Memorial Foundation, which relieved me of my teaching obligations in 1980–1. I must thank the staffs of the archives and libraries in which I worked, especially the Hoover Institution, whose financial support enabled me to work there during the summer of 1980. My gratitude extends much further. Gordon Craig, Gerald Feldman, Karl Holl, Paul Kennedy, Ray Birn, Robert Donia, Klaus Mattheier, Gerhard Weidenfeller, Dieter Düding, Wilhelm Deist, Geoff Eley, and Wolfram Fischer gave various forms of help and support. Hartmut Kaelble and Konrad Jarausch offered valued advice on the construction of my social-status scales. My colleagues and friends Tom Brady, Bob Berdahl, Stan Pierson, and Vernon Lidtke not only read the entire manuscript but shared with me their wisdom as I groped for a way to understand the world of the Pan-German League. My debt to Mary DeShazer is of a somewhat different order; it is none the less profound.

Listing the agencies and people to whom I owe such gratitude is a reminder of the extent to which preparing the book was a rewarding experience. During its gestation the book also bore witness to a great deal of grief among people whom I hold dear. The book is dedicated to those whose grief has pained me the most.

Eugene, Oregon
September 1982

For my boys

Prejudices, it is well known, are most difficult to eradicate from the heart whose soil has never been loosened or fertilized by education.

Charlotte Brontë, *Jane Eyre*

... gerade die Männer, die am deutschesten denken und fühlen, denen die Frau am heiligsten ist ...

Heinrich Class (1912)

List of Abbreviations

AA	*Auswärtiges Amt*
Abt.	*Abteilung*
ADB	*Alldeutsche Blätter*
ADV	*Alldeutscher Verband.* When this abbreviation follows ZStAP and precedes a number, it refers to a file in the *Bestand Alldeutscher Verband* in the *Zentrales Staatsarchiv* in Potsdam.
AHR	*American Historical Review*
ASG	*Archiv für Sozialgeschichte*
BA	*Bundesarchiv*, Coblenz
BAMA	*Bundesarchiv-Militärarchiv*, Freiburg i. B.
BBA	*Bergbauarchiv*, Bochum
CEH	*Central European History*
DB	*Deutschbund*
DFV	*Deutscher Flottenverein*
DHV	*Deutschnationaler Handlungsgehilfen-Verband*
DKG	*Deutsche Kolonialgesellschaft.* When this abbreviation follows ZStAP and precedes a number, it refers to a file in the *Bestand Deutsche Kolonialgesellschaft* in the *Zentrales Staatsarchiv* in Potsdam.
DKZ	*Deutsche Kolonialzeitung*
DOV	*Deutscher Ostmarkenverein*
DS	*Denkschrift*
GFA	*Sitzung des Geschäftsführenden Ausschusses des Alldeutschen Verbandes*
GG	*Geschichte und Gesellschaft*
GStA	*Geheimes Staatsarchiv*
GV	*Gobineau-Vereinigung*
HA/GHH	*Historisches Archiv der Gute-Hoffnungs-Hütte*, Oberhausen
HB	*Handbuch*
HZ	*Historische Zeitschrift*
JCH	*Journal of Contemporary History*
JMH	*Journal of Modern History*
KRgS	*Korrespondenz des Reichsverbandes gegen die Sozialdemokratie*
KRRW	Reichsarchiv, *Kriegsrüstung und Kriegswirtschaft*, 2 vols (Berlin, 1930)
LA	*Landesarchiv*
LR	*Landrat*
LRA	*Landratsamt*
MADV	*Mitteilungen des Allgemeinen Deutschen Verbandes*
MGM	*Militärgeschichtliche Mitteilungen*

MInn   *Ministerium des Innern*
NDB   *Neue deutsche Biographie*
NL   *Nachlass*
NPL   *Neue Politische Literatur*
Obpr.   *Oberpräsident; Oberpräsidium*
Ogr.   *Ortsgruppe*
OM   *Die Ostmark*
PAAA   *Politisches Archiv des Auswärtigen Amtes*, Bonn
RgS   *Reichsverband gegen die Sozialdemokratie*
RK   *Reichskanzlei*
RM   *Reichsmarineamt*
RS   *Rundschreiben*
StA   *Staatsarchiv*
StBR   *Stenographische Berichte über die Verhandlungen des Reichstages*
StdA   *Stadtarchiv*
StMin   *Staatsministerium*
UB   *Universitätsbibliothek*
VDA   *Allgemeiner Deutscher Schulverein (Verein für das Deutschtum im Auslande)*
VZG   *Vierteljahrshefte für Zeitgeschichte*
ZASV   *Zeitschrift des Allgemeinen Deutschen Sprachvereins*
ZfG   *Zeitschrift für Geschichtswissenschaft*
ZSg 1   *Zeitgeschichtliche Sammlung*
ZStAM   *Zentrales Staatsarchiv*, Merseburg
ZStAP   *Zentrales Staatsarchiv*, Potsdam

Note: Dates in the footnotes are listed according to the European convention of day–month–year. Thus 8.6.02 is 8 June 1902.

We Men Who Feel Most German

1 The Pan-German League as a Historical Problem

No country's modern history lies more in the shadow of catastrophe than Germany's. The need to understand the forces and circumstances that created and sustained the Third Reich has had a pervasive, sometimes overbearing influence on German historiography since 1945. This influence has been particularly marked in recent years in scholarship on the German Empire, whence troubling lines of continuity appear to run to the Third Reich. Perhaps most disturbingly, historians have documented the attempt of the Empire's ruling elites to defuse domestic social and political conflict by resorting to an aggressive and reckless foreign policy, consciously accepting the risk of a European war. Although this research has brought impressive results, some scholars have expressed concern lest the preoccupation with the origins of National Socialism implied in the search for continuity produce a distorted or unbalanced picture of the Empire. As Hans-Günther Zmarzlik has argued, Imperial Germany boasted institutions and achievements that were positive and progressive by any standard, and not all lines of continuity out of the Empire led ineluctably into the Third Reich.[1] Zmarzlik's point is doubtless well taken, but no amount of emphasis on the positive achievements in the Empire's history is likely to dislodge certain other features of this history from the prominent place they have occupied in discussions of the origins of National Socialism.

The most troubling case in point is the Pan-German League. Demands which this organization proclaimed years before Hitler surfaced in German politics were a chilling anticipation of the programs which the National Socialists attempted to put into practice. Pan-Germans called for the consolidation of Germans throughout the world; for Germans who resided in continental Europe, leaders of the League proposed to construct a giant central-European state, which would include large swaths of territory cut out of western Russia and eastern France (and emptied of their native inhabitants), in order to provide raw materials, commercial outlets, strategic security, and living space for a burgeoning German population. That this venture would require general war was self-evident. The Pan-German League was, in addition, at the forefront in promoting racist antisemitism in Imperial Germany. Leading Pan-Germans publicly advocated not only the exclusion of Jews from public life in Germany, but the suppression of socialists, ethnic minorities, and assorted other groups of people whom the League identified as enemies of the race.

The Pan-German League was the object of heated controversy long before the National Socialists appropriated its demands into their own program. The extravagance of these demands, as well as the energy with which the Pan-Germans pursued them, guaranteed the League a prominent place in the politics of Imperial Germany before the war. The League's critics, at home and in other countries, warned of its power and charged that it enjoyed the financial backing of German heavy industry, that it had ready access to the men who ruled in Berlin, and that it used its influence to help prepare a war of aggression. Germany's rulers, on the other hand, found the Pan-German League a source of growing concern once the organization began, in the name of patriotism and the national interest, to mobilize a broadly based opposition to the government's own policies.

The prominence of the Pan-German League in the politics of Imperial Germany, charges that the organization secretly inspired German foreign policy in the years before the war, and the resemblance of the League's demands to programs that led to the horrors of the Nazi era have all made this organization one of the most intensively studied phenomena in modern German history. At least a dozen monographs and dissertations have been devoted to it, and countless other studies have dealt extensively with its activities. Paradoxically, though, the Pan-German League remains in crucial respects an enigma. Fundamental questions remain open about its dynamism and the appeal of its radical nationalism in Imperial Germany. One of the difficulties has been the League's very notoriety. Its controversial role in the origins of the war and its association with National Socialism have riveted the attention of historians rather narrowly to questions of the League's ideology, program, and its influence in the shaping of official policy. Understanding the broader sources of the League's appeal – and its influence – will require going beyond the questions that have traditionally occupied the many authors who have participated in the historiographical controversy over the Pan-German League. First, however, this controversy, which is itself of no little historical interest, deserves a brief survey.

'True Germans who show the world the real Prussian soul'

The controversy originated in the realm of propaganda soon after the organization was formally founded in 1891. The League's program was no secret, and foreign journalists quickly sounded the alarm. The series of colonial disputes between Germany and the Western powers, which began over South Africa and flared up several times over Morocco, provided occasions for close scrutiny of the organization which the London *Times* called the *'enfant terrible* of German chauvinism'.[2] French journalists went further, charging that the Pan-German League was working with the full connivance and support of the German government, that it controlled the major political parties, and that its program accurately reflected German public opinion.[3] Nor were foreign journalists alone in their concern over the apparent power and influence of the League; statesmen, particularly those in Great Britain, shared it.[4]

Regardless of whether the German government did in fact have ties to the Pan-German League, officials in Berlin were embarrassed by the League's propaganda and the publicity it was receiving in other countries.[5] They responded, either personally or in inspired articles in the press, with assurances that the League was not to be taken seriously, that it consisted of a handful of fanatics who exercised no appreciable influence either on public opinion or in the corridors of power.[6] By now the basic issue that was to dominate the historiography of the Pan-German League had been defined: was the League an insignificant collection of what Theodor Mommsen dismissed in 1902 as 'national fools', or did its ideas find wide popular support and ultimately inspire official policy?[7]

With the outbreak of war in 1914 debate over this issue quickly escalated. Propagandists in the entente countries attempted, with considerable success, to portray the Pan-German League as the evil spirit behind the government's war aims, the symbol and quintessential expression of Prussian militarism and an endemic lust for power.[8] The German government was again genuinely embarrassed by these charges, but once it took the wraps off the war-aims debate in 1916, neither it nor those who advocated a moderate peace could do much effectively to counteract enemy allegations that the Pan-Germans were the people who mattered in Germany.[9]

The victory of the entente powers in the fall of 1918 temporarily resolved the question of the significance of the Pan-German League. The judgments that had informed Western war propaganda were now codified into international law in the Treaty of Versailles. The debate continued, however, after the war in the context of the heated controversy over war guilt. The fact that the Pan-German League continued to play an active role in the politics of the Weimar Republic only added to the controversy.

None the less, as historians and memoirists joined the debate in the 1920s, the League was, as Ludwig Dehio has observed, 'sent into the wilderness', and writers concluded that its role and importance in prewar Germany had been grotesquely exaggerated.[10] In 1924 the first study of the Pan-German League appeared from the pen of an academic historian. Significantly, its author was an American, and the study itself was a symptom of the rethinking taking place in this country about the origins of the European war and the wisdom of American participation in it. Mildred Wertheimer's dissertation was but one product of Carlton Hayes's pathbreaking seminar at Columbia on the influence of nationalism in recent European history.[11] It was also a very important piece of scholarship; in some respects it is still the best history of the League. Particularly valuable were her careful descriptions of the League's structure and social composition. Given the political atmosphere in which she wrote and the limited sources available to her, however, Wertheimer's conclusions were predictable. Her attempts to gain access to the League's records were unsuccessful, so her research rested exclusively on the League's published material, practically all of which she located, and on interviews with prominent Germans, among them Paul Rohrbach and Hans Delbrück, whose deprecatory views about the League were already well known.[12]

Wertheimer's conclusions squared entirely with contentions originally made by the Imperial German government itself. The Pan-German League was, she argued, 'an insignificant bunch of fanatics' (p. 186), a 'small, relatively unimportant but very noisy' organization (p. 154). She could find no evidence of any large-scale financial support from industrial or any other sources, and allegations of vital connections between the League and the German government she found 'entirely preposterous' (p. 159). The League was, she contended, more an embarrassment than an aid to the government, for it stirred up unfounded suspicions of German intentions all over the world.

One finds in Wertheimer's study the undertones of the theme to which Carlton Hayes's seminar was devoted, the proposition that the disease of intolerant nationalism had caused the European war, but that the disease had been a general European phenomenon. The Pan-German League, Wertheimer noted, had counterparts in all European countries and deserved no more blame than the others for poisoning the international atmosphere. Indeed, she discovered the Pan-Germans to be anything but the devils depicted in the propaganda of war. They were for the most part ordinary folks who could be found almost anywhere, 'jovial middle-class Germans' (p. 112), who, though naive in their politics, inspired some genuine sympathy: they were motivated by 'real sincerity' and their activities were imbued with a 'certain "family" spirit' (p. 83). Having portrayed the League in terms an American audience could appreciate, Wertheimer concluded with a plea for international understanding. 'The Pan-German League is an excellent example of the type of nationalist association which has done much to develop the spirit of intolerant nationalism in the world today. It is this spirit which makes infinitely more dangerous the "international anarchy" of our day' (p. 218).

Wertheimer's dissertation was an important document in the general reassessment of the war-guilt problem which was taking place in the 1920s on both sides of the Atlantic. Her study made it possible to minimize the significance of the most radical voice of prewar German nationalism, and her influence was evident in the work of other 'revisionist' historians. Sidney Fay, who had been one of the readers of her dissertation, spoke of Pan-Germanism in one breath with *révanchisme* and Pan-Slavism as general underlying causes of the war.[13] Harry Elmer Barnes was more blunt. Citing Wertheimer, he noted that the Pan-German League had 'less influence over the German government than our American societies [That is, the National Security League and the American Defense Society] had over the foreign policy of Woodrow Wilson from 1913–1916'.[14]

The historiography of the Pan-German League had another strain in the aftermath of the First World War. The seminal document of what might be called this 'German-national' historiography appeared in 1920 with the publication of the League's official history of its prewar activity.[15] Its author was Otto Bonhard, the editor of the League's journal, who had access to the League's records as well as to its leading personalities. Although his sources were more intimate than Wertheimer's, his conclusions about the significance of the League in prewar Germany were in many respects the same. In Bonhard's view, too, the League's role had been enormously exaggerated in hostile propaganda. Its membership very restricted, the

League had had to contend with the persistent opposition of those in power and with the 'mistrust of broad and respected circles of people' (p. 32). From this observation, however, Bonhard proceeded in a different direction than Wertheimer. Instead of using the admitted weakness of the League to moderate the guilt of the German government for what had happened in 1914, he used this weakness to underscore the German government's guilt for what had happened in 1918. Wertheimer attributed the League's weakness to the eccentric fanaticism of its members; this conclusion Bonhard rejected, arguing that the League had been correct in its perception of the foreign and domestic perils which had threatened the German Empire, and that the failure of the League to exert more influence was due to the ignorance and ill will of leading German statesmen, to the comfortable indifference of the populace, and, most ominously, to the machinations of treacherous elements close to the seat of power. To the League, then, had fallen the thankless role of independently pursuing the dictates of conscience and insight, despite the ridicule and hatred this role brought.

Bonhard's book was less interesting for what it revealed about the League's past than for what it announced about the organization's aspirations for the future. The war had been bitter-sweet vindication for its programs, and the League was calling in accounts, laying claim to leadership in the national opposition now forming against the Weimer Republic. A dramatic increase in the League's membership at the war's end seemed to give credence to Bonhard's belief that out of the organization would emerge 'the future educators' of the German people: 'So opens up the prospect that a stock of leaders will increasingly take form, a strong fundament [*tragfähige Schicht*] of honest men, who may self-confidently and energetically show the German people the ways to rise anew' (p. 231).

Mildred Wertheimer used the history of the Pan-German League to draw the lesson that, in the modern world, war was unnecessary, the product of misunderstandings fostered by small groups of fanatics. German-national writers, following Otto Bonhard, drew from the history of the League a different lesson. The League's demands, vindicated by recent history, represented in their view the only valid program for a 'national government' which was destined to succeed the republic.[16] This contention became more pointed as a mass-based national opposition to the republic began to take shape in the late 1920s. In 1930 another Pan-German writer, Franz Sontag, published a biographical survey of the leaders of this national opposition. He gave pride of place to Heinrich Class, the League's chairman, emphasizing that aside from the younger generation of leaders, anyone of importance in the national opposition had been connected in one way or another with the League. 'So whether many people wish to admit it or not', Sontag insisted, 'the Pan-German League has become, with respect both to the ideas and the personalities involved, the nursery and advanced school of our entire national life.'[17]

Implicit in Sontag's survey was more than a little concern about this 'younger generation' of nationalists, especially those associated with Hitler, with whom the Pan-German League's relationship had grown increasingly cool. This concern ran like a red thread through Heinrich Class's memoirs, which appeared late in 1932, when the victory of the national opposition seemed imminent.[18] These memoirs are an essential source for the history of the League, a revealing and in some respects remarkably candid account of Class's activities before the war. Without abandoning the image invoked in Bonhard's account, of the lonely and disregarded prophet of the prewar period, Class revealed that the League had by no means been as insignificant as Wertheimer's dissertation had contended. He disclosed the extensive nature of contacts between the League and the German Foreign Office on the eve of the Agadir crisis in 1911. He also revealed the instrumental role of the League in mobilizing broad popular sentiment in favor of the two huge army bills of 1912 and 1913. Class's principal concern in his memoirs, however, was to refute charges that the Pan-German League was out of date in the 1930s, that its claim to national leadership had been superseded by those of the more radical forces in the National Socialist Party. Accordingly, Class's account of the inner workings of the League emphasized his own role as leader of a younger generation of radical nationalists, who took power from an older, more moderate group of men in 1908, when Class became chairman. Determined to force the government into more aggressive policies by means of uncompromising opposition, these men could, according to Class, also take credit for propagating scientific theories of racism and an awareness of the full dimensions of the 'Jewish problem'. Standing on the threshold of power, but in a large crowd in which he no longer enjoyed much respect, Class commemorated the history of the 'creators and original pioneers of this [national] political movement'. He confessed, not without some pathos, that because 'I belong among these pioneers, I should be permitted to establish my contribution to the emergence and growth of this movement' (foreword).

As in many other areas, the year 1933 marked a *caesura* in the German-national historiography of the Pan-German League. If earlier writers had emphasized the League's insignificance in the prewar era in order to stake its claims to a significant role in the 'new' Germany, historians of the Third Reich used the League's insignificance before the war to justify its continued insignificance after the Nazi seizure of power. The Pan-German League was tolerated as an independent organization until 1939 (a rare honor in Hitler's Germany), but the Gestapo did keep an eye on its activities. In truth, the League had become a museum piece once Hitler took power, and the historiography of the Third Reich clearly reflected the organization's new status, as well as the image Hitler's regime wished to present of itself.[19]

The most extended and competent statement of the new orthodoxy was the dissertation of Lothar Werner, which was published in 1935.[20] Based on no new sources, it provided little fresh information about the League's activities, but it did cast these activities in a new light. Werner admitted at the outset that the purpose of his study was 'to emphasize clearly the gulf between "Pan-Germanism" and National Socialism' (p. 7). National Socialism, he insisted, represented a fundamentally different phenomenon, the product of the war and the struggles of the postwar period. Werner then shuffled themes from the earlier historiography of the League. Drawing from Bonhard and Class, he paid tribute to the League's pioneering mission before the war, although he carefully downplayed the importance of Class's contacts with the government. Paradoxically, Werner also joined Wertheimer in criticizing the League for its lack of tact and restraint, which, he observed, provoked suspicions of German intentions abroad and made life difficult for Germany's statesmen.

Werner followed Wertheimer's description of the League's membership, too, both in its composition and limited size. But here the two authors parted ways, for times had changed. Wertheimer had pointed to the eccentricity of the League to explain its limited appeal; Werner discovered in the League's composition not only the cause of its limited appeal, but also the principal characteristic that distinguished the Pan-Germans from the National Socialists. The League consisted of 'a small group of people extremely well educated in politics and history, who came socially almost exclusively from the bourgeois [*bürgerlichen*] *Mittelstand*' (p. 282). In this social exclusivity lay the key to the League's impotence in the prewar Germany. Unlike the National Socialists, claimed Werner, the League overlooked the need to appeal to the masses by 'attempting with all means to find a just solution for growing social tensions, instead of passing over them "inattentively"' (ibid.).

Werner's view of the League, which on the whole accorded better with Wertheimer's than with Bonhard's, served the regime's pose as the great conciliator of social tension and the effective advocate of Germany's national interests. This view appeared in other dissertations written during the Third Reich. These examined several aspects of the League's activities, including its position on colonial policy and its role in the naval agitation.[21] Like Werner, their authors praised the League's honorable intentions and ideals, but emphasized the organization's minimal impact, which they attributed to its narrow fanaticism and tactlessness.

If the Pan-German League's role in preparing the way for Hitler received but grudging recognition from historians of the Third Reich, this role appeared in an altogether different light after 1945. Now the attempt of German historians to 'come to terms with their past' (in the exercise known in German as *Vergangenheitsbewältigung*) meant confronting the problem of how far the origins of National Socialism ran back into that past. The programmatic similarities between the Pan-German League and the National Socialists were very disquieting, for they suggested that prior to 1914 the intentions of the German government and the tenor of German public opinion might have been much less innocent than the interwar historiography had concluded. So, in the aftermath of the Second World War, the need became acute to reassess the significance of the League.

That the picture did not initially change much was due to the reluctance of West German historians to admit that the roots of National Socialism extended deep into the Imperial period. These historians also found serviceable elements in the existing historiography of the League with which they could reconstruct a past that was acceptable, at least until 1914. Alfred Kruck's dissertation, which appeared in 1954, revealed how the project could be accomplished.[22] His study contained large amounts of new information, for he was the first scholar to carry the history of the League beyond 1918.[23] He was also able to interview Heinrich Class, by now a very old and bitter man, and to use a lengthy memorandum that Class had prepared about his activities after the outbreak of war in 1914. On the Imperial period, though, Kruck had little new to offer beyond a revised interpretation of the League's significance. In this revision one can still discern the influence of earlier historians, particularly of Mildred Wertheimer. In Kruck's view, the Pan-German League was a group of misguided fanatics, whose most serious failing was their misunderstanding and perversion of the legacy of Bismarck. Bismarck, Kruck argued, had understood the limits that Germany's precarious international position imposed upon both the substance and methods of the country's foreign policy; the Pan-German League abandoned all caution and sense of proportion, obstructed the peaceful expansion of German power and influence, and encouraged belligerence in Paris and St Petersburg. This view of the League was, like Wertheimer's, the one originally advocated by the Imperial German government. As a moral, Kruck endorsed the charges made by the German chancellor in 1915, that the League 'unfortunately coupled its national will with such a lack of political insight that even in the period before the war it frequently made the business of politics more difficult' (p. 75).

The activities of this group of fanatics appeared far less innocuous in 1954 than they had in 1924, and Kruck departed significantly from Wertheimer in his appraisal of the League's influence. He concluded that the League's demands found broad resonance in German public opinion. This conclusion of course carried the uncomfortable implication, which foreign propagandists had drawn before and during the First World War, that the Pan-German League expressed the true aggressive inclinations of most Germans. To resist this charge, Kruck resorted to a device frequently employed by German historians after 1945: he demonized the League and portrayed it as a small group of extraordinarily skilled propagandists, who led large segments of the German people astray of the Bismarckian tradition.

By arguing that the League had, in this manner, 'gravely wronged the German people' (pp. 218–19), Kruck was able to deal with the organization just as other West German historians were dealing with the phenomenon of National Socialism. He depicted it as an alien force which imposed a disastrous program on the well-intentioned but unsuspecting masses of Germans. This *apologia*, which many scholars outside West Germany regarded with a skepticism well expressed in the term *Bundesgeschichte*, no doubt served important civic functions in the Federal Republic. It informed, in any event, a great deal of the literature on the Pan-German League which appeared in the first two decades after the Second World War.[24] The political conditions that made this view of the League cordial to West German historians gradually receded, however; and in the 1960s the image of the organization was recast again in a historiographical upheaval which attempted to rectify not only the failings of *Bundesgeschichte*, but those of another earlier historiographical tradition as well.

'Representatives of the most reactionary wing of the ruling class'

All the studies surveyed to this point defined the problem of the Pan-German League's significance in terms of its influence on foreign policy and public opinion, or in the case of those written after 1933, in terms of elements of continuity between the League and National Socialism. This definition of the problem confined these studies to political and – particularly in connection with the question of continuity – intellectual history.[25] The question of *cui bono*, of the economic interests the Pan-German League might have served, was raised initially by Social Democrats and Communists, whose political motives seemed to discredit their arguments. Mildred Wertheimer's research further discouraged the attempt to locate the ultimate significance of the League's activity in the realm of material interest, for she could find no evidence to support allegations that heavy industry had bankrolled the organization. Class's memoirs reinforced this conclusion. He admitted that the coal baron Emil Kirdorf had occasionally made modest contributions to the League; but Class insisted that the many small contributions of members had financed most of the League's activities.

The first major breakthrough to a new level of analysis came in the late 1920s, in the work of Eckart Kehr. In his research into imperialist agitation in Germany at the turn of the century, Kehr revealed his debt to Marxist historiography. He accepted Wertheimer's judgment about the lack of financial ties between the League and heavy industry, but went on to show that this was not the whole story. In a now classic study of the popular crusade to build the German battle fleet, Kehr documented the manner in which heavy industry underwrote naval agitation for its own transparent interests.[26] This conclusion cast the Pan-German League's activity in a different light. Regardless of how little industrial money flowed into the organization's coffers, the League did stand undeniably at the ideological forefront of the naval agitation; it provided Tirpitz and his supporters with ideas that were propagated to serve industrial interests and to reinforce domestic political stability and the social *status quo*. Kehr accordingly characterized the Pan-German League as a 'political and ideological Holding-company, which delivered "intellectual" [*geistige*] weapons to the other agitational societies like the Colonial Society, the Navy League, and later the Defense League'.[27] Kehr's findings indicated the danger of studying the Pan-German League in isolation. They suggested that the influence and significance of this organization could only be determined indirectly, by analyzing first its ties to other patriotic societies and then the impact on German society and politics of the agitation of all these organizations.

Kehr was unable to follow these leads before his untimely death in 1933, but his work has been very influential, not the least in undermining the view held by Western revisionists and German-nationalists alike that the League had been of minimal importance before the war. In his study of European imperialism, which first appeared in 1935 and was dedicated to Kehr, George Hallgarten appropriated Kehr's view of the League's significance.

The organization was the most unrestrained expression of what Hallgarten called the 'spirit and will for power' which underlay German imperialism. Ultimately, and in ways many Pan-Germans themselves never realized, these ideas served the interests of German industry, so Hallgarten described the League as the 'vanguard [*Vortruppe*] of industry'.[28] The influence of Kehr was also perceptible in the dissertation of Pauline Anderson, which appeared on the eve of the second war on the theme of anti-English sentiment in Imperial Germany.[29] Emphasizing the importance of the naval agitation and the importance of the Pan-German League in this agitation, Anderson brought American historiography on the League full circle, as she repudiated Wertheimer's thesis that the organization's impact had been insignificant.

Kehr's influence remained dormant in the West for the next quarter century, while the line of analysis that identified material interest as the ultimate criterion of a political organization's significance was enshrined as orthodoxy in the German Democratic Republic. The study that represented the corner-stone of Marxist–Leninist historiography on the Pan-German League appeared just as the GDR was being founded. Its author was the renowned historian of the German working class, Jürgen Kuczynski.[30] It was a remarkable book, no less an attempt at *Vergangenheitsbewältigung* than Kruck's. Although Kuczynski was a historical materialist, his was an intensely moralistic book. Its format was a survey of the major patriotic societies in Imperial Germany, which Kuczynski insisted were all tied to industrial interests and prepared the way ideologically for Hitler. The tone of the book was one of outrage and scarcely controlled disgust. The subjects of his work he described as 'chauvinistic, uncultured [*kulturlose*], reactionary organizations, nauseous in their immoral demagoguery and the self-assuredness [*Sicherheit*] of their propaganda' (p. 6); their program he characterized as 'the arrogant policy of domination, the barbarous presumption of uncultivated so-called supermen hungry for power' (p. 92). If this rhetoric were not enough to betray the fact that Kuczynski was trying to deal with a moral problem, his line of analysis certainly was. This line was similar to Kruck's. Kuczynski too resorted to the demonization of the patriotic societies, especially the Pan-German League, which he labeled the 'most important and influential of all' (p. 9), the 'cover organization' which coordinated the activities of the others. Like Kruck, Kuczynski insisted that these organizations were in no sense indicative of any 'general aggressive spirit that resides in the German people' (p. 6); they were instead small groups of supremely clever and powerful agents, a 'propaganda clique or oligarchy' (p. 312), which controlled government policy and deluded the German masses into supporting monstrous plans for an aggressive war.

Here Kuczynski and Kruck parted company, for Kuczynski had more to say about the forces in whose service the Pan-German League and other patriotic societies labored. These were the forces of monopoly capitalism, principally the coal, iron, and steel industries of the Rhineland and Westphalia. On the strength of what Kehr and Class had revealed about the relationship between heavy industry and the patriotic societies, Kuczynski concluded that these societies were 'propaganda tools of monopoly capitalism itself' (p. 6).

Kuczynski's study displayed a tendency in Marxist–Leninist historiography that has limited insights that the materialist perspective might otherwise have afforded into the history of the Pan-German League. Historians in the GDR have tended to hypostacize monopoly capitalism, to turn it into an agent with a will of its own, whose dynamics require no further analysis. The drawbacks of this approach were evident in Kuczynski's attempt to analyze the social complexion of the Pan-German League's membership. Like previous historians, he discovered that teachers and public officials were heavily represented, but unlike previous historians, he tried to explain why. These people were singled out, Kuczynski explained, 'in precisely the cleverest way for a propaganda organization of monopoly capitalism which was to work among the middle classes [*Bürgertum*], especially among the lower and middle strata . . . [These persons] were chosen so that one could have a very great ideological influence with only a few members' (p. 9). One sees here its anonymous and all-pervasive power preserved in the passive voice, only the hand of monopoly capitalism, at work choosing people. This line of reasoning fully obscured the problem of why the human beings who joined the Pan-German League did so.

Subsequent Marxist–Leninist accounts of the Pan-German League have retained the analytical framework Kuczynski laid down. The League remains an extremely influential 'cover organization', which directed the work of other propaganda groups, controlled the men who shaped official policy, and did so in the interest of monopoly capitalism. Variations on this theme have added nuances, principally a definition of the ruling class broadened to include Junkers and bankers. This phalanx remains, however, foreign to the masses of Germans, who were mobilized into its service by the clever deceptions of a sophisticated propaganda network.[31]

The work of one East German scholar, Edgar Hartwig, occupies a special place in the history of the Pan-German League. In 1908 the league established an archive. Bonhard and Class (though none of the other authors) had access to it in writing their histories. In 1942, several years after the League's dissolution, Class handed the archive over to the *Reichsarchiv*, where it was presumed destroyed in the massive air raids on Potsdam in April 1945.[32] In fact the archive survived the war, and in the early 1960s it became accessible at what was then called the *Deutsches Zentralarchiv* in Potsdam. Hartwig's dissertation was the first scholarly work on the League to exploit this resource.[33] Hartwig provided a wealth of new detail about the internal workings of the organization. He also shed new light on the League's ties to the Foreign Office and on the role of Emil Kirdorf. However, all this detail he stuffed into the standard conceptual model and expounded in heavy-handed jargon. Kirdorf's participation was a sign that the 'Ruhr monopoly, its power increased to enormous proportions, was putting the Pan-German League more directly in the service of its policy of forcing a struggle to divide up the world anew' (p. 176). Class's contacts with the Foreign Office merely confirmed what other Marxist-Leninist historians had argued, that the League never really stood in opposition to the government, that any disagreements were minor and over tactics, and that the League was thus 'an influential political force, which helped align [*mitbestimmte*] the policy of the state in the interest of the most aggressive and reactionary segments of the monopolistic bourgeoisie' (p. 145).

Hartwig's dissertation, which he completed in 1966, was the last in the series of monographs that dealt exclusively with the history of the Pan-German League. The organization has remained a subject of great interest to historians, however, particularly in light of the revival in the Federal Republic in the 1960s of the debate over the origins of the First World War.

'The Empire's modern opinion-managers'

Little need be said here about the impact of Fritz Fischer's book on German aims in the First World War, the controversy the book unleashed, or the historiographical reorientation it encouraged among younger West German historians.[34] It suffices to note that Fischer's thesis posited the virtual identity between the aims of the German government, both before and during the war, and the program of the Pan-German League. While this conclusion was hardly novel to anyone following the literature being published in the GDR, its espousal by a West German historian had far-reaching consequences, not the least of which was an intensive reexamination, of the role of the Pan-German League in the structure of Imperial German politics. The influence of Marx was palpable in this reexamination but it was tempered by the influence of Eckart Kehr, whom West German historians rediscovered in the 1960s, as well as by the influence of Max Weber. Historians now investigated more closely the extent of the Pan-German League's influence; they examined its ties to various powerful interest groups and, through these groups, to the German government itself. While many of the specific conclusions of Fischer and his students remain in dispute, few historians doubt any longer that the Pan-German League played an important role in the German political system on the eve of the war. Its aggressive ideology provided the rallying cry behind which the parties of the right and the major heavy-industrial and agrarian interest groups attempted to consolidate their forces in the aftermath of the disastrous federal elections of 1912.[35]

The Pan-German League has also occupied a critical place in a general reinterpretation of the German Empire, which emerged in the early 1970s as a synthesis of the research done in the previous decade. The central concepts in this synthesis, whose leading spokesman has been Hans-Ulrich Wehler, are social imperialism and the plebiscitary mobilization of popular opinion as a substitute for genuine parliamentary rule.[36] As these concepts suggest, the emphasis falls on techniques of political management and manipulation used by elite groups, who clung to political power but were threatened by socialism and democratization. These groups attempted, so runs the argument, to divert social and political tension outward by pursuing an aggressive foreign policy, which included acquiring a colonial empire and constructing a battle fleet. In hopes of securing support for their policies, these elites attempted to bring pressure on a reluctant Reichstag and to mobilize popular opinion directly by means of various extra-parliamentary *Verbände*. In the workings of this socio-political system, the Pan-German League served as an instrument of rule, an agency through which dominant elites manipulated public opinion. Borrowing from Kehr, Wehler called the League the "'Holding [Company]'" of militant prewar nationalism', an organization intimately tied to important interest groups and other propaganda organizations; the function of all of these was the 'mobilization of plebiscitary approval for certain government policies, both during and independent of electoral campaigns'.[37] This view has informed many other recent works that have touched on the activity of the Pan-German League – its role in the colonial and naval propaganda, its influence in the press, and its ties to the political parties.[38]

This interpretation of the German Empire has been very attractive to West German historians. While it owes a great deal to Marx, it is more flexible than the kind of Marxism one encounters east of the Elbe River, and it can accommodate other theoretical models, such as modernization theory, interest-group theory, and non-Marxist theories of economic growth and business cycles.[39] None the less, this interpretation has not been immune to criticism. The principal contribution of Wheler and others who followed Fischer has been to turn attention to the realms of society and the economy, but most of their work has continued to focus on the state and the formulation of policy; the 'new' history in the Federal Republic has been chiefly devoted to the social history of politics, albeit with a much broader appreciation for the forces that impinged upon the political realm. Wehler in particular has been charged with purveying an overly managerial model of politics, in which the emphasis remains on the state, or more specifically on the machinations of the social groups that controlled the state.[40] These criticisms do speak to the analytical difficulties that this interpretation poses for an understanding of the Pan-German League – difficulties that are much the same as those posed by the Marxist–Leninist model. The League still functions as the agency of the ruling classes; the definition of the ruling classes is merely more flexible, and the manner in which the League served these interests is more thoroughly elucidated. It is still impossible, however, to explain the League's appeal, its ability to mobilize broad sectors of German society, without recourse to the same super-sophisticated propaganda apparatus that the East Germans have invoked. Leaders of the League typified, in Wehler's view, 'the modern opinion manager', and this fact largely explains their success.[41] Finally, like the East German Marxists, proponents of the 'Wehler model' are compelled, because of their emphasis on techniques of stabilizing the political system, to minimise the tensions between the League and the German government, or to reduce these tensions to the level of tactical disagreements.

It is a mistake to characterize Wehler's view of the Empire as a 'new orthodoxy'. Wehler would be the last one to make this claim, for he himself is too aware of directions of research that are undermining facets of his picture of the Empire. Recent research on the Pan-German League and other patriotic societies certainly indicates that modifications are in order. Several scholars have stressed the vehemence of the Pan-German League's hostility to the government and have concluded that the radical nationalism the League embodied and the success of its popular mobilization ultimately did less to stabilize the social and political *status quo* than to undermine it.[42] That patriotic societies were anything but pliant tools for manipulation in the service of government policies has emerged clearly from recent studies of the popular campaign to support construction of the navy and of the popular protests against the Boer War,[43]

Wehler's most persistent critic has been the English historian Geoff Eley, who along with a number of his compatriots has challenged the proposition that one can adequately understand Imperial German politics from Wehler's perspective, from 'the top down'.[44] Borrowing concepts and methods from British social history, Eley and the others have argued that society and politics in Imperial Germany must instead be analyzed at the grass-roots level and that this perspective will reveal a new dynamism, the self-mobilization of popular forces, which Imperial Germany's elites could not manipulate and which Wehler's model cannot comprehend.

Eley's most extended argument in favor of this alternative to Wehler's interpretation is his recently published book on the radical right in Imperial German politics.[45] I have expressed opinions elsewhere about this book.[46] Here I wish to emphasize its importance. Eley's rejection of the emphasis in Wehler's model on manipulation and mobilization from above has led him in search of new factors to explain the League's appeal. He has thus confronted a question that every previous historian of the League either disregarded or evaded: why did the organization attract into its ranks the kinds of people it did? Eley's argument, in brief, is that after 1890 the 'subordinate classes' became mobilized in the political arena. Some sectors of these classes – peasants, workers, and Catholics – were assimilated into mass organizations affiliated with established political parties. Another sector, however, the 'Protestant petty-bourgeoisie of teachers, professional men, moderately successful businessmen and middling civil-servants' (p. 67), found no comparable reception in the most logical place, the National Liberal Party. Instead, these people found that participation in the National Liberal Party was governed by the 'ingrained etiquette of *Honoratiorenpolitik*' (p. 184), which denied them access to positions of power and influence in the party. Frustrated, they found refuge and opportunity in patriotic societies like the Pan-German League and the Navy League, from which they mobilized a populist offensive against the entire system of traditional party politics.

Eley's provocative argument fails, in my opinion, especially with respect to the Pan-German League. This failure is due in part to his imprecise definitions of critical concepts, such as 'subordinate classes' and 'petty-bourgeoisie', but even more because Eley has not followed lines of research logically implied by his own thesis. These would have taken him, ironically, right down to where he and his friends have been urging historians of the German Empire to go – to the grass roots, to an analysis of just who was active in the patriotic societies at the local level and the nature of their relationship at that level to the National Liberal Party. Another scholar has recently argued that the National Liberal Party in fact succeeded very well in accommodating the patriotic societies.[47] Eley's attempt to locate the sources of the Pan-German League's appeal in frustrations created in a dynamically changing political system is none the less a pioneering effort, and it highlights questions about the League that can no longer be neglected.

Plan of the Study

The Pan-German League has inspired a large literature, in which the emphasis has fallen on several problems – the League's significance as an influence on official policies and as an index of public opinion, the material interests served by its activity, and the function of the organization in the politics of Imperial Germany. Although this literature has shed a great deal of light on the Pan-German League, the problems that it has addressed will remain unresolved until more fundamental questions are confronted.

The most fundamental question concerns the sources of the Pan-German League's appeal to certain social groups. Most of the League's historians have surveyed the social composition of the organization but have not asked why these groups of people were more attracted than others to the League's program and ideology. Citing the League's skillful propaganda or its success in deluding Germans is simply no answer to the question.

A second question is related to the first. It concerns the dynamics of popular mobilization and the tension between the Pan-German League and official authority in Imperial Germany. Most historians since the Second World War have minimized the significance of the tension. Eley's research has challenged this conclusion. His discussion of the relationship between the 'old' right of the political parties and the 'new' right which was mobilized in the patriotic societies suggests that the antagonism between the Pan-German League and the government involved fundamental differences of political philosophy and style. I find Eley's argument compelling, but I believe that an analysis of this antagonism must delve more deeply into the dynamics of popular mobilization in the name of causes like patriotism, which were highly charged emotionally and susceptible to an uncontrollable momentum. Questions about the dynamics of mobilizing popular forces point back, of course, to the question of the Pan-German League's appeal to specific social groups.

Because neither the sources of the League's appeal nor the dynamics of its popular mobilization have been sufficiently explored, the old question of the League's influence in German society and politics remains – for all the printed pages devoted to it – open. Nor has the contention really been put to the test that the League acted as the ideological 'holding company' and coordinator of the activities of other patriotic societies. Nor is it yet fully clear how the League put pressure on the German government.

These questions are enormously complicated. The most perplexing difficulty is evident in even a glance at the literature published by the Pan-German League itself. This literature reveals a high level of emotional intensity and suggests the play of forces in the League's perception of society and politics that were not altogether rational.[48] The possibility that the League's appeal and activity were even partially energized by non-rational forces raises fundamental analytical problems, for the recent histories of the League have all been informed by what one might call a 'common-sense, rationalistic interest-psychology'.[49] The role of the League in German politics has been cast in the context of the interests or calculated strategies of powerful groups of people, be they ruthless monopoly capitalists bent upon conquest, aristocrats plotting to frustrate parliamentary reform, or high-ranking soldiers planning preventive war. Even Eley's analysis deals with the ambitions of popular groups seeking alternative means to represent their interests. As a gesture to the play of popular emotions, historians have done little more than allude to the manner in which the masses were misled, deluded, or otherwise seduced away from the pursuit of their genuine interests.

I am convinced that a high degree of emotionalism, prejudice, and anxiety was a hallmark of the Pan-German League and that in order to understand these forces, a heuristic alternative to models built exclusively on interest-psychology must be found.[50] Finding a practical alternative is the real problem. Freudian analysis, the principal strain of what today passes under the name of 'psychohistory', is a tempting possibility. I have tried elsewhere to analyze a nationalist ideology, which was similar to the Pan-German League's, by using projection as the core concept.[51] I found it impossible, however, given the evidence, to show why an ideology built on projection – an ego-defense mechanism stimulated by a variety of intra-psychic tensions whose character can usually be analyzed only in therapy – should have appealed to a hundred thousand Germans who joined the organization that espoused this ideology. Freudian psychology may well hold the key to understanding the appeal of aggressive ideologies like that of the Pan-German League, but in the present case, limitations of evidence pose insuperable obstacles.[52]

A more accessible level of analysis lies at the intersection of psychology, or more specifically social psychology, and cultural anthropology. Here the distinction between rational and non-rational behavior is less analytically important, but concepts drawn from the two disciplines make it possible to comprehend modes of behavior that are beyond the conceptual range of conventional interest psychology.[53] And, in a way psychoanalysis cannot, cultural anthropology, in team with social psychology, can address other unanswered questions about the history of the Pan-German League, for it illuminates the transition from individual attitudes and ideology to the sphere of social action and political mobilization.

This study of the Pan-German League accordingly focuses on the pivotal realm of culture. The premise of the study is that an analysis of the League's cultural significance must precede the study of its political significance. The basic question the study poses is: what did activity in the Pan-German League *mean* to the people who were active?

As I shall use it, the concept of culture speaks directly to this question. Culture is the symbolic organization of social experience. The concept refers to the manner in which people lend meaning to their lives by structuring their experiences symbolically – not only in the creative works they patronize and admire as 'high culture', but in the ideologies and beliefs they hold, the formal and informal rituals and conventions they observe, and in the very language they use.[54] The radical nationalism which found expression in the Pan-German League was a phenomenon whose symbolic dimension is the key to its significance.

To approach the history of the Pan-German League from this direction is to follow several routes. It is necessary, in the first place, to scrutinize anew what members of the Pan-German League wrote and said. A new survey of the League's literature is needed not so much to spell out programs and demands, for other historians have done this abundantly; rather, the survey is necessary in order to probe more deeply into the ideological context in which these programs and demands were rooted. It is also important to analyze the language – the recurrent images, metaphors, and other symbols – in which the League's members structured and expressed their concerns, anxieties, aspirations, their perceptions of social and political reality, and – certainly not least important – their representations of themselves. These pre-eminently self-conscious features of the League's literature provide a basis for analysis of the League's membership. I propose to follow, up to a point, the lead of Klaus Theweleit who, in his wonderfully outrageous study of the imagery in the literature that came out of the Free-Corps movement, noted that 'up until now, the Fascists have been asked too little about Fascism, and those who claim to have seen through it . . . have been asked too much'.[55] Theweleit's study is outrageous because he tried to use this imagery as the basis for psychoanalysis. The goal of this study is, for reasons I have specified, more modest. I hope to link or to establish homologies between the symbols and images in the Pan-German League's literature and experiences common to the social groups heavily represented in the League's active membership.[56]

It is thus also essential to determine more precisely which social groups were heavily represented in the Pan-German League. This undertaking requires ascertaining, as far as the evidence allows, not only the identities of the active Pan-Germans, but the nature of their activity in the organization and as much as possible about their positions in the economy and society.[57]

Finally, it is important to examine the institutional realm in which activity in the Pan-German League took place. The League was a voluntary association that comprised over a hundred local chapters. These functioned like many other voluntary associations; they were arenas in which common experiences, anxieties, and aspirations were articulated, reinforced, and preserved in rituals, customs, and other forms of common behavior.[58] Furthermore, in the Pan-German League, the local *Verein* was the arena in which a critical transformation took place, in what some West German historians are now calling a 'base process'.[59] Not only were experiences, anxieties, and aspirations structured and expressed symbolically; they were also politicized and channeled into concerted action.

Focusing on the activity of the Pan-German League at the grass-roots level of the local *Verein* has other analytical advantages. It brings a new perspective on the question of the League's influence in German politics.

This influence was due in large part to the success of political mobilization, and the basic units in the process of mobilization were the League's local chapters. Here at the local level, too, the related question of the League's influence over other patriotic societies comes into sharper focus, for these other societies also comprised hundreds of chapters, which coexisted and interacted with those of the Pan-German League in localities throughout the country.

Although I shall pursue a number of new questions about the history of the Pan-German League, my answers will not rest on any dramatic new source material. I have drawn on material in West German as well as East German archives, but the documentary foundation of this study is not significantly broader than Edgar Hartwig's; it includes the archive of the Pan-German League and the organization's own literature, especially its journal, the *Alldeutsche Blätter*. I have concentrated, however, on facets of this source material that Hartwig and other historians of the League have neglected. I have paid particular attention to the correspondence in the archive between the local chapters and national headquarters and on the thousands of reports which the local chapters published in the League's journal about their activities.

Because the history of the Pan-German League has already been narrated often, I can cover certain phases of the story briefly and concentrate on the problems I have chosen to isolate. The organization of the study reflects this concentration. The first part consists of Chapters 2 and 3 and sets the background. Chapter 2 examines the social and political context in which patriotic societies took shape in the German Empire, while Chapter 3 narrates the early history of the Pan-German League, from its origins in 1886 until its rift with the German government shortly after the turn of the century. The second and principal part of the study comprises Chapters 4–9 and is devoted to an analysis of the cultural significance of the Pan-German League. Here I shall analyze, within the framework I have outlined, the League's ideology, the social complexion of its active membership, and the character and cultural significance of its activities. I shall investigate a range of factors – cultural, psychological, regional, confessional, and ethnic – that promoted interest in the Pan-German League among specific social groups and in certain parts of the country. In considering the dynamics of political mobilization, I shall examine the relationship between the Pan-German League and other voluntary associations, not only patriotic societies, but an array of cultural and political *Vereine* with which the League came constantly in contact. In the third part of the study, in Chapters 10 and 11, the narrative resumes as the backdrop for consideration of a number of additional problems. Chapter 10 deals with the period of roughly 1902–10 and emphasizes the growing stridency of the League's opposition to the government and the manifold financial, organizational, and ideological consequences of this opposition. Chapter 11 treats the final years before the outbreak of war and examines the League's mobilization of a broad national opposition to the German government.

Notes

1   Hans-Günther Zmarzlik, 'Das Kaiserreich als Einbahnstrasse?', in Karl Holl and Günther List (eds), *Liberalismus und imperialistischer Staat: Der Imperialismus als Problem liberalen Parteien in Deutschland 1890–1914* (Göttingen, 1975), pp. 62–71; cf. Thomas Nipperdey, 'Wehlers "Kaiserreich": Ein kritische Auseinandersetzung', in *Gesellschaft, Kultur, Theorie: Gesammelte Aufsätze zur neueren Geschichte* (Göttingen, 1976), pp. 360–89.

2   'Der Alldeutsche Verband und die Auslandspresse', ADB (1899), 354; ADB (1898), 229–30.

3   'Die Tätigkeit des Alldeutschen Verbandes in der Marokkofrage in französischer Beleuchtung', ADB (1905), 256–7; ADB (1906), 310–11; ADB (1913), 249–50; cf. Paul Vergnet, *La France en danger: L'oeuvre des pangermanistes* (Paris, 1913).

4   The most famous piece of evidence is the Crowe memorandum of January 1910. See G. P. Gooch and Harold Temperley (eds), *British Documents on the Origins of the War*, 11 vols (London, 1926–38), Vol. 6, no. 208; cf. Goschen to Grey, Berlin, 11.4.10, ibid., no. 344.

5   ZStAP, RK 1415, Sitzung des königlichen Staatsministeriums, Berlin, 13.2.09. See in addition, PAAA, Deutschland 169, Bd. 2, which contains many entries that reflect the concern of the German Foreign Office about the League.

6   ADB (1902), 261; ADB (1909), 389–90; ADB (1913), 1–2.

7   ADB (1902), 373.

8   For example: Roland G. Usher, *Pan-Germanism* (London, 1914); André Chéradame, *Le Plan pangermaniste démasqué* (Paris, 1916).

9   See Martin Wenck, *Alldeutsche Taktik* (Jena, 1917).

10   Ludwig Dehio, 'Thoughts on Germany's mission, 1900–1918', *Germany and World Politics in the Twentieth Century* (London, 1965), p. 91.

11   Mildred S. Wertheimer, *The Pan-German League, 1890–1914* (New York, 1924).

12   Hans Delbrück, 'Die Alldeutschen', *Vor und nach dem Weltkriege: Politsche und historische Aufsätze 1902–1925* (Berlin, 1926), pp. 397–403; Martin Hobohm and Paul Rohrbach, *Die Alldeutschen* (Berlin, 1919).

13   Sidney B. Fay, *The Origins of the World War*, 2 vols (New York, 1928–30), Vol. 1, p. 44.

14   Harry Elmer Barnes, *The Genesis of the World War* (New York, 1926), p. 52.

15   Otto Bonhard, *Geschichte des Alldeutschen Verbandes* (Berlin, 1920).

16   See Hans Herzfeld, *Die deutsche Rüstungspolitik vor dem Weltkriege* (Bonn and Leipzig, 1923), e.g. p. 81.

17   Junius Alter [pseud. Franz Sontag], *Nationalisten: Deutschlands nationales Führetum der Nachkriegszeit* (Leipzig, 1930), pp. 13–14.

18   Heinrich Class, *Wider den Strom* (Leipzig, 1932).

19   Jürgen Kuczynski, *Studien zur Geschichte des deutschen Imperialismus*, Vol. 2, *Propagandaorganisationen des Monopolkapitals* (Berlin, 1950), p. 115.

20   Lothar Werner, *Der Alldeutsche Verband 1890–1918* (Berlin, 1935).

21   Josefine Hussmann, 'Die Alldeutschen und die Flottenfrage' (Diss. phil., Freiburg, 1945); Dietrich Jung, 'Der Alldeutsche Verband und die Marokkofrage' (Diss. phil., Bonn, 1934); Siegfried Wehner, 'Der Alldeutsche Verband und die deutsche Kolonialpolitik der Vorkriegszeit' (Diss. phil., Greifswald, 1935); cf. Erich Schwinn, 'Die Arbeit des deutschen Wehrvereins und die Wehrlage Deutschlands vor dem Weltkriege' (Diss. phil., Heidelberg, 1940); Joseph Müller, *Die Entwicklung des Rassenantisemitismus in den letzten Jahrzehnten des 19. Jahrhunderts* (Berlin, 1940); Max Robert Gerstenhauer, *Der völkische Gedanke in Vergangenheit und Zukunft: Aus der Geschichte der völkischen Bewegung* (Leipzig, 1933).

22   Alfred Kruck, *Geschichte des alldeutschen Verbandes 1890–1939* (Wiesbaden, 1954).

23   See now though Brewster S. Chamberlain, 'The enemy on the right: the *Alldeutsche Verband* and the Weimar Republic, 1918–1926' (PhD Diss., University of Maryland, 1972); Willi Krebs, 'Der Alldeutsche Verband in den Jahren 1918 bis 1939: ein politisches Instrument des deutschen Imperialismus' (Diss. phil., Berlin, 1970).

24   For example: Ludwig Freisel, 'Das Bismarckbild der Alldeutschen: Bismarck im Bewusstsein des Alldeutschen Verbandes von 1890 bis 1933. Ein Beitrag zum Bismarckverständnis des deutschen Nationalismus' (Diss. phil., Würzburg, 1964); Dirk

Oncken, 'Das Problem des Lebensraums in der deutschen Politik vor 1914' (Diss. phil., Freiburg i.B., 1948); Dietrich Schwonder, *Bevor Hitler kam: Eine historische Studie* (Hanover, 1964).

25   The analyses of the 'continuity problem' by Anglo-American historians also fit into this tradition: see Rohan D'O. Butler, *The Roots of National Socialism, 1783–1933* (London, 1941); Fritz Stern, *The Politics of Cultural Despair: A Study in the Rise of the Germanic Ideology* (Berkeley, Calif. and Los Angeles, 1961).

26   Eckart Kehr, *Schlachtflottenbau und Parteipolitik 1894–1901: Versuch eines Querschnitts durch die innenpolitischen, sozialen und ideologischen Voraussetzungen des deutschen Imperialismus* (Berlin, 1930).

27   Kehr, 'Soziale und finanzielle Grundlagen der Tirpitzschen Flottenpropaganda', in *Der Primat der Innenpolitik: Gesammelte Aufsätze zur preussisch–deutschen Sozialgeschichte im 19. und 20. Jahrhundert* (ed. Hans-Ulrich Wehler) (Frankfurt a. M., 1965), p. 144.

28   George W. F. Hallgarten, *Imperialismus vor 1914: Die soziologischen Grundlagen der Aussenpolitik europäischer Grossmächte vor dem ersten Weltkrieg*, 2nd edn (Munich, 1963), esp. Vol. 2, pp. 19–23.

29   Pauline Relyea Anderson, *The Background of Anti-English Feeling in Germany, 1890–1902* (Washington, DC, 1939), esp. pp. 194–210.

30   Jürgen Kuczynski, *Studien zur Geschichte des deutschen Imperialismus*, Vol. 2, *Propagandaorganisationen des MonopolKapitals* (Berlin, 1950).

31   See Kurt Stenkewitz, *Gegen Bajonett und Dividende: Die politische Krise in Deutschland am Vorabend des ersten Weltkrieges* (Berlin, 1960), esp. p. 43; Fritz Klein *et al.*, *Deutschland im Ersten Weltkrieg*, 3 vols (Berlin, 1968–70), esp. Vol. 1, pp. 134–5; Adam Galos *et al.*, *Die Hakatisten: Der Deutsche Ostmarken-Verein (1893–1934). Ein Beitrag zur Geschichte der Ostpolitik des deutschen Imperialismus* (Berlin, 1966), p. 22; cf. A. S. Jerussalimski, *Die Aussenpolitik und die Diplomatie des deutschen Imperialismus am Ende des 19. Jahrhunderts* (Berlin, 1954), pp. 31–2, 67–8, 426, 463.

32   At least this is what Kruck – and presumably Class – believed: see Kruck, p. vi. On the archive see also Class, *Strom*, p. 130; ZStAP, ADV 29.

33   Edgar Hartwig, 'Zur Politik und Entwicklung des Alldeutschen Verbandes von seiner Gründung bis zum Beginn des Ersten Weltkrieges (1891–1914)' (Diss. phil., Jena, 1966); cf. Hartwig, 'Alldeutscher Verband (ADV) 1891–1939', in Dieter Fricke *et al.* (eds), *Die bürgerlichen Parteien in Deutschland: Handbuch der Geschichte der bürgerlichen Parteien und anderer bürgerlicher Interessenorganisationen vom Vormärz bis zum Jahre 1945*, 2 vols (Berlin, 1968–70), Vol. 1, pp. 1–26.

34   Fritz Fischer, *Griff nach der Weltmacht: Die Kriegszielpolitik des kaiserlichen Deutschland 1914/1918* (Düsseldorf, 1961); see Richard J. Evans, 'Introduction: Wilhelm II's Germany and the historians,' in Evans (ed.), *Society and Politics in Wilhelmine Germany* (New York, 1978), pp. 11–39.

35   Dirk Stegmann, *Die Erben Bismarcks: Parteien und Verbände in der Spätphase des Wilhelminischen Deutschlands. Sammlungspolitik 1897–1918* (Cologne and Berlin, 1970); Fritz Fischer, *Krieg der Illusionen: Die deutsche Politik von 1911 bis 1914* (Düsseldorf, 1969); cf. Gustav Schmidt, 'Innenpolitische Blockbildungen am Vorabend des Ersten Weltkrieges', *Aus Politik und Zeitgeschichte* (Beilage zum *Parlament*), no. 20 (1972), pp. 3–32.

36   Hans-Ulrich Wehler, *Das Deutsche Kaiserreich 1871–1918* (Göttingen, 1973); Wehler, *Bismarck und der Imperialismus* (Cologne and Berlin, 1969); Michael Stürmer, *Regierung und Reichstag im Bismarckstaat 1871–1880: Cäsarismus oder Parlamentarismus* (Düsseldorf, 1974).

37   Wehler, *Kaiserreich*, pp. 92–3.

38   Jürg Meyer, 'Die Propaganda der deutschen Flottenbewegung' (Diss. phil., Berne, 1967); Paul M. Kennedy, *The Samoan Tangle: A Study in Anglo-German Relations, 1878–1900* (New York, 1974), p. 264; Dankwart Guratzsch, *Macht durch Organisation: Die Grundlegung des Hugenbergischen Presseimperiums* (Düsseldorf, 1974); Anthony J. O'Donnell, 'National Liberalism and the mass politics of the German right, 1890–1907' (PhD Diss., Princeton University, 1973); Peter Hampe, 'Sozioökonomische und psychische Hintergründe der bildungsbürgerlichen Imperialbegeisterung', in Klaus Vondung (ed.), *Das wilhelminische Bildungsbürgertum: Zur Sozialgeschichte seiner Ideen* (Göttingen,

1976), p. 71; Jürgen Kocka, *Klassengesellschaft im Krieg 1914–1918* (Göttingen, 1973), p. 10.

39 See Jürgen Kocka, 'Theory and social history: recent developments in West Germany', *Social Research*, vol. 47 (1980), pp. 426–57.

40 Some of this criticism strikes me as unfair and polemical. See Evans's introductory essay in *Society and Politics*; Geoff Eley, 'Die "Kehreits" und das Kaiserreich: Bemerkungen zu einer aktuellen Kontroverse', GG, vol. 4 (1978), pp. 91–107.

41 Wehler, *Kaiserreich*, p. 93.

42 Konrad Schilling, 'Beiträge zu einer Geschichte des radikalen Nationalismus in der wilhelminischen Aera 1890–1909: Die Entstehung des radikalen Nationalismus, seine Einflussnahme auf die innere und äussere Politik des Deutschen Reiches und die Stellung von Regierung und Reichstag zu seiner politischen und publizistischen Tätigkeit' (Diss. phil., Cologne, 1968); Harmut Pogge von Strandmann, 'Nationale Verbände zwischen Weltpolitik und Kontinentalpolitik', in Herbert Schottelius and Wilhelm Deist (eds), *Marine und Marinepolitik im kaiserlichen Deutschland 1871–1914* (Düsseldorf, 1972), p. 301; Peter-Christian Witt, 'Innenpolitik und Imperialismus in der Vorgeschichte des 1. Weltkrieges', in Holl and List, *Liberalismus und imperialistischer Staat*, pp. 10–17.

43 Vokker R. Berghahn, *Der Tirpitz-Plan: Genesis und Verfall einer innenpolitischen Krisenstrategie unter Wilhelm II* (Düsseldorf, 1971); Wilhelm Deist, *Flottenpolitik und Flottenpropaganda: Das Nachrichtenbüro des Reichsmarineamts 1897–1914* (Stuttgart, 1976); Deist, 'Reichsmarineamt und Flottenverein 1903–1906', in Schottelius and Deist, *Marine und Marinepolitik*, pp. 296–317; Geoff Eley, 'The German Navy League in German politics, 1898–1908' (Diss. phil., Brighton, Sussex, 1974); Ullrich Kröll, *Die internationale Buren-Agitation 1899–1902: Haltung der Oeffentlichkeit und Agitation zugunsten der Buren in Deutschland, Frankreich und den Niederlanden während des Burenkrieges* (Münster, 1973), pp. 67–82.

44 Richard J. Evans (ed.), *Society and Politics in Wilhelmine Germany* (New York, 1978).

45 Geoff Eley, *Reshaping the German Right: Radical Nationalism and Political Change after Bismarck* (New Haven, Conn. and London, 1980).

46 AHR, vol. 86 (1981), pp. 159–60.

47 O'Donnell, 'National Liberalism'.

48 This is the conclusion recently reached by a young German historian, who used the communications theory of Karl Deutsch to argue that perceptual distortion was evident in the League's commentary on Hungarian politics: Günter Schödl, *Alldeutscher Verband und deutsche Minderheitenpolitik in Ungarn 1890–1914: Zur Geschichte des deutschen 'extremen Nationalismus'* (Frankfurt a. M., 1978).

49 See Peter Gay, *Art and Act: On Causes in History – Manet, Gropius, Mondrian* (New York, 1976), p. 21.

50 See Alisdair MacIntyre, 'Rationality and the explanation of action', in *Against the Self-Images of the Age: Essays on Ideology and Philosophy* (New York, 1971), pp. 244–59; cf. Gerald Izenberg, 'Psychohistory and intellectual history', *History and Theory*, vol. 14 (1975), pp. 139–55.

51 Roger Chickering, 'Der "Deutsche Wehrverein" und die Reform der deutschen Armee 1912–1914', MGM, no. 1 (1979), pp. 7–33.

52 The recent strictures of Hans-Ulrich Wehler impress me as well taken: 'Geschichtswissenschaft und "Psychohistorie"', *Innsbrucker Historische Studien*, vol. 1 (1978), pp. 201–13; cf. Wehler, 'Psychonalysis and history', *Social Research*, vol. 47 (1980), pp. 519–36; Dirk Blasius, 'Psychohistorie und Sozialgeschichte', ASG, vol. 17 (1977), pp. 383–403.

53 See Clifford Geertz, 'Ideology as a cultural system', in *The Interpretation of Cultures: Selected Essays* (New York, 1973), pp. 193–233.

54 This understanding of culture is indebted to many sources. See especially E. P. Thompson, 'The poverty of theory or an orrery of errors', in *The Poverty of Theory and Other Essays* (New York and London, 1978), pp. 1–210; Thompson, *The Making of the English Working Class* (New York, 1963); Raymond Williams, *Culture and Society, 1780–1950* (New York, 1958); Raymond Williams, *Marxism and Literature* (Oxford, 1977); Richard Johnson, 'Culture and the historians', in J. Clarke *et al.* (eds), *Working-Class Culture: Studies in History and Theory* (New York, 1979), pp. 41–71; William H. Sewell, Jr, *Work*

and Revolution in France: The Language of Labor from the Old Regime to 1848 (Cambridge, 1980), esp. pp. 9–13; Thomas Nipperdey, 'Die anthropologische Dimension der Geschichtswissenschaft', in *Gesellschaft, Kultur, Theorie*, pp. 33–58; Wolf Lepenies, 'Arbeiterkultur: Wissenschaftssoziologische Ammerkungen zur Konjunktur eines Begriffs', GG, vol. 5 (1979), pp. 125–36; Wolf Lepenies, 'Probleme einer historischen Anthropologie', in Reinhard Rürup (ed.), *Historische Sozialwissenschaft: Beiträge zur Einführung in die Forschungspraxis* (Göttingen, 1977), pp. 126–59.

55   Klaus Theweleit, *Männerphantasien: Frauen, Fluten, Körper, Geschichte* (Frankfurt a. M., 1977), p. 119.

56   See Klaus Vondung, 'Probleme einer Sozialgeschichte der Ideen', in Vondung, *Bildungsbürgertum*, pp. 13–15; Peter Hampe, 'Sozioökonomische und psychische Hintergründe der bildungsbürgerlichen Imperialbegeisterung', ibid., pp. 70–1. For sensible observations on the problematic relationship between psychopathology and the historical analysis of imagery see: Thompson, *Making*, pp. 49–50 (in criticizing Norman Cohn), and J. P. Stern, *Hitler: The Führer and the People* (Berkeley, Calif. and Los Angeles, 1975), p. 16 (on the phenomenon of psycho-Hitleriana).

57   See Konrad H. Jarausch, 'Die Alldeutschen und die Regierung Bethmann Hollwegs: Eine Denkschrift Kurt Riezlers vom Herbst 1916', VZG, vol. 21 (1973), p. 441, n. 25.

58   Hermann Bausinger, 'Vereine als Gegenstand volkskundlicher Forschung', *Zeitschrift für Volkskunde*, vol. 55 (1959), pp. 98–104; Heinz Schmitt, *Das Vereinsleben der Stadt Weinheim an der Bergstrasse* (Weinheim, 1963), p. 208.

59   Dieter Groh, 'Base-processes and the problem of organization: outline of a social history research project', *Social History*, vol. 4 (1979), p. 277.

2 Patriotic Societies in Bismarckian Germany

The recent historiography of the Pan-German League has confuted the thesis of Mildred Wertheimer and other American revisionist historians of the 1920s that the organization had minimal influence. However, another point that American historians argued in the 1920s is incontestable: Germans had no monopoly on patriotic societies in the decades prior to the First World War. Abstracting from an abundance of examples, one might define these societies as voluntary associations whose primary purpose was to mobilize the members of a given national group, irrespective of class, rank, or confession, in support of national symbols and what were called 'national causes'. The Pan-German League had, by this definition, counterparts in virtually every country in Europe, as well as in the United States – in organizations such as the Primrose League, the *Action française*, the Navy League of the United States, and the *Societa Nazionale Dante Alighieri*.

Comparative study of these organizations would be rewarding, and until it occurs, generalizations about them must remain impressionistic and tentative. With this caveat, the prewar patriotic societies did seem everywhere to display a number of similarities. Most obviously, their programs and demands were alike. Everywhere they called for military preparedness, the uncompromising defense of national interests, the pursuit of empire, and the building of the navies universally regarded as the *sine qua non* of a successful imperial venture. The generalization is also safe that the appearance of these patriotic groups represented an aspect of the growing democratization of Western societies, of the 'participation revolution' of the late nineteenth century, the intrusion of the masses into the political arena, or, to use Hans Rosenberg's expression, the development of a 'political mass market'.[1] These societies appear, however, to have appealed to specific sectors of this mass market. Their memberships comprised in the main people of the middle class, whose distinguishing characteristics were education or the possession of commercial or industrial capital, even if only on a modest scale.[2] This characteristic suggests that however idealistic their inspiration, a function of patriotic societies everywhere was to defend the status conferred by property and education against the threat posed by other social strata, which were themselves mobilized in the late nineteenth century but which had neither property nor education.

These generalizations cannot take the study of patriotic societies very far, for the history of these organizations is unintelligible if divorced from the national contexts in which each of them operated. Their appeal, success, influence, and significance varied greatly from one country to another, affected by manifold differences of context – social tension, political structure, confessional and ethnic conflict, and political culture. The history of patriotic societies in England was no less intimately tied to the efforts of the Tory Party to adapt to a mass constituency than was the history of such societies in France related to the issues of royalism and the status of the Catholic church. In Germany, too, the history of patriotic societies was decisively colored by a number of factors unique to the national context.

The Incubation of Patriotic Societies in Imperial Germany

Voluntary associations that served patriotic goals had a long history in Germany even before unification. Numerous student corporations, shooting clubs, choral and gymnastic societies, and other organizations effectively promoted the idea of unification; their achievement, in fact, was to elevate the nation to the status of a popular symbol.[3] In so far as these associations appealed to specific constituencies (such as students) or nurtured patriotism as an adjunct to pursuing other ends (such as choral recreation), they were of a different order than the patriotic societies which were founded after unification. The later societies appealed to all Germans and defended patriotic causes as their primary goal.

In Imperial Germany major patriotic societies first appeared in the 1880s, but their political impact and significance were conditioned by forces and circumstances that developed during the first decade of the Empire's existence. The first of these was the character of the Imperial German political system, which took shape in the 1870s, the product of both the constitution and political evolution in the first years of the new regime. The constitution of 1871 severely limited the power of the democratically elected federal parliament, by lodging primary jurisdiction over domestic affairs with the individual *Länder* (most of whose parliaments were not democratically elected), by carefully excluding control over foreign and military policy from the competence of the Reichstag, and by failing to make federal ministers responsible to this body. As Michael Stürmer has shown, the federal chancellor also took great pains, in the first years of the new Empire, to stifle tendencies that might imply the upgrading of the Reichstag's status, be these in the direction of enlarging the competence of the parliament or of establishing *de facto* ministerial dependence on a single stable parliamentary coalition.[4] Another aspect of this campaign to attenuate the development of a genuine parliamentary system was Bismarck's resort to quasi-plebiscitary intimidation of the Reichstag; in a manner that suggested parallels to the regime of Louis Napoleon, he attempted on several occasions, most blatantly in the elections of 1878, to mobilize public opinion directly in order to produce a pliable Reichstag.[5]

The limited power of the Reichstag diminished the status of the political parties which inhabited it and led quickly to the establishment of an alternative system of political representation and influence. Although extra-parliamentary pressure groups of many descriptions appeared throughout Europe at the end of the century, the peculiarities of the political system lent them special importance in Imperial Germany. Because the political parties proved to be only one avenue for the articulation of interests, and often a not very effective one at that, these extra-parliamentary *Verbände* soon made their presence felt in the offices of government agencies, of political leaders, and in the forum of public opinion, where they represented the interests of their assorted constituencies in questions of tax and tariff reform, social policy, military contracts, and countless other matters.[6]

The significance of the *Verbände* extended well beyond their lobbying. They soon developed into what Thomas Nipperdey has called a 'secondary system of social power'.[7] More than the political parties, these groups were vehicles of political mobilization in the 'participation revolution' of the late nineteenth century. Many of them had memberships far larger than most of the political parties. The *Verbände* thus quickly found a role in the plebiscitary politics of the German Empire, for they were in a position to mobilize their formidable constituencies, often with the connivance of the government, in order to exert popular pressure on the Reichstag. This role had unfortunate effects, however. The political mobilization that took place under their aegis was usually oriented toward the parochial interests of the major subgroups of German society – those associated with agriculture, industrial or commercial capital, industrial labor, and Catholicism.[8] Because the *Verbände* were immune to the need for parliamentary compromise, their pursuit of their constituents' interests worked less to integrate the subgroups for which they spoke than to perpetuate the cleavages which divided them.

In this constellation of social and political power, the foundations of which had been well laid by 1880, patriotic societies were to play a special role. Once major issues of direct patriotic significance appeared in the forum of political debate, the logic of the German political system encouraged the formation of extra-parliamentary groups to serve as protagonists. Patriotic societies would operate in much the same manner as other *Verbände*, but their status and significance in the German system were in some respects unique, for the constituency whose interests they claimed directly to serve was that of all Germans. Because they sought to mobilize broad support in various national issues, patriotic societies were ideally suited for plebiscitary use. Indeed, their significance would stand in direct relation to the political importance of just these national issues as sources of domestic consensus and integration in a society which was jarred in the late nineteenth century by prodigious growth and dislocation – a society whose divisions on the most fundamental political issues were epitomized in (though by no means limited to) the spread of the Social Democratic labor movement, which was ideologically committed to the overthrow of the whole Bismarckian system.

The characteristics of the Imperial German political system attached special significance to extra-parliamentary organizations, while the failure of this system to generate domestic political consensus put a premium on national issues as an alternative source of cohesion. The establishment of the

German Empire also vitally affected the character of the national issues that were to occupy patriotic societies. Simply stated, the foundation of the German Empire in 1871 created as many problems with respect to German national consciousness as it solved.[9] The nationalism officially propagated in the new Empire was a civic religion; the national community that was to be the object of civic loyalty was coterminous with the new political entity that had emerged in the heart of Europe.[10] Although it could build on political traditions that extended at least as far back as 1848, this 'official nationalism' had shallow roots. The symbolism of the new nation-state was meager and included, as Theodor Schieder has pointed out, little more than a flag, an army (which was not really national), and the monarchy.[11] Even the question of what, beyond the defense of the new national frontiers, lay within the purview of the national interest remained initially ill defined. In these circumstances, one of the primary challenges the new national government faced was to create the symbols, traditions, and values to buttress a national self-consciousness focused on the Reich. To this end the government used all its resources, from the schoolroom and pulpit to the academic community and the ministries in Berlin. No one, however, was more central in this undertaking than Bismarck, who, because of the role he had played in the founding of the Reich, emerged as the principal custodian of the grail of national symbols, in which he himself occupied a leading position. For the duration of his tenure in office, Bismarck remained unchallenged as a symbol of German national identity and interest; his was in fact the power to determine the very connotations of the word 'national', and he exercised this power frequently, as he brandished the word to defend his own policies and political friends while using the label *Reichsfeind* to attack his enemies.[12]

Even more than his formidable political power, Bismarck's status as a national symbol gave ascendency to a rather narrow, political definition of the 'German nation' during the first two decades after the *Reichsgründung*. This cataclysmic event in 1871, however, itself ensured the development, within the German Empire, of rival symbols and forms of national consciousness, which, though initially no match for those officially enshrined, were to become far more potent after the departure of the Great Man.

The root of the rivalry lay in the fact that the official nationalism seemed to do violence to the most compelling of all symbols of national unity. Millions of people whose first language was German lived outside Imperial Germany, throughout Central Europe and in scattered colonies of settlers in the United States, Canada, and Latin America. The events of 1870–1 had a profound impact on many of these Germans; identification with the accomplishments of the powerful new state was a source of pride, but because most of these people were not citizens of the Reich, their view of the national community tended to be cultural and ethnic rather than political, except in so far as a *grossdeutsch* political tradition survived the year 1866.[13] This more inclusive ethnic definition of the German nation clashed with Bismarck's own, and the chancellor displayed a conspicuous disinterest in the affairs of German-speaking people outside the Empire, whom he regarded as a potential threat to his attempts to stabilize the settlements of 1866 and 1871.[14] The Imperial constitution reflected Bismarck's attitude; it provided that the citizenship of any German would lapse automatically after ten consecutive years' residence outside the Reich.

Indifference toward Germans outside the Reich became increasingly difficult to maintain, in large part because of the impact that the foundation of the German Empire itself had on emerging patterns of ethnic conflict in Central and Eastern Europe. German unification encouraged the development of ethnic consciousness not only among Germans outside the Empire, but among many other groups as well – Magyars, Czechs, Poles, Italians, and Slovenes, to name only some of the major ones. This process was already well underway in 1871, and it was lent impetus not only by the unification of the German states, but by social and economic change in Central Europe at the end of the century, which produced large-scale demographic redistribution and brought ethnic groups into increasing contact, self-awareness, and conflict.

This ethnic conflict was an enormously complex phenomenon.[15] In some cases, as in Russia and Hungary, it involved deliberate attempts by governments to enforce the language and customs of a dominant nationality in schools, churches, and public business.[16] In other areas the struggle went on under the cover of more tolerant official policies, but it was scarcely less bitter. Germans were involved practically everywhere in one capacity or another, but their role was most conspicuous in two areas in which they had laid claim to be the dominant ethnic group, in the Cisleithanian lands of the Habsburg monarchy and in the German Empire itself.[17]

In Austria, Germans made up the largest single national group, and their hegemony over the others was an established fact, anchored in German domination of the civilian and military bureaucracies and in the status of German as the official language of the land. Although the Austro-German government's tolerance for ethnic diversity was magnanimous by comparison to Magyar rule in the monarchy's Transleithanian lands, German hegemony came under attack on many fronts. The prototypical and most intense confrontation was between Germans and Czechs in Bohemia, Moravia, and Austrian Silesia. Here the motive force was the development of coal-mining and a textile industry (both of which were largely under German ownership and management) and the demographic changes this development occasioned, principally the large-scale movement of cheap Czech labor from the mid-lands into German areas near the perimeter of the monarchy. The resulting ethnic tension transcended class cleavages, however; it not only brought Czech industrial workers into conflict with German managers, but farm workers into conflict with landowners, Czech and German merchants into competition for customers, and the educated of both national groups into a struggle for administrative positions and public office.[18] At stake was the integrity of ethnic groups as cultural entities; the recurrent issue was language, the most conspicuous mark of ethnic identity. Professor Kann has called this conflict over language 'dreary', but to the participants it was hardly that.[19] It was intensive and it flared up everywhere questions of language were even remotely touched – in elections to municipal councils, local school boards, and church vestries, in land sales and savings banks, and in mixed marriages.

To the north the patterns were similar. The German Empire hosted three major ethnic minorities, whose claims for cultural autonomy or political severance from the new state were sources of growing tension after 1871. The most serious confrontation, because the minority was the largest and most geographically mobile, was between Germans and Poles in the Prussian eastern provinces, but the character of this antagonism differed mainly in degree from tensions between Germans and Danes in North Schleswig and between Germans and French in Alsace-Lorraine. Again the main motive forces were economic change and the demographic movements this change produced. The demand for farm labor to work the great estates in the Prussian east attracted Polish immigration from Russia, while the growing demand for cheap industrial labor in the coal mines of the Ruhr extended the Polish migratory movement from eastern to western Germany.[20] The policy of the German government with regard to Poles, as well as to the Danes and French, was Germanization, but the government pursued the policy with varying degrees of intensity and applied it inconsistently. In the north and east the policy included the attempt to promote German landholding, but as in the Habsburg monarchy, the principal issue was language, specifically the attempt to enforce the use of German in official business, schools, churches, and public meetings. The response of the minorities was to resist this policy by every legal means, and occasionally more.

In both the German Empire and Austria the ethnic conflict called forth its own characteristic form of social organization, the *Schutzvereine*, or national protective association. These organizations sprang up among every ethnic group in central Europe, and the range of their activities was extremely diversified. Some, like the Polish Marcinkowsky Association, provided professional training and economic assistance to their co-nationals, in the form of mortgage subsidies, grants, and low-interest loans. Many of these associations were in fact no more than credit unions, savings banks, or consumer cooperatives. Others supported schools, museums, and other cultural institutions for their co-nationals. Still others, such as the reading circles and choral and gymnastic societies, might be more appropriately classified as cultural societies, except that one of their purposes was to promote contact, cohesion, and self-awareness among members of the same ethnic group.[21] These associations encompassed hundreds of thousands of people, and they constituted the institutional framework of ethnic conflict throughout Central Europe.

The patterns of ethnic struggle that emerged in Central Europe in the 1870s had a vital impact on patriotic societies that appeared in the German Empire in ensuing decades, as did the institutions of this ethnic struggle. With only a few exceptions, patriotic societies in Imperial Germany were to be centrally concerned with Germans who lived on the periphery or outside of the Empire, specifically with the effort to preserve a sense of ethnic identity among these people as they came in contact with other cultures. This concentration reflected a concept of the German nation that was broader in its definition and symbolism than Bismarck's, so that a certain tension between these patriotic societies and the German government was implicit from the beginning. In addition, many of these organizations imbibed their goals and their style in emulation of the *Schutzvereine*. This feature served further to distinguish patriotic societies from other *Verbände* in the German political system. Not only did these societies engage, like other *Verbände*, in direct lobbying and the mobilization of public opinion, but they also took on a broad variety of what they called 'practical activities' designed to support the economic position and cultural cohesion of Germans outside the Reich. Much of their activity, then, consisted of a running, small-scale war with the protective associations and cultural institutions of other ethnic groups throughout the world.

Patriotic Societies of the First Generation

Hans Rosenberg has argued that the 'Great Depression', the long-term economic down-swing which began in central Europe in 1873, conditioned social, political, diplomatic, and cultural developments in this part of the world for the next quarter century.[22] Rosenberg's provocative thesis has come under fire for being deterministic and too schematic, but in some areas its validity is difficult to dispute. One can certainly trace the founding of patriotic societies in Imperial Germany directly to this economic trend, for its effects were to make Germans in the Empire acutely aware of Germans outside of it.

One of the reasons why Rosenberg's thesis about the centrality of economic crisis is plausible is that so many people were conscious of a crisis. Hans-Ulrich Wehler has documented the prolonged public discussion which took place in Germany after 1873 about the causes and implications of the economic down-turn.[23] Although the discussion was fed from many sources and reflected diverse concerns and interests, a consensus emerged rapidly. At the root of the problem, so ran the argument, lay overproduction, the incapacity of the German domestic market to absorb the products of an expanded industrial plant. The economic consequence, documented vividly in growth statistics, was stagnation; the social repercussions promised to be more foreboding – reduced wages, strikes, unemployment, and violent disorder. In the lugubrious atmosphere of the mid- and late 1870s publicists also turned to another phenomenon which now struck them as far more alarming than it had before. *Auswanderung*, the emigration overseas each year of tens of thousands of Germans, had begun to take on massive proportions decades earlier without arousing much concern in Germany over its social or political implications. Paradoxically, even as migration dropped off significantly in the 1870s, writers began to view it as the direct consequence of economic stagnation and social unrest, and they equated the phenomenon with an irredeemable loss of manpower and talent for the fatherland.[24]

General agreement reigned not only about the origins and likely repercussions of the economic crisis which Germany confronted, but also about a solution to the problem. Empire emerged as the antidote to all social, economic, and demographic facets of the crisis. The stimulus afforded to German industry and commerce by imperial markets and products would reinvigorate the German economy and reduce social tension. Empire would also solve the problem of emigration, not by curtailing it but rather by redirecting it into new areas, where the establishment of settlement colonies would protect emigrant Germans from the threat of assimilation into foreign cultures, enabling them to retain both their ethnic identity and their ties to the fatherland. These themes were the subjects of a flood of literature which appeared in the late 1870s from the pens of influential publicists such as Ernst von Weber, Wilhelm Hübbe-Schleiden, and Friedrich Fabri, whose tract, *Does Germany Need Colonies? (Bedarf Deutschland Kolonien?)*, which appeared in 1878, was the most influential of all.[25] The ideas of these writers constituted an unabashed program of social imperialism: a domestic crisis, which threatened to bring far-reaching changes to the structure of social and political power in Germany, was to be defused by exporting it.

The virtue of this program was its broad appeal. It spoke directly to the interests of export merchants and industrialists. It also appealed to masses of people, chiefly civil servants and small businessmen, whose anxieties derived from social insecurities born of the depression. If the economic benefits of empire extolled by colonial publicists attracted the one group of people, the other responded more to the 'emigrationist' vision of settlement colonies as new centers of opportunity abroad and a vent for social tension at home.[26]

It is difficult to overstate the importance of this ideological consensus in the development of national self-consciousness in Imperial Germany. Fabri and the other publicists of the 1870s characterized imperial expansion as something far more than a venture to serve the interests of select entrepreneurs and émigrés; they identified empire as a national symbol and an issue which would have vital consequences for the interests, integrity, and survival of the entire national unit. No less significant was the change that the ideology of social imperialism implied in the definition of the national unit itself. The emigrationist argument was particularly emphatic that the strength and vitality of the Reich were inextricably linked to the fate of Germans living abroad and that the assimilation of these people into other cultures represented an irreparable loss to the German nation. The German nation, in other words, could no longer be coterminous with the frontiers of the Reich; the nation comprehended people who spoke German and carried German culture everywhere in the world. And although most of the discussion of Germans outside the Reich was devoted to overseas emigration, the concept of the German nation inherent in the emigrationist literature clearly included German-speaking people living elsewhere in Europe as well. In sum, the discussion surrounding the economic crisis of the 1870s produced an ideological consensus on a necessary solution, but this solution required a redefinition of the national symbolism. These symbols now included empire, culture, and language; they implied a vastly broadened perspective on the definition of national issues, as well as on the definition of the national community itself.

This broadened perspective marked the popular agitation that began during the 1870s in favor of overseas expansion. The agitation took many forms, from the entreaties of chambers of commerce and other merchant associations to the activities of local geographical societies and other organizations that were founded to promote interest in the fate of Germans who had emigrated. Because expansion could only take place with the intervention or support of the state, all of this agitation was ultimately directed toward Berlin, and its ultimate goal was the modification of the official symbols of the nation.

The most important of the groups to appear in this period was the Central Association for Commercial Geography and German Interests Abroad (*Zentralverein für Handelsgeographie und deutsche Interessen im Auslande*).[27] It was founded in Berlin in 1878, and its leading personality was the statistician Robert Jannasch. Its program was a synthesis of the most common economic and emigrationist arguments in favor of overseas expansion: German settlements abroad, their numbers multiplied and their contacts with the German homeland assiduously cultivated, were to become the secure foundation for German commercial expansion. The appeal of this synthetic program was evident in the establishment of similar groups in other cities, including Barmen, Chemnitz, Munich, Würzburg, Jena, Kassel, and, in view of later developments most significantly, in Leipzig, where another statistician, Ernst Hasse, founded the Association for Commercial Geography and Colonial Policy (*Verein für Handelsgeographie und Kolonialpolitik*). Each of these groups, which maintained a loose affiliation with the Central Association in Berlin, brought together two rather distinct social groups – on the one hand, merchants, bankers, industrial exporters, and other businessmen who were attracted by the commercial or social benefits of imperial expansion, and, on the other hand, academics whose primary interest lay in the cultural and demographic implications of emigration.

This loose organizational network provided the bases for the first two major patriotic societies in Imperial Germany. One of these owed its immediate origins to the impact of the Great Depression in Austria. Here the economic slump had by 1879 undermined the political position of the German liberals, the upper-middle-class advocates not only of industrial capitalism with minimal state interference, but of administrative centralism, which meant the continued hegemony of the Germans who dominated the central bureaucracy. Elections in 1879 revealed the liberals' weakened position and occasioned a fundamental reorientation in Austrian politics, with the formation of the so-called 'Iron Ring' of the new premier, Eduard von Taafe.[28] The props of this new parliamentary configuration were assorted anti-liberal groups, including representatives of the Czech minority, whose support the Taafe ministry purchased with concessions to their demands for autonomy, including establishment of a Czech university in Prague and a language ordinance whose effect was to place Czech on virtually an equal footing with German as the administrative language in Bohemia and Moravia.

Taafe could scarcely have foreseen the vehemence of the reaction his policies provoked among large groups of Germans, who were alarmed over what appeared to be a generalized assault on their culture and their dominant role in the monarchy. The initial center of the storm was the university in Vienna, where a group of recent graduates, including Viktor Adler, Heinrich Friedjung, and Engelbert Pernerstorfer – a remarkable troika whose subsequent careers became radically divergent – established in May 1880 the German School Association (*Deutscher Schulverein*). The purpose of the organization was to lend financial support to the construction of German schools 'on our linguistic frontiers and in linguistically mixed areas', where, the founders noted, 'thousands upon thousands of children of German parents grow up without a German school and hence are lost to the German people'.[29] The dramatic growth of the School Association was symptomatic of how widely their anxiety was shared among Austrian Germans. By early 1881 22,000 people had joined, and the group's membership continued to expand rapidly for the next several years; in 1887 it stood at 120,000 in 1,174 local chapters throughout Austria.[30]

The national protest in which the School Association was born reverberated for decades in the Habsburg monarchy, soon radicalized under the leadership of men such as Georg von Schönerer and Karl Lueger, who had been present, though only in minor capacities, at the founding of the School Association. The reverberations also extended immediately across the frontier into Germany, where interest in the Austrian crisis was widespread. Large amounts of money flowed from Germany into the coffers of the School Association; citizens of the Reich became members, and in a number of German cities local chapters were formed. The role of mediator and coordinator fell to the Central Association for Commercial Geography in Berlin, which in June 1881 acceded to the School Association as a chapter and used its own network to encourage the formation of local chapters in some fifty other German cities.

Difficulties soon arose, however, which made it necessary to reorganize the German chapters independently of the Austrian parent. In the first place, the intentions of the German groups were significantly broader than those of the Austrians. The Austrian School Association limited the range of its support to areas in the Austrian sector of the monarchy; the Germans proposed in addition to support German schools not only in the Hungarian part of the monarchy, but throughout the world. The Germans' interests coincided, that is, with their imperial aspirations, which most Austro-Germans did not share. If philosophical differences with the Austrians raised the possibility of establishing an independent school association in Germany, a court decision, which interpreted the Austrian law of associations to forbid Austrian organizations from establishing local chapters in foreign countries, made this step unavoidable.

Accordingly, on 15 August 1881 the General German School Association (*Allgemeiner Deutscher Schulverein*) was founded in Berlin.[31] In part because local groups had already been in contact with Vienna or tied to the Central Association in Berlin, the growth of the new organization in Germany was rapid. In 1883 membership stood at over 9,000, and there were seventy-six local chapters; by the end of the decade the General

German School Association comprised nearly 40,000 members and 356 chapters.[32] Expansion did not take place without friction, however. The plans of the Berlin group called for a centralized organization, with the seat of power in Berlin itself, as it was in the Central Association. These plans ran aground on particularist suspicions among groups outside Prussia, especially in the Kingdom of Saxony, where interest in the work of the School Association was very strong because of the geographical proximity of the Habsburg territories, and in Baden, a center from which emigration had earlier radiated. Because of this resistance, the School Association remained decentralized. The local chapters were autonomous, empowered not only to retain most of revenues they raised through dues, but to undertake support work independent of central headquarters in Berlin.

The goal of the School Association, as announced in its statutes, was 'to preserve for Germandom those Germans living outside the Reich and to support them as much as possible in their efforts to remain German or to become German again'. The means envisaged were considerably more modest than this ambitious goal might have suggested. The association was to 'support and, if circumstances dictate, construct German schools and libraries, furnish German books, distribute appropriate literature, [and] place and support German teachers'.[33] The organization chose thus to cast a blind eye to the possible political ramifications of its program and to limit its activities to cultural support. This strategy was encouraged by the autonomy of the local chapters, which made it difficult for the School Association to speak with a single voice on political issues. The strategy also conformed to the philosophy of Richard Boeckh, who was the organization's most eloquent and articulate ideologue during the first two decades of its existence. Boeckh was a Herderian. He regarded the German nation as but one of many ethnic units, a cultural community defined by the bonds of language, but one with no prior claims over others.[34] This vision appeared increasingly anachronistic in an age of militant ethnic conflict, but the militance of the School Association remained relatively muted in the period before the war. Although the organization did engage in some propaganda as an advocate of the interests of Germans abroad, the focus of its activity remained in the field of raising money for the practical purposes of school support.

The founding and initial expansion of the School Association in the early 1880s coincided with the intensification of the economic slump and an upsurge in emigration. These phenomena in turn stimulated the organizational consolidation of the colonial movement. As in the case of the School Association, the Central Association for Commercial Geography played a leading role, but it was eventually swallowed into a larger national organization.

The history of the colonial movement in the 1880s has been recounted many times, so it is necessary here only to mention the highlights.[35] The proliferation of local societies to promote colonial expansion suggested the need for a stronger organizational framework than the Central Association could provide. The need became more acute after 1881, when Friedrich Fabri founded the West German Association for Colonization and Export

(*Westdeutscher Verein für Kolonisation und Export*) in order to emphasize the interest of Westphalian businessmen in colonies. At the same time, the colonial movement took on political overtones in a manner the school-support movement never did, for it became linked to the fate of the National Liberal Party, at a time when this party, its ranks decimated in the secession crisis, found itself badly in need of a new integrating issue.[36]

A coalition of National Liberal Party leaders, spokesmen of north and west German export interests, and colonial publicists provided the initiative for the first amalgamation within the colonial movement with the founding, in Frankfurt, of the German Colonial Association (*Deutscher Kolonial-verein*) in December 1882. Well aware that the preservation of a broad popular coalition demanded careful balancing of economic and emigrationist arguments, leaders of the new organization branded colonial expansion a national issue, citing every plausible reason – 'the need to expand our markets, the growing significance of overseas trade, the deep impact of emigration on our social and economic life [and] the national interest in maintaining a lasting and firm tie between our excess population [*überschüssige Kräfte*] and the Fatherland'[37] The goal of the new organization was to promote colonial expansion by means of mobilizing popular sentiment in favor of it.

Within a year the Colonial Association had incorporated most of the existing colonial societies into its ranks. But the future of the organization, and indeed of the entire colonial movement, was decisively affected by the actions of the German government. Bismarck's colonial policy has been the topic of a long debate, out of which a number of conclusions have emerged. Although the chancellor was not directly involved in the founding of the Colonial Association, he was well aware of the developing colonial movement and ever alive to the possibility of exploiting it politically. Whether or not he regarded the acquisition of colonies as an attractive strategy for defusing the domestic tension occasioned by the depression is a good deal less clear than is his contempt for the idea that colonies were essential as outlets for emigration. In all likelihood, Bismarck viewed colonialism skeptically, and when he did move in 1884–5 to establish German colonial claims in West Africa and the Pacific, his decision was influenced little, if at all, by the arguments of the Colonial Association; the decision was instead the product of Bismarck's calculations about domestic politics, specifically his seizing the opportunity to isolate the left-liberals, who were known to oppose formal colonies because of the expense, and to reinforce a parliamentary coalition among the parties of the right.

Whatever his calculations, Bismarck's move to acquire colonies had the most far-reaching ramifications for the history of patriotic societies in Germany. In establishing the colonies and in defending this decision in the press and the Reichstag, Bismarck seemed to confirm the proposition that the colonial publicists had long been advocating – that empire was a national issue and that the development of the German nation had not come to a conclusion in 1871. By lending the incalculable authority and prestige of his *imprimatur* to these propositions, Bismarck appeared to incorporate empire into the shrine of national symbols and with it a conception of the German nation that looked far beyond the frontiers of the Reich.

Bismarck's action produced immediate results, some of them unanticipated and uncomfortable. The growth of the Colonial Association accelerated rapidly in an atmosphere of adventure and accomplishment, and in anticipation of further colonial acquisitions. By early 1885 membership stood at more than 10,000.[38] The Colonial Association also now found a rival. The new organization was the brain-child of the most colorful and troubling personality in the history of the German colonial movement. Carl Peters's psycho-biography would be a fascinating study; until it appears, there seems to be little reason to dispute the judgment of Fritz Ferdinand Müller, who, upon surveying the amalgam of sado-masochism, delusions of grandeur, self-doubt, and irrepressible ambition in his personality, pronounced Peters a psychopath.[39] He was, in any event, an extremely erratic and obstreperous man. Animated by visions of a 'German India' – a vast German empire in East Africa, which would serve the needs of German settlers and traders and would become the foundation of German world power – Peters and a group of friends established the Society for German Colonization (*Gesellschaft für deutsche Kolonisation*) in the spring of 1884. Unlike the Colonial Association, whose activities emphasized propaganda, Peters's organization was founded in order actually to establish colonies; the role of its membership was accordingly to fund Peters's own expeditions to East Africa. Largely because the Colonial Association's leaders believed Peters to be an irresponsible adventurer (and they were right), they withheld financial support from him, so he was reduced to relying on contributions from the small businessmen and subaltern officials who attended the rallies he staged and made up the bulk of his society's membership.

With this support Peters did in fact lead a team to East Africa late in 1884, where he signed a series of treaties with tribal chieftains proclaiming German sovereignty over large tracts of land.[40] The problem was that Peters acted without the approval of the German government; indeed, he simply ignored a directive to desist from Bismarck, who was growing increasingly uneasy about possible diplomatic complications with England. At home, though, Peters's adventures had made him a hero in the colonial movement, and Bismarck found himself compelled in February 1885 to declare a German protectorate over the areas Peters had claimed.

Bismarck was getting the first taste of a problem that was to plague his successors. He discovered the difficulty of harnessing people like Peters, who claimed to act in the national interest (and Bismarck himself had just declared empire to be in the national interest) and who enjoyed loud popular support. In trying to put reins on Peters, Bismarck found allies in the larger mercantile and industrial interests that dominated the rival Colonial Association. Peters's vulnerability was his need for more money to continue his work in Africa. After lengthy negotiations Bismarck provided it, but at a considerable price. In 1887 the German government chartered the German East Africa Company as the official concession company to develop and trade in the region. The charter provided that Peters and his friends were to be shareholders, but they were swamped by the infusion of large amounts of money from Hamburg and Westphalia.

The involvement of big commercial and industrial interests in financing the East African venture also robbed Peters's society of its raison d'être and paved the way for the final consolidation of the colonial movement. In 1887 Peters's group merged with the Colonial Association to form the German Colonial Society (*Deutsche Kolonialgesellschaft*), which comprised a membership of 15,000. It was, however, an unequal partnership, for the same interests that had controlled the Colonial Association emerged in the leading positions in the new Colonial Society. Like its predecessors, the Colonial Society attempted to balance economic and emigrationist arguments in its program and propaganda; this balance reflected the divergent interests that coalesced in the Colonial Society, for while the men in the leadership were plainly interested in empire for money, most of the members were more receptive to emigrationist arguments.[41]

Both the German School Association and the German Colonial Society took form against the backdrop of dramatic events outside the German Empire. The third patriotic society founded in the 1880s was the product of the same new national self-consciousness, but its origins were less dramatic. Concern in Germany over the threat to the German language extended beyond the initial outrage which arose in reaction to Taafe's linguistic concessions to the Czechs. This concern was reflected as well in a growing sensitivity about the purity and integrity of the German language itself. Several local societies for the protection of the German language were already in existence in 1885, when Hermann Riegel, an art historian and director of the ducal museum in Braunschweig, issued a public appeal for a national society. In January 1886 the General German Language Association (*Allgemeiner Deutscher Sprachverein*) was established, with Riegel as chairman, for the purpose of 'fostering the genuine spirit and unique essence of the German language, awakening love and understanding for the mother tongue, and activating a sense of its purity, correctness, clarity, and beauty'.[42] In the first instance, the organization proposed to purge the language of all unnecessary foreign words or expressions. This was evidently an appealing idea, for the association underwent a rapid expansion during the first years of its existence. By 1887 it had 7,000 members organized in ninety local chapters; in 1890 the membership stood at 12,000.[43] Like the School Association, the Language Association formally eschewed political activity; it concentrated on publishing scholarly studies and drawing attention to the intrusion of foreign words into the manifold phases of public and private life. Merchants and bankers overeager to court foreign customers, government officials (especially diplomats in their devotion to French phrases), the military (whose system of ranks betrayed French influence too), and even sportsmen who found 'tennis' a more appealing game than *Rasenballspiel* all felt the indignation of the guardians of the language who congregated in the *Sprachverein*.

As innocuous as the Language Association's activities might have appeared, it was idle to call them non-political. No less than the work of the School Association, the campaign of the Language Association had far-reaching political implications, for this campaign was also underlain by a concept of the German nation that was based on language and hence transcended the frontiers of the Reich. It was no accident that in 1906 the organization had twenty-four chapters in Austria–Hungary, one in Switzerland, and three in the United States.[44]

Although they were founded to serve different goals, the three patriotic societies which appeared in the 1880s had a great deal in common. Most apparent was the social complexion of their memberships. While the proportions of the configuration varied among the three, the same kinds of people predominated in each, and their distinguishing characteristics were wealth or a university education (see Appendix, Tables 5.6, 5.7, 5.8). Businessmen were a little more prominent in the Colonial Society, where the prospect of profits from empire no doubt appealed to the holders of commercial and industrial capital. The academically educated were more conspicuous in the School Association and the Language Association, and they included university-trained teachers, professionals, and civil servants. An analysis of the attraction of academics to these organizations is more complicated than explaining the presence of businessmen in the Colonial Society, for the profit motive played no significant role in the campaigns to defend the language and support schools. Because this analysis also bears directly on the Pan-German League, it is best postponed. It would, in any event, be misleading to draw too great a distinction between the Colonial Society and the other two organizations. Businessmen could be found in the School and Language Associations, while men of academic education were also prominent in the Colonial Society.

This social convergence corresponded to ideological affinities among the three organizations. Excepting those who admitted that they were only interested in empire for profit, the people who molded public thinking about empire spoke no less emphatically of defending German culture than did the men who sent money to schools in the Habsburg monarchy or protested against listing entrees in French on the menus of German restaurants. In this respect, the chief differences among the three societies were less social or ideological than in the geographical emphasis of their concern. The Colonial Society focused on overseas areas, arguing that the creation of settlement colonies would protect the bearers of German culture from assimilation. The School Association concentrated on the Habsburg monarchy, where the ethnic conflict was both most proximate and intense, while the Language Association found plenty to do at home. However, even the lines that marked geographical regions of concentration were fluid. The Language Association had chapters in German communities overseas, the School Association supported German schools in Latin America, and leaders of the Colonial Society were also interested in Eastern and Central Europe, both for the prospects this area offered for economic penetration and – in an era when the word *Lebensraum* had not taken on the connotations it suffers today – because the area seemed eminently suited for German settlement colonies.[45]

All three of the new patriotic societies shared a common conception of the German nation and invoked a broadened national symbolism. In the ideologies of all three the German nation comprised the entirety of the German *Volk*, an ethnic unit defined by language and culture. This definition linked the fate of Germans in the Reich with that of Germans everywhere else in the world. That this vision could only with the greatest difficulty be confined to the realm of culture and that in an age of ethnic conflict it had ultimately to raise questions of power and of Germany's role in international politics was evident to many people. Not the least of these was Bismarck, who well recognized the challenge this vision posed to the official image of the *Staatsnation* and the difficulties it would raise in Germany's relations to the other powers.[46] Bismarck himself, however, was substantially responsible for the growing currency of a rival image of the nation. Whatever his own motives, his decision to acquire colonies in 1884–5 seemed to endorse a broader, ethnic view of the nation. So too did the laws he pushed through the Prussian diet in 1886, which marked the beginning of a new phase of the policy of Germanizing ethnic minorities – a phase whose chief characteristic was the attempt to establish German settlement colonies in the predominantly Polish areas of the country and, in this manner, to promote German culture by contesting the economic foundations of a rival culture.

Bismarck was running a great risk. In invoking the symbols and imagery of a new concept of the nation, he gained a large body of articulate and enthusiastic popular support, which he used to strengthen his hand vis-à-vis the Reichstag. The difficulty was that this popular enthusiasm could turn against the government once official policy no longer conformed to the expectations of the newly mobilized popular forces. Each of the patriotic societies represented *in potentia* a sorcerer's apprentice, and the problems of keeping them under control were apparent even during Bismarck's tenure in office. For the most part he succeeded, owing largely to the power he exercised as guardian of national symbols in Imperial Germany; it was simply inconceivable to call Bismarck unpatriotic in public. Bismarck was aided by the professed determination of the School and Language Associations to remain out of politics. The latter organization was more successful, and for its efforts was rewarded with the conspicuous encouragement of the German government, as many top officials documented, by joining the Language Association, their opinion that it was a proper and worthy patriotic undertaking. The School Association received no such encouragement, even though its decentralization kept its political profile low; the organization could not plausibly contend that subsidizing schools in Hungary, within the jurisdiction of a foreign ministry of public instruction, was an unpolitical act. As a consequence, Bismarck instructed officials to avoid any action that might be construed as governmental endorsement of the School Association's work.[47]

The colonial movement presented much more serious problems. The organizations that mobilized popular support in favor of empire made no pretense of abjuring politics; and when, after 1886, Bismarck made it clear that he was no longer interested in expanding Germany's colonial domains, he dealt a major blow to the expectations of the people who had vocally supported him earlier. Mounting frustrations in the Colonial Society produced open criticism of the chancellor, which leaders of the society, particularly Fabri, attempted to mute and keep 'calm, factual' and 'sober'.[48] Tensions between Bismarck and the Colonial Society nevertheless mounted; they peaked in 1889, when the chancellor again, with an eye to a possible clash with England, disavowed the attempt of Carl Peters to extend German holdings in East Africa.[49] These tensions played a role in Bismarck's fall from power in early 1890, in so far as they lowered the chancellor's stock among the *Kartell* parties in the Reichstag, in which the Colonial Society was well represented.[50]

Ironically, however, even as the antagonism mounted between Bismarck and the Colonial Society, a relationship was growing that would in the future enable Bismarck's successors to silence opposition to official policy within the Colonial Society and to control the organization effectively.[51] German policy with respect to administering the new colonial holdings took shape during the last years of Bismarck's chancellorship. The hallmark of this policy was to concentrate administrative responsibility in private hands and to reduce the public role – and cost – to a minimum, restricted mainly to the preservation of order. To this end, the government encouraged the formation of private joint-stock companies, such as the German East Africa Company, to develop the colonies economically, and it offered these companies a broad range of lucrative land and mining concessions, monopolies, state contracts, and subsidies, often with no conditions attached.[52] The men who came to dominate the national leadership of the Colonial Society were the managers and leading shareholders of the colonial companies, and they needed no instruction on the advantages of close cooperation with the government, especially once the Colonial Society itself began as a corporate body in the 1890s to engage, with the blessings of the government, in a number of 'practical activities'. These included construction of harbor facilities, railroads, and irrigation projects in the colonies, the establishment of steamship lines to the colonies, and the promotion of German emigration to colonial areas.

The relationship that developed between the German government and the Colonial Society, now the lobby for the colonial companies, was very cozy. The government, most immediately the Colonial Section of the Foreign Office, relied on the Colonial Society to raise private capital for investment in the colonies, to disseminate information for prospective settlers, and to lobby in support of government policies in the Reichstag.[53] Leaders of the Colonial Society were regular advisors to the Colonial Section on all matters of policy, including the colonial budget and tariffs; representatives of the society also dominated the *Kolonialrat*, the board of citizens established in 1890 to advise the Foreign Office on colonial policy.[54]

The ties that evolved in the 1890s between the government and the German Colonial Society amounted to a condominium, and they made the expression of sustained antagonism toward the government virtually impossible within the society. After 1890 the Colonial Society supported the government's policies consistently, even when these policies seemed to work to the detriment of German colonial interests and were in fact being so criticized by other patriotic organizations. Opposition did, to be sure, survive in some of the local chapters, but the structure of the organization was authoritarian enough that the national leadership could, without much difficulty, move, sometimes at the urging of the Foreign Office, to suppress it.[55]

The patriotic societies founded in the 1880s were to remain comparatively docile for the rest of the prewar period, but the early history of these societies revealed sources of great potential friction between them and the German government. At issue was the definition and custodianship of the symbols of the nation. While the German government sought to define the nation politically, as a *Staatsnation* within the frontiers of 1871, the Colonial Society, the School Association, and the Language Association all appropriated an alternative symbolism as they defined the German nation in the more comprehensive terms of language, culture, ethnicity, and empire. Excepting only a brief episode in the mid-1880s, during which Bismarck appeared to endorse the arguments of the colonial enthusiasts, the government rejected the alternative symbolism and, in keeping with the centrality of the monarchy in the symbolism of the *Staatsnation*, asserted its own exclusive authority to define the national symbols. The rivalry of symbolisms thus implied a rivalry over custodianship of the national symbols themselves. This rivalry between the government and the patriotic societies remained for the most part quiet during the 1880s, for a number of reasons. The structure of the societies that were established in this decade and the goals they set for themselves encouraged their docility; but so too did the fact that their incubation occurred during Bismarck's chancellorship. As the patriarch of the new nation-state, Bismarck stood practically above attack in the realm of national issues. He remained the unrivalled custodian of the national symbols, and his authority was unchallengeable in defining and interpreting the national catechism. However, the enormous potential for opposition, which resided in the mobilization of popular forces in the name of emotionally laden symbols, became actualized immediately after Bismarck's departure from power in 1890.

Notes

1 Hans Rosenberg, *Grosse Depression und Bismarckzeit: Wirtschaftsablauf, Gesellschaft und Politik in Mitteleuropa* (Berlin, 1967), pp. 120–1; James J. Sheehan, *German Liberalism in the Nineteenth Century* (Chicago, Ill., 1978), p. 275; cf. Hans-Ulrich Wehler, 'Zur Funktion und Struktur der nationalen Kampfverbände im Kaiserreich', in Werner Conze et al. (eds). *Modernisierung und nationale Gesellschaft im ausgehenden 18 und 19. Jahrhundert* (Berlin, 1979), pp. 113–23.

2 See Eugen Weber, *Action française: Royalism and Reaction in Twentieth Century France* (Stanford, Calif., 1962), pp. 63–4; Salvatore Saladino, 'Italy', in Hans Rogger and Eugen Weber (eds). *The European Right: A Historical Profile* (Berkeley, Calif. and Los Angeles, 1966), p. 231; Armin Rappaport, *The Navy League of the United States* (Detroit, Mich., 1962); Paul M. Kennedy and Anthony J. Nicholls (eds), *Nationalist and Racialist Movements in Britain and Germany before 1914* (London, 1980).

3 See George L. Mosse, *The Nationalization of the Masses: Political Symbolism and Mass Movements in Germany from the Napoleonic Wars through the Third Reich* (New York, 1975).

4 Stürmer, *Regierung und Reichstag*.

5   See in addition to ibid., pp. 311–12: H. Gollwitzer, 'Der Cäsarismus Napoleons III. im Widerhall der öffentlichen Meinung Deutschlands', *HZ*, vol. 173 (1952), pp. 23–75; Ernst Engelberg, 'Zur Entstehung und historischen Stellung des preussisch-deutschen Bonapartismus', in Fritz Klein and Joachim Streisand (eds), *Beiträge zum neuen Geschichtsbild: Zum 60. Geburtstag von Alfed Meusel* (Berlin, 1956), pp. 236–51; Dieter Groh, 'Caesarismus: Napoleonismus, Bonapartismus, Führer, Chef, Imperialismus', in Otto Brunner *et al.* (eds), *Geschichtliche Grundbegriffe: Historisches Lexikon zur politisch-sozialen Sprache in Deutschland* (Stuttgart, 1972–), Vol. 1, pp. 726–71.

6   Thomas Nipperdey, 'Interessenverbände und Parteien in Deutschland vor dem Ersten Weltkrieg', in *Gesellschaft, Kultur, Theorie*, pp. 319–37. On the role of these organizations see Helmut Böhme, *Deutschlands Weg zur Grossmacht: Studien zum Verhältnis von Wirtschaft und Staat während der Reichsgrundüngszeit 1848–1881* (Cologne, 1966), pp. 341–409; Wolfram Fischer, 'Staatsverwaltung und Interessenverbände im Deutschen Reich', in Michael Stürmer (ed.), *Das kaiserliche Deutschland: Politik und Gesellschaft* (Düsseldorf, 1970), pp. 340–77; Fritz Blaich, *Staat und Verbände in Deutschland zwischen 1871 und 1945* (Wiesbaden, 1979), esp. pp. 5–51.

7   Thomas Nipperdey, 'Interessenverbände', p. 324.

8   M. Rainer Lepsius, 'Parteiensystem und Sozialstruktur: zum Problem der Demokratisierung der deutschen Gesellschaft', in *Wirtschaft, Geschichte und Wirtschaftsgeschichte: Festschrift zum 65. Geburtstag von Friedrich Lütge* (Stuttgart, 1966), pp. 371–93.

9   See James J. Sheehan, 'What is German history? reflections on the role of the *nation* in German history and historiography', *JMH*, vol. 53 (1981), pp. 1–23.

10 Theodor Schieder, *Das Deutsche Reich von 1871 als Nationalstaat* (Cologne and Opladen, 1961), esp. pp. 25, 52, 86.

11 ibid., pp. 72–87.

12 Klaus J. Bade, *Friedrich Fabri und der Imperialismus in der Bismarckzeit: Revolution – Depression – Expansion* (Freiburg, 1975), p. 77.

13 Schieder, *Nationalstaat*, pp. 48–51; Klaus Urner, *Die Deutschen in der Schweiz: Von den Anfängen der Kolonienbildung bis zum Ausbruch des Ersten Weltkrieges* (Frauenfeld and Stuttgart, 1976), p. 46.

14 ibid., pp. 31, 47.

15 The best schematic survey remains Oscar Jaszi, *The Dissolution of the Habsburg Monarchy* (Chicago, Ill., and London, 1929); see also Robert A. Kann, *The Multinational Empire: Nationalism and National Reform in the Habsburg Monarchy, 1848–1918*, 2 vols (New York, 1950); Richard Charmatz, *Oesterreichs innere Geschichte von 1848 bis 1907*, 2 vols (Leipzig, 1911–12).

16 Michael H. Haltzel, 'The Russification of the Baltic Germans: a dysfunctional aspect of imperial modernization', in Arvid Ziedonis, Jr, *et al.* (eds), *Baltic History* (Colombus, Ohio, 1974), pp. 143–52.

17 See Hermann Ullmann, *Pioniere Europas: Die volksdeutsche Bewegung und ihre Lehren* (Munich, 1956), pp. 15–24.

18 Jaszi, pp. 248–70, 283–97; cf. Karl Türk, *Böhmen, Mähren und Schlesien* (Munich, 1898), p. 58.

19 Kann, Vol. 1, p. 192.

20 The literature on this subject is enormous. The most recent works include: Roland Baier, *Der deutsche Osten als soziale Frage* (Cologne and Vienna, (1979), pp. 1–90; William W. Hagen, *Germans, Poles and Jews: The Nationality Conflict in the Prussian East, 1772–1914* (Chicago, 1980); Hans-Ulrich Wehler, 'Die Polen im Ruhrgebiet bis 1918', *Vierteljahrshefte für Sozial- und Wirtschaftsgeschichte*, vol. 48 (1961), pp. 203–35; Richard C. Murphy, 'The Polish trade union in the Ruhr coal field:Labor organization and ethnicity in Wilhelmian Germany', *CEH*, vol. 11 (1978), pp. 335–47; Christoph Klessmann, *Polnische Bergarbeiter im Ruhrgebiet 1870–1945: Soziale Integration und nationale Subkultur einer Minderheit in der deutschen Industriegesellschaft* (Göttingen, 1978). On North Schleswig see Oswald Hauser, 'Obrigkeitsstaat und demokratisches Prinzip im Nationalitätenkampf. Preussen in Nordschleswig', *HZ*, vol. 192 (1962), pp. 318–61. And on Alsace-Lorraine, Dan P. Silverman, *Reluctant Union: Alsace-Lorraine and Imperial Germany, 1871–1918* (University Park and London, 1972).

21 See Franz Guntram Schultheiss, *Deutschnationales Vereinswesen: Ein Beitrag zur*

Geschichte deutschen Nationalgefühls (Munich, 1897); Christian Petzet, *Die presussischen Ostmarken* (Munich, 1898), pp. 22, 35; Erwin Barta and Karl Bell, *Geschichte der Schutzarbeit am deutschen Volkstum* (Dresden, 1930); Hagen, pp. 225–65.

22 Rosenberg, *Grosse Depression und Bismarckzeit.*
23 Wehler, *Bismarck und der Imperialismus*, pp. 112–57.
24 Mack Walker, *Germany and the Emigration, 1816–1885* (Cambridge, Mass., 1964), pp. 175–227.
25 Bade, pp. 67–104; Wehler, *Bismarck und der Imperialismus*, pp. 142–54; Woodruff D. Smith, 'The ideology of German colonialism, 1840–1918' (PhD Diss., University of Chicago, 1974), pp. 85–190; Smith, 'The ideology of German colonialism, 1840–1906', JMH, vol. 46 (1974), pp. 645–52.
26 Smith, 'Ideology', JMH, pp. 645–50; Bade, p. 23.
27 See ibid., pp. 102–5; Schultheiss, *Vereinswesen*, pp. 25–8; Gerhard Weidenfeller, *VDA: Verein für das Deutschtum im Ausland. Allgemeiner Deutscher Schulverein (1881–1918). Ein Beitrag zur Geschichte des deutschen Nationalismus und Imperialismus im Kaiserreich* (Berne and Frankfurt a. M., 1976), pp. 141–54.
28 See Kahn, pp. 200–5; William A. Jenks, *Austria under the Iron Ring, 1879–1893* (Charlottesville, Va, 1965).
29 Quoted in Weidenfeller, p. 111; cf. Schultheiss, *Vereinswesen*, pp. 34–43; William J. McGrath, *Dionysian Art and Populist Politics in Austria* (New Haven, Conn. and London, 1974), pp. 168–9.
30 Schultheiss, *Vereinswesen*, p. 40. In 1912 there were 2,300 local chapters with 190,000 members.
31 Weidenfeller, *VDA*, is now the standard work. See also Günter Haude and Kurt Possekel, 'Verein für das Deutschtum im Ausland (VDA) 1881–1945', in Fricke, *Handbuch*, Vol. 2, pp. 716–29; Karl Bell, 'Geschichte des Vereins für das Deutschtum im Ausland', in Bartha and Bell, pp. 101–201; Schultheiss, *Vereinswesen*, pp. 45–48.
32 Weidenfeller, pp. 214–15.
33 ibid., pp. 176–8.
34 ibid., pp. 156–65; Schieder, *Nationalstaat*, pp. 27, 51.
35 Klaus Klauss, 'Die deutsche Kolonialgesellschaft und die deutsche Kolonialpolitik von den Anfängen bis 1895' (Diss. phil., Berlin, 1966); Richard Victor Pierard, 'The German Colonial Society, 1882–1914' (PhD Diss., State University of Iowa, 1964); Willibald von Stuemer and Erich Duems, *Fünfzig Jahre Deutsche Kolonialgesellschaft 1882–1932* (Berlin, 1932); Helmut Müller and Hans-Joachim Fieber, 'Deutsche Kolonialgesellschaft (DKG) 1982 (1887)–1933', in Fricke, *Handbuch*, Vol. 1, pp. 390–407; Fritz Ferdinand Müller. *Deutschland – Zanzibar – Ostafrika: Geschichte einer deutschen Kolonialeroberung 1884–1890* (Berlin, 1959); Woodruff D. Smith, *The German Colonial Empire* (Chapel Hill, NC, 1978), pp. 3–47; Wehler, *Bismarck und der Imperialismus*, esp. pp. 158–68; Bade, esp. pp. 136–85.
36 Dan S. White, *The Splintered Party: National Liberalism in Hessen and the Reich, 1867–1918* (Cambridge, Mass., 1976), p. 119.
37 Quoted in Bade, pp. 176–7.
38 ibid., p. 246.
39 Müller, *Deutschland – Zanzibar – Ostafrika*, p. 97; cf. Wehler, *Bismarck und der Imperialismus*, pp. 336–9; Henry Bair, 'Carl Peters and German colonialism' (PhD Diss., Stanford University, 1968).
40 For a discussion of the recent literature on this episode and on the broader topic of German colonialism in Africa see Jost Dülffer, 'Deutsche Kolonialherrschaft in Afrika', NPL, vol. 26 (1981), pp. 458–73.
41 Bade, pp. 197–309; Smith, 'Ideology', JMH, pp. 651–2.
42 ZStAM, Rep. 77, Tit. 1053 Nr. 241, Bd. 1, Satzungen des Allgemeinen Deutschen Sprachvereins. There is no history of the Language Association, but see Schultheiss, *Vereinswesen*, pp. 73–5; Hermann Dunger, 'Hermann Riegel, der Stifter des Allgem. Deutschen Sprachvereins', ZASV, vol. 16 (1901), pp. 67–72, 102–107; Dunger, *Die deutsche Sprachbewegung und der allgemeine deutsche Sprachverein 1885–1910: Festschrift zur 25. Jahrfeier des allgemeinen deutschen Sprachvereins* (Berlin, 1910).
43 Schultheiss, *Vereinswesen*, p. 74.

44 ZASV, vol. 21 (1906), pp. 246–54.
45 Smith, 'Ideology', JMH, p. 657.
46 Schieder, *Nationalstaat*, pp. 50–1; cf. Klauss, pp. 202–3.
47 ZStAP, AA Nr. 38402, Rottenberg RS, Berlin, 16.12.82.
48 Bade, pp. 246–8; cf. Schilling, pp. 22–6.
49 Pierard, pp. 126–7; Klauss, pp. 208–17.
50 Bade, pp. 26, 318, 344; cf. J. C. G. Roehl, 'The disintegration of the *Kartell* and Bismarck's fall from power, 1887–1890', *Historical Journal*, vol. 9 (1966), pp. 60–89.
51 See Roger Chickering, 'Patriotic societies and German foreign policy, 1890–1914', *International History Review*, vol. 1 (1979), pp. 473–77.
52 Mary Evelyn Townsend, *The Rise and Fall of Germany's Colonial Empire, 1884–1918* (New York, 1930), pp. 169–71; Smith, *Colonial Empire*, pp. 40–51.
53 Klauss, pp. 118–19; Pierard, pp. 272–4.
54 ZStAP, DKG Nr. 136, Kolonialabteilung 1897–1903; Klauss, pp. 123–6; Pierard, pp. 141–2, 267; Hartmut Pogge von Strandmann, 'The Kolonialrat: its significance and influence on German politics from 1890 to 1906' (Diss. phil., Oxford, 1970).
55 ZStAP, DKG Nr. 139, Johann Albrecht to Hohenlohe-Schillingsfürst, 24.12.94; DKG Nr. 655, Sachse to Johann Albrecht, 5.1.00.

3 The Formation and Early Development of the Pan–German League, 1886–1902

By 1890 the agitation of the three new patriotic societies had helped bring currency to a conception of the German nation that was based on ethnicity and transcended the political frontiers of the Reich. This ethnic or '*völkisch*' nationalism also found nurture in several other large organizations during the 1880s, most importantly in the national networks of the gymnastic and choral societies, in the *Evangelischer Bund*, and in the militantly nationalistic *Vereine deutscher Studenten*.[1] That the tensions between this *völkisch* nationalism and the officially endorsed conception of the *Staatsnation* did not produce open opposition to the government was due in no small part to the immense power that Bismarck, the most prominent advocate of the ideology of the *Staatsnation*, enjoyed himself as a national symbol. Yet even while Bismarck remained in office, there were signs of where advocacy of *völkisch* nationalism might lead once he departed.

The General German League, 1886–93

By the end of the 1880s most of the organizations that made up the colonial movement had been amalgamated in the German Colonial Society, but no analogous consolidation had taken place among the Colonial Society and the other patriotic societies, despite the social similarities and ideological affinities that linked all these organizations. The possibility of an amalgamation was obvious, though, and in 1886 an attempt was made. The failure of the attempt was enlightening and of far-reaching importance for the subsequent history of patriotic societies in Imperial Germany.

The venture was doomed from the start, for its moving spirit was the most volatile of the patriotic societies, the Society for German Colonization, and the prominence of Carl Peters in the undertaking provoked well-grounded suspicions among the other organizations. In the spring of 1886 Peters and a group of his associates began to plan a congress of representatives of all the major patriotic societies; its purpose was to be defining common national goals and creating a common cover-organization. Immediately the planners encountered problems. Neither the Colonial Association nor the School Association would join in sponsoring the congress, for they calculated that Peters hoped to use it and any new organization that might arise out of it to raise money for his own continued expeditions to East Africa.[2]

The other organizations were also uncomfortable with some of the ideas expressed by Peters's group. However clearly these ideas inhered in a broadened conception of the German nation, they had political implications that the leaders of the other societies were not willing to draw. 'Germandom all over the world', read one public announcement of the congress, 'is beginning again to think seriously about its great common Fatherland, and the urge is everywhere becoming alive to establish a closer union [*Zusammenschluss*] with fellow Germans [*Landesleute*] at home.'[3] This proposition was unobjectionable, as was the call for closer economic and cultural ties between the Reich and Germans abroad. However, even as it abjured any interest in politics, the announcement disclosed the fundamental threat that the new nationalism posed to the old. 'The responsibilities we face in this area are not political; governments need not concern themselves with carrying them out. They are instead general national responsibilities, and the people have to demonstrate themselves, in carrying them out, how much moral power resides in the people.' It is difficult to overstate the importance of this assertion. It was an open challenge to the government's exclusive claim to control the national symbols, an unambiguous statement of the contradiction between Bismarck's concept of the nation-state, which was authoritarian in tendency and lodged ultimate responsibility for defining and defending the national interest in the state, and *völkisch* nationalism, which was populist in tendency and lodged this responsibility in the hands of representatives of the *Volk* itself.[4] The ideological foundations of a national opposition to official authority were here already in evidence.

Despite the reservations of the School Association and the Colonial Association, Peters and his friends did convoke the congress, which met in Berlin in September 1886, attended by some 600 people. It proceeded without incident, as delegates explored the dimensions of the new 'national questions' which had been defined in the past ten years – colonial policy, emigration, and the vigorous defense of the German language and culture abroad. The culmination of the congress was the founding of the General German League for Representation of German-National Interests (*Allgemeiner Deutscher Verband zur Vertretung Deutsch-Nationaler Interessen*), a cover-organization to coordinate the activities of all other societies whose goals were promoting 'German-national interests directly or indirectly'.[5]

This General German League was stillborn. Its true purpose was not difficult to discern; the new group was, as its historian has observed, 'in the final analysis merely a broadened version of the Society for German Colonization'.[6] Of the twenty-five men who sat on the executive committee, fifteen were from Peters's organization; the Colonial Association and School Association refused to become involved. The failure of the General German Association was due in part to organizational rivalries – the phenomenon that the Germans called *Verbandspatriotismus* – which were to frustrate subsequent attempts to unify the patriotic societies on a national scale. Other factors contributed to the failure. Peters soon returned to Africa, so the new organization lost its main source of energy. When he later returned to Germany, he found his Society for German Colonization itself absorbed into the new German Colonial Society. Moreover, the kind of militance that Peters's organization embodied did not, in 1886, find much resonance beyond the confines of Peters's own circle. The tensions between Bismarck and the Colonial Society did not reach a head for another few years.

Yet the militance, the suspicion of the government, and the combative perspective on world politics which animated the General German League did survive, as did sentiment in favor of unifying all the patriotic societies. Although their voice was fairly submerged within the Colonial Society, the militants of the colonial movement found an organ in 1888 with the establishment of the *Deutsches Wochenblatt*, whose editor, Otto Arendt, and whose principal contributors, including Ernst Hasse, the banker Karl von der Heydt, and Julius Graf von Mirbach-Sorquitten, were all associates of Peters and had been among the organizers of the congress of 1886.[7] And in 1890 the political situation in Germany changed so basically that a national opposition to the government, which was implicit in the views of these men, could organize.

The dismissal of Bismarck from the chancellorship in 1890 marked a break in the political history of the German Empire second in significance only to the start of the war in 1914. Criticism of the German government on national issues had been stifled as long as Bismarck continued to exercise power. His dismissal – both the fact and the circumstances – changed the situation in the most fundamental way. Bismarck himself now went into opposition against the 'New Course' of his successor, Leo von Caprivi, and the young emperor.[8] Henceforth there would be two poles of national authority in Germany, the one symbolized by the emperor and his government and the other by the former chancellor. And Bismarck, whatever his views about the patriotic societies and about their ideas of the German nation in the 1880s, did not hesitate now to make common cause with them as long as it served his own political interests to do so.[9] Ironically, Bismarck in retirement endowed with his own enormous symbolic capital a populistic 'German-national' ideology which he had, as chancellor, resolutely opposed; and he became himself the symbol and focal point of a national opposition to the policies of his successors.

This opposition was an increasingly important feature of German politics in the 1890s, for Bismarck's dismissal coincided with the onset of a period of profound economic, social, and political change. The lapse of the anti-socialist laws in 1890 and then the massive acceleration of German industrial growth opened the way for the intrusion of the socialist labor movement into the political arena. The mobilization of the urban working classes was, however, but one facet of a broader current, in which new social groups became self-conscious and organized for political action.[10] In part as a response to the threat of the socialist movement, Catholics, peasants, and small-property owners congregated in their own mass-based voluntary associations, through which they began to bring pressure on the established political parties.

The Caprivi government presided over the initial phases of these structural changes, many of which it sought to encourage or exploit – by means, for instance, of tariff reform to promote industrial growth, liberalized social legislation to discourage the growth of the Social Democratic Party by means other than repression, and concessions to Catholics in order to win their support in the Reichstag. These policies had their victims as well as their beneficiaries, however, and the Caprivi years were marked by intense political antagonism, in which the government itself was one of the principal contenders.

The antagonism was played out in the rhetoric of national issues, as both proponents and opponents of the government's policies attempted to appropriate the national symbolism for their positions. In this contest the government was at a disadvantage, for the opponents of its policies now had at their disposal a national symbol more powerful than even the government itself. From his lair in Friedrichsruh, which had the aura of a national shrine even before his death in 1898, and in the newspapers to which he had access, Bismarck dispensed his endorsement to a number of new organizations that appeared in the early 1890s with the immediate goal of challenging policies of the Caprivi government. Agrarian opposition to the commercial treaties which the government was negotiating took militant form in the Agrarian League (*Bund der Landwirte*), a huge organization which, though geographically concentrated in East Elbia (where it was populated by peasants but dominated by large Conservative landholders), exerted a powerful influence in agricultural areas throughout most of the rest of the country.[11] The moderation of Prussian policy toward ethnic minorities in North Schleswig and the eastern provinces also called forth militant organizations for the defense of German interests in these areas – first, in 1891, with the founding of the German Association for North Schleswig (*Deutscher Verein für das nördliche Schleswig*) and then, in 1894, in the much larger Society for the Eastern Marches (*Deutscher Ostmarken-verein*).[12] Anxieties fostered by the growth of the Social Democratic Party after its legalization led directly, in 1893, to the formation of the German-National Commercial Employees Union (*Deutschnationaler Handlungsgehilfen-Verband*), which by the eve of the war had succeeded in organizing more than 100,000 commercial white-collar workers.[13]

The organizations that sprang up in opposition to the New Course displayed great diversity, particularly if one includes the antisemitic political parties, which underwent a resurgence during this period.[14] Not all of them were, strictly defined, patriotic societies. The Agrarian League and the Commercial Employees Union fell more properly under the rubric of interest group. All of these organizations, however, used the symbolism and rhetoric of nationalism in speaking for social groups threatened by trends that the Caprivi government's policies appeared to promote – German residents near the northern and eastern frontiers, landholders large and small, artisans and other small business-people, and white-collar workers. If one agrees to subsume the policies of the Caprivi government under the heading of 'modernization', Peter Leibenguth's characterization of these new organizations seems apt: they were 'collective movements [*Sammlungs-bewegungen*] of a modern current of protest cast in anti-modern terms'.[15] While they made use of modern techniques of political mobilization outside the terrain of the established parties, they exploited anxieties that grew out of rapid urbanization, industrialization, the mobilization of the urban working classes, and the drive for emancipation among Germany's ethnic minorities.

Some of these generalizations also apply to the patriotic societies founded in the 1880s; the colonial movement can be seen as the attempt of people threatened by a crisis of modernization – in this case a cyclical down-turn – to use modern tools of popular mobilization to avert or divert it. But the new generation of organizations, which took form after 1890, differed from the older patriotic societies. Although the level of tension between them and the government vacillated during the next twenty years, the new organizations were more vocal and explicit in the manner they claimed to discern the true interest of the German nation and disputed the claim of the government to be the sole representative of the national cause. Custodianship of national symbols and values was now in dispute, in a situation made conceivable only by the dichotomization of authority brought on by the fall of Bismarck, who now lent the force of his symbolic authority to the new organizations.[16]

Of all the new organizations, the one that most dramatically illustrated the problems inherent in the new situation was the patriotic society that was born in ferocious protest against the Caprivi government's colonial policy. On 24 June 1890 the government published the draft of a treaty it had just concluded with Great Britain. The treaty provided for British cession of the island of Heligoland in return for Germany's relinquishing claims to the islands of Zanzibar and Pemba off the coast of East Africa, the coastal settlement of Witu in Kenya, and substantial areas in southern Kenya and Uganda that had hitherto been in dispute. Whatever the strategic advantages in the acquisition of Heligoland, the treaty could not have been a more demonstrative negative gesture toward the colonial movement. It not only handed over to Britain much of the territory seized by Peters and the other explorer-heroes of the 1880s, but it also announced the abandonment of future German claims to colonial expansion in East Africa.[17]

Amidst lively debate over the treaty in the press, the German Colonial Society convened at the end of June in Cologne to address the issue at its annual congress.[18] None of the delegates were pleased about developments, and those who had been associated with the Society for German Colonization were furious. It was, however, a sign of how far the ties between the Colonial Society and the government had already grown that the society's leaders decided to limit their protest to a mild and carefully worded expression of disappointment over the treaty.[19] The Colonial Society was clearly not an organization capable of vigorous opposition to official policy.

But one was on the way. Even as the congress of the Colonial Society was agonizing in Cologne about how to respond to the Heligoland treaty, prominent newspapers throughout the country, among them the *Kölnische Zeitung*, printed a manifesto, entitled 'Germany Awaken!' The document not only denounced the treaty in the strongest terms, calling it a new Olmütz, but called explicitly for counter-measures: 'Shall this treaty become reality? No, no, and again no! The German people should rise up unanimously and declare that this treaty is unacceptable.' Announcing that what Germany had achieved in 1871 was 'too little in comparison to the horrible sacrifices in blood it cost us' and that the country urgently needed more territory, the manifesto noted that the other powers were partitioning the world while Germany looked idly on. In these circumstances, it concluded, even the most loyal Germans were forced to recognize that 'there are circumstances in which it is the most holy obligation to the Fatherland to respond to a measure of the government with a resolute [*mannhaft*] and decisive "no"!'[20]

This document, which in its tone and pugnacity rivaled anything Carl Peters had written, was the work of several Germans who resided in Zurich, chiefly an ophthalmologist by the name of Adolf Fick. Predictably, it struck a resonant chord among Peters's supporters in the Colonial Society, who began to consider reviving the General German League of 1886. Preparations took shape in the summer of 1890 around two poles. The first was Zurich, where hundreds of letters endorsing the manifesto flowed in from the Reich and elsewhere. The other pole was Hanover, where a still obscure but highly energetic and persuasive young civil servant, Alfred Hugenberg, took the lead in contacting people, many of whom were already active in other patriotic societies. On 28 September 1890 a group of eight men, including Hugenberg and Johannes Wislicenus, who was professor of chemistry in Leipzig and Fick's father-in-law, met in Frankfurt to discuss the project. Here they decided to enter into negotiations with Peters, who was the logical man to lead the organization.

Peters agreed early in 1891 and mobilized his allies behind the project to create an organization like that of 1886, but this time 'with broader goals and forms appropriate to the times'.[21] Just what these might be was the main topic of discussion at a meeting in Berlin on 9 April 1891, which officially constituted the organization and baptized it simply the 'General German League' (*Allgemeiner Deutscher Verband*). Peters led the meeting, which was attended by members of the Reichstag and Prussian diet, university professors, high officials, and west German businessmen. They agreed that the goals of the league were to be broadly defined, in order to synthesize in a single program the ideas of imperial expansion and ethnic solidarity among Germans throughout the world. Accordingly, the program called for:

(1) Activation of patriotic consciousness at home and combating all tendencies opposed to national [*völkisch*] development.
(2) Fostering and support of German ethnic [*deutsch-völkisch*] aspirations in all countries in which members of our people have to fight for the affirmation of their distinctiveness, and the consolidation of all Germans around the world for these ends.
(3) Promotion of an active and effective policy of German power in Europe and overseas, especially the continuation of the German colonial movement toward tangible results.[22]

The organization that emerged out of this meeting was clearly the direct product of frustration in the colonial movement, but it was a great deal more. It was designed to mobilize a broad range of disaffection over official policies and, more specifically, to consolidate into a single group the more militant sectors of the other patriotic societies – those not reluctant to oppose the government should circumstances warrant it. The symbol of 'Germandom everywhere on earth' was comprehensive enough to appeal to members of the School and Language Associations as well as the Colonial Society.[23] And in the language of the League's program this symbol also implied the possibility of German's expansion on the European continent as a central goal.

The composition of the national leadership of the General German League was a reflection of the groups that the new organization brought together. Initially the dominant group was the disaffected sector of the Colonial Society, many of whom had financial interests in east Africa and had long been close to Peters. This group included Karl von der Heydt, Alexander Lucas, who was director of the German East Africa Company, Hübbe-Schleiden, Theodor Reismann-Grone, Wilhelm Schroeder-Poggelow, Paul Simons, Ernst von Eynern, Friedrich Krupp, Emil Kirdorf, and Fabri.[24] The second principal group consisted of what might be called 'German-national academics', highly educated men, some of them university professors, whose interest in German activity abroad was less financial than cultural and who had been active in the School and Language Associations. Prominent among these were Ernst Hasse, Adolf Lehr, Paul and Johannes Wislicenus, and Ludwig Ennereccus. The prevailing political persuasion in both these groups was National Liberal, but the founders of the League included several leaders of the Conservative and Free Conservative parties, who hoped to use the new organization more than incidentally as a forum of opposition to the government's program of tariff reform. Wilhelm von Kardorff, Hermann Graf Arnim-Muskau, and Mirbach-Sorquitten were prominent in this group.[25] The final major component in the leadership of the new organization consisted of Germans residing abroad, although they were not, for evident reasons, numerous at the founding meeting. The German community in Zurich, led by Adolf Fick, was the most active.

Because Carl Peters soon left for Africa once again, Heydt became chairman of the General German League as it began its activities in the spring of 1891. Lucas was named treasurer and Hans von Eycken general secretary and editor of the organization's newsletter. An executive committee and an honorific national board of directors, both drawn predominantly from the ranks of those who had attended the founding congress, made up the rest of the national leadership.

The first problem the new League confronted was the question of its own structure. On the urging of Hugenberg, the national leadership decided to emulate the other patriotic societies, despite the competition the practice would provoke, and to set up chapters, or at least contact men (*Vertrauensmänner*) in as many localities as possible throughout the country.[26] In another respect, the League's structure was initially modeled more after the School Association than the Colonial Society; in order to create as broad as possible a basis of active local support, decentralization was to be the key. The first chapter was established in Berlin, and by the summer of 1891 it had attracted over 500 members.[27] It proved more difficult to set up chapters elsewhere in Germany, where the League had to rely on the energy and dedication of any men whom it could recruit as local leaders. By early 1892 chapters had taken root in Hamburg, Hildesheim, Heidelberg, and Essen. The pattern was similar everywhere. One of the national leaders – Hugenberg in the case of Hildesheim, Reismann-Grone in Essen – organized rallies to commemorate a patriotic occasion, such as Bismarck's birthday in April, at which membership cards were hawked and local people pressed into positions of leadership.[28] In this manner ten local chapters were established in Germany by the middle of 1893, their size varying from 1,600 in Berlin to thirty in Pritzwalk.[29]

Opposition to the Caprivi government made creation of the new League possible, and the organization's leaders sought immediately to legitimize its role by obtaining the endorsement of Bismarck, who had himself gone on record against the Heligoland treaty – shamelessly, for this treaty was, as Caprivi himself had pleaded, entirely in accord with the tendencies of Bismarck's own colonial policy. Representatives of the League made the ritual pilgrimage to Friedrichsruh, where, they assured the membership, Bismarck 'took note with great interest of the activities and expansion of the League'.[30] The League's publicists portrayed the former chancellor as the inspiration for the organization and all the policies it was itself now advocating.[31] The success of this courtship was finally sealed in 1895, when Bismarck agreed to become an honorary member of the League.[32]

The new organization was in a position to capitalize on a number of other developments during the early 1890s. The deterioration of the relationship between Russia and Germany after the lapse of the Reinsurance treaty, the acceleration of Russification in Poland and the Baltic provinces, and growing ethnic tension in Austria–Hungary all had direct implications for German communities outside the Reich and lent credibility to the League's demand for more forceful protection of their interests.[33] The tenor of Caprivi's colonial policy, which was set by the Heligoland treaty, made plausible the League's contention that the government needed to be prodded. In this atmosphere of frustration and concern the local chapters of the League frequently developed around a core of disgruntled members of the Colonial Society or School Association.[34]

Given these favorable circumstances, it is perhaps surprising that the General German League did not develop more rapidly during the first three years of its existence. In fact, these were years of crisis, in which the very survival of the organization was constantly in question. It was an apt comment on the real situation that the League could boast fewer local chapters in Germany than abroad. Outside the Reich chapters were founded in fifteen cities, including Brussels, Christiania, Lausanne, San José in Costa Rica, and Cairo; in these cities they usually comprised members of the resident German communities who came together with the encouragement of the German embassy or consulate.[35] Within Germany, though, it was by no means clear how many people actually belonged to the League or where they lived. In 1892, 21,000 membership cards were in circulation, but certainly no more than a quarter of these had been purchased with membership dues.[36]

The General German League faced a variety of difficulties. Association laws restricted recruitment in some states, particularly in Bavaria and the Kingdom of Saxony. These laws forbade national political organizations to maintain formal ties to local chapters, and officials in these states routinely classified the League as a political organization.[37] Other problems stemmed from the decision to make the League's appeal as broad as possible and to keep the organization decentralized. Dues were set very low, at 1 Mark, of which the local chapters kept half. The strategy failed to attract the masses of members who were anticipated, and it also failed to provide sufficient revenues to cover the most basic expenses, such as postage and secretarial help, to say nothing of sustained propaganda.[38] The bulk of the revenues came from the pockets of some 400 men who purchased lifetime memberships for 20 Marks apiece.[39] Publication of the newsletter was sporadic, so lines of communication between the local chapters and the national leadership were weak. For most of the first three years of its existence, the General German League thus consisted primarily of a couple of hundred people in the Berlin chapter.

These people could not get along. Immediately after the chapter's establishment they faced divisive questions about the organization's make-up. It was perhaps inevitable that an organization which took shape in the political atmosphere of Berlin in the early 1890s and which styled itself the representative of patriotic interests would have to confront the issue of whether Jews had any role in it. Opinion was sharply divided between those members with ties to the Conservative and antisemitic parties, who insisted on the statutory exclusion of Jews from the League, and those, most of whom were National Liberal in inclination, who rejected this idea.[40] The dispute almost led to the dissolution of the Berlin chapter before it was resolved against the antisemites; but the tensions did result in a substantial loss of membership and made it difficult for the Berlin group to exercise any national leadership.

So too did the renewal of debate over the League's mission and structure in 1893. This time the issue was the proposal of Heydt and Schroeder-Poggelow to transform the League into a political party, a *Nationalpartei*, which would build on foundations putatively laid by Bismarck and become a 'union of all patriots, not on the basis of a feckless program of mediation' – an obvious allusion to the New Course – 'but a firm and decisive intervention [*Auftreten*]'.[41] The proposal brought further controversy into the League, for Hugenberg and others defended the original concept of an organization above the parties. The dispute also antagonized members of the League who had strong ties to the existing parties, and many of these men dropped out of the League before the idea of a new political party was quietly dropped.

The cumulative result of administrative disorganization, financial crisis, and disunity in the leading chapter was to bring the General German League to the verge of collapse in the spring of 1893, when (as far as anyone could determine) membership fell below 4,000. Having concluded that administrative overhaul was the only alternative to disbanding the League, members of the national board of directors met in Berlin early in July 1893 to face the problem. The meeting laid the foundations for the League's resurgence under new leadership and a new name.

The Pan-German League: Consolidation, Expansion, and Competition, 1894–9

The first conclusion to emerge from this meeting was that Heydt and Eycken had been unable to provide energetic leadership. They now resigned. Heydt's place as national chairman fell to the man who would occupy the chair for the next fourteen years and exercise a decisive influence on the League's development. Ernst Hasse was born in 1846 in the town of Leulitz in the Kingdom of Saxony, where his father was pastor. After serving with the Saxon army in the Bohemian campaign of 1866, he began studies at the university in Leipzig, first in theology, then in law. War interrupted his studies in 1870, and he was wounded several times during the siege of Paris. In 1873 he transferred to the university in Berlin, where he studied statistics with Ernst Engel. Returning to Leipzig with a doctorate in 1875, Hasse became director of the Saxon Statistical Bureau, a post he held for the rest of his life. Ten years later he resumed academic work, taking his *Habilitation* in Leipzig, where he was named *ausserordentlicher* professor and and began to lecture on statistics. He also lectured on colonial policy, a subject in which he had developed a consuming interest after his return to Leipzig. In 1879 he founded the Leipzig Association for Commercial Geography and Colonial Policy, and in the 1880s he was a leading figure in the colonial movement during its consolidation, sitting on the national board of directors of the Colonial Society. He was also active in the Leipzig chapter of the School Association.[42]

Hasse's dedication to both imperial expansion and the defense of German culture abroad epitomized the currents that combined to form the General German League. His temperament well befit the militance that distinguished the League from the earlier patriotic societies. He was a man of boundless but humorless enthusiasm, volatility, and impatience. His was a limited and rigid intelligence, but he was also disarming in his openness. Bernhard von Bülow called him, only half disparagingly, one of the most candid souls he had ever met.[43] These qualities made him a tireless leader of the League, but they also made him extremely sensitive to criticism, unable to understand the calculations of people (like Bülow) less guileless than he, and prone to fight back at little provocation.

Hasse's residence in Leipzig posed problems for an organization headquartered in Berlin, and these problems were only partially resolved while Hasse was sitting in the Reichstag as a National Liberal between 1893 and 1903. To supervise the routine administration of the League, Hasse chose, as successor to Eycken in the office of national secretary in Berlin, his friend and associate Adolf Lehr.[44] Seven years older than Hasse, Lehr had been trained as an industrial chemist and engineer. He served in these capacities with a number of firms before his appointment in 1875 to direct the *Allgemeine-Unfalls-Versicherungs-Bank* in Leipzig. His path did not cross Hasse's for another thirteen years, when the enactment of a federal program of a social insurance made necessary the liquidation of Lehr's bank. Lehr then decided to take a doctorate. In 1888 he appeared as a 49-year-old student in Hasse's seminar on statistics, and the two men soon became fast friends. Because Lehr was wealthy, he was able to move to Berlin in 1894 to run the affairs of the League, as both secretary and deputy chairman, with only a modest salary. In 1898 he too won a seat in the Reichstag (as a National Liberal from a Saxon district), which he occupied until his death in 1901.

Lehr was a good complement to Hasse. 'In fact', Hasse once recalled, 'Lehr was my mentor and my moderator.'[45] Having spent much of his life in managerial positions, Lehr was more flexible and open to compromise than Hasse. He developed a reputation among government officials as the leader of the moderates within the League, but his differences with Hasse were temperamental rather than philosophical; on all fundamental issues they agreed.

Lehr's appointment was one of the conditions Hasse laid down when he agreed to accept the chairmanship of the League. He insisted on more. The organization was over 5,000 Marks in debt, its revenues entirely inadequate. To deal with this problem, Hasse persuaded Heydt and other wealthy members to pledge a fixed amount of money for the next three years to a 'Guaranty Fund', which collected a sum in excess of 8,000 Marks each year and made possible the elimination of the debts.[46] This expedient provided only a short-term solution, though; with the expiration of the Guaranty Fund in 1899 the financial problems returned, only partially mitigated by the decision in 1897 to raise the dues from 1 to 2 Marks.[47]

Financial concerns were related to the organizational changes Hasse initiated. He insisted on establishing closer ties between the local chapters and the national leadership; the principal avenue was to be a new weekly journal, the *Alldeutsche Blätter*, which began publication in 1894 on the strength of a subsidy from Heydt and a subscription charge of 4 Marks for all members who chose to take it.[48] Hasse also pressed the local chapters to keep more systematic accounts and records of their membership, and to send regular reports on their activities to Berlin. More than any changes in the formal structure of the League, however, Hasse and Lehr brought a new spirit of dedication and energy to the top of the organization, and this spirit percolated down into some of the local chapters.

Finally, the organization changed its name. This decision symbolized a new beginning, but it was also necessary in order to avoid confusion with another small organization in Berlin, the General German Association (*Allgemeiner Deutscher Verein*), about which little is known, except that its leader was Albert von Levetzow, the president of the Reichstag.[49] In mid-1894 Hasse's group absorbed Levetzow's, and the General German League officially became the Pan-German League (*Alldeutscher Verband*).

These changes did produce some encouraging results in 1894 and 1895. Membership rose from 5,600 in mid-1894 to 7,715 at the end of the next year; subscriptions to the journal increased from 2,200 to 3,586.[50] The financial deficit disappeared. Eleven local chapters were founded or revived. Most of the thirty-three locals that the League comprised at the end of 1894 were still abroad, but most of the membership lived in Germany.[51]

The modesty of these gains disabused most of the national leaders of the idea that the Pan-German League would ever become a mass-based cover-organization for all German patriots.[52] Yet this perception of the League's limited popular appeal did not accompany a restriction of the range of the organization's concerns. Unlike the Colonial Society and School Association, which confined themselves to well-defined areas of activity, the Pan-German League claimed prior jurisdiction in all national issues, from colonies to the Polish problem, from the protection of Austro-Germans to the attack on foreign words. All this it combined with noisy attacks on the government, one of whose spokesmen, the Foreign Minister Alfred Marschall von Bieberstein, once characterized the organization as simply a 'gathering point for accusations and complaints'.[53] Hasse realized that the diffuseness of the League's program not only invited such remarks but was one of the causes of the League's weakness.[54] It is an apt comment on the political mentality of the League's leaders, though, that they resisted attempts to limit the scope of their organization's programmatic jurisdiction.

The formation of a rival organization imposed some limitation on them, however. One of the chief areas of the League's interest during the early 1890s was the situation in the Prussian eastern provinces, specifically the threat posed to Germans in the area by the Caprivi government's liberalizing the policy of Germanization.[55] The establishment in September 1894 of the Society for the Eastern Marches presented the League with a formidable rival which focused its attention exclusively on the Polish problem. The society was well backed financially by the large landowners close to its three founders, Ferdinand von Hansemann, Hermann Kennemann, and Heinrich von Tiedemann-Seeheim. Actively encouraged by the Prussian bureaucracy after the fall of Caprivi and the resumption of more intensive Germanization, the organization quickly spread a network of local chapters throughout the provinces of Posen, West Prussia, and Silesia, through which it not only coordinated an intense anti-Polish propaganda campaign, but undertook to support German landholders and businessmen financially.

Clearly the Pan-German League could not compete in this part of the country, and a division of labor between the two patriotic societies seemed the logical solution for both. It was difficult to reach. Buoyed by its initial success, the Eastern Marches Society announced, to the alarm of the Pan-Germans, that it intended not to restrict its work to the Prussian east, but to establish chapters all over the country – a decision which could only result in direct competition with the Pan-German League.[56] Negotiations to prevent this competition fell through, and the Eastern Marches Society did take up agitation in western Germany. Its leaders soon discovered, however, that with the exception of areas such as the Ruhr, into which Polish labor had immigrated, interest in the Polish problem was not acute west of the Elbe River.[57] Conversely, the Pan-German League found itself all but excluded from the Prussian east; the League did not, however, draw the programmatic consequences and eliminate or deemphasize Polish policy among its concerns. Neither organization abandoned its pretensions to invade the territory of the other, but by 1897 an informal truce had set in; henceforth the Eastern Marches Society concentrated its organizational effort in the east while the League worked primarily west of the Elbe.[58]

The expansion of the Pan-German League became dramatic once the organization found a compelling national issue on which to concentrate its activity. Paradoxically, the League's benefactor was the brunt of its criticism, the German government. The management of national symbols had become problematic with Bismarck in opposition, particularly since the emperor and Caprivi themselves recognized the value of Bismarck's own use of social imperialism and his techniques of rallying public opinion directly on national issues.[59] Just how problematic the situation could become was evident in 1893, when the government orchestrated a campaign in favor of a program of expansion and reform in the army – always one of the most powerful national symbols – only to find Bismarck criticizing aspects of the program.[60] Even after his public reconciliation with Bismarck in 1894, the monarch's position as custodian of national symbols was insecure. One strategy for reinforcing it was to create, or resurrect, a symbol that would be directly associated with the monarchy.

The circumstances that led to the popular campaign in favor of a navy were very complicated. They included strategic considerations, the emperor's infatuation with the idea of a battle fleet to rival Great Britain's, inter- and intra-agency rivalries in Berlin, the calculation that construction of the fleet would have a stabilizing impact on German domestic politics, and diplomatic tension between Germany and Britain over South Africa, which set in after the Jameson raid late in December 1895.[61] The most dramatic signal of the emperor's intentions came on 18 January 1896, when, on the occasion of the twenty-fifth anniversary of the founding of the German Empire, William announced that the 'German Empire has become a world empire. Everywhere in the most distant parts of the earth live thousands of our compatriots. German wares, German knowledge, German industriousness go overseas. The value of what Germany has put on the sea numbers in the thousands of millions. You, gentlemen, face the grave obligation of helping Me to incorporate this greater German Empire firmly into our homeland.'[62] In the context of contemporary discussion, the hints about the urgency of expanding the German navy could scarcely have been more clear. The impact of the emperor's remarks on the Pan-German League was electrifying, and well might the organization's leaders boast that in these remarks 'we find the program of the League'.[63] The emperor appropriated, in any event, a broadened conception of the German nation implicit in the idea of *Weltpolitik*; and he incorporated empire and a battle fleet into the symbolism over which the monarchy claimed custody.

In the aftermath of the emperor's speech the agitators of the Pan-German League discovered an enormous popular receptivity to the idea of a naval build-up. Lecturers accustomed to speaking in half-empty halls now faced overflowing crowds. Local chapters that had ceased to exist except on paper awoke to resume activity; dozens of new chapters were established on the strength of naval rallies.[64] The enthusiasm at these rallies was so great that a

remarkably large amount of money was donated for an even more
remarkable undertaking – to help build a warship. By the end of 1896 the
Pan-German League had received over 11,000 Marks both from Germany
and abroad for this purpose.[65]

The Pan-German League did not create this popular enthusiasm, but it
certainly exploited and helped to mobilize it. Membership in the League rose
from about 7,700 at the end of 1895 to 9,443 at the end of 1896 and to over
10,000 in the next four months.[66] Nor was the League alone in mobilizing
this sentiment. The Colonial Society, discouraged and stagnant after 1890 in
the face of the government's evident disinterest in colonies, also found the
navy to be a galvanizing issue, which in the course of 1896 alone produced a
10-percent growth in membership.[67] The Pan-German League, however,
emerged early as the most energetic and enthusiastic organization; its
speakers and publicists were the men who most conspicuously and tirelessly
disseminated the arguments in favor of making Germany a naval power.[68]

The popular agitation in favor of naval expansion was of great interest to
agencies of the German government, as was the leading orchestrator of the
agitation. The relationship that took shape during the naval campaign
between the Pan-German League and the government was an early
indication of problems that would subsequently become acute: officials
attempted to exploit the League in mobilizing opinion and in inter-agency
competition, only to learn that the Pan-Germans were difficult to control
and that their agitation could get out of hand.

The popular agitation became in 1896 an element in a dispute within the
Geman naval leadership itself, between those who favored construction of a
battle fleet based on capital ships and those who questioned both the
military and political wisdom of this project and favored instead a more
modest build-up, with the emphasis on the construction of cruisers, whose
strength was thought to be in coastal defense and the protection of
commerce. The battle-fleet conception found its leading spokesman in the
Chief of the Naval Cabinet, Gustav von Senden-Bibran, and in Alfred
Tirpitz, then the Chief of the Naval Staff; their ideas accorded with the
sympathies of the emperor, who was a devotee of the theories of Alfred
Thayer Mahan. The main advocate of the more restricted program was the
Secretary of the Imperial Naval Office, Friedrich Hollmann.[69]

The one group of officials was more comfortable than the other with the
activity of the Pan-German League, even though the League itself had, in
1896, developed no specific conception of the fleet it wanted built. Early in
1896 Senden met with Hugenberg and expressed his sympathy for a plan for
country-wide agitation in favor of spending 200 million Marks on the fleet –
a plan that envisaged, if necessary, dissolving the Reichstag and a change of
chancellors.[70] This contact lapsed, however, once Hollmann learned of it.
Hollmann himself appreciated the utility of patriotic societies, as long as
'they set as their goal the propagation of an awareness and interest in the
navy'.[71] This goal did not, in Hollmann's eyes, include raising money to build
warships. The Naval Secretary's anxiousness about the Pan-German League
was evident in the tone in which he rejected the more than 10,000 Marks
which the League offered him in October 1896; such donations, he

explained, would be better spent on some navy-related charity, such as the *Frauengabe Berlin-Elberfeld*.[72] Undeterred, the League submitted early in February 1897 a proposal for systematic cooperation to Hollmann's office. 'We must join forces', Hasse urged, 'in order to force the government to submit a new, far-reaching plan of naval construction, which would be either accepted or rejected *en bloc* – with the possibility of dissolving the Reichstag.' Then, in an ominous allusion to the Prussian constitutional crisis of the 1860s, Hasse warned that 'if the manouver fails, the emperor must display the same awareness of his duty as did his grandfather'. The fleet that the League proposed to construct was to be larger than the Russian and two-thirds the size of the French fleet. With such a navy, Hasse concluded, 'a basis would be laid for Germany's world domination [*Weltherrschaft*]'.[73] Hasse was candid enough to admit to Hollmann that the League's cooperation with the Naval Office and its advocacy of such radical demands would enable the organization to remain at the vanguard of the popular naval movement. Hollmann was none the less opposed to all aspects of the proposal, but his own position was undermined when the Reichstag rejected parts of the modest program he submitted early in 1897.

Hollmann's successor as Naval Secretary was much more alive to the potential of the kind of campaign the Pan-German League was proposing. It is no exaggeration to describe the role that Alfred Tirpitz assumed in 1897 as propaganda minister.[74] He promptly restructured the Naval Office, adding a 'Section for Information and General Parliamentary Affairs', commonly known as the Information Bureau (*Nachrichtenbüro*).[75] This agency, headed by August von Heeringen, became the orchestrator of a massive campaign both to awaken popular support for a battle fleet, which now officially became the goal of German naval policy, and – in a manner clearly anticipated in the thinking of the Pan-German League – to bring irresistible pressure on the Reichstag to pass the necessary appropriations.[76] Subsidized by official monies and by contributions from interested sectors of commerce and industry (many of whom had also been prominent in the colonial movement), the Information Bureau developed what the agency's historian has called a 'huge propaganda apparatus', with ties to journals and newspapers around the country.[77] Heeringen recruited professors and naval officers to lecture and write about the need for a large fleet; the flood of lectures and pamphlets was channeled toward strategic groups, for whom every conceivable argument was adduced, from industrial growth to the material benefits that would allegedly accrue to workers, and from Germany's cultural mission in the world to the need to protect settlement colonies abroad.[78]

The patriotic societies figured large in the calculations of the Information Bureau. Heeringen's office remained in touch with the leaders of the Colonial Society and, after some initial hesitation because of its radicalism, with the Pan-German League, where Lehr was the primary contact.[79] The Information Bureau supplied the patriotic societies with pamphlets, information and subsidies for their own pamphlets, reserve officers for lectures, and slides to be shown at rallies.[80]

The campaign soon reached a new stage of intensity. After the passage of

Tirpitz's first naval bill in March 1898 and the exacerbation of diplomatic tension between Germany and Britain over South Africa and Samoa, an atmosphere prevailed in Germany in which the agitation of the Pan-German League enjoyed unprecedented success. The League grew dramatically, encouraged not only by the support of the Naval Office but by the availability of the money which Hollmann had turned down and which the League now diverted to purposes of propaganda. Membership increased from just over 10,000 early in 1897 to more than 17,000 a year and a half later. New chapters appeared throughout central, western, and southern Germany, particularly in the Kingdom of Saxony, where, as in Bavaria, the liberalization of association laws removed obstacles that had earlier blocked the League's growth. During the same year and a half, the number of local groups in Germany grew from just over forty to more than one hundred. Rallies were frequently attended by more than a thousand people; they featured travelling speakers (often supplied by the Naval Office), who illustrated their talks with slides (also supplied by the Naval Office). In the enthusiasm and excitement, stimulated in part by the technological novelty of the slides, the chapters thrived. In Kassel the local group, on the verge of collapse early in 1897, suddenly revived late in the year at a large rally.[81] The chapter in Constance, which boasted a membership of sixty-three at the end of 1897, expanded on the strength of several *Flottenversammlungen* to 170 just over a year later.[82] These chapters only typified developments elsewhere.

The dramatic and unanticipated growth of the Pan-German League made necessary some organizational changes. In order to coordinate regionally the appearances of travelling lecturers, chapters began to form district associations (*Gauverbände*); these provided an intermediate administrative level between the locals and national headquarters in Berlin, where most of the agitation was coordinated.[83] By mid-1899 district associations had appeared in areas where the naval campaign had been particularly successful – in Thuringia, Hessen, and Westphalia (where the *Gauverband Berg und Mark* coordinated the activities of chapters in Barmen, Düsseldorf, Elberfeld, Hagen, and several other cities).[84]

The naval campaign not only promoted cooperation among the League's chapters; it made for closer relations among patriotic societies, especially between the League and the Colonial Society, which itself underwent dramatic growth after 1897.[85] Cooperation helped defray the costs of rallies, which were usually so well attended that both organizations could recruit members. One patriotic society suffered, though, in the naval campaign. The Eastern Marches Society now found its recruiting efforts stifled in western Germany, where enthusiasm over the navy overwhelmed concern about the activity of Poles in Posen and West Prussia.[86]

Throughout the first stages of the naval campaign, relations between the Pan-German League and the Naval Office remained relatively unstrained. Pamphlets published under the League's auspices by its official publisher, the J. F. Lehmann *Verlag* in Munich, reproduced information and arguments generated in the Information Bureau.[87] The only signs of potential friction were in the shrill tone of some of the League's literature and in hints that Tirpitz's bills represented the barest minimum of what was needed.[88] After passage of the first naval bill, the League called immediately for another, and when, late in 1899, a second bill was announced, the League's spokesmen, though enthusiastic, could not resist criticizing its limited size.[89]

Tirpitz was shrewd enough to recognize the problems of relying on an organization such as the Pan-German League, whose own vitality seemed to depend upon keeping popular enthusiasm at a fever-pitch. Tirpitz himself had other concerns. His plan for constructing the fleet rested on the assumption that the build-up would have to proceed in carefully calculated stages, in order to ensure the support of the Catholic Center Party in the Reichstag and in order not to alarm the British during the initial stages of the build-up.[90] The possibility that popular patriotic enthusiasm could overwhelm these calculations and increase the pace of construction made Tirpitz wary of the Pan-German League; it also made him receptive to the idea of a new patriotic society to promote the navy, one whose agitation the Naval Office could itself control.

The initiative for founding the German Navy League (*Deutscher Flottenverein*) did not come from Tirpitz's office, but from a group of men associated with the heavy-industrial pressure group, the Central Association of German Industrialists (*Centralverband deutscher Industrieller*), many of whom had already contributed money to Tirpitz's campaign.[91] With the quiet encouragement of the Naval Office, whose primary concern was that any new popular organization lobbying for the navy remain in reliable hands, a group of industrialists, merchants, and shipbuilders officially constituted the Navy League in April 1898, shortly after the Reichstag had passed the first naval bill. The real locus of power in the organization was indicated in the fact that its executive secretary was a journalist, Viktor Schweinburg, who was known to have close ties to the *Centralverband* and to Friedrich Krupp.

Tirpitz could be comfortable with the new Navy League. Its leaders insisted that the role of their organization would be loyally to support the building program of the Naval Office and, in general, to educate the German people about naval matters. Because this conception conformed so well to his own views about the proper role of a patriotic society, Tirpitz supported the new group with all the means at his disposal. These were considerable. It was a matter of policy that the federal and Prussian bureaucracies were to support organizations deemed to serve worthy patriotic causes.[92] With Tirpitz's blessing, these bureaucracies now came so thoroughly to the aid of the Navy League that they turned the organization into something different than other patriotic societies in Imperial Germany: it became virtually a semi-public institution. The federal and Prussian ministries of the interior and most of the Prussian bureaucracy treated Schweinburg to full cooperation.[93] Instructions went out from Berlin to all *Oberpräsidenten* in Prussia to recruit prominent citizens to lead committees charged with establishing provincial federations of the Navy League.[94] The *Oberpräsidenten* in turn instructed the *Regierungen* and *Landräte* in their provinces to encourage formation of local chapters and, to this end, the *Landräte* mobilized local officials, particularly those in the railroad and postal services, in their administrative districts.[95] Officialdom in other German states emulated the Prussian example. Here too the initiative for setting up the infrastructure of the Navy League passed from state offices to mayors and other local officials.[96] To emphasize the official grace in which the new organization stood, as well as to ensure its political reliability, the government showered orders and distinctions on the men who were active in it; prominent members of the German royal houses were persuaded to become protectors of the state and provincial federations, while Prince Heinrich of Prussia, the emperor's brother, became the Navy League's national protector.[97]

The result of this breath-taking display of official support was to create an enormous organization, which easily outnumbered all the other patriotic societies combined. By 1902 membership in the German Navy League stood at more than a quarter million – a figure that was in part the product of the low annual dues, only 50 *Pfennige*, which the organization charged.[98] Revenues from membership dues were none the less lavish, and they made agitation possible on a scale with which neither the Colonial Society nor the Pan-German League could compete.

Because they had no appreciation for the calculations that led Tirpitz to foster another patriotic society, the Pan-Germans resented the establishment of the Navy League and the official favors it received. Spokesmen for the Pan-German League argued, with good reason, that their own organization had been an effective leader of the naval agitation and that another patriotic society was worse than superfluous, for it would fractionalize the naval movement.[99] They were also hurt when still another organization invaded an area of their strength, this time German communities abroad. In June 1898 the Central Association of German Navy Leagues Abroad (*Hauptverband Deutscher Flottenvereine im Auslande*) was founded, largely under the auspices of the Colonial Society; this organization also enjoyed the encouragement of the government, though not on such a massive scale as the Navy League, through the avenue of German embassies and consulates.[100]

Fragmentation of the naval movement did not occur, however. Dues were so low in the Navy League that many people could afford memberships in it and another patriotic society. Because popular enthusiasm was so widespread, the three major societies involved in the naval agitation were able to cooperate. That this cooperation could produce formidable pressure became apparent during the campaign in favor of Tirpitz's second naval bill early in 1900. From the Pan-German League came the idea of a petition 'with a colossal number of signatures', which 'would be of aid to the government in the desired manner against possible opposition in the Reichstag'.[101] Lehr then approached Heeringen in the Information Bureau with the idea, and the two agreed that the coordinated efforts of all the patriotic societies were needed to produce enough signatures – Lehr calculated a minimum of 100,000 – to have an impact.[102] The Lehmann *Verlag* became the central clearing house, as thousands of petititons were sent out for distribution at naval rallies sponsored by the Pan-German

League, the Colonial Society, and the Navy League. At the time of the bill's passage, early in June 1900, petitions had arrived in Berlin bearing nearly 300,000 signatures.[103]

The swift passage of the navy law of 1900 would doubtless have occurred even had the Reichstag not seen the mountains of petitions the patriotic societies submitted. Yet the petitions did indicate how effectively these organizations were learning to mobilize public opinion on national issues. The naval campaign also marked a high-point in cooperation between the Pan-German League and the government; with one notable exception, the League's mobilization of patriotism would henceforth run contrary to the intentions of leading agencies of the German government. In fact, the seeds of this conflict had already begun to sprout during the years of the naval agitation.

The Development of a National Opposition, 1899–1902

A critical posture toward the policies of the German government was an inherent characteristic of the Pan-German League from the day of its founding. This posture implied a conflict with the government over custodianship of national symbols and the authority to define the national interest. The availability of Bismarck as an alternative pole of national authority made opposition on patriotic grounds possible, but the fall of Caprivi in 1894 and the abatement of the 'Bismarck fronde', of which the League had been one of the most vocal components, made it far more difficult. So too did the active attempt to associate the monarchy with the dramatic new national symbol taking shape in Germany's shipyards. Then, in 1898, when Bismarck died, he disappeared as a rival pole of national authority and was himself apotheosized as a national symbol – in a shrine the monarch could henceforth claim to guard alone. In these circumstances, criticism of government policy on national issues became more difficult and uncomfortable, for it came dangerously close to criticism of the monarchy itself and all that the monarchy symbolized.

Criticism of the monarchy or even the monarch was, however, not the intent of the Pan-German League. The League's position was not to oppose the monarchy's authority but rather to insist on a kind of joint custodianship over the national symbols, an arrangement in which the monarch would, in questions of the national interest, seek and heed the advice of those who represented the *Volk* – a role that leaders of the League claimed themselves to perform. Even when they denounced the government's policies, these men emphasized their loyalty and insisted that their criticism was only 'advice for positive improvements given by honorable patriots' and that the criticism was directed neither at the institution of the monarchy nor the person of the monarch, but rather at the Reichstag or the ministers who were constitutionally charged with advising the monarch.[104] The Pan-German League's opposition was reluctant. The organization would no doubt have preferred to cooperate with the government as it did during the naval campaign; it valued the occasional contacts it developed with officials, and it was gratified when its demands were embodied in policy.[105] However, given the extravagance of these demands, government after government was to prove wanting and become the brunt of the League's attacks. And because these attacks focused on national issues, the implication became difficult to evade that the League was challenging not only the wisdom of the emperor's ministers, but their authority – and ultimately the authority and custodial power of the monarch himself over the national symbols.

Although these problems did not culminate until the *Daily Telegraph* affair in 1908, they were defined before the turn of the century, during the tenure in office of Bernhard von Bülow. As the research of Peter Winzen has confirmed, many of Bülow's ideas were consistent with the program of the Pan-German League.[106] Like the Pan-Germans, Bülow anticipated Germany's becoming a 'world power', which meant challenging British colonial and naval supremacy. Bülow also believed in exploiting national issues – he called it 'beating the national drum' – to promote domestic stability; he believed in mobilizing public opinion on these issues to bring pressure onto the Reichstag and in using patriotic societies as agents in this mobilization.[107] These similarities in conception explain the enthusiasm with which the Pan-Germans greeted most of Bülow's actions while he was Foreign Minister and then, in 1900, his elevation to the chancellorship.[108]

More telling in the long run, however, were the differences between Bülow and the Pan-Germans. Bülow's conceptual world was governed by the category of power; he had no sympathy for ethnicity as a guide to policy. When he thought of expansion, he meant colonies overseas, not the continental expansion, undertaken in the name of consolidating the German community in Europe, which became a central feature of the program of the Pan-German League; such expansion, Bülow calculated, would merely enlarge the number of unhappy Catholics ruled from Berlin. In addition, an important difference of perspective made relations between Bülow and the League increasingly hostile. Bülow was fond of recounting an exchange that he had with Hasse in the Reichstag, which epitomized the problem. To Bülow's charge that the League's agitation was creating diplomatic complications for Germany with England, Hasse replied: 'As a representative of the people it is my right and my duty to express the real sentiments of the German people. It is Your Excellency's duty because you are the Minister, to see that our foreign relations do not suffer as a result.'[109] This, of course, was easier said than done; and the shrill agitation of the League became an increasing source of embarrassment to Bülow, just as the constraints that considerations of diplomacy imposed on him became an increasing source of frustration to the Pan-Germans. Bülow was especially sensitive when Anglo-German relations were at stake, for it was of critical importance to him and Tirpitz that these relations remain as amicable as possible during the early phases of the German naval build-up. Anglophobia, however, was one of the primary sources of the Pan-German League's success.[110]

The anti-British thrust of the naval campaign was unavoidable, and although Bülow, like Tirpitz, was annoyed at the tone of some of the Pan-German League's propaganda, the two sides worked in relative harmony on the issue of the navy. The navy was, however, not the only issue on which the League capitalized during the last years of the century; and the League's exploitation of these other issues, some of which also had anti-British overtones, brought it into conflict with Bülow's diplomatic plans.

Two issues were of particular importance. The first concerned the Habsburg monarchy. In 1897 Austrian politics again erupted when the prime minister, Casimir Badeni, attempted to forge a parliamentary alliance similar to Taafe's Iron Ring, by means of additional concessions to the Czech minority in the form of language ordinances which required civil servants in Bohemia and Moravia to speak Czech as well as German. These ordinances revived the ethnic conflict in the Habsburg monarchy with unprecedented ferocity. The most outspoken opponents of the ordinances were a group of parliamentary deputies, led by Georg von Schönerer and Karl-Hermann Wolf, who also called themselves Pan-Germans although they were not organizationally tied to the Pan-German League in Germany.[111] The League did, however, become involved in the conflict. Its publicists advanced the provocative argument that defending Germans in the Habsburg territories might require dissolving the monarchy and annexing its Cisleithanian lands to Germany.[112] Protests against the Badeni ordinances became the main theme at large rallies. The League also lent its support, though unofficially, to the so-called '*Los-von-Rom*' movement – the attempt sponsored by the *Evangelischer Bund* to organize the defection of Austro-Germans from the Catholic church, an institution alleged to be an accomplice in the subjugation of Germans in the monarchy.[113]

The protests over the Badeni ordinances, which coincided with the growing excitement over the navy, served to reemphasize ethnicity as a foundation of the Pan-German League's program. At the same time, the League found another issue, which combined like no other the questions of ethnicity and imperialism. Interest in the Boer uprising against British domination was intense in Germany after the emperor's famous telegram of congratulation to Paul Kruger at the end of 1895. The Pan-German League took a special interest in the matter, though, once its publicists concluded that the Boers made up part of the German nation. 'The Boers are German in blood (in descent), in language, in national character, and in all the rest of their ethnicity [*Volkstum*]', one writer announced in 1896. 'In South Africa too we have ethnic German territory [*deutscher Volksboden*] – as genuine as in Flanders or Holstein [*sic*].'[114]

The outbreak of war between Britain and the Boer republics in the fall of 1899 was the signal for a popular campaign in Germany even more extensive than the naval agitation. Styling itself as the 'carrier and interpreter of general sympathy for the brave little brother-nation of Boers', the League tapped the unexpectedly broad current of popular protest in Germany against the British war effort.[115] Most of the hundreds of thousands of Germans who attended rallies in support of the Boers did not share all facets of the League's perception of the conflict, particularly the idea of an ethnic community among Germans and Boers and the proposition that the Boer republics lay on German soil. However, even if their significance was only to give expression to what one report described as growing anger and profound outrage over the 'brutal, illegal acts of violence perpetrated by English policy in South Africa', these rallies were impressive.[116] The audiences were larger than the League had ever encountered before, often numbering several thousands of people. The meeting held in Plauen on 18 January 1901 stands as a good example. The local chapter of the League filled the meeting hall with 900 people, turning another 600 away. After a short speech from the local leader and communal singing of '*Deutschland, Deutschland über alles*', the lectures began. The first, on the subject of 'England against Germany', was the prelude to the main attraction of the evening, an account of combat in South Africa, which a Boer officer delivered in his native idiom with the aid of a local translator. Finally, an Austro-German from Bohemia appeared on the platform to speak of the plight of Germans in the Habsburg monarchy, after which a resolution was passed condemning both the British and Austrian governments.[117] The enormous audiences, the presence of Boer soldiers and others who had seen action in the war, the careful orchestration of the agenda, the inclusion of themes, like the Austrian problem, that were central to the Pan-German program, and the passage of formula resolutions at the meeting's conclusion characterized this agitation everywhere in Germany and demonstrated how well the League was learning techniques of mobilization.[118]

The League now also found it possible to undertake its own 'practical' support work. The rallies ritually included passing the plate for donations to the Boer cause, and the income was enormous. To coordinate the fund-raising, the central headquarters of the League issued an appeal for a 'Boer Collection' (*Burensammlung*) in October 1899; within six months over 200,000 Marks had flowed in, and at the end of the Boer conflict, in 1902, the League had collected more than a half million Marks.[119] Most of this money the League channeled through Holland to Boer organizations for charitable purposes, but some of it the League retained for its own agitation, particularly for sending veterans of the war to local chapters, where they proved to be great attractions at meetings.

The result of all this excitement was to bring the Pan-German League to the peak of its prewar strength. Many of those who attended the rallies not only gave money to the Boers, but joined the League amidst the enthusiasm. Existing local chapters grew to several times their previous size; dozens of new ones were founded in the wake of Boer rallies. Shortly before the protests began in earnest, in April 1899, the organization comprised 157 locals; at least fifty new chapters owed their origins to the Boer protests, for early in 1902 the figure stood at 215. Membership rose during the same period from 19,400 to 22,300.[120] Implicit in these statistics was a lesson not lost on the organization's leadership: the excitement generated by international tension worked to the benefit of the League, and the League hence had a corporate interest in keeping this excitement at a high pitch.

The excitement quickly brought the League into conflict with the government. Although it officially endorsed the German government's policy of neutrality in the Boer War, the League soon began to criticize what it charged was the government's favoritism toward England.[121] In any event, the desire of the German government to remain on good terms with the British government created a situation in which a clash with the Pan-German League was unavoidable. The Anglophobia fanned at the rallies that the League convoked to protest the Boer War became a source of growing concern to the British government and growing annoyance to the German government, especially as numerous other incidents, which crowded the years 1898–1900 (most significantly the Anglo-German dispute over Samoa), swelled the volume of the Pan-German League's criticism of German policy.[122]

Some of this criticism Bülow found unobjectionable, if not opportune. The League's demands for the fleet, even if they exceeded what the Naval Office thought feasible at the time, enabled the government to pose as if it were being driven, against its own will, by the force of popular opinion. But when the League's criticism was no longer consistent with the intent of Bülow's own policies, it became a real problem. Bülow was thus worried not only about the hostility the League was sowing against England, but about the League's involvement in Austrian affairs, particularly its practice of sending Austrian Pan-Germans around the country as celebrated guests to speak before local chapters, where their lectures always featured criticism of the Habsburg government.

The difficulty Bülow faced was that he could not easily muzzle the Pan-German League. Unlike the Navy League, the Pan-Germans were unbeholden to the government for bureaucratic beneficence, nor were they in the government's debt for financial favors, as was the Colonial Society – an organization in which a wink from the government sufficed to stifle criticism in connection with the Boer War.[123] Bülow did, however, try several devices to bring pressure on the Pan-Germans. When protests arrived in the Foreign Office from the Austrian government over the manner in which Austrian Pan-Germans were using their tours in Germany as a forum to criticize the policies of the Austrian government, Bülow mobilized the Prussian Ministry of the Interior and Prussian missions in other German states in order to supervise the meetings in which Austrians were speaking and on occasion to have the local police shut these meetings down.[124]

This tactic was less practical as a means of restraining the expression of sympathy for the Boers – a phenomenon far more popularly based and less narrowly associated with the Pan-German League. So Bülow tried a number of other tactics. The first was to cultivate people in the Pan-German League's leadership who were thought to be moderate, in the hope that these men would restrain the radicals. Arnim-Muskau, Udo von Stolberg-Wernigerode, who were the two leading Conservatives in the League's leadership, and Reismann-Grone all received overtures in 1900; the first two men were receptive to Bülow's pleas (Reismann-Grone was not), but their efforts to tone down the League's criticism were a failure and resulted only in their own resignations from the executive committee.[125] Their failure left Bülow with no choice but to humiliate the League publicly, a strategem to which he had already been resorting with increasing frequency. Newspapers known to have close ties to the government, such as the

Kölnische Zeitung, the *Berliner Neueste Nachrichten*, and the *Münchner Allgemeine Zeitung*, had begun in 1898 to run articles about the League, the thrust of which was to portray its leaders as a group of 'colonial supermen', '*Superlativalldeutschen*' – men full of all the best intentions but no feel for the realities of foreign policy.[126]

The culmination of this strategem came in 1900. Tensions between the League and the government peaked when Bülow refused to hold an official reception in Berlin for Paul Kruger, who was on a European tour late in 1900. No pressure from Bülow, however, could prevent the Pan-German League first from staging a gala reception for Kruger in Cologne and then sending a delegation to pay honor to him at The Hague.[127] The reverberations from the Kruger incidents extended into the Reichstag on 12 December 1900, when Hasse and Bülow faced off. Hasse attacked first. Beginning with the failure of the German government to make the gesture of receiving Kruger, Hasse went on first to denounce German policy in the South African war and then to condemn the entire course of German foreign policy since the fall of Bismarck. The government, Hasse concluded, had lost all touch with the mood of the German people.[128] Bülow then took the floor and showed that he was more than a match for Hasse. So significant were his remarks in defining the Pan-German League's subsequent self-image that they deserve to be cited at some length.[129] Bülow assumed the posture of the responsible statesman, who had to face pressures of which the Pan-Germans could have no conception. Hasse and his friends, according to Bülow, could thus well indulge in the sentimentality that guided their views of the Boers. 'Hasse has not spoken without a certain excitement, nor without pathos – noble pathos', Bülow conceded. 'It has also interested me to see how merrily Herr Hasse has been splashing around in the blue waves of the boundless ocean of the politics of conjecture [*Konjekturalpolitik*]'. The lines of Bülow's strategy were already clear, but more was to come. Pointing out that Hasse's support of Kruger put him in the same camp with the Social Democrats, Bülow addressed the League's claim, as the representative of German public opinion, to exercise custody over the national symbols:

> Public opinion is the strong current that ought to drive the wheels of the mill of the state. However, when this current threatens to drive the wheels in the wrong direction or even to destroy them, then it is the obligation of any government worthy of that name to oppose that current, regardless of any unpopularity it may incur. There are greater garlands than those the Pan-German League has to bestow, namely the consciousness that one is being guided simply and exclusively by the genuine and lasting interests of the nation.

Bülow's final blow included the formula which was to haunt the League throughout the prewar period. 'I cannot', he proclaimed, 'conduct foreign policy from the standpoint of pure moral philosophy – Bismarck did not either – nor can I from the perspective of the beer hall [*Bierbank*].'

The humiliation of Hasse and the Pan-German League was complete. Bülow's contention that the government stood above public opinion in questions of foreign policy was less painful than the sarcastic tone of his remarks and his intimation that the League was a group of men who were not to be taken seriously. The most humiliating thing about Bülow's response to Hasse was, as one member later observed, that it was 'rude' (*unvornehm*).[130] It was also effective. *Bierbankpolitik* – a word that raised images of burghers pounding their fists on the tables of beer halls, their patriotic ire increasing in measure with the alcohol they consumed – now surfaced everywhere in the governmentalist press: 'Pan-German' became a formula word to connote any crazy scheme in foreign policy.[131] As a further sign of the disgrace of the League, the German Colonial Society now began publicly to snub it.[132]

One of the reasons why Bülow's remarks stung so much was that they were true. The rapid growth of the League at the end of the 1890s was in fact accompanied by the flow of great quantities of spirits in public halls around the country. But if Bülow hoped that calling a spade a spade would undermine Hasse's position and make the League more docile, he was disappointed. The local chapters rallied immediately to Hasse's defense, expressing their gratitude for his 'manly intervention' (*mannhaftes Auftreten*) in the Reichstag.[133] Nor did Bülow's attack seem on the surface to have any impact on the Pan-German League's growth, which continued, on the strength of the protest rallies during the on-going Boer War, until the middle of 1901.

Yet Bülow's public humiliation of the League did mark a turning point in the history of the organization. Like no previous incident, it signalled a definitive break with the government and pushed the League toward a more radical position of opposition, from which the organization would claim exclusive custody of national symbols and deny the government's authority and competence to guide the nation's fate.

The cost of taking this position soon proved to be high. Many members of the League were uncomfortable with the growing hostility toward official authority, and in the months following the scene in the Reichstag large numbers resigned, their departure initially concealed in the influx occasioned by the continuing war in South Africa.[134] As the likelihood of a British victory in the war became apparent, though, an absolute drop in the League's membership set in.

Those who remained in the Pan-German League were for the most part the militants who were willing to accept the public image of an organization whose mission was to oppose the government regardless of the consequences. The defection of the more moderate elements from both the national and local leadership left behind a group of men under whose influence the League's criticism became more outspoken and bitter, as the organization adopted more consciously the self-image of the only true spokesman of the nation. Ultimately this role involved the attempt to forge a broad coalition of opposition to the government, whose policies, leaders of the League now concluded, were leading the country toward catastrophe.

Two events early in the new century well symbolized the beginning of a new phase in the League's history. The first was the death of Lehr in 1901. This event eliminated another of the moderating influences in the national leadership, for Lehr was succeeded as deputy chairman by Heinrich Class, the leader of the local chapter in Mainz, a younger man who possessed none of Lehr's patience or tact and who began to draw out the more impulsive side of Hasse. Class was soon joined in the national leadership by other younger men who shared his loathing for the Bülow government.

The second event was the final defeat of the Boers in mid-1902. Not only did this event remove one of the principal sources of the Pan-German League's success, but it left behind deep resentments over the role which the German government had played in the war. These resentments were to figure heavily in the League's adjustment to the crisis it was about to face. 'When we look back on the course of the Boer War, it is difficult for us to control our bitter feelings', wrote Paul Samassa, the editor of the League's journal. If there was any consolation, it lay in the ability which the League had demonstrated to mobilize large numbers of people. 'Because of the conflict between the feelings of the German people and the policy of the government', Samassa concluded, 'the feeling of co-responsibility for the fate of our own people was awakened in broad circles of people – people who otherwise have remained aloof from political activity and have found it almost a burden.'[135]

Samassa's perceptions were widely shared in the League's leadership. They also point to problems in the history of the Pan-German League that must now be confronted before the narrative can be extended into the organization's years of crisis. These problems have to do with the sources and contours of the League's view of politics, the reasons why this view appealed to specific circles of Germans, and the dynamics of a patriotic crusade which, when frustrated, turned openly against official authority.

Notes

1 Hans-Joachim Rothe, 'Deutscher Sängerbund (DSB) 1862–1945', in Fricke, *Handbuch*, Vol. 1, pp. 541–53; Eberhard Jeran, 'Deutsche Turnerschaft (DT) 1868–1936', ibid., pp. 605–19; Werner Methfessel, 'Evangelischer Bund zur Wahrung der deutsch-protestantischen Interessen (EB) seit 1886', ibid., pp. 787–91; Hans Winkel, 'Kyffhäuserverband der Vereine deutscher Studenten (KVDS) 1881–1919', ibid., Vol. 2, pp. 313–19. Dieter Düding is doing a study of the development of *völkisch* nationalism in these organizations during the 1880s.

2 ZStAP, DKG 255, Bericht über die am 27.4.86 . . . stattgehabte Sitzung der Kommission zur Feststellung eines Aufrufes zu einem 'Allgemeinen Deutschen Kongress zur Förderung überseeischer Interessen'; Falkenstein to Peters and Kersten, Berlin, 5.5.86. The most extensive account of the congress is in Müller, *Deutschland, Zanzibar, Ostafrika*, pp. 177–91; cf. Werner, pp. 24–7.

3 ZStAP, DKG 255, Allgemeiner Deutscher Kongress zu Berlin; cf. Karl Peters, 'Alldeutschland (1886)', in *Gesammelte Schriften* (ed. Walter Frank), 3 vols (Munich, 1943–4), Vol. 3, pp. 275–8.

4 See Eley, *Reshaping*, pp. 184–205.

5 Pierard, pp. 86–8; cf. ADB (1907), 105.

6 Müller, *Deutschland, Zanzibar, Ostafrika*, p. 188.

7 ZStAP, ADV 2, *Deutsches Wochenblatt* (2.6.92), Verzeichnis von Mitarbeitern; Schilling, pp. 24–5; cf. Klauss, p. 207.

8 The best discussion of the changes occasioned by the fall of Bismarck is Peter Leibenguth, 'Modernisierungskrisis des Kaiserreichs an der Schwelle zum wilhelminischen

Imperialismus: politische Probleme der Aera Caprivi (1890–1894)' (Diss. phil., Cologne, 1975), esp. pp. 270–1; cf. J. Alden Nichols, *Germany after Bismarck: The Caprivi Era, 1890–1894* (Cambridge, Mass., 1958), esp. pp. 29–46; J. C. G. Röhl, *Germany without Bismarck: The Crisis of Government in the Second Reich, 1890–1900* (Berkeley, Calif. and Los Angeles, 1967), esp. pp. 13–26.

9   See Manfred Hauk, *Bismarck ohne Amt: Fürst Bismarck nach seiner Entlassung 1890–1898* (Munich, 1977); Wolfgang Stribrny, *Bismarck und die deutsche Politik nach seiner Entlassung (1890–1898)* (Paderborn, 1976); Werner Pöls, 'Bismarckverehrung und Bismarcklegende als innenpolitisches Problem der Wilhelminischen Zeit', *Jahrbuch für die Geschichte Mittel- und Ostdeutschlands*, vol. 20 (1971), pp. 183–201; cf. Johannes Penzler, *Fürst Bismarck nach seiner Entlassung*, 7 vols (Leipzig, 1897–8).

10   Eley, *Reshaping*, esp. pp. 1–40.

11   Hans-Jürgen Puhle, *Agrarische Interessenpolitik und preussischer Konservatismus im Wilhelminischen Reich (1893–1914): Ein Beitrag zur Analyse des Nationalismus in Deutschland am Beispiel des Bundes der Landwirte und der Deutsch-Konservativen Partei* (Hanover, 1967); S. R. Tirrell, *German Agrarian Politics after Bismarck's Fall* (New York, 1951).

12   On the *Ostmarkenverein* see Galos *et al.*, *Die Hakatisten*; Felix-Heinrich Gentzen, 'Deutscher Ostmarkenverein (DOV) 1894–1935', in Fricke, *Handbuch*, Vol. 1, pp. 502–12; Richard W. Tims, *Germanizing Prussian Poland: The H.K.T. Society and the Struggle for the Eastern Marches in the German Empire, 1894–1919* (New York, 1941). There is no study of the *Deutscher Verein für das nördliche Schleswig*, but see ZStAM, Rep. 77, Tit. 1103 Nr. 3, Der deutsche Verein für das nördliche Schleswig 1892–1905; Alexander Scharff, 'Deutsche Ordnungsgedanken zum völkischen Leben in Nordschleswig vor 1914', in *Schleswig-Holstein in der deutschen und nordeuropäischen Geschichte* (Stuttgart, 1969), pp. 9–42; Galos, p. 23.

13   Iris Hamel, *Völkischer Verband und nationale Gewerkschaft: Der Deutschnationale Handlungsgehilfen-Verband 1893–1933* (Frankfurt a. M., 1967); Siegwart Böttger and Werner Fritsch, 'Deutschnationaler Handlungsgehiflenverband (DHV) 1893–1934', in Fricke, *Handbuch*, Vol. 1, pp. 702–14.

14   The literature on the antisemitic parties is enormous. Two recent works have full references: Peter G. J. Pulzer, *The Rise of Political Anti-Semitism in Germany and Austria* (New York, 1964); Richard S. Levy, *The Downfall of the Anti-Semitic Political Parties in Imperial Germany* (New Haven, Conn. and London, 1975).

15   Leibenguth, pp. 320–1.

16   ADB (1894), 157; Eley, *Reshaping*, pp. 176–7; Martin Broszat, 'Die antisemitische Bewegung im Wilhelminischen Deutschland' (Diss. phil., Cologne, 1952), p. 124; Oncken, 'Lebensraum', p. 39.

17   See Jack Richard Dukes, 'Helgoland, Zanzibar, East Africa: colonialism in German politics, 1884–1890' (PhD Diss., University of Illinois, 1970).

18   See Manfred Sell, 'Die deutsche öffentliche Meinung und das Helgolandabkommen im Jahre 1890' (Diss. phil., Cologne, 1926).

19   DKZ (1890), 177–81; Klauss, p. 240; Pierard, pp. 135–8; Smith, 'Ideology', pp. 344–5.

20   The full text is in Bonhard, pp. 233–7 (Anlage 1). On the founding of the General German League in 1891 see ibid., pp. 1–4; Werner, pp. 27–34; Wertheimer, pp. 22–48.

21   Bonhard, p. 3.

22   ibid., p. 4.

23   MADV (1.6.91), 1–2.

24   Klauss, pp. 242–4; Bade, pp. 352–3.

25   O'Donnell, p. 313; Leibenguth, p. 264; Eley, *Reshaping*, p. 49.

26   Guratzsch, pp. 22–6, 60–1. Although Kruck exaggerates when he calls Hugenberg 'the real father of the Pan-German movement' (p. 8), the man did play a significant role in shaping the structure of the organization.

27   ZStAP, ADV 2, Arendt RS, An die Mitglieder des Vorstandes des Allgemeinen Deutschen Verbandes, June 1891.

28   MADV (21.5.92), 47–8.

29   ZStAP, ADV 3, Verzeichnis der Ortsgruppen, 10.7.93.

30 MADV (21.5.92), 46.
31 ADV (1894), 58; cf. Freisel, *passim*; Leibenguth, pp. 267-8.
32 Bonhard, p. 205.
33 Schödl, p. 13.
34 As in Hildesheim: MADV (1.9.93), 96.
35 ZStAP, ADV 3, Verzeichnis der Ortsgruppen, 10.7.93; cf. MADV (15.11.92), 82-4.
36 MADV (1.8.93), 83-4.
37 Schultheiss, *Vereinswesen*, p. 77.
38 ZStAP, ADV 3, Bericht des Herrn van Eycken an der Vorstandssitzung vom 5.7.93; Bonhard, p. 5.
39 MADV (24.10.91), 23; MADV (19.1.92), 35.
40 ZStAP, ADV 183, Wislicenus to Hasse, Berlin, 5.9.93, 8.9.93; MADV (8.7.92), 67.
41 ZAtAP, ADV 3, Heydt and Schroeder-Poggelow RS, Berlin, 23.1.93; cf. Eley, *Reshaping*, pp. 49-50.
42 ZStAP, ADV 369, Hasse's Lebenslauf; *Hasse als Politiker* (Leipzig, 1898); ADB (1906), 45-7; ADB (1908), 18-20, 26-30; Hans-Günther Zmarzlik, 'Ernst Hasse', NDB, vol. 8, pp. 39-40.
43 Bernhard von Bülow, *Memoirs of Prince von Bülow*, 4 vols (Boston, Mass., 1931-2), Vol. 3, p. 353; Wertheimer, p. 45, n. 4.
44 ADB (1901), 498.
45 ZStAP, ADV 369, Hasse to Lehmann, Leipzig, 29.12.07.
46 ZStAP, ADV 3, Hasse RS, Berlin, 4.2.94.
47 ZStAP, ADV 13, Vorstands- und Ausschussitzung Protokoll, Düsseldorf, 13.12.97; ADB (1898), 3.
48 ZStAP, ADV 3, Hasse RS, 18.8.93.
49 ibid., Hasse to Levetzow, Berlin, 7.6.94; Hasse RS, Berlin, 8.6.94; ADB (1894), 109.
50 ADB (1897), 80.
51 ADB (1894), 153, 211-12; ADB (1895), 77-9.
52 ADB (1898), 3; ADB (1906), 73.
53 ADB (1895), 37-40.
54 ZStAP, ADV 3, Hasse RS, Leipzig, 18.8.93; ADB (1894), 1-2.
55 ZStAP, ADV 10, GFA, Berlin, 17.4.96; ADV 3, Hasse RS, Leipzig, 27.5.94; ADB (1894), 42-3, 65-6, 154.
56 BBA, 55/8 7010 (GEBAG), ADV Präsidium und GFA RS, Berlin, 6.10.94; ZStAP, ADV 8, GFA, Berlin, 21.10.94; ADB (1894), 177, 197-8.
57 ZStAM, Rep. 195 Nr. 90, Tiedemann to Binzer, Berlin, 16.12.94, 29.12.94.
58 ADB (1897), 125-6; Galos, p. 106.
59 Leibenguth, p. 293; O'Donnell, pp. 433-53.
60 Otto Hammann, *Der neue Kurs: Erinnerungen* (Berlin, 1918), pp. 72-3; August Keim, *Erlebtes und Erstrebtes: Lebenserinnerungen von Generalleutnant Keim* (Hanover, 1925), pp. 50-67; Nichols, p. 242; Röhl, *Germany*, p. 111; cf. Kruck, p. 50.
61 Berghahn, *Tirpitz-Plan*, 90-108; Kehr, *Schlachtflottenbau*, pp. 34-61; Schilling, pp. 61-85.
62 *Schulthess' Europäischer Geschichtskalender*, Vol. 37 (1896), pp. 12-13.
63 ADB (1896), 101-3.
64 ADB (1906), 51, 56, 72, 84.
65 ADB (1896), 10-11; ADB (1897), 89-92.
66 ADB (1896), 41-2; ADB (1897), 80. See Appendix, Figures 10.1, 10.2.
67 ZStAP, DKG 731, DS über voraussichtlichen Mitgliederbestand ... 30.13.95; DKZ (1896), 33-4, 41-2, 49-51, 97-8; Pierard, pp. 169-70, 176.
68 The most peripatetic of the League's agitators was Bruno Weyer, a retired naval officer and director of the *Mosel-Dampfschifffahrts-AG* in Coblence. ADB (1896), 33-5; Schilling, pp. 70-1.
69 Berghahn, *Tirpitz-Plan*, pp. 90-107; cf. Jonathan Steinberg, *Yesterday's Deterrent: Tirpitz and the Birth of the German Battle Fleet* (New York, 1965), pp. 97-124.
70 StBR (18.3.96), 1532, 1541; cf. Schilling, p. 75; Jerusalimski, p. 426.
71 BAMA, RM 3/v Nr. 88, Hollmann to Hohenlohe, Berlin, 11.3.95.
72 ADB (1896), 205-6.

73   BAMA, RM 3/v Nr. 88, Meinungsbild aus Süddeutschland, February 1897.
74   Meyer, 'Propaganda', p. 25.
75   Deist, *Flottenpolitik*, esp. pp. 71–145.
76   ibid., pp. 118–29; Meyer, 'Propaganda', pp. 26, 138; cf. Kehr, *Schlachtflottenbau*, p. 72.
77   Deist, *Flottenpolitik*, pp. 81–2; Meyer, 'Propaganda', pp. 37, 144.
78   ibid., pp. 41–107; Kehr, *Schlachtflottenbau*, pp. 208–379.
79   ZStAP, ADV 45, GFA, Leipzig, 7–8.10.04; Class, *Strom*, p. 83; ZStAP, DKG 244, Bericht über die Sitzung des Komitees für den Flottenwerbungs-Fond, Berlin, 8.10.97; DKG 248, Sachse to Strauch, Berlin, 23.5.00; Meyer, 'Propaganda', pp. 34–35.
80   ZStAP, ADV 184, ADV RS, Berlin, 5.12.99; BAMA, RM 3/v Nr. 9904, Geiser to Witzleben, Berlin, 4.11.02; ibid., Nr. 10405, Heeringen to Maschke, *et al.*, Berlin, 25.11.99.
81   ADB (1904), 358.
82   ADB (1899), 98.
83   ADB (1901), 350.
84   ADB (1898), 167; ADB (1899), 174–5, 262.
85   ZStAP, DKG 509, Bericht über die Sitzung des Ausschusses, 1.2.07.
86   Galos, p. 57.
87   Bruno Weyer, *Deutschlands Seegefahren: Der Verfall der deutschen Flotte und ihr geplanter Wiederaufbau* (Munich, 1898); cf. Hussmann, esp. pp. 38–65; Gary D. Stark, *Entrepreneurs of Ideology: Neoconservative Publishers in Germany, 1890–1933* (Chapel Hill, NC, 1981), pp. 111–24.
88   ZStAM, 2.2.1. Nr. 15370, ADV, 'Wo liegt das Sedan der Zukunft?' (1899); ADB (1898), 49–50.
89   ADB (1898), 85; ADB (1899), 381–2, 441–4; ADB (1900), 34.
90   Berghahn, *Tirpitz-Plan*, esp. pp. 90–201.
91   On the Navy League see Geoff Eley, 'Navy League'; Eley, *Reshaping*; Deist, *Flottenpolitik*; Amandus Wulf, 'Deutscher Flottenverein (DFV) 1898–1934', in Fricke, *Handbuch*, Vol. 1, pp. 432–7.
92   ZStAM, Rep. 77, Tit. 871 Nr. 1, Adhib. IV, Erlass des Staatsministeriums, 12.4.98.
93   ibid., Rep. 77, Tit. 662 Nr. 104, Reichsamt des Innern to Preussisches MInn, Berlin, 20.8.98; Starkowski to Schweinburg, Berlin, 9.6.98.
94   LA Koblenz, Obpr. Rheinprovinz Nr. 9661, Recke to Hasse, 28.7.98; ZStAM, Rep. 77, Tit. 662 Nr. 104, Obpr. Hessen-Nassau to MInn, 17.10.98.
95   StA Münster, Obpr. Nr. 3797, Schweinburg to Studt, Berlin, 29.3.99; Studt to Regierungspräsidenten der Provinz, 18.7.99; ibid., Kreis Unna, LRA Nr. 1062.
96   StA Bremen, v.2 Nr. 202, Wied to Pauli, 25.7.98; Eley, 'Navy League', pp. 125–6.
97   ZStAP, RK 2261, Vorschläge ... zur Verleihung allerhöchster Auszeichungen an Personen, die sich um die Bestrebungen des Deutschen Flottenvereins verdient gemacht haben sollen.
98   ZStAP, RK 2261, Jahresbericht des DFV für das Jahr 1903.
99   ADB (1898), 137–8.
100 ZStAP, AA Nr. 22668, Tirpitz to Sachse, Berlin, 8.4.98; Sachse to Bülow, 8.5.98; Satzungen des Hauptverbandes Deutscher Flottenvereine im Auslande (Berlin, 1898); ADB (1898), 128.
101 ZStAP, ADV 15, Dessauer to Hasse, Munich, 29.10.99.
102 ibid., Lehr to Hasse, Berlin, 2.11.99.
103 BAMA, RM 3/v Nr. 10407; ADB (1900), 109, 169, 213–15.
104 ZStAP, ADV 15, Hasse RS, Leipzig, 7.11.99; ADB (1898), 286.
105 Schilling, pp. 75, 86–115.
106 Peter Winzen, *Bülows Weltmachtkonzept: Untersuchungen zur Frühphase seiner Aussenpolitik 1897–1901* (Boppard a. R., 1977); Winzen, 'Prince Bülow's Weltmachtpolitik', *Australian Journal of Politics and History*, vol. 22 (1976), pp. 227–42.
107 'The national moment must always be pushed into the foreground by means of setting a national mission [*nationale Aufgaben*], so that the national idea never ceases to motivate and bind the parties': Bernhard von Bülow, *Deutsche Politik* (Berlin, 1916), p. 211; Bülow, *Memoirs*, Vol. 1, p. 68; cf. O'Donnell, pp. 373–4.

108 ADB (1900), 430; ADB (1903), 339.

109 Bülow, *Memoirs*, Vol. 1, p. 549.

110 On the problem of Anglo-German relations at the turn of the century see now especially Paul Kennedy, *The Rise of the Anglo-German Antagonism, 1860–1914* (London, 1980), pp. 223–50, 361–85, 410–31.

111 Andrew G. Whiteside, *The Socialism of Fools: Georg Ritter von Schönerer and Austrian Pan-Germanism* (Berkeley, Calif. and Los Angeles, 1975), pp. 257–9.

112 Schödl, pp. 39–44.

113 Whiteside, pp. 205–10, 243–62.

114 ADB (1896), 151–2.

115 ADB (1900), 176. On the protests in Germany against the Boer War see Kröll, pp. 67–81; Anderson, *Background*, pp. 285–360.

116 ADB (1900), 34–5.

117 ADB (1901), 73.

118 e.g. ADB (1899), 332, 349, 357, 365–7, 386–8.

119 ZStAP, ADV 185, Stand der Burensammlung am 13.5.01; ADB (1902), 93; Kröll, p. 77.

120 ZStAP, ADV 188, Fischer, Erläuterungen, p. 12; ADB (1899), 141.

121 Kröll, pp. 36–40.

122 ADB (1899), 136–41, 257–8, 403; cf. Kennedy, *Samoan Tangle*, p. 267.

123 ZStAP, DKG 139, Johann Albrecht to Hohenlohe-Schillingsfürst, Berlin, 24.12.99; DKG 655, Sachse to Johann Albrecht, 5.1.00.

124 ZStAM, Rep. 77, Tit. 662 Nr. 133, MInn RS to sämtliche Oberpräsidenten, Berlin, 26.8.99; Rotenhahn to William, Berlin, 11.11.97; PAAA, Deutschland Nr. 169, Bd. 1, Richthofen to Gesandten Darmstadt, Berlin, 23.9.00; ADB (1897), 241; ADB (1899), 58–9, 121–2.

125 PAAA, Deutschland Nr. 169, Bd. 1, William to Arnim-Muskau, 7.12.00; Klehmet to Stolberg-Wernigerode, Berlin, 12.1.01; Klaus Werner Schmidt, 'Die "Rheinisch-Westfälische Zeitung" und ihr Verleger Reismann-Grone', *Beiträge zur Geschichte Dortmunds und der Grafschaft Mark*, vol. 69 (1974), p. 311; Bonhard, pp. 210–11; cf. Siegfried von Kardorff, *Wilhelm von Kardorff: Ein nationaler Parlamentarier im Zeitalter Bismarcks und Wilhelms II. 1828–1907* (Berlin, 1936), pp. 343–4.

126 ADB (1898), 249–50, 253; ADB (1899), 353–4, 264; ADB (1900), 403–5.

127 ADB (1900), 489–90, 503, 505; cf. Kröll, p. 44.

128 StBR (12.12.00), 469–73.

129 ibid., pp. 474–5; cf. Schilling, p. 135; Bülow, *Memoirs*, Vol. 1, pp. 548–9.

130 Class, *Strom*, pp. 60–1.

131 ADB (1900), 520–1, 525–8.

132 ZStAP, ADV 33, GFA, Eisenach, 23/24.5.02; ADB (1902), 206.

133 ADB (1901), 6–8, 35–6.

134 ZStAP, ADV 185, Hasse to Ogr. Annaberg-Buchholz, Leipzig, 8.10.01; ADB (1901), 108, 260, 332; ADB (1902), 43.

135 ADB (1902), 197–9.

4 Ideology

Even during the years of its early activity the Pan-German League demonstrated the characteristics that made it the object of such controversy and alarm in Germany and elsewhere. The organization championed an extravagant and aggressive program, which seemed to call for unrestrained building of warships to challenge the British, the demise of the Habsburg monarchy, and constructing an empire to comprehend an ethnic community so far-flung that it embraced Boers in South Africa. In mobilizing support for these and other patriotic causes, the League displayed an evidently uncontrollable dynamism which led it, in the name of patriotism, into open conflict with the German government.

Studying the roots of the Pan-German League's controversial behavior requires suspending the narrative in favor of a different kind of analysis. The next several chapters will be devoted to the study of the cultural context within which the League operated; they will address the problem of why the men who attended the League's rallies and became active in the organization found this behavior meaningful. These chapters will explore the character of the beliefs, concerns, and anxieties the Pan-Germans harbored, the kinds of people they were, the question of why the League's program and activities appealed to them, and the avenues through which they translated their beliefs, concerns, and anxieties into effective political action. The analysis begins, in the present chapter, in the intellectual world of the Pan-German League, the realm in which one finds not only the extravagant contours of the organization's program, but more subtle images and themes which provide hints about the concerns that made this program attractive to certain kinds of people.

Despite the controversy that surrounds it, the concept of ideology is, for several reasons, the best description of this intellectual world. The concept suggests, in the first place, a highly structured belief system, a systematized representation of reality.[1] Ideology is 'political cosmology', in which the word 'political' pertains in the broad sense to power relationships in and among social groups. Ideology thus connotes intellectual system, the attempt to bring conceptual order to a world in which questions of power are being debated. This order comprehends the temporal as well as the spatial dimensions of the social world. It involves an interpretation of the past (of the derivation of power relationships), an analysis of the present (either to justify or to repudiate these relationships), and a set of precepts and imperatives for future conduct. Ideology makes political action meaningful by rooting it in the context of an intelligible past and present and a desirable future.[2]

Jean-Paul Sartre has written of antisemitism as a 'passion and a conception of the world'.[3] His characterization is true of ideology in general. Ideology differs from concepts such as belief and opinion, not only in being more systematic and comprehensive – which is what Sartre meant by a 'conception of the world' – but in so far as it demands – as a 'passion' – more than casual commitment to its validity. The term 'secular religion', which several commentators have used to describe ideology, emphasizes this point. Like theology, ideology is a tightly articulated system, with limited tolerance for ambiguity, skepticism, or dispute.

One additional element in the concept of ideology deserves particular emphasis. Ideology is an eminently self-conscious system of thought. It is no coincidence that ideologies arise commonly within social groups whose values are being challenged in confrontation with other groups; in the systems they formulate, ideologists develop images of themselves and of their own groups as well as of the groups that threaten them.[4] Often this self-consciousness is not the most conspicuous dimension of ideology, but it is accessible in the symbolism, metaphors, rhetoric, and imagery of which ideology is constructed. E. P. Thompson has alluded to this dimension in speaking of the 'psychic energy stored – and released – in language'.[5] And in a somewhat different context, J. P. Stern has referred to ideological statements as the 'public presentation of intimate thinking'.[6] Construing ideology in this manner, attempting to connect intimate thinking with an intellectual system publicly professed is not without risk, and the risk increases in geometric ratio to the level of intimacy being analyzed. It is, none the less, essential to bear in mind the symbolic riches contained – and often disguised – in these systems.

The analysis of the Pan-German League's ideology will deal first with the organization's program and the broader view of history and politics that underlay it. The analysis will then turn to another part of what one might call, with Peter Berger and Thomas Luckmann, the League's 'symbolic universe'; it will examine the self-conscious realm in which more fundamental anxieties and aspirations found guarded expression.[7]

The Program

An obvious objection remains to using the concept of ideology in connection with the beliefs of the Pan-Germans. The diffuseness of the League's interests lends the impression that the organization's program lacked any system or concentration.[8] It is tempting to conclude with Professor Whiteside, who has dealt with the evidently no less disheveled program of the Austrian Pan-Germans, that the views of the League were a 'congolomerate that defies logical analysis'.[9] Other historians have reached similar conclusions about such views and prefer to speak of a 'feeling and mood', of a 'feeling of discontent that had no clear source or goal', rather than of a systematic view of politics that would justify the label of ideology.[10]

The objection is plausible, but it overlooks the enormous effort leaders of the Pan-German League devoted to systematizing their program and outlook. These men recognized the liabilities posed by their diffuse concerns, and their

efforts to systematize their views represented a response to this problem. The
search for what they referred to as the 'key' to political change, for 'theoretical
clarity', or 'fundamental premises with the status of dogma' – in other words,
the search for ideology – demonstrated how difficult it was for them to harbor
'feelings of discontent' in an intellectually unordered context.[11] 'We have
always felt the need to arrive at a unified view of the world', wrote Paul
Samassa in 1908.[12] And the Pan-Germans did formulate what another leader
proudly called a 'self-contained [*geschlossene*] national *Weltanschauung*'.[13] It
is a system of thought which does not defy logical analysis.

Admittedly, it is not easy to find any single coherent statement of this
ideology. The Pan-Germans possessed no seminal documents analogous to
the writings of Marx and Engels. Ernst Hasse was the League's most
influential and systematic ideologist until his death in 1908. He formulated his
views in countless public lectures and in articles he wrote for the League's
journal and publication elsewhere. Fragments of what was to be Hasse's
comprehensive treatise on politics appeared separately between 1905 and
1908 under the title of *Deutsche Politik*.[14] A number of other pieces of
literature were of particular importance in articulating the League's ideology.
These included the pamphlet series, *Kampf um das Deutschtum*, in which
writers surveyed the condition of Germans throughout the world, and two
pseudonymous books by Hasse's successor as the League's chairman,
Heinrich Class – his *Deutsche Geschichte*, which supplied the League with a
coherent if unoriginal schema of historical analysis, and his manifesto of 1912,
Wenn ich der Kaiser wär'.[15] Beyond these sources, the Pan-German League's
ideology must be pieced together out of a myriad of fragments, commentary
by leaders of the organization in speeches, in pamphlets which the League
published officially or semi-officially, and in articles by a large number of
members in the *Alldeutsche Blätter*.[16] Although by no means free of
contradictory details, these fragments do come together with remarkable
coherence.

The basic premise in the Pan-German League's ideology was that German
national development was incomplete, that it had not reached its fulfillment in
1871. The critical deficiency in the German Empire was that it was not a
genuine *Nationalstaat*: its frontiers failed to comprehend the German nation.
The Reich of 1871 accordingly could never be more than a *Vorstaat*, a
preliminary, albeit necessary phase, during which forces were maturing that
would push the process of national development to completion.[17] This
premise implied two further propositions, which reflected ideas that had
dominated the early history of patriotic societies in the German Empire and
found synthesis in the ideology of the League. These propositions were the
central importance of ethnicity in human affairs and the urgency of imperial
expansion.

The Pan-German League was a foremost advocate of the variety of
nationalism known both to contemporaries and to subsequent historians as
völkisch. The distinguishing feature of this variety was to challenge the
proposition, advanced in Marxist and other materialist doctrines, that human
existence was governed by economic forces and that the fundamental unit of
human organization was social class. Pan-Germans insisted that human life

was instead founded on groups (*Völker*) that were ethnically defined – by language, culture, tradition, and race (this last concept remained until shortly before Hasse's death ill defined and unsystematic in the thinking of the League's ideologists). Ethnicity, belonging to one of these units, was an existential fact, the most natural and genuine characteristic of any human being. However, of more programmatic relevance than the psychological dimensions of ethnicity were its political implications. In the eyes of the Pan-Germans, a natural, eternal, and pre-political bond of unity existed among all people born into a given ethnic unit; the function of politics, of the state, was merely to give organized expression and protection to the ethnic community.[18] The claims of the *Volk* were accordingly higher than those of the state. Political society was fluid, the ethnic community transcendent and eternal. 'The only thing that possesses stability in the flux of a thousand years of development is the *Volk*', Hasse wrote. 'States, as conglomerations of ethnic groups, come and go; and even more transitory are political constitutions and social conditions.'[19] Hasse's observations were directed at the German constitution of 1871, which, he was convinced, would eventually disappear. For although political units were transitory phenomena, the greatest goal of political evolution – the closest approximation to political perfection – was identity between *Volk* and *Staat*.

The emphasis in the League's ideology on ethnicity as the foundation of national identity betrayed the influence of the ethnic conflicts of the 1880s. These conflicts were no less evident in another of the Pan-Germans' beliefs: ethnic communities existed in a perpetual state of conflict, frequently violent. At stake was the survival of each group as an ethnic unit; each accordingly found itself in a struggle for its very existence.[20] In this struggle, Hasse and other Pan-German leaders were convinced, an ethnic community had but one avenue to survival, and this was expansion.[21] On the subject of expansion, lines of reasoning came to the fore that originated in the colonial movement of the 1880s. The principal threat to the *Volk*, the Pan-Germans argued, was strangulation for want of outlets for surplus population and areas for economic growth. An expanding economy and population growth made territorial expansion ineluctable. The Pan-Germans did not, however, like many in the Colonial Society, restrict their gaze to overseas areas. Emphasizing the fluidity of politics, Hasse and the others pointed out that the world was everywhere being constantly repartitioned, and that the survival of the German ethnic community demanded the mobilization of all its power in a genuinely national state and then the occupation of more land wherever on earth this land might become available.[22]

Imperial rivalries of the late nineteenth century were also reflected in the Pan-Germans' vision of the character of the impending struggle. This was to involve four great antagonists, and the prize was to be power and domination on a worldwide scale. The four contenders were Great Britain, backed by the immense resources of its empire, the United States on the strength of its economic might, Russia, with the support of the rest of the Slavic community in Europe, and finally the German nation.[23] For Germans the risks were greater than for the others, because of their strategic vulnerability in the heart of Europe, their ethnic dispersion, and because of the economic disadvantages they faced for having arrived late in the race for empire. None the less, failure to enter the struggle, Pan-Germans insisted, would result in Germany's fall to a second-rank power, like France, and its eventual extinction as an ethnic unit.

The Pan-Germans' most controversial project derived directly from their beliefs about ethnic conflict and the impending struggle for world power. This project was to be simultaneously the fulfillment of the political development of the German *Volk* and the necessary precondition for successful competition around the world with the other international giants. The Pan-Germans were by no means the only people in Wilhelmine Germany to be fascinated with the idea of establishing some form of central European union under German domination, but their project was the most grandiose.[24] It was informed by the constant interplay of ethnic and economic considerations; if the one set determined the extent and political significance of the *Mitteleuropa* union, the other underlined its urgency and the role it would play in the struggle for world power. The basic idea was that the borders of the German state were to expand to include all areas of the European continent in which Germans were the dominant ethnic element. This expansion would, its proponents contended, represent the natural culmination of German national development; it would both enlarge enormously the German *Wirtschafts-gebiet* and provide the most logical territorial outlets into which the German population could be redistributed.[25]

However logically conceived, the project raised theoretical problems. It was by no means clear which parts of Central Europe the consolidated areas were to comprehend. This problem sprang directly from another: the Pan-Germans found it difficult to define precisely who was German. That people whose first language was German belonged in the union seemed clear enough, but prominent spokesmen in the League insisted that common linguistic roots also made the Flemish and Dutch populations components of the German ethnic community and hence that the lands in which these people lived represented *deutscher Volksboden* – a realm which also included, in the eyes of most Pan-German leaders, areas which Germans had once colonized in the Habsburg monarchy and in Baltic Russia.[26] The logic of this argument suggested that the German ethnic community was ultimately a Germanic unity, which would include, in addition, Scandinavians and Anglo-Saxons. By the turn of the century, however, after the experiences of the Boer War, the growing rivalry with the United States, and ethnic tensions with Danes in North Schleswig, this broader vision, which the League's ideologists referred to as *Pan-Germanismus* in distinction to *Alldeutschtum*, had lost much of its appeal.[27]

The dimensions of the Pan-Germans' vision were nevertheless breath-taking. The German community in *Mitteleuropa* was, by general consensus in the League, to include the German Empire, the Habsburg lands, Switzerland, Holland, Luxemburg, Belgium, and – less out of ethnic considerations than because it lay at the mouth of the Danube – Romania.[28] The League made no secret of its expectation that full political unity would be the end result, although in the short run political unity appeared impractical, owing not the least to the resistance of Swiss Germans and Flemish separatists to the idea.[29] Even the possibility of a direct annexation of the Cisleithanian

Habsburg territories, which surfaced during the uproar over the Badeni decrees, faded after the turn of the century because the idea found little support in Austria beyond the circles of the Austrian Pan-Germans.[30] The creation of the great German political unit, the *Nationalstaat* in Central Europe, would therefore, most Pan-Germans agreed, be the product of extended evolution, impelled by the logic of ethnic solidarity, economic pressure, and, should it prove ultimately necessary, military force. The first step was to be the establishment of a Central European customs union, similar in form to the *Zollverein*.[31] Its destiny would be similar to that of the *Zollverein* too: the bonds of dependency so created would prepare the way for the creation of community-wide legal and political institutions.

The centrality of this project in the program of the Pan-German League sometimes left the impression that the organization had opted for a course of continental expansion at the expense of acquiring colonies overseas.[32] The Central European state was, to be sure, to guarantee the ethnic integrity as well as the economic vitality of the German nation; in this sense it was, probably for most Pan-Germans, the primary goal.[33] Its construction did not, however, by any means rule out pursuit of *Weltpolitik*; the Central European state was in fact the indispensable precondition of an effective colonial policy overseas. The new state would be far more formidable than the old in the worldwide struggle between Germany and its antagonists. Consolidation with Belgium and Holland would bring to the German nation the colonial holdings of these two states; revenues produced by a common community-wide tariff were to be used to construct the fleet needed to enforce German colonial claims.[34] And the combined economic resources of the new state would enable Germans to compete around the world with their British and American rivals. Having the requisite military and economic power, the German nation would, for purposes of further settlement and economic support, at last build an overseas empire commensurate with the nation's continental power.

The specific demands that the Pan-German League raised all derived from this vision. The supremacy of ethnicity in human affairs and the inevitability of conflict for world power were the propositions that determined the perspective of the League on all contemporary issues. So fundamental were these propositions that the range of issues they comprehended was extremely broad, as one leader revealed in answering the question, 'What is national?' He replied:

Everything that relates to the preservation, promotion, future, and greatness of our people and Reich is national; that means that national questions of the first order are: the army, the navy, colonies, Germanization of the Prussian eastern provinces and North Schleswig, de-Latinization [*Entwelschung*] of Alsace-Lorraine, honorable representation of the German Empire, protection of Germans, preservation of the citizenship and civil rights of Germans abroad, cultivation of the German language and German schools abroad, combating the treacherous [*vaterlandslose*] Social Democrats, *und so weiter*.[35]

Given this broad definition of their concerns, it is not surprising that contemporaries and historians alike have found the Pan-Germans' program diffuse. In every area, however, the League's position was to advocate policies calculated to promote the *Nationalstaat* they envisaged.[36] At home, the League called for making the existing Reich more national, by suppressing the use of languages other than German. As long as they defined language as the chief determinant of ethnicity, Pan-Germans advocated the imposition of the German language on ethnic minorities living in Germany, as well as the undercutting of their cultural and economic positions by means of population redistribution.[37] Building the *Nationalstaat* also implied the unremitting support of German ethnic consciousness everywhere on earth, particularly in the Habsburg monarchy, which was to be one of the core areas of the new state and where the supremacy of the German element seemed most immediately threatened. The worldwide aspirations of the new state required the vigorous quest for colonial empire overseas; and this quest demanded a navy.

Enough has been written about the location of the Pan-German League's program along the intellectual pedigree of National Socialism that little more need be said here. The vision of the League unambiguously anticipated the program of the Nazis, to the point of including a *Stufenplan*, in which continental hegemony was to be the foundation for worldwide empire.[38] The documentable intellectual sources of the Pan-Germans' program include most of the people commonly featured in the gallery of precursors of National Socialism – Friedrich List for the commercial consolidation of Central Europe,[39] Paul de Lagarde and Julius Langbehn for the aggressive belief in the mission of the German ethnic community,[40] a vulgarized Nietzsche for the glorification of power,[41] Charles Darwin and especially Heinrich von Treitschke for the vision of world politics as perpetual conflict.[42] The *grossdeutsch* political tradition also occupied a conspicuous place in the League's ideology.[43]

Although they were more effectively disguised than other sources, offshoots of the German liberal tradition were fundamental in the ideology of the Pan-German League.[44] Establishment of the German Empire in 1871 dealt a severe blow to the aspirations of liberals to popular representation in shaping foreign policy, but these aspirations lived on, not only among the left-liberal political parties. The rivalries in the 1880s between the government and the patriotic societies were a sign of the persistence of these aspirations in groups whose political inclinations were National Liberal. The Pan-German League's program was the most unrestrained statement of the same populism which had animated the older societies. Demands for popular representation resurfaced in rival claims to custodianship over the national symbols, in the proposition that the *Volk* and not the state was the ultimate repository of national authority, and in the demand that the government heed the voice of public opinion, as articulated by the Pan-German League, in questions of national policy.

Several other points about the League's program deserve comment. The first concerns the extent to which the Pan-Germans represented an eccentric or unique phenomenon in Wilhelmine Germany. One can argue that the League's program expressed the aspirations of broad segments of the German middle class, that the organization was, in Dirk Oncken's words, 'the actual carrier of the idea of world power in the German public'.[45] As popular enthusiasm over colonies in the 1880s and over the navy in the 1890s demonstrated, the idea that Germany's mission was to exercise power on a worldwide scale was hardly the exclusive property of the Pan-German League. Nor was active concern for the fate of Germans outside the Reich. Yet the Pan-German League was, in important respects, a distinctive phenomenon. Its distinctiveness lay in the radical single-mindedness with which its leaders combined all these more popular issues into a single systematic view of the world and pursued the logic of their position to the point of active opposition to the government. The League's program was unique, in other words, to the extent that it was ideological, that it rested upon a tightly articulated and rigid view of the world, one which prescribed a difficult and frequently unpopular course of political action.

The ideology of the Pan-German League was a national religion, which displayed structural parallels with the Christian vision of fall and redemption. The event that Pan-Germans regarded as the analogue of the fall in German history was the Thirty Years' War, the catastrophe which brought political fragmentation, cultural stagnation, and the beginnings of the diaspora of emigrant Germans throughout Europe. To Bismarck fell, in the Pan-Germans' view, the role of national Messiah, in the sense of both redeeming the nation from the consequences of the fall and offering the promise of regeneration in the true *Nationalstaat* of the future. The year 1871 accordingly marked the beginning of the penultimate phase of German history, the mobilization of the nation's forces, and the spreading of the German Gospel in preparation for redemption in national unity and world power.

The word 'redemption' (*Erlösung*) may seem contrived in this context, for, as Roy Pascal has observed in connection with German literature of this period, it is loaded with metaphysical overtones.[46] The word appeared constantly in the literature of the Pan-German League, however, as did others with explicit religious connotations, such as 'diaspora' and 'Gospel'.[47] The frequent religious allusions and the structural similarities to the Christian cosmology betrayed the emotional intensity of the Pan-German League's ideology. The intensity cannot be adequately captured in a bloodless analysis of the logical cohesion of the League's program; the intensity, and the anxieties that underlay it, were more apparent in the imagery which pervaded the ideology.

Outposts amidst the flood

The imagery in the literature of the Pan-German League was very rich, and religious metaphors were but one of the funds from which Pan-German writers drew. The imagery and the rhetoric in which the League's ideology was couched revealed a great deal about the emotional implications of the League's program. In this rhetorical or semeiological realm – in the images and metaphors in which they depicted who they were and what they aspired to do – lay indications of the central concerns which occupied the Pan-Germans.

Theirs was foremost a rhetoric of conflict. They devoted an enormous volume of literature to ethnic struggle, for they described conflict everywhere, although for evident reasons most of their commentary dealt with the situation in Austria-Hungary. One of the first pronouncements that the League issued set the tone: 'Recent history means nothing other than the struggle of *everyone against Germandom*.'[48] The italics betrayed the anonymous author's inability to squeeze any more emphasis out of the words available to him. Words like 'struggle of desperation' (*Verzweiflungskampf*) and annihilation (*Vernichtung*) also made their appearance early to reveal how rapidly the level of rhetorical intensity had escalated.[49]

Pan-German writers employed a variety of images to describe ethnic conflict. Military imagery was one of the more obvious genres. Germans, embattled by hostile ethnic groups, were 'soldiers in our army, which is only too small'; the task at hand was hence the 'mobilization' of larger forces.[50] In the military idiom, the confrontation between Danes and Germans in North Schleswig became a 'situation of revolutionary war'; in the Prussian east, on the other hand, the struggle was 'nothing short of real war' (*ein regelrechter Krieg*).[51] Medical pathology was another source of images that Pan-Germans used to describe the threat their antagonists posed. To portray the Polish minority, for instance, they invoked the image of a cancer, suggesting propensities to grow imperceptibly but with fatal irresistibly.[52]

Of all the imagery with which Pan-German writers and speakers described ethnic conflict, the most common involved the play of elemental forces, especially water. 'The conditions in the *Ostmark* and in Austria-Hungary have deteriorated to the point where all Germans must join together today', warned one leader in 1908, 'in order to resist the impact of the flood tide [*Hochflut*] of Slavic and other foreign peoples.'[53] In the Prussian east the danger was 'an advancing Polish flood', which threatened to 'inundate [*überschwemmen*] the provinces with foreigners'.[54] In South Tirol it was an 'Italian flood', which 'surged around' (*umbrandet*) German settlements in the area.[55] In Carinthia, where the flood was Slovene, it menacingly 'washed around' German landholdings in the provinces.[56] Further to the north, in Bohemia, the Czech flood 'approached ever closer to the borders' of Germany.[57] In fact, the flood tide of enemies had already penetrated into the heart of the Reich, in the form of the 'growing inundation of our fatherland with foreigners', of 'overflooding by elements who speak more than one language [*gemischtsprächige*]', or in the form of the 'overflooding of German technical universities with disagreeable foreigners'.[58]

Variations on the theme of the flood included the image of the storm, both directly, as in the 'storm flood of nationalities in the Habsburg monarchy', and in the figurative sense, as in storming a fortress (*anstürmen*).[59] Germans in Austria confronted the 'on-storming masses of people hostile to them', or a 'Slavic onslaught [*Ansturm*], which threatens to annihilate everything German'; in the federal elections of 1903, the city of Leipzig faced the 'burst of the waves of the on-storming revolutionary party'.[60] Streams, another related image, appeared repeatedly in the Pan-German literature too. One writer warned, for example, of the 'wild Slavic stream' in Austria, which, if not resisted, would soon 'break devastatingly into the Reich'.[61] Another drew attention to the 'Stream of Italian immigrants' into South Tirol, which, he noted, had recently 'risen significantly [*angeschwollen*]'.[62]

Examples could be multiplied to emphasize how attractive Pan-German writers and speakers found the imagery of water. Their preference for it was pronounced, even though alternative images were available to them to symbolize the threat. The imagery of conflagration, for instance, appeared only occasionally, albeit colorfully. Thus did one writer describe revolutionary events in the Russian Baltic provinces in 1905–6: 'As in house-fires the small blue flames flitter above the roof, disappear, and return until they spot the places where they take hold, so too did the revolutionary movement dart about the land, at first unsure and tentative.'[63] But while the imagery of fire had many of the same connotations as water, it was less appealing to the Pan-Germans, although one can only speculate why. Both fire and flooding became uncontrollable; both penetrated and demolished. Fire, however, was not normally the result of natural causes; and flooding, unlike fire, usually left something behind, to be taken over from these who had been driven out. Polish communities could take root, springing up 'like mushrooms after the rain' in soil inhabited by Germans before the flood.[64] In addition, water flowed; its impact spread, through in-fluence (*Beeinflussung*), initially in subtle ways.[65]

The feature of the watery imagery that appealed most to the Pan-Germans was, in any event, the connotation of forces beyond control. Flooding, storms, and streams symbolized the advance of elemental forces, which penetrated ineluctably and destroyed positions occupied by Germans. On only a few occasions did Pan-Germans speak positively of storms or currents, and even on these occasions the phenomena retained their elemental power. A resolute policy with respect to Austria's ethnic minorities could thus work like a 'purifying storm [*Gewitter*] in the intolerable humidity of the present European situation'.[66] Much more commonly, storms, streams, and floods were destructive, turbid (*trüb*), and they unleashed forces that broke bounds.[67]

Pan-Germans described the forces threatening Germans throughout the world in much the same terms as they would a natural catastophe.[68] The imagery they employed to describe the Germans who were facing the catastrophe was not entirely consistent metaphorically with flooding and storm, but it was none the less effective. The dominant image was that of the outpost (*Vorposten*), on guard against the initial signs of danger, charged with serving as the first line of resistance. If the flood connoted hostile forces out of control, the outpost symbolized solidity, rootedness, and control. The specific imagery varied widely. Pan-German writers spoke of forward walls (*Vormauer*), a fortress (*Burg* or *Festung*), outer forts (*Aussenforts*), and outworks (*Vorwerke*), all of which were drawn from a military idiom.[69] Other commentators adapted the imagery to the metaphors of water. The outposts now became dams, dikes (*Schutzwälle*), roofs against the storm, or rocks (*Felsen*); most commonly, however, they became islands in the hostile sea.[70] The city of Budweis in Bohemia, a center of the struggle between Czechs and Germans, was thus, in the words of one observer, 'an island of the German language [*Sprachinsel*], ever more powerfully overflooded by the Czech bay, which sends out streams [*ausbuchtet*] in all directions'.[71]

The Germans who inhabited this 'island empire of German colonies in Eastern Europe', or who manned the 'posts around which the battle rages', were the heroic pioneers (*Vorkämpfer*) of the German cause.[72] Theirs was a lonely, dangerous, but elite role. Selected to provide the first line of defense, they operated bravely at a distance from the citadel of the German community, the Reich itself; they faced the risk of being fully isolated, left in the lurch, and abandoned to the flood.[73] The facts of distance and separation, and the attendant risks, defined the pioneer, for the image applied not only to Germans living in Eastern Europe, but to German officials isolated in the ethnically troubled parts of the Reich, and to German settlers and businessmen overseas.[74]

It is not difficult to discern at least one deeper level of meaning beneath the imagery in this literature. Outposts and pioneers were self-images of the Pan-German League. In its efforts to awaken national awareness and to encourage a forceful foreign policy, the League was, its spokesmen assured the membership, performing 'pioneer services' or 'pioneer work'.[75] The local chapter in Posen, revivified after several years of inactivity, announced to the rest of the League in 1904 that once again German men were 'at their posts' in Posen.[76] Pan-German writers described both themselves and the pioneers in the field with the same formula words, especially with the word '*wacker*', which carries connotations of both bravery and honesty.[77] In the imagery of the flood, the mission of the League was to be a rock in the sea, a lighthouse, or an island.[78]

The idea of distance or separation, which was essential to the role of the pioneer, also figured in the League's self-image. Here the distance was less geographical than temporal or emotional. Years of opposition to the German government left an ideological imprint, in the idea that the League's mission was to act as a national 'pacemaker' or 'pathbreaker', in the sense of anticipating policies before their time had come.[79] 'We are really nothing but people who have arisen a little earlier than many of our contemporaries who continue to sleep', as one commentator put it.[80] This role separated the League from the main 'stream of conventional attitudes' and compelled its members (for the water was everywhere) to 'swim against public opinion'.[81]

The role of national pioneer was difficult and lonely. It was only partially eased by the realization that being the 'conscience of the German people' required temporary divergence from popular attitudes, but that the role would ultimately be vindicated with the general acceptance of the League's views.[82] Still, the heroism implied in this posture had accents of martyrdom, particularly after the tension with the government became severe. In 1909, for example, a speaker encouraged members of the chapter in Eisleben not to grow weary of their national responsibilities, even if 'progress was only slow and they were persecuted [*angefeindet*] on all sides'.[83] Speakers at other rallies urged members to persevere in the face of 'hate-filled, mendacious persecution of the League', 'fanatical opposition', or the 'scorn and ridicule' of their opponents in Germany.[84]

The theme of martyrdom casts the flood metaphor into another perspective. The metaphor is loaded with religious and emotional connotations. In Christian imagery it is a Satanic force. Freudian psychoanalysts have noted how it stimulates ambivalent feelings of fascination, attraction, and danger.[85] Common to both the Freudian and Christian symbolism is the idea that the flood represents powerful forces which resist confinement in their proper limits, be these limits defined as moral precepts or ego injunctions.

Well might the Pan-Germans have found the metaphor of the flood attractive to describe their enemies, who they were convinced were advancing everywhere. These enemies included nearly everyone in the world who was not a German, as well as many people who were. The list was headed by all the non-German ethnic groups in Central Europe, foremost among them the Poles and Czechs. The category extended to all people who were nationals of Germany's rivals, actual or potential – English, French, Russians, Americans, Italians, and Japanese. It included Germans whose patriotic credentials were tainted in any manner with international loyalties, particularly Catholics and socialists.

Disparate as the groups were that fell into the Pan-Germans' category of enemy, they were in several respects united. All of them were powerful, dangerous, supremely clever, and they all shared a common motive – hatred of everything German. Everywhere they looked, Pan-German commentators saw the same forces at work. 'Precisely at this moment', wrote one of them in connection with a conflict between German and French students at the university of Lausanne in 1908, 'one sees how on all sides hatred of Germandom becomes apparent.'[86] Among the Catholic clergy it was a 'fanatical hatred of Protestantism and ferocious ridicule of every patriotic feeling', in Italy it was a 'scarcely contained resentment [*Groll*] of us Germans', in the Prussian east it was a 'demonic hatred of Prussia and its government', while in the city of Prague, Czech 'mania and hatred' celebrated 'their wildest orgies'.[87] Consumed with hatred, these omnipresent enemies shied from nothing in their attack: they were fanatical, shameless, unscrupulous, 'simultaneously insidious [*heimtückisch*] and brutal', perseverant, ruthless, given to violence, and they interpreted attempts at conciliation by Germans only as signs of weakness.[88]

Because they saw their enemies in this light, Pan-German writers had only a limited understanding of the causes of animosity toward Germans. But the limitations of their understanding were themselves enlightening. The most common explanation was well formulated by a speaker in 1910, who concluded at the League's annual congress that 'we have as many enemies as we count those who envy us'.[89] The concept of envy was extremely attractive to Pan-Germans, for it provided an analysis that not only absolved Germans of any responsibility for the hostility they faced, but made this very hostility a cause for self-respect. The concept also had broader implications. Envy connoted a desire for something to which one was not entitled or, more broadly, an unwillingness to accept limitations legitimately imposed. In this sense, envy was generically related to other qualities Pan-Germans identified in the motivation of their enemies. Prominent among these were lack of respect for Germans, arrogance, unruliness (*Ungeberdigkeit*), impudence (*Frechheit*), haughtiness (*Hochmut*), presumption (*Ueppigkeit* or *Anmassung*), immoderation (*Masslosigkeit*), ill breeding (*Unerzogenheit*), impatience, and impertinence (*Unverschämtheit*).[90] All these characteristics shared the sense of transgression against appropriate constraint, order, or authority. So too did two other, more psychologically charged words which occupied a prominent place in the vocabulary of the Pan-Germans: these were 'penetrate' (*eindringen*) and 'violate' (*vergewältigen*). Foreign firms penetrated the German market, foreign words (*sprachliche Eindringlinge*) the German language.[91] Czechs lured German children into their schools, one alarmed writer observed, 'in order to commit on them an act of the most brutal spiritual [*geistige*] national violation'.[92]

The countless variations in the Pan-German literature on the theme of transgression against limit, the constant imagery of this theme in the flood, reflected these writers' ultimate concern. Above all, they feared the total breakdown of legitimate constraint and order. Their most foreboding vision was the triumph of the flood, the overwhelming of outposts abandoned to their fate, and then the fall of the now isolated citadel itself. The result would be the disappearance of limit, restraint, and order – chaos, in a word, the most frightening situation imaginable. And imagine it these writers did. As he watched the turmoil in Austria at the turn of the century, one writer was convinced he was witnessing the penultimate phase of the drama:

> It is as if all the joy of life had disappeared from this [German] people; nothing concerns them any more except the thought of their ethnic identity [*Volkstum*]. Business comes to a standstill. Wherever men congregate they speak of the yoke the Slavs are preparing for them; and at home, by the hearth, the housewife tries in vain to soothe her husband's brow, strained with anxiety, anger, and fear [*sorgen- und grollgefürchtete!*]. Something like stifling sultriness that precedes the storm burdens the land, and everyone has the feeling that it will only take a spark to unleash a storm of unfathomable violence. Whom will it annihilate?[93]

A more pertinent question was *what* would the storm annihilate. The answer was the very concept of order. 'Chaos knows no crown', wrote Heinrich Class with respect to the monarchical order. 'If it breaks in over the German people, it is going to swallow everything that stands out [*alles ragende*].'[94]

The concept of order underlay the symbolism in the Pan-German literature; it was the key to understanding the League's political cosmology. Anxiety over the disorder sown by ethnic conflict was a *Leitmotif*, varied endlessly. Another motif, subject to less variation, was the Pan-Germans' vision of a specific kind of order.

Order, Culture, and Authority

The imagery in the ideology of the Pan-German League betrayed a paramount concern for order. The flood symbolized the overwhelming of legitimately prescribed confines, transgression against proper limit – in sum, disorder, whose culmination was chaos. The outposts and the pioneers who occupied them stood for resistance to disorder, for discipline, stability, and the preservation of a proper system of confines.

The symbolism extended further. The concept of order implied a stable regularity in human affairs, a clearly defined pattern of relations among people or groups of people who were, by definition, not equal. The ideas of regularity and stability, which were basic to order, demanded that patterns of precedence and subordination be cemented by authority and deference. Order comprehended, that is, both the claim of the superordinated to represent or to have prior access to some source of strength or truth, and the disciplined recognition by the subordinated of the validity of this claim.[95] Authority and discipline buttressed the order of relationships among all elements of a social or political system, for they defined legitimate spheres of existence and activity, the proper bounds of aspiration and ambition. In the Pan-German League's idiom, the concept of order dictated that those people entitled to exercise authority, *'die Obrigkeit'* in the abstract, enjoy attitudes of 'reverence and deference' (*Ehrfurcht und Ehrerbietung*) from those who stood under this authority.[96] The negation of order was of course the principle of insubordination, the abandonment of deference, of the proper limits imposed by order, and the repudiation of the authority of those in positions of superordination.

In the literature of the Pan-German League the flood symbolized the negating, destructive principle of insubordination, which began in its early stages with the subtle undermining of authority and culminated, if unchecked, in swamping the whole structure of order. Conversely, the pioneers represented authority as well as order. Their claim to authority derived from their advanced, exposed position; as vanguards of the nation, they stood out as leaders, men who had been the first to perceive the patterns of ethnic conflict which were the stuff of history, and who foresaw the impending struggle for national survival.

Order meant for the Pan-German League specific patterns of authority and precedence. Although they ultimately merged, these patterns applied to two realms of human organization, the ethnic and the social. That ethnic conflict was an inevitable feature of human history was axiomatic in the Pan-Germans' view of the world. However, this proposition was not easily reconciled with another, which implied that ethnic conflict was somehow contrary to the proper order of things, which dictated that nations were unequal and that the German nation stood atop the ethnic hierarchy. Pan-German writers variously invoked nature, history, and providence to fortify their claim that of all the ethnic groups in the world, the Germans were the superior and hence entitled to exercise authority, precedence, and domination (*Herrschaft*) over others.[97]

This claim was bold, but Pan-Germans could adduce specific criteria to measure the quality of ethnic groups. 'We are the best warrior nation in the world', proclaimed one writer at the turn of the century. This virtue was evidently not sufficient, though, for he went on to insist that 'we are the ablest [*tüchtigste*] nation in all areas of knowledge and the fine arts. We are the best settlers, the best seafarers, even the best businessmen.'[98] Other writers subsumed these virtues under the heading of 'culture', which they construed to be the collective achievement of the *Volk*, the expression of its soul and worth.[99] The most obvious and tangible manifestations of *Kultur* were science and the advancement of knowledge (all of which Germans designated *Wissenschaft*), art, technology, commerce, and a series of qualities that characterized people who could be said to be 'civilized' (to partake of *Gesittung*), such as intelligence, diligence, and sincerity (*Redlichkeit*).[100] The concept of culture also had important political connotations. The Cologne chapter alluded to these when, late in 1908, it passed a resolution endorsing the proposition that the Austrian state owed its 'existence and endurance [*Bestand*] exclusively to German culture'.[101] In this respect, culture was practically synonymous with political order: it connoted collective traits that were *'staatsschöpferisch und staatserhaltend'* – traits, that is, which promoted and sustained stable relationships of power and authority in a unified state.[102]

The superiority of German culture, of those 'noble characteristics' which constituted the 'most precious spiritual blossom of the human race', entitled the German nation to authority and precedence in the ordered structure of relations among the nationalities of the world.[103] The subordinate position of other ethnic groups was justified by the inferiority of their cultures, specifically in the case of other ethnic groups in Central and Eastern Europe (and here the lessons of 1871 were evident), by their inability to create political order in their own states.[104] Pan-Germans insisted in fact that the culture these other ethnic groups had attained in the past they owed primarily to German settlers, colonizers, and missionaries. The role of Germans had historically been to serve as precepts, as 'pioneers of all culture', or, in the more earthy expression preferred by some writers, as 'ethnic fertilizer' (*Volksdünger*) for others.[105] Prominent among the benefits brought by Germans during this process of 'elevating barbarians to cultured nations' were the virtues and institutions necessary for political order, such as legislation, administration, and a system of justice.[106]

In the final analysis, Pan-Germans believed, the root of ethnic struggle was the insubordination of other nationalities, their refusal to acknowledge the superiority of German culture and the respect and authority to which this superiority entitled the German *Volk*. One image used to express this belief was that of rebellious students threatening their teacher – as desperate an act of disorder as Germans could imagine.[107] But hostility toward Germans implied not only the rejection of their precedence in the ethnic order of the world, but the repudiation of the principle of ethnic order itself. 'Hatred of Germans', wrote one commentator on the basis of his experiences in Hungary, 'is the sign of a true renegade.'[108] Only in this light can one understand why the United States presented such a foreboding spectacle to the Pan-Germans. The fact that Germans did not occupy the positions of leadership to which their cultural contributions entitled them was far less frightening than the fact that Germans (and others) were losing their very ethnic identity, that in the United States, in the 'mass grave of Germandom', the very idea of ethnicity, and hence of ethnic order, had been undermined.

Into this morass emigrant Germans were sucked, sank, were abandoned and forgotten.[109] The melting pot was ethnic chaos.

Because the Pan-Germans held ethnicity to be the basic feature of human affairs, they insisted that social order was a derivative of it and that culture implied a series of social postulates as well. The preservation of the dominant position of the German *Volk* in the ethnic order demanded social order within the ethnic unit. Social order in turn implied harmony, cohesion, and balance among all the component groups of German society, the acceptance by each of its proper sphere, and a general sense of contentedness (*Neidlosigkeit*).[110]

In the eyes of the Pan-Germans, social order further implied specific patterns and roles. At the foundation, as the 'firmest pillar of Germandom', stood the peasantry.[111] In extolling the virtues of the peasantry – its diligence, piety, simplicity, and the modesty of its pretensions – the Pan-Germans had a lot of company in Imperial Germany.[112] Their own appreciation of the peasantry was in part the result of their involvement in the ethnic struggle in eastern Prussia, which they concluded could only be won through massive settlement of German peasants on middle-sized plots in the Polish provinces.[113] However, the virtues that the Pan-Germans found embodied in the German peasantry had broader implications for social order; the peasant represented culture in its most intuitive and innocent form. As he surveyed German peasant colonies in Russia, one writer was impressed at how 'German order and neatness [*Sauberkeit*] characterized the villages and houses, German diligence makes the villages prosper in peaceful times, so they serve as models to others'.[114] In Russia, as elsewhere, the German peasant represented the *Volkspionier* who displayed most instinctively the traits that distinguished German culture. Not surprisingly, these peasant traits had direct political relevance; they included 'national reliability', a sense of order (albeit with a certain – admirable – obstinacy), and a sufficient feeling of their own importance that peasants were content with their social station.[115] The stability, rootedness, and independence afforded them by small property holdings and a close relationship to the soil preserved these traits in peasants and made them appreciate, like no other social group, the importance of order.

Only a little less emphatic was the tribute the Pan-Germans paid to the *Mittelstand*. In their view this social group included artisans, handicraftsmen, and other small businessmen – people who resembled the peasantry in their independence, their possession of modest amounts of property, and in the attitudes they were presumed to hold about the importance of social order and stability.[116] The *Mittelstand* was accordingly another of the most secure repositories of German culture; it too could lay claim, in the Pan-German vision, to the status of 'backbone of the nation'.[117]

One of the principal marks of the virtue and reliability of both these social groups was their devotion to the family, an institution in which Pan-Germans descried social order in microcosm. The family was an 'auxiliary and military community [*Hilfs- und Kampfgenossenschaft*] in the stream of life'.[118] A realm where each member had her or his structured role, the family was the essential 'precondition for the healthy durability of the nation', the breeding ground of national virtues, prominent among which the Pan-German writers identified 'domestic discipline and order'.[119]

As the most reliable props for attitudes and institutions essential to the preservation of social order, the peasantry and *Mittelstand* were to enjoy special status within this order – but not at the top. In the Pan-German vision, the role of elite in the social order and the national community was reserved instead for another group, whose relationship to German culture was of a different character than that of peasants or artisans. The essential role of interpreting, refining, and mediating German culture was the most esteemed of all, and it entitled those who performed it to the authority of national leadership. These were the men whose access to culture was most immediate, conscious, and creative, by virtue of their being 'cultured'. The distinguishing mark of these men was their *Bildung*, a concept difficult to translate from the German, for it simultaneously connoted culture and a special kind of education which is perhaps best described by the word 'cultivation'. *Bildung* meant a general education of the whole person, training not only in academic subjects, particularly classical languages, but in 'taste, judgment, and intellect'; it implied a certain autonomy and nobility of character unavailable to people without it. And it normally required a university education.[120]

In their admiration for *Bildung* and the values it connoted, the Pan-Germans were hardly unique in Imperial Germany. Most of their contemporaries did not, however, draw the same political conclusions as they did. The simultaneity of meaning in the word *Bildung* reflected a critical juncture in the Pan-Germans' view of order. The juncture implied that the only men with a full appreciation for German culture were those who had absorbed it directly in the course of their university education. Trained to value 'higher spiritual development' and to 'comprehend the great continuities of national development', the academically educated were the 'spiritual leaders of the *Volk*', men entitled to elite positions of political authority and to dispense culture for the satisfaction of 'the spiritual hunger of the *Volk*'.[121] Cultivation brought entitlement to authority. It was also a sign of achievement and bore witness to the bonds that linked the elite to the broader groups that constituted the pillars of the nation; for the men of *Bildung* were themselves often distinguished children of the *Mittelstand*. Their achievement, culture, national consciousness, and their insight into the patterns of history put them at the apex of the social order; theirs was the role of pioneer, vanguard, and leader *par excellence*.

Culture was the governing principle of order; access to culture brought entitlement to precedence and authority. This principle applied, in the Pan-Germans' view, to ethnic as well as to social relationships. Germans could lay claim to *Herrschaft* over other nationalities by virtue of their superior culture, while the academically educated were entitled to exercise authority within the German *Volk* by virtue of the mediating role they played with respect to this same culture. In the final analysis, though, the association between culture and order was tautological. Pan-Germans identified culture with order, or rather with specific patterns of social and ethnic subordination. The distinguishing characteristics of culture were precisely those habits of mind presumed to buttress these patterns of order – a want of pretension and an appreciation for limit, regularity, and stability.

It has become commonplace to discuss the Pan-Germans' ideas about order in the context of 'cultural despair', a tradition of general hostility to modernity and the search for a harmonic order by resurrecting the simple virtues of a more pristine past. Although there is some truth to this view, it is too simple.[122] The faith the Pan-Germans placed in the peasantry and the *Mittelstand*, the political quietism they found so attractive in these social groups, was consistent with this view, as was their glorification of a system of general education which pedagogical reformers were already attacking at the turn of the century as out of date. Yet the concept of 'cultural despair' fails to comprehend several important facets of the Pan-German League's view of the world. Until the turn of the century, the accents in its ideology were optimistic, as the success of the naval campaign made its predictions about national fulfillment in the future seem plausible. The enthusiasm of the League for the navy pointed as well to an appreciation of industrial power which did not square with a longing for a pre-industrial past.[123] The Pan-Germans' vision of order was broad enough to reconcile industry and agriculture, modern and 'pre-modern' sectors of society; it was necessary only that each occupy its proper sphere.[124]

The principal justification for inserting the Pan-Germans into the tradition of cultural despair is their acute sensitivity about forces contained in industrialization which threatened to destroy not only the delicate balance between industry and agriculture, but the whole structure of social and ethnic order. Order was linked, in the Pan-Germans' thinking, to rootedness, which normally meant ownership of at least a small piece of property. In so far as the social change associated with industrialization tended to cut these roots and to create a propertyless working class in big cities, it had dangerous ramifications. Mobility off the countryside was in fact one of 'the fundamental evils of our national life', Hasse lamented, for it created not only social unrest but ethnic disorientation.[125] People caught up in this process lost 'the tie to their German ethnicity', observed another writer.[126] One is reminded here of the forebodings that the Pan-Germans expressed about the ethnic disorder of the United States: peasants who wandered into the social chaos of the big cities lost touch with their sense of order, their culture, and hence their ethnic identity.[127]

Many of the schemes that the Pan-Germans advocated reflected a concern about the evils of urbanization, rootlessness, and social disorder. In the Prussian east and in North Schleswig, they promoted what amounted to a program of land reform, the large-scale settlement of an independent German peasantry; to this end, they even advocated breaking up large estates in the east that were worked by a landless (and usually Polish) proletariat. Pan-Germans also advocated various programs to bail out small businessmen. And, in speaking of the need for colonies, most of them were unsympathetic to the claims of the companies which were turning profits; they subscribed instead to the emigrationist argument that settlements abroad were essential as future bases for an independent German peasantry.[128]

The League's ideologists professed sympathy for social reform, but their ideas were anchored in a socially conservative populism – in the conviction that preserving social order demanded the support and revitalization of the backbone of 'the people', which meant in the first instance the peasantry and artisanal *Mittelstand*. Pan-German theorists were far less comfortable discussing the plight of the industrial working class in the cities. The cultural values that ensured the cohesion of the social order were naturally to apply to this class too. Industrial workers were to display punctuality and discipline; they were to be 'extremely diligent' and, probably more important, 'unpretentious' (*anspruchslos*).[129] Their just rewards were the fortunes of a 'disciplined clan of workers' (*Arbeiterstamm*) such as the one the Pan-Germans thought they had found in the small iron- and steel-processing plants in Remscheid (where the League congregated for its convention in 1913): many of these 'simple men' had, as one speaker noted, managed to 'work their way up to proud heights', although he did not specify what these were.[130] None the less, large sectors of the working class refused to accept the place the Pan-Germans prescribed for them in the social order. Their ingratitude and pretentiousness knew no bounds. 'The benevolent hand of bourgeois society' they rejected 'ungratefully and coarsely'.[131] They had forgotten the virtue of frugality: it was pointless to give them higher wages, one writer complained, for they would only squander these on luxuries, such as 'more expensive walking sticks, more elegant prams, and modern hats' – luxuries which, the writer did not have to add, were appropriate to some social stations, but certainly not theirs.[132]

The source of this problem lay, Pan-Germans believed, only partially in the rootlessness and temptations of the big city. The principal cause of the workers' disrespect for order lay in a foreboding phenomenon. To the Pan-Germans, Social Democracy was simply the most ominous thing conceivable, the original evil, the repudiation of order.[133] It was a Mephistophelian force, 'the spirit of abnegation' (*der Geist, der immer verneint*), of indiscipline, dissension, destruction, and discontent, the mortal enemy not only of property and social order, but of the principle of ethnicity as well.[134] For the Pan-Germans, Social Democracy was the most palpable manifestation of the flood; it was the very spirit of chaos.[135]

The Pan-German League was understandably troubled when on several occasions, such as during the Boer War, its criticism of the German government ran parallel to that of the German Social Democratic Party. These parallels highlighted an apparent contradiction in the League's position: it was not immediately clear how a group of men whose view of the world so emphasized order and authority could openly challenge the authority of the German government on national issues. This is one of the central problems in the history of the Pan-German League, and its resolution must take place on several levels of analysis. Here an ideological explanation is pertinent. Pan-Germans believed that the preservation of social order was contingent upon asserting German authority in the ethnic order or, to put it in slightly different terms, that the national consciousness essential to a stable social order demanded an aggressive foreign policy. They concluded, definitively after the Boer War, that the German government, as it was then staffed, was too weak and indecisive to conduct the policies necessary to check the forces of disorder at home and abroad.[136] It was a measure of their concern that these men could, for entirely patriotic reasons, call into question the government's exclusive guardianship of the national interest and demand that they themselves, as the spokesmen of the will of the *Volk*, be consulted in the determination of policy. Resisting the forces of disorder demanded that the authority of the pioneers be recognized.[137] To deserve this recognition, however, the pioneers had themselves constantly to document their personal qualifications.

Bismarck and Hamlet

In 1900 the *Alldeutsche Blätter* revealed a new masthead. It depicted a single Teutonic warrior, clad in armor and winged helmet, standing beside an oak tree situated atop a cliff overlooking the sea. The warrior's gaze carried out toward the rising sun, over the sea and the ships that were seen sailing on it. Entwined among the branches of the oak was a banner bearing the League's motto, 'Remember that you are a German!' (*Gedenke, dass du ein Deutscher bist!*).

The imagery was not exactly subtle. The high cliffs and the oak symbolized order, defense, and stability; the sea, though calm and subject to a degree of human control (in the ships), threatened to become the flood once the sun, which indicated optimism, disappeared behind storm clouds. The lone warrior was of course the pioneer – exposed, living in danger, but vigilant at his outpost. In its heavy symbolism, the glorification of the Teutonic past, and in the knight's heroic posture, which smacked none the less of sentimentality, one finds typified the aesthetic sensitivities the League's writers cultivated.[138] To dismiss it all as only so much kitsch, however, would be to overlook the messages this symbolism conveyed about the self-understanding of those who read the League's literature. The warrior figure was particularly suggestive psychologically, for it embodied attitudes and character traits that the Pan-German writers held to be essential to German identity.

The problem of identity was one to which the Pan-Germans devoted a great deal of attention, both as an individual and a collective phenomenon. They held that identity and ethnicity were inseparable, indeed that ethnicity was prior to identity.[139] The language one spoke was more than an appurtenance or something that one could, for convenience's sake, 'shed like a coat'; it constituted a fundamental part of every person's psychological make-up and, for Germans at least, 'the most holy' component of one's being.[140] 'He who knows not whether his character [*Art*] is German or French suffers from an imperfection that limits his entire development', was the dictum of one writer.[141] His sentiments were shared by another, who spoke more suggestively of the 'national asexuality' of the Social Democrats.[142] In the same vein, still another writer condemned the very concept of bilinguality, which was being promoted in some circles in Alsace-Lorraine, as calculated to breed 'national hermaphrodites'.[143]

Collective identity, no less than personal identity, was the product of ethnicity. It was self-evident to Pan-Germans that certain collective traits defined the essence of any ethnic unit and were central features of any nation's culture. In speaking of their own essential national characteristics, these writers isolated a long list of traits, most of them exemplary as befit the claims they were making for the German nation. The list included German daring, German bravery, a German sense of freedom and independence (which bordered on obstinacy but which did not exclude German discipline), German honor, German loyalty, German courage, German simplicity, German pride, and German conscientiousness.[144] There was, however, another, darker side of the German character. This comprised traits which, however laudable in an individual, were dangerous in their collective manifestation. Prominent among these were proclivities toward self-deprecation, cosmopolitanism, innocent complaisance and sentimentality, too much 'concern for the welfare and plight' of other nations, inordinate patience, and a tendency to become lost in profound, other-worldly meditation.[145] These characteristics were commonly associated, in the Pan-German literature, with the virtuous but naive and dreamy figure of the 'German Michel' or with Hamlet, who was not German, but was evidently Germanic enough to epitomize the perils of indecision and overscrupulousness.[146]

The question is not germane whether these characteristics bore any semblance to reality or whether they were even compatible with one another (although it is challenging to imagine Germans who were simultaneously obstinate, disciplined, proud, self-deprecating, simple and yet given to intellectual profundity). Of greater interest is the fact that the character traits which most disturbed the Pan-Germans represented the psychological equivalent of social disorder. These traits implied, above all, lack of control. Sentimentality, complaisance, and naiveté all suggested want of direction, of awareness, or an inability to take seriously forces that threatened, impinged, or penetrated. Hamlet's problem was his inability to seize control; his critical failing was his wooliheadedness (the German word, *Verschwommenheit*, is much more suggestive, for it retains the implications of being overcome by water).[147] Lack of control connoted passivity, femininity, and dependence upon external circumstances, the danger of 'resignedly and inactively letting the future break in over us', as Hasse phrased it, appealing again to the watery metaphor.[148]

Given this analysis of personality, the psychology in the ideology of the Pan-German League emphasized, as the analogue to the achievement of culture, the quest for self-transcendence, the effort to overcome essential German traits that were ill-suited to the rigors of ethnic struggle and defending social order. 'We want to be the hammer, not the anvil', was the slogan to which Pan-German writers appealed in describing the virtues in need of cultivation. These virtues connoted control, autonomy, independence, strength, masculinity, and self-assertion.[149] Germans were to be self-conscious, energetic,[150] self-aware (*selbstbewusst*), willfully perseverant, tough (*zähig*), purposeful (*zielbewusst*), steady (*stetig*), and, if necessary, ruthless (*rücksichtslos*).[151] Above all, they were to be earnest – a characteristic which seemed in the Pan-German literature to subsume all the rest in its implication of self-control and awareness of the imperatives of a situation fraught with peril.

Pan-German writers were convinced that one did not have to look far to see these virtues embodied, nor will psychologists accustomed to thinking in terms of projection be surprised at where they looked. All of Germany's enemies had achieved them. 'Let us learn from our opponents' was accordingly the best plan of action; or, as another writer put it, more lyrically, *'Willst du dich selber erkennen,/So sieh, wie die Andern es treiben!'*[152] As the ultimate model of national virtue and the epitome of the pioneer, however, the Pan-Germans claimed one of their own.

Inevitably, this was Bismarck. The adulation of the Pan-German League for the former chancellor was boundless. It reached, in fact, the point of deification, and the annual pilgrimages Pan-Germans made to Bismarck's tomb were as replete with liturgical rituals as any religious service.[153] Bismarck was 'the very quintessence of Germandom', the 'teacher of the German people'; he was also featured in the watery metaphor, as the 'great helmsman' who did not fear the storm as he guided the ship of state *Germania*.[154] He was, in addition, the embodiment of the more domestic virtues, as members of the League learned at the lectures they attended on subjects such as 'Bismarck as a Human Being and Father' and 'Bismarck as Husband'.[155] But the most important reasons why Pan-Germans worshipped the man, collected portraits of him, helped build monuments and museums to his memory, and poured over the literature being published about him were the personal traits that Bismarck had turned into public virtues – his moral strength, toughness, vigilance, purposefulness, and his supreme control over the political situation.[156]

Bismarck was, however, in some respects too removed and perfect to serve as the model pioneer. A more comfortable precept, because he embodied human weakness in a way the image of Bismarck could not, was the figure of the 'loyal Ekkehard', the hero of Josef Viktor von Scheffel's historical novel of the same name. An intrepid leader in battle, Ekkehard was naive and oblivious of the machinations of his envious enemies. Banished into exile, he overcame these personal flaws and returned to become the emperor's trusted adviser. Elements in this story of course ran parallel to Bismarck's own career, and Pan-Germans often referred to Bismarck as the 'Ekkehard of the German people'.[157] But the image was also one they used to describe the psychological and political drama they saw themselves acting out. Ekkehard symbolized pioneering leadership inadequately appreciated, the transcending of personal weakness, and final vindication as trusted advisers to the policy-makers.[158]

Those who had, like Ekkehard, successfully dealt with the flaws in their make-up and had achieved the virtues demanded of the pioneer were, in the analysis of the Pan-Germans, fulfilled, 'whole men', 'genuine personalities'; they could lay claim to 'character'.[159] In the opinion of Heinrich Class, who had an acute eye for this kind of 'character', Ludwig Possehl, the immensely wealthy Lübeck merchant, was one such, 'a *Herrenmensch* through and through, ruthless in the pursuit of his own advantage but willing to make any sacrifice for the good of the whole community [*dem grossen Ganzen*]'.[160] The industrialist Wilhelm Kollmann, another of Class's friends, deserved the attribution of 'character' on the strength alone of having broken a wine bottle over the head of Bismarck's critic, Maximilian Harden.[161]

The psychology of Pan-Germanism was intimately tied to the vision of order and conflict in society and politics. 'Character' was the psychological equivalent of culture; it entitled those who had achieved it to authority and positions of leadership.[162] Conversely, 'character' was the guarantee of order, of the stable structure in which legitimate authority was recognized. Of German diplomacy the League demanded 'character'; foreign policy was to be informed by brutal but 'healthy national egoism' which inspired fear among Germany's enemies and compelled respect for German authority throughout the world.[163] Ego was to be recognized as an ethnic as well as a psychological category: control, autonomy, independence, and initiative were as indispensable to the fulfillment of the German nation as they were to the individuals who collectively constituted it.[164]

The dependency in the Pan-Germans' ideology between psychology and socio-ethnic categories of order and conflict was mutual. Preservation of social and ethnic order had psychological ramifications: it impinged directly upon personal feelings, for ultimately at issue was psychological order, a sense of personal identity and control. A strong, assertive foreign policy was not only the essential condition and guarantee of order; it created self-respect, feelings of honor, high prestige, and repute (*Ansehen*) for the German nation and for all those who had identified with it (pre-eminently, of course, its pioneers).[165] Conversely, the consequences of a weak and passive policy – one without character – were in the end psychological; they included self-abnegation [*Selbstentäusserung*], humiliation, lack of respect, and, most painfully, an acute sense of shame.[166] Shame was in fact the principal feeling awakened among Pan-Germans as they responded to international events. Comparisons between the navies of Germany and other countries, for instance, provoked a sense of 'surprise and shame'.[167] The marriage of a Hessian princess to the heir-apparent to the Russian throne in 1894 stimulated feelings of 'shame and humiliation'.[168]

The Pan-Germans' view of the world had several dimensions, linked by a number of correlates. The focus of the League's program was on a strong foreign policy, which was to eventuate in the creation of a Central European nation-state, but the ramifications of a strong foreign policy were manifold. Its inspiration and ultimate consequences were psychological. Informed by the personal traits that made up 'character', a strong foreign policy solidified ethnic order in the world, allowing the nation with entitlement to precedence by virtue of its culture to exercise authority. Strong foreign policy also solidified the social order within the nation; it provided common national goals to promote cohesion and allowed the men who were entitled to precedence by virtue of their culture, *Bildung*, and character, to exercise authority. Finally, a strong foreign policy created a sense of psychological order; it inspired feelings of self-respect, honor, and personal control.

These several dimensions of the Pan-Germans' ideology were entwined within the national symbolism and within the imagery of the pioneer, outposts, and the flood. *Deutschtum*, the German nation, the language, empire, Bismarck, and the navy all symbolized order. The League's program called for the aggressive defense of these symbols, in the creation of a great Central-European nation-state with a wordwide empire. Creating this nation-state was to be more than a political achievement, however. It represented the ultimate dike against the flood, that counter-symbol of disorder in all its ethnic, social, and psychological manifestations. The political unification of the German nation symbolized the stabilization of order and the vindication of the pioneer's claims to precedence, for that elite figure embodied the noble features of German culture, and his 'character' was the emblem of having achieved psychological order and control.

The Pan-German League's claim to protect the national symbols was finally a claim to interpret them, to define just what these symbols stood for. The League's interpretation emphasized the concepts and values of order, control, culture, education, property, and achievement. The prominence of these concepts and values was not fortuitous, for the symbolism in the ideology of the Pan-German League reflected the experience of the social group that made up most of the organization's active membership.

Notes

1   See Vondung, 'Probleme einer Sozialgeschichte der Ideen', p. 13; Kurt Lenk, *'Volk und Staat': Strukturwandel politischer Ideologien im 19. und 20. Jahrhundert* (Stuttgart, 1971), p. 17; Peter Berger, Brigitte Berger, and Hansfried Kellner, *The Homeless Mind: Modernization and Consciousness* (New York, 1974), pp. 159–60.
2   Geertz, esp. pp. 207–19.
3   Jean-Paul Sartre, *Anti-Semite and Jew* (New York, 1965), p. 17.
4   Peter Berger and Thomas Luckmann, *The Social Construction of Reality* (New York, 1976), pp. 107–8; Hans Gerth and C. Wright Mills, *Character and Social Structure: The Psychology of Social Institutions* (London, 1954), pp. 287–94.
5   Thompson, *Making of the Working Class*, p. 50.
6   Stern, *Hitler*, p. 16.
7   Berger and Luckmann, pp. 85–118.
8   Gerhard Schulz, 'Imperialismus im 19. Jahrhundert', *Das Zeitalter der Gesellschaft: Aufsätze zur politischen Sozialgeschichte der Neuzeit* (Munich, 1969), p. 159.
9   Whiteside, p. 301.
10 See Stern, *Cultural Despair*, p. 213; Arno J. Mayer, *Dynamics of Counterrevolution in Europe, 1870–1956: An Analytical Framework* (New York, 1971), p. 53..
11 ZStAP, ADV 45, GFA, Leipzig, 7/8.10.04; MADV (June 1891), 2; ADV (1904), 146–9.
12 ADB (1908), 94–6.
13 ADB (1911), 424–6; cf. ADB (1905), 177–8; ADB (1914), 146; Werner, p. 62.
14 *Das Deutsche Reich als Nationalstaat* (Munich, 1905); *Die Besiedlung des deutschen Volksbodens* (Munich, 1905); *Deutsche Grenzpolitik* (Munich, 1905); *Die Zukunft des deutschen Volkstums* (Munich, 1907); *Weltpolitik, Imperialismus und Kolonialpolitik* (Munich, 1908); cf. ADB (1904), 448–9.
15 Einhart [pseud. Heinrich Class], *Deutsche Geschichte* (Leipzig, 1909); cf. ADB (1909), 133–4; Daniel Frymann [pseud. Heinrich Class], *Wenn ich der Kaiser wär': Politische Wahrheiten und Notwendigkeiten* (Leipzig, 1912).
16 A great number of pamphlets appeared in the decades prior to the war which, because of the extravagance of their demands, were attributed to the Pan-German League, but for which the organization was not responsible. I have confined my analysis to the literature that can be linked directly to the League. See Hobohm and Rohrbach, p. 6; Hartwig, 'Entwicklung', pp. 52–3; Gerstenhauer, p. 11.
17 ADB (1894), 149–50; ADB (1902), 448–9; Bonhard, p. 13, n. 1.
18 ADB (1902), 117; Frymann/Class, *Kaiserbuch*, pp. 133–4.

19   Hasse, *Weltpolitik, Imperialismus und Kolonialpolitik*, p. 60; cf. Hasse, *Nationalstaat*, p. 50;
     Hasse, *Besiedlung*, p. 60; ADB (1897), 117; ADB (1902), 179–80; ADB (1911), 311–12.
20   Hasse, *Weltpolitik, Imperialismus und Kolonialpolitik*, p. 48; Fritz Bley, *Die Weltstellung
     des Deutschtums* (Munich, 1897), p. 24; ADB (1899), 299. A few isolated representatives
     of the Herderian tradition, men who hoped that the relationship among ethnic groups could
     be one of 'noble and fruitful competition', could be found in the Pan-German League. They
     were not, however, very numerous: see Jakob Hunziker, *Schweiz* (Munich, 1898), p. 60.
21   Hasse, *Weltpolitik, Imperialismus und Kolonialpolitik*, pp. 1, 63; Hasse, *Besiedlung*, p. 126;
     ADB (1901), 231.
22   Hasse, *Weltpolitik, Imperialismus und Kolonialpolitik*, pp. 4, 54; Bley, *Weltstellung*, p. 10;
     ADB (1896), 172.
23   Hasse, *Weltpolitik, Imperialismus und Kolonialpolitik*, p. 58; ADB (1894), 5–7; ADB
     (1895), 9; ADB (1899), 150; ADB (1901), 204–5.
24   Henry Cord Meyer, *Mitteleuropa in German Thought and Action, 1815–1945* (The Hague,
     1955), pp. 82–115.
25   Hasse, *Grenzpolitik*, pp. 167–74; Hasse, *Weltpolitik, Imperialismus und Kolonialpolitik*,
     pp. 51, 65; ADB (1897), 223–4.
26   [Ernst Hasse], *Grossdeutschland und Mitteleuropa um das Jahr 1950 von einem
     Alldeutschen* (Berlin, 1895); cf. Hasse, *Grenzpolitik*, pp. 155–6; Fritz Bley, *Die alldeutsche
     Bewegung und die Niederlande* (Munich, 1897); ADB (1894), 22–3; ADB (1895), 40–1,
     189–90.
27   ADB (1902), 117–19, 186; ADB (1904), 258–9; Wertheimer, p. 96; Werner, p. 57.
28   Hasse, *Weltpolitik, Imperialismus und Kolonialpolitik*, pp. 49–50; ADB (1903), 12–13;
     ADB (1910), 295.
29   ADB (1895), 161; ADB (1897), 130–1, 133–4; ADB (1902), 398; Urner, pp. 70, 498.
30   ADB (1898), 145, 229–30; ADB (1899), 77–8, 93–4; ADB (1900), 245–7; ADB (1903),
     401–3. On the problem of the Pan-German League and Austria see Schödl, esp. pp. 35–44.
31   ZStAP, ADV 188, Reismann-Grone to Hasse, Essen, 9.1.04; ADB (1894), 175; ADB
     (1904), 19–20; Hasse, *Weltpolitik, Imperialismus und Kolonialpolitik*, pp. 48–50.
32   ADB (1899), 193–4.
33   Hasse, *Grenzpolitik*, pp. 161, 167.
34   Hasse, *Weltpolitik, Imperialismus und Kolonialpolitik*, pp. 50–2; Bley, *Niederlande*, p. 6.
35   ADB (1907), 308.
36   For general surveys see: *Zwanzig Jahre alldeutscher Arbeit und Kämpfe* (Leipzig, 1910);
     Bonhard, pp. 50–132; cf. Hasse, *Nationalstaat*, pp. 49–78.
37   Hasse, *Nationalstaat*, pp. 58–9.
38   See Klaus Hildebrand, *Vom Reich zum Weltreich: Hitler, NSDAP und koloniale Frage
     1919–1945* (Munich, 1969).
39   ADB (1896), 235–6.
40   ADB (1904), 381–2; Stern, *Cultural Despair*, p. 216.
41   The influence of Nietzsche was particularly apparent in the writings of Fritz Bley:
     Weltstellung, pp. 5–7, 26; cf. Gerstenhauer, p. 12; Bonhard, p. 187.
42   Treitschke never joined the League, but his intellectual influence was so great that Bonhard
     called him 'more or less the father of the Pan-German League': p. 176; cf. ADB (1906),
     133–4; Class, *Strom*, pp. 15–16; Hasse, *Besiedlung*, p. 2.
43   Schieder, pp. 50–1.
44   See ADB (1897), 241; ADB (1898), 5–7; ADB (1900), 123, 368, 525–8.
45   Oncken, 'Lebensraum', p. 50; cf. Schilling, p. 403.
46   Roy Pascal, *From Naturalism to Expressionism: German Literature and Society, 1880–1918*
     (London, 1973), pp. 171–4, 194–7; cf. Stern, *Cultural Despair*, pp. 2–3.
47   ZStAP, ADV 7, Vorstandssitzung, Frankfurt a. M., 30.11.12; ADB (1895), 133; ADB
     (1896), 99; ADB (1897), 67–8; ADB (1898), 84.
48   MADV (June 1891), 2.
49   ADB (1898), 99; ADB (1899), 245.
50   ADB (1908), 9–10.
51   ADB (1898), 274; ADB (1911), 199.
52   Petzet, p. 53; ADB (1901), 95.
53   ADB (1908), 407; cf. ADB (1896), 14–15.

54 Alfred Hugenberg, *Streiflichter aus Vergangenheit und Gegenwart* (Berlin, 1927), pp. 280–85; Hasse, *Besiedlung*, p. 112; ADB (1894), 44; ADB (1902), 218–20.
55 ADB (1900), 51; ADB (1905), 14–15; ADB (1912), 51.
56 ADB (1909), 433–5.
57 ADB (1911), 100.
58 ADB (1904), 78; ADB (1907), 384–6; ADB (1909), 150.
59 ADB (1897), 101–2; ADB (1901), 129–30.
60 ADB (1897), 101–2; ADB (1898), 271; ADB (1903), 215; ADB (1908), 18–19.
61 ADB (1894), 20.
62 ADB (1900), 259–60.
63 ADB (1906), 353–5; cf. ADB (1908), 430.
64 ADB (1903), 94; ADB (1911), 360–1.
65 ADB (1898), 216–17.
66 ADB (1914), 277–8; cf. MADV (15.11.93), 125–6.
67 Türk, p. 55; ADB (1894), 41–2.
68 ADB (1895), 97–8; ADB (1900), 113.
69 P. Hofmann von Wellenhof, *Steiermark, Kärnten, Krain und Küstenland* (Munich, 1899), p. 101; Türk, p. 56; ADB (1907), 92–3, 158; ADB (1909), 189–90.
70 ADB (1896), 5; ADB (1897), 273; ADB (1907), 277–8; ADB (1908), 441.
71 Schultheiss, *Vereinswesen*, p. 49; cf. Schultheiss, *Deutschtum und Magyarisierung in Ungarn und Siebenbürgen* (Munich, 1898), p. 58; ADB (1895), 43; ADB (1902), 185–92; ADB (1908), 447; ADB (1909), 146.
72 Hofmann von Wellenhof, p. 2; ADB (1900), 533.
73 ZStAP, ADV 3, Hasse RS, Leipzig, 18.8.93; ADB (1894), 14–15; ADB (1896), 121–2; ADB (1904), 406; ADB (1905), 351.
74 Wilhelm Wintzer, *Die Deutschen im tropischen Amerika* (Munich, 1900), pp. 60, 74; ADB (1894), 149–50; ADB (1909), 322; ADB (1913), 372.
75 ADB (1904), 199; ADB (1907), 299–300.
76 ADB (1904), 239, 358.
77 ADB (1898), 277–8; ADB (1899), 131.
78 ADB (1909), 100; ADB (1911), 174.
79 ADB (1905), 158; ADB (1909), 357–8, 397–8.
80 ADB (1905), 117.
81 ADB (1898), 103–4, 137–8; ADB (1904), 94–5.
82 ADB (1898), 185; ADB (1904), 196–7.
83 ADB (1909), 11.
84 ADB (1896), 237–8; ADB (1905), 357; ADB (1910), 183; cf. ADB (1897), 209–20; ADB (1903), 46; ADB (1905), 61–2; ADB (1914), 123.
85 See Theweleit, pp. 290–4.
86 ADB (1908), 149–50.
87 Petzet, p. 26; ADB (1894), 133; ADB (1906), 397; ADB (1907), 439–40.
88 For a sample see ADB (1894), 166; ADB (1896), 15, 87; ADB (1897), 211–12, 281–2; ADB (1901), 430.
89 ADB (1910), 328–9.
90 For example: Hofmann von Wellenhof, p. 102; ADB (1894), 102–3; ADB (1903), 22–3; ADB (1904), 286, 348–9, 357; ADB (1905), 29–31, 204; ADB (1911), 257–8; ADB (1912), 313–14.
91 ADB (1899), 422; ADB (1906), 55.
92 Türk, p. 60; ADB (1899), 422; ADB (1906), 55.
93 ADB (1898), 281–2.
94 Frymann/Class, *Kaiserbuch*, pp. 219–20.
95 See Richard Sennett, *Authority* (New York, 1980), esp. pp. 4, 10, 17–19, 194; cf. Georg Simmel, 'Superordination and subordination', in *The Sociology of Georg Simmel*, ed. Kurt H. Wolff (New York and London, 1950), pp. 181–303.
96 ADB (1903), 349–54.
97 Türk, p. 63; Bley, *Weltstellung*, p. 48; ADB (1900), 1–2; ADB (1902), 398; ADB (1907), 354.
98 Bley, *Weltstellung*, p. 21.

99 Hasse, *Zukunft*, pp. 165–8.
100 Schultheiss, *Magyarisierung*, p. 85; Hofmann von Wellenhof, p. 104; ADB (1894), 121–2; ADB (1905), 297; ADB (1908), 411.
101 ADB (1908), 447.
102 ADB (1898), 5–7; ADB (1899), 61–2; ADB (1907), 297–300.
103 Bley, *Weltstellung*, p. 29; ADB (1894), 74–5; ADB (1909), 182–3.
104 ADB (1902), 11–12.
105 Theodor Basler, *Das Deutschtum in Russland* (Munich, 1911), p. 13; Schultheiss, *Magyarisierung*, p. 92; Hasse, *Besiedlung*, p. 109; ADB (1894), 149–50; ADB (1897), 255–6.
106 Petzet, p. 15; Hasse, *Weltpolitik, Imperialismus und Kolonialpolitik*, p. 57.
107 Hofmann von Wellenhof, pp. 2, 25.
108 Schultheiss, *Magyarisierung*, p. 73; cf. ADB (1895), 95.
109 Julius Goebel, *Das Deutschtum in den Vereinigten Staaten von Nord-Amerika* (Munich, 1904); Bley, *Welstellung*, p. 45; ADB (1901), 178; ADB (1904), 397; ADB (1909), 266–7.
110 Frymann/Class, *Kaiserbuch*, pp. 50–1, 65–8; ADB (1896), 235–6; ADB (1897), 118.
111 ADB (1901), 277–8.
112 Klaus Bergmann, *Agrarromantik und Grossstadtfeindschaft* (Meisenheim, 1970), pp. 33–163; cf. Gustav Schmoller, *Was verstehen wir unter dem Mittelstande? Hat er im 19. Jahrhundert zu- oder abgenommen?* (Göttingen, 1897), pp. 20–1; Stern, *Cultural Despair*, p. 189.
113 Hugenberg, *Streiflichter*, pp. 280–97; ADB (1899), 145–7.
114 Basler, p. 33.
115 Schultheiss, *Magyarisierung*, p. 63; ADB (1907), 267–9.
116 ADB (1907), 1–3; ADB (1909), 143; ADB (1913), 412.
117 ZStAP, ADV 329, Hasse's politisches Glaubensbekenntnis; Türk, p. 71; ADB (1897), 30–1.
118 ADB (1905), 215–16.
119 Hofmann von Wellenhof, pp. 1–2; ADB (1909), 333–5, 354.
120 Charles E. McClelland, *State, Society and University in Germany, 1700–1914* (Cambridge, 1980), pp. 60, 97; Fritz K. Ringer, *Education and Society in Modern Europe* (Bloomington, Ind., 1979), pp. 20–1; cf. Walter Horace Bruford, *The German Tradition of Self-Cultivation: 'Bildung' from Humboldt to Thomas Mann* (Cambridge, 1975).
121 Frymann/Class, *Kaiserbuch*, pp. 110–12; Class, *Strom*, p. 19; Bonhard, p. 212; ADB (1903), 193–4; ADB (1907), 234; ADB (1908), 94–6; ADB (1910), 320. *Bildung* was also dangerous in the wrong hands. The sectors of rival ethnic groups whom the Pan-Germans most feared were those whom education had made into cultural leaders: see Petzet, p. 21; ADB (1897), 15–16; ADB (1902), 187; ADB (1906), 382.
122 See Stern, *Cultural Despair*, esp. pp. 213–16; George L. Mosse, *The Crisis of German Ideology: Intellectual Origins of the Third Reich* (New York, 1964), esp. pp. 218–25.
123 ADB (1896), 161–2; ADB (1907), 426.
124 Hasse, *Zukunft*, p. 95; cf. Hasse, *Weltpolitik, Imperialismus und Kolonialpolitik*, pp. 54–5; ADB (1897), 161–2; ADB (1901), 65.
125 ADB (1895), 173–4.
126 Basler, p. 26; cf. ADB (1908), 323–5; Frymann/Class, *Kaiserbuch*, pp. 20–6.
127 Hasse, *Besiedlung*, p. 123; ADB (1907), 234; ADB (1908), 179.
128 Smith, *Colonial Empire*, p. 131; ADB (1904), 429; ADB (1907), 157; ADB (1908), 231–3, 240–3; ADB (1912), 138.
129 ADB (1901), 72–3; ADB (1910), 254–5.
130 ADB (1913), 423.
131 Hasse, *Zukunft*, p. 108.
132 ADB (1913), 121–3.
133 ADB (1903), 342.
134 ADB (1904), 213; ADB (1906), 286–8, 350, 353–5; ADB (1907), 17–18.
135 Frymann/Class, *Kaiserbuch*, 38, 52–5; ADB (1908), 199–200.
136 ADB (1908), 409; ADB (1911), 141–2.
137 ZStAP, ADV 3, Hasse RS, Leipzig, 27.5.94; cf. ADB (1911), 315.

138 Favorite literary figures included Josef Viktor von Scheffel, Ernst von Wildenbruch, and Felix Dahn. Of Dahn one member wrote that his 'poetic creations touch our [Pan-German] efforts in the most intimate way', for his works evoked feelings of 'German consciousness, German pride, enthusiasm': ADB (1899), 45–7.

139 ADB (1895), 109–10.

140 ADB (1897), 101–2; ADB (1908), 188–9, 367.

141 Julius Petersen, *Das Deutschtum in Elsass-Lothringen* (Munich, 1902), p. 109.

142 ADB (1911), 238.

143 Frymann/Class, *Kaiserbuch*, pp. 83–4.

144 For examples: Türk, p. 69; Frymann/Class, *Kaiserbuch*, p. 30; ADB (1899), 94, 225; ADB (1902), 117–19, 190–1; ADB (1908), 114, 216–17.

145 Türk, p. 82; Bley, *Weltstellung*, p. 21; ADB (1899), 350; ADB (1901), 21–2; ADB (1907), 434; ADB (1912), 217–18, 341–3.

146 Türk, p. 80; ADB (1903), 101–2; ADB (1908), 193–4; ADB (1912), 50, 233–4. In Bayreuth the figure of Siegfried represented the same traits: Geoffrey G. Field, *Evangelist of Race: The Germanic Vision of Houston Stewart Chamberlain* (New York, 1981), p. 150.

147 See ADB (1898), 43–4.

148 BAMA, RM 3/v Nr. 88, Meinungsbild aus Süddeutschland, February 1897; cf. Frymann/Class, *Kaiserbuch*, p. 123; Bley, *Weltstellung*, p. 6; ADB (1902), 469–70; ADB (1909), 333–5.

149 Bley, *Weltstellung*, pp. 10–11; Frymann/Class, *Kaiserbuch*, p. 102; ADB (1899), 58; ADB (1909), 354; ADB (1912), 202–3.

150 The irony of some of the advertisements in the League's journal was extraordinary. In 1902 subscribers were instructed on how to become energetic. *'Wie werde ich energisch?'* asked the ad. *'Durch die epochemachende Methode Liébault-Lévy [sic!]. Radikale Heilung von Energielosigkeit, Zerstreutheit, Niedergeschlagenheit, Schwermut, Hoffnungslosigkeit, Angstzuständen, Kopfleiden, Gedächtnisschwäche, Schlaflosigkeit, Verdauungs- und Darmstörungen und allgemeiner Nervenschwache. Misserfolge ausgeschlossen'*: ADB (1902), 80.

151 Hofmann von Wellenhof, p. 3; Bonhard, p. 19; MADV, Beilage zu Nr. 7 (15.11.92); ADB (1897), 241; ADB (1899), 257–8; ADB (1899), 251–2; ADB (1901), 362; ADB (1902), 450–1; ADB (1904), 174; ADB (1910), 320.

152 ADB (1894), 101–2; ADB (1909), 344–5; cf. ADB (1910), 291; Petzet, p. 66.

153 ADB (1896), 221; ADB (1899), 337–9; ADB (1901), 332; ADB (1910), 121–2; cf. Wenck, p. 31; Freisel, p. 28.

154 ADB (1895), 65–8; ADB (1897), 241–2; ADB (1902), 435; ADB (1904), 118.

155 ADB (1901), 143, 398; ADB (1910), 183.

156 Hasse's hobby was collecting portraits of Bismarck. See ADB (1904), 339–41; ADB (1909), 397; cf. Ernst zu Reventlow, *Was würde Bismarck sagen?* (Berlin, 1909).

157 ADB (1894), 90; ADB (1903), 333.

158 Bonhard, p. 19.

159 ADB (1896), 188; ADB (1902), 174, 453–8; ADB (1904), 387–9; cf. ADB (1899), 364; ADB (1908), 409; ADB (1913), 31.

160 Class, *Strom*, p. 231.

161 ibid., pp. 288–9.

162 ADB (1896), 1; ADB (1900), 92–3; Frymann/Class, *Kaiserbuch*, pp. 112–14.

163 ibid., pp. 108–10; ADB (1899), 1; ADB (1905), 434–6; ADB (1910), 328–9.

164 Bley, *Weltstellung*, p. 45; cf. MADV (1 June 1891), 1–2; ADB (1898), 216–17; ADB (1899), 86–8.

165 Hofmann von Wellenhof, p. 103; ADB (1894), 29–31; ADB (1895), 189; ADB (1896), 47–8; ADB (1911), 43; ADB (1912), 363.

166 Petzet, p. 26; Petersen, p. 121; ADB (1899), 117, 330–1; ADB (1900), 243–4; ADB (1908), 89–90; ADB (1908), 373–4.

167 ADB (1897), 103.

168 ADB (1894), 82–3.

5 Social Foundations of Ideology

'It is the very essence of the symbols of culture that they are ambiguous', Abner Cohen has recently written, adding that 'Their meaning is charged in the course of social action'.[1] Symbols, to put this proposition into slightly different terms, lend structure to social experience; their ambiguity betrays and reinforces the diversity of experience in any complex society. In Imperial Germany not all social groups regarded empire as the positive symbol of culture and order; for some groups empire was a matter of indifference, with practically no symbolic connotations at all, while for others it symbolized foolhardy adventurism, the extension of brutal oppression abroad, or the bankruptcy of a social system which could not survive without expansion. Although the Pan-German League claimed to speak in the name of the entire German nation, it could not evade the ambiguity of the national symbolism; and the manner in which the organization interpreted empire and the other national symbols reflected a specific social experience.

The Pan-German League: a Social Profile

The idea of transcendence occupied a central place in the ideology of the Pan-German League. Not only were the pioneers to transcend the flaws thought to reside in the German national character, but the ethnic community of which the League spoke was to transcend parochial loyalties among Germans, be these social, political, regional, or confessional in character. Germans were to put aside all these loyalties and to 'join together in common national love [*Volksliebe*], in common love for the essence of that which is German'.[2] The Pan-German League itself was to be the instrument of this transcendent community. The League's mission was to accord ethnicity its proper place in the hierarchy of human values, to awaken ethnic instincts in Germans everywhere on earth, and to win acceptance for the proposition that 'the most important thing is simply being German'.[3] 'The Pan-German League', read one early circular, 'is neither conservative nor liberal, neither Catholic nor Protestant, neither antisemitic nor philosemitic; it is simply *German*.'[4] Or, as another writer put it, the League was 'interested in the German *qua* German'.[5]

The emphasis on a transcendent ethnic community implied a number of things about the sociology of the Pan-German League itself. Because membership in the organization was to be limited only by ethnicity, the

League would, its founders anticipated, be a massive organization.[6] It would, in addition, be socially comprehensive; it would comprise people of the most diverse descriptions who were bound only by the essential tie of common ethnicity – 'the scholar in his quiet study', as one writer rhapsodized, 'the merchant in the midst of his business pursuits, the artisan at his bench and anvil, and the simple peasant behind his plow'.[7]

The Pan-German League failed to realize these goals. Both its size and social diversity remained far more limited than the pretensions of the organization's founders would have required. The idea that the League could achieve a mass membership evaporated shortly after the turn of the century, when the number of members began to decline steadily after reaching a peak of a little over 23,000. And just a glance at this membership revealed how empty was the hope that the League would appeal to a socially comprehensive audience.

Mildred Wertheimer noted more than a half century ago that the Pan-German League drew most of its members and its cadres of local leaders from a narrow social pool.[8] Her findings have stood the test of time, but it is now appropriate to pose anew the question of just who was active in the League, both because a much larger population can be generated for study and because new forms of analysis shed a different light on some of her major findings. A full description of the procedures I used in this analysis is in the Appendix, along with the complete statistical apparatus. In order to keep to a minimum the clutter of numbers in the text, I shall extract only the pertinent statistical fragments.

Analysis of the men who held local office in the Pan-German League suggests that the organization was overwhelmingly urban and middle class in character (see Appendix, Tables 5.1, 5.2, 5.10). Fewer than 2 percent of these men made their livings in agricultural pursuits. Barely 2 percent were noble, and only about 1 percent could be described as working class, even in the sense of being employed in artisanal trades. The League might have extolled the virtues of the peasantry and handicrafts, but these social groups did not play an active role in the organization.

The League drew the cadres of its local leaders almost exclusively from men engaged in occupations clearly identifiable as middle class. About 20 percent were owners of industrial capital, management personnel in industrial firms, or skilled professionals in industry. Approximately another 20 percent worked in the commercial sector, where they were engaged as independent merchants (*Kaufleute*), bankers, or as top- or mid-level commercial employees (*Angestellten*). The most striking feature of the League's cadres, because it was not apparent in earlier statistics, is that well over half of the local leaders came from an occupational category that comprehended public service and the professions. Nearly the majority of the League's local leadership consisted in fact of teachers, civil servants, doctors, and lawyers.

This last finding deserves some comment. The occupational categories devised by the German census-takers, which I have used in this breakdown, often concealed more than they disclosed. In this case, though, the category of service and professions – one in which the Pan-German League was vastly overrepresented – reveals the two most salient characteristics of the organization's local leadership: most of them worked for public agencies and most were academically educated. Nearly 50 percent of the local leaders were on the public payroll. Almost half of these were university and high-school teachers, with the other half made up in roughly equal proportions of judges, officials in the postal and telegraph service, in mining and construction, religion, the military, and in the so-called general or political administration (see Appendix, Table 5.3). The proportion of the League's leadership involved in public service swells to more than half with the inclusion of two other categories. The first is parliamentarians serving in federal, state, or local bodies. The other is a group of men who held positions that one might describe as 'semi-public' (*beamtenähnlich*); these included notaries and the lawyers, doctors, and businessmen who had been granted the honorific title of '*Rat*' (*Justizrat, Sanitäts-* or *Medizinalrat, Kommerzienrat*).[9]

Of the public officials in the Pan-German League's local leadership, about three-quarters occupied positions that demanded an academic education as qualification. Only slightly smaller was the percentage of all the League's local leaders who were academically educated. Statistical precision is more difficult in the case of occupations in the private sector; it is clear, however, that most of the men in the private professions – the lawyers, architects, pharmacists, and physicians – were academically educated. In any event, close to two-thirds of the League's local leaders probably had an academic education. Most of them appear to have attended a university, where they were trained to be public officials, lawyers, physicians, journalists, pharmacists, and chemists. A much smaller number probably attended *Technische Hochschulen*, where they studied architecture or engineering, while another small group appear to have attended agricultural or artistic academies. In addition, nearly a quarter of the local leaders held a doctorate.

Little evidence survives about the ages of the local leaders. A sample of the men who held national office yields some additional information, although the issue remains to be confronted of how representative the national leadership was. The evidence suggests the presence in the national leadership of two cohorts (see Appendix, Table 5.4). One (about 30 percent) comprised men in their later middle age, those who were older than 55 at the turn of the century. A considerably larger group of men (over 60 percent) was born after 1850. The events of 1866–71 were of crucial psychological importance to both groups, though the perspective of each on these events was different. The older group, the leading figure of whom was Hasse, had grown to political maturity before or during the *Reichsgründung*, some in fact as soldiers during the campaigns. Many of these men were liberals, for whom the events of 1866–71 meant not only the achievement of national unity (albeit in truncated form), but the frustration of their aspirations for genuine representation in government. These aspirations never entirely disappeared, even in the authoritarian climate of Bismarck's chancellorship, but were channeled into the populism of ethnic nationalism.

The older group of Pan-German leaders was more resigned to frustration than the younger. The leading figure in the latter group was Heinrich Class, who was born in 1868. These men were too young to have participated in the founding of the Empire, although most of them were old enough to have vivid memories of the event. Alfred Hugenberg, who was 6 in 1871, described as his 'primal political experience' the victory procession of German troops into his home-city of Hanover – the 'soldiers, guilds, colorful costumes, carts, horses, flags'.[10] These men grew to political maturity (or at least to majority) amidst the optimism and exuberance of the early years of the new Empire, but many of them were troubled by the fact that they had been only spectators at the birth. 'I was fourteen', Robert Krause, a leader in the Cologne chapter, recalled of the German victory at Sedan, 'old enough to regret that I too could not march against the *Erbfeind*.'[11] For Krause and others of his generation, one might speculate that the embrace of ethnic nationalism represented an opportunity to deal with these feelings of regret (or perhaps even shame), to participate actively in Germany's continuing development, and to complete what the earlier generation had initiated.

It is impossible to determine which of these two cohorts corresponded to a majority of the League's local leaders, although fragmentary evidence invites the speculation that most of the local leaders were born after 1850. The frequency with which the theme of redeeming the debt owed to the previous generation recurs in the Pan-German literature suggests as much.[12] So does the fact that only a tiny minority of the local leaders was retired.[13]

Biographical information about the national leaders suggests another reason for receptivity to ethnic nationalism. Many of these leaders had had significant experience outside Germany. They were born outside the frontiers of 1871, resided, traveled extensively, or were educated abroad, or married women who were not citizens of the Reich (see Appendix, Table 5.5). Johannes Wislicenus lived between the ages of 18 and 21 in the United States, where his father had fled in 1853 to avoid arrest for subversive activity in Halle; the younger Wislicenus then spent an additional sixteen years in Zurich.[14] His son-in-law, Adolf Fick, another of the League's founding fathers, was not only a leading figure in the German colony in Zurich, but had earlier practiced medicine for several years in the Transvaal.[15] Paul Samassa was born in Austria.[16] Theodor Basler, one of Samassa's successors as editor of the *Alldeutsche Blätter*, resided for a number of years in Russia.[17] Alfred Geiser, who succeeded Lehr as national secretary, married into one of the leading German families in Riga.[18] The list could be extended indefinitely to show how many of the League's national Leaders had had significant contacts abroad. Unfortunately, no comparable evidence on the local leaders exists, although it is likely that many of them, like the chairman of the chapter in Düsseldorf – a man by the name of Schlegtendahl who had lived for several years in Rio Grande de Sul – had foreign experience too.[19]

Whatever their ages or the extent of their foreign experience, the local leaders of the Pan-Germans were recruited overwhelmingly from the propertied and well-educated middle class – especially from the latter. The question is apt, however, whether this profile was unique to the League. One might well argue that the kinds of people who made up the bulk of the League's cadres could not only be found in positions of leadership in other patriotic societies, but that they were, as one historian has suggested, 'classic "joiners"', who populated and led a broad range of voluntary associations and that 'exactly the same sort of people' were, for example, in the German Peace Society.[20]

It is possible to test this argument, with respect both to other patriotic societies in Imperial Germany (with which the League was generally on cordial terms) and to the Peace Society (with which it was not) (see Appendix, Tables 5.6, 5.7, 5.8). At first glance, the social make-up of all these organizations does appear remarkably similar to that of the Pan-German League. All of them were overwhelmingly middle class in composition; people in agricultural occupations and industrial workers were conspicuous in their absence. In each of these organizations the category of service and professions comprised by far the largest occupational group (between half and three-quarters of the total), while owners and white-collar employees in the industrial and commercial sectors made up the bulk of the rest of the cadres. In addition, a very large proportion of the leaders of these organizations was academically educated, and a comparably large proportion was publicly employed.

However, these similarities between the League and the other organizations conceal significant differences of social status and position in public administration. On these bases, the local leaders of the Pan-German League were, in the first place, on the average, men of significantly higher status than the leaders of the German Peace Society. This conclusion is based on a number of indices. Substantially more academically educated officials, academically educated teachers, and wealthy businessmen populated the cadres of the League than the Peace Society. Conversely, there were significantly more teachers without academic qualifications in the Peace Society. A large number of women appeared in the Peace Society's leadership, but none at all in the Pan-German League's. It is difficult to gauge the significance of this statistic, for a woman's status, while assuredly not very high in a political organization in Imperial Germany, was related to her husband's, and this was, in most cases, impossible to determine. Significantly fewer of the Peace Society's leaders were academically educated, held a doctorate, or were publicly employed. Finally, leaders of the Peace Society who were on the public payroll tended to occupy lower positions than their counterparts in the Pan-German League. In light of these figures, the conclusion still appears justified that the Peace Society was 'drawn from a non-rural, middle to lower-middle class constituency – that it consisted of people who, in the words of one police report, "belong to the middle *Bürgerstand*, but occupy no prominent position in society"'.[21]

This characterization does not hold for the Pan-German League, nor for the other patriotic societies. Most of these societies more closely resembled the League than they did the Peace Society with respect to the status of their local leaders and the level of the positions they tended to hold in the public bureaucracy. Two patriotic societies, however, displayed important and enlightening contrasts to the Pan-German League. The German Colonial Society and the German Navy League recruited their cadres from a group of men whose status and administrative positions were significantly higher than those of the Pan-German League's local leaders. Men whose prestige could be described as top-level – generals in the army, the highest public officials, university professors, and the wealthiest merchants and industrialists – were much more in evidence in the Colonial Society and Navy League than they were in the Pan-German League.

Comparing the local leadership of the Pan-German League with that of the Navy League and Colonial Society, on the one hand, and with that of the Peace Society, on the other, suggests the upper and lower bounds that defined the distinctive social position of most of the Pan-German League's local leaders. They were clearly not lower-middle class, so their receptivity to extreme nationalism cannot be explained by theories that isolate the anxieties of downwardly mobile sectors of this class. The sectors usually associated with this theory, the 'old *Mittelstand*' of artisans, peasants, and small businessmen, as well as the 'new *Mittelstand*' of white-collar workers, were simply not prominent among the local leaders of the Pan-German League.[22] Nor were people of great wealth; nor were members of the highest echelons of Germany's social and political elites.[23] These kinds of people found the moderate posture of the Colonial Society and Navy League more congenial to their tastes.

Leaders of the Pan-German League were fond of calling themselves members of the *Mittelstand*.[24] This self-characterization reflected the ideological imperative of maintaining a link to the peasants, artisans, and small businessmen who the Pan-Germans claimed made up the 'backbone of the nation' more than it did any commonality of social station, background, or interest. In fact, the whole category of *Mittelstand* possessed greater ideological than social significance in Imperial Germany; and even Gustav Schmoller, who put together perhaps the most discriminating contemporary analysis of the concept, was not altogether free of the desire to create an ideological unity in the face of social conflict.[25] None the less, Schmoller's analysis does come as close as any to locating the specific social stratum from which the Pan-German League drew the great majority of its local leaders. This stratum was what Schmoller labeled the 'higher [*oberer*] *Mittelstand*' – a group of about 2·75 million families, 'mid-level land-holders and entrepreneurs, most higher officials, and many sectors of the liberal professions'. This group, for which the English-language term 'upper-middle class' is probably the most appropriate, occupied an intermediate position, in Schmoller's schema, between the 250,000 families who made up the real elite of German society, and the group Schmoller designated the 'lower *Mittelstand*' – some 3·75 million families of smaller landholders, businessmen, and lower officials. Schmoller' categories are attractive in so far as they tend to correspond to differences in social complexion among the German Peace Society, the Colonial Society and Navy League, and the Pan-German League.

The question remains of the extent to which the local leadership of the Pan-German League was representative of the rank and file. The question is difficult to answer, owing to the fact that practically no membership lists survive, and the largest of those that do is almost certainly atypical (see

Appendix, Tables 5.9, 5.10, 5.11). To judge from the scant information, more of the rank and file held occupations in the industrial and commercial sectors than did the local leaders; conversely, fewer members than local leaders were employed in the area of service and the professions. In only one case, however, was this discrepancy dramatic, in Hamburg, where the mercantile sector was, for obvious reasons, enormously overrepresented; it comprised more than two-thirds of the entire membership. This case notwithstanding, the local leadership appears to have been reasonably representative of the rank and file with respect to occupational classification.

Comparing the social status of the membership with that of the local leaders is even more difficult, for the extant membership lists yield very little evidence. Comparing the membership lists with information about the leaders of the same chapters produces some consistent conclusions, but their statistical basis is so narrow that they must be regarded as tentative. The social profile of the rank and file does not appear to be significantly different than that of the local leadership; the rank and file consisted of people in the same kinds of occupations as the leadership, except that they were slightly less likely to have been academically educated or hold a doctorate or to be publicly employed. Their social status was a little below the average of the local leadership, and they tended slightly to hold lower positions when publicly employed.

The social profile of the Pan-German League displayed a number of distinct characteristics. Although the evidence makes conclusions more tentative about the rank and file than about the cadres of local leaders, the Pan-Germans were recruited predominantly from those strata of the German middle class whose distinguishing marks were *Bildung* or *Besitz*. Businessmen played a prominent role, but the most salient characteristic of the men in the Pan-German League was academic education, which in turn served usually as a credential for a career in the public service. These features of the League's social profile suggest the nature of the common social experience which was structured and given meaning in a militant ideology of ethnic nationalism.

Custodians of Culture and Authority

Analyzing the relationship between the ideology and the social profile of the Pan-German League raises questions about why people chose to become active in this organization. Why were specific social groups particularly susceptible? Did the League's ideology and interpretation of the national symbolism correspond in some special way to their anxieties and aspirations? Or did they become active in the League for other reasons that had little to do with the program or ideology?

Two possible theories about why people joined the Pan-German League prove to be ungrounded. Men on the public payroll did not become active in the organization in response to any systematic pressure from their superiors or in hopes of promoting their careers by documenting their patriotism in this manner. In this respect, the League differed from the Eastern Marches Society and especially the Navy League, many of whose local leaders were public officials whose superiors encouraged them to join.[26] The Pan-German League never enjoyed this kind of encouragement. Activity in it was not an avenue toward career advancement in public bureaucracies, although conversely nothing beyond a few isolated instances suggests that activity in the Pan-German League was an obstacle to advancement either.[27]

If considerations of career advancement did not figure large in motivating people to become active in the Pan-German League, neither did calculations of profit. Some men did, no doubt, have direct monetary considerations in mind, but this group was not large. It included a few men, such as Otto Oehlerking in Düsseldorf and Gustav Neuhaus in Bochum, who advocated an aggressive colonial policy because they had business interests in Africa.[28] The motives of Fritz Möller, who was chairman of the chapter in Zella and whose firm manufactured firearms, were probably not entirely disinterested either. Another group of men whose activity in the League probably sprang from calculations of economic interest were the scattered businessmen who hoped to attract customers among the membership. The League's journal regularly ran advertisements for firms owned by Pan-Germans whose patriotism was to help recommend their wares or services.[29] One special category of businessmen for whom these considerations were doubtless central consisted of booksellers, such as Hans Ewich in Duisburg, who sold culture as a commodity from his 'large store of patriotic works'.[30] Finally, some proprietors of local inns and *Gasthäuser* had an obvious interest in being active in the Pan-German League. For a man like Hermann Lass in Frankfurt am Main, having his '*Kölner Hof*' designated the local chapter's official *Vereinslokal* assured a regular group of indulging patrons.[31]

Calculations of interest, either in the sense of profit or career advancement, do not explain why a vast majority of the League's local leaders became active. Most of them were not involved in occupations in which profit was a consideration, nor did the public agencies for which most of them worked encourage activity in the League. The features of the League's social profile raise the more fundamental question of whether 'interest', advantage, or rational calculation – the categories conventionally employed to link ideology and social reality – are in fact of much use in analyzing the appeal of the Pan-German League to most of the men who were active in it. Certainly the concept of interest must be more broadly understood than is commonly the case in Marxist-Leninist historiography. It must comprehend aspirations and concerns that have less to do with profit than with status and social survival, and it must be modified sufficiently to deal with an ideology informed less by calculations of advantage than by anxiety.[32]

As Clifford Geertz has argued, these modifications push the anemic psychology of an 'interest theory' of ideology too far.[33] An alternative, which Geertz calls 'strain theory', is more useful in dealing with a phenomenon like the Pan-German League. Without denying correlations between ideology and social groups, this theory recognizes that social existence involves insecurities and anxieties as well as the pursuit of advantage, and accordingly that the analytical link between ideology and society is more psychologically complex than the rationalization of social interest.

Unlike interest theory, which conceives of ideology as a more or less conscious attempt to disguise or obfuscate the pursuit of interest, strain theory assumes that ideology bears a direct, albeit symptomatic relationship to what people actually believe. This assumption poses one of the difficulties in using strain theory to analyze a historical phenomenon like the Pan-German League: the theory assumes that the Pan-Germans took the ideology seriously and that their participation in the organization was motivated by ideological considerations. This assumption is difficult to demonstrate. Sociological research suggests that most people join voluntary associations because of an interest in the goals of the organization.[34] In the case of the Pan-German League, however, one suspects that for many members this interest was only casual and did not signify much commitment to the ideology. Many people joined the League on the spur of the moment, at the emotional climax of a rally, when membership lists were passed around the room.[35] Most of these people did not then become dedicated members. They renewed their membership reluctantly, if at all, fled the organization at the suggestion that dues be raised, did not bother to subscribe to the journal, and were unfamiliar with much of the League's program.[36]

The cadres of local leaders would appear *prima facie* to have taken participation in the League – and by implication the organization's program and ideology – more seriously. These were the men who donated their time, energy, and sometimes their money to serving in local office. Yet the commitment of many of these men appears to have been rather casual too. Their average period in office seems to have been about two or three years, and many of the offices were honorific positions which required practically nothing of the men who occupied them.

That at least one group of Pan-Germans genuinely subscribed to the League's ideology seems indisputable. This group comprised the core of real activists, the men whose participation in local office was long-term. These men were the 'pillars of the League', who founded the local groups and conscientiously performed the time-consuming tasks required to keep them functioning.[37] They included men such as Franz Winterstein in Kassel, Hans Scupin in Halle, Adolf Findeisen in Plauen, Hermann Doebel in Mülheim, Max Baumann and Fritz Reuter in Cologne, and the Calmbach brothers, Christian and Heinrich, in Swabia.

If service in local office for an extended period of time – more than five years – be taken as the criterion of selection, this group of activists included about 500 men. Their social profile provides an interesting comparison with that of all the local leaders (see Appendix, Tables, 5.9, 5.10, 5.11). The occupations of these long-term activists were concentrated slightly less heavily in the industrial and commercial sectors, slightly more heavily in the service and professional sector. They tended as well to be a little more heavily concentrated in the top-level and high-status occupations; their average position in the public bureaucracies was also slightly higher than that of all the local leaders.[38] The significance of the comparison, however, lies less in these rather small discrepancies than in the fact that the long-term activists were more likely to display precisely the two characteristics that most distinguished the cadres as a whole: a greater proportion of them had an academic education and were publicly employed.

If any features of the social profile of the Pan-German League's local leadership were associated with receptivity to the organization's ideology, they were academic education and public employment. These two characteristics placed most of the local leaders into an esteemed group and entitled them to a distinguished role in Imperial German society. It made them *Honoratioren*.

The category of 'notable' was by no means unique to German society and politics in the second half of the nineteenth century. But the relative rigidity of status distinctions in Germany makes it possible to speak of a more formally delineated group in Germany than in England or France. While the word *Honoratioren* usually connoted the elites of smaller cities and towns, localities of all sizes featured circles of men whose role was community leadership and who enjoyed, because of this role, high status and prestige. These were the 'first circles of society', the 'best circles of the city', and the 'most respected men' in a locality.[39] By the last decades of the nineteenth century qualification for these roles had been rather formally defined by social background: most of the men who occupied them were distinguished by birth, wealth, or education (with birth declining in importance as one moved west).

The role of notables was defined, however, not so much socially, by common background, as it was culturally, by the role of custodianship. The notables were the men who represented the dominant political and social institutions in Germany and who embodied, defended, and disseminated the values and conventions that supported these institutions. The traditional core of the notables, in the west at least, comprised the custodians of authority, the representatives of the state, who occupied the higher echelons of public bureaucracies – the leading officials, judges, pedagogues, churchmen, and soldiers in communities around the country.

In most cases, though, the custodial role of these men extended further. The academic training most of them boasted as qualification for high public office made them simultaneously custodians of culture. These were the 'cultivated' men in localities throughout Germany, men whose *Bildung* both stood as a mark of their achievement and conferred on them a kind of grace.[40] Cultivation, or what one sociologist has called possession of 'cultural capital', entitled these men to represent the values, virtues, and attitudes that culture was thought to prescribe and to guard the integrity of its symbols, prominent among which was the state itself.[41] Their role included the transmission of culture, both in the literal sense of what they did in the classroom or pulpit, and by the authority of their example.

By the late nineteenth century the circles of the notables, traditionally the realm of the *Bildungsbürgertum*, had broadened to accommodate the economic change the country had been undergoing since the middle of the century. These circles now increasingly included the *Besitzbürgertum*, the custodians of the country's wealth and economic vitality – the leading manufacturers, merchants, and bankers in localities around the country, as well as the leading landowners. In the case of these economic leaders, as in the case of the political and cultural leaders, custodial roles reflected the power these men exercised in their communities. If the custodial role of the academically educated officials corresponded to the political and cultural power they wielded, the custodial role of the business leaders reflected power over the health of local economies.[42]

Relations among the sectors of the notables were by no means free of friction; none the less, the common interests, concerns, habits, and attitudes – what some historians might call the common mentality – imposed on them by their custodial role were sufficiently salient that in many communities they constituted a fairly coherent group. Their common mark was a consciousness of their own role and of the authority, prerogatives, and obligations this role imposed on them. They were the superordinated stratum of what might be described as a 'deference community', in which claims for precedence derived from both the formal and informal authority they embodied.[43] Their role accorded them social advantage, high status, and prestige, which in some communities bordered on awe.[44] The role transformed them, in the western part of the country, into a kind of *ersatz* nobility, just as it imposed on them a sense of *noblesse oblige* toward their subordinates.[45]

The commonalities among the notables were evident in many ways. These men dominated local politics in Germany through networks of formal associations and informal ties. They occupied both electoral and honorific office in city councils, school boards, church vestries, and on the boards of poor houses and other charitable associations. They were also the 'occasional politicians' about whom Max Weber wrote in his famous essay on 'Politics as a Vocation'.[46] While they were not involved in party politics as a full-time vocation, they commanded the resources (both cultural and economic) and the free time to exert a dominant influence in local affairs of the political parties.[47] The commonalities often extended to life-style. They intermarried. They observed, in public at least, the canons of personal behavior thought proper to their station. They ran in the same social circles, were members of the same social clubs and other voluntary associations.[48]

Although the position of notables was defined by commonalities of role, life-style, and by formal and informal patterns of deference, the rigidity of the category ought not to be overestimated. It was, in some respects, a paradox. Elites are, by definition, exclusive, but exclusivity relates to context. Socially, the character of the notables varied considerably throughout Germany. 'The most important people' in small places like Altena, Creuzberg, or the Hessian village of Niederflörsheim were of a different social complexion than the municipal elites in cities such as Berlin, Hamburg, Cologne, or Munich. In the small towns the *Honoratioren* usually included a handful of people with an academic education, who would be found in the church, the school, the doctor's office, or the office of the *Amtsmann*; they also included lower officials, the more substantial landowners, and leading businessmen, who might be no more than artisans.[49] Were there a garrison in the vicinity, the notables would include the officer corps. Most of the people of these descriptions would have no claim to the role of notables in the larger cities, or if they did by virtue of their education, they would be consigned to the lower echelons of the group. In the big cities, the category of 'leading businessmen' included some of the richest men in the country, and 'leading officials' included the *Regierungspräsident*, the president of the *Oberlandesgericht*, and the *Oberbürgermeister*.

The heterogeneity of the men who laid claim to the role of notables not only reflected the diversity of local context. Even within the same community, the circle of notables was diversifying by the end of the nineteenth century. The principal cause of the growing diversity was the expansion in the numbers of people who possessed the essential qualifications for the role. Economic growth broadened the commercial and industrial elites, adding to them a group of highly skilled and highly paid managers and technical officials. Economic growth and the social change it brought in its wake were also the driving mechanisms behind the dramatic expansion of the public sector in Germany; this expansion opened new occupational opportunities for the academically educated and led to a significant growth in the numbers (if not the percentage) of Germans receiving academic training.[50] The areas traditionally in the public sector grew to include technical services, such as the railways and public construction, health, social welfare, and industrial regulation; at the same time, secondary education – the prelude to academic training – grew dramatically. The professions also grew dramatically during the same period and in response to the same pressures. The corps of highly trained professionals was in many respects a satellite of the public sector in Germany; they were trained in the same academic institutions as higher public officials and had constant contact with the public sector, both in performing services for it and in the public licensing and supervision that was becoming increasingly part of their professional experience.[51]

These changes broadened the numbers and diversity of the people who could lay claim to the high status implied by the role of notable. In fact, however, diversification meant that status distinctions not only defined barriers between the category of notables and the rest of German society, but increasingly segmented this category itself. Thomas Nipperdey has used the expression 'broader stratum of *Honoratioren*' to suggest that although access to the circle of notables was normally restricted to men of *Bildung und Besitz*, some members of the circle were more peripheral than others.[52] These were, as a rule, the large number of 'new' men who now entered the circle alongside those in careers traditionally associated with elite roles – officials in the general administration, judges, and established businessmen. These new men were younger or engaged in careers that were relatively new, either in the public sector or in professional careers whose status had only recently been enhanced with academic qualification. That this expansion involved tension among the notables was inevitable. Many of the new arrivals were upwardly mobile, men of lower social background whose fathers had not been academically trained.[53] Others had academic credentials that were tainted; they had attended *Technische Hochschulen*, which in the eyes of the university graduates remained second-class academic institutions even after the upgrading of their status which came in 1899 in the form of the right to confer the doctoral degree.[54] Nor was the alliance of *Bildung und Besitz* fully without friction, and the changes in the size and complexion of the business elites prompted many of the traditional custodians of culture to agonize over the growing power of wealth in German society.[55]

The impulse for the radical nationalism of the Pan-German League came from pressures and strains within the circles of notables in Imperial Germany. The most important exponents of this ideology were men who had recently (in either a figurative or literal sense) arrived in the peripheries of this esteemed group of custodians. The social profile of the local leaders of the Pan-German League reveals that most of them occupied a common location in the structure of social, political, and cultural power in Imperial Germany. Almost two-thirds of them belonged to but four categories (see Appendix, Table 5.11). These categories were defined by sufficient wealth or education, or a sufficiently high bureaucratic position that the men in them could be reckoned among the 'leading circles' of most communities in the country, but not by enough wealth, education, or bureaucratic position that these men could be considered among the highest echelons of the notables. The first category comprised academically educated public officials from the apprentice rank of *Assessor* up to the rank of *Regierungsrat* and *Landgerichtsrat* – men whose bureaucratic position entitled them to salaries of up to but not more than 9,500 Marks in the Prussian scale of 1897. The second group were the academically educated teachers below the rank of university professor, principally the *Oberlehrer*, professors, and administrators of various secondary schools – *Gymnasien*, *Realgymnasien*, and *Realschulen*. The third major category from which the League's cadres came were the academically trained professionals, the lawyers, doctors, physicians, architects, chemists, and engineers. Finally – and this is the least precise and reliable category – the League's local leadership was drawn heavily from 'substantial businessmen' and management personnel – people who designated themselves industrialist, factory owner, banker, and *Prokurist*. These men were probably wealthy, but not extraordinarily so: it is doubtful that the net worth of many of them exceeded half a million Marks.[56]

Most of these notables in the Pan-German League laid claim to this role by virtue of their education rather than their wealth. The League was principally a phenomenon of the *Bildungsbürgertum*; the distinguishing characteristics of most of its local leaders was their claim to represent authority or culture (or both). Significantly, however, the League's cadres consisted largely of what might be called 'new custodians'. The cadres contained a large proportion of public bureaucrats, who as representatives of the state and as instruments of public *Herrschaft* could lay claim to the role of custodians of authority. Few of these men, however, were from the traditional core fields of the civil service, the so-called general or political administration and the judiciary (or the military). Most of the public officials came instead from fields such as finance, secondary education, and the technical services, which had burgeoned at the end of the nineteenth century, but whose members were still regarded as a cut below 'real' *Beamten* and whose salaries reflected this fact.[57] Here again comparison of the Pan-German League with the Colonial Society and Navy League is instructive (see Appendix, Table 5.12). Of the leaders of the Colonial Society who were on the public payroll, well over half pursued careers in the 'core areas' of political administration and justice or the military. Nearly half of the local leaders of the Navy League who were publicly employed were to be found in these areas. The corresponding figure for the Pan-German League was just 20 percent. Conversely, fewer than a third of the local leaders in the Colonial Society, and only about 40 percent in the Navy League, worked in the less traditional or expanding fields, as opposed to more than three-quarters of the public officials in the Pan-German League. In addition, nearly 40 percent of the publicly employed leaders in the Colonial Society and 30 percent in the Navy League occupied top-level bureaucratic positions; the corresponding figure for the Pan-German League's local leaders was only about 7 percent.

The public officials in the Pan-German League tended to work in less prestigious sectors of the bureaucracy and to occupy positions which, in the full context of careers in the public sector, were high-level yet a step below the top level. That their positions subjected them to various forms of intrabureaucratic discrimination was nowhere more graphically demonstrated than in the example of the *Oberlehrer*, the academically educated secondary-school teachers, who alone made up almost a fifth of the Pan-German League's local leadership. The ethos of this profession emphasized that its members were not only *Herrschaftsträger* but the custodians *par excellence* of German culture. As one American observer reported in 1914, on the strength of extensive interviews with leaders of the profession, the *Oberlehrer* had 'become the *Kulturbeamter* at large'. His function was 'to make the culture of the university available to society'; he 'receives, unifies, assimilates, and transmits, both in instruction and in the example of his whole mental and moral attitude'.[58] As the more recent research of Hartmut Titze and others has shown, however, a painful discrepancy remained between these teachers' perceptions of their own significance and their status within the public service.[59] Probably more than any other part of the public sector, secondary teaching was an avenue of social mobility for the sons of lower-middle-class families. Their backgrounds proved to be a liability in several ways, though. Their incomes suffered from a general prejudice among ministries of education against these *Aufsteiger*. Economic relief came, in Prussia at least, in 1909 when their salary scales were raised, but this relief did not bring acceptance of the *Oberlehrer* as a peer among colleagues of equivalent rank in other branches of the civil service, to say nothing of university professors. Nor was their position made any more comfortable by the fact that their students came, as a rule, from families of higher social standing than they themselves.

In so far as invidious comparisons with reference groups cast a shadow on social or professional pretensions, the experience of the *Oberlehrer* resembled that of members of other branches of the public sector, such as the technical services. It also resembled the experience of several other occupational groups heavily represented in the League's cadres. Professionalization meant that physicians, pharmacists, chemists, architects, and, to a smaller extent, engineers had academic training. Academic training was of great importance to members of these professions, not only because of the enormous prestige it carried, but paradoxically as a defense against the threat professionalization posed to their status. Industrial growth and reorganization, as well as the technological advances that accompanied it, threatened to turn chemists, architects, engineers, and even journalists into 'mere' salaried employees, while pharmacists, no longer able to compete with industry in the manufacture of drugs, faced reduction in status to that of 'mere' retailers.[60] Physicians faced something akin to this threat in the growing public supervision of their profession, particularly with the spread of the institution of the *Krankenkasse*.[61] For those who had it, an academic degree brought a sense of continued professional distinctiveness. It did not, however, bring status equal to the reference group to which they all looked, the jurists in the public bureaucracy.[62]

It is of course impossible to determine the extent to which these pressures bore specifically on the professionals and public officials who led the Pan-German League. It is, however, possible to perceive in the ideology of the League a reflection of precisely these pressures and an appeal to the professional ethos of all these groups. In its unabashed elitism, this ideology was a paean to the notables of Wilhelmine Germany, particularly to the men who claimed this role by virtue of their education. These men were, the League's ideologists proclaimed, the true pioneers of Germandom, the 'thinking, independent men of judgment', who were qualified because of their *Bildung* to be the pillars of the community, the 'spiritual leaders of the *Volk*', 'models of patriotism', and an 'example of how loyally to fulfill national obligations'.[63] These obligations included ensuring, by enlightened policies and example, social peace and the purveying of culture – in assimilable quantities – to the less cultivated strata of the nation.[64]

Emil Lederer observed many years ago that one of the functions of ideology was to postulate an identity between individual and general interest. 'The general interest', he noted laconically, 'is always motivation, but never motive.'[65] Without conceding that 'interest' is the proper word to describe what was being articulated, it is fair to say that the League's ideology appealed not only to the general elitist consciousness of the notables, but specifically to various constituents of this group.

The ideological appeal to the ethos of the educated public bureaucrat was the most transparent. As Jane Caplan has recently argued, one should accept only with caution generalizations about the German bureaucratic ethos, with its emphasis on transcending particular interests, service to the common good, discipline, and unity of purpose; this ethos was at least as much an injunction as it was a description of reality.[66] None the less, the homologies between this ethos and the ideology of the League were far-reaching. The League's vision of harmonious order, its emphasis on the disciplined acceptance of a clearly articulated, hierarchical structure of roles, both ethnic and social, was a bureaucratic ideal, while the academic qualifications the League's spokesmen cited for the superordinated roles in this structure were just those that governed public bureaucracies in Imperial Germany.[67] If their cultural roles made them instruments of authority or 'producers of the state', public officials were, in the Pan-Germans' vision, apotheosized into 'supporting pillars of the Reich', models of patriotic commitment, and the chosen vanguard in the ethnic struggle.[68] This idealization included the teachers whose cultural roles were not only to be custodians of public authority, like other *Beamte*, but guardians and disseminators of German culture. This elite role imposed on them, Pan-Germans observed, the obligation to serve as national *Lehrmeister*, to enlighten not only their students but the whole nation with ethnic consciousness and patriotic virtue.[69]

In elevating the educated *Honoratioren* to the role of elite in the ethnic community, the League's ideologists also made room for the independent professionals. Academic education, they insisted, distinguished these men too as custodians of culture.[70] The League appealed in addition to two cardinal tenets in the occupational ethos of these groups, as it extolled the virtues of independence and achievement, and placed these virtues in the catalogue of qualifications for elite status in the Pan-German vision of order. The emphasis on independence, which was calculated to appeal to physicians, pharmacists, architects, and especially to lawyers not in the public employ (all of whom made up about a sixth of the League's local leadership), became an increasingly prominent feature in the League's ideology as the rift with the government grew wider and independence became synonymous with opposition.[71] The emphasis on ability, as demonstrated in achievement, encompassed *Bildung* in general but was of particular importance to the technical professionals, such as the engineers and chemists, whose occupational ethos was founded on the proposition that achievement brought entitlement to precedence.[72]

Finally, the Pan-German vision appealed to the ethos of the businessmen. The national elite was to comprehend the notables of wealth, particularly those 'worthy and diligent' *Handelspioniere*, who had risked their wealth and livelihoods to extend German wealth and commerce around the globe, and in this manner to lay the material foundations for the expansion of German culture.[73] Emphasizing the entitlement that came with independence and achievement also had obvious relevance for the many *Kaufleute* and *Fabrikanten* who populated the League. Wealth was, Pan-German ideologists observed, a mark of achievement, an emblem which brought prestige, inspired emulation, and imposed upon those who wore it – those 'pillars of the national economy', those who 'manned the outposts of *bürgerliche Gesellschaft*' – the obligations as well as the status of leadership in both the social and the ethnic order.[74]

Despite gestures to their professional ethos, however, the notables of the *Besitzbürgertum* were junior partners in the Pan-German vision of the elite. In this vision, ideology and social reality converged, for the elite roles idealized in the ideology were to fall to precisely the kinds of people who made up most of the League's cadres of local leaders and, in all likelihood, most of the membership as well. The pioneers were the men whose academic education or participation in public office entitled them in fact to custodial roles over culture or authority in Imperial Germany. One of the salient themes in the Pan-German League's ideology was an obsession with control and the preservation of culture and order in the face of threatening forces. It was no coincidence that the men who found this ideology appealing were those who actually represented culture and performed the roles of social control in Imperial Germany.

Homologies between the Pan-German League's ideological vision and the social roles played by most of the organization's local leaders suggest why some groups were receptive to this ideology. The ideology was a symbolic representation and an idealization of a specific social experience. The ideology appealed in the first instance to the stratum of the German middle class whose experience was conditioned by academic education, the exercise of custodial roles over authority and culture, and the expectations of precedence, as well as the strains, these roles entailed.

Yet these homologies pose as many problems as they resolve. The salience of the themes of order, authority, and control in the ideology of the Pan-German League corresponded to the prominence of men in the organization who represented the state and all the authority and order it symbolized. Logically, the League's ideology ought in the last analysis to have been a variety of what some commentators have called 'statolatry', a doctrine that idealized and accepted uncritically the power and prerogatives of the state.[75] Establishing links between ideology and social experience cannot alone explain the militant impulse in the Pan-German League, which resulted not only in the formulation of an aggressive program of foreign-policy demands, but in bitter and uncontrollable opposition to the German government. Understanding this aggressive impulse requires exploring additional features of the Pan-German League's ideology and then a cautious appeal to psychology.

Notes

1   Abner Cohen, *The Politics of Elite Culture: Explorations in the Dramaturgy of Power in a Modern African Society* (Berkeley, Calif. and Los Angeles, 1981), p. 215.
2   ADB (1910), 317.
3   Frymann/Class, *Kaiserbuch*, pp. 55–1.
4   BBA, 55/8 7010 (GBAG), ADV RS, Berlin, 6.10.94.
5   MADV, Beilage zu Nr. 7 (15.11.92).
6   ADB (1894), 1–2; ADB (1898), 3.
7   ADB (1897), 101–2; cf. ADB (1898), 84; ADB (1900), 34; ADB (1908), 320–3.
8   Wertheimer, pp. 53–72.
9   Hansjoachim Henning, *Das westdeutsche Bürgertum in der Epoche der Hochindustrialisierung 1860–1914: Soziales Verhalten und soziale Strukturen. Das Bildungsbürgertum in den preussischen Westprovinzen* (Wiesbaden, 1972), pp. 310, 354.
10 Hugenberg, *Streiflichter*, p. 198; Guratzsch, p. 22.
11 ADB (1910), 297–8.
12 MADV (1.2.91), 1–2; ADB (1906), 82, 83; ADB (1910), 273–5; ADB (1914), 63, 67.

13 'The chapter has not yet taken root in the leading circles of Görlitz, but consists overwhelmingly of younger academics, technicians, and businessmen': ZStAP, ADV 188, Geiser to Hasse, 29.3.04; cf. ADB (1897), 125–6. Galos's team has calculated that the average age of the leadership of the *Ostmarkenverein* was about 45 in 1894. This does not seem an unreasonable estimate for the Pan-German League either: Galos, p. 82.

14 ADB (1902), 453–8.

15 PAAA, Deutschland 169, Bd. 2, Generalkonsul Zurich to Bülow, Zurich, 18.7.04.

16 ZStAP, ADV 408, Class to Kiderlen-Wächter, Mainz, 12.1.11; ADB (1902), 141–2.

17 ADB (1911), 95.

18 ADB (1905), 168. Among other prominent Pan-Germans with significant foreign experience in their backgrounds were Reismann-Grone (studies in England and France), Karl Klingemann (a pastorate in Alexandria, residence in Switzerland), Hermann Gerhard (a pastorate in a German community in America), Paul Dehn (residence in the Balkans), and Leopold von Vietinghoff-Scheel (birth in Russia).

19 ADB (1905), 41. This was true too of Max von Klitzing, chairman of the chapter in Cologne, who resided abroad for sixteen years: ZStAP, ADV 193, Klitzing to Normann, Cologne, 27.7.09.

20 Eley, *Reshaping*, p. 122, n. 53.

21 Roger Chickering, *Imperial Germany and a World without War: The Peace Movement and German Society, 1892–1914* (Princeton, NJ, 1975), p. 75. The Hamburg police, who were responsible for the report Eley cites, described those in attendance at a Pan-German meeting as 'all members of the better strata [*Stände*]': StAH, Politsche Polizei, V 452, Bd. 1, Polizeiliche Bericht, 18.11.03.

22 See Shulamit Volkov, *The Rise of Popular Antimodernism in Germany: The Urban Master Artisans, 1873–1896* (Princeton, NJ, 1978), esp. pp. 123–31.

23 The correspondence between the League's headquarters and the chapters in connection with raising money for a '*Bismarck-Sammlung*' in 1913 is very instructive: ZStAP, ADV 626. In practically every case, the local chairman could name only a handful in his group whom he would describe as '*reich*' or even '*wohlabend*'. Hartwig's generalization thus strikes me as misinformed: 'there were a considerable number of monopoly capitalists, mid-level capitalists dependent on monopoly capital, and several hundred Junkers as members'; Hartwig, 'Alldeutscher Verband', p. 5; cf. ADB (1908), 320–3.

24 ADB (1902), 395–6; cf. Werner, pp. 62–3.

25 Schmoller, pp. 29–31; see too the discussion of the whole *Mittelstand* problem in David Blackbourn, 'The *Mittelstand* in German society and politics, 1871–1914', *Social History*, no. 4 (January 1977), pp. 409–34.

26 Galos, pp. 78–9; Henning, *Bürgertum*, p. 179.

27 ZStAP, ADV 195, Klingemann to Class, Essen, 28.5.11; ADB (1911), 95; Gerstenhauer, pp. 29–30.

28 ADB (1899), 119; ADB (1904), 286; ADB (1911), 10–11.

29 For example: 'Consider the fact that there are Pan-German craftsmen too. One of them is named Rudolf Schwarzmann, furniture-manufacturer and cabinet-maker in Mainz': ADB (1903), 400; ADB (1913), 183. Other patriotic societies also had to deal with these kinds of people. In 1904 an official of the Eastern Marches Society complained of a certain Müller in the village of Konitz, a disreputable man 'who used to be into antisemitism and wants now to get into patriotism, purely for his own business interests [*Reklamenrück-sichten*]': ZStAM, Rep. 195 Nr. 115, Vosburg Reisebericht, 1.3.04; cf. Schmitt, *Vereinsleben*, p. 61.

30 ADB (1912), 420.

31 ADB (1902), 270; ADB (1913), 39.

32 See Jerussalimski, p. 463; Paul Massing, *Rehearsal for Destruction: A Study of Political Anti-Semitism in Imperial Germany* (New York, 1949), p. 76; Christina von Seggern, 'The Alldeutscher Verband and the German Nationalstaat' (PhD diss., University of Minnesota, 1974), pp. iv, 26; Emil Lederer, 'Klasseninteressen, Interessenverbände und Parlamentarismus', in *Kapitalismus, Klassenstruktur und Probleme der Demokratie in Deutschland 1910–1940*, ed. Jürgen Kocka (Göttingen, 1979), pp. 33 –50.

33 Geertz, 'Ideology as a cultural system', pp. 201–6.

34 Schmitt, *Vereinsleben*, p. 94.

35 ZStAP, ADV 57, GFA, Berlin, 17–18.11.06.

36 ZStAP, ADV 95, GFA, Berlin, 4.7.14; ADB (1898), 177–8; ADB (1901), 410; ADB (1904), 72.

37 ZStAP, ADV 43, GFA, Gotha, 9–10.4.04, Reismann-Grone DS, Zur Lage des Verbandes.

38 The correlation between length of service in local office and mean social status was not significant ($r = +0.14$), nor was the correlation between length of service and mean public administrative position ($r = +0.11$).

39 BAMA, RM 3/v Nr. 9911, Eisendendecher to AA, Karlsruhe, 6.2.12; ADB (1903), 5, 413–14; ADB (1909), 71.

40 Ringer, p. 20.

41 Pierre Bourdieu, *Outline of a Theory of Practice* (Cambridge, 1977), p. 187.

42 David F. Crew, *Town in the Ruhr: A Social History of Bochum* (New York, 1979), p. 145.

43 Sheehan, *Liberalism*, p. 142; White, p. 45.

44 Volkov, pp. 129, 135.

45 Henning, *Bürgertum*, p. 484; White, p. 50.

46 Weber, 'Politics as a vocation', in *From Max Weber: Essays in Sociology*, eds H. H. Gerth and C. Wright Mills (New York, 1946), pp. 77–128.

47 White, pp. 40–1; O'Donnell, pp. 22–5; Eley, *Reshaping*, pp. 19–40; Sheehan, *Liberalism*, p. 164; and especially Thomas Nipperdey, *Die Organisation der deutschen Parteien vor 1918* (Düsseldorf, 1961), pp. 42, 86–109.

48 Henning, *Bürgertum*, pp. 310, 423, 487–91.

49 ZStAP, ADV 186, Class to Hasse, Mainz, 22.12.02; ADV 193, Gerhard to Class, Berlin, 27.1.09; ADV 626, Balser to Vietinghoff-Scheel, 7.12.13; ADB (1899), 150; ZStAM, Rep. 195 Nr. 62, Schmidt to DOV, Creuzberg, 14.11.04; Nipperdey, *Organisation*, p. 50; cf. Nipperdey, 'Die Organisation der bürgerlichen Parteien in Deutschland vor 1918', HZ, vol. 185 (1958), p. 595.

50 Ringer, pp. 53–4, 76.

51 Henning, *Bürgertum*, p. 415; Ringer, p. 36.

52 Nipperdey, 'Organisation', pp. 564–5.

53 Hartmut Kaelble, 'Social mobility in Germany, 1900–1960', JMH, vol. 50 (1978), p. 451.

54 Ringer, p. 297; Klaus Vondung, 'Zur Lage der Gebildeten in der Wilhelminischen Zeit', in Vondung, *Bildungsbürgertum*, pp. 27–8.

55 Werner Jochmann, 'Struktur und Funktion des deutschen Antisemitismus', in Werner E. Mosse (ed.), *Juden im Wilhelminischen Deutschland 1890–1914* (Tübingen, 1976), p. 404.

56 See ZStAP, ADV 626, Grell to Vietinghoff-Scheel, Potsdam, 4.12.13.

57 See Henning, p. 316; Folkert Meyer, *Schule der Untertanen: Lehrer und Politik in Preussen 1848–1900* (Hamburg, 1976), p. 122.

58 William Setchel Learned, *The Oberlehrer: A Study of the Social and Professional Evolution of the German Schoolmaster* (Cambridge, Mass., 1914), p. 75.

59 Hartmut Titze, 'Die soziale und geistige Umbildung des preussischen Oberlehrerstandes von 1870 bis 1914', *Zeitschrift für Pädagogik*, 14. Beilage (1977), pp. 107–28.

60 Lothar Burchardt, 'Professionalisierung oder Berufskonstuktion? Das Beispiel des Chemikers im Wilhelminischen Deutschland', GG, vol. 6 (1980), pp. 326–48; Gerd Hortleder, *Das Gesellschaftsbild des Ingenieurs: Zum politischen Verhalten der Technischen Intelligenz in Deutschland* (Frankfurt a. M., 1970), p. 40; Harald E. Kuhn, *Soziologie der Apotheker: Ein Beitrag zur Soziologie des Gesundheitswesens* (Stuttgart, 1963), pp. 50, 57, 60, 76.

61 Claudia Huerkamp, 'Aerzte und Professionalisierung in Deutschland: Ueberlegungen zum Wandel des Arztberufs im 19. Jahrhundert', GG, vol. 6 (1980), pp. 361, 373–75.

62 Hortleder, p. 42; Henning, *Bürgertum*, p. 425.

63 ZStAP, ADV 45, GFA, Leipzig, 7–8.10.04, Hopf RS, Dresden, 7.9.04; ADB (1903), 193; ADB (1908), 18–19; ADB (1911), 349–50.

64 ADB (1894), 24, 112; ADB (1907), 50–2.

65 Lederer, 'Klasseninteressen', p. 39.

66 Jane Caplan, '"The imaginary universality of particular interests": the "tradition" of the civil service in Germany history', *Social History*, vol. 4 (1979), pp. 303–4. See Otto Hintze, 'Der Beamtenstand', in *Soziologie und Geschichte: Gesammelte Abhandlungen zur*

Soziologie, Politik und Theorie der Geschichte, ed. Gerhard Oestreich, 2nd edn (Göttingen, 1964), pp. 66–125; Max Weber, 'Bureaucracy', in Gerth and Mills, pp. 196–204; Albert Lotz *Geschichte des deutschen Beamtentums* (Berlin, 1909), pp. 1–20.

67 Talcott Parsons, 'Democracy and social structure in pre-Nazi Germany', in *Essays in Sociological Theory* (Glencoe, Ill., 1954), pp. 104–23; Robert K. Merton, 'Bureaucratic structure and personality', *Social Forces*, vol. 18 (1940), pp. 560–8; Heinz Fick, *Der deutsche Militarismus der Vorkriegszeit: Ein Beitrag zur Soziologie des Militarismus* (Potsdam, 1932), pp. 67–76; cf. Michael Stephen Steinberg, *Sabres and Brown Shirts: The German Students' Path to National Socialism, 1918–1935* (Chicago, 1977), p. 60.

68 Petzet, p. 64; Türk, p. 57; Petersen, p. 133; ADB (1899), 147; ADB (1901), 418; ADB (1909), 58; ADB (1910), 243–5; cf. Emil Lederer, 'Die Angestellten im Wilhelminischen Reich', in *Kapitalismus*, p. 54; Herbert von Borch, *Obrigkeit und widerstand: Zur politischen Soziologie des Beamtentums* (Tübingen, 1954), pp. 21–2.

69 Petzet, p. 41; Frymann/Class, *Kaiserbuch*, pp. 108–10; ADB (1902), 448–9; ADB (1908), 66–8; ADB (1913), 325–6.

70 Basler, p. 13; ADB (1895), 109–10.

71 ZStAP, ADV 585, Class to Bethmann Hollweg, Mainz, 19.8.09; ADB (1901), 96; cf. Class, *Strom*, p. 29; DKZ (1903), 8.

72 ADB (1910), 66; Hortleder, pp. 43–4, 73–4; Jürgen Kocka, *Unternehmerverwaltung und Angestelltenschaft am Beispiel Siemens 1847–1914: Zum Verhältnis von Kapitalismus und Bürokratie in der deutschen Industrialisierung* (Stuttgart, 1969), pp. 531–3.

73 Wintzer, esp. pp. 1–2, 60, 74; Petzet, p. 47; ADB (1909), 418; ADB (1911), 119–21.

74 ZStAP, ADV 2, ADV Aufruf, April 1891; Frymann/Class, *Kaiserbuch*, pp. 16, 29–30, 122. The allusion to the outposts came from Max Röttger, the chairman of the *Centralverband deutscher Industrieller*: Klaus Saul, *Staat, Industrie, Arbeiterbewegung im Kaiserreich: Zur Innen- und Aussenpolitik des wilhelminischen Deutschlands 1903–1914* (Düsseldorf, 1974), p. 326.

75 Nicos Poulantzas, *Fascism and Dictatorship: The Third International and the Problem of Fascism* (London, 1974), p. 243.

6 Ideology and Psychology

'It may perhaps seem curious to the outsider', wrote a Pan-German author of the situation in Styria, 'that a small people like the Slovenes, with scarcely more than a million souls, could seriously threaten the position of the great German people.'[1] It does seem curious. So does the alarm shown by Franz Winterstein, the leader of the League's chapter in Kassel, who, upon learning that the Bohemian String Quartet was going to perform the music of Dvořák, Tschaikowsky, and Josef Suk at a concert in his city, protested to the concert's organizers about the cultural pollution they were encouraging and threatened them with a boycott.[2] Curious too was the behavior of Adolf Fick, who vacationed in Alsace in order to check the progress of Germanization by counting French and German headstones in local cemeteries.[3] This behavior and the anxieties it reflected might be dismissed as idiosyncratic, were it not for the fact that these men were held up for emulation in the pages of the *Alldeutsche Blätter*, a journal devoted to an ideology that made their behavior appear not only laudable but imperative.

This kind of behavior, the anxieties and exaggerated apprehensions in the ideology of the Pan-German League, the militancy of the organization, and its uncontrollable impulse to opposition against official authority all betrayed a dynamism that is no less critical to the history of the organization than it is difficult for the historian to analyze with much confidence. Identifying the social foundations of ideology, the homologies that made the symbolism in the League's vision attractive to specific social groups, does not fully explain this dynamism. In fact, these homologies and the social composition of the Pan-German League would seem instead to have implied an uncritical devotion to the authority of the state. The effort to understand the dynamism of the organization requires venturing into the less historically accessible realm of psychology and recognizing that the social experience of the men who were active in the Pan-German League was emotionally difficult, that it involved psychological strains which colored their behavior and their view of the world.

A World of Enemies

The ideology of the Pan-German League was a vivid vision of fear. The symbolism of the flood, the premonitions of catastrophe, the obsession with enemies, the anxieties about disorder, about the failure of authority and loss of control, all suggest a view of the world which, if not pathological, was at least psychologically problematic. This impression is confirmed in other features of the Pan-Germans' ideology, which betrayed the extent to which their anxieties affected their perception of events.

It needs no further emphasis that a cardinal tenet in the Pan-Germans' ideology was the presence everywhere of enemies. At a deeper level than the programmatic, this conviction lent structure to the ideology, once the Pan-Germans had concluded that however diverse these enemies appeared, they were all ultimately linked in a single conspiracy, united in its hostility to Germans. This conspiracy, which one writer referred to as a 'league [*Gesellschaftsverband*] against Germans in all zones and realms', united Poles with Czechs, Czechs with Russians, Poles and Czechs with socialists, Catholics with socialists, Russia with Japan, and ultimately all of these, and many more, with one another.[4] 'Enemies all around us' (*Feinde ringsum*) was more than a slogan; it was a premise. 'A broadly based conspiracy has developed with the aim of harming Germandom', was the analysis of one leader in 1908.[5] The situation had not improved in the view of another, who concluded several years later that 'the enemies of Germans [*Deutschfeinde*] throughout the world are holding together'.[6]

Opinions differed among the League's publicists on the precise nature of the ties that bound the nation's enemies together. These men all agreed, however, that the conspiracy was animated by cunning agents – 'agitators and seducers' all the more powerful and dangerous for their anonymity.[7] These agents were 'uncommonly clever'; they worked by stealth, slowly to subvert the integrity of Germandom, and the repertory of their skills included extraordinary adaptability, 'concealing their ultimate aims', posing 'behind the mask of harmlessness', remaining 'behind the scenes', and violence.[8] They had also succeeded in 'wonderfully organizing' their forces, establishing networks and secret ties, and eliminating internal opposition to their power.[9]

Some of these agents were identifiable. Pan-Germans saw the hand of the Jesuits, that 'general staff of the battle order which is mobilized against the German Empire', everywhere at work.[10] They attributed similar powers and intentions to the British monarch, Edward VII.[11] Evidence of the presence of other agents was less distinct but no less alarming, as the local chapter in Eisleben attested in 1903, when it laid out a series of lectures on the 'three internationals which endanger Germandom'. These were, in close if improbable alliance, the Black International of ultramontanism, the Red International of socialism, and the Gold International of high finance.[12]

The tendency of the League's writers to descry supremely unified hostile forces was evident in the very language they used. These linguistic purists thought nothing about desecrating the language with dreadful neologisms which reified abstract concepts and the most diverse collections of people. '*Slaventum*', '*Angelsachsentum*', '*Engländertum*', '*Polentum*', '*Jesuitismus*', and even '*Fremdtum*' (these words do not lose much in translation as 'Slavdom', 'Anglo-Saxondom', 'Englishdom', 'Poledom', 'Jesuitism', and 'foreigndom') conveyed the impression of large blocks organized by superhuman agents who tolerated no dissent.[13] These writers also emphasized, by their frequent use of the passive voice and the impersonal pronoun '*man*', the impression of anonymous forces difficult to identify.

Because they were convinced of the existence of a comprehensive conspiracy directed against the German nation, Pan-German observers were chronically suspicious and hypersensitive about all of its possible manifestations. Alert to attempts by their enemies to bluff and deceive them or, as one writer put it, 'to throw sand in our eyes', they found traces of the conspiracy in many unlikely places – in the pathetic German peace movement, in the French foreign legion, in the docile Casubian minority, and in the appearance of a handful of Poles in southern Brazil.[14] A favorite pastime of these people was to pour over demographic statistics to confirm their fears about the deterioration of the Germans' position in various parts of Europe; not even statistics that appeared to belie their fears could fool them, however.[15]

The world of the Pan-Germans was an arena of titanic conflict which, in the final analysis, reduced to the struggle of Germans against all their enemies. This vision was colored by what one might call political manicheanism; history and politics were a morality play, which pitted Germans against everyone else and whose dénouement would come in war.[16] To the moralists in the League who conceived it, the script tolerated no ambiguity or neutrality. Their search for intellectual order led them to divide the world rigidly into categories of friends and enemies. And even if the latter far outnumbered the former, the schema at least afforded the League's ideologists that degree of control that comes from having perceived the truth.

The ideology of the Pan-German League stands as a classic example of the kind of thinking that has in recent years spawned a tradition in historical writing in which historians have joined hands with psychoanalysts in the attempt to analyze political and social movements under the rubric of a 'paranoid style', a 'paranoid orientation', or something similar.[17] The League's ideology displayed all the standard symptoms that these writers have identified in the 'paranoid syndrome' – the preoccupation with enemies, the tendency to group these together in an all-embracing conspiracy, delusions of grandeur, hypersensitivity, dichotomization, and militant intensity.[18]

It is tempting to join these writers in appropriating from psychoanalysis the concept of paranoia to analyze the views and behaviors of the Pan-German League. Not only the conspiratorial thinking and militant suspicion, but the obviously problematic relationship to authority and the anxieties over loss of control, which protrude so vividly in the ideology, could thus be read, with little imaginative effort, as symptoms. Tracing the etiology of these symptoms requires more imagination, but the analysis would emphasize that the Pan-Germans were collectively employing an ego-defense mechanism in order to control threatening libidinal forces (which were probably the product of an unresolved Oedipal complex), by projecting these forces onto outside objects; these objects the Pan-Germans in turn perceived as the threatening forces in a hostile conspiracy.[19]

I have found the problems inherent in this line of analysis insuperable. It attributes collectively to a large group of men a defense mechanism which is, by definition, a profoundly personal phenomenon, one whose etiology and workings are complex and can be analyzed, if at all, only under therapeutic conditions unavailable to historians. The concept of paranoia is also troubling in so far as it connotes pathological emotional problems. It treats ideology as symptomatic of illness and implies that the people who articulated and subscribed to it were severely disturbed. Some of the Pan-Germans might well have been mentally ill – *vide* Carl Peters – but the vast majority of the men who harbored these ideological views appear, by any clinical definition, to have been entirely normal, functional members of their communities.

Yet for all the problems it raises, the concept of a paranoid style, if used cautiously, brings important insights into the history of an organization like the Pan-German League. The concept's principal virtue is that it suggests the extent to which the League's world-view and behavior reflected the play of powerful anxieties and other emotional forces. These forces had two effects of particular significance. They produced, in the first place, severe perceptual distortion. Because Pan-Germans perceived and understood history in terms of ethnic conflict and conspiracies, they blocked out information that indicated that their antagonists were themselves weak and that the groups that appeared to make up a monolithic conspiracy were themselves the victims of social, political, and ethnic conflict.[20] In addition, the imperatives that resided in the Pan-Germans' anxious vision were emotionally compelling. These imperatives prescribed vigilance and the pursuit of ruthless and aggressive policies. They allowed no laxity or compromise in the defense of the nation's integrity in a world of enemies; and they pushed the men who shared the vision into the position of opposing official authority in Germany. The category of enemies was so comprehensive that it invited inclusion – if only as unwitting accomplices – of anyone who failed to share the Pan-Germans' view of the world. The League's oppositon to the German government thus rested ultimately upon the frightening belief that the men who conducted the country's policies were abetting the conspiracy among Germany's enemies.

The real problem with using the concept of a paranoid style is that it usually points to a level of psychological analysis so deep that it is inaccessible to historians. The ideology and behavior of the Pan-Germans unquestionably had a powerful emotional dimension, but the precise derivation, character, and intrapsychic function of the emotional drives that produced this behavior and receptivity to ideology in individual Pan-Germans must remain hidden to historians. This is not to abandon the effort to understand the problem of why these men thought and behaved as they did; it is rather to suggest that if historians wish to address the problem at all, they must do so at a different level of analysis.

Toward a Social Psychology of Radical Nationalism

The limitations of psychohistory have been sufficiently noted that they need not be rehearsed here.[21] The use by historians of explanatory categories drawn from psychology has frequently rested upon such shaky evidence that skeptics have had little difficulty in dismissing the results of the venture as conjecture. The analysis that follows is probably not going to convert the skeptics, but two considerations recommend it. The first is that the Pan-German League presents an instance in which, to use the words of Tim Mason (one of the skeptics), 'more mundane explanations do not match the extreme character of the behavior under discussion'.[22] The behavior under discussion here is the receptivity to the notables in the Pan-German League for a militant ideology which prescribed opposition to official authority and which was charged with anxieties, an obsession with enemies, and a pronounced tendency toward rigid, conspiratorial thinking. And it is difficult indeed to see how one can explain this behavior without resort to psychology.

The second consideration which recommends a psychological approach to the Pan-German League is the availability of a model which, while admittedly vulnerable to some of the objections traditionally raised against psychohistory, offers historians the opportunity to link psychology and social history in a manner that most varieties of psychohistory, which have taken their analytical categories directly from Freudian theories of personality, have not. The model rests upon sociological and psychological concepts that are compatible and open, to a certain extent, to empirical verification. Parsonian role theory has supplied the sociology of the model; the psychology draws heavily from the developmental theories of Erik Erikson, in which the emphasis falls less upon the shaping of personality in ontogenetic, intrapsychic conflicts than upon the development of identity in the constant interaction between personality and social and cultural roles and norms.[23]

Simply stated, the model is based upon the premise that the psychological process of building identity is not exclusively ontogenetic, that it continues throughout a person's life, and that social roles and cultural symbols encountered in adult life continue to have critical psychological significance. These symbols and roles are internalized: they are invested with emotional energy and incorporated into the system of ego-ideals and object-relations out of which identity and self-esteem are constructed.[24] Throughout a person's life an essential link accordingly exists between culture and society, on the one hand, and personal identity on the other. From this premise the conclusion follows that social or cultural upheavals or discontinuities are bound to have psychological consequences for large groups of people. Challenges to the validity of cultural symbols or the inability to act out accustomed social roles produces a blow to what psychologists call the 'narcissistic integrity' of the people affected and make necessary what Fred Weinstein and Gerald Platt have referred to as 'restitutional measures' – psychological adjustments of a broad possible range, including the search for new ideal objects, the codification of regressive fantasies in ideology, or relapse into apathy.[25] The point to be stressed is that when social and cultural dislocations challenge the personal identity and self-esteem of large numbers of people, the psychological responses can be highly emotional and difficult to predict, although social and cultural conditions – for example, the availability of culturally sanctioned objects for aggression – can decisively affect the character of the restitutional measures to which people resort.

The appeal of this model is that it provides a social and cultural dimension for a psychological explanation of modes of thinking and behavior in the Pan-German League – modes that are impossible to understand in the more conventional terms of interest psychology. Most of the activists in the organization were men who, as custodians of authority and culture, performed prestigious roles in German society. These roles were 'objective' in the sense that they were culturally assigned to men who were academically educated and who represented the state in the higher realms of the public bureaucracy. That these roles also had psychological significance for the men who performed them, that these roles provided self-concepts and sources of self-esteem, is a conclusion invited by common sense and empirical research on elites in other cultures; and the Pan-Germans' literature bore witness to it as well.[26] The symbolism in this literature related directly to these roles. The *Vorkämpfer* or pioneer symbolized the custodial roles these men saw themselves playing. *Deutschtum*, the German nation, and all the other national symbols represented everything over which they believed they had custody – culture, authority, and order.

The cultural objects and the roles that Pan-Germans coded symbolically as pioneers, *Deutschtum*, empire, the navy, and all the rest, were internalized. In the sense specified by Roy Shafer, the pioneer was an ideal self-representation, and the national symbols were ideal-objects.[27] All these ideals were emotionally vested components of the self-concepts of Pan-German leaders. The national symbols prescribed identification with a collectivity and a structured system of social and ethnic relations; the pioneer prescribed identification with cultural role. Just as performance of the custodial roles was culturally a source of status and prestige, identification with the ideals associated with these roles was psychologically a source of self-image, self-concept, and self-esteem.[28]

Identification with these ideals was of special psychological importance for men whose relationship to the custodial roles and objects associated with them was in some way marginal or otherwise problematic. This generalization applies to several of the groups heavily represented in the cadres of the Pan-German League. The first were those with prolonged exposure to a foreign environment, people whose ethnic identity was insecure for having incubated in a state of tension with the cultural environment in which they were born, grew up, studied, resided, or into which they married.

The second group consisted of those for whom a self-image of pioneer was insecure by virtue of their being new arrivals in the esteemed ranks of the custodians. These 'new pioneers' included the professionals with academic credentials but without the status of public officials and the public officials in the less traditional sectors of the bureaucracy. Although it is impossible to determine from available evidence, it is probable that many of these people were also upwardly mobile socially, so that their situation bears marks of the phenomenon that the sociologists call 'status inconsistency' or 'status lag'.[29] To the extent that these men were recent arrivals in roles that carried high status, their self-concepts tended to be tenuous and insecure; the status and respect these roles implied were clouded by incommensurate social background or by credentials that had yet to find unqualified acceptance. Ludwig Kuhlenbeck was a classic example of the problem. The son of a locksmith, he took the major step up the social ladder when he earned a university degree in law. He was haunted, however, by the insecurities of his social background: convinced that he was not being accorded due respect by his peers, he became insufferably defensive. After his irascibility had cost him the chance to pursue an academic career in Germany, he settled first for a career as an attorney and then for a teaching post at the French university in Lausanne, where his feelings of isolation and lack of respect only grew. Finally, his provocations of his French students led to his dismissal in 1908, when he returned to Germany to find company in the Pan-German League's chapter in Naumburg.[30]

Kuhlenbeck's career exuded marginality – the social marginality of the upwardly mobile, the cultural marginality of the new custodian, and the geographical marginality of residence abroad. Elements of career frustration also contributed to his insecurity, and the evidence suggests that Kuhlenbeck was not alone in having this problem. High-ranking military officers who were active in the League had also experienced career frustration. Many of them, including August Keim, Eduard von Liebert, and Alfred Breusing, were either non-noble or came from backgrounds that made social mobility a distinct feature of their careers (Liebert's father was a major). Their backgrounds made them ill at ease with the social conservatism they encountered in the officer corps, and they retired in clouded circumstances.[31] Career frustrations clearly figured in the background of another former officer of much higher social station, Ernst Graf zu Reventlow, who before becoming active in the League had been forced out of the navy when he married a dance-hall singer.[32] The suspicion is also as difficult to suppress as it is to document that many of the attorneys, prominent among them Heinrich Class, had been unable to find careers in the more prestigious ranks of the civil service.[33]

Whether or not it was complicated by any of these circumstances, the role of custodian was, by definition, culturally insecure in a period of rapid change such as that which beset Germany after 1890.[34] To the extent that these men represented authority and dominant cultural values, they were, in an objective sense, on the first line of defense when these values and the structure of authority came under attack. It is unnecessary to describe this change in any detail here, for it is the basic theme of German history in the Wilhelmine era, and it was played out in many different realms. Several facets of it particularly emphasized the vulnerability of the custodians. The challenge posed by the political mobilization of the urban working classes was especially troubling, for it was the most fundamental, directed against the entire social order and structure of political authority. The mass mobilization of peasants and Catholics represented another attack on bastions of political authority traditionally controlled by *Honoratioren* around the country.[35] The demands of ethnic minorities for autonomy or independence challenged German authority along the periphery of the

Reich. The growing weight of industry in German society, which had occasioned much of the social and political ferment, had more diffuse cultural implications as well, principally in drawing into question the very relevance of *Bildung* as traditionally conceived and hence the entitlement to precedence and authority that it gave to those who had it.[36]

These trends are not only abundantly recounted in the history books; they were dramatically in evidence in the Pan-German League's literature, where they were collectively symbolized as the flood and were subjected to a process of interpretation and distortion which leaves little doubt that these men were psychologically as well as culturally vulnerable. The challenges they encountered to the cultural roles they played and to the values they represented were at the same time psychological threats to the internalized roles and ideal-objects on which their self-images and esteem rested. The cultural challenges produced, in other words, psychological tension in the form of conflicts between ego-ideals and the reality these men experienced.[37]

This psychological tension specifically involved threats to national symbols internalized as ideal-objects and to expectations created by role models internalized as ego-ideals. Threats perceived to national symbols from whatever source – from ethnic or international rivals, domestic enemies, or even an anemic German foreign policy – had direct emotional repercussions. So too did the strains that inhered in the role of custodian. The role demanded that its occupants enjoy deference, that their claims to authority and precedence be recognized. The perception that their authority was instead being challenged – by socialists, ethnic minorities, and many other groups – was emotionally traumatic, especially for the men who were new arrivals, and hence insecure, in the custodial roles.

The most telling clues to the nature of the psychological strains that Pan-Germans experienced are the repeated allusions in their writings and lectures to the related themes of abandonment and shame. Shame connotes a particular kind of stress. It is distinct from guilt, which arises when moral injunctions (or, in the idiom of psychoanalysis, the demands of the super-ego) are unmet. Shame, by contrast, arises when, to quote a leading authority, the 'goals and images of the ego-ideal are not reached', or when self-concept, which is molded from these ideal goals and images, is discrepant with cultural reality. If guilt instills the fear of punishment, shame gives rise to the fear of being exposed, isolated, and abandoned.[38]

One index of the centrality of such fears was the frequency with which Pan-Germans admitted their feelings of shame as they evaluated their nation's standing in the world. Exposure, isolation, and abandonment were, in addition, hallmarks of the symbolism in the League's ideology. Surrounded by the flood, the island outposts faced the dreaded risk of being fully cut off and abandoned to hostile forces. The essential characteristics of the pioneer were, in the last analysis, his separation, isolation, precarious exposure, and his loneliness. 'No horror today is like the loneliness of those who are not heard', Class confessed in 1912, 'the moral, spiritual, political loneliness of all of those' – and here he meant his fellow pioneers in the League – 'who are aware of the real condition of our fatherland and its people and who have the courage no longer to delude themselves.'[39]

The vision that Class, Hasse, and other leaders of the League articulated in an effort to come to terms with their feelings of shame and loneliness was an emotionally charged 'restitutional measure', a representation of reality, a central feature of which was a conspiracy among the enemies of authority and culture throughout the world. The nature of the deeper psychological needs served by the vision – many features of which psychologists would no doubt describe as neurotic – must remain obscure. In its basic contours, though, this vision resembled belief-systems observed among highly prejudiced people in other cultures.[40] The social and cultural position of these prejudiced people also appears to have corresponded to that of the Pan-Germans, at least to the extent that they too were often members of marginal groups disoriented during periods of rapid social change. Like the Pan-Germans, they seized upon belief-systems characterized by a rigid schematization of reality, aggressive attitudes against out-groups, a high level of anxiety, and a low tolerance for ambiguity – all of which resulted in militance and perceptual distortion.[41] The Pan-Germans, like these other prejudiced people, found in their ideological vision an element of intellectual control, which made possible the maintenance of self-esteem as it reconciled ego-ideal and experienced reality.[42] The pioneer was an admirable figure precisely because of all the hostility he faced.

In 1899 Julius Lenzmann, a deputy of the Progressive Party, attempted to analyze the roots of radical nationalism for his colleagues in the Reichstag. The phenomenon represented, he observed, 'the self-seeking employment of a purported patriotism to satisfy egotistical needs'.[43] Stripped of its polemical intent, his analysis had an element of truth, at least with respect to leaders of the Pan-German League. A substantial proportion of these men belonged to what might, with little exaggeration, be described as a 'crisis stratum'.[44] Their role was to defend culture and authority in Imperial Germany at a time when prodigious social change made this role difficult, both culturally and psychologically. The fact that most of these men were new arrivals in the role intensified their insecurities and increased their receptivity to the radical nationalism of the Pan-German vision.

The resort to psychology provides a plausible explanation for the appeal of the Pan-Germans' anxiety-laden vision of the world, and it underscores the emotional dimension of their reactions to political events. None the less, the limitations of this analysis must be emphasized. Beyond the fact that its evidentiary foundations are weak, an obvious problem remains. The logic of the analysis implies that the psychological tensions to which the Pan-Germans' ideology and behavior were a response inhered in the role of custodian. However, the great majority of the men who performed these roles in Imperial Germany were not in the Pan-German League. Psychological needs that arose out of cultural strain might well have motivated some notables to become active in the organization, but more tangible factors affected the extent to which such psychological needs generally resulted in a decision to join the Pan-German League.

Notes

1   Hofmann von Wellenhof, p. 4.
2   ADB (1910), 6; cf. ADB (1909), 213.
3   ADB (1908), 187–8.
4   Türk, p. 78; ADB (1894), 21–2; ADB (1895), 163; ADB (1902), 121–2; ADB (1904), 337–8; ADB (1907), 33–5.
5   ADB (1908), 107–8.
6   ADB (1911), 426.
7   ADB (1896), 222, 231–2; ADB (1901), 281; ADB (1907), 1–3.
8   e.g. Türk, p. 68; ADB (1894), 65–6; ADB (1903), 414; ADB (1905), 121–3; ADB (1907), 234; ADB (1909), 270–1, 376; ADB (1910), 242–3.
9   Petzet, p. 66; ADB (1895), 85–6; ADB (1898), 17; ADB (1904), 334.
10 ADB (1898), 5–7; ADB (1904), 116; ADB (1909), 142.
11 ADB (1909), 1–2, 9–11; ADB (1910), 166–8.
12 ADB (1903), 386–7.
13 ADB (1895), 115–16; ADB (1897), 139; ADB (1899), 349; ADB (1904), 67.
14 ADB (1900), 32–3; ADB (1909), 2–5; ADB (1911), 164–6; ADB (1912), 161–2; ADB (1913), 409–10;, ADB (1914), 98.
15 See Petzet, p. 40; ADB (1894), 214; ADB (1903), 186–8; ADB (1908), 367.
16 Hasse, *Zukunft*, p. 132.
17 See especially Richard Hofstadter, 'The paranoid style in American politics', in *The Paranoid Style in American Politics and Other Essays* (New York, 1967), pp. 3–40; David Shapiro, *Neurotic Styles* (New York, 1965), pp. 54–107; David W. Swanson *et al.*, *The Paranoid* (Boston, Mass., 1970).
18 See C. W. Miller 'The paranoid syndrome', *A.M.A. Archives of Neurology and Psychiatry*, vol. 45 (1941), pp. 953–63; H. S. Sullivan, 'The paranoid dynamism', in *Clinical Studies in Psychiatry* (New York, 1956), p. 145; Norman A. Cameron, 'The paranoid pseudo-community', *American Journal of Sociology*, vol. 49 (1943), pp. 32–8; Cameron, 'The paranoid pseudo-community revisited', ibid., vol. 64 (1959), pp. 52–8.
19 See Jules Nydes, 'The paranoid-masochistic character', *Psychoanalytic Review*, vol. 50 (Summer 1963), p. 57; Norman A. Cameron, 'Paranoid conditions and paranoia', in Silvano Arieti (ed.), *American Handbook of Psychiatry*, 3rd edn, 6 vols (New York, 1974–5), Vol. 3, pp. 676–94.
20 This was not always true. Some of the League's literature contained astute and sensitive analyses of the ethnic conflict. See Petersen, *Deutschtum in Elsass-Lorthringen*; cf. ADB (1902), 438–40; ADB (1903), 323–4; ADB (1909), 67–9; ADB (1910), 306–7. On the problem of perceptual distortion in the League's view of politics see Schödl, pp. 223–33.
21 See Wehler, 'Geschichtswissenschaft und "Psychohistorie"', pp. 201–13; Wehler, 'Zum Verhältnis von Geschichtswissenschaft und Psychoanalyse', HZ, vol. 209 (1969), pp. 529–54.
22 T. W. Mason, 'Women in Nazi Germany', *History Workshop*, no. 2 (1977), p. 27.
23 The most cogent presentation of this model is Fred Weinstein and Gerald M. Platt, *Psychoanalytic Sociology: An Essay on the Interpretation of Historical Data and the Phenomena of Collective Behavior* (Baltimore, Md and London, 1973); see also Edith Jacobsen, *The Self and the Object World* (New York, 1964), pp. 185, 196–7; M. K. Opler, 'Cultural anthropology and social psychiatry', *American Journal of Psychiatry*, vol. 113 (1956), pp. 304–9; Alex Inkeles, 'Some sociological observations on culture and personality studies', in Clyde Kluckhohn and Henry A. Murray (eds), *Personality in Nature, Society, and Culture*, 2nd edn (New York, 1956), pp. 577–92.
24 See Abner Cohen, *Two-Dimensional Man: An Essay on the Anthropology of Power and Symbolism in Complex Society* (Berkeley, Calif. and Los Angeles, 1974), esp. pp. 54–60.
25 Weinstein and Platt, pp. 107–8.
26 See Harriett Moore and Gerhard Kleinig, 'Das soziale Selbstbild der Gesellschaftsschichten in Deutschland, *Kölner Zeitschrift für Soziologie und Sozialwissenschaft*, vol. 12 (1960), pp. 86–119; cf. Hans P. Dreitzel, *Elitebegriffe und Sozialstruktur: Eine Soziologische Begriffsanalyse* (Stuttgart, 1962), pp. 139–45.

27   Roy Shafter, 'Ideals, the ego ideal, and the ideal self', in Robert R. Holt (ed.), *Motives and Thought: Psychoanalytic Essays in Honor of David Rappaport* (New York, 1967), pp. 150–4; cf. G. Piers and M. B. Singer, *Shame and Guilt: A Psychoanalytic and a Cultural Study* (Springfield, Ill., 1953), p. 14.

28   See Jeanne N. Knutson, *The Human Basis of the Polity: A Psychological Study of Political Men* (Chicago and New York, 1972), esp. pp. 28–69; Stanislav V. Kasl, 'Status inconsistency: some conceptual and methodological considerations,' in John P. Robinson *et al.*, *Measures of Occupational Attitudes and Occupational Characteristics* (University of Michigan, Institute for Social Research, 1969), p. 378; Thomas Luckmann and Peter L. Berger, 'Social mobility and personal identity', *Archives européennes de sociologie*, vol. 5 (1964), p. 335; cf. Hintze, p. 72; Gerth and Mills, p. 185.

29   See Joseph Greenblum and Leonard I. Pearlin, 'Vertical mobility and prejudice: a socio-psychological analysis', in Reinhard Bendix and Seymor Martin Lipset (eds), *Class, Status, and Power: A Reader in Social Stratification* (Glencoe, Ill., 1953), pp. 480–91; Kasl, pp. 377–99; Mayer, *Dynamics*, p. 51; Ira S. Rohter, 'Social and psychological determinants of radical rightism', in Robert A. Schönberger (ed.), *The American Right Wing: Readings in Political Behavior* (New York, 1969), pp. 213–17.

30   Urner, pp. 506–14; Ludwig Kuhlenbeck, *Lausanne: Ein Wort zur Berichtigung und Abwehr* (Munich, 1908).

31   Keim, *Erlebtes und Erstrebtes*; Eduard von Liebert, *Aus einem bewegten Leben: Erinnerungen* (Munich, 1925); Class, *Strom*, pp. 242–6; cf. Chickering, 'Wehrverein', pp. 9–10.

32   Horst Boog, 'Graf Ernst zu Reventlow (1869–1943): Eine Studie zur Krise der deutschen Geschichte seit dem Ende des 19. Jahrhunderts' (Diss. phil., Heidelberg, 1965), pp. 100–11.

33   Class, *Strom*, p. 29, denies this emphatically.

34   See Dietrich Rüschemeyer, 'Modernisierung und die Gebildeten im Kaiserlichen Deutschland', *Kölner Zeitschrift für Soziologie und Sozialpsychologie*, vol. 16 (Sonderheft 1972), p. 519.

35   Eley, *Reshaping*, esp. pp. 19–40.

36   Vondung, 'Zur Lage', p. 30; Jochmann, p. 404; Wehler, 'Zur Funktion und Struktur', p. 117.

37   See Shafer, p. 169.

38   Piers and Singer, esp. pp. 11–16; cf. Helen Merrell Lynd, *On Shame and the Search for Identity* (New York, 1958), esp. pp. 56–7, 66.

39   Frymann/Class, *Kaiserbuch*, pp. 234–5; cf. Stern, *Cultural Despair*, pp. 2–3.

40   See especially Gordon W. Allport, *The Nature of Prejudice* (Cambridge, Mass., 1954); Bruno Bettelheim and Morris Janowitz, *Dynamics of Prejudice: A Psychological and Sociological Study of Veterans* (New York, 1950); Milton Rokeach, *The Open and Closed Mind: Investigations into the Nature of Belief Systems and Personality Systems* (London, 1960); Peter Heintz, *Soziale Vorurteile: Ein Problem der Persönlichkeit, der Kultur und der Gesellschaft* (Cologne, 1957); T. W. Adorno *et al.*, *The Authoritarian Personality* (New York, 1950).

41   See Laurence S. Kubie, 'The nature of the neurotic process', in Arieti, *American Handbook of Psychiatry*, Vol. 3, pp. 3–16; John C. Nemiah, 'Anxiety: signal, symptom, and syndrome', ibid., pp. 91–109.

42   Rohter, pp. 198–9, 230–2; Hans Toth, *The Social Psychology of Social Movements* (Indianapolis, Ind., 1965), pp. 52–3, 69–70; Willy Baranger, 'The ego and the function of ideology', *International Journal of Psycho-Analysis*, vol. 39 (1958), p. 191; cf. Bourdieu, p. 164.

43   StBR (18.2.99), 953–4; cf. Schilling, p. 52; Stern, *Cultural Despair*, p. 254.

44   See Mayer, *Dynamics*, p. 60.

7 A Favorable Climate

The ideology of the Pan-German League reflected the social experience of a group of men who performed custodial roles over culture and authority in Imperial Germany. The aggressiveness, hypersensivity, and militance of the ideology, and the League's dynamism were products of psychological strains that these roles imposed upon the men who performed them. However, emphasizing the broad social, cultural, and psychological foundations of radical nationalism leaves an incomplete picture of both the League's appeal and the dynamism which would by the eve of war turn the organization into a major political force in Imperial Germany. In order to study more fully the sources of the League's appeal and dynamism, and to pose in somewhat different terms the question of what activity in the organization meant to the men who were active, the analysis must turn now to the Pan-German League at the grass-roots level.

The Pan-German League was a social organization. Its constituent units were several hundred local chapters (*Ortsgruppen*) throughout the country. These local groups were the real foundation of the League, and within their confines took place most of the organization's activities. The next three chapters will focus on these groups. The present chapter explores patterns of regional diversity in their strength in order to suggest how local conditions affected the Pan-German League's appeal. Chapter 8 will investigate the dynamics of the internal life of the *Ortsgruppen*, particularly the manner in which the customs and rituals which the local groups nurtured during the demonstration of patriotism further reflected the social experience of the people who made up most of the membership. Finally, Chapter 9 will examine the place of the Pan-German League's local groups in the networks of voluntary associations which underpinned middle-class cultural life in Imperial Germany and which eventually provided channels for mobilizing a national opposition to the German government.

Most of the local chapters of the Pan-German League were born in similar circumstances, in public meetings convened to celebrate a patriotic occasion or to hear a speech on a patriotic topic by a visiting speaker of some note. The underlying theme of the meeting was invariably the need for an organization to keep patriotic sentiment alive in the community, and just as invariably the meeting concluded with a motion from the floor to establish a chapter of the Pan-German League.

Orchestrating this ritual was also a standard process. The initiative came usually from one of the League's leading figures or traveling speakers, such as Alfred Geiser, Lehr's successor as national executive secretary, who developed the techniques of founding local groups into an art. The critical step was to make contact with people known to enjoy the 'necessary respect' in a community, in the calculation that the networks of colleagues, friends, and relatives in which these people circulated would bring together a group large enough to constitute the core of the chapter.[1] Access to the mayor, the *Landrat*, some higher official, or the community's representative in the Reichstag was a great asset. Ernst Bassermann, who represented Mannheim in the Reichstag, was instrumental in attracting over a hundred people into the League's chapter in his city, while the very presence of high officials at meetings contributed substantially to the success of groups in Bochum, Kassel, and Magdeburg.[2] Public officials were also frequently of value because of their professional contacts. A number of local groups grew up around a core of *Oberlehrer* who knew each other professionally. The city of Ratibor in Silesia was the classic example of this phenomenon; here four teachers at the Royal Evangelical Gymnasium were the heart of the chapter.[3] The moving force behind the establishment of the chapter in Bochum was a factory inspector by the name of Kuchenbuch, who proselytized 'with fiery zeal' throughout the geographical jurisdiction of his office, using his professional contacts to set up chapters in nearby communities.[4] Judges in local *Amtsgerichte* and public surveyors were also assets because of the wide range of contacts they made during the travels which their work demanded.[5]

Once a local committee of sufficient size and social standing had been brought together, the public meeting was the next item on the agenda. Its success was contingent upon a number of things, including careful planning, which meant sufficient advertising, having the right people in attendance, selecting the proper meeting hall, and timing the pitch for membership.[6] The timing of the meeting itself was also important. Like other patriotic societies, which employed the same techniques, the Pan-German League quickly learned that meetings were most likely to draw large crowds in an atmosphere of international crisis or patriotic excitement.[7] The dramatic growth of the organization at the turn of the century was demonstration of this truth, as was the fact that the subsequent decline in membership came after the end of the Boer war, during a period when international tension subsided and the League found it more difficult to define what its leaders called 'great goals'.[8]

Although the circumstances of their births were usually similar, the Pan-German League's local chapters displayed considerable diversity in appeal, interest, social composition, and vitality. Each of them had, to some extent, to adapt to local conditions.[9] The program of the League was broad enough in scope that the locals could emphasize different phases of it in making their appeals. The navy and an aggressive colonial policy were the points of emphasis in the activities of chapters in Hamburg, Lübeck, Kiel, and Berlin; in Berlin, in fact, the chapter served as a center of opposition to the leadership of the German Colonial Society.[10] Chapters in Silesia paid more attention to the Polish problem than did those to the west, while the groups in Saxony focused their attention on ethnic conflict in the Habsburg monarchy.[11] Although the League's membership was drawn from the same broad social groups throughout the country, the proportions of the mixture reflected differences of local appeal. The business community was particularly well represented in chapters in commercial and industrial centers, such as Hamburg and Mülheim. In Hessen, on the other hand, several of the smaller chapters were made up almost entirely of peasants mobilized by activists from larger groups in Mainz and Worms, which were in turn dominated by public officials.

In no respect, though, was there more variety among the local chapters than in their vitality. Almost 400 chapters were in existence at one time or another. Some of them, such as those in Hamburg, Dresden, Leipzig, Bonn, Cologne, and Kassel, were large, counting memberships of several hundred people, and very active. The *Ortsgruppe* in Mainz, which stood as a model of vitality, had in 1901–2 a membership of more than 600, including 350 which it had recruited from villages in the surrounding countryside; it staged at least one major meeting each month during this period, and in the summer of 1901 it organized an excursion for its members and their families to the Niederwald.[12]

The chapter in Mainz was by no means typical, however. The majority of these groups – more than two-thirds – existed only on paper or were dormant on all but select occasions. After an auspicious beginning at the founding meeting, most of these collapsed as soon as the routine set in of organizing meetings, collecting dues, arranging for distribution of the journal, and keeping in touch with national headquarters.[13] Those that survived did so on the strength of the work of a handful of activists, who, for all practical purposes, constituted the entirety of the chapters except on those occasions when a prominent lecturer from outside or an international incident briefly breathed in a little life.[14]

The variety of success among different local chapters poses an interesting problem. One obvious explanation for it is that chapters took hold and thrived in those communities where 'suitable personalities' were to be found. This description applied to men who possessed both the requisite status in their communities and the time, energy, and dedication to look after the details of keeping the chapter alive. The category included a man like Dr Lampe, an *Oberlehrer* in Posen, who, upon his transfer to Droyssig in 1898, promptly set up a chapter in his new home town, or like Dr. Halfmann, another *Oberlehrer*, who did the same when he was transferred from Eisleben to Itzehoe.[15] Without these activists to serve as the 'souls of the *Ortsgruppe*', few chapters would have survived anywhere.[16]

Yet citing the presence of these men in a given locality to explain the vitality of the League's chapter begs the question. Potential activists could be found practically everywhere in the country, but local circumstances were not everywhere conducive to their activism. The experience of one eager organizer illustrated this truth well. Scouring the plains of Farther Pomerania trying to set up chapters, he discovered that the local gentry would not even talk to him. A small group of middle-class landholders were mildly interested, but when he began to speak of the practical business of founding a chapter, 'they all began', he complained, 'quietly to smile, almost with a sense of sympathy'. In these circles he soon became known – no longer with much sympathy – as a nuisance. 'the national doctor'.[17] Clearly, if men like this were to be persuaded to shoulder the burdens of local leadership, they needed encouragement and support – in the form of other men who were willing to help, sufficient numbers of people to participate regularly in activities, and some appreciation for the work they were doing, be this in the local papers or even among friends and colleagues.

Some German communities provided a more supportive climate than others. It is possible to determine roughly which communities these were, using as an index the reports the local chapters submitted, at the repeated behest of national headquarters, on their activities.[18] This index is by no means precise, for many of the local activities doubtless went unreported. None the less, counting the reports each local sent in during the last fifteen years before the war does confirm a conclusion suggested by the lamentations of the national leadership, that only a small proportion of the chapters, at the most about sixty, were consistently active.[19] And a closer look at the communities in which chapters were most active reveals some interesting patterns (see map).

Most of these communities were large. Twenty-seven had populations of over 100,000, and another twenty had more than 20,000 inhabitants. Although the observation probably needs little emphasis, the size of the community was of more than peripheral relevance for the vitality of the local chapter: larger cities offered larger pools from which to draw members. The size of the pool was in fact critical to the survival of the League in communities where it faced competition from chapters of other patriotic societies (as it frequently did).

Another generalization applies to practically every community in which chapters of the League thrived. Given the occupational profile of the organization, it is no surprise that the active chapters were located in administrative centers (*Beamtenstädte*). Their size and the scale of their administrative operations varied enormously – from Berlin, the administrative hub of the entire country, to little places like Altenkirchen, which, as a *Kreisort*, was the site of a *Landratsamt*, an *Amtsgericht*, and customs and tax offices. The presence in these communities of administrative agencies of all descriptions – courts, offices of mining, construction, and school inspection, garrisons, regional and provincial administrative bodies (*Landratsämter*, *Hauptamtsmannschaften*, *Bezirksregierungen*, *Oberpräsidien*), or state ministries – made available to the League's organizers a large corps of precisely the kinds of men whose concerns the League sought to represent. Linked by both personal and professional ties, these public officials made up the pool from which both the leadership and membership of local chapters could be drawn.

A problem remains. Administrative centers existed throughout Germany, but the distribution of the communities in which the League was active suggests that the organization's appeal was geographically restricted. Clearly, regional conditions affected the League's chances of success. The truth of this observation is best demonstrated in the areas where the organization enjoyed its least success.

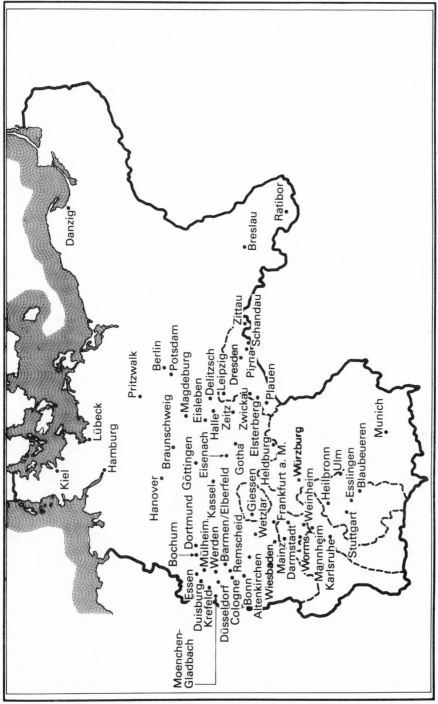

Active chapters of the Pan-German League, 1899–1914

The Pan-German League in the East and South

In Prussia there were but three consistently active local chapters east of Berlin – in Danzig, Breslau, and Ratibor. In Bavaria only two were worth mentioning, in Munich and Würzburg, while in Württemberg the League was active only in Stuttgart, Ulm, Esslingen, Heilbronn, and Blaubeuren. To the west, in Baden, the lone active chapters were in Karlsruhe and Mannheim; and in Alsace-Lorraine there were none.

The causes of the League's conspicuous weakness in the east and south were several. In the Prussian east ethnic conflict and militant nationalism were endemic, but the League failed to exploit the situation because it faced two powerful rivals. The advantages enjoyed by the Eastern Marches Society have already been mentioned. Well financed, efficiently organized, supported by public agencies, and dedicated to a single cause – the Germanization of the Prussian east – this society was more able than the Pan-German League to speak to the immediate concerns of officials and businessmen in this part of the country. While the Eastern Marches Society drew potential support away from the Pan-German League in the towns and cities of the east, the countryside was even more hopeless. It was the domain of the Agrarian League, an organization with which the League was on bad terms throughout most of the prewar period, owing chiefly to the League's insistence that Germanization of the east required expropriation of large estates worked by Polish labor. The men who controlled the Agrarian League were themselves large landowners, and many of them employed cheap Polish labor on their estates, so they resisted the attempts of the Pan-German League to organize in the east. For all practical purposes, then, the Prussian east was barren soil for the Pan-German League. The only chapter of any note, aside from those already mentioned, was in Posen, a large administrative center, which for a few years supported the League (as well as a large and active chapter of the Eastern Marches Society), chiefly on the strength of the navy agitation and the protests over the Boer war. After 1904, however, this chapter collapsed and was not heard from again.

The weakness of the Pan-German League in south Germany was due to different circumstances. Here the principal obstacle was the strength of Catholicism. In its ideology as well as in its composition, the Pan-German League was, protests to the contrary notwithstanding, a distinctly Protestant phenomenon. This was in some respects a curious fact, for the *Grossdeutsch* tradition, which the League inherited, had had a clear Catholic accent, and the realization of the Pan-German vision in Central Europe would have made Catholics a majority in the new state.[20] Such calculations were altogether lost on the League's ideologists, for whom the legacy of the *Kulturkampf* provided the governing credo and who insisted that the international ties of the Roman church made it an un-German institution.[21] Although it usually surfaced in thin disguise as attacks on the Jesuits or ultramontanism, anti-Catholicism was a central strain in the League's ideology.[22] Most of the Poles and French people living near the eastern and western frontiers of the Reich were Catholic, as were most of the subject nationalities in the Habsburg monarchy. The fact that the Catholic clergy played a central role in nurturing ethnic consciousness among these groups placed it high on the Pan-Germans' list of enemies. The parliamentary behavior of the Center Party, particularly its apparent hesitancy over the naval build-up and then its exploitation of the colonial scandals, only confirmed the view of most Pan-Germans that political Catholicism was scarcely less threatening then Social Democracy. Contradictory evidence, indications that German Catholics were themselves becoming increasingly alarmed after the turn of the century over foreign threats to the country, did not register on the Pan-Germans.[23]

Instead, the Pan-German League repeatedly documented its anti-Catholicism by conspicuous, if unofficial, association with organizations and causes that were red flags to the German church and to the Center Party. The League's policy of cooperating with the *Evangelischer Bund* was already a matter of record when the *Los-von-Rom* movement demonstrated it anew at the turn of the century.[24] Austrian Pan-Germans spearheaded this attempt to organize a secession from the Catholic church, but the *Bund* mobilized support for the campaign within Germany. The Pan-German League decided, after considerable debate, neither to support nor to repudiate the campaign formally, but it did give its blessing to individual members who wished to become involved.[25] Many of them did, most prominently Julius Lehmann, the League's publisher in Munich, who was also a leader of the *Evangelischer Bund* and the coordinator of the entire effort in Germany.[26] After the *Los-von-Rom* movement died out with little success in Austria, relations between the League and the *Bund* remained warm, as did the League's enthusiasm for undermining the political power of the Center Party. To this end, it applauded the foundation in 1907 of the *Deutsche Vereinigung*, an organization of so-called 'national Catholics' in western Germany, who came together to obstruct what they considered the party's growing liberalization and increased subservience to Rome.[27] The Pan-German League also supported the efforts of the ex-Jesuit Paul von Hoensbroech, whose *Antiultramontaner Reichsverband* challenged not only the position of the Center Party, but also the teachings of the church itself.[28] Although the Pan-German League chose not to accede to the urgings of some of its members and establish formal ties with Hoensbroech's organization, Hoensbroech himself spoke frequently to the League's chapters on the Jesuit peril, a subject on which he was naturally reputed to be an expert.[29]

Because the League maintained ties to notorious Catholic-baiters like Hoensbroech and Lehmann and because it could not disguise the anti-Catholic themes in its ideology, the organization's spokesmen were hard pressed to sound credible when they issued assurances that the League stood for parity among German Catholics and Protestants, that it recognized no confessional cleavages among Germans, and that it welcomed both Catholics and Protestants into its ranks.[30] Most of the German Catholic press was undeceived; in fact, the Pan-German League was in the eyes of many Catholics the very symbol of the lingering spirit of the *Kulturkampf*, and the Catholic press, most loudly Karl Bachem's liberal *Kölnische Volkszeitung*, engaged the League in a running feud.[31]

The structure of the Pan-German League reflected this antagonism. Very few Catholics joined the organization, although it is impossible to determine precisely how few.[32] In heavily Catholic areas, such as Upper Bavaria, Lower Franconia, Upper Swabia, and Silesia, it proved impossible to establish chapters with any durability. The notables here were themselves Catholic or, if they were Protestant, they were reluctant to antagonize the Catholics who made up the majority of the population in these areas.[33] The only major exceptions to this pattern were cities, such as Munich, Würzburg, and Breslau, which, despite lying in heavily Catholic regions, included substantial Protestant minorities (Breslau in fact had a Protestant majority). This generalization applies as well to the active Pan-German chapters in Catholic areas to the north, in the Rhineland and Westphalia. In cities such as Bonn, Cologne, Düsseldorf, Moenchen-Gladbach, and Bochum, the League also drew its active members from a corps of Protestant notables who made up, so to speak, a large Protestant island in a Catholic sea. Yet the lot of even these chapters was frequently difficult. As long as the political culture in the community was predominantly Catholic, and even in cities where the Protestant minority was substantial, the *Ortsgruppen* tended to be small, and they complained repeatedly of their isolation.[34]

Catholicism was not the only reason for the weakness of the Pan-German League in south Germany. Even in the predominantly Protestant parts of northern Württemberg and Baden, only a handful of chapters exhibited any vitality. In 1905 only about 600 people in all of Württemberg belonged to the League.[35] The principal cause of this situation was the strength of democratic left-liberalism among non-Catholic sectors of the middle class in this part of the country. At first glance, this need not have been an insuperable obstacle, for the populism of the Pan-German League's program could be used to support demands for democratic reform. Several of the League's leaders in south Germany, such as Friedrich Fick in Würzburg (a cousin of Adolf Fick), were in fact democrats who argued that popular influence in the formulation of foreign policy ought to be institutionalized in the Reichstag.[36]

None the less, the points of conflict between the Pan-Germans and south German democrats were numerous. Most Pan-Germans refused to draw the institutional consequences of their populism, calculating, like many other political groups, that democratization would work chiefly to the advantage of the socialists. Moreover, the position of the left-liberals on most questions of foreign policy clashed frontally with that of the Pan-German League. Animated by a spirit of internationalism, which in some circles bordered on pacifism, left-liberals, particularly the south Germans who congregated under the banner of the German People's Party, viewed expenditures on the army, navy, and colonies with suspicion.[37] Swabian provincialism was a major element in this suspicion, and it limited the Pan-Germans' success in other ways as well. Potential activists in this part of the country discovered that the local population could be interested in the fate of Swabians who had emigrated centuries earlier to Hungary, but not in much else that the League had to offer.[38] Suspicion of outsiders also obstructed the work of the League in Swabia in so far as many of the potential local leaders were officials who had transferred into the region and whose alien roots were obvious the moment they opened their mouths to speak.[39]

In these circumstances the League found little support. When Geiser arrived in Reutlingen in 1904 to set up a chapter, he encountered all the difficulties the region had to offer.[40] Despite its reputation as 'the ugliest nest of democrats in Württemberg', Geiser was confident of finding a core of 'nationally reliable elements' in the city. The problem was to find a chairman. The leader of the local People's Party at first consented, but criticism in the local press persuaded him to hand the office over to his son-in-law, the town pharmacist, who soon thereafter moved away. Geiser then tried the dentist and a doctor at a nearby asylum, but they were both north Germans and did not enjoy the confidence of the local folks. Finally, a teacher at the local *Oberrealschule* agreed to become chairman, and for the next several years a small group did meet sporadically.

Reutlingen was one of the stronger chapters in the southwest. Others were located in larger administrative centers such as Stuttgart, Karlsruhe, Mannheim, and Heilbronn, but even these suffered chronically from scant local interest which jeopardized their survival.[41] They usually subsisted around a core of teachers at *Gymnasien* or *Lateinschulen* and a handful of businessmen and professionals, a few of them left-liberals.[42] The experience in Swabia also demonstrated the limits of what a single dedicated activist could do. That there were chapters at all in most of the south German communities was due in the first instance to the tireless agitation of Heinrich and Christian Calmbach, too. *Oberhlehrer* whose successive transfers around the region could be traced in the successive appearance of Pan-German chapters in Ulm, Nienbürg, Heilbronn, Blaubeuren, Esslingen, and Cannstatt.[43] The left-liberal political climate in these places kept the Calmbachs isolated, however; and if they survived the departure of the Calmbach who founded them, most of these chapters remained anemic.

The reasons for the League's complete failure in Alsace-Lorraine were obvious. Convinced that French agitation was preparing the way for the eventual return of the provinces to France, the League advocated making them a part of Prussia to ensure more direct and effective control from Berlin.[44] This demand was calculated to appeal to practically no one in the provinces themselves – not even to the public officials sent there from other parts of Germany, most of whom recognized the wisdom of not antagonizing the local population gratuitously.[45]

The weakness of the Pan-German League in south Germany was due to the inhospitality of the political climate throughout most of this region. In communities in which Catholicism or left-liberalism was the dominant political force, notables who might have been inclined toward activity in the Pan-German League remained isolated and discouraged. Few people attended the organization's meetings regularly or volunteered to help with administration, and most of the community, including the leading newspapers, either reacted hostily or took no notice of what the Pan-Germans were doing. The only major exceptions to this pattern were the communities, such as Munich, with a large and self-conscious Protestant minority, or those such as Stuttgart, Esslingen, and Mannheim, in which the strength of left-liberalism among the Protestant middle class was, for one reason or another, minimal. These patterns explain not only the weakness of the League in some parts of the country; they help account for the organization's strength in others.

Regional Strongholds

The communities that supported most of the strong chapters of the Pan-German League lay around the perimeter of the state of Prussia. These communities fell into three categories. The first were the coastal cities of Danzig, Lübeck, Hamburg, and Kiel. The second were the large industrial centers of northwestern Prussia, the most important of which were Dortmund, Duisburg, Bochum, Essen, Barmen, Krefeld, Mülheim, and Düsseldorf. The third and most numerous group were a belt of cities that extended from the Grand Duchy of Hessen in the west through Thuringia and the Prussian province of Saxony into the Kingdom of Saxony in the east. In this belt were the largest and most active chapters in the country, including those in Mainz, Kassel, Halle, Plauen, Dresden, Eisleben, and Leipzig.

The diversity of these three groups of cities suggests the risks of explaining the vitality of the Pan-German League's chapters in the light of regional social or economic conditions. Local chapters appear to have thrived in mercantile as well as industrial centers, and in communities whose economies were dominated by heavy as well as by light industry. None the less, certain generalizations do apply to most of the cities in all these categories.

In the first place, the generalization bears repetition that whatever the emphasis of their local economies, these communities were all administrative centers. Hamburg, Darmstadt, Gotha, and Dresden were capitals of federal states; Danzig, Düsseldorf, Eisenach, Kassel, Cologne, Magdeburg, Mainz, and Zwickau were seats of district administrations (*Bezirksregierungen* or their equivalents in states other than Prussia), while Bochum, Bonn, Dortmund, Eisleben, Halle, Plauen, and Zeitz were centers of county administration. All these communities were, in sum, places where public officials made up an important part of the circles of notables.

In the second place, most of these communities lay in areas that were heavily Protestant. Those that did not, such as Cologne, Bonn, Düsseldorf, and Moenchen-Gladbach, had Protestant minorities of sufficient size that they insulated their members against the social isolation that membership in the Pan-German League might otherwise have entailed.

Finally, communities in all three groups displayed a similar political configuration. Nearly every one of them lay in a federal electoral district in which the Social Democratic Party had, by 1903, either won the seat or was a close second. Socialist strength was concentrated either within municipal boundaries, as it was in the large centers of industry, or it lay in outlying areas, as in the case of some of the smaller communities in Saxony. In either event, the situation was complicated by the fact that municipal elections were still governed by restrictive suffrage, so that non-socialist blocks were able to cling to local power despite being in a decided minority.[46] And in most of these localities, the non-socialist voters came together under the banner of the National Liberal Party. In fact, the concentration of the most active chapters of the Pan-German League corresponded closely to the electoral geography of National Liberalism, particularly in the common areas of strength in the central belt.

This correspondence was no coincidence. The National Liberals were a party in search of an identity, or rather of a common ground on which to integrate a constituency of businessmen large and small, professionals, officials, and peasants, which it had traditionally served but which, as the research of Dan White has shown in the case of Hessen, was becoming increasingly fragmented.[47] In these circumstances, the symbols and slogans of aggressive nationalism – the navy, empire, and anti-socialism – assumed critical importance for the internal cohesion of the party itself, as well as for the cohesion of the non-socialist forces throughout this part of the country.

Thus, despite their extreme diversity in other respects, the communities in which the Pan-German League was most vigorous exhibited a number of similarities. Most were Protestant administrative centers in which the socialist challenge was immediate. Well might the notables here too have felt like islands surrounded by a sea of hostile forces, and well might they have appealed to aggressive nationalism to consolidate the 'forces of order'. For notables who were clinging to local power, aggressive nationalism seemed to be a key to political survival.

While these common features fostered a climate conducive to chapters of the Pan-German League, the character of these chapters varied among the three categories of communities. The northern seaports represented something of an anomaly in the general pattern of Pan-German strength, in so far as a vested interest in free trade inclined the non-socialist forces toward the Progressive Party rather than the National Liberals. Colonial expansion and the navy were causes around which these forces could rally, however, and broad enthusiasm for these causes generated an atmosphere favorable to the Pan-German League, particularly in Hamburg, where the chapter included hundreds of export merchants, many of whom had served apprenticeships overseas.[48] In Hamburg, too, there was a substantial pocket of National Liberal sentiment, which was served by the *Hamburger Nachrichten*, one of the League's most vocal supporters. Of the other northern ports, Lübeck boasted the largest chapter; it attracted not only a complement of *Oberlehrer*, harbor officials, and merchants, but a number of leading local politicians, including Ludwig Possehl.[49] Chapters in Kiel and Danzig, though active, were small.

The industrial and commercial centers of the northwest usually supported large groups of National Liberals – even in cities such as Essen, Krefeld, Dortmund, Düsseldorf, and Moenchen-Gladbach, where the majority of the non-socialist population was Catholic. Chapters of the League grew up in these cities around a core of teachers and public officials, substantial industrialists and *Kaufleute*, and high-level commercial and industrial *Angestellten*. Anti-socialism was the dominant *motif* in most of these chapters, and in some of the Ruhr cities – Essen, Mülheim, Bochum, and Dortmund – the immigration of Polish workers, who were Catholic, enhanced the League's appeal as it compounded social with confessional and ethnic tension.[50]

The central belt of the country from Hessen to Saxony was the principal locus of the Pan-Germans' strength. Chapters in this area were not only larger as a percentage of local population, but they were, as a rule, more vigorous than chapters elsewhere. Their vitality was due to several circumstances. Unlike the cities of the northwest, whose economies were dominated by large-scale heavy industry, most of the communities in the central belt featured more mixed economies; industry was usually light, organized in smaller firms which engaged in the manufacture or processing of chemicals, instruments, light machinery, precious metals, or foodstuffs. The middle class remained, as a result, more broadly based and diverse, while the ascendancy of socialism was more recent and less massive, confined to the larger cities and the mining or industrial centers.

In the Grand Duchy of Hessen the social composition of the League most closely recreated the full range of the traditional National Liberal coalition. Chapters in Mainz and Worms formed the axis of the League in Hessen. Both recruited their members among professionals, teachers, and other public officials (particularly, in Mainz, from the *Eisenbahndirektion*); both chapters were centers of networks of smaller groups that spread out into the surrounding countryside and attracted peasants and vintners who had traditionally voted National Liberal.[51] In their ability to attract peasants, though, the Hessian chapters were practically unique.[52]

To the east in this central belt the Pan-German League's strength rested not only on increasingly beleaguered pockets of National Liberal support, but on ethnic tension. Nowhere was the League stronger than in the Kingdom of Saxony, an area that was adjacent to Bohemia and the ethnic struggles that raged there. Although it was by no means as extensive as Polish immigration into eastern Prussia, the influx of Czechs into Saxony, particularly the immigration of cheap Czech labor into the industrial centers of Dresden and Leipzig, was sufficient to feed anxiety; so was the fact that Saxony served as a transit station for Polish, Jewish, and other migration out of Galicia and areas to the east.[53] The salience of anxiety over immigration into the area gave the League's chapters in Saxony the imprint of a regional protective society, like the Eastern Marches Society or the German Association for North Schleswig.

Chapters in Dresden and Leipzig were among the largest and most active in the country. Over a thousand Pan-Germans populated the chapter in Leipzig in 1901; about half as many were to be found in Dresden.[54] The teachers, officials, professionals, and businessmen who were active in these chapters included some of the leading figures in the non-socialist political block, which in these cities comprised an alliance of National Liberals and antisemitic groups.[55] In Leipzig this alliance and the Pan-German League both enjoyed the enthusiastic support of the *Leipziger Neueste Nachrichten*, whose editor was Ernst Hasse's friend Paul Liman.

Most remarkable was the strength of the Pan-German League in smaller

Saxon communities, particularly in the western region of the kingdom known as the Vogtland. The anchor of these groups was in Plauen, where local conditions were in many respects ideal for the Pan-German League. Situated less than 20 kilometers from the Bohemian border, the city was heavily Protestant and a center of county administration. It was famous for its textile processing, especially its embroidery. The mechanization of embroidering and the development of a machine industry to feed the textile mills resulted in the dramatic growth of the city at the end of the century and in a socialist majority in the federal elections after 1903. The non-socialist voting block was divided between the National Liberals and the Progressives who spoke for the textile exporters. The two sectors cooperated, however, to secure a precarious hold on municipal power.

The chapter of the Pan-German League in Plauen was not only very large (over 400 in a city of 100,000); it was extraordinarily active – so much so that it was held up as a model *Ortsgruppe*.[56] In raising money for patriotic causes it was unsurpassed, and when the occasion demanded, the group could mobilize audiences in excess of a thousand people.[57] The vitality of the chapter was the product of social and ethnic tensions, which in Plauen reinforced one another because of the immigration of Czech labor.[58] In these circumstances, the rhetoric of ethnic struggle adapted easily to the campaign against the socialists, and the Pan-German League became a leading force in the consolidation of the non-socialist forces. Merchants were the dominant element in the chapter, and a number of them held seats on the city council.[59]

Local conditions in Plauen – the strength of Protestantism and National Liberalism and the compounding effect of social and ethnic antagonism – resembled those in other communities that hosted active chapters of the Pan-German League. Most of these communities shared another common characteristic whose significance is more difficult to gauge: they lay outside the state of Prussia or in areas recently incorporated into that state.[60] These areas probably provided more fertile soil for the ethnic nationalism that emerged at the end of the nineteenth century as a rival to the Borussian nationalism being officially cultivated in Berlin. Another, more speculative theory is that for some men, roots in the more peripheral, non-Prussian states led to a problematic psychological relationship with the new Empire which Prussian arms had created, and that this relationship was eventually resolved in exaggerated nationalism.[61]

Chapters of the Pan-German League thrived in one other kind of local environment. The conditions that prevailed in these localities proved in fact to be the most propitious of all; and they outweighed even the most severe regional liabilities the League had to face.

Gaudeamus igitur

No feature of a German community more affected the vitality and shaped the character of a chapter of the Pan-German League than did the presence of an institution of higher learning. In Leipzig, Dresden, Giessen, Darmstadt, Braunschweig, Göttingen, and Hanover, support from a university or *Technische Hochschule* enhanced already favorable conditions.[62] In other parts of the country, where the climate was less favorable, institutions of higher learning were the primary (and sometimes the only) foundations of the local chapters. Without the support provided by these institutions, chapters would probably not have survived in Danzig, Königsberg, Bonn, Heidelberg, Breslau, Karlsruhe, Würzburg, or even Munich.[63]

This support took a specific form. University professors did not, as a rule, provide it, for few were active in the League. Only thirty-seven university professors served in the League's cadres between 1891 and 1914. This fact belies the impression conveyed by the association of several prominent academic scholars with the League, among them Ernst Haeckel, Karl Lamprecht, Max Weber, Theodor Schiemann, Dietrich Schäfer, and Otto Hoetzsch.[64] In most cases their association was casual. Weber, who was interested in the League because he shared some of its views about the Polish problem, soon lost touch, as did Haeckel and Lamprecht, two political eccentrics who later turned up in the peace movement.[65] Other professors also proved unreliable candidates for positions of local leadership in the League, for they were usually too busy and quickly lost interest. When they did consent to participate in local meetings, though, they were a great asset, for their very presence lent, as one reporter remarked of a meeting in Göttingen in 1901, an 'imposing and uplifting' aura to the whole event.[66] Aware themselves of the impression they made, professors who spoke at Pan-German meetings used the occasions to pontificate on topics related to their own expertise, much as they would lecture to an audience of students.[67]

These professors read their audiences well. In the university cities, those who attended Pan-German meetings were often in fact principally students, and their presence was the key to the success of a large number of the League's chapters. Student interest had many roots, in the social backgrounds of the young men who attended academic institutions in Imperial Germany, as well as in the nature of the university experience itself. The work of Konrad Jarausch explores the broader dimensions of this problem.[68] Here it suffices to point out one obvious reason for the receptivity of students for the program and ideology of the Pan-German League. These students were apprentice custodians of culture and authority, trainees for the elite roles in Imperial German society. Arrogant elitism and the xenophobia that derived from it made academic students at home in the Pan-German League. Not only did the organization's ideology idealize and seek to fortify the custodial roles the students expected to assume, but Pan-German meetings were ritual celebrations of the students' xenophobia. Leaders of the League went, in addition, out of their way to defend the corporate interests of German students, in protesting, for instance, against the intrusion of 'inferior colleagues [i.e. students] from abroad', whose presence at German academic institutions could only 'diminish the status [*Ansehen*] of the whole *Stand* to which the student is proud to belong'.[69]

Student participation in the League was usually a collective phenomenon. Large numbers of them appeared at meetings bedecked in the colors of their corporations. Their presence not only assured the financial success of events at which admission was charged, but it added an element of festivity, particularly when, after the lectures, conviviality took over and the student groups displayed their talents in song and ritual drinking.[70] Many student groups joined chapters of the League as corporate members. This status, purchased for a blanket fee, entitled all the members of the corporation to the rights and privileges of membership in the League, including a corporate vote and, in many chapters, representation on the board of local officers. In Stuttgart several *Burschenschaften* from the *Technische Hochschule*, including *Alemania*, *Ghibellinia*, and *Ulmia*, were members of the League's chapter, as was the *Korps Bavaria* and the *Akademischer Liederkranz Schwaben*.[71] The chapter in Göttingen had eight student groups as corporate members, while representatives of these groups sat on boards of local officers in Braunschweig and Heidelberg.[72] While *Burschenschaften* were affiliating with local chapters of the League all over the country, the national organization, the *Deutsche Burschenschaft*, which represented over 3,000 German students, also affiliated corporately with the Pan-German League.[73]

Although student groups of many descriptions were prominent features at Pan-German meetings, the enthusiasm of the *Burschenschaften* was particularly marked. The evidence is too scant to permit more than speculation about the roots of this special enthusiasm. The *Burschenschaften* had a long tradition of *grossdeutsch* nationalism which accorded well with the messages that students heard when they came together with the Pan-Germans. The statistics that Konrad Jarausch has compiled on student organizations in Marburg suggest another reason for the special affinity: *Burschenschaftler* were, to a greater extent than the members of most other kinds of student groups, the sons of academically educated public officials.

The enthusiasm of the *Burschenschaften* for the Pan-German League was surpassed only by that of one other category of student organization. To judge by their program and goals, the local chapters of the so-called *Kyffhäuserverband* of the Associations of German Students (*Vereine deutscher Studenten*) were practically indistinguishable from those of the Pan-German League; their members were merely younger.[74] These associations were the most ferocious expression of the radical nationalism of German academic students, for their activity was unalloyed by the pomp and frivolity that characterized the *Burschenschaften* and other corporations, although these other student organizations did, to be sure, often participate in the Associations of German Students. Like the Pan-German League, the Associations defined their jurisdiction as 'everywhere the German nation is to be found', adding only that 'it goes without saying that the German nation extends beyond the frontiers of the Reich'.[75] And like the Pan-German League, the Associations both encouraged political activism among their members and – if the statistics for Marburg are representative – drew a disproportionate share of their membership from men who pursued teaching careers.

The close relations between the League and the Associations of German Students took a number of forms. Members of the *Vereine* participated at League meetings and sat on boards of local officers.[76] Like the

Burschenschaft, the entire *Kyffhäuserverband* was a corporate member of the Pan-German League. A number of prominent members of the League, including Hasse, were honorary members or *Alte Herren* of the Associations. Alfred Geiser, who had been active in the Association in Göttingen, attempted to exploit his student ties to the benefit of the League. During his recruiting tours he used directories of the Associations in deciding whom to contact, and several of these men became the props of their chapters.[77] Geiser was also editor of the 'national handbook' which the Associations published to provide a 'foundation of the political education [*Bildung*]' of their members. The authors whom Geiser selected to write on vital topics such as 'voluntary associations that threaten Germans' (*deutschfeindliches Vereinswesen*) were, almost without exception, prominent Pan-Germans.[78]

The popularity of the Pan-German League among German students was significant for a number of reasons, and it will be germane when consideration turns to the sources of Pan-German influence in German society. Here it is pertinent to note that a vigorous student population was but one of the factors that affected the political climate in communities where chapters of the Pan-German League thrived. These communities were similar in so far as social, political, confessional, or ethnic conditions produced a climate in which the imagery of outposts amidst a sea of hostile forces was relevant to the social experience of a block of Protestant notables (or aspiring notables). Chapters of the League thus tended to be active in administrative centers in Protestant parts of the country (or in Catholic cities with large Protestant minorities) and in areas where rapid industrialization fostered social tensions, particularly where social and ethnic tensions compounded each other.

The study of the Pan-German League's appeal in Imperial Germany can now descend to another level, at which the individual chapters actually operated and where the social and cultural conditions that encouraged the League took on life and color. Investigating the League in action at this level reveals additional sources of the organization's appeal, as well as some of the sources of its influence.

Notes

1   ZStAP, ADV 188, Fischer, Erläuterungen, p. 21; ADB (1898), 147–8; ADB (1902), 279; ADB (1911), 62.
2   ADB (1898), 239, 269; ADB (1900), 122; ADB (1910), 55.
3   ZStAP, ADV 188, Geiser to Hasse, 29.3.04; ADB (1905), 366; ADB (1909), 87.
4   ZStAP, ADV 188, Geiser to Hasse, Berlin, 22.3.04.
5   ZStAP, ADV 188, Geiser to Hasse, 23.5.04.
6   ZStAP, ADV 195, Class RS, Mainz, 12.8.11.
7   ZStAP, DKG 731, DS über voraussichtlichen Mitgliederbestand . . . 20.12.94; ZStAP, Rep. 195 Nr. 42, Geschäftsstelle Danzig to DOV, Danzig, 17.11.13; cf. ADB (1904), 110; ADB (1907), 297–300.
8   ZStAP, ADV 43, GFA, Gotha, 9–10.4.04; Wenck, p. 28.
9   ADB (1898), 21; cf. Schmitt, *Weinheim*, pp. 20, 61.
10 ADB (1903), 247; ADB (1904), 124–5; ADB (1905), 35–6; ADB (1907), 433; cf.

Ekkehard Böhm, *Ueberseehandel und Flottenbau: Hanseatische Kaufmannschaft und deutsche Seerüstung 1879–1902* (Düsseldorf, 1972), pp. 67–70.

11 ZStAP, ADV 43, GFA, Gotha, 9–10.4.04, Eingegangene Antworten auf die Rundfragen . . . Niemann-Barmen, 11.4.04.

12 ADB (1902), 125.

13 For example: ZStAP, ADV 626, Reutzel to Vietinghof-Scheel, Heppenheim, 2.12.13; ADB (1899), 14.

14 ZStAP, ADV 187, Hasse to Regel, Leipzig, 25.11.03; ADV 188, Hasse to Spitzner, Leipzig, 19.5.04; ADB (1903), 445.

15 ADB (1898), 286; ADB (1904), 66.

16 ADB (1903), 330.

17 ADB (1895), 195–6.

18 ADB (1905), 137; ADB (1910), 98; ADB (1912), 202.

19 ZStAP, ADV 70, GFA, Eisenach, 17.4.09, p. 24; ADB (1902), 127; ADB (1904), 441–2.

20 Theodor Reismann-Grone, *Der Erdenkrieg und die Alldeutschen* (Mülheim, 1920), p. 75.

21 Richard Graf du Moulin-Eckart, *Deutschland und Rom* (Munich, 1904); Hasse, *Nationalstaat*, pp. 64–5; ADB (1904), 287.

22 See Christoph Weber, *Der 'Fall Spahn' (1901): Ein Beitrag zur Wissenschafts- und Kulturdiskussion im ausgehenden 19. Jahrhundert* (Rome, 1980), p. 12.

23 See Rudolf Morsey, 'Die deutschen Katholiken und der Nationalstaat zwischen Kulturkampf und Erstem Weltkrieg', *Historisches Jahrbuch*, vol. 90 (1970), pp. 31–64.

24 ZStAP, ADV 183, Hasse RS, Leipzig, 7.7.96.

25 ZStAP, ADV 22, GFA, Leipzig, 8–9.9.00, Hasse RS, Zur konfessionellen Frage.

26 Whiteside, pp. 205–10, 243–62.

27 See Herbert Gottwald, 'Deutsche Vereinigung (DV) 1908–1933', in Fricke, *Handbuch*, Vol. 1, pp. 629–32; Klaus J. Mattheier, 'Drei Führungsorganisationen der wirtschaftsfriedlich-nationalen Arbeiterbewegung', *Rheinische Vierteljahrsblätter*, vol. 37 (1973), pp. 244–75.

28 Herbert Gottwald, 'Antiultramontaner Reichsverband (AUR) 1906–1920', in Fricke, *Handbuch*, Vol. 1, pp. 41–3.

29 ZStAP, ADV 7, Vorstandssitzung, Berlin, 10.2.07; ADV 622, *passim*; ADB (1907), 50–2; ADB (1912), 88.

30 Hugenberg, pp. 298–9; ADB (1896), 153–4.

31 ADB (1899), 283–4; ADB (1903), 73; ADB (1905), 378; ADB (1906), 17–19; ADB (1907), 70.

32 Werner, p. 66; cf. ZStAP, ADV 188, Geiser to Hasse, 29.3.04; Hasse to Ogr. Altenkirchen, 26.4.04.

33 ZStAP, ADV 187, Bericht des Geschäftsführers Geiser über seine Reise in der bayerischen Pfalz zur Gewinnung von Anknüpfungen für eine alldeutsche Werbetätigkeit v. 27.6.03; ADV 188, Geiser to Hasse, 29.3.04; ADB (1904), 91.

34 ZStAP, ADV 196, Ilges to Class, Cologne, 31.5.12; ADV 197, Lehmann to Class, Munich, 23.4.13; DKG 509, Lehmann to Johann Albrecht, Munich, 22.12.06; ADB (1905), 384; ADB (1909), 27.

35 ADB (1905), 358.

36 ZStAP, ADV 196, F. Fick to Class, Würzburg, 8.12.12; cf. ADB (1894), 29–31; ADB (1895), 46–7; Class, *Strom*, p. 50.

37 See Klaus Simon, *Die württembergischen Demokraten: Ihre Stellung und Arbeit im Parteien- und Verfassungssystem in Württemberg und im Deutschen Reich* (Stuttgart, 1969); James Clark Hunt, *The People's Party in Württemberg and Southern Germany, 1890—1914* (Stuttgart, 1975); Chickering, *Imperial Germany and a World without War*, pp. 245–8.

38 ZStAP, ADV 188, Geiser to Hasse, Berlin, 23.5.04; ADB (1904), 179; ADB (1908), 431.

39 ZStAP, ADV 15, Lehr to Hasse, Stuttgart, 30.10.99; ADV 196, Calmbach to Class, Magdeburg, 23.12.12. Although it was most pronounced in Swabia, provincialism was a problem for the League in other parts of the country too. One member complained of the difficulty of finding the right person to lead the chapter in Naumburg, whose inhabitants, he reported, 'speak faultless Saxon and regard it as the only proper language for cultivated central Europeans': ZStAP, ADV 197, Flitner to Class, Weissenfels. 27.1.13.

40 ZStAP, ADV 188, Geiser to Hasse, Berlin, 23.5.04.
41 ZStAP, ADV 57, Boesser to ADV, Karlsruhe, 28.10.06; ADV 195, Calmbach to ADV, Esslingen, 10.2.11; ADB (1902), 126.
42 ZStAP, ADV 196, Class to Wolf, Mainz, 3.3.10; Fick to Class, Würzburg, 16.12.10; ADV 196, Calmbach to Class, Magdeburg, 23.12.12; cf. ADB (1907), 102–3.
43 ZStAP, NL Gebsattel 1, Class to Gebsattel, Mainz, 23.7.14; ADV 188, Geiser to Hasse, Berlin, 23.5.04; Class, *Strom*, p. 134; ADB (1912), 202.
44 ADB (1910), 326–7; ADB (1911), 50–1.
45 The Pan-Germans' difficulties in the *Reichsland* were similar to the Colonial Society's, only more extreme: ZStAP, DKG 719, Abt. Mülhausen to DKG, 28.11.94; Abt. Strassburg to DKG, 15.12.95; cf. ADB (1913), 440–1; Silverman, esp. pp. 65–90.
46 James J. Sheehan, 'Liberalism and the city in nineteenth-century Germany', *Past and Present*, no. 51 (May 1971), pp. 116–37; Sheehan, *Liberalism*, p. 230; Heinrich Heffter, *Die deutsche Selbstverwaltung im 19. Jahrhundert: Geschichte der Ideen und Institutionen* (Stuttgart, 1950), pp. 605–22.
47 White, *Splintered Party*, esp. pp. 23–50.
48 Böhm, pp. 12, 67–70.
49 ibid., pp. 69–70; ADB (1907), 247.
50 See Wehler, 'Die Polen im Ruhrgebiet', pp. 219–36.
51 ZStAP, ADV 187, Class RS, Finthen bei Mainz, 22.7.03; ADB (1900), 122; ADB (1902), 90; ADB (1903), 5–6, 143; ADB (1904), 126–7.
52 ZStAP, ADV 188, Geiser to Hasse, Berlin, 25.5.04; ADB (1907), 174.
53 ADB (1895), 63; ADB (1900), 408–9; ADB (1905), 250; ADB (1906), 285; ADB (1909), 166, 383–4; ADB (1910), 6; ADB (1911), 114; ADB (1913), 78.
54 ADB (1901), 286, 545; ADB (1905), 18; ADB (1907), 238.
55 ADB (1904), 311; Jochmann, p. 55.
56 ADB (1903), 329; ADB (1912), 47.
57 ADB (1906), 114–15; ADB (1907), 71, 107.
58 ADB (1898), 69–70; ADB (1900), 238; ADB (1903), 344.
59 ADB (1905), 408.
60 Kruck, p. 4.
61 Evidence in the biographies of Reventlow, who was born in Holstein, and Keim, a Hessian, supports this theory; see Boog, esp. p. 27; Class, *Strom*, pp. 157–8.
62 See ADB (1898), 278; ADB (1902), 251; ADB (1905), 102; ADB (1912), 433.
63 ZStAP, ADV 197, Lehmann to Class, Munich, 2.5.13; ADV 188, Geiser to Hasse, 29.3.04; ADB (1900), 495; ADB (1904), 75; ADB (1905), 207, 233; ADB (1914), 63.
64 Deitrich Schäfter, *Mein Leben* (Berlin and Leipzig, 1926), pp. 150–4; Klaus Meyer, *Theodor Schiemann als politischer Publizist* (Frankfurt a. M. and Hamburg, 1956); Gerd Voight, *Otto Hoetzsch 1876–1946: Wissenschaft und Politik im Leben eines deutschen Historikers* (Berlin, 1978).
65 ADB (1897), 76; ADB (1899), 107; Chickering, *Imperial Germany and a World without War*, pp. 127, 137–9; Alfred Kelly, *The Descent of Darwin: The Popularization of Darwinism in Germany, 1860–1914* (Chapel Hill, NC, 1981), pp. 112–14.
66 ADB (1901), 120.
67 See McClelland, p. 318; Sheehan, *Liberalism*, p. 234.
68 I am grateful to Konrad Jarausch for allowing me to read his manuscript, 'Academic illiberalism: students, society, and politics in Imperial Germany', which the Princeton University Press has recently published. I have drawn particularly from chapters 5 and 6 of this manuscript. See also Jarausch, 'Liberal education as illiberal socialization: the case of students in Imperial Germany', JMH, vol. 50 (1978), pp. 609–30.
69 ADB (1904), 85–6.
70 ADB (1897), 104, 117; ADB (1899), 414; ADB (1901), 308; ADB (1902), 262.
71 ZStAP, ADV 626, Ogr. Stuttgart, Mitgliederliste; ADB (1902), 460; ADB (1903), 126.
72 ADB (1903), 62, 98; ADB (1908), 38; ADB (1913), 139.
73 ZStAP, ADV 194, Pohl to Class, Essen, 22.3.10; ADV 241, Uebersicht über Mitgliederzahl und Beitragsleistung der dem ADV körperschaftlich beigetretenen Vereine; cf. ADB (1894), 209–10.

74 See Winkel, pp. 313–18; Jarausch, 'Socialization', pp. 621–2; Jochmann, pp. 415, 428; Detlev Grieswelle, 'Antisemitismus in deutschen Studentenverbindungen des 19. Jahrhunderts', in *Student und Hochschule im 19. Jahrhundert: Studien und Materialien* (Göttingen, 1975), pp. 366–79.
75 Quoted in Winkel, p. 316.
76 ADB (1898), 294; ADB (1902), 53; ADB (1914), 63.
77 ZStAP, ADV 187, Bericht des Geschäftsführers ... 27.6.03; ADV 188, Geiser to Hasse, 19.3.04.
78 Alfred Geiser (ed.), *Deutsches Reich und Volk: Ein nationales Handbuch*, 2 vols (Munich, 1910). The publisher was J. F. Lehmann. cf. ADB (1910), 381.

8 Social Experience in a 'German-National Public Realm'

The local chapters were the centers of life in the Pan-German League. Members congregated here to participate in a variety of activities designed to promote ethnic consciousness and unity among Germans. The most common activities were meetings in which members heard speeches or lectures on patriotic themes, usually chosen for their current interest, from South Africa to China and from the plight of Germans in Hungary to the growing menace of socialism at home.[1] The chapters sponsored a number of charitable activities too: they sent money, books, clothing, and other articles (such as Christmas trees) to people whom they identified as 'oppressed Germans' abroad. The more active chapters also organized tours, reading rooms stocked with patriotic literature, bazaars, and expositions.

By all outward appearances, these were mundane social activities, of no particular historical importance. However, appearances deceive: these activities were of the greatest significance. They were the basic elements in the process of translating ideology into practice. Pan-German meetings were the ritualistic complement of ideology. When Pan-Germans congregated, they invoked the national symbolism, reinforced the values and customs implied in their own interpretation of this symbolism, and collectively exorcised the anxieties that inhered in their troubled view of the world. These activities provided, in addition, rudimentary political form to the Pan-Germans' efforts to defend their values and customs and to relieve their anxieties. The meetings of the local chapters were, in sum, a pivotal forum, in which the imperatives inherent in the ideology were first ritually affirmed and then translated into a program of political action.

Spontaneity and Structure in the Local Chapters

In order to judge the significance of what took place at Pan-German meetings, it is necessary to look beyond these activities themselves to the manner in which they were represented. The chapters regularly sent reports to national headquarters describing, often in great detail, the activities in which they had participated. These reports make fascinating reading (at first), and they belong to a genre all their own. A few more or less random examples will suffice to give the general idea.

In 1899 the chapter in Rheydt celebrated Bismarck's birthday with a festival attended by nearly 900 people. The highlight of the event was the oration delivered by a Dr Johannes from Cologne. According to the report, he delivered a 'vivid picture of the great departed figure and made a deep impression, which was manifest at the end of the speech in loud applause. After a concluding word from the chairman of the chapter, the edifying festival closed with everyone singing *"Deutschland, Deutschland über alles"*.[2]

Several years later the chapter in Wiesbaden organized a summer excursion to the Niederwald. Upon their arrival the members listened to a speech from a Dr Spamer, which the reporter characterized as 'profoundly thought out and conveyed with passionate enthusiasm [*hohe Begeisterung*] and the deepest love for the Fatherland'. Dr Spamer was evidently an electrifying orator, for, the reporter went on to observe, 'his words, spoken from heart to heart, resonated truly not only among those participating in the excursion, but among other Germans who happened by accident to be there; and practically interminable, thunderous applause rewarded the speaker for his meaningful and magnificent words'.[3]

Neither Dr Johannes nor Dr Spamer was a match for Karl-Hermann Wolf, the Austrian Pan-German, who in 1909 dazzled an audience in Darmstadt. 'Wolf's superb oratorical talents drove his listeners repeatedly to jubilations of stormy applause [*stürmischer Beifallsjubel*]', according to the report. 'First employing caustic scorn, then righteous anger to grip all hearts and to empassion the audience with its poetic vitality, his vivid speaking style held the entire meeting in breathless tension, which was released at the end of the speech in frantic applause.'[4] On another occasion the same speaker reportedly delivered a 'fiery speech conveyed with splendid humor, drastic earthiness, and heart-wrenching earnestness'. Here too the audience responded with 'stormy, interminable applause'.[5]

To judge from the reports that appeared in the *Alldeutsche Blätter*, these were by no means unusual occasions. Speeches were almost invariably breathtaking events, 'captivating and patriotically empassioned', 'streaming forth from a German heart', and 'glowing with patriotism', with 'real fire', or with 'the breath of warm, patriotic passion'.[6] The people privileged to hear these speeches did so invariably with an 'indescribable storm' of applause, 'heart-bracing enthusiasm', 'shouts of *Heil!* at every mention of German virtue or German success', or with 'constantly repeated, storming applause and shouts of *Heil!* which went on for minutes'.[7] Meetings of the chapters, according to the reports, inspired 'edifying feelings' and 'renewed enthusiasm' for the Pan-German cause.[8] Life in the locals was 'animated and purposeful'; the members devoted 'their entire interest to the Pan-German cause'; the journal was 'awaited with baited breath, read with joy'.[9] Boards of local officers were chosen spontaneously, by acclamation, while the resolutions they framed were immediately approved, 'unanimously and as if with one mind [*einstimmig und einmutig*]'.[10]

The more one reads these reports, the more difficult it is to resist the impression that they were written according to a single formula to which every reporter had access. Adjectives like 'passionate', 'splendid', 'tasteful', 'convincing', 'lively', 'purposeful', 'earnest', and 'surging' were reduced to formula-words suitable interchangeably to describe speeches, moods, applause, visages, and atmosphere at these meetings.

The monotony of fiery, earnest remarks and swelling applause in these reports was broken only by intermittent glimpses of what probably happened in reality. That some of the lectures were interminably boring, lasting well past midnight, is a fair deduction from reports that the speaker's remarks were 'concise but exhaustive'; another reporter invited the same conclusion when, after enduring a lecture on the theme 'Man as Creator of the Cultural Landscape' (which took up with battles between prehistoric monsters and concluded, considerably later, with the 'utility of German colonization'), he confessed that 'the speaker presented a survey of cultural history which was so rapid and of such rich material that it was sometimes difficult to follow him'.[11] Of course, even at the conclusion of these ordeals, the audience broke automatically into 'roaring applause'. Or, if the audience's reaction were not enthusiastic, an explanation for their behavior was always available. At one rally in the Teutoberg forest in the spring of 1901, for instance, the mood of the audience was evidently surly, in part because the weather was unseasonably hot. 'In keeping with the quiet, ponderous [*schwerflüssig*] manner of the Lower Germans, honest enthusiasm was not expressed in spirited storms of applause', the report admitted; the honest enthusiasm was 'none the less evident in the entire demeanor of the participants, who held out for two hours, like a wall, under the warm spring sun in exemplary order and profound earnestness'.[12] On rare occasions, the reporters dropped all the pretentious formulas and described events with complete candor. The results offer such a refreshing respite from the monotony of formula enthusiasm that they are almost worth the wait. The best example is the tired lament which a reporter sent in about conditions in Offenbach in 1904. The meeting was poorly attended, he began, 'like all the previous ones':

> Last year's chairman gave a thorough report of our activities, efforts, and successes, but the picture he unrolled suffered from the impression of dispiritedness. Our population, which is otherwise active and patriotic, has displayed a distaste for all political and idealistic questions, and their attitude has, in general, limited the salutary activation of Pan-German interests. The financial report could not be given because the treasurer (who is also having disagreements with the district leadership) was sick; but it will be read at the next meeting. Then came elections to the board of officers. The chairman resigned his office, which he had taken over only temporarily in an emergency, because he is too busy with other things.[13]

For every such jewel, thousands of glowing reports bore witness to patriotic exuberance and limitless devotion. So caught up in the atmosphere were some of the reporters that they became sensitized to the aesthetic dimensions of the events they were describing. The account one reporter submitted of another excursion to the Niederwald suggested one of Anton von Werner's heroic canvasses. 'It was', he wrote,

> a unique picture, full of life: the closed ranks of participants crowded around the oak-bedecked podium, in front of which representatives of student corporations formed an honor-guard with unsheathed swords. The eye wandered, as if in drunken joy, over the blessed fields of the

Rhine district, far out to the distant blue heights of the Kaiserstuhl, before sinking back in earnest passion into the powerful noble features of the towering Neiderwald monument.[14]

Reports of other summer excursions also invoked patriotic landscapes. An outing to the island of Heligoland was rife with symbolic connotations, which did not escape the artist's eye of the reporter, who described the Pan-German visitors 'united in an hour of festive-earnest enthusiasm' on the 'island of rock surrounded by raging waves'.[15] The storm, a hazard of the German summer climate, was almost as common a feature in the Pan-Germans' excursions as it was in their ideology. Like latter-day romantics, though, the reporters could capture the aesthetic element in even these situations. When torrents of rain descended on the hapless members of the Pritzwalk chapter, who were on an outing to Schwerin in the summer of 1907, the reporter commented, recalling the lines of Goethe's *'Wanderers Sturmlied'*, that 'Jupiter Pluvius opened his floodgates'.[16] No matter how torrential the storm, though, the mood during the excursions remained, as always, elevated, honest and brave, enthusiastic, united, and determined.

As folklorists have discovered, this stilted language has been common to many forms of associational life in Germany – so common, in fact, that it has its own designation as *Vereinssprache* or *Vereinsdeutsch*.[17] It is a vernacular, the product of an organization's need to justify its own existence and define its mission in terms compelling enough to attract and retain members. Language plays, in sum, a critical role in the life of a voluntary association; and for all the kitsch and bathos, it reveals a great deal about the organization's self-image.

In the case of the Pan-German League, the language in which the local chapters reported their activities spoke volumes about the organization's aspirations. This language conveyed the image of a group of people united in a profound collective experience. The national enthusiasm that defined this experience was elemental – as elemental as the forces that threatened Germans around the world – and it was spontaneous. It transported those whom it animated into a transcendent realm of national consciousness, in which speakers achieved inspired heights of oratorical brilliance and their listeners, acutely attuned to the truths being conveyed, responded in spontaneous unison, whether these truths elicited anger, outrage, earnestness, joy, or levity. Involvement in this experience had a rejuvenating, cleansing, therapeutic effect on the participants.[18] The spontaneous unanimity of thought and feeling overwhelmed the individual will and private concerns.[19]

It is not difficult to see what was happening here. These events were all taking place in what Erving Goffman has catalogued as a theatrical frame.[20] They were performances, although appearances were slightly misleading. The performers were not the speakers on the podium, and the audience was not the group of people who cheered at every mention of German virtue. Everyone at the meeting or on the excursion was on stage. All of them were performing a ritual, the purpose of which was to reinforce and document collective beliefs.[21] The content of the speeches was largely irrelevant, for they did little more than reformulate the beliefs. The role of the orator was analogous to that of an orchestral conductor, to interpret and restate beliefs and to preside over their collective expression.

The real 'audience region', to use Goffman's expression again, lay elsewhere. It comprised the people who read the reports of these events, both the members of the Pan-German League, who read the reports in the organization's journal, and the non-members who read similar accounts in the press. The function of these events was acclamatory and demonstrative. Not only were they designed to affirm the patriotic commitment of the participants; they were directed self-consciously outward, to the doubters and unconverted. 'In the unanimously composed resolutions, the internal unity [*Geschlossenheit*] of the League was manifested outward [*trat nach aussen hin in die Erscheinung*].'²² Such formulations appeared constantly to indicate just whom the League's leaders hoped to inspire. 'The League's congress should be attended by as many people as possible', read one directive, 'so that the very event in its own right [*an und für sich*] makes an effective outward impression by virtue of the large number of participants.'²³ 'We must constantly show that we are around', was the analysis of the chapter in Kassel, and Class made the same point when he observed that publishing an appeal for membership in the press was really only 'an act by which the Pan-German League manifests its presence'.²⁴

The audience at whom all these demonstrations were ultimately directed was the entire German public, and their goal was ultimately the transformation of the character of this public. The purpose of the demonstrations was to eliminate the audience region altogether, or rather to draw the entire German public into the region of the performers. The whole existing public realm of parties, institutions, associations, and public customs – a realm rent by social and political conflict, confessional tension, and ethnic unrest – was to be transformed into a new phenomenon, which one might call a 'German-national public' (*Deutschnationale Oeffentlichkeit*) – a term whose cumbersome adjective is necessary for the connotations it carries. This transformed public realm was to be constituted by a consensus on the primacy of ethnic solidarity, a devotion to the national symbols and to the values and imperatives that these symbols implied. The public sphere was accordingly to be restructured, social reality transcended; each German was to be treated solely as an ethnic being. Access to the German-national public was to be governed, to paraphrase Jürgen Habermas, by the 'parity of being German' (*Parität des bloss deutschen*).²⁵ Distinctions of birth, status, occupation, or confession were irrelevant in this realm; and all issues and conflicts incompatible with the imperatives of ethnic solidarity were to be banished. Because ethnicity was a basic instinct and the national symbols so compelling, however, the consensus in the German-national public realm would be comprehensive and overpowering, as well as free and spontaneous. Political discourse would be similarly transformed, subsumed under the national moment, which constituted the very stuff of politics. Recognition of this principle was the defining condition of politics in the German-national public realm, where ethnic solidarity elevated political discourse onto a level of compelling unanimity.

The accounts published about the Pan-German League's activities were thus at the same time a description of a German-national public realm already being experienced, albeit in microcosm, and a prescription for restructuring the entire public sphere in Germany. The reports told of a realm in which social and religious distinctions had disappeared, where high-ranking military officers could rub shoulders with the simple folk, and where 'men of all classes – workers, officials, clergymen and peasants' had come together to support patriotic causes.[26] When Germans entered this realm, they underwent a metamorphosis. They were 'torn out of barren absorption in ... individual troubles and class anxieties of the moment', out of 'idle nausea over the distractedness and insipidity of our current political life', and were 'released [*erlöst*] by the fresh and powerful force of national will'.[27] In this realm, disagreements, if any, were confined to peripheral matters, for consensus reigned on all 'important political questions and basic propositions', the most basic of which was that ethnicity was the constitutive force in human life and that it provided the prism through which all political questions were to be analyzed.[28]

The German-national public was a phenomenon full of paradox and contradiction, and the analytical difficulties the concept poses will be addressed later in the present chapter. Here it is important to emphasize that the public realm described in the Pan-Germans' reports was in large part an ideological vision, an idealized representation of experience, which was colored no less by aspiration and pretension than by social and cultural reality. The reality of life in chapters of the Pan-German League in fact belied many of the impressions conveyed in the reports. Pan-German meetings did not bring together men of diverse social and confessional backgrounds. Nor were the meetings characterized by automatic consensus or spontaneous outbursts of patriotic emotion. Indeed, to a group of men for whom order and control were of such fundamental psychological importance as they were for the Pan-Germans, any show of spontaneity would have been threatening precisely to the extent that it was genuine, hence uncontrolled and independent of authority in its genesis.

Little took place at the meetings of the Pan-German League, however, that was not controlled. The meetings were tightly structured around an elaborate agenda, which prescribed everything, including the point at which the spontaneous venting of feelings was to occur. Typically the meetings opened with the performance of patriotic pieces of music by a band, ensemble, or chorus. The next item was the greeting to those present from the chairman of the chapter, followed by more music, any business matters in need of consideration, and then the principal speech, at the conclusion of which time was usually reserved for questions from the floor, and time was always reserved for '*nichtendewollende nationale Begeisterung*'.[29] The next phase of the meeting was devoted to the careful exploitation of the patriotic enthusiasm so engineered. A resolution, if appropriate, was passed by acclaim, and an officer of the League delivered the pitch to join, as membership lists, along with collection plates, patriotic literature, and assorted trinkets for sale circulated among those in attendance.[30]

These meetings were meticulously structured rites devoted to acting out the spontaneous bonds that were to unite men of patriotic dedication and to driving out the enemies that threatened them.[31] All the elements in the ritual had their proper roles – even the reports, which were themselves carefully structured documents.[32] These rituals ran with a 'punctuality and reliability' that made their organizers proud.[33] The sequence of events was planned like a liturgy, and virtually nothing was left to spontaneity.

Even the expression of emotion was canalized by the heavy use of symbolic trappings. Although their appreciation for the use of these trappings was rudimentary in comparison to that of the generation of radical nationalists who followed them, leaders of the Pan-German League understood the importance of 'every outward sign that symbolizes the unity of the Reich'.[34] They bedecked their meeting halls with pictures, busts, flags, and banners.[35] The Bismarck *motif*, which after the chancellor's dismissal could connote opposition to government policy, was dominant in this symbolism – sometimes at the expense of official symbols of patriotism.[36] At the League's annual meeting in 1904 in the Colosseum in Lübeck, for example, the walls were covered with colorful flags and laurel branches, while above and directly behind the podium the audience beheld a 'magnificent group of plants', in the middle of which stood, beneath a sheaf of 'mighty palm branches', a bust of Bismarck. A bust of the emperor, by contrast, was to be found on the floor of the dais, behind the podium, amidst a group of flowers in which, the reporter had to emphasize, it was at least visible.[37] Other activities that the League sponsored featured more dramatic symbolism. Nocturnal festivals were a prominent part of the League's ritualistic repertory, staged usually at the base of the Bismarck towers which dotted the landscape after the chancellor's death, or at some other appropriate monument. The festivals emphasized fire to symbolize the vitality of the German 'spirit and character' – a huge bonfire during the festival itself, followed by fireworks, and a torchlight procession down from the tower.[38]

In another respect, the public realm of the Pan-German League diverged significantly in reality from the spontaneous sphere of national consensus that it was reported to be. The reports said very little about the formal structure of authority in the German-national public. Instead they left the impression that the exercise of authority was practically irrelevant. Consensus was free and spontaneous, needing no formal coercion or encouragement. Leaders appeared usually only in minor roles in the reports; they were chosen by spontaneous acclamation, and the functions they performed were more or less peripheral. Authority was so omnipresent that it became inconspicuous; the structure of roles it prescribed was so self-evident that these roles were freely and automatically accepted by all present.

The actual situation in the chapters was otherwise. The structure of authority was highly formalized, as befit both the demands of the police and the determination of the League's leaders to leave nothing out of control. Like other political associations, the chapters of the League had to draw up elaborate bylaws, which regulated all facets of their existence, from payment of dues to the holding of at least one general meeting every year and the disposition of assets in the event of the chapter's formal dissolution. The bylaws also laid down procedures for electing a board of local officers, which in most group comprised a chairman, secretary, treasurer (and usually deputies for all three of these officers), and an advisory committee composed of men called *Beisitzer*. Although the situation varied among the chapters, the office of chairman was normally the one with the power, particularly if the incumbent were determined to use it. The secretary and treasurer usually had less power in office than burdens, for they were responsible for the correspondence and money – matters which, if taken seriously, involved extensive contact with both the members of the chapter and national headquarters. The post of deputy chairman was usually decorative, as was the advisory committee, which also contained the representatives of organizations, such as the local student groups, which were corporate members of the chapter.[39]

In theory any male German could occupy any post. The impression lent by the reports was that conventional status distinctions were suspended in the German-national public and that elections to positions of leadership and authority depended exclusively on what Hasse called a 'willingness to sacrifice in the national cause [*nationale Opferwilligkeit*]'[40] This impression was erroneous. Although local elections were nominally democratic, they usually produced a distinct hierarchy of authority – a hierarchy which, as one might infer from the League's ideology, was measured in traditional German middle-class criteria of status, particularly education. The fragmentary statistics based on surviving membership lists suggest that officers of the local chapters were on the whole – if only slightly – better educated, wealthier, more likely to be publicly employed, and more highly placed in the public sector than were the rank and file (see Appendix, Table 5.9). More complete statistics on the local officers reveal the hierarchy more clearly (see Appendix, Table 8.1). Comparing the men who held the most visible posts of chairman and deputy chairman with those who held the less conspicuous and more dreary offices of secretary and treasurer shows that the former enjoyed, as a rule, significantly higher social status: they were more likely to be noble, have been academically educated, hold a doctorate, be publicly employed, and hold a high position in the public sector. Instances abounded in which academic credentials were the barrier that separated the chairman and his deputy from the other officers. In the town of Altdöbern in 1899 the chairman was an *Oberlehrer* and the secretary a teacher in the *Volksschule*. In Dieringhausen in 1900 a physician held the chair, assisted as secretary by a subaltern official in the post office. The board of officers in the chapter in Schwerin in 1901 included as chairman an academically educated archivist, as secretary a subaltern official in the postal administration, and as treasurer a minor clerk. The most grotesque example of the hierarchical tendencies within the local groups was in Marburg, where in 1894 the chairman and most of the members of the decorative advisory committee were professors at the university; the secretary was an *Oberlehrer*, while as a gesture to the ideal of social breadth, the safe post of deputy secretary was given to a mechanic who worked at the university.[41] Marburg was an extreme case, but it exemplified a general pattern. Altogether in only about

3 percent of the cases were the offices of chairman or deputy chairman in the hands of men undistinguished by an academic education or substantial wealth, and most of these cases were in chapters in smaller towns.

This hierarchical pattern was of course not unique to the Pan-German League, nor for that matter to voluntary associations in Imperial Germany. Harold Nicolson once wrote, in connection with a subcommittee of the London Library on which he was serving, of the importance of dividing the labor between a 'man of eminence' and a 'man who attends meetings' (Nicolson, though himself not exactly obscure, took the busy-job, for in this subcommittee the standard of eminence was T. S. Eliot).[42] Like many other societies, the Pan-German League was alive to the importance of having such men of eminence in conspicuous positions in the chapters. Many times the activities these men performed were less important than their very presence, which was itself a kind of *Vereinspropaganda*.[43] To have men of high status represent the organization in the public eye guaranteed respectability and served as a drawing card. Within the organization, the status of these men tended to reinforce the authority of the leadership and to guarantee the cohesion of the chapter. In many chapters, finding a chairman with the social qualifications to command the respect of the membership was essential to survival. The chapter in Breslau, for instance, tottered on the brink of collapse because its chairman, Max Koch, though an eminent literary scholar at the university, was a Jew.[44]

The persistence of social hierarchy combined with other features of the internal life of the chapters to produce an exclusivity which also contradicted the image presented in the reports of broad solidarity and enthusiastic participation. Despite the higher prestige normally associated with holding office in the locals, members were reluctant to take on the burdens. Although the truth of this principle was universally recognized, it was rarely uttered, except in an occasional lapse, such as the report submitted from Dortmund in 1901. This year's general meeting 'was unfortunately, as usual, very poorly attended', the report sighed, 'probably because many members feared that they would be immediately elected onto the board of officers'.[45] This reluctance tended in turn to encourage elitism among the group of activists who did occupy leading positions. In many chapters a caste spirit developed, as the board of officers made major decisions on matters of policy and procedure, coopted their peers to serve alongside them, and then presented their decisions to the membership in the form of resolutions and slates of candidates for acclamatory endorsement.[46] That authority lay properly in the hands of an elite in the German-national public was suggested even in the arrangement of the meeting halls. The front of the room was the domain of the *Vorstandstisch*; at this table, which was often mounted on a dais, the board of officers sat alone, looking down at the assembled rank and file.

In none of these respects was the Pan-German League unique among voluntary associations in Imperial Germany. It differed from others only to the extent that its ideology and the image it presented in its reports seemed to emphasize genuine community and participation while denying the validity of traditional status distinctions in a German-national public realm.

Tension thus festered in the League between the ideal of spontaneous community and the reality of a highly formalized structure of authority consciously patterned after traditional status distinctions. Most members probably saw no contradiction between community and status, between *Zusammengehörigkeitsgefühl* and *Standesbewusstsein*, in part because they themselves possessed the requisites of high status, in part too because the League's ritual was so calculated to charm the contradiction away.[47] Occasionally, however, it did surface in complaints about the exclusive atmosphere among the academically educated, which lent the impression that, as one member complained, 'in order to be respected, one must at least have a doctorate'.[48] Resentment also surfaced in some embarrassing incidents. One of these, in 1912, involved the reluctance of members of the chapter in Magdeburg to send as their representative to a national meeting a man who was only a postal secretary.[49] National headquarters quickly intervened to resolve the dispute, but only by issuing a pronouncement that was transparently a lie. 'Naturally for us being human does not require an academic degree', was the dictum. 'Whoever is filled with love and concern for our *Volk* and is ready to work is welcome; we do not recognize distinctions of occupation or class [*Stand*]. Attitude and its testing in action are decisive – and every comrade [*Gesinnungsgenosse*] is equally entitled.'[50]

The reports of impulsive outbursts of national enthusiasm and spontaneous acclamation of principle invite the same skepticism as does this pronouncement. Everything about the local organization of the Pan-German League was expressly designed to exclude real spontaneity and impulse – dangerous forces to people anxious about their own authority. Indeed, the only genuine spontaneity at these meetings came when a spat occurred, occasioned by disagreements among members and officers (which were rare and registered in the reports as a 'lively exchange of views'), or when enemies, usually in the form of socialists or Hanoverian autonomists, invaded the meetings.[51] These were ugly aberrations. On most occasions, control was the watchword in the chapters, and it extended even to the more informal activities the League sponsored.

Sociability and Patriotism

After a poorly attended meeting early in 1907 in Plauen, the reporter drew the lesson that it was 'very well advised to deal now and then at meetings with matters that do not directly relate to Pan-German concerns'.[52] The other chapters hardly needed this advice, for most of the activities they sponsored touched, at least at first glance, only peripherally on matters related to program and ideology. It often seemed as if immediate 'Pan-German concerns' were a bitter pill, which required a great deal of sweetening before being swallowed.

The sweetening came in many flavors. Speakers embellished their lectures with slides and occasionally with the more novel spectacle of motion pictures to excite and hold the interest of their audiences.[53] Artistic embellishment served the same purpose. Plays and *tableaux vivants* featuring members of the chapter or local companies of actors were effective in stimulating patriotic indignation, with scenes, for example, from the Boer War.[54] Poetry was serviceable too, Poetic 'admonishments to concord' and assorted treasures from the chest of patriotic lyric and *Heimatsdichtung* were regular items on the agendas of Pan-German meetings, sometimes recited by a man designated *Vereinsdichter*.[55] The principal representatives of these poetic genres, which are not common among the anthologies any more (for good reason), included such figures as Heinrich Gutberlet, Fritz Bley, Arthur Rehbein (a member of the chapter in Cologne who wrote under the name of Atz von Rhyn), Wilhelm Rohmeder, and Richard Deye, a man whose poems the Pan-Germans described as 'beautiful blossoms in the garden of German lyric, filled with fresh, youthful enthusiasm for the German Fatherland'.[56] Most of this poetry was at least a small cut above the collective lyrical efforts of the rank and file, a genre for which a single stanza – from a longer poem dedicated to Paul Kruger from members of the chapter in Werden – can stand alone (and untranslated) as testimony:

> Heil dem Vater seines Volkes
> Der im heiligen Gottesstreit
> Für der Erde höchste Güter
> Heldenmutig sich geweiht.[57]

Many of the themes treated in the lectures themselves were only incidental to the program or ideology of the League and were calculated in the first instance to entertain. 'Cultural themes' included lectures on art, literature, and music (particularly the music of Richard Wagner), illustrated with slides, readings, or musical accompaniment.[58] Travel lectures were popular too, especially if the traveler offering his impressions of China or Spain (and incidentally the lot of Germans in these lands) were a member of the chapter.[59]

At the conclusion of most Pan-German meetings all pretense of serious business disappeared, as the agenda turned to what was commonly called the 'sociable part' of the evening – the part in which, as the reporter noted of a meeting in Bonn in 1901, 'pleasure claimed its due'.[60] The pleasure, which often went on for hours, included musical offerings from a local band or chorus, a great deal of toasting, particularly if students were present, and community singing, for which the League published an *Alldeutsches Liederbuch* featuring patriotic songs in which 'German yearning, German love of country and freedom, *Wanderlust*, and sociability find their most profound and comprehensive expression'.[61]

Other activities in which the League's chapters engaged were openly devoted to entertainment and sociability alone. The highpoint of the year for the more active chapters was sponsoring some kind of gala, such as a summer excursion, a Christmas bazaar, or, more commonly, an 'evening of entertainment' (*Volksunterhaltungsabend*). On these occasions the only mention of the Pan-German League itself came in short opening remarks or a *Festrede*, which was only the prologue to the fun. Concerts, drama, gymnastic exhibitions, and often a banquet were staples at these festivals. The character of the event was dependent upon local tradition. The chapter in Pritzwalk favored, despite the risk of rain, the summer excursion into the surrounding Mecklenburg countryside, while the group in Dresden organized summer outings across the border into Bohemia.[62] Boat trips up and down the Rhine were features of the summer excursions for some of the chapters in the west. In Lübeck the chapter was renowned for its *Trachtenfest* and Christmas bazaar, which culminated in an enormous dance.[63] The atmosphere in Berlin was more high-society, and the favorite forms of pure entertainment were the formal concert, banquet, and ball.[64] The atmosphere in the few rural chapters was naturally different, but patriotic festivals adapted to it. In 1907 a 'rural festival *mit Spiel und Tanz*' sponsored by the chapter in Heldburg in Sachsen-Meiningen was evidently a great success among the local peasants, one of whose wives was overheard to exclaim, '*den Abend wars schöner als zur Kirchweih*' (and this was no small compliment).[65]

Probably the better part of the interaction among members of the Pan-German League was devoted exclusively to sociability. The typical *Ortsgruppe* did not meet formally more than a half-dozen times a year. Members gathered much more frequently, however, in what were referred to as 'casual get-togethers' (*zwangslose Zusammenkünfte*). These were nothing more than weekly or bi-weekly sessions around the *Stammtisch* at a local tavern. The only formal connection between these sessions and the League was the chapters' attempt to publicize and exploit them as '*Alldeutsche Stammtischabende*'; the topics discussed over cigars and *Schnaps* were never confined to (or, for that matter, one suspects, even primarily concerned with) ideology. The Pan-Germans gathered at their *Stammtisch* weekly on Fridays in Eisenach, Mondays in Eisleben, Tuesdays in Barmen and Bonn. In Schandau the members were invited to drop by after work every evening. In Coblenz they met at the pub only every other Friday evening, but members were urged to compensate for this infrequency by their 'zealous participation'.[66] In Doebeln, Elsterberg, Cologne, Magdeburg, Hildesheim, and other communities, members participated zealously in skat and bowling. Members of the Dresden chapter were not content merely to meet for an '*Alldeutscher Kegelabend*'; instead they set up an '*Alldeutsche Kegelvereinigung*', replete with its own bylaws and board of officers.[67]

In some cities the sociability of the *Stammtisch* flourished to the point that the chapter negotiated an agreement with a tavern owner who was willing to see his establishment, or part of it, designated the *Vereinslokal*. The agreement was usually beneficial for both parties. For the *Wirt* it offered steady customers in return for minor commitments, such as reduced fees for the use of his rooms for formal meetings, an occasional discount on food and drink, subscribing to the *Alldeutsche Blätter*, or making the journal and other patriotic literature (supplied by the chapter) available for reading.[68] For the Pan-Germans the arrangement offered a regular point of social contact, providing that the *Gasthaus* was well chosen. It certainly was in Plauen; it was situated next to the railway station, so that visiting

Pan-Germans could conveniently stop by and chat with members of the local chapter, who, a reporter assured the rest of the membership, were to be found there 'almost for sure every evening'.[69] In Danzig the chapter met, both formally and informally, in the *Gasthof 'Zur Hoffnung'* in the *Krebsmarkt*; the group in Langenburg established a 'Pan-German Room' in the *Gasthaus 'Zur Vogtei'*, while in Schmalkalden the Pan-Germans met in *Gathmanns Alldeutsche Bierstube*.[70] In Berlin, in accordance with local custom, the chapter established a *Verbandskneipe* on the Bellevuestrasse and fitted it out with trinkets from the colonies and patriotic reading material; in 1913, however, the chapter had to move to larger quarters in the *Belle-Alliance-Kasino* – an establishment whose foreign name evidently posed no problem.[71] Nor was the name of the locale a problem for the Pan-Germans in Dresden, who first set themselves up in the *Hotel de France* and later moved to quarters in the British Hotel.[72]

Sociability was a central part of life in the Pan-German League, and its prominence raises a number of questions. The League was not unique among voluntary associations in exploiting recreation to make business more palatable. In fact, so many voluntary organizations of such diverse descriptions have cultivated (and still cultivate) sociability among their members that some scholars have concluded that people join these groups principally because the sociability offered speaks to their affiliative needs and that the programs and goals of these associations are of secondary importance.[73] For some men membership in the Pan-German League doubtless fit this pattern; they were lured into the organization because their drinking friends had joined it or because the chapter of the Pan-German League (rather than, say, the Antivivisection *Verein*) happened to meet in their favorite tavern on the evenings when they escaped home after dinner.

Sociability had a more complex role, however, in the Pan-German League than in many other voluntary associations, for the ideology of this organization lent special psychological and political significance to even the most innocuous forms of social intercourse. Whether or not it conforms to any human sociable instinct or need, sociability within a group of people who share certain beliefs or fears does serve important psychological functions. It provides a network of social interchange and support, which reinforces collective beliefs and, to the extent that self-images derive from these collective beliefs, reaffirms the symbols and ideals that constitute personal identity.[74] The reinforcement and reaffirmation accompany the breaking down of the social distance among people who hold similar beliefs. If the ideological propositions that they ritually reaffirmed were any indication, the Pan-Germans felt acutely the isolation and distance that the role of pioneer entailed, and they regarded sociability as an essential means for overcoming it. The evidence suggests that the Pan-Germans, at least those who spoke for the organization, were lonely men whose attempts to establish close contacts among their fellow patriots betokened psychological needs deeper than the desire to assure unanimity for the sake of impressing the public. Their goal was to establish bonds among members that reached below common convictions to the plane of personal sympathy and friendship. The purpose of the recreational activity was, as one leader put it, 'gradually to transform the *Gesinnungsgenossen* in the Pan-German League into real friends'.[75] Chapter meetings, if properly arranged, offered opportunities for close 'mutual friendships [*Anschlüsse*]' among members rather than 'merely loose contacts'.[76] The German-national public was to be a realm in which Germans cared about one another as human beings, where 'close relations among friends' were forged by a 'measure of personal sympathy' and where 'one felt among brothers'.[77] To encourage this kind of contact, the League also published lists of when and where chapters met around the country, in hopes that traveling members would view chapters away from home as places where they could relieve their loneliness in the company of real friends.[78]

This reaching out for genuine friendship was not without an element of pathos, for the few more intimate glimpses into life among the Pan-Germans which survive among the documents suggest that the effort usually failed. Correspondence among the League's leaders reveals that only in the rarest instances did they succeed in breaking through the ultimate barrier to real friendship that was preserved in the use of the formal *'Sie'* in address. The familiar *'Du'* was restricted in Pan-German usage to situations in which the distance between the addresser and addressee was so great that there could be no misunderstanding; Bismarck and Germans abroad as an abstract category were safe, as was Ernst Hasse, though only after he was dead.[79] Among the quick, Heinrich Class and a handful of others were on familiar terms or addressed one another as 'dear friend', but in the prevalent pattern all the proprieties and distance of formal address survived.[80]

The attempt to overcome social and psychological distance among members and to establish true human bonds among them did not exhaust the role of sociability in the Pan-German League. No less important were the political connotations of *Geselligkeit*. 'Entering into personal relationships' described its function from only one perspective; from another, sociability promoted 'united feelings of [national] solidarity'.[81] Describing the phenomenon in these latter terms immediately 'keyed' it – to use Goffman's terms once again – into the region of politics.[82] Here the simplest forms of social contact, from friendly greetings to the exchange of postage stamps, solidified the bonds of ethnic consciousness among Germans.[83] Here too the most innocuous forms of recreation were translated into occasions fraught with political overtones. Sociability provided opportunity for refreshment and relaxation from the serious business of ethnic struggle, but it resulted ultimately in rededication and renewed energy.[84] Festive occasions were calculated, from this perspective, 'to make our hearts receptive to all great things, to prepare the spirits for the heroic [*mannhaft*] deed, [and] to raise souls to the proudest heights'.[85] Although the Pan-Germans were not alone in their appreciation of the political dimension of sociability (the Imperial German government was alive to it too), no one sought more self-consciously to exploit it.[86] The immediate goal of sociability was to produce a joyous mood, in which psychological and social barrers to human contact among Germans would vanish; ultimately, however, the purpose of joy was strength.[87]

The politicization of sociability in the Pan-German League extended to humor and drink, those of its features that might appear to mark conviviality in its purest form. The role of humor, like that of recreation and entertainment, was to provide relief and refreshment from the ardors of ethnic struggle. Humor meant temporary relaxation of defenses, a momentary retreat from the earnestness and control demanded of the pioneer. It was usually described in the reports as 'sunny' or 'healthy'; it inspired optimism among the participants at the meetings.[88]

Humor did not come easily to the Pan-Germans, however. They were not, as a rule, able to appreciate the irony or to tolerate the ambiguity on which much humor depends. Laughter in Pan-German meetings was often itself a defense, a nervous response to the discomfort of ambiguity. For by humor Pan-Germans really meant ridicule: 'Phrases like international brotherhood, perpetual peace, cultivating "humanity" were rendered suitably laughable [*wurden der verdienten Lächerlichkeit preisgegeben*].'[89] Satire they regarded as subversive; its subtlety was foreign to them, particularly when they themselves were its objects, as they were frequently in the pages of *Simplicissimus*, a journal on which Pan-Germans wasted none of their own meager reserves of humor when they called it a 'fanatical, traitorous, inflammatory, smutty rag'.[90]

The Pan-Germans were much more comfortable with alcoholic spirits. The flow of beer, *Schnaps*, wine, and champagne began as soon as the meetings opened, and it continued for hours. Meeting halls were normally arranged so that participants were seated at tables, where they could comfortably smoke and drink during the speeches and formal entertainment, as well as during the 'sociable part' of the evening. They used the opportunity to consume prodigious quantities of spirits. The people who participated in the excursion to the Niederwald after the annual congress in 1907 probably held the record. Their odyssey began at their midday meal, where 'good German wine' sustained the festive mood. The afternoon found them visiting a wine cellar in Assmannshausen and testing the product, whereupon they repaired to a nearby tavern to enjoy 'several hours of fun and liquid refreshment' – there is simply no adequate translation for the word '*feuchtfröhlich*' with which the reporter described these hours – 'on the sunny Rhine'. The boat trip back up the Rhine found them still in the 'merriest mood', which they preserved to the 'sounds of German songs and the clinking of glasses'. Upon their return to Wiesbaden, several of these pioneers managed to find their way to yet another tavern for a 'farewell drink'.[91] Because most Pan-German meetings did not last this long, the consumption was usually less staggering, though probably not by a lot. The chapter in Hofgeismar, with less than a hundred souls, raised 78 Marks by taxing its members 5 *Pfennige* per half liter of beer during a handful of meetings in 1905–6; the mathematics suggest that average consumption was more than 2 liters per person per evening.[92]

By the later stages of the meetings, the halls reeked of beer and tobacco, and the mood was supremely conducive to frenzied outbursts of whatever patriotic feelings the occasion appeared to demand.[93] An atmosphere now reigned which Thomas Mann once derided as patriotism '*mit Bieremphase*' and which his brother captured in the famous tavern scene in his novel *Der*

Untertan.[94] Innumerable 'stirring' toasts, to God, country, and to 'the speaker who has grown thirsty', occupied the participants well into the small hours of the morning.[95]

The consumption of alcoholic beverages had a cultural and political significance that extended beyond the stimulation of patriotic emotion. The imbibing, like the banquets, was an act of commensality, one of the most universal symbolic conventions to document and reinforce community solidarity.[96] The Pan-Germans were particularly alive to the symbolic importance of drinking together, for they regarded alcoholic beverages as products of a nation's culture, evidence of a culture's quality. It was accordingly essential that Pan-Germans indulge in 'German wine/bestowed by Father Rhine' (whose producer, in this case, happened to be a member of the League) and that they sample the wines produced by German colonists in Hungary.[97] In the German-national public realm even the consumption of spirits was thus politicized. This spectacle reached its height in the controversy over pilsner beer, in which the Pan-German League was a principal protagonist. In response to a campaign waged by Czech protective societies to boycott German businesses in Bohemia, the Pan-German League declared a boycott on all pilsner beer early in 1909.[98] Chapters encouraged the taverns they frequented to stop importing it for use. It was a measure of how much beer the Pan-Germans drank that cries of anguish soon were heard from German-owned breweries of pilsner beer in Bohemia.[99]

All the merry-making in which the League indulged did leave behind some bad conscience. A handful of abstainers, whose spokesman was Adolf Fick in Zurich, regarded the consumption of alcohol at Pan-German meetings as a squandering of national wealth at best, at worst a symptom of national disease.[100] But Fick's views on this subject were not widely shared. Of more general concern was the charge that most of the organization's activities were trivial, calculated only to appeal to the baser inclinations of that peculiarly German philistine, the *Spiessbürger*.[101] When Bülow described the Pan-Germans in the Reichstag as *Bierbankpolitiker*, he lent this charge enduring popular currency. Whether or not the image was apt (and it is difficult to believe that it was not), the Pan-German League was in no position to change the rituals its members performed at their meetings. These rituals flowed largely from pre-existing traditions of the middle-class tavern culture in Germany; the League's own contribution was the attempt to politicize them. Here, as in a number of other respects, the activities of the Pan-German League reflected faithfully the cultural milieu in which the organization had taken root. These activities served, in other words, to elevate into ritual ideals conventions and traditions that were essential features of the social experience of the people who participated at these meetings.

Private Virtue and the German-National Public Realm

As sociologists have come to use it, the term 'public realm' stands by definition in contrast to the private sphere of home, family, and domestic

life. In an earlier era this strict separation might have described at least a
bourgeois ideal, but in the twentieth century it has ceased to describe any
cultural reality. The domestic sphere has lost whatever immunities it once
enjoyed to the global implications of the issues debated in the public realm
and to the technology that has carried the public realm physically into the
private. The German-national public of the Pan-German League was, by
today's standards, the child of a technologically primitive culture, but its
ideological claims already extended far into the private realm. Obligations
imposed by ethnic solidarity, which governed the German-national public,
were not suspended at the conclusion of Pan-German meetings; they
followed the patriot home, where they were to inspire the private aspects of
his life.

The comprehensive nature of these obligations was immediately evident
in the rhetoric of the speeches at meetings. 'Being Pan-German', one leader
told a large audience in 1909, 'means embracing the whole German nation
in ardent love, it means loving the German character, language, and
breeding [*Gesittung*] above everything else, and it means being personally
imbued with German character and spirit.'[102] The controlling word here was
'personally': the set of attitudes held up for emulation was valid for all facets
of personal behavior and domestic life.

That the German-national public realm exerted claims on the whole
person was implied too in more subtle ways. The *Alldeutsche Blätter*
regularly ran a feature called the 'Pan-German Family Bulletin Board'
(*Alldeutsche Familientafel*), in which members announced events of
personal importance – engagements and marriages, deaths of loved ones,
and births of children (the male babies were invariably 'robust' [*kräftig*] or
'sturdy' [*stramm*], while the girls were usually described more modestly as
'sprightly' [*munter*]). Inclusion of these vital statistics was calculated in the
first instance to draw members closer together, to make them feel like 'one
big common family' by creating bonds of personal interest and sympathy.[103]
Beyond what they suggested about the Pan-Germans' search for closer
personal ties, the items on this 'bulletin board' attested to the public
relevance of the most private joys and sorrows.

Obligations incurred in the public realm thus defined private virtue as
well. They prescribed what Germans should have in their homes. Everything
was to be 'tasteful'. Furnishings would ideally be coordinated in the Gothic
style.[104] On the walls of German rooms one would find portraits of Bismarck
and the emperor, and the works of patriotic artists such as Franz von
Lenbach, Paul Bennecke, and Anton von Werner, whose creations would
'raise and strengthen the spirit' of the inhabitants of the home.[105] In their
bookshelves Germans were to have (alongside their issues of the *Alldeutsche
Blätter*) patriotic journals, patriotic fiction (some of it especially for the
children), and the great German classics.[106] Germans whose tastes were
properly honed would allow no trace in their bookshelves of modernist
writers like Ibsen, Tolstoy, and Strindberg, whose bewildering works
undermined a healthy German appreciation of art.[107] Perhaps to guarantee
that the encounter with the bookshelf would be an uplifting experience,
Pan-Germans were encouraged to buy small porcelain Bismarck-towers,

suitable for use as flower vases or just for decoration, on the bookshelf, table, or anywhere else around the room.[108]

Patriotic obligation invaded the home not only as canons of taste in art, reading, and home furnishing. It prescribed that Pan-Germans wear suits, shirts, collars, and ties made of German cloth, and brooches and pins with the League's motto inscribed on them.[109] It required that they light their tobacco with matches similarly inscribed and that they use postcards and envelopes with the League's seal on them and that they affix special 'defense seals' (*Wehrschatzmarken*) on their letters.[110] Patriotic obligation extended to what Pan-Germans ate, smoked, and smeared on their bodies. They were, whenever possible, to purchase coffee, chocolate, cigars, palm oil, and soaps from the colonies.[111] Obligation extended even to the language they used, in the private as well as the public realm; foreign words were scarcely less objectionable than Strindberg in translation.[112] Nor could Pan-Germans escape the obligations of patriotism by fleeing their homes for vacation. They were to vacation among German communities in embattled areas of Europe and to eat and sleep in *Gasthäuser* whose proprietors spoke German, made German publications and stationery available to their guests, used German menus in the dining room, and rendered accounts in German; while traveling, Pan-Germans were to speak their own language everywhere – even when foreigners feigned an inability to understand them, although these touchy situations 'naturally' demanded, as one commentator warned, 'a tactful lack of pushiness'.[113]

The term 'patriotic obligation' may well be misleading in this connection if it is allowed to imply a one-way intrusion of imperatives from the public sphere into the private. In the German-national public of the Pan-German League, these imperatives were themselves faithful reflections of the private virtues cherished by the social stratum that made up most of the League's membership. Speaking German while vacationing outside the country could only be of concern to people who were accustomed to making these excursions, just as the purchase of collars and ties cut from German cloth or of palm oil from the colonies had no relevance whatsoever for some classes of people in Imperial Germany.

The patriotism of the Pan-German League apotheosized the values, virtues, and mores of the German upper-middle class. The League's ideology was a paean to the education and wealth that governed status in these circles; the private obligations this patriotism seemed to impose were those that middle-class tastes and customs demanded. The Pan-German meetings were also geared to the traditions of the social group that provided most of the membership – even to the point of timing. Because they realized that no one would attend, local leaders did not schedule regular meetings on Sundays (the day of the family outing) or during the summer.[114] Most chapters scheduled but one special outing during the summer, and they tailored it to include enough recreation that it would not diminish the spirit of the summer season.

In no respect, however, were the League's activities a more faithful reflection of the private mores of its membership than in the role these activities assigned to women. On the subject of women the Pan-German credo included a number of propositions which revealed the extent to which the properly ordered ethnic community depended upon a well-run middle-class household. 'The foundation of living together in the great community of the *Volk* and its state', wrote Heinrich Class, summarizing the views of most of the League, 'is living together in the small circle of the family.'[115] Here, under the 'intimate roof of the family', the feminine spirit found the essential 'conditions for its full and free development'.[116] This development was to be 'full and free', but within the confines prescribed by the feminine character and by domestic and patriotic virtue (which again happened to coincide). Warmth, goodness, loyalty, love, endurance, patience, and purity were the quintessential virtues of the German woman; 'the tender German feminine heart' was the profound repository of 'love for house, home, and Fatherland'.[117] These characteristics suited the German women for her role as faithful supporter of her husband, diligent educator of German youth, and custodian of the shrine of German domesticity.[118] Class, who claimed to be married to one such domestic angel, once described the obligations of this role in some detail. The German woman was to 'keep her house holy and clean', he wrote – adding quickly, lest he be misunderstood, 'from all subversive influences'. She was 'to draw the clearest line between herself and everything impure; let no book, no newspaper enter the house if it could be contagious; let no guest be tolerated who is not unobjectionable [*unantastbar*]; let no company be kept in which the spirit of moral purity does not reign'.[119]

The performance of these duties was time-consuming and, if properly done, left the German woman with little opportunity for an appearance in the public realm. Some Pan-Germans objected in fact to the idea that women could play a public role at all. One of them was Reventlow, who as editor of the *Alldeutsche Blätter* wrote in 1909 that he held a woman's taking an 'active and public position on any public issue whatsoever (and especially on foreign policy) to be pernicious under all circumstances'.[120] Reventlow's views were a little extreme, for the protests they brought suggested that most Pan-Germans were willing to concede some public role to women, providing that women managed to 'preserve the bounds of noble femininity'.[121] These bounds seemed safely to comprehend charities for patriotic causes and even the kind of heroic support given by Boer women to their menfolk during the war against the British.[122] These same bounds of noble femininity were carefully drawn, however, to exclude the kind of public activity associated with the names of Lily Braun, Klara Zetkin, and Rosa Luxemburg – dangerous women, who were given to 'boundless, venomous political fanaticism' (an unfeminine trait) – or with the name of Bertha von Suttner, whose more feminine vice was her 'other-worldly soft-headed [*weichlich*] swooning after peace'.[123] The causes these women championed of course threatened the Pan-Germans' concepts of social and ethnic order, but scarcely less objectionable was the spectacle of women who refused to observe their appropriate limitations: it is significant, in this respect, that Pan-Germans opposed suffrage for even the most patriotic of women.[124]

The role allotted to women in the Pan-German League reflected this grudging approval of limited sorties out of the domestic realm. Women were an important part of Pan-German activities. They paid admission charges and filled seats in halls that otherwise would have remained half-empty. Retaining their interest was thus an important concern. Among the functions of the 'sociable part' of the meetings was to provide the women with the kind of light patriotic amusement thought to appeal to them. Toasts 'to the women' were standard features of the ritual; these and other references to women were also the principal occasions for humor, as if the men were masking their nervousness over the presence of women in their earnest midst. 'That some unavoidable serious [*ernst*] matters for review did not impair our sense for harmless cheer', read a report from Eutin, 'was demonstrated by a humorous challenge to the women to participate in our work.'[125] Like the bazaars and summer outings, the institution of the 'family evening' was devised in part to give the wives and children of the members their own place in the organization's activities.

The role of women in the 'serious business' of the League was a more touchy problem. They did attend the lectures, some of which, as one reporter wrote, were 'so entertainingly structured and presented that even the women ... followed the remarks with the most eager attentiveness, right through to the end'.[126] Some women presented lectures themselves. These women were, for the most part, conservative femininists (most feminists in Imperial Germany cannot be described in any other way), who shared the League's views on the proper scope of women's activism.[127] The impression they made was particularly lasting if they deported themselves appropriately on the podium. One who did was a 'brave, engaging' woman who spoke to the chapter in Göttingen on the role played by the pioneering wives of German settlers during the uprising in Southwest Africa: her description of her experiences, the reporter commented, was 'plain, unpretentious, and hence all the more charming [*anziehend*]'.[128]

None the less, until 1902 women were not permitted to attend the League's national conventions, nor for most of the prewar period were they allowed to join the organization as regular members (to say nothing of occupying positions of leadership).[129] Laws of association kept women out of chapters in most states until 1908, when passage of the federal law of association removed the legal barriers. Leaders of the League then had to confront the issue themselves, and in 1910 they decided that women still could not become regular members, although they did not enforce this ruling when a handful of women subsequently joined chapters.[130]

The Pan-German League was more retrograde in its handling of the 'women's question' than the other patriotic societies, which saw the wisdom at least of establishing special auxiliaries to coordinate charitable activities for the colonies or for Germans abroad or to promote interest in the navy among German women. The possibility of setting up an analogous organization in the Pan-German League surfaced briefly on several occasions, when it appeared that women might defect (along with their husbands) to other societies which offered women's auxiliaries.[131] Principle prevailed, however. The only women's organizations the League would tolerate (and not without suspicion) were local auxiliaries attached to chapters in Berlin and Danzig.[132] Made up principally of the wives and daughters of members of the two chapters, these groups carefully limited the range of their activities to the unobjectionable: they collected money and gifts for German orphanages in the east, held afternoon teas, and organized Christmas balls, at which the women dressed up in *Trachten* indigenous to German settlements around the world.[133]

The place of women in the German-national public realm, no less than the place of sociability, was defined and regulated in a manner that reflected the middle-class traditions which underlay radical nationalism in Imperial Germany. In this respect, too, the image of free and spontaneous consensus belied the reality of highly structured rituals in the local chapters. And in the performance of these rituals the chapters were themselves but parts of a more comprehensive structure of authority.

The Public Obligations of Patriotism

Had the activities of the local chapters taken place in isolation, they would be of greater interest to folklorists than to historians of German society and politics. These activities did not, of course, take place in isolation; the local chapters that sponsored them were parts of broader local networks of associations (to be considered in the next chapter) and cells in a national organization through which these activities were orchestrated for the greatest political effect.

At first appearance, the Pan-German League was democratically organized at the national level. To judge from the national bylaws the key institution was the national board of directors (*Vorstand*), a body of about 200 men composed of the representatives of the local chapters (after 1903 one for every hundred dues-paying members in a given chapter) and other men selected by co-optation.[134] The national board of directors was responsible for determining the position of the Pan-German League 'on all basic questions' (including changes in the bylaws) and for selecting, from its own numbers, the members of the two higher agencies, the executive committee (*geschäftsführender Ausschuss*) and the praesidium (*Hauptleitung*).

The democratic trappings were a facade. The structure of power at the top of the Pan-German League resembled in actuality a series of concentric circles, in which the smaller the circle the greater the exclusivity and access to real power.[135] The national board was the largest circle. The executive committee, which consisted of about twenty men serving three-year terms, was the agency that actually formulated the League's policies on most issues. The praesidium was made up of about a half-dozen men drawn from the executive committee and included the chairman and vice-chairman of the League. The praesidium consisted in fact of a small circle of the chairman's closest confidants. The power of the men at the top rested on their rights of co-optation, which guaranteed that the flow of authority downward was always greater than the nominal influence from below. For all intents and purposes, the praesidium chose the executive committee, and the executive committee in turn chose most of the national board.[136]

The consolidation of power at the top of the League was not an automatic process. Hasse was long an advocate of decentralization, for he believed that the health of the organization demanded more than a cosmetic role for the chapters in shaping policy.[137] The same dynamics that bred elitism among the officers of the chapters, however, encouraged the increasing centralization of power at the national level. Many of the chapters proved uninterested in exercising the influence the bylaws afforded them: they failed to nominate representatives to the national board or to make their views known in other ways.[138] The men who composed the elites within the active chapters were usually co-opted into one or more of the national agencies, where they themselves began to see the advantages of continued centralization.

In the authoritarian distribution of power, the League as a whole looked like the individual chapters writ large. Important decisions were made at the top, usually in the executive committee. The annual conventions (which were open to the entire membership), and, for that matter, the semi-annual meetings of the national board were no less thoroughly orchestrated than the local meetings in order to provide acclamatory approval for policies already determined.[139]

The structure of authority in the national organization resembled that of the local chapters in one other important respect. It too conformed to a hierarchy, the measures of which were the same middle-class standards of status that patterned the holding of office in the chapters. Statistics on the men who sat on the national board of directors in 1899 (a randomly chosen year) and all the men who were in the executive committee from 1891 to 1914 reveal these hierarchical tendencies clearly (see Appendix, Table 8.1). A significantly higher proportion of national directors than local officers were noble, had an academic education, held a doctorate, and worked for public agencies; their mean social status and public administrative positions too were appreciably higher. And by most of these indices, the men on the executive committee ranked higher still. The same considerations that recommended having people of high social rank in positions of prominence in the chapters of course operated at the national level. *Dekorationspersonen*, people whose only contribution to the organization was to lend it their prestige by appearing at an occasional meeting, populated all the national agencies, particularly the board of directors, whose principal function was cosmetic.[140]

The sense of being an elite was very pronounced among the upper echelons of the Pan-German League. When Class recalled the intellectual 'heights on which the deliberations moved' in the executive committee, he revealed at least as much about the self-conscious elitism of this body as he did about the general level of education of the men who sat in it.[141] Meetings of the national agencies were set in first-class restaurants and hotels – a practice which occasioned some resentment among the chapters but which continued anyway, because the national leaders determined that the League 'had to make as distinguished an appearance as possible'.[142] Given this atmosphere at the top, the members of the chapter in Magdeburg might well have wondered about the propriety of sending a postal secretary as their representative.

Yet for all the elitism and authoritarianism at the top, the leadership remained sensitive to the sentiments of the chapters. The practice of co-opting the leading activists from the chapters into the national governing bodies not only ensured that the active chapters had a voice at the top, but provided the avenue through which the activistic impulse from the chapters was translated into policy. In addition, the national leadership consulted regularly with leaders of the chapters, particularly before making decisions with a direct bearing on them. The executive committee consulted, for example, with the chapter in Braunschweig before taking positions on questions that related to Hanoverian separatism.[143]

None the less, the flow of authority from the top down in the Pan-German League was ensured not only by provisions in the organization's bylaws but by patterns of deference that were rooted in the broader culture of the German middle class. It was of great importance that the authority of the national leadership be buttressed in this way, for preserving the impression of spontaneous consensus in the German-national public, or what the League called a 'unified position' (*geschlossenes Auftreten*), demanded extensive coordination and the drawing of narrow limits on disagreement.[144]

The executive committee was normally the agency which determined the League's policies. It met several times a year, but it was small enough that it could be convened quickly in a crisis. Its deliberations were secret. Once the executive committee had determined the League's position, this body had a wide range of devices available for mobilizing a consensus within the broader realms of the organization. Usually the process began with the orchestration of approval for the committee's position by acclaim at meetings of the national board of directors or the general membership. Communications to the chapters took place directly as well, in the form of memoranda which laid down the general lines that lectures were to follow, suggested formulas for resolutions that were to pass unanimously at the meetings' conclusions, and recommended techniques for making the chapters' views known to the press and public officials.[145] When hundreds of chapters simultaneously sent identical telegrams of support to the Naval Office in 1897, or when they passed virtually identical resolutions defending Hasse against Bülow's attacks in the Reichstag in 1900, it was no coincidence.[146] It was in fact, although the national leadership was unhappy with a term that so belied the image they were trying to convey, patriotic exuberance 'by command'.[147]

In order further to ensure unity of views, the League's office sent lecturers on tours of the chapters. Some of these men, such as the Boer officers, or Eduard von Liebert, were real celebrities, whose presence at a local rally was arranged in order not only to deliver the truth from Berlin but to reinvigorate the chapters in a manner that emphasized their debt to the national organization.[148] Official publications, including the journal and several pamphlet series, also provided regular channels of communication through which the positions and policies determined by the national leadership informed the activities of the chapters.

While the apparatus existed for communicating decisions made at the top quickly throughout the entire organization, the decision-making process itself posed some interesting problems. In theory, decision-making in the German-national public realm was spontaneous: the principles implied by the national consensus were self-evident on all major issues, in need only of articulation and communication. In fact, the need to preserve the appearance of spontaneous consensus made it difficult for the League's leaders to deal with the disagreement and dissent that decision-making inevitably provoked. In this respect, the Pan-German League was more uncomfortable than the Social Democratic Party, which was no less committed to the pursuit of ideological truth and consensus, but still managed to vent its doctrinal debates in public.

The confidential meetings of the executive committee were the only recognized forum for genuine debate on major issues. The protocols of these meetings reveal, though, that consensus was frequently difficult to build, owing not the least to the passionate intolerance of many of the men who composed the committee.[149] Hasse hoped that consensus would emerge automatically during the committee's deliberations, but he soon found it necessary to bring order to the meetings by adopting parliamentary procedures. Given the League's suspicion of democratization and the parliamentary tradition, there was more than a little irony in the fact that the position of the organization in several major controversies was determined by a close head-count in the executive committee.[150] One of the additional virtues of having formal rules of procedure was that they could be manipulated to minimize the influence of dissenters.[151]

Some questions the leadership was unable to debate at all without provoking 'furious opposition' in one faction or another.[152] Views were very outspoken and just as divided in matters that related to confession (particularly over whether the League should officially endorse anti-Catholic organizations), to the priority the League should assign to continental or overseas expansion, and to questions of support for specific candidates or parties during electoral campaigns.[153] Unless these issues involved fundamental principles, the policy of the leadership was simply to leave them alone.[154]

The only debates aired publicly with the sanction of the executive committee involved questions minor enough that they did not threaten basic programmatic tenets. The dialogue was none the less often shrill, for the rules of discourse in the German-national public realm demanded that each of the opposing sides in any question appropriate national symbols in its own defense. One episode, in itself rather trivial, illustrated well the problems that decision-making posed in this realm. The League faced repeatedly the question of publicly endorsing the use of Gothic or Roman script. The executive committee was reluctant to take a stand and cleared the matter for public discussion. The debate proved to be much stormier than anticipated, erupting regularly in the pages of the *Alldeutsche Blätter* over a period of years. The proponents of *Fraktur* claimed it as a national cultural institution in danger of extermination, full not only of beauty but – and this claim was supposed to be decisive – character; the proponents of Roman script pointed out, with no less passion, that Germans abroad were not being trained to use Gothic and that German culture would be more compelling abroad if it were legible.[155] The debate eventually ran down, less because of resolution than exhaustion, with the leadership assuring the rank and file that one could advocate either position and still be a good German.[156]

The ferocity of the debate over Gothic script demonstrated the risks of submitting more fundamental questions to public discussion: to do so was to invite chaos in the German-national public realm. The cardinal sin in the Pan-German League was accordingly the public airing of views contrary to those determined by the leadership in 'important political questions'.[157] This practice was apostasy, a breach of the discipline and order imposed by consensus in the German-national public, and it was punishable by formal exclusion from the League.[158]

Whenever they occurred, public breaches of discipline were traumatic events. It is remarkable, however, how infrequently they occurred. With the exception of several celebrated instances, to be considered below, debate in the League remained well within the prescribed limits. This fact suggests that for all the manipulation that went into its articulation and expression, the consensus in the Pan-German League's German-national public realm was to a significant degree genuine. When he pronounced that 'in all circles of the Pan-German League there reigns complete and unconditional agreement on fundamental political views', Class was no doubt indulging in the bombast that reigned at Pan-German meetings; yet he was not exaggerating much.[159]

The combination of manipulation with genuine consensus was one of the several interrelated paradoxes about the Pan-German League's German-national public. The League's leadership carefully engineered the expression of opinion, but the leaders could not have remained long out of step with the basic views and concerns of the members, who had only to cease paying their dues to leave. The public consensus was artificial only in the extravagance of the rhetoric in which it found expression; and even this rhetoric spoke to ideals and aspirations generally shared among the League's membership. The consensus lay latent in the concerns, anxieties, traditions, and values – in sum, in the social experience – of the beleaguered stratum of the educated German middle class which made up most of the League's membership. The role of manipulation in the German-national public realm was not to generate the consensus, but rather to articulate it – to translate common anxieties about the challenge to authority, culture, and order into an effective political voice, which called for recognition of the ethnic foundations of history and politics, appreciation for Germany's precarious position in the world, and forceful policies to deal with the nation's many enemies at home and abroad.

A second paradox relates to what might be called the phenomenology of the German-national public realm. This realm seemed to hover somewhere between reality and ideological fantasy; the term 'German-national public realm' can apply to both an aspiration never fully realized and to a social and cultural phenomenon ritually reaffirmed every time the Pan-Germans congregated. The roots of this paradox lie in the very concept of the public realm (*Oeffentlichkeit*) itself. Classically defined, the public realm is the sphere of associations, institutions, and activities bounded on the one side by the private sphere of society (the family and the marketplace) and on the other by the state; the public is the realm in which the needs of society are mediated and impressed upon the state as a general consensus called public opinion. The problem, as Marx and his followers have been quick to demonstrate, is that this public realm is both a socio-cultural phenomenon and an ideological fiction whose origins lie in the early modern period, when the liberal bourgeoisie claimed to speak in the name of a general consensus and clothed its own aspirations in the mantle of public opinion.[160]

Oskar Negt and Alexander Kluge have offered a resolution of this paradox, arguing that the very definition of the public realm is class-bound, that the character of the public realm is a product of social experience, a dimension of class consciousness. The public realm, they write, is the 'general social horizon of experience, which comprehends that which is real or purportedly relevant for all members of society'.[161] In a class society, however, there must be as many public realms as there are classes.

The conclusions of Negt and Kluge pertain to the German-national public of the Pan-German League. This realm had both an ideological and social dimension. It was, on the one hand, an idealized vision of spontaneous consensus and common worship of the national symbols; but it corresponded to a group of men whose devotion to the consensus and the national symbols was genuine – a group who comprised, so to speak, a field defined by common participation in this public realm.[162] The fact that these men were socially so similar betrays the extent to which the German-national public was culturally the product of the experience of a specific stratum of Imperial German society. This realm reflected not only the traditions, values, and anxieties of this stratum, but its aspiration to speak for German society – the German nation – as a whole.

The German-national public realm was a paradox in one further respect. In the sense that Habermas uses the terms, this public was both critical and acclamatory.[163] Its acclaim for the policies of the leadership was engineered through a number of channels. Yet despite the fact that it appropriated the same patriotic symbols and claimed to speak in the same national interest as did the German government, this German-national public remained genuinely independent of official influence, and the policies acclaimed in it were increasingly critical of policies officially pursued.

This final paradox is worth emphasizing in light of recent controversy over the relative weight of self-mobilization and manipulation from above in the history of social and political movements in Imperial Germany.[164] The history of the Pan-German League illustrates a basic truth about the dynamics of political mobilization in the modern period, that no matter how genuine the activistic impulse from the grass roots, some degree of manipulation is essential to channel this impulse into an effective political force. To restate the paradox more bluntly: to be effective even a self-mobilized movement must be manipulated, or, specifically in the case of the radical nationalism that animated the Pan-German League, to be effectively critical the public realm had to some degree to be acclamatory.

Of course, the essential question is: who does the manipulating? In the Pan-German League the manipulation remained entirely in-house, and the organization resisted more successfully than the other major patriotic societies the attempts of agencies of the German government to establish channels of official manipulation. This unique independence made possible the League's outspoken criticism of the government, and it also complicated the organization's relationship with the other patriotic societies.

Notes

1 Changing patterns of popular interest are evident in the statistics on lectures reported by the locals to national headquarters. In 1901 the most common topics were the navy and the war in South Africa; in 1906 the Herero uprising was most frequently the subject, and the next year this distinction went to the plight of Baltic Germans: ADB (1901), 353; ADB (1906), 210; ADB (1907), 173.
2 ADB (1899), 129–30.
3 ADB (1907), 327–9.
4 ADB (1909), 86–7.
5 ADB (1900), 247.
6 ADB (1896), 169–72; ADB (1899), 91, 389; ADB (1900), 395; ADB (1909), 71.
7 ADB (1898), 9; ADB (1899), 434; ADB (1901), 121; ADB (1904), 365; ADB (1907), 426; ADB (1908), 411.
8 ADB (1895), 101–2; ADB (1903), 455; ADB (1913), 119.
9 ADB (1897), 34–5; ADB (1900), 104.
10 ZStAP, ADV 195, Baumann to Steller, Cologne, 13.9.11; ADV (1911), 175, 223.
11 ADB (1904), 81; ADB (1907), 311–17; ADB (1909), 128; ADB (1910), 55, 191; ADB (1911), 10.
12 ADB (1901), 282–3.
13 ADB (1904), 67; cf. ADB (1903), 445.
14 ADB (1900), 248–9; cf. ADB (1899), 388–9.
15 ADB (1898), 309–10.
16 ADB (1907), 222–3; cf. ADB (1900), 322; ADB (1904), 238–9; ADB (1909), 354.
17 See especially Hermann Freudenthal, *Vereine in Hamburg: ein Beitrag zur Geschichte und Volkskunde der Geselligkeit* (Hamburg, 1968), pp. 514–57.
18 ADB (1904), 165; cf. Frymann/Class, *Kaiserbuch*, pp. 68–9.
19 ADB (1895), 11; ADB (1901), 50.
20 Erving Goffman, *Frame Analysis: An Essay on the Organization of Experience* (New York, 1974), pp. 124–55.
21 Bourdieu, p. 167. In this sense, I think George Mosse is wrong when he writes that patriotic festivals gradually excluded popular participation: *Nationalization of the Masses*, pp. 91–2.
22 ADB (1910), 311.
23 ADB (1908), 397–8.
24 ZStAP, ADV 83, GFA, Berlin, 17–18.2.12; ADB (1904), 142; cf. ADB (1894), 72; ADB (1896), 37–8; ADB (1901), 96; ADB (1911), 424–6.
25 Jürgen Habermas, *Strukturwandel der Oeffentlichkeit: Untersuchung zu einer Kategorie der bürgerlichen Gesellschaft* (Neuwied and Berlin, 1962), p. 52.
26 ADB (1894), 112; ADB (1900), 152; ADB (1904), 81; ADB (1910), 91; ADB (1913), 71.
27 ADB (1894), 199–200; ADB (1898), 84.
28 See Bley, *Weltstellung*, p. 48; ADB (1900), 198, 367–8; ADB (1907), 410; ADB (1901), 89–90.
29 For examples: ADB (1895), 20; ADB (1898), 172; cf. ZStAP, ADV 7, Vorstandssitzung, Hamburg, 3.4.10; ADB (1898), 21; ADB (1907), 370; cf. Paul Luther, *Deutsche Volksabende: Ein Handbuch für Volksunterhaltungsabende. Für die Praxis zusammengestellt* (Berlin, 1898).

30 HA/GHH 300127/8, Sperlin to Woltmann, Bochum, 8.4.13; StAH, Pol. Polizei, V452 Bd. 1, Polizeiliche Bericht, 18.11.04; ZStAP, ADV 195, Class RS, Mainz, 12.8.11; ADB (1903), 223; ADB (1904), 427.
31 See Freudenthal, p. 484; Sennett, pp. 4, 10.
32 ADB (1900), 122; ADB (1912), 202; cf. ZStAM, Rep. 195 Nr. 50, DOV to Matthias, Berlin, 18.3.09.
33 ZStAP, ADV 197, Walbaum to Class, Göttingen, 16.3.13.
34 ADB (1897), 74.
35 ADB (1901), 250; ADB (1905), 51; ADB (1913), 420.
36 See Thomas Nipperdey, 'Nationalidee und Nationaldenkmal in Deutschland im 19. Jahrhundert', in *Gesellschaft, Kultur, Theorie*, pp. 133–73; Schieder, p. 73.
37 ADB (1904), 197; cf. ADB (1902), 97–8; ADB (1904), 134.
38 ADB (1899), 130; ADB (1904), 238; ADB (1906), 294–5; ADB (1910), 224; ADB (1911), 255; ADB (1914), 259.
39 For some of the variations see ZStAP, ADV 188, Geiser to Hasse, Berlin, 23.5.04; ADB (1900), 65, 103, 508; ADB (1902), 69; ADB (1903), 126.
40 ZStAP, ADV 185, Hasse to Fabricius, Leipzig, 1.10.01.
41 ADB (1894), 68.
42 Harold Nicolson, *The Later Years, 1945–1962* (New York, 1968), p. 211.
43 StdA Wuppertal, P III 186, DKG Abt. Elberfeld to Funck, Elberfeld, 27.4.04.
44 ZStAP, ADV 188, Geiser to Hasse, 29.3.04; cf. ADV 57, GFA, Berlin, 17–18.11.06; ADB (1902), 279; Nipperdey, *Organisation*, pp. 76–7.
45 ADB (1909), 123.
46 The best documentation of this *Kastengeist* emerged from the Eastern Marches Society in the pamphlet by Hans Semrau, *Der Deutsche Ostmarkenverein und die völkische Erziehung in der Ostmarkdeutschen* (Lissa, 1907), pp. 3–17; cf. ZStAM, Rep. 195 Nr 10, Reisebericht Pillau, 19.1.13; Galos, p. 159. The documents leave no doubt, however, that similar conditions existed in the Pan-German League: ZStAP, ADV 182, Wislicenus to Hasse, Berlin, 5.9.93; ADB (1895), 43; ADB (1904), 94–5; ADB (1912), 122; ADB (1914), 142. And in the Navy League: BAMA, RM 3/v Nr. 9911, Hollweg to Tirpitz, Berlin, 12.6.12.
47 See ADB (1903), 149–50; cf. Raymond Firth, *Symbols: Public and Private* (Ithaca, NY, 1973), p. 177; Pascal, p. 295; Klaus Vondung, *Magie und Manipulation: Ideologischer Kult und politische Religion des Nationalsozialismus* (Göttingen, 1971).
48 ADB (1904), 398; ADB (1907), 383–5.
49 ZStAP, ADV 196, Koecher to Class, Magdeburg, 27.10.12.
50 ZStAP, ADV 196, Class to Koecher, Mainz, 28.10.12.
51 For example: ADB (1904), 134, 408; ADB (1907), 105–6, 198–9; ADB (1908), 169–70, 173–7; ADB (1909), 111; ADB (1911), 319.
52 ADB (1907), 87; cf. OM (1904), 18.
53 ZStAP, ADV 43, GFA, Gotha, 9–10.4.04, Eingegangen Antworten . . . (Neumann); ADV 187, Bericht des Geschäftsführers Geiser über seine Reise in der bayrischen Pfalz . . . 27.6.03; ADB (1899), 98; cf. ZStAP, DKG 710, Abt. Bamberg to DKG, 21.11.94; ZStAM, Rep. 195 Nr. 116, Schreiber Reisebericht, Forsthausen, 12.10.07.
54 ADB (1899), 423; ADB (1902), 173; ADB (1902), 231.
55 ADB (1910), 83.
56 ADB (1896), 196; ADB (1898), 4; ADB (1899), 45–7; ADB (1909), 123; ADB (1910), 191.
57 ADB (1900), 508–9.
58 ADB (1894), 80; ADB (1899), 31; ADB (1901), 260.
59 ADB (1899), 58; ADB (1906), 154.
60 ADB (1901), 389; cf. ADB (1914), 227.
61 ADB (1902), 449–50.
62 ADB (1903), 263; ADB (1905), 290; ADB (1906), 243.
63 ADB (1902), 459.
64 ZStAP. ADV 182, Ogr. Berlin, Vaterländischer Eröffnungs-Abend, 6.10.93; MADV (19.1.92), 38; ADB (1914), 103.
65 ADB (1907), 410.
66 ADB (1901), 74, 389; ADB (1909), 15.

67 ADB (1902), 202.
68 ADB (1901), 247; ADB (1904), 324.
69 ZStAP, ADV 193, Gerhard to Class, Berlin, 27.1.09; ADV 195, Class RS, Mainz, 12.8.11; ADB (1900), 154.
70 ADV HB (1908), p. 19; ADB (1900), 197–8; ADB (1903), 73.
71 MADV (19.1.92), 38–9; ADB (1913), 153.
72 ADV HB (1905), p. 14; ADB (1906), 312.
73 See Freudenthal, pp. 11, 20–6; Schmitt, pp. 91–4; Urner, p. 515. Two recent studies of patriotic organizations in England and France point to sociability as the main attraction: H. Cunningham, *The Volunteer Force* (London, 1975), pp. 103–26; Antoine Prost, *Les Anciens Combattants et la société française 1914–1939*, 3 vols (Paris, 1977), esp. Vol. 2, pp. 135–7, 181–200. On the phenomenon of *Geselligkeit* see Georg Simmel's thought-provoking essay, 'Die Geselligkeit (Beispiel der Reinen- oder Formalen-soziologie)', in *Grundfragen der Soziologie: Individuum und Gesellschaft* (Berlin and Leipzig, 1917). The essay is in English translation in Kurt H. Wolff (ed.), *The Sociology of Georg Simmel* (New York and London, 1950), pp. 40–57.
74 See Rohter, pp. 198–9; Bourdieu, p. 167; Freudenthal, p. 16; Nipperdey, 'Verein als soziale Struktur', pp. 5–6; Luckman and Berger, pp. 342–3; Gerth and Mills, p. 86; Cohen, *Two-Dimensional Man*, p. 55.
75 ZStAP, ADV 195, Pohl to Class, Berlin 31.3.11; cf. George L. Mosse, 'Friendship and nationhood: about the promise and failure of German nationalism', JCH, vol. 17 (1982), pp. 351–67.
76 ADB (1901), 501.
77 Class, *Strom*, p. 131; ADB (1899), 370; ADB (1900), 94; ADB (1908), 52–3; ADB (1912), 246–7.
78 ADB (1897), 160; ADB (1901), 9.
79 ADB (1899), 337–9; ADB (1900), 393; ADB (1901), 412; ADB (1909), 24–5.
80 Class was on familiar terms with Karl Klingemann and Philipp Bonhard. Heinrich Pohl, Paul Simons, Karl Itzenplitz, Ernst Graf zu Reventlow, Theodor Reismann-Grone, and Heinrich Calmbach were in the circle of Class's 'dear friends'.
81 ADB (1900), 94; ADB (1912), 246–7.
82 See Goffman, pp. 43–4.
83 ZStAP, ADV 43, GFA, Gotha, 9–10.4.04, Eingegangene Antworten ... (Reismann-Grone); ADB (1898), 59–60.
84 ADB (1901), 237; ADB (1904), 165, 347; ADB (1907), 131–2.
85 ADB (1913), 363–4.
86 ZStAM, Rep. 77 Tit. 871 Nr. 1, Adh. 2, Bd. 1, Wilamowitz to MInn, Posen, 30.8.98.
87 ADB (1900), 122.
88 ADB (1898), 191; ADB (1908), 68–9; ADB (1914), 146–7, 194.
89 ADB (1909), 123; cf. ADB (1902), 399.
90 ADB (1900), 369; ADB (1908), 328; ADB (1911), 113–14.
91 ADB (1907), 327–9.
92 ADB (1906), 90–1.
93 ZStAP, ADV 187, Fischer to Hasse, Marburg, 13.11.03.
94 *Thomas Mann–Heinrich Mann Briefwechsel 1900–1949* (Frankfurt a. M., 1969), p 66.
95 ADB (1900), 495; ADB (1901), 271.
96 See Cohen, *Elite Culture*, p. 211.
97 ADB (1900), 199; ADB (1903), 397.
98 ADB (1909), 29.
99 ADB (1909), 414.
100 ADB (1898), 155; ADB (1905), 54–5; ADB (1911), 234–6.
101 Bley, *Weltmachtstellung*, pp. 35, 42; ADB (1895), 126–7; ADB (1910), 273–5; Werner, p. 71; cf. Hermann Glaser, *Spiesserideologie: Von der Zerstörung des deutschen Geistes im 19. und 20. Jahrhundert* (Freidburg i. B., 1964), p. 244.
102 ADB (1909), 321.
103 See OM (1905), 70.
104 ADB (1912), 195.
105 ADB (1898), 175; ADB (1903), 111; ADB (1905), 58.

106 ADB (1895), 92; ADB (1896), 141–2; ADB (1898), 239, 277–8; ADB (1903), 358; ADB (1908), 125–6.
107 ADB (1894), 87–8.
108 ADB (1906), 368.
109 ZStAP, ADV 188, Fischer, Erläuterungen, p. 16; ADB (1898), 90; (1913), 8.
110 ADB (1899), 95, 323; ADB (1907), 181; ADB (1913), 48.
111 ADB (1898), 256; ADB (1900), 498; ADB (1902), 26; ADB (1904), 6.
112 ADB (1897), 257–8; ADB (1902), 449–50; ADB (1911), 27.
113 ADB (1899), 246, 444; ADB (1903), 254–5; ADB (1907), 234–9.
114 ZStAP, ADV 188, Calmbach to Class, Esslingen, 22.1.04; DKG 244, Bornhaupt to Kusserow, Berlin, 25.11.99, 3.3.00; ADB (1901), 271; cf. ADB (1897), 132; ADB (1904), 135.
115 Class/Frymann, *Kaiserbuch*, pp. 116–18.
116 ADB (1900), 254.
117 ADB (1897), 125; ADB (1912), 434; *Die Wehr* (December 1912), 4–5.
118 ADB (1908), 216–17, 288–90; ADB (1910), 190; ADB (1912), 382–3.
119 Frymann/Class, *Kaiserbuch*, pp. 118–22; Class, *Strom*, p. 238. On the image of the domestic angel and its implications see Sandra M. Gilbert and Susan Gubar, *The Madwoman in the Attic: The Woman Writer and the Nineteenth-Century Literary Imagination* (New Haven, Conn., and London, 1979), esp. pp. 17–27.
120 ADB (1909), 370–1. Another writer, who preferred anonymity, had earlier cited with approval a remark attributed to Lessing that 'the best woman is the one of whom the least is said': ADB (1894), 13–14.
121 ADB (1911), 307.
122 ADB (1900), 142–4.
123 ADB (1907), 167, 180–1; ADB (1909), 333–5.
124 Frymann/Class, *Kaiserbuch*, pp. 51–2.
125 ADB (1903), 247; cf. ADB (1902), 262; ADB (1914), 47.
126 ADB (1907), 215–16; cf. ADB (1903), 5; ADB (1907), 426.
127 ADB (1908), 444–5; ADB (1910), 406. See Richard J. Evans. *The Feminist Movement in Germany, 1894–1933* (London, 1976), esp. pp. 22, 147–8, 175–82.
128 ADB (1908), 68–9.
129 ZStAP, ADV 33, GFA, Eisenach, 23–24.5.02.
130 UB Freiburg, NL Schemann IV B, Liebert to Schemann, Berlin, 25.9.10; ADB (1912), 131, 418.
131 ZStAP, ADV 59, GFA, Berlin, 11–12.5.07; ADB (1897), 100; ADB (1907), 161–2.
132 ZStAP, ADV 93, GFA, Berlin, 10.1.14; ADB (1910), 7.
133 ADV HB (1915), p. 16; ADB (1903), 33; ADB (1905), 27; ADB (1908), 130.
134 *Alldeutsches Werbe- und Merkbüchlein* (Munich, 1899), pp. 5–8; ADV HB (1915), pp. 3–8; cf. Wertheimer, pp. 49–53; Werner, p. 68; Wenck, pp. 3–4.
135 ADB (1902), 185; Wertheimer, pp. 114–15.
136 ZStAP, ADV 2, Vorstand RS, Essen, 13.4.91.
137 ZStAP, ADV 183, Hasse RS, Leipzig, 20.10.00.
138 ZStAP, ADV 187, Hasse to Klee, Leipzig, 11.11.03; ADV 188, Fischer, Erläuterungen, p. 19; ADB (1902), 127; ADB (1904), 441–3; ADB (1905), 111.
139 ZStAP, ADV 192, Class to Reventlow, Mainz, 15.7.08; Itzenplitz to Class, Mülheim, 22.12.08; ADV 195, Baumann to Steller, Cologne, 13.9.11.
140 ZStAP, ADV 188, Hasse to Class, Leipzig, 2.1.04.
141 Class, *Strom*, p. 78; cf. ibid., pp. 239–40; ADB (1904), 347.
142 ZStAP, ADV 7, Vorstandssitzung, Hamburg, 3.4.10; ADV 74, GFA, Hamburg, 2.4.10.
143 ZStAP, ADV 33, GFA, Eisenach, 23–24.5.02; ADV 44, GFA, Lübeck, 27.5.04; ADV 49, GFA, Worms, 15–16.5.05.
144 ADB (1898), 103–4.
145 ZStAP, ADV 45, GFA, Leipzig, 7–8.10.04; ADV 192, Reventlow to Class, Charlottenburg, 30.5.08.
146 ZStAP, ADV 179, Hasse RS, Berlin, 1.3.97; ADB (1901), 108; cf. ADB (1901), 491; ADB (1904), 30; ADB (1908), 62.
147 ADB (1901), 511–12.

148 ZStAP, ADV 188, Fischer, Erläuterungen, p. 21; ADB (1904), 302–3, 310; ADB (1905), 439.
149 Class, *Strom*, p. 90. The notorious hotheads on the executive committee included Class, Reventlow, Liebert, August Keim, and Richard Graf du Moulin-Eckart.
150 ZStAP, ADV 29, GFA, Leipzig, 30–31.8.01; ADV 45, GFA, Leipzig, 7–8.10.04; ADV 67, GFA, Berlin, 4–5.11.08.
151 ZStAP, ADV 7, Vorstandssitzung, Berlin, 10.2.07; Vorstandssitzung, Braunschweig, 1.12.12; Reismann-Grone, *Erdenkrieg*, pp. 67–9.
152 ZStAP, ADV 192, Reventlow to Class, Charlottenburg, 4.6.08.
153 ADB (1902), 186.
154 ZStAP, ADV 48, GFA, Göttingen, 15.4.05; ADB (1902), 119.
155 ADB (1894), 143–4; ADB (1902), 339–40, 356–7, 365–6; ADB (1911), 174.
156 ADB (1909), 246.
157 ZStAP, ADV 45, GFA, Leipzig, 7–8.10.04, Hasse RS, Leipzig, 15.9.04; ADV 57, GFA, Berlin, 17–18.11.06; ADV 192, Reventlow to Class, Charlottenburg, 29.4.08; ADB (1904), 118; ADB (1913), 159; ADB (1914), 266–7.
158 ZStAP, ADV 89, GFA, Berlin, 3.7.13; ADV 92, GFA, Remscheid, 6.12.13; ADV 309, Class to Breusing, Mainz, 25.10.13 [?].
159 ADB (1901), 24–5.
160 See Habermas, esp. pp. 144–58.
161 Oskar Negt and Alexander Kluge, *Oeffentlichkeit und Erfahrung: Zur Organisations-analyse von bürgerlicher und proletarischer Oeffentlichkeit* (Frankfurt a. M., 1972), p. 18; cf. Peter Brückner *et al.*, 'Perspectives on the fascist public sphere', *New German Critique*, vol. 11 (1977), pp. 94–132.
162 See Richard Johnson, 'Three problematics: elements of a theory of working-class culture', in J. Clarke *et al.* (eds), *Working-Class Culture: Studies in History and Theory* (New York, 1979), p. 236.
163 Habermas, pp. 233–50; cf. Bade, p. 168.
164 Wolfgang Mock, '"Manipulation von oben" oder Selbstorganisation an der Basis? Einige neuere Ansätze in der englischen Historiographie zur Geschichte des deutschen Kaisserreiches', HZ, vol. 232 (1981), pp. 358–75.

9 The Scope of the German-National Public Realm

In Imperial Germany the public realm was constituted principally in the form of voluntary associations. Tens of thousands of these *Vereine* were founded after 1890 to serve every conceivable purpose and to bring together the devotees of every conceivable pastime, from group singing or the cultivation of carrier pigeons to religious charity or the training of police dogs. Every German community boasted a plethora of them. The town of Weinheim an der Bergstrasse, with a population of 12,500 in 1905, hosted more than a hundred different *Vereine*.[1] The small town of Freienwalde, which lay to the northeast of Berlin, had more than fifty such associations for its 7,000 inhabitants in 1894, while Cronberg im Taunus, a town of 3,200 souls, was infested with forty-two in 1912.[2] In 1898 the city of Naumburg had six religious associations, five women's groups, nine veterans' organizations, five gymnastic societies, and dozens of others of various descriptions to serve the 20,000 people who lived there.[3] It is reasonably certain that few healthy adult male Germans escaped membership in one or more of these organizations at some time in their lives; and some Germans belonged to a staggering number of them. Although he was doubtless not a typical example, Hasse once complained of the burdens he faced as a member of fifty-three different *Vereine*.[4]

The proliferation of voluntary associations was one of the most remarkable cultural phenomena of the Wilhelmine epoch. It inspired scholarly investigation, satirical poetry, jokes, and even its own label in the word *Vereinsmeierei*, whose meaning is best captured in the saying, then current, that 'whenever three Germans get together they form a *Verein*'.[5] The phenomenon was also a facet of social change in Germany at the end of the nineteenth century. Most of the new associations were urban, formed to meet the affiliative needs of the dramatically growing numbers of Germans residing in cities.[6] More specifically, the proliferation of voluntary associations was due in no small part to the polarization of class relationships in urbanized Germany. The rift between the socialist labor movement and the rest of German society at the end of the century was institutionalized in the establishment of all manner of voluntary associations that catered to a working-class constituency.[7]

In other respects, too, although not as radically as in the case of the socialist working class, voluntary associations reproduced and reinforced the segmentation of Imperial German society. Indeed, each of the major segments of this society was delineated in large part by voluntary associations – the cooperatives and political action groups (such as the

Agrarian League) which defended both the social existence and the cultural traditions of rural Protestant Germany, the trade unions and parish auxiliaries which kept alive a corporate consciousness among German Catholics, and the social clubs of the Protestant middle class.[8] Voluntary associations tended, in addition, to underpin the vertical stratification of the various segments of German society. Either by design or custom, most of these associations became preserves of specific social strata. These strata were in fact partially defined by their social contacts and the manner in which they managed their leisure time in the organizations to which they belonged. Selecting the proper *Verein* was accordingly a serious undertaking for anyone with social pretensions, who had to take care to associate with organizations that enjoyed 'a certain prestige and respect' and were frequented by 'the better sectors of the public'.[9]

Voluntary associations of all descriptions also had tremendous political significance. This truth has lain buried for decades beneath the famous thesis of the 'unpolitical German' – a thesis that has rested to a large extent on the purportedly non-political character of German associational life.[10] To be fair to its proponents, the thesis reflects (in addition to the self-image of some German intellectuals and literary figures) a peculiarly American view of what politics means; but if one defines politics as the process by which questions of public power and policy are debated and resolved, voluntary associations were the most important political medium in Imperial Germany. For most Germans they provided, in the first place, the principal access to the public realm in which political questions were at issue.[11] Moreover, by virtue of the multiple affiliations of their members, voluntary associations were interwoven in intricate webs; these linked the more overtly political organizations, such as the Agrarian League, with groups like the choral societies or *gesellige Vereine* which on the surface had no political significance at all.[12] These links made voluntary associations of practically every description available for politicization and turned them into the basic cells of political mobilization in Imperial Germany.[13] The best testimony to the truth of this proposition comes from the two masters of political mobilization in modern German history. Bismarck regarded voluntary associations with suspicion regardless of their goals. 'All *Vereine*', he wrote in 1887 to Prince William, 'in which entry and activity depend upon the individual members themselves, their good will and personal intentions, can be used very effectively as tools of attack and destruction, but not for construction and preservation.'[14] Hitler agreed. His government moved swiftly in the first months of the *Machtergreifung* to remove all points around which organized opposition might crystalize by destroying the autonomy of voluntary associations whether they were immediately political or not.[15]

The principles of political mobilization had not changed much from the days of Bismarck to those of Hitler. But the style of politics in Germany had. The ground-rules of the political process in Imperial Germany corresponded to the character of the voluntary associations that participated in it. It was, with remarkably few aberrations, an ordered process, conditioned by the demands of the police who supervised it, as well as by a sense of propriety which, though middle-class in inspiration, prevailed in the politics of the other sectors of German society too. Formal bylaws and procedures, lectures, resolutions, petitions, and an occasional big rally were the hallmarks of the process. Violence and terror were foreign to it. These limitations of style extended to those features of the Imperial German political landscape that seem most clearly to have prefigured the National Socialists. Many of the propaganda techniques employed by the Imperial Naval Office and other agencies of the German government might well have anticipated the plebiscitary style of the Nazis, but Tirpitz and other officials geared their propaganda to the associational conditions they found: building the battle fleet was debated not on the streets, but around the *Stammtisch*.[16] The Pan-German League anticipated the Nazis in much of its program and rhetoric, but never in its political style. Significantly, the League was uncomfortable with Georg von Schönerer and the Austrian Pan-Germans, precisely because the political tactics of these men did include violence.[17]

In the galaxy of voluntary associations in Imperial Germany, the Pan-German League represented but one small star. It resembled most *Vereine* in drawing its members from a distinctive segment and stratum of German society, in making its members at least potentially available for political mobilization, and in observing the prevailing proprieties of style. The Pan-German League also resembled a number of voluntary associations in many additional respects.

The Pan-German League and Other Patriotic Societies

To extend the astronomical metaphor, the Pan-German League belonged to a large constellation, which comprised dozens of voluntary associations that served what were called 'national goals'. These associations included six major patriotic societies, which were nominally open to all Germans without respect to confession or class; in addition to the Pan-German League, these were the School Association, the Colonial Society, the Language Association, the Eastern Marches Society, and the Navy League. The label 'national organization' comprehended as well countless other associations whose membership, appeal, and goals were more restricted. These groups included the women's auxiliaries of the big patriotic societies, religious organizations, veterans' associations, student groups, patriotic youth and workers' organizations, genealogical societies, antisemitic groups, and sectarian organizations like the *Deutscher Bund für Regeneration*, which were devoted to causes still exotic and populated by men still considered cranks.[18]

The six major patriotic societies were the core of what contemporaries called the 'national' or 'German-national movement'. They were all remarkably similar. The extent of their similarity can perhaps be best appreciated in a few more or less random samples from the reports in which chapters of each of these societies described their activities.

Like the Pan-German League, the Colonial Society capitalized on opposition to the Boer War in Germany. Early in 1900 the society's chapter in Aschaffenburg heard a lecture on political conditions in the Transvaal.

The lecture, according to the report, 'proceeded in an edifying manner [*nahm einen erhebenden Verlauf*]'. At its conclusion the assembled guests 'joined enthusiastically in cheering the German fatherland, and the elevated, patriotic mood found warm expression as everyone sang together "*Deutschland, Deutschland über alles*"'.[19]

Several years later the chapter of the Eastern Marches Society in the Silesian town of Wollstein held a late-summer festival. Although the weather was bad, some 700 people attended, including representatives of the society's chapters in other towns around the county. The festival opened with music, whereupon the chairman of the host chapter greeted the participants 'with warm words and pointed out that the purpose of the festival was to strengthen in the society's members the consciousness that they constitute a large family to which the defense of home and hearth has been entrusted'. After the deputy *Landrat* had delivered an 'enthusiastically received toast to the Kaiser', the principal speaker described, 'in stirring fashion, the blessed [*segensreich*] influence of German settlers and the solicitude of the House of Hohenzollern in the Eastern Marches'. In concluding, the report emphasized that the 'elevated mood of the participants was not influenced by the disfavor shown by the weather'.[20]

Meetings of chapters of the Language Association emphasized specialized themes, but these meetings had the same effect on their participants as did those of other patriotic societies. In Kassel in 1912, for example, the Language Association's chapter sponsored a 'dialect evening'. The meeting opened as the chairman greeted the guests and demanded of them 'energetic assistance in the fight against foreign words [*Fremdwörterwesen*] and against everything un-German'. The highlight of the evening was a series of readings in dialects indigenous to various parts of Germany and Austria. According to the report, the audience 'followed with the most excited interest the presentations, some of which provoked considerable merriment, and thanked the readers with rich applause'.[21]

Many of the activities sponsored by chapters of the Navy League also had a distinctive flare, for this organization had resources unavailable to the others. The effect, however, was familiar. 'As in previous years', read the report which the Navy League's group in Essen submitted about activities in 1909, the festivals that featured motion pictures 'were the most actively in demand; on occasion the crowd was so large that hundreds of people had to be turned back at the doors'. Altogether some 40,000 people attended these festivals, but, lest one get the impression that the throngs were there for the technological novelty of motion pictures rather than because of glowing enthusiasm for the navy, the reporter hastened to add that the participants were all 'elevated in patriotic spirit by speech and song'.[22]

Finally, although the School Association was primarily interested in raising money for Germans abroad, its chapters appreciated the importance of the proper mood at their meetings. Late in 1909 the newly founded chapter in Bayreuth inaugurated its activities with a public lecture by a German delegate to the Bohemian diet in Prague. The lecture was received with 'grateful enthusiasm', whereupon the musicians struck up '*Deutschland, Deutschland über alles*' and everyone rose to sing it. The entertainment that followed was 'immensely successful'. At the end of the meeting a spokesman for the chapter thanked the guest speaker for his 'splendid words' and assured him that the chapter would 'remain mindful of his admonishments' about the Slav peril and would 'translate them into action'. The whole evening, the reporter concluded, 'proceeded in a harmonious manner and represented an uplifting demonstration for the German nation'.[23]

Citing additional examples would merely belabor the point that all these reports were describing the same phenomenon. No less than in the Pan-German League, the meetings of the other patriotic societies summoned up a German-national public realm, which transformed every German who entered it as it suspended class distinctions and parochial loyalties, generating spontaneous unanimity of thought and emotion in the defense of national symbols. In fact, to judge from the format of the meetings and from the rhetoric of the speeches, toasts, resolutions, and the reports, it would be difficult to distinguish one patriotic society from another.[24] Nor were these similarities superficial; they reflected commonalities of ideology and mentality, social structure, and geographical distribution.

The patriotic societies defended different components of the same network of national symbols. The navy, the colonies, the language, and Germans struggling to preserve their ethnic integrity all ultimately meshed with one another to symbolize the defense of culture, authority, and order at home and abroad. The patriotic societies shared a common fear of threats to these symbols. The ideologies of all these organizations were informed by a common vision of conflict between the forces of order and disorder, whether this conflict be played out in terms of rivalry for naval power and empire, or in the progressive subversion of one language and culture by another.

The same images and metaphors surfaced in the programmatic literature of all these associations, where they bore witness to common anxieties. Cunning and unscrupulous enemies abounded, portrayed frequently – especially in the literature of the Eastern Marches Society and the School Association – in the imagery of the flood. The figure of the pioneer and the preoccupation with the ideas of distance and isolation were prominent in the literature of the other societies too. In the case of the School Association the metaphorical tradition was practically identical with that of the Pan-German League: the pioneers were the lonely champions of German culture in Central and Eastern Europe. In the Eastern Marches Society the metaphors were more geographically specific and applied to the efforts of Germans to beat back the flood of Poles in the Prussian east. The Language Association made free use of the same imagery, as it appointed itself the vanguard in the defense of the language against foreign intrusions from all sides. In the Colonial Society's literature the pioneers were the intrepid German merchants and settlers who brought culture to the distant wilds of the empire. The Navy League appropriated much of the Colonial Society's imagery in arguing that a fleet was essential for the spread and protection of German culture overseas.

The ideologies of these patriotic societies appealed in addition to the same kinds of people. Every organization drew its cadres overwhelmingly from the propertied and educated middle class (see Appendix, Tables 5.6, 5.7, 5.8). Although the proportions of the mixture varied among the societies, academically educated public officials and teachers, professionals, and military officers made up an absolute majority of the local leadership in all of them; and these people presumably were representative of the rank and file as well, with the probable exception of the more broadly based Navy League.[25]

Although conclusive generalizations must await more systematic comparison of these organizations, the ideological and sociological similarities among them suggest that the same cultural and psychological dynamics that underlay radical nationalism in the Pan-German League were at work in the other societies too. All were populated in the first instance by custodians of culture and authority. These men found in a generalized, aggressive antipathy to outgroups a vision which spoke to the confusions and anxieties they were experiencing, as rapid social and cultural change bred challenges to their authority.

The patriotic societies were similar in another respect. Excepting the Eastern Marches Society, which was concentrated in the cities and towns of the east, they exhibited the same patterns of regional distribution; all were strong in the central belt from Hessen to Saxony.[26] The same social and confessional conditions that encouraged large and active chapters of the Pan-German League worked to the benefit of the other societies. Their chapters, too, were strong in administrative centers in Protestant parts of the country, where the threat posed by socialists to bastions of power, especially to bastions traditionally occupied by National Liberals, was immediate. And Catholics were nearly as rare in the other societies as they were in the Pan-German League.[27]

Despite the fundamental similarities among the patriotic societies, their political postures were different, in some cases dramatically. The Pan-German League was unique among these organizations in its consistent and outspoken opposition to the German government. The roots of this divergence among the patriotic societies extended back into the 1880s, into the debates over the definition of the German nation and whether ultimate national authority resided in the monarchy which ruled within the frontiers of 1871 or in the ethnically defined *Volk*, which transcended these frontiers. While the tension between the political and ethnic definitions of the nation never disappeared entirely, the domestication of most of the patriotic societies in the 1890s seemed to resolve the issue in favor of the monarchy, whose own place in the shrine of national symbols became that of supreme custodian. The monarchy served, that is, not only itself as the symbol of national integrity, order, and authority, but it claimed the exclusive authority to tend all the other national symbols – not only those, like the colonies, which were associated with the monarchy from their creation, but also cultural symbols, such as the language, which operated well beyond the scope of the monarchy's political authority.

Apart from the Pan-German League, in which opposition to monarchical authority became increasingly explicit, this interpretation of the monarchy's role found general acceptance among the patriotic societies. Beyond the area known as *Kulturpolitik*, the School and Language Associations abandoned the realm of politics, but if they did take positions of immediate political consequence, they normally supported the government. The Colonial Society, the Eastern Marches Society, and the Navy League all adopted a 'governmentalist' posture most of the time. The Colonial Society in particular consistently followed what might be called an official line, gearing its propaganda and activities to official policy, whatever the vagaries of this policy might prescribe. The Eastern Marches Society was less reluctant to criticize the government, but did so rarely in public. For a short while the Navy League provided the one other exception to this pattern; its support for official policy was punctuated, between 1905 and 1908, by a major crisis (to be considered below), during which its challenge to the government's authority to determine naval policy rivalled that of the Pan-German League.

The docility of patriotic societies was not a foregone conclusion.[28] The ideologies, programs, and styles of all of them implied at least a latent tension with the government, for all were potentially rival custodians of the national symbols. Speaking in the name of the nation, all had been founded on the proposition that patriotic causes, from building the fleet to prohibiting languages other than German at public meetings, could be served by mobilizing popular sentiment in their support. However, in exploiting this support the government ran the risk of creating sorcerer's apprentices, in so far as the process involved playing on popular anxieties and the manipulation of emotionally laden symbols. Particularly in the event that official policies seemed to work to the detriment of the national symbols which these organizations served, the danger arose that patriotic activism could turn against the government and challenge its custodial authority.

The key to the docility of most of the patriotic societies lay in structural features in each organization that made difficult the venting of patriotic activism in public criticism of official authority. The bylaws of both the Language and School Associations limited the purview of these organizations' activities to areas in which direct confrontation with official authority was unlikely. The potential for friction was greater in the case of the School Association, whose subsidizing of German schools abroad did on occasion raise problems with the Foreign Office; however, the extreme decentralization of the organization, the fact that its local chapters were for all intents and purposes independent institutions of eleemosynary patriotism, made it difficult for the national organization to mobilize any sustained opposition to the government.

The potential for friction with the government was still greater in the cases of the Colonial Society, Eastern Marches Society, and the Navy League, for they all dealt with controversial issues of immediate political consequence. That this potential did not result in more public criticism was due to the channels which the government had built into each of these organizations and which made possible the stifling of patriotic activism whenever it threatened to turn into public criticism of official policies. The extensive, lucrative system of concessions which linked the government to the national leadership of the Colonial Society gave the top echelons of this organization a powerful incentive to heed the entreaties of high officials and to silence criticism of the government coming up from the chapters. In the Eastern Marches Society and the Navy League the channel of government influence lay in the massive encouragement each organization had enjoyed, during its incubation, from bureaucrats acting in a semi-official capacity. The debt owed by the Navy League to official favors was especially obvious, but the success of the Eastern Marches Society owed only a little less to the systematic encouragement of the Prussian bureaucracy in the eastern provinces. The penetration of both organizations by the bureaucratic apparatus continued to make the expression of criticism difficult.

In many respects, then, the Pan-German League was unique among the patriotic societies in Wilhelmine Germany. Its program was the most broad and systematic; the organization did not, like the School and Language Associations, eschew issues of direct political importance. The League's program embraced, in fact, the issues of primary concern to all the other societies. Furthermore, the Pan-German League differed fundamentally from the Colonial Society, the Eastern Marches Society, and the Navy League, in that the government had built no regular channels of influence into it through which to mute the expression of criticism. The Pan-German League remained genuinely independent of official control, so that the political expression of emotions and anxieties mobilized at the local level could be more radical than in any other patriotic society. Unattenuated by official pressure, the voice of the Pan-German League was less reluctant to dispute the claim of the monarchy to preside over the national symbols.

All these points of similarity and contrast combined to govern relations between the Pan-German League and the other patriotic societies on both the national and local levels. The contrasts and points of collision figured more prominently at the national level, where ideological differences and the question of ties to official agencies were focused. At the local level, on the other hand, the social, ideological, and cultural similarities among the patriotic societies weighed more heavily.

At the national level, the Pan-German League's relationship was most cordial with the Language and School Associations, the two organizations whose programs were the most restricted and whose own renunciation of political activity made for complementarity of roles with the Pan-Germans. The League was content to concentrate its own efforts elsewhere while the Language Association took over primary responsibility for hunting down foreign words.[29] The League and the School Association quickly accommodated one another's programs, leaving the subsidization of most schools abroad to the School Association and support for other German organizations, as well as most of the political agitation on behalf of Germans abroad, to the League.[30] Encouraged by this comfortable division of labor, the ties between the League and the School Association grew very close. In 1908–9, in fact, the possibility of a merger of the two organizations surfaced briefly; it did not materialize, but the transfer of Alfred Geiser from his position of executive secretary in the League to a similar job with the School Association in 1908 guaranteed that the two societies would continue to act in concert.[31]

Relations between the League and the other societies were more clouded by direct competition. Although the League and the Eastern Marches Society had reached an implicit understanding by the turn of the century about the areas of the country each was to cover, relations between the two organizations were far from the 'hearty and undisturbed friendship' which an official of the Eastern Marches Society claimed them to be.[32] In part the trouble stemmed from personal animosity between the autocratic leader of the Eastern Marches Society, Heinrich von Tiedemann, and the League's principal advisor on Polish affairs, Alfred Hugenberg, whom Tiedemann regarded as a 'pie-eyed [*schwärmerisch*] idealist'.[33] Hugenberg's idealism was the moving force behind the League's adopting positions in the Polish question that were more radical than those that the Eastern Marches Society, an organization more attuned to the dictates of official policy, was willing to endorse. As early as 1899 the League called publicly for the suspension of the constitutionally guaranteed principle of equality before the law in Prussia, in order to prepare the way for restricting the rights of Poles to own property.[34] Several years later the Eastern Marches Society adopted this demand too (and it was put into law in 1908), but the fact that the League had been in the vanguard did nothing to diminish the rivalry between the two organizations.[35]

More threatening to the League than its rivalry with the Eastern Marches Society over the Polish question was its competition with other patriotic societies in exploiting popular excitement over the issues of empire and the navy – the issues to which the League owed its dramatic growth in the late 1890s. With the exception of several brief episodes of collaboration, relations between the Pan-German League and the Colonial Society were consistently bad. The League was originally born in the early 1890s as a rival colonial society, and although the scope of its interests expanded, the League continued to denounce the Colonial Society for its anemic advocacy of colonial expansion and its cozy relations with the government. The greatest source of tension was the extensive concessions that bound the Colonial Society and the government. Nowhere was the populism that animated the Pan-German League more evident than in the organization's denunciation of the speculative profits this system was bringing, particularly in Southwest Africa, not only to the colonial companies whose directors controlled the Colonial Society, but to the Colonial Society itself as a corporate investor.[36] The League's attack touched a nerve in the Colonial Society, and the attack was motivated in no small part by resentment in the League over the riches and other official favors the Colonial Society reaped from what one of the League's leaders called its '*Dekorationspolitik*'.[37] In its own defense, the Colonial Society only exacerbated the resentment and ill will by publicly treating the League like an unmannered child.[38]

The relations between the Pan-German League and the Navy League vacillated. For most of the prewar period the Navy League was, like the Colonial Society, a '*Regierungsbildung mit Serenissimus-Kultus*', in the untranslatable words of one bitter Pan-German – an organization so dependent on the good will of the government for its existence that any radical departures from serene endorsement of official policy were inconceivable.[39] As a consequence, relations between the two organizations remained cool, except for the period of crisis during which the Navy League itself attacked the government's policies and prerogatives.

With special organizations at work in all the major sub-fields that its own program comprehended, the Pan-German League had constantly to emphasize its own unique ideological profile. Running feuds with other patriotic societies contributed substantially to the character of this profile. Years of criticizing other groups for their want of resolve and independence from the government cast a new light on the image of the pioneer in the Pan-German League. The image implied service in the vanguard of the national cause, independent and out ahead of both the government and the more docile patriotic societies. The League was the pioneer among pioneers.[40] This role entitled the organization, its spokesmen claimed, to prior authority on all national issues. The League accordingly comprised the unadulterated core of patriotic Germans, next to whom the other societies represented but groups in a diaspora; its comprehensive program made the League in addition the 'natural center' or point of crystallization for patriotism properly conceived and hence the logical foundation for a broad coalition of patriotic organizations.[41]

Maintaining the profile of the true pioneer weighed heavily on the League's leadership. On many occasions the decision about the position the League was to adopt hinged on the need to demonstrate the organization's independence and its role in the vanguard. The role required that the League pose demands that were more radical than those of the other patriotic societies – more ships than the Navy League advocated, more colonial annexations than the Colonial Society wanted, and more radical measures against the Poles than the Eastern Marches Society thought advisable.[42]

The League's profile did tend to broaden the ideological distance between it and the other patriotic societies, but the result was not invariably beneficial. While the League's leaders thought in terms of pioneering service to the nation, the salient features of organization's public image were its radicalism, the extremism of its program, its hostility to the government, and its irresponsibility. Especially once the German government began systematically to promote this image, the League's calculated advocacy of extreme positions ran the risk of casting the organization as a group of eccentric chauvinists.[43]

While programmatic and ideological disputes set the tone for relations among the patriotic societies at the national level, a different set of circumstances operated at the local level. Here a single truth governed the situation: all the patriotic societies had to appeal to the same group of people, and as patriotic societies shot up 'like mushrooms out of the ground', as one patriot in Bamberg described the problem, they found themselves competing for a limited pool of potential activists and members.[44] The problem was not so much economic, for most people from these social strata could afford to pay dues to several patriotic societies; it was a question of the time, energy, and the interest that people could devote to more than one organization, particularly when patriotic societies had to contend with all manner of other associations for their members' attention and when, despite the concerted efforts of the national leaderships, the ideological distinctions among patriotic organizations were not always clear and many Germans believed that membership in just (any) one was sufficient.[45]

German cities and towns thus became arenas in which the logic of *Verbandsimperialismus* was played out in a running struggle among the patriotic societies – a struggle that seemed hardly to befit the ideal of national solidarity they all claimed to serve. An organization's appeal to the distinctive merits of its own program or ideology often counted for less in this competition than the skill with which it exploited other more mundane features of German associational life. The patriotic societies vied with one another to make their meetings the most interesting and attractive. The group that succeeded in bringing in the most prominent speaker, or in tapping the best tavern as a meeting hall, or in appearing to be the best organized, or in displaying the most colorful literature could achieve a decisive advantage.[46] One of the reasons why the Navy League was such a formidable competitor was that the assets at its disposal allowed it to charge the lowest dues of all the patriotic societies and to outfit its travelling lecturers with motion pictures for showing at meetings.[47] Occasionally, tactics in the competition included the exchange of public recrimination, subversion of one group by another, and the outright rustling of members.[48]

The eventual outcome of the competition depended upon the local context in which it took place. The organizers of all the patriotic societies encountered the same experiences as the Pan-German League's. In most communities the number of members they initially attracted was less important than the kinds of people these were. The object was to win the allegiance of men who, as one organizer for the Navy League counseled, 'enjoy a certain influence among their fellow citizens', men whose standing in the pool of local notables would attract others, like satellites, into the organization and keep them there.[49] In Worms the Pan-German League occupied a dominant position among the patriotic societies, in large part because it succeeded in enlisting into its ranks Cornelius Heyl zu Herrnsheim, who was the single most important political figure in Hessen.[50] The fortunes of patriotic societies in Cologne fluctuated as they competed for the allegiance of Wilhelm von Recklinghausen, a wealthy merchant who was active first in the Colonial Society in 1890, then became chairman of the School Association, joined the board of directors of the Pan-German League in 1899, and took on a leading role in the local chapter of the Eastern Marches Society several years later.[51]

When organizers of patriotic societies arrived in a community, they often discovered that these influential notables were already organized, either in a chapter of another patriotic society or in some other voluntary association that placed rival claims on the loyalty of its members. When Geiser appeared in Lauf, in northern Bavaria, in 1904, he discovered that the town's 'national element' was already in the camp of the Navy League.[52] In Stuttgart the main obstacle to the activity of all the patriotic societies was the *Württembergischer Verein für Handelsgeographie*; originally founded in the 1880s, it was well established as the club of the best groups of people in

Stuttgart when, in the 1890s, other patriotic societies attempted to challenge its dominant position.[53] In Greifswald the situation was similar; here the local Geographical Society served as *the* patriotic society in the community.[54] In other communities, such as Paderborn and Konstadt, the *Bürgerverein*, nominally only a social club, was the dominant middle-class association, and it resisted the incursions of the patriotic societies.[55]

Breaking the monopoly of groups already established was a difficult undertaking, and in the dynamics of local competition prior presence could be decisive. Once a society became established in a community, the group loyalties it created were hard to break, if only because of inertia. One of the reasons why the Eastern Marches Society failed to recruit more successfully in the west was that other societies had beaten it into community after community.[56] That the Navy League was able to do so well, in spite of its late start, was due to its massive resources and the official endorsement it enjoyed.

The proliferation of patriotic societies and their competition in localities around the country meant that the notables for whose loyalty these organizations vied were under a great deal of pressure to support all manner of patriotic causes. The fragmentary evidence that survives indicates that a man like Recklinghausen in Cologne, who was an officer in four different patriotic societies, was unusual. Most of these people chose to become active in only one. Of the slightly more than 2,000 men whom I have identified as local leaders in patriotic societies in twenty-five communities, less than 6 percent were officers in more than one group, although this figure would no doubt be higher if more complete information were available on the cadres of the School Association.[57] It is more difficult to determine whether many notables chose to be officers in one group and only members in another, or simply members in more than one patriotic society. Of the 753 members in the Hamburg chapter of the Pan-German League in 1901, only eight were officers of other patriotic societies in Hamburg at one time or another, while the corresponding figures for Stuttgart were seven of 117.

Only for Hamburg do multiple membership lists survive for the patriotic societies. Comparing them suggests that most people chose to belong to only one, although the lists reveal some interesting patterns of cross-affiliation (see Appendix, Table 9.1). The membership lists of the Hamburg chapters of the Pan-German League, Colonial Society, School Association, Language Association, and Navy League had a combined total of 5,767 names (more than half of them in the Navy League). In just under 1,500 instances the same name appeared on two or more lists; and in just over 300 cases it appeared on three or more. Accordingly, about one patriot in eleven or twelve was a member of more than one society in Hamburg.[58] The School Association had the greatest percent of members with multiple memberships, the Navy League the least. The Pan-German League had the largest number of activists who were members of three or more societies, and it shared these activists most frequently with the massive Navy League, least frequently with its bitter rival, the Colonial Society.

Because the pool of potential members was limited, and because the number of activists willing to contribute their time and energy to more than one patriotic society was even more limited, the virtues of cooperation among the patriotic societies at the local level were compelling, although the fact that each organization jealously guarded its own corporate identity placed limits on their cooperation and made outright consolidation impossible. The principal stimulus to cooperation was economic. Staging patriotic meetings could be expensive: a meeting hall had to be rented, flyers and other forms of advertising had to be printed and disseminated, and the speaker, if he were coming from outside, had to be paid.[59] By pooling their resources, patriotic societies could not only share the expenses and administrative burdens, but could avert the psychological as well as the financial catastrophe of a half-empty meeting hall.[60] The advantages of cooperation were particularly impressed upon the small group of activists, like Recklinghausen, or Paul Winter in Hamburg, or professors Clauss and Barthelmess in Ulm, or Winterstein in Kassel, or Friedrich Hopf in Dresden, who were the moving spirits in the local chapters of several patriotic societies and whose lives were made less complicated by arranging meetings that served their several constituencies at the same time. Similarities of program and ideology made selecting themes for these joint meetings easy. The navy motif attracted Pan-Germans and members of the Colonial Society, as well as friends of the Navy League. The same was true of colonies, while the theme of oppressed German minorities abroad appealed to everyone in one way or another. One final consideration weighed heavily in encouraging cooperation, particularly at the turn of the century when the intrusion of the Navy League posed a threat to all the others. By arranging some kind of truce, patriotic societies diminished the risk of their members deserting to competitors.[61]

The liabilities of continued competition were already apparent when, at the turn of the century, a number of issues prompted cooperation by making even more salient the symbols that these societies shared. Building the navy was one issue; even more compelling, because it combined the symbols of imperial power and ethnic unity, was the Boer War.[62] But the greatest impetus to join forces came with the death of Bismarck in 1898 and the commemorative activities that soon followed. Bismarck was symbol supreme to every patriotic organization in Germany, the putative champion of the goals each promoted. As the campaign took hold to build monuments in his honor in the form of towers on hillsides throughout the country, the patriotic societies were in the vanguard. Coming together in the committees set up to raise the money, they quickly saw the merits of working together on a more lasting basis.[63] Thereafter the annual *Bismarckfeier* in April was the occasion for joint celebrations among the patriotic societies, as were other patriotic holidays, such as the anniversary of the founding of the Reich on 18 January and the *Sedantag* on 2 September.[64] In many communities cooperation among the patriotic societies was encouraged by public officials, who worked through these organizations in arranging local public festivals.[65]

Cooperation among the patriotic societies of a community took several forms. In many localities the societies simply agreed from time to time to hold joint meetings, which they promoted together. In other places they agreed on a mutually profitable division of labor and cemented it by becoming corporate members of one another or by delegating representatives to sit on one another's board of officers.[66] In Ratibor, for example, the survival of the Pan-German League was due in no small degree to its cooperation with the local chapter of the Eastern Marches Society; the Pan-Germans left the Polish problem to the Eastern Marches Society, while the two groups alternately sponsored big festivals.[67] In other communities patriotic societies offered one another reduced rates of admission to their meetings.[68] In Hamburg and Pritzwalk, and doubtless in many other places as well, members of several patriotic societies sat at the same *Stammtisch*.[69]

In a number of communities cooperation reached the point of being institutionalized. In Potsdam, Lübeck, Posen, Dresden, Barmen, Kassel, Berlin, Erfurt, Göttingen, and several other cities, the patriotic societies put on regular joint meetings called 'German Evenings' (*Deutsche Abende*).[70] To coordinate the arrangements, they established cover-organizations, usually called 'leagues of patriotic associations' (*Verbände vaterländischer Vereine*) and composed of representatives of the participating groups.[71] The situation in Barmen was typical. Five patriotic societies agreed to sponsor a series of five lectures, with each of the groups responsible for selecting the speaker and theme for one; members of each participating society purchased a series ticket at a reduced price.[72] Elsewhere patriotic societies arranged bazaars and summer outings together or set up common reading rooms. The institution of the 'German Evening' reached its height in Potsdam, where in 1897–8 the Pan-German League, Colonial Society, Eastern Marches Society, and the School and Language Associations met jointly thirty-four times.[73] Cooperation tended everywhere to have salutary effects on all the participating organizations. It made possible the staging of larger and more impressive rallies, which enhanced the public profiles of all the groups and, in most communities, added to all their memberships.[74]

Considerations of survival recommended the subduing of rivalries among patriotic societies and their forming loose cartels at the local level. At the national level the patriotic societies were unable to establish any analogous arrangement. Here cooperation remained limited to consultation from time to time among national officers, the sending of representatives to one another's national congresses, and the occasional undertaking of joint charitable activities.[75] Projects to institutionalize this cooperation, in the form of a single national congress, a common charitable fund, or a cartel to promote more regular communication, foundered repeatedly on the suspicions among the national leaders of all the societies and on their determination to sacrifice none of their own organization's identity.[76] Antagonisms among these societies were sometimes so intense at the national level that they inhibited cooperation at the local level. Relations between the Pan-German League and the Colonial Society, respectively the most radical and the most staid of the patriotic societies, were so strained at the national level that chapters of the Colonial Society refused, probably on orders from Berlin, on a number of occasions to participate with the League in the 'German Evenings'.[77]

It has become commonplace to interpret the Pan-German League's cooperation with other patriotic societies at the local level as the avenue through which it spread its influence into other, less radical organizations. This view, which both Franz Sontag and Eckart Kehr initially popularized, implies that the League was the most virulent of the patriotic societies – the most radical, active, and effective.[78] The League was assuredly the most radical, and in many (though by no means all) communities it was also the most active. But the popular view both overrates the effectiveness of the League's infiltration and underrates the commonality of views among the patriotic societies. The Pan-Germans did aspire to infiltrate and radicalize chapters of the more moderate groups, particularly in the Navy League and Colonial Society.[79] At times they succeeded, but just as often they failed, as the persistence of rivalries at the local level made other groups reluctant to adopt positions associated with the Pan-German League.[80]

None the less, the significance of these rivalries should not be overplayed either. The patriotic societies in Imperial Germany were involved in a common venture. Their cooperation in communities around the country revealed the extent to which they all invoked and participated in the same German-national public realm – a realm defined by consensus on a broad range of issues and a commitment to defending a common set of national symbols. The social affinities among the patriotic societies – the prominence in all of them of the academically educated – betrayed the extent to which this public realm was a cultural product of a specific social experience. The men who congregated in this realm were custodians of culture and authority. They were convinced that Germany faced a world of enemies, both at home and abroad, that struggle was the basic law of politics, and that upon Germany's success in this struggle depended not only the country's survival and security, but ultimately the integrity of its culture and the structure of domestic authority.

The point at which consensus ended in the German-national public realm was the question of monarchical authority. Here the Pan-German League stood, so to speak, with one foot outside the consensus as it argued that the protection of the national symbols could *in extremis* justify active opposition to the government, that the defense of authority could require challenging official authority. For most of the prewar period the League was isolated in this view. To anticipate, though, the German-national public underwent radicalization on the eve of the war, and the consensus broadened to accept the League's position. The radicalization was due not to the infiltration by the Pan-German League of the other patriotic societies, but rather to the alarming impact of outside events. The League's contribution was nevertheless crucial: it was to provide the program in which the radicalization of the German-national public could find expression. And the political force exerted in the wake of this radicalization was all the more compelling because the scope of the German-national public realm extended far beyond the patriotic societies.

Patriotic Societies and Other Voluntary Associations

The proliferation of voluntary associations in Germany at the turn of the century and the fact that many Germans were members of dozens of these organizations created a situation in which the potential for political mobilization was high. Every sector of German society bore witness to this potential to one degree or another. The mobilization of the socialist labor movement depended to a large degree on the multiplication and growth of all manner of voluntary associations.[81] This process had analogues in the mobilization of peasant associations by the Agrarian League and in the relationship between the Center Party and a network of Catholic voluntary associations, particularly the *Volksverein für das katholische Deutschland*.[82] The closest analogue within the urban Protestant middle class was the mobilication that took place in the name of the national cause, a process spearheaded by the patriotic societies.

Like political mobilization in other sectors of German society, the mobilization of patriotism in the Protestant middle class began in the personal networks that linked Germans in the private as well as the public sphere – as relatives, friends, parishioners, colleagues, and members of voluntary associations.[83] Chapters of the patriotic societies grew up around the personal networks of influential notables. In Mainz the pivotal figure was Heinrich Class, who as a lawyer had contacts among local judicial officials; his nephew's brother worked in the office of public construction and had acquaintances among the local architects. With Class's encouragement a small group of these men formed an antisemitic group, which during the naval agitation became the core of a new chapter of the Pan-German League.[84] The League's chapter in Hoyerswerda grew around a nucleus of men who worked in the local *Amtsgericht*. The chapter of the Eastern Marches Society in Elberfeld, like many chapters of the Colonial Society, consisted of the friends and colleagues of the man who served as chairman.[85] The Colonial Society's chapter in Wiesbaden orginated around a handful of men who frequented the same tavern.[86] Because they well recognized the dynamics of the situation, organizers in all the patriotic societies recommended recruitment among friends and acquaintances as the most effective technique.[87]

The personal networks of the men who were active in the patriotic societies extended into other voluntary organizations of all descriptions. These other organizations provided channels for broadening mobilization. Personal contacts could be exploited to produce new members for the patriotic societies, or, if interest were great enough, entire organizations could be drawn loosely into the orbit of the patriotic societies by means of participation at patriotic festivals, corporate affiliations, or subscriptions to patriotic newsletters.

Predictably, patriotic societies had the greatest success in mobilizing voluntary associations that catered to the same educated and wealthy stratum of the middle class. The range of these organizations was broad, from cultural societies like the *Deutscher Schillerbund* in Ulm or the *Allgemeiner Plattdeutsch-Verband* in Essen, to recreational organizations such as the *Deutsch–österreichischer Alpenverband* and assorted sport clubs.[88] They also included religious organizations, most significantly the *Evangelischer Bund*, whose anti-Catholicism and anti-socialism were spearheaded by the Protestant clergy in the Catholic west, where chapters of the organization were frequent participants at activities sponsored by patriotic societies.[89]

Patriotic societies were also successful in exploiting the ties of their members to social clubs, casinos, *Bürgervereine*, and, in the mercantile sector, to *Kaufmännische Vereine*. These contacts resulted in the frequent participation of these organizations alongside the patriotic societies in national festivals and their corporate affiliation with many chapters of patriotic societies.[90] In some locations winning over these associations was vital to the survival of patriotic societies. In the town of Kybnitz in Silesia, for example, the *Kaufmännischer Verein* provided the Colonial Society with the bulk of its membership, while the vitality of the Pan-German League in Mülheim was due in no small part to the support of the local *Kaufmännischer Verein*.[91]

The social center of gravity of the patriotic societies, and of the personal networks of their members, was located in the upper-middle class. The activities in which these societies participated also attracted a number of large organizations whose social complexion was more heavily lower-middle class. These organizations were not, by strict definition, patriotic societies, for they had specific primary goals and appealed to specific constituencies.[92] For a number of reasons, though, which related to their histories or social composition, extreme nationalism was a central characteristic of all of these organizations, and it drew them into the German-national public realm.

Theories that emphasize downward social mobility, or the threat of it, are more convincing in explaining the receptivity of lower-middle-class groups to radical nationalism than they are in accounting for the behavior of the better-established people who gathered in the patriotic societies. Nationalism served different functions for different social groups. Participation in the German-national public realm could, in other words, be motivated by a variety of social experiences. For small businessmen and white-collar employees, the defense of culture and authority was not so important in itself, for these people could not, as a rule, credibly claim to represent culture or authority in Imperial Germany; it was rather a symbol of the social distance that separated these people from the blue-collar labor force. In proportion as the objective measures of this distance (chiefly income and property-holding) diminished, and as the socialist labor movement publicly abandoned the national symbols, these same symbols became increasingly important in defining the social existence and in lending meaning to the social experience of large sectors of the urban *Mittelstand*.[93] The attempt to emphasize social distance from the manual labor force also encouraged these lower-middle-class groups to emulate the cultural practices of the upper-middle class, so that the values and traditions nurtured in the German-national public realm – the careful structuring of authority on the basis of education and wealth, the modes of sociability, and the station of women – were both familiar and agreeable to them.

The group to which these generalizations appear most clearly to apply was the army of clerks and other commercial employees who organized in the *Deutschnationaler Handlungs-Gehilfenverband*. The members of this organization, who on the eve of the war numbered more than 160,000, embraced radical nationalism in all of its manifestations, from antisemitism to extravagant demands for building the navy. The Commercial Employees' Union was a regular participant alongside the patriotic societies at 'German Evenings' and other national festivals.[94] It maintained cordial relations with all the patriotic societies, but it had the closest ties to the most radical of them.[95] At the national level, the union was long a corporate member of the Pan-German League, while local chapters of the union joined the League's chapters in Schandau, Tilsit, Würzburg, Giessen, Plauen, and many other communities.[96] Relations cooled only a little at the national level, when in 1910 Hans Bechly became chairman of the union and undertook to emphasize its non-partisanship by withdrawing its corporate membership in all other organizations, including the Pan-German League.[97]

It is more difficult to generalize about the social complexion and the motivations of the veterans' associations (*Kriegervereine*), which made up the most numerous sector of the German-national public.[98] The composition and political disposition of the many thousands of local veterans' associations varied from region to region. In the areas where the patriotic societies were strongest, lower-ranking civil servants, artisans and other small businessmen, and salaried employees constituted most of the membership – along with enough blue-collar workers that the civilian and military officials charged with supervising the *Kriegervereine* were preoccupied with using these organizations to combat socialism. This undertaking involved the effort to keep socialists out of them and to employ the associations – sometimes against the inclination of their own memberships – as agencies of popular education in patriotism. Large contingents from the *Kriegervereine*, with flags and often in uniform, joined the patriotic societies at officially sponsored national festivals. Participation in these events was often mandatory, but many local veterans' groups chose to associate with the patriotic societies on other occasions as well, perhaps because their leaders, in contrast with their rank and file, were usually wealthy and educated men who held reserve commissions and were active in patriotic societies. Because they were purportedly non-political, veterans' groups eschewed corporate membership in the Pan-German League and most other patriotic societies, in part too because they calculated that their advocacy of national causes like the navy would be more effective if it were independent.[99] They cooperated, in any event, with the patriotic societies in many other ways, as sponsors of 'German Evenings' and other festivals and as members of local leagues of patriotic associations.[100]

The presence at patriotic festivals of veterans' associations in full regalia was one of the main attractions of these events. Another was the gymnastic exhibitions that were regularly featured to symbolize the physical vitality of the nation. The prominence of these displays in the ritual of the festivals was but one of the reasons for the close ties between local gymnastic societies and other patriotic organizations. Like the veterans' associations, gymnastic societies drew the bulk of their membership from the lower-middle class (except in academic centers, where they also comprised large numbers of students), but they were led by local *Honoratioren* with ties to the patriotic societies. The receptivity of these organizations to ethnic nationalism owed much to the *grossdeutsch* tradition in which the German gymnastic movement had grown up in the middle of the nineteenth century. In the Imperial period, ethnic nationalism merged easily with anti-socialism, which became a prominent feature of the program of the gymnastic federation after the defection of working-class gymnasts to their own societies once the anti-socialist laws lapsed in 1890. Like the veterans' associations too, local gymnastic societies did not confine their cooperation with other patriotic organizations to officially sponsored festivals. In many communities they joined with patriotic societies in leagues of patriotic associations.[101]

The nether social reaches of the German-national public were inhabited by workers' associations of several descriptions. All had been founded with the encouragement of employers or the state and in opposition to the socialist unions; the symbols of patriotism, particularly the ideal of domestic unity (read: concord between capital and labor) accordingly served as alternatives to the socialist vision of class struggle.[102] Many of these workers belonged to company unions, whose participation in national festivals was due less to the patriotism of their members than to the fact that the men who employed and organized these workers belonged to patriotic societies.[103] In 1904, when the chapter of the Eastern Marches Society in the Silesian town of Radoschau held a festival to celebrate the tenth anniversary of its founding, the reporter pointed out, because it was unusual, that a large number of miners were among the participants. Their presence could 'be attributed to the fact that the higher mining officials also came', he remarked in all seriousness, 'for experience has shown that not even the best festive offerings exert as much attractive power on the people of our town as does the good example of the "higher circles"'.[104] No one offered a better example than Wilhelm Kollmann, the director of the *Bismarckhütte* near Kattowitz in Silesia, who led his workers into a local chapter of the Pan-German League just as he led them to the polls.[105]

Pressures similar in character, if not quite so direct, figured in the ties between patriotic societies and the Evangelical trade unions. The political and social philosophy of these organizations was largely that of the Conservative Party, and their leadership was usually in the hands of local notables who belonged to the patriotic societies. Particularly in parts of the country that were predominantly Catholic, Evangelical unions were prominent fixtures in the German-national public, as participants in festivals and meetings, and as corporate members of chapters of patriotic societies.[106]

One other category of workers' association was also linked to the German-national public realm. The so-called national or patriotic workers' associations resembled the Evangelical and company unions both in their docility and in the fact that their leadership was in the hands of notables, many of whom belonged to the patriotic societies. A large number of these national unions owed their founding to the work of the Imperial League against Social Democracy (*Reichsverband gegen die Sozialdemokratie*), an organization created in the aftermath of the federal elections of 1903, which saw alarming socialist gains.[107] The Imperial League was an interesting addition to the team of 'national organizations' in Imperial Germany. It resembled the patriotic societies in many respects. Its leadership was in the hands of the same kinds of people. In fact, its national chairman, Eduard von Liebert, was a prominent figure in both the Colonial Society and the Pan-German League, while its executive secretary was Albert Bovenschen, who before joining Liebert in the Imperial League had been executive secretary in the Eastern Marches Society. Like the patriotic societies, the Imperial League stood guard over one component of the system of national symbols, in this case the ideal of industrial peace or, more negatively, anti-socialism. However, after a desultory attempt, soon abandoned, to emulate the others in setting up an infrastructure of local chapters, the Imperial League turned its attention to two other spheres of activity, in which it concentrated until the war.[108] The first of these was a campaign, encouraged and financially supported by both industrial employers and the German government, to publish and distribute anti-socialist literature among workers.[109] The other sphere was establishing patriotic unions and coaxing them in to the German-national public, as participants in national festivals and corporate members of patriotic societies.[110]

Despite the encouragement of the state, employers, and the Imperial League against Social Democracy, workers did not make up a significant component of the German-national public. Veterans' associations and other organizations of a lower-middle-class complexion provided most of the members, but the tenor in this public realm was set by men of the wealthier and better-educated middle class who led the patriotic societies and controlled many of the other organizations. These men also dominated the organs through which the voice of the German-national public was transmitted directly into the arena of party politics.

The German-National Public Realm and the Structure of Party Politics

The multiplication of voluntary associations of all descriptions after 1890 was but one facet of the mobilization of new groups in Imperial German society; this mobilization produced as well a restructuring of the political parties. These began to shed their character as alliance of local committees of 'occasional politicians' – notables who were linked together more in loose personal networks than in formal political organizations and who joined forces only during electoral campaigns, when they worked to secure office for one of their own.[111] After 1890 the parties began to develop more ramified and permanent infrastructures geared to the demands of keeping mass constituencies loyal. Local, regional, and national offices, staffed by full-time political professionals, became the marks of party organization. So too did alliances between the parties and popular interest groups. Although nominally independent, these groups served as auxiliaries to the parties, for the issues around which they mobilized their own constituencies corresponded to positions articulated in the programs of the political parties. In establishing an extensive party bureaucracy and in using the free trade unions to mobilize working-class support, the Social Democrats provided the impetus for the transformation of party politics in other sectors of German society. In fear of losing their own constituencies to the Social Democrats, the Catholic Center and Conservative parties quickly responded, the one by working through the *Volksverein*, the other through the Agrarian League.

While none of the non-socialist parties entirely shed the character of *Honoratiorenpartei* before the war, the two liberal parties were the slowest in adjusting to the new forms of politics and in abandoning the traditional loose-knit structure of local committees of notables.[112] One reason was the liberals' deep-seated distaste for the kind of bureaucratic regimentation the new mass politics appeared to require. The National Liberals, however, had other compelling reasons to prefer the traditional system of associations of notables: the system continued to work, because it was particularly endemic to the constituency to which this party appealed. Political mobilization of this constituency was principally a question of forging alliances among local associations of notables. And in this process, the National Liberals found their own auxiliaries in the patriotic societies and other organizations that made up the German-national public.[113]

The patriotic societies professed to be non-partisan organizations, willing to support any of the 'reliably national parties'.[114] Their understanding of this description was restrictive, however, and in practice it excluded the Social Democrats, Progressives, and Catholics. The major exception to this pattern was the Navy League, which did make a concerted attempt to court Catholics, but this attempt was the result of official pressure, and the resistance it encountered among the activists nearly tore the organization apart. The other patriotic societies spared themselves the ordeal and maintained ties only to the parties that Bismarck had blessed with the designation of 'parties of order' – National Liberals, Free Conservatives, Conservatives, and Antisemites.

In those parts of the country in which more than one of these parties was strong, patriotic societies drew their leaders and members from all of them and encouraged the cooperation of these parties in a kind of local anti-socialist, anti-Catholic *Sammlung*. The role of mediator fell chiefly to the Eastern Marches Society, most of whose chapters lay in the east, where they attempted to mediate between local organizations of the National Liberal and Conservative parties.[115] Nowhere, however, did the patriotic societies play a more prominent political role than in Dresden. Here the league of patriotic associations simply changed its name during elections to the 'National Electoral Committee'.[116] Its component groups included, in addition to all the major patriotic societies, the local committees of the National Liberal, Conservative, and antisemitic Reform parties. Anti-socialism, reaffirmed annually at gigantic rallies to celebrate the founding of the Empire, was the cement that held this coalition together, and while the block failed to keep Dresden's three Reichstag seats out of the hands of the Social Democrats, it did retain control of the municipal government.

Because the patriotic societies were concentrated most heavily in central and western Germany, the party to which they were most closely tied was the National Liberal. In fact, the National Liberals, more than any other party, represented the political arm of the German-national public. The reasons for this state of affairs were several. The campaign to defend national symbols was the principal bond with which the party tried to hold together its increasingly diversified and fragmented constituency. Although the rhetoric of the campaign was intended to appeal to all sectors of German society, it consisted of politically charged code-words, which, when deciphered, implied specific positions on the salient issues of German party politics. And these positions corresponded in most instances to the program of the National Liberal Party.[117] National security, building a navy, colonial expansion, combating socialism, and protecting Germans abroad all raised touchy issues of constitutional jurisdiction, finance and taxation, the distribution of property, diplomacy, and civil rights. The priority National Liberals assigned to the defense of national symbols translated into specific political demands, which reflected a belief in the sanctity of property and order, in commercial and industrial enterprise as the principal source of the nation's strength and well-being, and in the obligation of a strong central government actively to encourage the nation's well-being.

The affinities between the patriotic societies and the National Liberal Party were more than programmatic. The local committees that were the backbone of the party drew their memberships from the same sectors of the populace as did the patriotic societies, and the party's activities observed the same cultural traditions.[118] In many instances the National Liberal committees were made up precisely of the same people who led chapters of the patriotic societies. In the twenty-five communities I selected for survey, the board of local officers of the National Liberal committee included one or more leaders of the patriotic societies in seventeen.[119] Extant membership lists for patriotic societies indicate that the overlap was even more extensive. In Stuttgart, three of the four men who sat on the board of officers of the National Liberal *Ortsverein* in 1907 were members of the Pan-German League. In Hamburg, the directing committee of the National Liberal *Reichstagswahlverein von 1884* included forty-seven men, of whom twenty-one belonged to the Pan-German League, Colonial Society, School Association, the Language Association, or the Navy League.

A large number of top party leaders and parliamentarians were members of patriotic societies too, but the cross-affiliations at the local level were a more telling index of the ties between the National Liberal Party and the patriotic societies.[120] National Liberal clubs and local associations of *Jungliberalen* were regular participants at national rallies of all kinds, and they frequently joined the chapters of one or more patriotic societies in sponsoring them.[121] The symbiotic relationship between the patriotic societies and the National Liberal Party was particularly evident at times of elections, when the same men, in their capacity as leaders of the National Liberal clubs, first selected candidates and then, in their capacity as leaders of patriotic societies, mobilized support for them.[122] In some communities the National Liberal electoral committees were virtually identical with one or more chapters of the patriotic societies. The conspicuous association of the National Liberals with patriotic activities added a further political dimension to these activities, just as it provided the party with its principal channel for mobilizing a large constituency. The National Liberal clubs were thus pivotal agencies in transferring the defense of middle-class values and traditions from the *Stammtisch* to the field of party politics.

The local committees of the National Liberal Party represented the most immediate political dimension of one of the central cultural phenomena in Imperial Germany. The German-national public realm was rooted in a formidable network of associations. At the center of this network stood the Pan-German League and the other patriotic societies. Linked to them by common members, corporate affiliations, and cooperation in local leagues of patriotic associations were the National Liberal committees, student organizations, upper-middle-class cultural and professional clubs, and a host of other organizations that were larger and had broader social appeal – chapters of the Commercial Employees' Union, veterans' associations, gymnastic societies, and a few workers' organizations. The boundaries of this network of associations were set by class, confession, and region, and they worked to exclude Catholics, peasants, and workers with socialist leanings.

It is difficult to estimate the numerical extent of this public realm, principally because of multiple memberships. Over a hundred organizations, with a total membership in excess of 130,000, were corporately affiliated with the Pan-German League in 1905, although the Commercial Employees' Union accounted for most of these members.[123] The Navy League, far and away the largest of the patriotic societies, had a membership of well over 300,000 in 1913, and the organizations that were corporately affiliated with it numbered just under 800,000.[124] On the eve of the war there were more than 32,000 separate veterans' associations, with close to 3 million members.[125]

These figures must be interpreted with care. Aside from the problem of multiple memberships, it is difficult to judge what significance to assign to the corporate membership of one association in another, beyond some general sympathy in one for the goals of the other. The most that can be said is that the programs of the patriotic societies found resonance in a broad, interconnected network of associations and that the people potentially available for mobilization in the name of these programs probably numbered in the hundreds of thousands.[126]

The significance of this conclusion is more apparent at the local level. In communities throughout the land, although particularly in the central and western regions, a large block of people, known variously as the 'German-national movement', 'the national middle class', or the 'German movement' – the phenomenon designated in this study as the German-national public – was organized in a network of associations, which invoked the primacy of national symbols in politics.[127] In Magdeburg, according to contemporary estimates, seventeen such associations had a total membership of about 4,100 people; in Würzburg, eighty-eight such associations were active, many of them student groups.[128] In Essen these associations could mobilize some 2,000 people, while in Dresden the patriotic societies and their friends counted about 25,000.[129] The importance of the phenomenon, however, lay in more than the numbers. The block of associations that made up the German-national public realm included the most respected and influential members of countless German communities – leading public officials, professionals, and businessmen, men who controlled the press, academically trained teachers who shaped coming generations of the country's elites, and the academic students who were being so shaped.

Several other features of this phenomenon deserve emphasis. In cities and towns throughout Germany these associations constituted a milieu in which large numbers of Germans pursued their social and cultural needs in a manner that emphasized the primacy of national symbols in politics. While the patriotic societies exploited the sociability of the upper-middle class, the *Kriegervereine* politicized the *Stammtisch* of the lower-middle class. Organizations near the periphery of this associational network politicized the use of leisure in other ways – in gymnastic societies, in swimming, bicycle, boating, and assorted other kinds of sport clubs, and in youth groups.[130]

The values and attitudes cultivated in this public realm were, for the most part, those of the dominant culture in Imperial Germany. Many of the associations that populated the German-national public – particularly the *Kriegervereine*, the Navy League, and the Eastern Marches Society – were subjected to the systematic influence of official agencies, which sought consciously to use these organizations as institutions for the political socialization of their members (and their members' children).[131] It is essential, however, to recognize, as did the men who led the patriotic organizations, that their milieu was a fairly discrete phenomenon, that the German-national public realm had limits.[132] This realm was in the last analysis devoted to appropriating the national symbols in defense of Protestant, urban, middle-class traditions and values; it did so in part by denying other sectors of German society, notably Catholics and socialist workers, access to these symbols in defense of their own traditions and values. It bears emphasis that in Imperial Germany several cultural traditions survived, that they were not well integrated, and that the German-national public supported but one of them.

It also bears emphasis that the radical nationalism that emerged out of this milieu was in potential conflict with dominant values officially encouraged. The play of activism in many of the organizations that made up the German-national public derived from the mobilization of anxieties not easily controlled, even with all the channels available to the government, should the government itself, for one reason or another, antagonize the patriotic sentiment in this realm.

Many political events thus intruded with a special force into the German-national public, a realm that was highly sensitive to the symbolic implications of political issues. Whether they concerned foreign or domestic themes, events or issues that appeared in any way to threaten the national symbols had far-flung cultural and psychological ramifications; they threatened ultimately a system of values, a way of life, and the self-esteem of the people who participated in this realm. The forces at work in the German-national public were emotionally volatile; they were also politically potent, for the organizational network that made up this realm offered the means for mobilizing a broad coalition in defense of threatened symbols.

Against this backdrop, the narrative history of the Pan-German League can now resume. By the turn of the century the League had already become the leading proponent of the view that defending the national symbols could demand challenging the government's authority to tend these symbols. Once political events and issues lent currency to the League's view, the organization emerged in the vanguard of a successful campaign to mobilize the German-national public in opposition to the government. But first, the Pan-German League nearly collapsed.

Notes

1 Schmitt, p. 30.
2 ZStAP, DKG 719, Abt. Freienwalde to DKG, 19.11.94; *Der Völker-Friede*, vol. 13 (1912), p. 30.
3 ZStAM, Rep. 195 Nr. 67, Mahr to DOV, Naumberg, 28.2.98. Marburg, a city of comparable size to Naumburg, boasted 292 *Vereine* in 1913: Rudy Koshar, 'Two "Nazisms": the social context of Nazi mobilization in Marburg and Tübingen,' *Social History*, vol. 7 (1982), p. 32.
4 ZStAP, ADV 188, Hasse to Dehn, Leipzig, 17.3.04; cf. Renate Mayntz, *Soziale Schichtung und sozialer Wandel in einer Industriegemeinde: Eine soziologische Untersuchung der Stadt Euskirchen* (Stuttgart, 1958), p. 241; Schmitt, p. 94; Schafer, pp. 150–4.
5 Franz Klein, *Das Organisationswesen der Gegenwart: Ein Grundriss* (Berlin, 1913); Schmitt, p. 63; Freudenthal, p. 446; Sheehan, *Liberalism*, p. 249. For the broader context see Thomas Nipperdey, 'Verein als soziale Struktur in Deutschland im späten 18. Jahrhundert und frühen 19. Jahrhundert', in Hartmut Boockmann *et al.*, *Geschichtswissenschaft und Vereinswesen im 19. Jahrhundert: Beiträge zur Geschichte historischer Forschung in Deutschland* (Göttingen, 1972), pp. 1–44.
6 Freudenthal, pp. 20–6.
7 Guenther Roth, *The Social Democrats in Imperial Germany: A Study of Working-Class Isolation and National Integration* (Totowa, NJ, 1963), esp. pp. 159–63, 221–32; cf. Hans Staudinger, *Individuum und Gemeinschaft in der Kulturorganisation des Vereins* (Jena, 1913), esp. pp. 97–8; Urner, p. 519.
8 Lepsius, pp. 371–93.
9 StdA Wuppertal, P III 79, DFV Ogr. Barmen to Evers, 13.3.05; ZStAP, ADV 83, GFA, Berlin, 17–18.2.12 (Reismann-Grone); cf. ADV 194, Weber to Bassler, Bochum, 21.7.10; Henning, *Bildungsbürgertum*, pp. 174, 182–3, 209, 303, 310, 359, 423, 491; Sheehan, *Liberalism*, pp. 151–2.
10 The most influential statement of this view has been Fritz Stern, 'The political consequences of the unpolitical German', most recently, although the author has now confessed some misgivings about it, in *The Failure of Illiberalism: Essays on the Political Culture of Modern Germany* (New York, 1972), pp. 3–25; see also Wertheimer, p. 112; Mosse, *Nationalization*, pp. 91–2; Stern, *Hitler*, p. 191. For a more recent commentary see Tony Judt, 'A clown in regal purple: social history and the historians', *History Workshop*, no. 7 (Spring 1979), pp. 69–94.
11 Karl H. Pähler, 'Verein und Sozialstruktur: Versuch einer soziologischen Analyse', *Archiv fur Rechts- und Sozialphilosophie*, vol. 42 (1956), p. 201.
12 See ADB (1907), 10–11; Petersen, p. 92; Schultheiss, *Vereinswesen*, pp. 80–1; Kröll, p. 77.

13 See Anthony Obershall, *Social Conflicts and Social Movements* (Englewood Cliffs, NJ, 1973), esp. pp. 124–5.

14 Quoted in Pähler, pp. 197–98.

15 William Sheridan Allen, *The Nazi Seizure of Power: The Experience of a Single German Town, 1930–1935* (Chicago, 1965), pp. 209–26.

16 Kehr, *Schlachtflottenbau*, p. 106; cf. Meyer, 'Propaganda', p. 26.

17 ADB (1897), 245; ADB (1904), 282; Whiteside, pp. 257–9. The visit of Boer generals to Berlin in 1902 occasioned some anxiety among the Pan-German leaders, because as Paul Samassa warned, 'in a city of a million inhabitants there is a mob around, which can all too easily take over the street': ADB (1902), 382.

18 For catalogues see Philipp Stauff, *Das deutsche Wehrbuch* (Wittenberg, 1912); Schultheiss, *Vereinswesen*.

19 DKZ (1900), 72.

20 OM (1905), 76.

21 ZASV (1912), 122.

22 LA Koblenz, Obpr. Nr. 9529, DFV Kreisgeschäftasstelle Essen, Tätigkeitsbericht, Essen, 24.2.10.

23 *Das Deutschtum im Ausland* (March 1910), 146.

24 ZStAM, Rep. 195 Nr. 18, Bd. 1, Ratschläge für die Schlesischen Vertrauensmänner des DOV, Breslau 1905; ZStAP, DKG 101, RS, Herrenabende (March 1902); StA Münster, Kreis Hattingen LRA 216, Allerlei Fingerzeige für Flottenvereins-Abende (Berlin, 1903); cf. Luther, *Deutsche Volksabende*.

25 See Eley, *Reshaping*, pp. 128–33.

26 Galos, p. 74; Eley, *Reshaping*, p. 127; Bade, pp. 308–9; cf. Sheehan, *Liberalism*, p. 246.

27 ZStAP, DKG 509, Hartrek to Abt. Trier, Trier, 7.2.07; DKG 719, Abt. Halberstadt to DKG, Halberstadt, 1.12.94; ZStAM, Rep. 195 Nr. 53, Berndt to DOV, Hamm, 31.10.00.

28 I have dealt with this problem in more detail in 'Patriotic societies and German foreign policy'.

29 ADB (1894), 152; ADB (1898), 185; ADB (1901), 412.

30 ZStAP, ADV 42, GFA, Berlin, 20.2.04; ADB (1895), 48; ADB (1900), 242; ADB (1909), 326.

31 ZStAP, ADV 86, GFA, Erfurt, 6.9.12; ADV 192, Hentig to Class, Berlin, 5.3.08; ADV 193, Geiser to Class, Berlin, n.d. [early 1909]; Class, *Strom*, pp. 52, 273; ADB (1910), 317.

32 ZStAM, Rep. 195 Nr. 31, Bovenschen to Schnur, Berlin, 11.2.02.

33 ZStAM, Rep. 195 Nr. 2, Hauptvorstandssitzung, 15.2.06; ADB (1898), 209; ADB (1899), 86–8, 201; cf. ADB (1899), 301–2.

34 ZStAM, Rep. 195 Nr. 90, Eidemann to Binzer, Berlin, 16.12.94; ZStAP, ADV 187, Hasse to Lehmann, Leipzig, 20.11.03.

35 The much smaller Association for North Schleswig limited its activities to the north and was no rival to the League. Relations between the two organizations were close: the two agreed on all matters of policy with respect to the Danish problem, and the Association was a corporate member of the League: see ADB (1894), 70–1.

36 The main culprit was the *Südwestafrikanische Siedlungsgesellschaft*, of which the Colonial Society was a major shareholder. By promoting land speculation, the company systematically drove up the price of land given to it by the government for 'development'; it then sold the land at inflated prices to settlers. See ADB (1904), 199; ADB (1907), 157.

37 ADB (1903), 249–50.

38 ZStAP, ADV 7, Vorstandssitzung, Eisenach, 25.5.02; ADB (1902), 206; ADB (1904), 273–4; Class, *Strom*, p. 85.

39 Reismann-Grone, p. 1.

40 See ADB (1898), 137–8; ADB (1904), 199.

41 ADB (1900), 189–90; ADB (1904), 109; ADB (1905), 55–7; ADB (1909), 254; ADB (1912), 19–21.

42 ZStAP, ADV 43, GFA, Gotha, 9–10.4.04; ADV 44, GFA, Lübeck, 27.5.04; ADV 59, Hasse to Itzenplitz, Leipzig, 20.4.07; ADV 198, Class to Niessner, 17.2.14; cf ADB (1908), 163.

43 ZStAP, ADV 195, Dieckmann to Class, Osnabrück, 12.4.11; ADB (1899), 300–31; ADB (1906), 77–8; ADB (1909), 430–2.

44 ZStAP, DKG 719, Abt., Bamberg to DKG, Bamberg, 21.11.94.

45 For examples: ZStAM, Rep. 195 Nr. 33, Schlegtendahl to DOV, Barmen, 22.10.98; Rep. 195 Nr. 49, Lucanus to Bovenschen, Gotha, 25.1.02; ZStAP, DKG 719, Abt. Bromberg to DKG, 28.11.94; Abt. Lübeck to DKG, 27.11.94; ADB (1900), 495.

46 ZStAM, Rep. 195 Nr. 44, Flex to DOV, Eisenach, 26.4.99; Rep. 195 Nr. 64, Schaumann to DOV, Lübeck, 13.11.06; ZStAP, ADV 195, Class RS, Mainz, 12.8.11; DKG 179, Abt. Löbau to DKG, 29.11.94; cf. ADB (1909), 254.

47 ZStAP, ADV 185, Section Mainz des DFV to ADV Ogr. Mainz, 20.5.01; DKG 653, Hoffmann DS, betreffend einen weiteren Ausbau der Organisation der DKG, 8.10.01.

48 ZStAM, Rep. 195 Nr. 48, Frohwein to DOV, Gleiwitz, 8.12.03; Rep. 195 Nr. 31, Reichardt to Bovenschen, Annaberg, 19.1.02; Rep. 195 Nr. 32, Dammholz to Bovenschen, Angermünde, 13.9.00; ZStAP, ADV 7, Vostandsstizung, 25.5.02; ADV 188, Hasse to Buchholtz, Leipzig, 1.3.04; Geiser to Hasse, Berlin, 23.5.04.

49 StA Münster, Kreis Hattingen, LRA 216, Allerlei Fingerzeige für Flottenvereins-Abende (Berlin, 1903); ZStAP, DKG 719, Abt. Hattingen to DKG, 1.12.94.

50 White, pp. 42–4; cf. Günther Kriegbaum, *Die parlamentarische Tätigkeit des Freiherrn C. W. Heyl zu Herrnsheim* (Meisenheim, 1962).

51 ZStAM, Rep. 195 Nr. 116, Schoultz Reisebericht (Köln), 31.5.14; cf. Rep. 195 Nr. 44, Bunge to DOV, Elberfeld, 28.3.00.

52 ZStAP, ADV 188, Geiser to Hasse, Berlin, 23.5.04.

53 ZStAP, DKG 719, Abt. Stuttgart to DKG, 22.11.94.

54 ZStAP, DKG 719, Abt. Greifswald to DKG, 22.11.94.

55 ZStAM, Rep. 195 Nr. 71, Hengesbach to Bovenschen, Paderborn, 2.3.02; ZStAP, ADV 188, Geiser to Hasse, 29.3.04.

56 Galos, p. 174.

57 This is, in any event, a rough figure, owing to the limited size of the sample of leaders from the School Association, and to the difficulty of identifying the same person in more than one society. Of the 2,093 leaders, 120 appear clearly to have been officers in more than one patriotic society, although not necessarily simultaneously. cf. ADB (1907), 5–6; ADB (1911), 47; Werner, p. 94. The situation in Munich suggests the likely impact of more complete statistics from the School Association. In the period 1895–8 eleven of the twenty-four men who served on the local board of officers were also officers of other patriotic societies in Munich: BA, ZSg 1, 142/3, VDA, Ogr. Munich, Jahresberichte 1895–8.

58 The statistical calculations necessary to arrive at this figure are a headache and involve the so-called 'inclusion/exclusion principle', which accounts for all the possible combinations of multiple memberships. I wish to thank Paul Speckman, statistician and colleague, for his help.

59 ZStAP, ADV 197, Baumann to Class, Bonn, 13.5.13; DKZ (1913), 862–3; ADB (1904), 210–12.

60 ZStAP, ADV 187, Hasse to Schmidt, Leipzig, 30.11.03.

61 e.g. ADB (1899), 31, 98.

62 ADB (1899), 107, 397–8; ADB (1900), 52; cf. Kröll, p. 75.

63 ADB (1899), 30–1, 51, 151; ADB (1900), 113, 485; ADB (1901), 97; ADB (1902), 222; cf. Nipperdey, 'Nationalidee und Nationaldenkmal', pp. 166–70.

64 StA Hamburg, A 440/27, Kap. 1, Bismarck-Kommers . . . 1.4.02; ADB (1904), 123–4, 153–4; ADB (1905), 18, 125, 166; ADB (1911), 159–60, 174.

65 GStA Dahlem, Rep. 6B Nr. 81, Stempel Aufzeichnung . . . Meseritz, 12.3.00; ADB (1897), 201–3; ADB (1900), 270–1; cf. Mosse, *Nationalization*, pp. 91–3.

66 e.g. OM (1912), 62; ADB (1904), 375.

67 ZStAP, ADV 188, Geiser to Hasse, 29.3.04.

68 ADB (1899), 358.

69 ADB (1899), 446; ADB (1904), 269–70.

70 ADB (1904), 210–12.

71 ZStAM, Rep. 195 Nr. 44, Satzungen des Deutschen Verbandes in Erfurt; cf. ADB (1904), 75; ADB (1905), 51.

72 ADB (1910), 183; cf. ADB (1900), 7–8, 454; ADB (1910), 15; ZASV (1914), 58–9.
73 ADB (1898), 219; ADB (1907), 346–7; cf. OM (1900), 7–8.
74 ADB (1900), 22; ADB (1901), 60; ADB (1908), 430–1.
75 e.g. ZStAM, Rep. 195 Nr. 228, Tiedemann DS, Seeheim, 12.8.12; ZStAP, ADV 3, Hasse to DKG, Berlin, 18.4.94; ADV 187, Arbeitsplan für das Büchereiwesen [December 1903].
76 ZStAM, Rep. 195 Nr. 228, Tiedemann to Ilges, Seeheim, 30.7.11; ZStAP, ADV 48, GFA, Göttingen, 15.4.05; ADV 78, GFA, Berlin, 28.1.11; ADV 188, Hasse RS, 24.3.04; UB Freiburg, NL Schemann IV A, Zwecke und Ziele der 'Deutschen Kanzlei'.
77 ADB (1911), 223; ADB (1912), 110–11; cf. ADB (1905), 102.
78 Alter, p. 17; cf. O'Donnell, p. 312; Guratzsch, pp. 60–1.
79 ZStAP, ADV 78, GFA, Berlin, 28.1.11; Reismann-Grone to Class, Essen, 28.12.10; ADV 188, Geiser to Hasse, Berlin, 22.3.04; ADB 197, Hofmeister to Class, Köln, 9.2.10.
80 ZStAM, Rep. 195 Nr. 60, Paul Steller, 'Alldeutsche Grosstaten', Köln, 14.2.14; DKZ (1900), 91.
81 See, in addition to Roth, Ursula Mittmann, *Fraktion und Partei: Eiin Vergleich von Zentrum und Sozialdemokratie im Kaiserreich* (Düsseldorf, 1976), pp. 140–206.
82 ibid., Puhle, *Agrarische Interessenpolitik*, esp. pp. 50–5, 143–55; David Blackbourn, *Class, Religion and Local Politics in Wilhelmine Germany: The Centre Party in Württemberg before 1914* (New Haven, Conn. and London, 1980), esp. pp. 100–19; Horstwalter Heitzer *Der Volksverein für das katholische Deutschland 1890–1918* (Mainz, 1979); Weber, *Spahn*, p. 181.
83 See Jeremy Boissevain, *Friends of My Friends: Networks, Manipulators and Coalitions* (Oxford, 1974); Jeremy Boissevain and J. Clyde Mitchell (eds), *Network Analysis: Studies in Human Interaction* (The Hague, 1973).
84 Class, *Strom*, pp. 30–4, 233.
85 ZStAM, Rep. 195 Nr. 44, Bunge to DOV, Elberfeld, 28.3.00; ZStAP, DKG 101, Aeusserung der Abt. Gnesen … 14.5.02; DKG 719, Abt. Hattingen to DKG, 1.12.94; Abt. Halberstadt to DKG, 1.12.94; cf. ADB (1898), 147–8.
86 ZStAP, DKG 719, Abt. Wiesbaden to DKG, 9.12.94.
87 e.g. ZASV (1908), 21; DKZ (1913), 862–3.
88 ADB (1904), 406; ADB (1910), 237–8; ADB (1911), 255; ADB (1912), 466.
89 ADB (1898), 278–9; ADB (1899), 238; ADB (1905), 84, 384; cf. Methfessel, p. 788.
90 ZStAP, DKG 730, Korporative Mitglieder, 1910 ff.
91 ZStAP, DKG 719, Abt. Kybnitz to DKG, 19.11.94; ADB (1903), 142; cf. ADB (1899), 107, 214; ADB (1900), 52; ADB (1904), 119; ADB (1905), 154; ADB (1906), 138; ADB (1914), 15.
92 See Staudinger, pp. 111–12, 120.
93 See especially Emil Lederer, *Die Privatangestellten in der modernen Wirtschaftsordnung* (Tübingen, 1912); Jürgen Kocka, 'The First World War and the "Mittelstand": German artisans and white-collar workers', JCH, vol. 8 (January 1973), pp. 101–24; Kocka, 'Zur Problematik der deutschen Angestellten 1914–1933', in Hans Mommsen *et al.* (eds), *Industrielles System und politische Entwicklung in der Weimarer Republik* (Düsseldorf, 1974), pp. 792–811; Kocka, *Unternehmensverwaltung*, esp. pp. 521–2; Arno J. Mayer, 'The lower middle class as a historical problem', JMH, vol. 47 (1975), pp. 4–36; and the strictures of David Blackbourn, 'The *Mittelstand* in German society and politics'.
94 ZStAM, Rep. 195 Nr. 47, Einladung des 'V.v.V.' [Verband vaterländischer Vereine], Cassel, November 1912; ZStAP, DKG 248, DHV to DKG Flottenkomitee, Hamburg, 29.12.99; ADB (1906), 285.
95 ADB (1899), 314; ADB (1900), 175; ADB (1901), 134; ADB (1908), 55–6.
96 ADB (1902), 251; ADB (1904), 498; ADB (1907), 202, 363; ADB (1912), 47; ADB (1914), 211.
97 ZStAP, ADV 195, Ilges to Class, Cologne, 17.8.11; Hamel, p. 119.
98 See Klaus Saul, 'Der "Deutsche Kriegerbund": Zur innenpolitischen Funktion eines "nationalen" Verbandes im kaiserlichen Deutschland', MGM, no. 2 (1969), pp. 95–159; Hansjoachim Henning, 'Kriegervereine in den preussischen Westprovinzen: Ein Beitrag zur preussischen Innenpolitik zwischen 1860 und 1914', *Rheinische Vierteljahrsblätter*, vol. 32 (1968), pp. 430–75.

99 BAMA, RM 3/v Nr. 9909, Spitz DS, Stellung der Kriegervereine zum DFV, February 1905.
100 ZStAP, DKG 245, Zeitschel to DKG, 25.3.98; DKZ (1900), 274; ADB (1900), 146; ADB (1901), 536; ADB (1904), 37, 119; ADB (1908), 430–1.
101 ZStAM, Rep. 195 Nr. 128, Verband nationaler Vereine von Gross-Berlin, Einladung ... ; ZStAP, ADV 188, Geiser to Hasse, 29.3.04 (Görlitz); ADB (1900), 64; ADB (1904), 153–4; ADB (1906), 224, 259.
102 Klaus Mattheier, *Die Gelben: Nationale Arbeiter zwischen Wirtschaftsfrieden und Streik* (Düsseldorf, 1973).
103 ZStAM, Rep, 195 Nr. 61, Bd. 1, Ogr, Königshütte, Jahresbericht pro 1903; ADB (1901), 332; ADB (1905), 66; ADB (1908), 396; cf. Schmitt, p. 31.
104 OM (1904), 114.
105 ADB (1895), 23.
106 HA/GHH 300127/8, Sperling to Woltmann, Bochum, 8.4.13; ADB (1898), 278–9; ADB (1899), 405; ADB (1900), 52; ADB (1906), 138.
107 Dieter Fricke, 'Der Reichsverband gegen die Sozialdemokratie von seiner Gründung bis zu den Reichstagswahlen von 1907', ZfG, vol. 7 (1959), pp. 237–80; Fricke, 'Reichsverband gegen die Sozialdemokratie (RgS) 1904–1918', in Fricke, *Handbuch*, Vol. 2, pp. 620–30; Mattheier, 'Drei Führungsorganisationen', pp. 246–58; Saul, *Staat, Industrie, Arbeiterbewegung*, pp. 115–32; Stegmann, *Erben*, pp. 47–50.
108 LA Schleswig, LRA Oldenburg Nr. 608, Liebert to Springer, 22.2.04; StA Hannover, LRA Zellerfeld Nr. 950, RgS, Verzeichnis der Mitglieder... 18.3.10; Saul, *Staat, Industrie und Arbeiterberegung*, p. 328.
109 ZStAP, RK 1395/2, *passim*.
110 UB Freiberg, NL Schemann II D, Nationaler Reichswahlverband (RgS, Körperschaftliche Mitglieder, April 1905); ZStAP, DKG 1092, Sartorius to DKG, 29.4.13; cf. ADB (1898), 9; ADB (1905), 210; ADB (1909), 105–6.
111 See Nipperdey, *Organisation*, esp. pp. 42–6, 75; Nipperdey, 'Organisation', p. 602; cf. Weber, 'Politics as vocation', pp. 83, 86.
112 Nipperdey, *Organisation*, pp. 86, 90, 94; Nipperdey, 'Organisation', pp. 559–60; Sheehan, *Liberalism*, pp. 151–2; Eley, *Reshaping*, pp. 19–40; cf. Blackbourn, *Class*, p. 114.
113 O'Donnell, *passim*.
114 ZStAP, ADV 534, Philipp Bonhard, DS betreffend die innenpolitische Tätigkeit des ADV, p. 9.
115 O'Donnell, p. 342; Galos, pp. 103–5.
116 ADB (1903), 191; ADB (1904), 100; ADB (1905), 18; ADB (1906), 25; ADB (1907), 131–2; KRgS (5.1.07), 3.
117 O'Donnell, p. 311; Sheehan, *Liberalism*, p. 276.
118 Nipperdey, *Organisation*, pp. 103–5; Sheehan, *Liberalism*; cf. Theodor Heuss, *Vorspiele des Lebens: Jugenderinnerungen* (Tübingen, 1953), pp. 280–1.
119 Information on the National Liberal committees was drawn from *Organisations-Handbuch der Nationalliberalen Partei des Deutschen Reiches* (Berlin, 1907); H. Kalkoff, *Organisationshandbuch der Nationalliberalen Partei des Deutschen Reiches 1912/13* (Berlin, 1912).
120 O'Donnell, pp. 313, 326; Bonhard, pp. 210–11.
121 For example: ADB (1901), 547 (Worms); ADB (1903), 73 (Crefeld); ADB (1906), 138 (Moenchen-Gladbach), 155 (Coblence); ADB (1908), 163 (Kempten), 446–7 (Heppenheim); ADB (1909), 86 (Bonn).
122 ZStAM, Rep. 195 Nr. 53, Berndt to DOV, Hamm, 31.10.00; ADB (1903), 330–1; ADB (1904), 81; ADB (1905), 408; ADB (1907), 47; ADB (1912), 79; ADB (1913), 372.
123 ZStAP, ADV 241, Uebersicht über Mitgliederzahl und Beitragsleistung der dem ADV körperschaftlich beigetretene Vereine; ADB (1906), 208.
124 Wulf, p. 432.
125 Winkel, p. 297.
126 See Alter, p. 17; O'Donnell, p. 311.
127 Allgemeines Staatsarchiv, Munich, MInn 73551, *Augsburger Postzeitung*, 24.2.00; Schieder, p. 77; cf. Leibenguth, p. 259; Rudolf Rüsten (ed.), *Was tut not? Ein Führer durch die gesamte Literatur der Deutschbewegung* (Leipzig, 1914).

128   ADB (1908), 38; ADB (1913), 353.
129   ADB (1905), 18; ADB (1914), 251.
130   ADB (1900), 217; ADB (1903), 295; cf. Werner Bethge, 'Bund Jungdeutschland (BJD) 1911–1933', in Fricke, *Handbuch*, Vol. 1, pp. 162–5; Klaus Saul, 'Der Kampf um die Jugend zwischen Volksschule und Kaserne: Ein Beitrag zur "Jugendpflege" im Wilhelminischen Reich 1890–1914', MGM, no. 1 (1971), pp. 97–143; cf. ADB (1911), 423–4.
131   Wehler, *Kaiserreich*, esp. pp. 164–5.
132   ZStAP, DKG 330, Karl A. Kuhn RS, Das Doppelspiel des Generals A. Keim; ADV 188, Liebert to Hasse, Charlottenburg, 17.10.04; ADV 192, Stössel to Class, Potsdam, 19.1.08; ADV 193, Gerhard to Class, Berlin, 2.2.09.

10   In the Wilderness

Although it was not entirely clear at the time, the celebrated encounter between Ernst Hasse and Bernhard von Bülow in the Reichstag late in 1900 signalled a turning point in the fortunes of the Pan-German League. The humiliated Hasse could take heart in the many letters of consolation and support which poured in to him from members of the League, who were themselves outraged at having been derided publicly as *Bierbankpolitiker*. One of these letters, though, from Ludwig Kuhlenbeck, offered a more sober thought. Kuhlenbeck wrote of an impending 'ordeal by fire', a 'bitter struggle which is going to lead to many an altercation within the League' and which would 'separate the chaff from the grain'.[1]

Kuhlenbeck's predictions were accurate. In the next years the Pan-German League plunged into its gravest crisis in the prewar period. Its relations with the government deteriorated to the point of an open and definitive break, and this trend raised anew ideological problems concerning the League's mission and its relationship to official authority. The deterioration of the League's relations with the government also had more immediate impact, for it brought about a large-scale exodus of members and a financial crisis that pushed the League to the brink of bankruptcy. In an atmosphere of frustration, bitterness, and demoralization, the leaders of the League resolved the crisis. The ideological and financial solutions upon which they seized transformed the organization into a more formidable and – in view of subsequent German history – a more ominous force in German politics in the years just prior to the war.

The Growing Rift with the Government

The membership of the Pan-German League reached a peak in 1901 at about 23,000, but a decline set in rapidly thereafter. By the end of 1903 membership was down nearly 4,000 (see Appendix, Figure 10.1). The principal cause of the decline was the abatement of popular protests over the Boer War, which came to an end in 1902. Continuing official and semi-official ridicule of the League, for which Bülow had set the tone, did nothing to decelerate the decline; it also enraged the League's leaders, who in fact blamed the organization's growing misfortunes in the first instance on what one embittered writer called the government's campaign 'systematically to discredit and ruin our League'.[2]

The year 1903 brought an event scarcely less discouraging than the end of the Boer War. Among the alternatives the League had considered to compensate for its diminished popular influence was to place its leading members into the Reichstag, where they could join forces with Hasse in future debates with the chancellor. During the elections to the Reichstag in 1903 the League exploited its ties to electoral committees of the 'national parties' to secure the nomination of most of its inner circle to Reichstag seats. Beside Hasse, who ran for reelection in his district in Leipzig, Class was the joint candidate of the National Liberals and the Agrarian League in the Hessian district of Bingen-Alzey; Karl Klingemann, a pastor and leader of the chapter in Essen, ran in his home city; Richard Graf du Moulin-Eckart, an officer of the chapter in Munich, ran in Erlangen-Fürth; and Fritz Bley, one of the organization's leading publicists, was a candidate in Kreuznach-Simmern. In Dresden, the League's chapter threw its support behind the 'national candidates' (all of whom belonged to the League) in all three of the city's electoral districts.

In view of the efforts the League expended during the elections of 1903, the results could not have been more depressing.[3] Not only did the Social Democrats emerge dramatically as the winners, picking up twenty-five seats, but every one of the men who campaigned with strong ties to the Pan-German League lost – including Hasse who, like all the Pan-Germans running in Dresden, fell to a socialist.[4] Hasse's loss was the most painful, for it not only deprived the League's leader of a parliamentary forum, but it revealed the extent to which association with the League had become a political liability. In a bitter campaign, Hasse had had to contend anew with charges that the League's quixotic program was a threat to a well-conceived foreign policy. These charges came not only from the socialists, but from the National Liberal *Nationale Zeitung* and the left-liberal who drained away much of Hasse's earlier support.[5]

The results of the elections weighed heavily as the League attempted, at its annual convention in Plauen in September 1903, to draw the programmatic consequences of its misfortune. Even before the elections, in fact, the executive committee had announced that the convention in Plauen would be devoted to an analysis of national developments since the turn of the century and an attempt to place them into broader perspective. Suitable speakers, the committee announced, were being sought.[6]

It was a measure of the alarm in the League's leading circles that the man assigned to present this analysis was Heinrich Class. Though only 35 years old, Class had by 1903 emerged as heir-apparent to Hasse, as well as the spokesman of the League's most radical faction, a group which had responded to the government's attacks with growing extravagance in its own demands and growing bitterness in its opposition to official policies. The son of a high-ranking Hessian judiciary official, Class had trained for a career in law, first in Berlin, where he, like many others of his generation, fell under the spell of Treitschke, and then in Giessen, where he put into practical application the antisemitism he had learned from Treitschke, as he participated in the campaigns of Otto Boeckel among the Hessian peasants. Class then settled in Mainz as an independent attorney. He also became active in an antisemitic society and the German Colonial Society, before he found in the Pan-German League a more suitable outlet for his ferocious energy. By the turn of the century he was the leading figure among the western chapters, and upon Lehr's death, Hasse named him vice-chairman of the League.[7]

To judge by his memoirs, as well as by his actions, Class was an intense, insecure, and lonely man. His loneliness he palliated by praise, as the virtue of independence, which in his own case meant obstinacy, impulsiveness, and pugnacious arrogance. Temperamentally he felt most secure in astounding others with the extremism of the views he was willing to defend. That this man so left his imprint on the Pan-German League was as much a symptom of the anxieties among the men who made up the organization as it was a tribute to his own tireless dedication to the cause.

Class's growing prominence in the League was the source of some concern in the executive committee, less because of his general outlook on politics than because of his impetuosity. Before he was allowed to deliver a speech that would be interpreted as the League's official position at the convention in Plauen, the committee screened his remarks and toned down a number of passages.[8] Class's speech in Plauen was none the less a provocative event; and because it so determined the position of the League during the rest of the prewar period, it deserves more than casual attention.

The speech was a confession of ideological faith, a statement of a world-view grown increasingly confused and in need of reorientation. Entitled 'Changes in the position of the German Empire in the world since the year 1890', the speech invoked new parallels with the Christian vision of the Fall and Redemption.[9] In 1890, at the time of Bismarck's dismissal, the country had stood at the apex of its power and prestige: Germany, according to Class, then enjoyed a 'condition of generally recognized external security [and] growing domestic consolidation'. German history since 1890, in Class's estimation, had been marked by steady decline. The process of squandering Bismarck's 'rich, practically inexhaustible legacy' began immediately, under Caprivi; it continued under the chancellorship of Hohenlohe, which Class condemned as an 'enormous, depressing failure', and it culminated under Bülow, whose feckless and confined view of world power was responsible for the catastrophe in South Africa.

In Class's eyes, the deterioration of Germany's position involved more than a series of diplomatic set-backs. The country had been repeatedly shamed. 'Where is the German citizen', he asked, 'who dares to say when abroad, "I am a German!" without being viewed as a nuisance or falling prey to the curse of ridicule?' 'We flatter everyone and turn them all into enemies, since no one believes any longer in our reliability and persistence.' Most alarming were the domestic ramifications of Germany's humiliation. A weak foreign policy had undermined order and respect for authority at home. The onslaught of the forces of chaos had been documented anew in the socialist victory in the recent elections, but Class was convinced that these elections were symptomatic of a general crisis of authority which had befallen the country. 'The prestige of the Imperial throne, of the dynasties, and the monarchy has sunk, the Reichstag has lost the respect of the people, and the office of chancellor has been robbed of its essential attributes.'

For a German patriot, these were strong words. Class actually skirted close to libel in imputing Germany's crisis to the systematic mismanagement of incompetent chancellors and, by implication, the monarch. Class's intent was to dispute openly the government's authority to preside exclusively over the determination of the national interest. His conclusion was thus provocative in the extreme: the preservation of stable authority and order in Germany demanded more vigorous definition and defense of the national interest, and hence the replacement of the supreme official custodians of authority by an elite responsive to the real source of authority, the German nation itself. 'We must liberate the moral forces in our *Volk*', Class concluded, 'to pursue a national policy which places the nation above the state when the two stand in contradiction.' And it needed no emphasis that this alternative elite comprised precisely the academically educated patriots who sat in Class's audience in Plauen.

Class's speech represented a departure not so much in its criticism of the course of German foreign policy as in its systematic condemnation of the government and its open repudiation of the government's claim to be the sole or even principal custodian of the national symbols.[10] In linking these symbols so centrally to the defense of domestic order and authority, Class also pointed out the ideological and psychological paradox of the national opposition which now for the first time was fully articulated: authority had to be preserved and regenerated by means of its own repudiation.

The circumstances of both its preparation and delivery indicated that Class's speech was to define the programmatic lines the Pan-German League would henceforth pursue. Those present at Plauen reacted in form, according to the report, with spontaneous acclaim, and they departed 'strengthened anew to work together as one for the Pan-German cause'.[11] To emphasize its importance, the executive committee published the speech as a pamphlet and arranged for its massive distribution – not only within the League itself but to members of parliamentary bodies throughout the country.[12]

The demonstration of support for Class's radical position was deceptive, however, for heated disagreements soon developed and spilled out into the public. While stronger chapters, such as those in Plauen and Eisleben, endorsed Class's manifesto, many others were uncomfortable with the posture of principled opposition which the League's program seemed now to proclaim.[13] Criticism of this posture came not only from the weaker groups in Baden and Württemberg, but from chapters such as those in Mülheim and Danzig, where the League was strong, active, and thought to be radical.[14] Evidence of dissatisfaction within the rank and file built up, in addition, in the continuing decline in membership.

Class's speech exacerbated rather than resolved the crisis in the League. His attempt to buoy spirits by emphasizing the organization's unique profile as the leader of a national opposition raised charges that the League stood only for negative criticism, that it could offer nothing practical or constructive as alternatives to official policy, and that it had condemned itself to isolation and impotence. The debate over the propriety of this new course extended during the next several years into the executive committee, where opinion was also divided between Class's supporters and those who had initially endorsed his position in Plauen only to regret their decision once the full consequences became apparent.

On the surface the debate in the Pan-German League was over tactics: could the organization achieve more by relentlessly attacking the government when official policies and programs failed to conform to the League's broad expectations, or should the organization be prepared to moderate its demands and seek, like the Navy League and Colonial Society, to work in concert with the agencies responsible for official policies and programs? In reality, the debate touched on more profound issues. These involved not only the corporate identity of the League, but the very symbolic content of patriotism in Wilhelmine Germany. In arguing for the wisdom of acting in at least tacit accord with the government, Class's opponents accepted the proposition that the network of patriotic symbols included, as one of its main components, the custodial power of the monarchy. Class and his supporters denied this proposition, arguing that custodial authority was vested elsewhere and that the mission of the Pan-German League was nothing less than to represent it.

In a series of crucial meetings in 1904, the executive committee confronted these issues and attempted to define anew what the Pan-German League stood for.[15] Discussion extended over the entire range of questions the League had traditionally incorporated into its program – colonial expansion and its relationship to the consolidation of Germans on the European continent, building the fleet, ethnic conflict in the Habsburg monarchy, protecting the language, and the threats of socialism and political Catholicism. The task of counteracting charges that the League was pursuing opposition for its own sake seemed to require reducing all these programmatic concerns to a coherent set of practical demands; but neither programmatic coherence nor a consensus on what was practical was easy to find. The debates within the executive committee proved to be painful, and they could not be restricted to the intimate confines of the committee itself. The propriety of the League's position was criticized not only in the chapters, but in the press, where respected leaders of the organization gave public expression to their apprehension over Class's course.[16] The controversy culminated late in 1904, when a delegate to a meeting of the national board of directors moved for a vote of no-confidence in Hasse.[17]

The ease with which this motion was defeated reflected the fact that the issues, while not yet fully settled, were well on their way to resolution by the end of 1904. Hasse was in Class's camp, as were most of the other members of the executive committee. The moderates were unable to devise a credible profile for the League as an alternative to Class's, which had the virtue of consistency with the League's previous positions, contained a coherent, if pessimistic view of politics, and which defined the League's mission in terms that made it distinctive among the patriotic societies. Class's position appealed temperamentally to the younger men who rallied behind him and Hasse on the committee – men such as Klingemann, Philipp Bonhard from Worms, Heinrich Calmbach, Karl Itzenplitz from Mülheim, Georg Freiherr von Stössel from Potsdam, Walter Simons from Meiningen, Gustav Petzoldt from Plauen, Reismann-Grone, and Samassa. For these men, like Class, the humiliation the League had suffered since the turn of the century from official and semi-official sources made the thought of cooperation with the government – at least one headed by Bernhard von Bülow – repugnant.

The ramifications of the League's growing radicalization now began to emerge. Class's view was that the League should be uncompromising in setting demands consistent with its own ultimate goals – no matter how radical these demands might seem; the organization was then to criticize the government relentlessly for its failure to enact policies to meet these demands. Class and his supporters were aware that this position entailed the risk of isolating the League still further and accelerating the depletion of its members. They calculated, however, that the core of fully committed Pan-Germans who remained would be their best asset once the government's weakness vindicated their own views – as they were confident it would.

The next three years put the radicals' calculations to the test. The conflict with the government grew more intense, aggravating the crisis in the League and encouraging the organization's radicalization. As criticism of the government's policies grew more blunt, officials responded with further public ridicule, which prompted more people to drop their membership as it intensified the bitterness of those who chose to stay.

The first clashes involved the issues of Morocco and the navy. Because other historians have already analyzed the League's positions on these issues, little need be added here beyond their impact on the League's internal evolution.[18] The subject of Morocco had loomed large in the discussions of the League's profile in the executive committee, as international tension kept the issue current. Calling for German acquisition of at least a portion of the country impressed the committee as the kind of practical demand the League needed – one which, while more extreme than anything the Colonial Society could be expected to advocate, might deflate accusations that the League stood only for opposition and provide an issue to mobilize the increasingly dispirited rank and file.[19] Class characteristically entertained hopes of much more. Arguing that the German people 'thirsts for a great mission which must have a liberating and healing effect', he proposed to the executive committee that the League call for German acquisition of the entire Atlantic coast of Morocco and large tracts of the hinterland – as a prelude to German penetration of South America and an eventual strategic confrontation with the United States.[20] The position the organization officially adopted was a little less extreme. Omitting all references to America, the committee called for German intervention in Morocco in order to claim the Atlantic coast, although it emphasized that this claim could be peacefully realized.[21]

Whatever the Kaiser's motivations in making his dramatic visit to Tangier in March 1905, the event itself appeared to signal the inauguration of just the kind of policy the Pan-Germans had been advocating, and they acclaimed it.[22] Only Class remained unconvinced, principally because the government justified its intervention in terms only of defending the Open Door. Class himself had publicly demanded the seizure of Moroccan territory, only to find Bülow explicitly rejecting this idea as irresponsible.

Class's bitter feelings were scarcely concealed in his insistence that the 'surprising change in our policy will bring the least desirable solution conceivable to the Moroccan question'. Class concluded his commentary with another charge directed close to a dangerous target: 'We fear that the Kaiser was poorly advised when he decided to go to Tangier, and we could only regret it if his Person were to be associated with the failure of policy.'[23] Class's cynicism was too much for even his most ardent supporters. Samassa delivered a public rebuke, as protests about Class's position flowed in from the chapters.[24] In the executive committee, Class found himself isolated, criticized for both his unrepentant negativism and his remarks about the emperor. Unable to accept criticism gracefully, Class threatened to resign before Hasse stepped in as mediator.[25]

The seriousness of this crisis in the leadership did not become public before events had vindicated Class. By the fall of 1905 it was clear that any German gains from involvement in Morocco were going to make a mockery of expectations inspired by the Kaiser's visit. In the Pan-Germans' eyes the whole venture – from the heralded intervention to the subsequent backing down – came to bear a distinct resemblance to the episode of the Kruger telegram and its dismal aftermath. Opinion in the League now rallied behind Class. 'We are not happy', wrote Samassa, in a tone very different than his earlier criticism of Class. 'Contrary to the reputation we unjustly enjoy of being unproductive grumblers [*unfruchtbare Nörgler*], we supported the regime.' It should thus come as no surprise, he concluded, if the League were to 'greet any such demonstrations in the future with skepticism'.[26] Hasse announced that Class had been right all along, and the Württemberg chapters, which had earlier chided Class for his 'all too sharp, uninformed criticism of the government', wired him in the aftermath of the Algeciras conference: 'In your condemnation of our fruitless Moroccan policy, you have unfortunately been right. We thank you for not allowing your judgment to be deceived by day-to-day vicissitudes.'[27]

Class had to overcome no such isolation as he attacked the manner in which the government was managing the naval build-up. As the League sought ways to reverse its decline, the navy had naturally figured as a potential issue to exploit. In hopes of reactivating the dynamic that had helped bring the League to the pinnacle of its strength at the turn of the century, the executive committee began, without consulting the Naval Office, early in 1904 to demand a major acceleration of the building program, most centrally the reduction by eight years of the period before which German capital ships were to be automatically replaced.[28] The specifics of the League's proposed program were not so important in themselves, but they revealed the Pan-Germans' determination to emphasize their own profile by outbidding the government and everyone else. Maintaining the posture of the 'only independent patriotic society' took on both urgency and credibility as evidence came to light, during the public controversy over a new naval law in 1905, that the Naval Office was attempting to muzzle both the Colonial Society and the Navy League.[29]

Publication of the government's proposal for a naval law late in 1905 coincided with the culmination of disillusionment in the Pan-German

League over the Moroccan venture. Given the mood in the League, Tirpitz's proposals could hardly have found approval, even though they initiated the construction of a *Dreadnought* class of German battleships and brought an escalation in the naval race of incalculable consequences.[30] The League simply rejected the Naval Office's authority to allow diplomatic and political considerations to affect the pace of the naval build-up: strategic considerations were paramount, and these the League claimed itself entitled to determine.[31] Tirpitz's proposals it proclaimed wanting, and to demonstrate its disapproval – and in hopes of using the issue to breathe life back into the chapters – it called a special national convention in Leipzig late in 1905. There the delegates heard Class, basking in his triumph in the Moroccan issue, reassert the League's prior claims to interpret the country's naval needs. 'Before anyone else, before the government and the parties, we recognized the need for a strong fleet and brought this need before the public.'[32]

Bernhard von Bülow watched with growing annoyance as the Pan-German attacks mounted against his policies and the government's claim to speak in the national interest. Bülow's appreciation of the problem was deeper than that of some other officials, who treated the Pan-Germans' behavior as a question of lack of 'tact and political insight'.[33] Yet Bülow did not appreciate the extent to which his own penchant for drumming up patriotic emotions over issues like Morocco created popular expectations which the apparently incoherent policies he chose to pursue could not but frustrate. The chancellor still proposed to deal with these frustrations, at least as they found vent in the Pan-German League, through a strategy of public humiliation, which his own wit, sarcasm, and flippancy made effective. He knew well where the Pan-Germans were sensitive. Early in 1905, for instance, he ridiculed the popular enthusiasm for the Boers at the turn of the century – a phenomenon that remained prominent in the shrine of the Pan-Germans's collective memory long after the enthusiasm had subsided – as much 'hurly–burly' (*Burenrummel*), not unlike the philhellenism of the previous century.[34]

The League's criticism of the outcome of the Moroccan crisis and the naval bill occasioned more concern, however, for the League's views were widely shared – in the press, in the parties of the right, and, most embarrassingly, in the Navy League which, despite all the safeguards the Naval Office had constructed, had fallen under the control of a group of men whose ideas about the building program were much the same as the Pan-Germans'. Bülow's counterattack on the Pan-German League was accordingly directed at a wider audience as well. It came late in 1906 in the Reichstag, in response to a telling interpellation by Ernst Bassermann on the subject of the general deterioration of Germany's international position. Replying that the situation was hardly as bleak as it appeared, Büllow paused to consider the Pan-German phenomenon once again. 'I well know that the efforts of the Pan-German League have the benefit of keeping national feelings alive and of counteracting the inclination of the German philistine toward wooly-headed cosmopolitanism or narrow-minded confessional politics.' Then, reportedly to the 'great amusement' of the parliamentarians, many of whom also recalled the scene with Hasse in 1900, Bülow confessed that 'I for my own part regret that the chairman of the Pan-German League has not returned to this exalted house'. Bülow then returned to the charge with which he had then confronted Hasse. There were, he admitted,

> warm-hearted patriots in this organization, but in questions of foreign policy, a clear head [*Klarheit des Kopfes*] counts for more than a warm heart, and the heart of the patriot ought to manifest itself not just in indiscriminate wrangling with all foreigners ... and even less in bold dreams about the future – dreams which only complicate things for us in the present and provoke mistrust of us everywhere.[35]

The Pan-Germans were livid, as much over the sweet venom in Bülow's tone as over the implication of his charges. Bülow had used the most public forum in the country to repudiate not only the Pan-Germans' authority to speak in the national interest, but their competence. Now, however, none of the League's leaders sat in the Reichstag to respond. An angry open letter, which Bülow did not deign to answer, provided no adequate outlet for the resentments that were accumulating in the League.[36]

These resentments were all the more acute because the League's clash with the government had escalated shortly before with the involvement of the emperor himself. At the League's convention in September 1906 Class had anticipated Bassermann's interpellation of Bülow, only in more pointed terms, with a bleak survey of Germany's declining position in the world. And as if to anticipate Bülow's defense of official authority, Class observed caustically that the country's leaders 'are no geniuses, but we believe that the greatness which they themselves lack can be compensated for by the political conviction and the national will of the nation which stands behind them'. According to Class, those who guided the state should be 'happy and thankful' for the patriotic societies that articulated this national will.[37] Within days, Class's remarks brought a curt rebuff from a source whose authority stood above attack – at least in 1906. 'I will not tolerate pessimistic alarmists [*Schwarzseher*]', William proclaimed in an unmistakable allusion to the Pan-Germans, 'and whoever is not suited to [positive] work, let him leave and seek, if he wants, a better country.'[38]

The final stage in the alienation of the Pan-German League from the official symbols of authority lasted another two years before it culminated in the League's open repudiation of the emperor's authority too. The elation occasioned by the patriotic frenzy during the elections of 1907 proved to be temporary, even though a member of the League's executive committee, Liebert, won a Reichstag seat. The crisis in the League, measured in the steady drop of membership and growing feelings of political isolation, continued to bear witness to Bülow's success in portraying the Pan-Germans as a group of well-meaning fools.

Bülow's political demise was thus a source of immense satisfaction to the League, but the incident late in 1908 that led to his resignation provoked one of the greatest traumas the League had to face. In its criticism of official policy, the League had aimed its attacks toward the chancellor, Foreign Minister, or other officials, but had tried to keep them a safe distance from the emperor.[39] Of course, compelling considerations recommended this discretion, although many Pan-Germans recognized that they were paying tribute to a fiction. Both the constitutional authority and the symbolic position of the monarch made him the supreme official representative of the nation and its interest; but more critically, the monarchy also symbolized the whole domestic structure of authority in Imperial Germany. To challenge the constitutional authority of the Kaiser was thus an endeavor fraught with symbolic connotations, of which the Pan-Germans were more painfully aware than most Germans.

The publication of the Kaiser's interview in the *Daily Telegraph* late in October 1908 pushed the Pan-German League over the brink.[40] The emperor's indiscretions were consternating enough in themselves, but they touched the League at a particularly tender point. William's revelations about his actions during the Boer War showed him to have been working repeatedly at cross-purposes with the League – in sabotaging the European tour of Paul Kruger, in resisting the idea of international intervention on behalf of the Boers, and, most astoundingly, in drawing up operational plans for a campaign against the Boer insurgents. Outrage in the League was general, and the major question was how radical the Pan-Germans' response would be. 'The words fail us to express the depths of our despondency, bitterness, and shame', wrote the editor of the *Alldeutsche Blätter*.[41] Words did not fail them long. Within a week the executive committee had called for another special national convention in Leipzig and had issued a manifesto that lacked nothing in bluntness. The emperor, it announced, did not have the 'essential qualities of a ruler' and had therefore to be excluded from the formulation of policy. The chancellor's independence was henceforth to be guaranteed by the support of a 'strong organized public opinion'.[42]

The advance to this extreme did not come easily for the League. Many on the executive committee opposed the strong language of the manifesto; and Liebert, whose position in the Imperial League against Social Democracy made him dependent on official good will, threatened to resign rather than sign the document.[43] Publication of the manifesto prompted several hundred members to quit the organization, although their loss was compensated by new members who joined in response to the manifesto.[44]

The manifesto laid bare the League's dilemma. Preserving the 'positive aspects of what the monarchy has created' seemed at last to require, as one local leader concluded, 'revolt against the monarch'.[45] Ultimate authority in national questions was to be taken from the monarchy and vested in the *Volk* – an uncomfortable proposition in so far as it implied the democratic reform of foreign policy. The League, however, had no more confidence in the Reichstag than in the emperor. The only viable alternative was accordingly a political organization in which the will of those strata specially qualified to represent the national will – principally, of course, the educated middle class – could find expression with respect to all essential 'national questions'.[46] Such an organization was naturally the Pan-German League itself. In response to its progressive alienation from the government, the organization was compelled to make explicit a conclusion implied by the logic of its views on society and politics. Entitlement to authority did not ultimately flow from the monarchy; the monarchy was instead to be only a symbol, devoid of substantive authority in national questions. Custodianship of the entire shrine of national symbols – including now the monarchy itself – was to rest in the hands of the German-national public, although just how this arrangement might be institutionalized remained unclear, for the League rejected the idea of changing the constitution. Germany in any event, as Class announced in the midst of the *Daily Telegraph* crisis, 'cannot allow itself to be thrown into misfortune through the blunders of a single person, and it is necessary to subject foreign policy to the strictest control of the public'.[47] In other words, the mission of the Pan-German League was to be 'bodyguard to the German nation and to the monarchy'.[48]

At the time its leader was making them, these pretensions seemed extravagant in the extreme, for the Pan-German League was on the verge of collapse. Years of mounting opposition had taken their toll in demoralization and the defection of thousands of members who were unable to tolerate the conflict with official authority that the League's position increasingly made explicit.[49] Their defection left the League both smaller and more radical, although its social complexion remained unchanged. Class's influence and power grew steadily after 1904, as Hasse's health deteriorated. When Hasse succumbed to typhus early in 1908, Class was already the virtual head of the League, and his election to the chairmanship was a foregone conclusion despite the reservations of a few remaining moderates in the executive committee.[50]

Class needed all his energies to save the Pan-German League during the first years of his chairmanship. Most immediately, the defection of so many members had left the finances of the organization in complete disarray. No less significant was the ideological disarray the League confronted, for the antagonism with the government and the repudiation of official authority created the compelling need for an alternative source of authority on which the League could base its entitlement to the custodial role it proposed to exercise.

The Financial Consequences of Opposition: the Business of Patriotism

The finances of the Pan-German League have been a subject of great interest to historians, particularly to those of a Marxist-Leninist persuasion who have charged that the organization was the tool of the monopoly capitalists. In recounting the history of the League it has been possible in this study to dispense so far with a detailed inquiry into this question. The narrative can proceed no longer without the inquiry, for the crisis that now threatened the League's survival most centrally involved money.

Patriotism in Imperial Germany was an eminently commercial phenomenon. The sentiments and emotions on which it fed, no less than the calculated interests that fed on it, encouraged the exchange of large amounts of money. The most impressive illustration of this truth was the fortune realized by select commercial and industrial interests which succeeded, by means of the German Colonial Society and its antecedent organizations, in attaching patriotic emotions to the symbol of empire and generating an enormous fund of capital, both private and public, for investment abroad. Ethnic struggle was no less a commercial venture. It too involved the mobilization of large amounts of money for investment in schools, libraries, real estate, commercial and industrial ventures, and in charitable undertakings among settlements of co-nationals around the world. Finally, mobilizing and sustaining the German-national public itself required financial underpinnings, and the process created opportunities which shrewd entrepreneurs, from publishers to tavern-owners, were quick to exploit.

The Pan-German League was the smallest of the major patriotic societies in Imperial Germany, and for most of the prewar period the scale of its operations remained comparatively restricted. The expenses involved in these operations were, however, fairly typical. The League was, in the first instance, a propaganda organization; most of its expenses related to the public dissemination of its ideology.[51] Publication and distribution of the *Alldeutsche Blätter* was the largest single expense.[52] To oversee the administration of the organization, the League hired an executive secretary, who ran the central office in Berlin (between 1903 and 1909 at the Steglitzerstrasse 77); the overhead costs of this office were the second largest expenditure in the budget. Most of the other expenses grew out of the attempt to establish local chapters and to keep existing ones alive by furnishing them with speakers and literature; the locals met most of their own expenses, however, by means of admission charges and contributions from members. Altogether, the regular expenses of the League's national organization ran between about 80,000 and 100,000 Marks a year after the turn of the century.

The League had another category of expenses. After the turn of the century the scope of its operations broadened, and it undertook various 'practical activities' in addition to propaganda, particularly in providing support for German communities in ethnically troubled areas. Encouraged by the success of the campaign to raise money for the Boers, the League funneled money and literature to German newspapers, schools, voluntary associations, and individual settlers in Central and Eastern Europe and overseas.[53] Some individual chapters also supported German communities abroad on a modest scale.[54] Although the League's support remained but a fraction of what the School Association provided to Germans abroad, this support did amount to about 10,000 Marks a year.[55] In addition, the League supplied, free of charge, copies of its journal to 200 libraries, reading rooms, clubs, schools, and pedagogical seminars in Germany and Austria-Hungary.[56]

Raising the money to meet all these expenses was a constant problem. The Pan-German League did not command a large and reliable source of income and could only gaze enviously at the Navy League, whose enormous membership generated ample funds even with low dues, and at the Colonial

Society, whose operations were lavishly financed not only by its investments, but by a public lottery, which it ran in cooperation with the state and which produced annual revenues in excess of 50,000 Marks.[57] By contrast, the Pan-German League was dependent for the bulk of its revenues on direct contributions from a relatively small membership. Revenues came chiefly in the form of annual dues and subscriptions to the journal. Membership in the League cost 2 Marks a year, in addition to whatever supplementary dues, usually between 1 and 2 Marks, the local chapters charged for their own operations. Subscription to the journal cost an additional 4 Marks a year, but only about a third of the members subscribed.[58] Revenues from dues and subscriptions were never enough to cover the regular costs of the propaganda campaign, so the organization was dependent for its survival on income from special funds raised predominantly among its wealthier members. The 'Guaranty Fund', to which Karl von der Heydt was the principal subscriber, sustained operations in the 1890s, but it expired in 1899. The rise in membership at the turn of the century brought relief, but when it began to taper off in 1901, the League was compelled once again to pass the hat for a special 'Operating and Agitational Fund', to which all members capable of donating 10 Marks a year were urged to contribute and which provided a little breathing room for the next three years.[59]

The League's support work was financially independent of its propaganda operations and was covered entirely by special funds. The costs of sending out free copies of the journal were covered by the interest revenue on a gift of 20,000 Marks from a benefactor in Bonn.[60] The principal source of money for the other support work was the so-called *Wehrschatz*, a fund created in 1903 out of annual pledges from wealthier members as well as from assorted gifts and other contributions.[61] During the first year and a half of the fund's existence, some 200 people pledged a total of about 20,000 Marks, and by the time of Hasse's death in 1908, the fund had grown to about 90,000 Marks.[62] Half the money was capitalized; the other half, in addition to the interest on the capital, was available for distribution at the discretion of the executive committee.

While Hasse was chairman, the League enjoyed no regular support from German commerce or industry.[63] Corporate funds of any description did not figure in the League's ledger, which, while Hasse was alive, recorded in any event the flow of comparatively insignificant amounts of money.[64] To be sure, the League's operations were dependent upon contributions from members of means, such as Heydt, Kollmann in Kattowitz, and the industrialist Paul Simons in Elberfeld. But these contributions reflected the personal inclinations of their donors, and their volume is easily exaggerated. To the extent that industrial and commercial money subsidized the mobilization of patriotism in Wilhelmine Germany, it worked through the Navy League and Colonial Society, whose less extravagant programs and whose official patronage made them better risks.[65]

Had the Pan-German League enjoyed any substantial support from German business, the organization would have been spared the financial ordeal that its antagonism to the government brought on. It is impossible to determine just how many members left the Pan-German League between

1902 and 1909, for the League's statisticians chose to publish figures only on those who had formally resigned, before the situation became so bleak that they ceased mentioning the figures altogether in 1907. Officially, membership dropped only about 4,500, from 23,000 to 18,500, between 1902 and 1906, but these figures did not deceive the accountants, who could calculate that in 1907 only about 14,000 people were paying dues.

The ramifications of the decline in membership were nearly devastating. Many of those who left and ceased paying dues were also subscribers to the journal, so another major source of income was curtailed.[66] As membership dropped, the local chapters found their own sources of income reduced; most of them were then forced to limit their activities, which only aggravated the problem by reducing their visibility.[67] Many collapsed. As chapters dwindled in numbers and size, the flow of membership dues to Berlin began to dry up, so that national headquarters faced a shortage in its own operating revenues. Late in 1902 arrears in payments from the chapters, which formally collected the dues, already stood at nearly 30,000 Marks (total revenues from membership dues in 1900 had been just over 40,000 Marks), and although some of these arrears were recovered, the deficit on this line of the budget continued to grow at an alarming rate.[68] Exhorting the patriotism of the chapters failed to help much in recovering the arrears; the idea of suing them for restitution also surfaced briefly as an indication of Hasse's desperation.[69] National headquarters tried to generate alternative sources of income, but appeals to the membership for special donations had disappointing results, in part because so many members had already contributed to the *Wehrschatz*, whose funds were restricted to support work.[70]

Neither supplementary sources of income nor budgetary cutbacks could arrest the deterioration of the League's financial situation, which by the time Class took over in 1908 had become calamitous.[71] Funds for covering the recurring and increasing deficits could only be found by drawing from the League's meager reserves, which had accumulated during the happier years of the Boer campaign, and, *in extremis*, by quietly draining money from the capital of the *Wehrschatz*.[72] By the beginning of 1909 even these expedients appeared exhausted, and the leaders of the Pan-German League prepared to declare bankruptcy.[73]

These were the darkest days in the prewar history of the Pan-German League. The culmination of the financial crisis coincided with the ideological crisis which came to a head in the *Daily Telegraph* affair. The turmoil in both the organization's finances and in its relationship to the official symbols of patriotism very nearly brought the end of the Pan-German League in 1909.

The resolution of the financial crisis came relatively swiftly. The unexpected success of a special head-tax among the members not only provided a little financial breathing-room early in 1909 but suggested that the forces that remained in the League were rallying behind the uncompromising stand of the leadership in the *Daily Telegraph* issue.[74] In April, in order to cut costs, the executive committee agreed to transfer national headquarters and the editorial offices of the journal to Class's home city of Mainz, where Class could run both directly with a reduced staff. These expedients bought time. Real relief came when the League found a new source of regular income.

The people on whom Class leaned most heavily in trying to salvage the League's finances were a group of members of the executive committee who resided in the Ruhr and Westphalia and who had contacts to some of the area's leading industrialists. This group included Reismann-Grone, who published the *Rheinisch-Westfälische Zeitung*, Paul Simons from Elberfeld, Wilhelm Niemann from Barmen, Adolf von der Nahmer, whose firm in Remscheid manufactured kitchenware, Itzenplitz, who operated a steamship company in Mülheim and was Hugo Stinnes's cousin, and Klingemann, who knew the Krupp family personally.[75] The efforts of these men to exploit their contacts proceeded slowly, but by the end of 1909 they were beginning to bear fruit.[76] The documents do not permit an exact reconstruction of the role of Emil Kirdorf and his coal syndicate in rescuing the Pan-German League. Kirdorf had long been a member of patriotic societies, including the Pan-German League which he had joined in the early 1890s; he made no significant financial contribution to the organization, however, and soon drifted away.[77] He did remain in contact with Reismann-Grone, who had served as executive officer in the *Bergbau-Verein*, and, through Stinnes, with Itzenplitz, By early 1910, principally through the mediation of Itzenplitz, Kirdorf announced his willingness to discuss renewing his association with the League and underwriting a substantial share of its costs.[78] In May 1910 Kirdorf and Class met for the first time. Kirdorf promised to 'use his influence in the associations of which he was a member on behalf of the Pan-German League, both with respect to recruiting and financial support'.[79] To seal the arrangement, Class put Kirdorf on the national board of directors, in the understanding that the coal baron would soon join the executive committee.[80]

The Pan-German League's financial problems now vanished overnight. It is not clear just how much money came in from the coal syndicate, or in what form, but by 1 July 1910 the League was not only free of debt but showed a surplus of close to 10,000 Marks; a month later Class confessed that the financial situation had improved 'more rapidly than could possibly have been anticipated'.[81] The situation improved yet again as another source of industrial funds materialized. The interest of the Krupp firm in patriotic causes lay chiefly in the navy, and Krupp money had helped launch the Navy League.[82] The firm had no contacts with the Pan-German League, except for Klingemann, until 1909, when Hugenberg became chairman of the firm's directorate. Hugenberg was one of the founding fathers of the Pan-German League; but he had found it prudent to resign from the executive committee in 1903, when he went to work for the Prussian Finance Ministry. He remained none the less in consultation with Hasse and Class, particularly with respect to the League's position in the Polish question, which he practically dictated.[83] Hugenberg's move to Essen in 1909 worked to the direct and lasting benefit of the League, for he used not only his influence with Krupp, but also his system of contacts with a number of other leading industrialists, prominent among them Wilhelm Hirsch, Stinnes, and Kirdorf, to consolidate and coordinate contributions from heavy industry to various national causes; and his loyalties to the Pan-German League affected his decisions about where this money would go.[84]

Hugenberg became the pivotal figure in the industrial financing of the Pan-German League. The two principal sources from which he drew were Kirdorf and Krupp, both of whom hoped to use the League to counteract what appeared, in the establishment of the *Hansabund* and in the evolution of the National Liberal party, to be the leftward drift of the German business community.[85] Efforts to pull other leading industrialists directly into the orbit of the Pan-German League were less successful. Because of his holdings in French mines, Stinnes, who met with Class in 1911, remained nervous about the Pan-Germans' aggressive demands in foreign policy, although he found their ideas on domestic policy to be attractive, particularly what one Pan-German described as their advocacy of a 'moderate tempo' in social policy.[86] The League's concept of a 'moderate tempo', which it documented through its association with the Imperial League against Social Democracy and the national workers' organizations and through its opposition to suffrage reform in Prussia and to a constitution for Alsace-Lorraine, was also the feature of the organization's program that appealed to Kirdorf, who was full of premonitions of general decay brought on by democratization.[87]

The heavy-industrial support for the League was substantial, and it came in through two channels. The first were direct subsidies, amounting to probably more than 50,000 Marks a year, to the League's operating account.[88] These funds enabled the League to cover all its regular expenses and to produce a sizable annual surplus. In addition, comparable amounts of money flowed annually through the mediation of Hugenberg into the *Wehrschatz*, usually on an *ad hoc* basis to support specific projects; Class also presented shopping lists directly to Kirdorf, as did Klingemann to Krupp.[89] Because of the industrialists' largesse, the Pan-Germans spent the last four years prior to the war (to use their own metaphor) swimming in money. Not only did the League's support for Germans abroad increase significantly, but the surplus in its operating budget made possible the resumption of recruiting and the establishment of new chapters.[90] Statistics are lacking, but by the eve of the war the membership appears to have crept back up to about 18,000.[91]

Of more fundamental significance than the modest resurgence in the membership was the transformation that the industrial money encouraged in the structure of the Pan-German League. The most telling indication of the change was the fact that the rank and file never learned who was paying the bills.[92] The industrial subsidy remained the carefully preserved secret of the executive committee, whose distance from the wider membership had already begun to grow once Class succeeded Hasse. The move to Mainz in 1909 fostered centralization and the authoritarian exercise of power in the League, for Class now presided over both the editing of the journal and the day-to-day administration of the organization, and his inclinations were more elitist and dictatorial than those of his predecessor.[93] For advice Class relied increasingly on the men of the executive committee who were closest, both geographically and in influence, to the industrial money and who came together in a special committee called the 'Rhenish-Westphalian agents' (*Rheinisch-westfälische Vertrauensmänner*).[94]

Class's principal advisor, though, was Hugenberg. The growing distance between the executive and the rank and file corresponded to a conception of the League that Hugenberg had long advocated. 'In the future the Pan-German League should be more Janus-faced than in the past', he had recommended in 1904. 'Inwardly, within a rather narrow circle, it should reveal its true face, as an association of people who ... want to do practical work and surreptitiously lay the cookoo's egg all over the place – without insisting, as *Vereine* conventionally do, on taking credit for it.' 'Next to this, and in second order of significance, stands the broadening of our organization. The broader organization is only a means to raise money and to make new contacts – the scraps we throw to the fellow-travellers and the foil we display outwardly.'[95] The unreliability of the chapters during the period of crisis encouraged the national leadership's low estimation of the broader membership, but the attempt to implement Hugenberg's ideas and to convert the executive committee into a more exclusive and autonomous 'national-political officer corps' remained unfeasible as long as the leadership was financially dependent on the chapters.[96] The industrial money severed the bond of dependency and relocated the center of gravity in the League's political activities. While the orchestration of enthusiasm and indignation, of acclamation and condemnation within the chapters did, to be sure, remain an essential feature of the organization's efforts to mobilize opinion, the leadership now resorted to new, more covert and expensive techniques. These included quiet subsidies to other, more broadly based organizations, underwriting publications by authors not publicly associated with the League, and cultivating contacts with leading editors and publishers, even to the point of buying into one major Berlin newspaper, *Die Post*, in 1910.[97]

The transformation that took place in the Pan-German League after 1910 makes it difficult indeed to quarrel with Marxist-Leninist historians who have argued that the League was the propaganda arm of the most reactionary and aggressive segment of German industry. Through Krupp, Kirdorf, and Hugenberg, the community of interest for which the League now began to speak extended into the leading circles of the *Centralverband deutscher Industrieller* and the Silesian magnates who dominated the Free Conservative Party.[98] The extreme hostility of these men to social and political reform fit easily into the ideology of the League; opposition to independent trade unions, to the extension of social insurance, and to suffrage reform blended into the rhetoric of national solidarity and preserving the structure of authority. Nor was it difficult for the Pan-Germans to accommodate the 'pillars of our national economy' alongside the guardians of German culture' in their definition of the national elite.[99]

As the shift in the accent of the League's propaganda became more difficult to ignore, it added a political dimension to the growing distance between the leadership and the rank and file. The dominant political orientation in the membership remained National Liberal, while that of the leadership drifted to the right and began to reflect the views of the men most involved in efforts to create a political block among the parties of the right.[100] That these efforts would entail some compromise of principle and the risk of antagonizing the rank and file was clear. One instance was the success of the League's Westphalian benefactors, who were concerned about cutting off a source of cheap labor, in persuading the executive committee to retreat from the League's traditional demand that Germany's eastern frontiers be closed to Polish immigration.[101]

The resolution of the League's financial crisis thus occasioned far-reaching structural changes in the organization, changes that were reflected in the program as well. More significant, however, were the programmatic changes that came in the wake of the ideological reorientation which the years of crisis had occasioned.

The Ideological Consequences of Opposition: the Embrace of Racist Antisemitism

The deepening antagonism between the Pan-German League and the German government nearly brought the League's demise through the erosion of its finances, but the antagonism had ideological and psychological repercussions as well. The conflict with official authority and the eventual repudiation of official symbols of authority raised anew and more urgently than ever before essential questions about the League's own role in the structure of authority and its own authority to guard the national symbols – questions which touched upon the organization's *raison d'être*. The resolution of this ideological crisis came more gradually than the resolution of the financial crisis, but its impact on the character of the Pan-German League was no less profound.

The onset of the period of crisis bred a new mood of pessimism in the Pan-German League and resulted initially in significant programmatic adjustments. The optimism fed at the turn of the century by the success of the naval agitation and the protests over the Boer War did not survive long the setbacks of the ensuing years. Pessimism rapidly set in, rooted in the fearsome perception that events were proceeding out of control. 'Precisely in the best, patriotic, and educated circles', Samassa wrote after the elections in 1903, in an obvious allusion to the League itself, 'there reigns a gloomy pessimism, the feeling that fate is going its own way and that the voice of a single individual cannot change much.'[102] As feelings of helplessness and despair became pervasive, the League's spokesmen struggled to comprehend their own plight, to bring it under ideological control, by casting it in the context of a generalized deterioration, not only of Germany's position in the world, but of national values, order, authority, and culture.

Despair over the course of the country's foreign policy quickly produced two modifications in the League's program. The outcome of the Moroccan crisis and disappointment over the naval bill of 1905 combined to suggest to Pan-German leaders the impossibility of colonial expansion overseas. Not only were the country's leaders evidently unwilling to push for the weapons essential for such a program, but the tentative initiatives the German government had undertaken in Morocco had succeeded only in uniting the country's rivals. At least in the near future, the Pan-Germans concluded, German colonial expansion would have thus to be directed elsewhere, to the south and east on the European continent.[103] At the same time, though, the country's diplomatic isolation seemed to make essential the survival of its one remaining ally, Austria-Hungary. Hence the League's leaders modified their view of the future of the Habsburg monarchy. During the uproar over the Badeni language ordinances, they had joined the Austrian Pan-Germans in predicting that the monarchy was about to collapse and in demanding that the western half be consolidated with the German Empire. This view the League now changed in favor of the position, argued most forcefully by Samassa, that the security of the German Empire demanded the stabilization of the Habsburg monarchy, even at the risk of abandoning German communities there to the Slavic threat.[104]

These adjustments in the League's program were responses to the perception that Germany was being diplomatically isolated. At the same time, the League's leaders had to contend with the ramifications of another, more painful kind of isolation – that of their own organization. The League had long claimed to speak in the name of the German nation. This claim rested on the proposition that as 'cultivated' Germans, the League's members enjoyed a special, prior, and creative relationship to German culture, which was the supreme and most essential expression of German ethnicity and national will. This special relationship entitled cultivated Germans to precedence in the structure of authority; it endowed them with the authority to exercise custodial roles over the national symbols and the national interest. Until the full rift with the government, the Pan-Germans were not compelled to explore the implications of this claim. It reflected a modified theory of popular sovereignty: an immediate tie to German culture made Pan-Germans the most genuine expression of the collective *Volkswille*. The Pan-Germans insisted, however, that these claims were not inconsistent with a structure of authority that rested on monarchical sovereignty; the authority of the monarchy itself, they argued, derived ultimately from the same source, the national will. Far from threatening one another, the authority of the national elite and that of the monarchy were mutually reinforcing.

This view remained implicit in the Pan-German League's commentary on German politics until the final break with the government in 1908. The League invoked the authority of the monarchy to buttress its own claim to authority in national questions. The role of pioneers for the German nation meant serving as the advance agents of the monarch's authority; the cause in which they labored was the monarch's own. The monarch was accordingly 'the leader of Pan-Germanism [*Alldeutschtum*]', the 'shining model of ceaseless, continuous work for the good of His *Volk*' (this latter description in 1905).[105] It was essential, for the integrity of the Pan-Germans' position, that the bonds that linked the pioneers to the source of official authority remain unbroken. For all the vigor of their criticism of the government, the tension itself was, by the Pan-Germans' own admission, extremely painful, for it threatened just these bonds.[106]

When the antagonism culminated with the direct and unambiguous involvement of the monarch, the ideological repercussions were far-reaching, and they laid bare the full ramifications of the League's problematic relationship to authority. The *Daily Telegraph* affair severed definitively the bond between the League and monarchical authority and, so to speak, left the pioneers themselves abandoned. No longer could they contend that their criticism of official policy ultimately served the positive purpose of buttressing authority; they were now open to the charge that they were undermining authority, that they stood only for negation, and that, like the Social Democrats, they labored in the service of the forces of chaos.[107] These charges were particularly painful because the steady erosion of the League's membership also made dubious the organization's claim to speak in the name of the *Volkswille* or, for that matter, any popular sentiment at all. The League thus appeared cut off from the other source from which it claimed authority. 'Persecuted and ridiculed from above and below', as one lecturer moaned early in 1909, the League seemed now to be isolated from any credible source of authority, their pretensions to stand for some higher national truth or wisdom repudiated.[108]

The symbolic impact of these cumulative blows and the break with the monarchy was staggering. In repudiating the authority of the monarchy, the Pan-Germans appeared to have assaulted the whole structure of authority which the network of national symbols signified and which the monarchy claimed to represent and uphold. The custodians of authority seemed to have forfeited their own custodial authority. Many members of the League responded to this ideological crisis by quitting the organization, documenting their prior commitment to the official symbols of authority. However, those who remained in the League reconstructed their ideology. They discovered a compelling new truth on which to base their claims to custodial roles – a source of authority that superseded both the monarchy and the *Volkswille*.

Historians are coming to appreciate a truth long known to psychologists, that antisemitism is a complex phenomenon, that it appeals to different kinds of people for different reasons.[109] When Paul Massing wrote years ago that antisemitism in the German Empire was principally a phenomenon of the socially insecure lower-middle class, fueled by resentment of the upper bourgeoisie, his description was not so much wrong as it was incomplete.[110] Antisemitism appealed as well, though for different reasons, to segments of the upper bourgeoisie itself. In this respect, the Pan-German League is of more than casual interest. While one could find men in it whose hatred and fear of Jews was probably pathological (one of them, for example, was given to counting Jews in the streets), the reasons for the general receptivity to antisemitism in the League had directly to do with the organization's crisis.[111] Once fully systematized and turned into a comprehensive racial philosophy of history and politics, and once endowed with the ultimate authority of science, antisemitism provided the League with a cogent new world-view – one which provided new underpinnings for the Pan-Germans' collective self-representation. The eternal and demonstrable verities of *Wissenschaft* brought back the element of conceptual control over the 'chaos of our spiritual life' to the pioneers who now enlisted in the service of science and claimed its authority.[112]

Antisemitism had several foci in Germany in the 1890s, but the Pan-German League could only with qualification be numbered among them. Antisemitism served then chiefly as an idiom of peasant and artisanal protest, and it was mobilized in the first instance by political parties and interest groups, most successfully by the Agrarian League; the phenomenon was not so prominently associated with the patriotic societies, where the prevailing influence was usually National Liberalism, whose supporters objected both to the political style of the antisemites and to the violence that exclusionary legislation, for which the antisemites were calling, would do to constitutionally guaranteed civil rights. This brake did not, however, free the patriotic societies from debates over the 'Jewish question'. Particularly the organizations that were directly involved in the ethnic struggles found that the very attempt to define German ethnicity raised the issue of the status of Jews.[113]

For the Pan-German League this issue was difficult from the start, for opinions within the organization were no less intense than they were divided.[114] One of the signatures under the manifesto 'Germany Awaken!', which appeared in 1890 and was the direct stimulus for the founding of the League, was that of Otto Lubarsch, a pathologist in Zurich, a friend of Adolf Fick, and a Jew. Many of the men who put the organization together during the next year were unimpressed by Lubarsch's patriotism; with direct ties to the antisemitic parties, these men insisted that Jews be excluded from the new organization.[115] The antisemites lost on this issue when Carl Peters opposed them, but the problem continued to unsettle the League during the first years of its existence.[116] In the two most important chapters, in Berlin and Hamburg, the efforts of antisemites to exclude Jews resulted in heated debate, which in Berlin nearly caused the dissolution of the chapter.[117]

In these two chapters, and in most of the others, the influence of the National Liberals prevailed. Jews were allowed to join. And to judge by their names, a handful of them did become active.[118] In most localities, though, their presence was only grudgingly tolerated, and even Hasse, whose commitment to liberal ideals had long been showing signs of erosion, confessed in 1901 that 'if we were to be consistent, we could not admit Jews into the Pan-German League'.[119]

In reality the antisemitism of the Pan-German League in the 1890s was anything but consistent, for it reflected the disparate sources that fed it. The teachings of Treitschke, in which the most salient features of the 'Jewish problem' were political and religious, funneled into the League through the *Vereine deutscher Studenten* and other student organizations.[120] Social resentments, which antisemitic politicians exploited, came in through the League's ties to the German-National Commercial Employees' Union and were reinforced by the presence in the League's ranks of antisemitic political leaders, including Max Liebermann von Sonnenberg, Wilhelm Lattmann, Ludwig Werner, Paul Förster, and Oswald Zimmermann.[121] The League's amalgam of antisemitism also betrayed the influence of the incipient racism being preached by some Austrian Pan-Germans.[122] All these sources combined to buttress the view of many Pan-Germans that Jews were foreign and hence dangerous to the German nation, that Judaism was a threat to German culture. Views in the League remained divided, however, on the questions of the foundations of Jewish distinctiveness, the specific character of the Jewish threat, and the suitable remedies.

This division of views reflected an unsystematic approach to the concept of race. The subject arose repeatedly in connection with the Pan-Germans' attempt to define ethnicity. A preponderance of opinion held that the determinants of ethnic identity were language, culture, and religion. Shortly after its founding, the League sought to clarify the issue in a public statement. 'Ethnicity [*das Volkstum*] ties a bond – spiritual, moral, and linguistic – around all Germans, wherever they may be.'[123] Ethnicity was not, in this definition, a congenital trait; it was instead a characteristic imprinted upon each individual by the culture in which he or she developed. Ethnicity was also an ethical category. For Germans, and presumably for members of other ethnic groups as well, the affirmation of one's ethnic identity was a matter of volition and moral obligation. This definition of ethnicity had implications for the policies the Pan-Germans advocated. In areas where Germans were the dominant ethnic group but faced minorities from other groups, a policy of assimilation appeared not only feasible but ethically imperative. In the Prussian east and the Austrian sector of the Habsburg monarchy, the League called during the 1890s for the Germanization of Poles and other minorities, principally by means of enforcing the use of the German language.[124] Assimilation was an avenue open, most Pan-Germans agreed at this time, to Jews too; their Germanization required the conscious choice to take on German ethnicity, which implied religious conversion as well as using the language.[125]

In most of these discussions, Pan-German writers used the term race simply as a synonym for ethnicity.[126] Even on occasions when they sought to use the term more precisely, it remained but an aspect of ethnicity, the physical expression – but never the determinant – of culture.[127] The word 'Aryan' also surfaced in casual usage in the early literature of the League, to describe any group of people, even Czechs or Hungarians of whom the League did not think highly, that was not Jewish.[128]

The contours of a comprehensive philosophy of racism were only beginning to appear in Germany in the 1890s. Its intellectual antecedents, in the writings of Eugen Dühring, Julius Langbehn, Paul de Lagarde, and others, are too familiar to require recounting here.[129] Of more immediate interest is an organization through which racist antisemitism began in the 1890s to feed into the Pan-German League. This organization was the creation of Friedrich Lange, the editor of the *Tägliche Rundschau*, who in the 1880s had been involved with Peters and the other original moving spirits behind the Pan-German League.[130] Although Lange himself never became active in the League, he shared with the Pan-Germans a world-view whose organizing principle was the superiority and historical mission of German ethnicity. Lange, who had been trained as a philosopher, concluded his search for conceptual order by constructing what amounted to a national religion, a synthesis of Christianity and the adulation of *Deutschtum*, with pronounced undertones of mysticism. The Christian virtue of love was to be perfected in its attachment to the German nation and its elevation to the governing principle of life among all Germans. 'Love of German ethnicity [*Deutschtum*] is the highest measure of all worth among the brothers and sisters', he wrote.

> Beyond this there is nothing among them that patience would not bear or improve, and nothing shall divide them among themselves – not riches or poverty, not rank or class [*Stand*], and each German shall feel the warming flame of community and become richer in the love of his brothers, because he is a good German.[131]

In its pathos, as well as in its eclectic content, Lange's national religion betrayed the influence of Lagarde. Lagarde's influence was evident in other features of Lange's thought, but the word pathos no longer seems appropriate to describe them. Lange was a passionate antisemite. Curiously, because it was inconsistent with his emphasis on the spiritual motif in the definition and fulfillment of ethnicity, Lange's antisemitism was racial. Although he held that the Jews constituted a *Volk* themselves, they were by nature the enemies of ethnicity in every other group of people on earth, and this characteristic resided, he insisted, in Jewish blood, where it was immune to spiritual purification through baptism. 'The Jewish *Volk*', Lange proclaimed, has been 'forever a mockery of other nations and a plague on practically all humanity, for wherever it comes, it spoils the earth of the fathers in every nation and sows weeds in every field'. With this proclamation Lange came to the practical imperatives of his national religion. 'With this Jewish nation let there be no treaty, no settlement; only in beating it back with all legal means and steadfast will can all healthy nations attest to their power.'[132]

Lange's contribution was to combine racist antisemitism with a comprehensive philosophy which compensated in fervor for its inconsistencies. In 1893 he began to proselytize. As a manifesto he published, with the title 'Pure Germandom' (*Reines Deutschtum*), a series of articles he had earlier written for the *Tägliche Rundschau*.[133] Lange also planned a newspaper to carry the national religion to the artisanal and peasant *Mittelstand*, which he, like other antisemites, regarded as the purest sector of the nation. Although these plans fell through, he did acquire his own paper when in 1896 he founded the *Deutsche Zeitung*.[134]

Finally, in order to spread his views, Lange established in 1894 a society with many features of a religious order. Risking the opprobrium of the linguistic purists, he called his organization the *Deutschbund* (a reasonable approximation in English might be Germanunion).[135] Unlike the patriotic societies, Lange's group was small and exclusive by calculation. Membership was by invitation and required a period of apprenticeship and a solemn oath. By the turn of the century the group comprised about 800 *Bundesbrüder* and thirty-five 'communities' around the country. The men who joined were the same kinds of academically educated teachers, officials, and professionals who predominated in the patriotic societies; a hint of the concerns that motivated them lay in Lange's claim that one of his organization's distinctive features was that its members 'recognized the authority of its leading men not only in practice but unconditionally in form as well'.[136] The unconditional authority was Lange's own. His goal was to assemble a group of men who would 'support and encourage one another through love' and who would serve as precepts for the rest of the German nation.[137]

The agitational activities of the *Deutschbund* were neither very extensive nor significant. They consisted of a few publications and the attempt to set up a handful of patriotic artisanal organizations.[138] Of more lasting importance was the manner in which the *Bundesbrüder* cultivated racist antisemitism in other voluntary associations to which they belonged. Foremost among these was the Pan-German League. The paucity of membership lists makes it impossible to determine the exact extent of the overlap between the two organizations, but it was significant. The most noteworthy case was in Mainz, where Heinrich Class set up a *Gemeinde* of the *Deutschbund* in 1894 and several years later led it collectively into the Pan-German League.[139] Members of the *Deutschbund* were also active in founding or sustaining chapters of the League in Dresden, Görlitz, Kassel, Worms, Karlsruhe, Gotha, and several other places.[140] In addition, the League underwrote Lange's newspaper.[141]

In the 1890s, however, the influence of the *Bundesbrüder* and other men who were groping their way towards a consistent philosophy of race remained limited in the Pan-German League. Lange's ideas were murky and sectarian, and like other emergent theories of race they were open to charges of methodological inconsistency – a deficiency to which the academics in the League were sensitive.[142] Nor were leaders of the League comfortable with the anti-Christian implications of theories that invoked biological determinism.[143] The chief opponents of racism in the League were Hasse and Lehr, whose doubts about the intellectual and analytical integrity of racial theories were compounded by their aversion to the antisemitic political parties. Together they resisted attempts by the racists to replace with a rigid biological definition the loose cultural concept of ethnicity which appeared in the League's program.[144]

The decline in the League's fortunes after 1901 changed radically the context in which racial theories were debated in the organization. The need to find a framework in which to analyze this decline and to resolve the problem of the League's relationship to authority enhanced greatly the organization's receptivity to theories which seemed to offer philosophical truth and ideological certainty. The final factor in the equation was the appearance of a new theory of race which seemed vastly superior to all the others, because it seemed endowed with the ultimate authority of science. Quite apart from the subsequent role of *Rassenwissenschaft* in German history, its intrusion into the Pan-German League is important enough to justify a brief excursus.

Few ideas have left such clear traces of their derivation, dispersion, and popularization as has the scientific theory of race that captivated the educated middle class in Germany after the turn of the twentieth century. The dubious honor of paternity belonged to a Frenchman. Count Arthur de Gobineau's *Essay on the Inequality of Human Races* was published nearly a half-century before anyone in the Pan-German League had heard of its author.[145] Gobineau purported, in brief, to have discovered the single principle that governed human history. All social and cultural change, he argued, could be reduced to a biological dynamic, to race-mixing. Race was not only prior to culture, but its determinant. Gobineau descried a primal hierarchy of human races, at whose upper reaches stood the white race; and at the very pinnacle stood the purest and most excellent branch of the white race, the Aryans, who by dint of their racial quality were the font and carrier of human culture, beauty, creativity, and virtue. In Gobineau's view, the teleology of history was cast in racial intermingling, which he believed to be inevitable and which resulted in increasing dilution of Aryan blood by inferior strains. The cultural consequence of this biological fact was the enervation of the sole source of human excellence and creativity. The end to which historical development pointed was accordingly a condition of general racial uniformity and cultural mediocrity.

About the validity of Gobineau's vision nothing need be added to Michael Biddiss's remark that 'his errors of method, his tautologies, his determinism, and his overcritical simplifications left many hostages to fortune'.[146] Several other features of this vision do deserve brief comment, though, for they contributed significantly to its subsequent appeal in the Pan-German League. Gobineau's was an all-embracing philosophy of history whose truth was, its author claimed, scientifically demonstrable. Race determined culture with calculable precision and regularity. Most of his *Essay* was devoted to describing, often in meticulous detail, the manner in which patterns of racial mixing had operated in shaping the cultural traits of civilizations throughout history. Gobineau's vision was, in addition, as somber as it was vast. The very mechanism of historical change, race-mixing, determined that the pattern of history was one of ineluctable degeneration.

Gobineau's work found virtually no popular resonance in Germany for the next forty years.[147] This is at first glance a curious fact, for Gobineau had insisted that the Germans and Scandinavians were the purest and most noble surviving descendants of the Aryans. However, not even the antisemites in Germany could find much to use. While Gobineau had no high opinion of Jews (he believed them to be contaminated with admixtures of the lowest race, the black), he assigned to them no particular historical significance.[148] A more significant obstacle to the popularization of Gobineau's thought in Germany was the fact that its determinism and pessimism were debilitating and made it unsuitable as an anchor for an ideology of political action.

The channel through which Gobineau's doctrines finally entered the realm of popular interest in Imperial Germany rid them of these deficiencies. The channel originated in Bayreuth. Richard Wagner met Gobineau in 1876 and thereafter immersed himself in the Frenchman's ideas.[149] Gobineau's theories of racial degeneration and Aryan superiority meshed well with Wagner's own Germanomania and his growing interest in the idea of cultural regeneration. Regeneration for Wagner was a cyclical process; it involved both a degenerative and a subsequent restorative impulse. Gobineau's theories served Wagner well as an analysis of the degenerative phase of human history; and at the point where Gobineau's pessimism seemed to undermine any thought of restoration, Wagner simply ignored it and continued his own speculations about an 'antidote' to arrest the decline of civilization. Nor was Wagner restrained by the fact that the kind of regeneration he envisaged was to be spiritual and religious, hence incompatible not only with the tenor but the biological premise of Gobineau's theory.

Gobineau's work was none the less required reading among Wagner's disciples in Bayreuth. One of these was Ludwig Schemann, a young bibliographer at the university library in Göttingen. Gobineau's *Essay* not only captivated Schemann; it changed his life. After delving further into the Frenchman's writings, Schemann resolved, with Wagner's encouragement, to devote himself to spreading the scientific gospel of race. He became, as he later confessed, 'deindividualized, the instrument of higher powers'.[150] After his health forced him to retire to Freiburg, Schemann began with the fervor of an apostle to raise money for the translation, publication, and popular distribution of Gobineau's writings. In 1894 he established the Gobineau Society (*Gobineau-Vereinigung*), a group consisting primarily at first of his acquaintances from the circle of Wagner's admirers who were willing to put up the money to finance the translation of the *Essay*, which Schemann himself was preparing.[151] In 1897 the first volume appeared, and by 1900 the German translation was complete in three volumes. Schemann now began almost single-handedly to purvey the volumes, through the Gobineau Society, to libraries around the country and to public officials.[152]

The version of Gobineau that Schemann purveyed was thoroughly Wagnerized. The influence of the Master was not so much apparent in Schemann's translation of the *Essay*, which was faithful, as in the exegesis of Gobineau's writings which Schemann undertook in his role as custodian of the Gobineau shrine in Germany. In Schemann's eyes, Gobineau's racial theory possessed not only scientific validity, but esthetic quality; it was to an understanding of history and society what Wagner's operas were to art, music, and drama – a monumental, all-embracing synthesis of everything that had preceded it.[153] Schemann followed Wagner in the ease with which he slid, in speaking of regeneration, from biological to spiritual and moral categories. Indeed, as he minimized the implications of Gobineau's pessimism for his German readers, Schemann left the impression that race derived from culture, rather than the other way around. Germans could take solace in the realization that they belonged to the 'relatively least degenerated race' and that – and here Schemann made sheer nonsense of Gobineau's insistence that intermingling inevitably resulted in degeneration – 'race-mixing has been the main physiological process in history, in proportion as the blood of the higher race has remained triumphant [*siegreich!*] in the mixture'.[154] But whether or not the higher race emerged victorious was, in Schemann's view, ultimately a moral and spiritual question. It involved a decision. As Schemann spelled it out in his inimitable prose:

If the Germanics [*Germanen*] in fact play the role in history that Gobineau saw for them, and if the Germans are still the ethnic element within the Germanic race [*Germanentum*] that has most consciously [*sic*] seized upon the racial heritage of the Germanics, then their mission for the future too would be so clearly indicated that even Gobineau's final prophecy does not need to exist [*existieren*] for them, to the extent that they feel, affirm, and activate themselves as Germanics. Abstract truth need not confuse in his concrete conduct a human being who feels Germanic and heroic [*einen germanisch-heroisch empfindenden Menschen*].[155]

The casualness with which Schemann blended biological determinism and moral imperatives in promoting Gobineau's writings made these writings attractive as a framework for the men who at the turn of the century were constructing a syncretic theory of race.[156] This endeavor took place, as two contemporary observers noted, 'in one of the most dangerous realms along the border of science and fantasy'.[157] Some of the men who participated in the effort possessed scientific credentials, most did not. The feat they as a group accomplished required, in any event, the ingenuity of dilettantes. They managed to fuse Gobineau's historical panorama, Wagner's theory of regeneration, antisemitism, and theories of natural selection drawn from Darwin. The infusion of Darwinism, for which most of the credit belongs to the anthropologist Ludwig Woltmann, was the leavening in the synthesis, for it provided these thinkers with a biological metaphor in which to discuss regeneration.[158] Regeneration would take place in the context of interracial struggle, in which the purest race would survive. Darwinism also made it possible to discard Gobineau's fatalism and, with the *imprimatur* of Schemann himself, to identify racial breeding as the key to arrest race-mixing and the cultural and physical degeneration still associated with it.[159]

These theorists did not, however, discard Gobineau's theory of an inherent, prehistorical hierarchy of races, despite its incompatibility with the logic of natural selection. The retention of this hierarchy enabled them to anchor antisemitism within the framework supplied by Gobineau and Wagner, and thus to furnish the German antisemites with what one of their number described as 'a powerful, decisive, scientific weapon'.[160] Racists had merely to follow Gobineau in installing the Germanic race atop the racial hierarchy as the purest remnant of the Aryans, and then to disregard Gobineau in casting Jews in a unique role that seemed to defy the laws of nature and history. The Jews emerged as the anti-race, the race that not only survived, but thrived in race-mixing, the very process that negated the integrity of blood and culture in other races.[161]

The contours of this synthesis emerged only gradually out of the research and speculation of a large number of people (by no means all of whom were Germans). One group, in which the names of Woltmann, the anthropologist and craniometrician Otto Ammon, Alfred Plötz, Alexander Tille, and Ludwig Wilser stood out, explored the biological implications of racial theory and became the founders of the eugenics movement and the 'science of sociobiology' in Germany.[162] A second group, which included Gustav Kosinna, Ernst Krause, Heinrich Driessmann, and Adolf Bartels, undertook cultural and historical studies to show the play of biological determinants. No complete and systematic statement of the new racial theory appeared in Germany before the war, in part because the synthesis was never completely stable (it is difficult to see how it ever could have been). The closest approximation to such a statement was Houston Stewart Chamberlain's monumental *Foundations of the Nineteenth Century*, whose sales figures demonstrated that, for all its inconsistencies and weaknesses, the scientific theory of race had enormous appeal.[163]

Nowhere did the theory have more appeal than in the Pan-German League. The fact that the final volume of Schemann's translation of the *Essay* appeared just as the League's fortunes began to decline was a coincidence; the fact that the ideas of Gobineau and his followers began at this time to resonate so broadly in the League was not. In direct proportion as the crisis in the League deepened, the 'intellectual current' of racial theories gathered strength; and, as Samassa announced in 1902, in the familiar imagery of water, this current came to 'dominate our national cultural life as an ever broader stream, emerging more and more from the undercurrent which it used to be, out onto the surface'.[164] The Pan-German League soon became in fact one of the leading agents in the development and spread of racial theories in Germany.

Well aware of its ideological potential, and in hopes that exposure to it would improve morale in the chapters, the League's leaders cleared the subject of racism for public debate.[165] Samassa and his successors turned the *Alldeutsche Blätter* over to racist authors of every stripe, from Adolf Lanz von Liebenfels, who presented his turbid thoughts on Aryan virtue, to Willibald Hentschel and Johannes Hering, who argued over whether the original home of the white race was at the North Pole or in the tropics of Oceania.[166] No major new piece of racist literature escaped the eye of the journal's reviewers, nor did a lot of the more obscure things, such as the study by one physician of the relationship between race and tooth decay.[167] The chapters began to receive a barrage of lectures, often by leading racists themselves, on a broad range of themes relating to the new science.[168] Speakers enlightened their audiences in lectures 'profoundly reasoned out and rich in content', on the teachings of Gobineau and other pioneers of racist philosophy, on the latest findings of sociobiological research, on the principles of racial breeding, on the role of the Aryans in history, on the customs of the Germanic tribes, on Wagner, and on the views of Lagarde.[169]

The growing prominence of these themes in the activities of the Pan-German League reflected the intimate ties that developed between the League and the men and organizations most responsible for constructing the theory of scientific racism in Germany. The most important of these ties were to Schemann and his Gobineau Society, from which lines of contact extended out to virtually every other racist organization in the country. Schemann knew the leading racist theoreticians personally, and his society served as a clearing house and bibliographical center for their literature.[170] He was in touch with all the patriotic societies too, but he quickly realized that the Pan-German League offered the most promising terrain.[171] Several leaders of the League, including Class, Heydt, and Schroeder-Poggelow, had been among the early patrons of the Gobineau Society, but the breakthrough did not come until 1902, when Samassa read the newly published translation of the *Essay* and began to promote it in the League's journal.[172] Shortly thereafter, in June 1902, the League joined the Gobineau Society as a corporate member and pledged 200 Marks a year – a major sum in Schemann's small budget.[173] Other leaders of the League then read Gobineau's writings 'with baited breath' and discovered 'an endless wealth of ideas and stimulating thoughts'.[174]

The League's leadership also promoted Gobineau among the chapters. From Schemann they procured a hundred copies of the *Essay*, one half of which went out on loan to the chapters, while the rest the League sent elsewhere in the German-national public – to the Eastern Marches Society, the Commercial Employees' Union, student associations, and to several other groups.[175] Despite its ponderous length, many Pan-Germans read the *Essay*, at least to judge from the number of lectures devoted to its exegesis in ensuing years and from the number of the League's members who joined the Gobineau Society.[176] Schemann reciprocated shortly before the war by setting up a chapter of the Pan-German League in Freiburg.[177]

Schemann's involvement with the Pan-German League solidified the League's ties to a number of other racist and antisemitic organizations to which Schemann had been close. The relationship of the *Deutschbund* to the League reached the point of virtual fusion. Lange managed to embrace scientific racism without fully abandoning religious mysticism; Gobineau he hailed now as a 'redeemer'.[178] His organization moved to the forefront of the campaign to spread the new gospel, where it joined forces with the Gobineau Society and the Pan-German League.[179] Cooperation with the League produced a modest increase in the number of *Bundesbrüder*, most of whom were Pan-Germans too. In chapters of the League in Darmstadt, Gotha, Jena, Kassel, Bochum, and Meiningen, the boards of officers were by 1910 in the hands of men who belonged to the *Deutschbund*.[180] The extent of the overlap was again documented when, in 1913, elections to the *Deutschbund*'s ten-man national directorate (called the *Bundeskammer*) produced six prominent Pan-Germans, including Paul Langhans from Gotha, who replaced Lange as *Bundeswart*, and Leopold Freiherr von Vietinghoff-Scheel, who was then serving as executive secretary to the Pan-German League.[181]

The spread of racist antisemitism also brought the League into contact with one of the founding fathers of the antisemitic movement in Germany. The popularization of Gobineau gave a new lease on life to Theodor Fritsch, who had long been a leading publicist for the antisemitic political parties but whose fortunes had fallen with theirs late in the 1890s.[182] In 1902 he founded a journal called the *Hammer*, in which he hoped, by means of propagating a scientific antisemitism, to provide a rallying point for the forces he had earlier served.[183] The journal never did enjoy a mass circulation, but a number of '*Hammer* communities' did form among the journal's readers in Berlin, Leipzig, Stuttgart, and Hamburg.[184] The fact that many of these people came from the ranks of the Commercial Employees' Union encouraged cooperation between the communities and the Pan-German League, as did Fritsch's ties to Schemann, Lange, Albert Ritter (who was one of the League's travelling lecturers), and to Class's friend Stössel.[185] When in 1910 these communities coalesced to form the *Reichshammerbund* for purposes of 'preserving and promoting a healthy, distinctive German character [*Eigenart*]', the chairman was Karl Hellwig, a retired colonel who sat on the board of officers in the League's chapter in Kassel.[186]

The network that spun out from the Pan-German League and tied together the propagators of scientific racism also comprehended leading lights in the racist movement, such as Ammon and Wilser, both of whom belonged to the League. It comprised as well more obscure racist organizations, such as *Bund für Heimatschutz* and the *Deutsche Gesellschaft für Vorgeschichte*.[187] Finally the network extended into the eugenics movement, to Alfred Plötz's *Deutsche Gesellschaft für Rassenhygene* and to the *Politisch-Anthropologische Revue*, whose editors, Woltmann and later Otto Schmidt-Gibichenfels, presented their findings to chapters of the Pan-German League.[188] Nor was it a coincidence that the League's publisher, J. F. Lehmann, was one of the leading producers of books on racial hygiene in Germany.[189]

The Pan-German League developed into the single most important public forum for the discussion of *Rassenwissenschaft* in Germany. Although the League never officially adopted racist antisemitism into its program, the axioms of racial theory blended easily and with increasing visibility into the ideology.[190] Although arguments persisted over some of the more arcane points, such as the original home of the Aryans, consensus reigned on the propositions that race – biological make-up – was the most fundamental factor operating in human affairs, that it determined ethnicity and culture, and that race-mixing was the dynamic of history. From Gobineau, Pan-Germans embraced the belief that the Aryans had stood at the top in the natural hierarchy of races and that the distinction of being the least polluted survivor of the Aryans belonged to the Germanic (or Nordic) race, of which the Germans made up the principal part.[191]

Apart from its claim to scientific validity, the most appealing feature of the scientific theory of race was its emphasis on the theme of regeneration, which enabled the Pan-Germans to contend with the pessimism that arose out of their organization's own crisis. Fusing Gobineau and Darwin led to the view that the inherent tendency in history was toward cultural degeneration, but that decisive intervention could still reverse, or at least arrest it. The crisis in the Pan-German League appeared accordingly as but an aspect of a broader process of cultural decay – a process that could be halted with the identification of its true cause. The cause that the Pan-Germans identified was the pollution of German blood; and the agent of pollution was the Jew.

After 1902 central themes in the League's ideology adapted to categories supplied by the theory of scientific racism.[192] Ethnic struggle in Central and Eastern Europe the Pan-Germans now cast in the irreconcilable terms of a

Rassenkampf between Germans and Slavs.[193] Race theory enabled the
League's publicists also to descry now the ultimate link among all the
nation's enemies. The influence of Jews they discovered everywhere – in
fomenting hatred of Germans among the Slavs, in undermining the German
family through the women's movement, in the peace movement, and even in
ultramontanism.[194] Jews were the animating power behind Social
Democracy.[195] They were, in sum, the agents of cultural degeneration in all
its forms. 'Leaders from a foreign race have filled the masses with foreign
ideas', one writer warned in 1912, pointing to the 'hundreds of canals and
small gutters' through which 'the materials of subversion push into our
innermost life [*in unser Inneres*] – through books and newspapers, novels
and songs, through satirical journals and motion pictures, through drama
and art'.[196]

The Jews now symbolized all that the Pan-German League most feared.
They were unleashing the flood. 'By virtue of their essence and instincts',
Jews embodied the spirit of chaos – not only the biological chaos of
race-mixing, but its product, the cultural chaos of insubordination,
negativism, and the repudiation of proper authority and order.[197] The
Pan-Germans' conceptions of order and authority thus also adapted easily to
the biological metaphor. With scientific reliability, they believed, race
determined entitlement to authority and elite roles in the proper order. In a
manner reminiscent of Gobineau's attempts to buttress the claims of his own
aristocratic class to preferment, leaders of the League adduced biological
factors to underpin the structure of authority, both in the world at large and
at home. Culture remained the criterion, but culture now became an index of
racial purity and quality. 'The Germanic peoples have the highest
culture-forming rank', one leader told the League's congress in 1913. 'The
more Germanic blood a *Volk* has in it, the more capable it is of producing
culture [*kulturfähig*].'[198] The international order, the apportionment of
power and influence in the world, ought, the Pan-Germans insisted, to
correspond to this racial hierarchy.

The principles governing the structure of authority at home, within the
German race, were the same. In this connection, the Pan-German writers
virtually equated racial superiority with *Bildung*, as they lodged, on the
authority of science, their own claims to precedence.[199] The pioneers served
the German race: they represented an 'aristocracy of personality', of 'blood
and *Geist*'.[200] They displayed the same essential attributes of character as the
old, racially unpolluted German tribesmen, who, in the judgment of one
Pan-German leader, had been 'healthy in body and soul, independently
minded and self-reliant, despising mundane values like goods and wealth,
filled with noble faith and genuine humanity'.[201]

The scientific theory of race finally lent chilling accents to the League's
demands. The growing importance of cultural degeneration in the League's
world-view brought on a new emphasis on domestic problems. The
suppression of ethnic minorities and other domestic enemies, not a new
demand in itself, appeared now in racial attire as the call for the protection of
the health and purity of the race, or, as one writer put it, for 'measures for the
ennoblement of the race'.[202] Racial health required the prevention, by all

legal means, of pollution by inferior blood. Leading Pan-Germans called accordingly for laws to forbid marriages of people who were crippled, blind, deaf, dumb, epileptic, alcoholic, retarded, tubercular, had criminal records, or had otherwise been institutionalized.[203] Most centrally, however, the 'ennoblement of the race' raised the 'Jewish problem', for whose 'happy solution' Edward von Liebert was, as he announced to his colleagues on the executive committee, 'personally prepared to undertake even the most "radical" measures'.[204] In the prewar years the range of the Pan-Germans' imagination did not extend beyond proposing to deprive the Jews of their civil rights, to limit their right to marry, and to refuse them access to hotels and restaurants, the armed forces, most professions, and ownership of agricultural property.[205]

No less foreboding were the accents that racial theory added to the Pan-Germans' thinking on foreign policy. In the logic of racial breeding, the quantity of racial stock was no less critical than its quality. According to this logic, the more numerous the superior race, the more secure was its purity and integrity, the less tempting or necessary was racial intermingling. 'Even if they live far abroad', one writer pointed out, 'the more Germans on earth, the more secure is the future of the German character, language, and culture [*Gesittung*]'.[206] Following this reasoning, the Pan-German League groped its way in the years before the war toward a comprehensive 'population policy'. The health of the race demanded measures to increase the birth rate, even at the risk of a wholesale intrusion into the private sphere – by such means as encouraging early marriages, combating infant mortality, prohibiting contraception, and setting up homes for illegitimate children.[207] Once pursued this far, though, the logic of racist theory led to a paradox. A high birth rate, though essential to the health of the race, encouraged overpopulation, which in turn threatened the health of the race by encouraging its concentration in the large urban centers of socialism and Jewish decadence. One solution was inescapable, formulated as unambiguously as one could wish by one leader who proclaimed that 'politics is a question of space'.[208] The paramount goal of German foreign policy had, the Pan-Germans concluded, to be forestalling the social, cultural, and racial consequences of overcrowding by finding *Lebensraum*, the land on which to settle the 'colossal surplus' already building up in the German race.[209]

This was no incidental theme in Pan-German literature. It surfaced with increasing frequency after 1904, when Class first spelled out the consequences of a population policy in a meeting of the executive committee. The only remaining question, he insisted, was where German expansion would take place.[210] Because the setbacks of 1905–6 seemed to rule out seizing settlement colonies overseas, Class and the other leaders turned their gaze to the east.[211] 'We need land' was the dictum of one of them, 'even if it is inhabited by foreigners, so that we can adapt it to our needs'.[212] Class himself went a step further. On the eve of the war he publicly proposed to evacuate large strips of land of their inhabitants in both European Russia and eastern France and to resettle these areas with Germans.[213]

Before it had reached these grotesque extremes, the Pan-Germans' attempt to enlist the theory of race to buttress authority and order had proved distasteful to many members, particularly in the chapters in the south. Some of the League's declining membership after 1902 was in fact a sign of protest over just this phase of the organization's radicalization.[214] Those who remained by 1909 could have had few qualms about the new accents in the League's activities, for racist antisemitism had not only become a dominant theme in the League's ideology, but the organization's broadening orbit and new financial strength turned it into the largest and most important medium for spreading the science of race into the German middle class.

The League's growing association with racist antisemitism provided a new dimension to the organization's profile as the most radical sector of the German-national public, and for a time it broadened the distance between the League and most of the other patriotic societies.[215] This evolution corresponded to the designs of the League's national leadership, which, even before the ascendency of Class, had fallen under control of racists. Even Hasse, who had once resisted racism, changed his views dramatically after he read Gobineau and Chamberlain.[216] The position of the leadership was signalled as early as 1905, when it commissioned Kuhlenbeck to speak to the national convention on the subject of race.[217] Thereafter, though especially after Class became chairman, the executive committee systematically encouraged the discussion of racism in the chapters, despite evidence of the League's isolation among the patriotic societies.

In the 'race question' the leadership tended to be more extreme than the rank and file. The distance between the leaders and the membership, which opened up in the wake of Class's centralization and the resolution of the financial crisis, was thus ideologically reinforced, although disagreements with the national leadership over the issues of race and antisemitism were never significant enough after 1909 to cause many members to leave. In any event, now that they had their own sources of money, Class and the rest of the executive committee could afford to risk antagonizing the rank and file. And by 1911 they had reason to believe that despite its costs, racism was going to increase dramatically the force they could mobilize in opposition to the government.

Notes

1   ZStAP, ADV 183, Kuhlenbeck to Hasse, Jena, 13.12.00.
2   ZStAP, ADV 43, GFA, 9–10.4.04, Eingegangene Antworten ... Reismann-Grone, Essen, 26.3.04.
3   ADB (1903), 233–4.
4   In the Reichstag of 1898, forty-five members had been in the League, although many chose not to advertise the fact. Ten of these men lost their seats in 1903: see Eley, *Reshaping*, p. 248.
5   ADB (1903), 131, 215; ADB (1908), 45–6; Wenck, p. 25.
6   ADB (1903), 189–90.
7   Class, *Strom*, esp. pp. 1–9; cf. Werner Conze, 'Heinrich Class', NDB. vol. 3, p. 263.
8   Class, *Strom*, pp. 92–5; cf. Bonhard, pp. 18–19.

9   ADB (1903), 331–44.
10 See ADB (1896), 121–2; ADB (1902), 469–70; cf. Bonhard, p. 18.
11 ADB (1903), 345–6.
12 Class, *Die Bilanz des neuen Kurses* (Munich, 1903); ZStAP, ADV 187, Hasse to Geschäftsstelle, Leipzig, 3.11.03.
13 ADB (1903), 386–7; ADB (1904), 358.
14 ZStAP, ADV 43, GFA, Gotha, 9–10.4.04, Reismann-Grone DS, Zur Lage des Verbandes; ADV 45, GFA, Leipzig, 7–8.10.04, Hopf RS, 7.9.04; ADB (1904), 134, 324.
15 ZStAP, ADV 43, GFA, Gotha, 9–10.4.04; ADV 44, GFA, Lübeck, 27.5.04; ADV 45, GFA, Leipzig, 7–8.10.04; ADV 188, Hasse RS, Kolonial-politische Forderungen, 31.1.04; Hasse RS, Ueberseeische oder Festlands-Politik?, Leipzig, 12.3.04; Hasse DS, Die Flottenfrage, Leipzig, 5.3.04.
16 ZStAP, ADV 45, GFA, Leipzig, 7–8.10.04, Lehmann RS, August 1904.
17 ZStAP, ADV 7, Vorstandssitzung, Berlin, 21.12.04; ADB (1904), 70–4.
18 Wehner, pp. 40–62; Oncken, 'Lebensraum', pp. 108–30; Werner, pp. 146–9, 159–66; Hussmann, pp. 38–54.
19 ZStAP, ADV 43, GFA, Gotha, 9–10.4.04, Liebert RS, Nächste Aufgaben; Sitzungsprotokoll–Marokko; cf. Oncken, 'Lebensraum', pp. 105–8; Pierard, pp. 246–7.
20 ZStAP, ADV 43, GFA, Gotha, 9–10.4.04, Class DS, Die Besitzergreifung Westmarokkos, 12.3.04.
21 ADB (1904), 113–14, 129–31; Heinrich Class, *Marokko verloren?* (Munich, 1904).
22 ADB (1905), 134–5. On the crisis that followed see Eugene N. Anderson, *The First Moroccan Crisis, 1904–1906* (Chicago, 1930); Kennedy, Antagonism, pp. 275–83.
23 ADB (1905), 105–6.
24 ADB (1905), 113–15, 166.
25 ZStAP, ADV 48, GFA, Göttingen, 15.4.05; ADV 49, GFA, Worms, 15–16.5.05; ADV 188, Hasse RS, Leipzig, 4.5.05; Class, *Strom*, pp. 109–12.
26 ADB (1905), 337–8.
27 ADB (1905), 358, 384–5; ADB (1906), 101, 109–11, 162–3.
28 ADB (1904), 129–31; ADB (1905), 213.
29 ZStAP, ADV 49, GFA, Worms, 15–16.5.05; ADV 188, Geiser to Hasse, 21.5.04.
30 Berghahn, *Tirpitz-Plan*, pp. 419–504.
31 ADB (1905), 80–1.
32 ADB (1905), 334–6; cf. ibid., pp. 399–401, 405–6, 430, 444–5; ADB (1906), 50.
33 PAAA, Deutschland 169, Bd. 3, Eisendecher to Bethmann Hollweg, Karlsruhe, 14.9.10; cf. ibid., Bd. 2, Richthofen to Generalkonsul Zürich, 15.7.04; Bülow, *Deutsche Politik*, p. 149.
34 ADB (1905), 97; cf. ADB (1904), 175.
35 StBR (14.11.06), 3630.
36 PAAA, Deutschland 169, Bd. 2, Tschirsky Notiz, 25.11.06; ADB (1906), 377–9.
37 ADB (1906), 286–8.
38 *Schulthess' Europäischer Geschichtskalender*, vol. 47, p. 161; ADB (1906), 305–9; ZStAP, ADV 57, GFA, Berlin, 17–18.11.06.
39 ZStAP, ADV 45, GFA, Leipzig, 7–8.10.04, Lehmann RS, Munich, August 1904; ADV 49, GFA, Worms, 15–16.5.05; ADB (1898), 286; ADB (1902), 403–5; ADB (1903), 344–5; ADB (1904), 93; ADB (1906), 361–2, 406; Class, *Strom*, pp. 92–5; Ernst Graf zu Reventlow, *Kaiser Wilhelm II und die Byzantiner* (Munich, 1906).
40 On the whole episode see Wilhelm Schüssler, *Die Daily-Telegraph-Affaire: Fürst Bülow, Kaiser Wilhelm und die Krise des zweiten Reiches 1908* (Göttingen, 1952); Eschenburg, pp. 131–75; and now Terence F. Cole, 'The *Daily Telegraph* affair and its aftermath: the Kaiser, Bülow and the Reichstag, 1908–1909', in John C. G. Röhl and Nicholaus Sombart (eds), *Kaiser Wilhelm II: New Interpretations* (Cambridge, 1982), pp. 249–68.
41 ADB (1908), 381–3, 389.
42 ZStAP, ADV 67, GFA, Berlin, 4–5.11.08.
43 ZStAP, ADV 192, Stössel to Class, Potsdam, 27.11.08.
44 ZStAP, ADV 68, GFA, Leipzig, 21.11.08; ADV 193, Ein- und Austritte . . . ; ADV 83, GFA, Berlin, 17–18.2.12.

45 ZStAP, ADV 67, Radebold to Class, Dortmund, 3.11.08.
46 ZStAP, ADV 67, GFA, Berlin, 4–5.11.08, Aufruf; cf. ADB (1908), 297–300.
47 ADB (1908), 395.
48 ADB (1910), 111.
49 e.g. ZStAP, ADV 57, GFA, Berlin, 17–18.11.06, Boeser to Hauptleitung, Karlsruhe, 28.10.06.
50 ZStAP, ADV 190, Hasse to Class, 18.12.06; ADB (1907), 270–71; ADB (1908), 52–3.
51 See Wertheimer, pp. 76–7 for a summary of the League's budget.
52 The League regularly sent a correspondence sheet with news briefs of patriotic interest to about thirty-five newspapers around the country: ZStAP, ADV 193, Zahlende Bezieher der Nationalen Korrespondenz vom 16.3.09.
53 ZStAP, ADV 188, Fischer, Erläuterungen ... Anlage: Uebersicht über die ausserordentlichen Ausgaben im Jahre 1903.
54 ADB (1901), 59.
55 In 1904 the School Association supported German communities abroad to the tune of over 100,000 Marks: BA, ZSg 1, 142/5, Gesamt-Uebersicht der Einnahmen und Ausgaben des Allgemeinen Deutschen Schulvereins im Jahre 1904.
56 ADB (1910), 109–10.
57 Chickering, 'Patriotic societies', pp. 474–6, 485.
58 ZStAP, ADV 95, GFA, Berlin, 4.7.14.
59 ZStAP, ADV 29, GFA, Leipzig, 30–31.8.01; ADV 188, Fischer, Erläuterungen, p. 26; ADB (1901), 410.
60 ADB (1897), 197–8; ADB (1899), 190.
61 ADB (1903), 330; Wertheimer, pp. 79–82.
62 ADB (1904), 130–1; ADB (1905), 226; ADB (1907), 365.
63 See Hans Jaeger, *Unternehmer in der deutschen Politik (1890–1918)* (Bonn, 1967), pp. 132–41.
64 These amounts were, however, significant enough that on more than one occasion they invited fraud. The most painful incident involved the League's investments in a bank established to make short-term credit available to German farmers who wished to settle in North Schleswig. The bank's founder discovered other uses for his investors' money before he was imprisoned for embezzlement: ADB (1901), 295–6; ADB (1903), 204, 399.
65 See Jaeger, pp. 141–7; Chickering, 'Patriotic societies', pp. 474–5, 483–4.
66 ZStAP, ADV 188, Fischer, Erläuterungen, pp. 8–9; ADB (1902), 82.
67 ZStAP, ADV 188, Geiser to Hasse, 21.5.04; ADV 192, Klitzing to Class, Cologne, 19.8.08; ADB (1904), 125; ADB (1907), 71.
68 ZStAP, ADV 192, Simons DS, Ortsgruppenrückstände, Godesberg, 12.12.08; ADB (1902), 351; ADB (1903), 19; ADB (1904), 247; ADB (1905), 299.
69 ZStAP, ADV 20, GFA, Berlin, 26–27.10.01.
70 ZStAP, ADV 188, Hasse to Samassa, Leipzig, 1.3.04; ADB (1905), 209–10; ADB (1909), 275–6.
71 ZStAP, ADV 193, Itzenplitz to Class, Mülheim, 8.1.09.
72 ZStAP, ADV 69, GFA, Berlin, 16–17.1.09; ADV 188, Fischer, Bemerkungen zu dem Kassenabschluss für Ende 1903.
73 ZStAP, ADV 192, Itzenplitz to Class, Mülheim, 22.12.08.
74 ZStAP, ADV 70, GFA, Eisenach, 17.4.09; ADV 193, Class to Klingemann, 12.2.09; ADB (1909), 274–6.
75 ZStAP, ADV 68, GFA, Leipzig, 21.11.08; ADV 192, Class to Stössel, Mainz, 8, 15.08; ADV 193, Klitzing to Class, Köln, 13.3.09.
76 ZStAP, ADV 193, Klingemann to Class, Essen, 12.4.09; ADV 411, Class to Itzenplitz, Mainz, 30.12.09.
77 ZStAM, Rep. 195 Nr. 48, Kirdorf to DOV, Gelsenkirchen, 20.11.94; BBA, 55/8 7015, Bismarck-Gesellschaft in Stendal, Liste der Beitrittserklärungen (December 1904); Klauss, p. 116; cf. Helmut Böhme, 'Emil Kirdorf: Ueberlegungen zu einer Unternehmerbiographie', *Tradition*, vol. 16 (1969), esp. p. 37, n. 105.
78 ZStAP, ADV 194, Class to Itzenplitz, Mainz, 20.2.10.
79 ZStAP, ADV 411, Class to Reventlow, Mainz, 7.5.10.

80 ZStAP, ADV 411, Kirdorf to Class, Streithof, 7.8.10.

81 ZStAP, ADV 194, Class to Simons, Mainz, 9.8.10; ADB (1910), 275–6.

82 Eley, 'Navy League', pp. 142–50.

83 BA, NL Hugenberg 1, Hugenberg to Class, Frankfurt, 8.5.08; ZStAP, ADV 395, Class to Hugenberg, Mainz, 11.12.09; Class, *Strom*, p. 47.

84 ZStAP, ADV 196, Stössel to Class, Potsdam, 5.10.12; ADV 197, Klingemann to Class, Coblenz, 13.2.13; ADV 322, Klingemann to Class, Essen, 14.7.11; Alter, pp. 145–6; Guratzsch, pp. 95–6; Heidrun Holzbach, *Das 'System Hugenberg': Die Organisation bürgerlicher Sammlungspolitik vor dem Aufstieg der NSDAP* (Stuttgart, 1981), pp. 52–4.

85 Hartmut Kaelble, *Industrielle Interessenpolitik in der Wilhelminischen Gesellschaft: Centralverband Deutscher Industrieller 1985–1914* (Berlin, 1967), pp. 155–63; Guratzsch, pp. 81–2, 186; Nipperdey, 'Interessenverbände', p. 331; cf. Siegfried Mielke, *Der Hansa-Bund für Gewerbe, Handel und Industrie 1909–1914: Der gescheiterte Versuch einer antifeudalen Sammlungspolitik* (Göttingen, 1976), esp. pp. 81–91. Kirdorf's support for the League was not to the taste of all his friends in the coal syndicate, some of whom feared for their holdings in France should the tie become known: ZStAP, ADV 197, Itzenplitz to Class, Mülheim, 9.5.13; ADV 408, Class to Pohl, 24.6.11; ADV 411, Kirdorf to Class, Mülheim, 19.12.11.

86 ZStAP, ADV 198, Hugenberg to Class, Essen, 27.7.14; Class, *Strom*, pp. 216–17; Jaeger, pp. 137–8. Paul Reusch of the Gute-Hoffnungs-Hütte was a member of the Pan-German League, but there is no evidence that he contributed more than 10 Marks a year: HA/GHH 30019326/16.

87 ZStAP, ADV 193, Klitzing to Normann, Köln, 27.7.09; ADV 411, Kirdorf to Class, Streithof, 7.8.10; Kirdorf to Class, Mülheim, 17.2.14; Class, *Strom*, pp. 247–9.

88 The annual budgets, which circulated confidentially within the executive committee after 1910, listed under income an item described only as 'withdrawals'. In 1911 this item, the bulk of which was certainly the industrial subsidy, amounted to nearly 53,000 Marks; in 1913 it was almost 64,000 Marks: ZStAP, ADV 84, 'Kassenbericht für das Jahr 1911', *Vertrauliche Mitteilungen*, no. 3 (13.3.12); UB Frieburg, NL Schemann, II D, 'Kassenbericht für das Jahr 1913', *Vertrauliche Mitteilungen*, no. 5 (15.6.14); ZStAP, ADV 84, GFA, Hannover, 13–14.4.12; ADV 92, GFA, Remscheid, 6.12.13; cf. O'Donnell, p. 327, n. 219; Kruck, p. 16.

89 By 1908 about 90,000 Marks had been donated to the *Wehrschatz*. During the next six years an additional 300,000 Marks flowed in. Not all of this was industrial money, but a lot was: BA, NL Hugenberg 10, Class to Kirdorf, Mainz, 2.6.14; ZStAP, ADV 197, Class to Schnauss, Mainz, 18.12.13; Klingemann to Class, 31.1.13; ADV 395, Class to Kirdorf, 2.6.14; ADB (1910), 19–20; ADB (1911), 125, 446; Wenck, p. 15; Schödl, p. 159.

90 ZStAP, ADV 7, Vorstandssitzung, Hamburg, 3.4.10; ADB (1910), 171, 275–6.

91 Hartwig, 'Zur Politik', p. 279.

92 ZStAP, ADV 197, Class to Schnauss, Mainz, 18.12.13. In his memoirs Class still lied about the extent of the industrialists' support: Class, *Strom*, pp. 247–9.

93 ZStAP, ADV 192, Class to Calmbach, Mainz, 18.2.08; Class, *Strom*, pp. 103–4, 130; cf. Hartwig, 'Zur Politik', pp. 144–5.

94 See Reismann-Grone, p. 45.

95 ZStAP, ADV 43, GFA, Gotha, 9–10.4.04, Eingegangene Antworten ... H.Z. DS, Nächste Aufgaben.

96 ZStAP, ADV 43, GFA, Gotha, 9–10.4.04, Neue Arbeitsprogramm; Class, *Strom*, p. 131; cf. Alter, pp. 15–16.

97 Guratzsch, pp. 257–60; cf. Friedrich Krutmann, 'Die Aussenpolitik in der Tageszeitung "Die Post" von 1890 bis 1914', (Diss. phil., Leipzig, 1933).

98 See Hallgarten, Vol. 2, p. 189; Kaelble, pp. 139–43.

99 ZStAP, ADV 411, Kirdorf to Class, Streithof, 7.8.10; Frymann/Class, *Kaiserbuch*, p. 16.

100 ZStAP, ADV 194, Class to Wolf, Mainz, 3.3.10; Ilges to Class, Cologne, 22.9.10; ADV 195, Dieckmann to Class, Osnabrück, 12.4.11.

101 ZStAP, ADV 197, Class to Schnauss, Mainz, 18.12.13; ADB (1911), 104–5; ADB (1913), 433–4.

102 ADB (1903), 193–4.

103 ADB (1905), 342; ADB (1906), 83; Pogge von Strandmann, 'Nationale Verbände', pp. 296–317.

104 ADB (1906), 173–5; Schödl, esp. pp. 39–44.

105 ZStAM, 2.2.1. Nr. 15370, ADV Ogr. Bonn to William, 28.10.99; ADB (1905), 41; cf. ADB (1900), 195–7; ADB (1904), 305.

106 ADB (1904), 192–3.

107 ADB (1909), 37–8.

108 ADB (1909), 70–1; cf. ADB (1907), 377–8.

109 Nathan W. Ackermann and Marie Jahoda, *Anti-Semitism and Emotional Disorder: A Psychoanalytic Interpretation* (New York, 1950), p. 25; Robert Gellately, *The Politics of Economic Despair: Shopkeepers and German Politics, 1890–1914* (Santa Barbara, Calif., 1974), p. 8; cf. Jochmann, pp. 439–72; Broszat, p. 4; Reinhard Rürup and Thomas Nipperdey, 'Antisemitismus–Entstehung, Funktion und Geschichte eines Begriffs', in Rürup, *Emanzipation und Antisemitismus: Studien zur 'Judenfrage' der bürgerlichen Gesellschaft* (Göttingen, 1975), esp. pp. 89–91.

110 Massing, esp. pp. 79–81, 99–108; cf. Field, p. 269.

111 In 1913 Konstantin von Gebsattel wrote to Class from St Moritz, where he was vacationing, 'I have here a good opportunity to observe the predominance of these vile people. Recently I encountered, within half an hour, twenty-three Christians and thirty-four Jews': ZStAP, NL Gebsattel 1, Gebsattel to Class, St Moritz, 23.7.14. On another occasion, though, Gebsattel insisted that he was no antisemite: NL Gebsattel 1, Gedanken über einen notwendigen Fortschritt der inneren Entwicklung Deutschland; cf. ADV 197, Liebig to Class, Giessen, 24.6.13.

112 See ADB (1902), 201; ADB (1912), 25–6; ADB (1913), 368–70.

113 On the School Association see Weidenfeller, pp. 227–31; and on the Eastern Marches Society, Galos, p. 107.

114 For surveys of antisemitism in the Pan-German League see Uwe Lohalm, *Völkischer Radikalismus: Die Geschichte des Deutschvölkischen Schutz- und Trutz-Bundes 1919–1923* (Hamburg, 1970), pp. 32–56; Pulzer, pp. 226–35.

115 ZStAP, ADV 661, Hasse to Ogr. Frankfurt, Leipzig, 23.8.01; Bonhard, pp. 97–9.

116 Kruck, p. 130.

117 StAH, Pol. Polizei V 452, Bd. 1, *Hamburgischer Correspondent*, Nr. 192, 16.3.92; ZStAP, ADV 182, Wislicenus to Hasse, Berlin, 5.9.93.

118 An Emanuel Rothschild appeared on the board of officers in the chapter in Coblenz in 1897, and an Alfred Israel was a member of the chapter in Hamburg in 1901. A more celebrated case was that of Max Koch, an eminent Wagner scholar at the university in Breslau and a baptized Jew, who chaired the local chapter before protest from the antisemites in the chapter convinced Hasse to elevate him into the national board of directors; ZStAP, ADV 188, Geiser to Hasse, 29.3.04.

119 ZStAP, ADV 661, Hasse to Viereck, Leipzig, 24.9.01

120 Griesewelle, pp. 366–79; Jochmann, p. 428; Class, *Strom*, p. 16.

121 ZStAP, ADV 30, GFA, Berlin, 26–27.10.01; Levy, p. 127; Broszat, pp. 127–9; cf. Class, *Strom*, p. 29.

122 Broszat, p. 122.

123 ZStAP, ADV 3, ADV Aufruf [November 1891?]; cf. ADB (1897), 233–4; ADB (1899), 37–8; ADB (1902), 459.

124 ADB (1894), 5–7; ADB (1898), 25; ADB (1900), 490–2; ADV, Gau Ruhr und Lippe, *Die Polen im Rheinisch-westfälischen Kohlenbezirke* (Munich, 1898).

125 ZStAP, ADV 2, Der Allgemeine Deutsche Verband und der Antisemitismus (19.8.91), on which Hasse's gloss reads: 'It can be left to a Jew to decide if he wants to be considered a Jew or not? Yes.' cf. Petzet, p. 10; Schultheiss, *Magyarisierung*, pp. 80–1.

126 ADB (1894), 42–3; ADB (1897), 242; ADB (1898), 53–4; ADB (1901), 308.

127 ZStAP, ADV 2, ADV Aufruf, April 1891; ADB (1894), 22–3; ADB (1897), 134.

128 Türk, p. 54; ADB (1897), 217–18.

129 See especially Patrik von zur Mühlen, *Rassenideologien: Geschichte und Hintergründe* (Berlin and Bonn-Bad Godesberg, 1977), pp. 32–51; Leon Poliakov, *The Aryan Myth: A History of Racist and Nationalist Ideas in Europe* (New York, 1974); George L. Mosse, *Toward the Final Solution: A History of European Racism* (New York, 1978); Jacques

Barzun, *Race: A Study in Superstition* (New York, 1937); Bronder, pp. 283–303; Mosse, *Crisis*, pp. 88–107; Stern, *Cultural Despair, passim.*

130 Friedrich Lange, *Reines Deutschtum: Grundzüge einer nationalen Weltanschauung*, 4th edn (Berlin, 1904), pp. 415–29; cf. A. Linnemann, 'Friedrich Lange und die Deutsche Zeitung' (Diss. phil., Berlin, 1938).

131 ZStAM, Rep. 77, Tit. 662 Nr. 91, Satzung des DB.

132 ibid.; cf. Gerstenhauer, p. 11; Stern *Cultural Despair*, p. 124.

133 *Reines Deutschtum: Grundzüge einer nationalen Weltanschauung* (Berlin, 1893).

134 Lange, *Reines Deutschtum* (1904), pp. 415–29.

135 There is no study of this organization, but see: ZStAM, Rep. 77, Tit. 662 Nr. 91, *passim*; Schultheiss, *Vereinswesen*, pp. 72–73; Lange, *Reines Deutschtum* (1904), pp. 347–414; Broszat, pp. 145–7; Pulzer, pp. 230–1; Lohalm, pp. 33–5.

136 Lange, *Reines Deutschtum* (1904), p. 351.

137 ibid., p. 355; ZStAM, Rep. 77, Tit. 662 Nr. 91, Verfassung und Regeln des DB.

138 ibid., pp. 347–8, 370–3.

139 Class, *Strom*, pp. 30–3, 37; Lohalm, p. 35.

140 ZStAP, ADV 188, Geiser to Hasse, 29.3.04; ADB (1901), 545; Lange, *Reines Deutschtum* (1904), pp. 374, 427.

141 ADB (1899), 309, 315. Lange's chief patron was Georg Freiherr von Stössel, who provided the money that enabled Lange to launch the *Deutsche Zeitung*.

142 ADB (1898), 83–4.

143 Hasse, *Nationalstaat*, p. 66; cf. Tal, p. 301.

144 ADB (1898), 133–5, 190; Gerstenhauer, pp. 11, 24.

145 *Essai sur l'inégalité des races humaines*, 4 vols (Paris, 1853–5). The best introduction in English to the work of Gobineau is Michael D. Biddiss, *The Father of Racist Ideology: The Social and Political Thought of Count Gobineau* (London, 1970); see also Hannah Arendt, *The Origins of Totalitarianism* (Cleveland, Ohio, and New York, 1958), pp. 170–5.

146 Biddiss, p. 265.

147 Manfred Steinkühler, 'Gobineau au jugement de ses contemporains d'Outre-Rhin' (Diss. phil., University of Paris, 1961).

148 Biddiss, p. 250; cf. Frymann/Class, *Kaiserbuch*, pp. 34–5.

149 Winfried Schüler, *Der Bayreuther Kreis von seiner Entstehung bis zum Ausgang der Wilhelminischen Aera: Wagnerkult und Kulturreform im Geiste völkischer Weltanschauung* (Münster, 1971), pp. 124, 237–8, 244; Ludwig Schemann, *Gobineaus Rassenwerk: Aktenstücke und Betrachtungen zur Geschichte und Kritik des Essai sur l'inegalité des races humaines* (Stuttgart, 1910), pp. 236–47; Biddiss, pp. 255–6; Field, pp. 152–4.

150 Ludwig Schemann, *Lebensfahrten eines Deutschen* (Leipzig and Hartenstein, 1925), p. 320; Schemann, *Rassenwerk*, p. 244; Schüler, pp. 104–5.

151 UB Freiburg, NL Schemann II D, Erster Bericht über die GV, Wilhelmshöhe, September 1895; cf. Schemann, *Fünfundzwanzig Jahre Gobineau-Vereinigung 1894/1919: Ein Rückblick* (Strasburg and Berlin, 1919), p. 31; Schemann, *Rassenwerk*, pp. 137–8; Hans von Wolzogen, 'Zur Gobineau-Bewegung', in *Aus deutscher Welt: Gesammelte Aufsätze über deutsche Art und Kultur* (Leipzig, 1910), pp. 102–11.

152 ZStAM, Rep. 195 Nr. 128, Schemann, Dritter Bericht über die GV, Nervi, 1898/9; UB Freiburg, NL Schemann IV B, Liebert to Schemann, Berlin [June 1910]; Lucanus to Schemann, Potsdam, 19.8.01; Vierter Bericht über die GV, Freiburg, July 1900; Badisches Generallandesarchiv, 60/1722, Dusig to Geheimes Kabinett, 30.12.01.

153 ZStAM, Rep. 195 Nr. 128, Schemann RS, An die Freunde und Verehrer des Grafen Gobineau, Freiburg, January 1900; Schemann, *Rassenwerk*, pp. xvii–xviii; Schüler, p. 59.

154 ZStAM, Rep. 195 Nr. 128, Schemann RS, Freiburg, Autumn 1897.

155 Schemann, *Rassenwerk*, pp. 249–50; cf. ADB (1902), 283–4.

156 See Mühlen, pp. 101–31.

157 Hobohm and Rohrbach, p. 129.

158 See Hedwig Conrad-Martius, *Utopien der Menschenzüchtung: Der Sozialdarwinismus und seine Folgen* (Munich, 1955); Hansjoachim W. Koch, *Der Sozialdarwinismus: Seine*

Genese und sein Einfluss auf das imperialistische Denken (Munich, 1973); Hans–Ulrich Wehler, 'Sozialdarwinismus im expandierenden Industriestaat', in Imanuel Geiss and Bernd Jürgen Wendt (eds), *Deutschland in der Weltpolitik des 19. und 20. Jahrhunderts* (Düsseldorf, 1974), pp. 132–43; Hans-Günther Zmarzlik, 'Der Sozialdarwinismus in Deutschland als geschichtliches Problem', VZG, vol. 11 (1963), pp. 246–73; Kelly, pp. 101–2.

159 ZStAM, Rep. 195 Nr. 128, Schemann RS, An die Freunde und Verehrer des Grafen Gobineau, Freiburg, January 1900; Schemann, *Rassenwerk*, pp. 253–4; cf. Gerstenhauer, pp. 37–8.

160 Schüler, p. 243.

161 Broszat, pp. 89–90.

162 See Loren R. Graham, 'Science and values: the eugenics movement in Germany and Russia in the 1920s', AHR, vol. 82 (1977), pp. 1133–65; cf. Michael Freeden, 'Eugenics and progressive thought: a study in ideological affinity', *The Historical Journal*, vol. 22 (1979), 645–71; Kelly, pp. 105–9.

163 Field, pp. 169–77. See also Roderick Stackelberg, *Idealism Debased: From Volkisch Ideology to National Socialism* (Kent, Ohio, 1981), pp. 105–31; Donald E. Thomas, Jr, 'Idealism, romanticism, and race: the "Weltanschauung" of Houston Stewart Chamberlain' (PhD Diss., University of Chicago, 1971).

164 ADB (1902), pp. 225–6.

165 ibid., pp. 233–4. Werner's contention that a 'thorough discussion' of the Jewish question 'began only during the war' is wrong: pp. 82–3.

166 ADB (1905), 379–81; ADB (1909), 155–6, 171–3, 179–80, 286–7.

167 For example: ADB (1905), 274–5; ADB (1906), 404–5; ADB (1907), 142; ADB (1913), 368–9.

168 ADB (1908), 379; ADB (1911), 447; ADB (1914), 91.

169 For example: ADB (1902), 43, 90, 114; ADB (1903), 191; ADB (1904), 91, 119, 372–3; ADB (1906), 105, 389; ADB (1907), 215; ADB (1908), 87; ADB (1910), 127.

170 UB Freiburg, NL Schemann II D, Sechster Bericht über die GV, Freiburg, September 1903; Schemann, *Lebensfahrten*, p. 296.

171 ZStAM, Rep. 195 Nr. 128, Raschdau to Bovenschen, 9.5.00; UB Freiburg, NL Schemann IV A, Bovenschen to Schemann, Berlin, 15.6.99; Schemann, *Rassenwerk*, pp. 252–3.

172 UB Freiburg, NL Schemann II D, Haller to Schemann, Leipzig, 18.3.02; GV 1894–5, Verzeichnis der Mitglieder, Gönner und Förderer; GV Juli 1900 bis Januar 1902, Verzeichnis der Mitglieder, Gönner und Förderer; ADB (1902), 225–6, 233–4, 283–4.

173 ZStAP, ADV 76, GFA, Berlin, 8.10.10; ADB (1902), 229.

174 UB Freiburg, NL Schemann IV B, Liebert to Schemann, Berlin, 16.3.10; ZStAP, ADV 194, Klingemann to Class, Essen, 23.12.10; cf. Hasse, *Zukunft*, p. 46.

175 UB Freiburg, NL Schemann II D, Class to Schemann, Mainz, 13.12.03, 27.10.04; ADB (1904), 83, 214; Class, *Strom*, p. 131.

176 UB Freiburg, NL Schemann II D, GV, September 1912–December 1914, Verzeichnis der Mitglieder, Gönner und Forderer.

177 UB Freiburg, NL Schemann II D, Schemann to Vietinghoff-Scheel, Freiburg, 17.10.13.

178 Schemann, *Rassenwerk*, p. 260.

179 UB Freiburg, NL Schemann II D, Schemann RS, Freiburg, May 1910; ADB (1906), 73.

180 BA, ZSg 1, E/105, Stammrolle des Deutschbundes; UB Freiburg, NL Schemann IV A, Belde to Schemann, Cologne, 2.2.08, Düsseldorf, 31.1.12; cf. ADB (1909), 423.

181 StA Hamburg, Politische Polizei, S4669, *Deutsch-Soziale Blätter*, Nr. 44, 31.5.13.

182 See Pulzer, esp. pp. 33–55, 197; Levy, pp. 37–9, 235–6.

183 Theodor Fritsch, 'Aus der Entstehungszeit des "Hammer" ', in *Festschrift zum fünfundzwanzigjährigen Bestehen des Hammer* (Leipzig, 1926), pp. 7–18; Lohalm, pp. 56–66.

184 Willibald Schulze, 'Aus den Jugendtagen des Hammerbundes, Hamburg and Anderes', *Hammer-Festschrift*, pp. 69–73.

185 ZStAP, ADV 661, Fritsch to Stössel, Leipzig, 22.12.08; Fritsch to Schemann, 3.2.08, in *Hammer-Festschrift*, pp. 84–5; Schemann, *Rassenwerk*, p. 262; Lange, *Reines Deutschtum* (1904), p. 373; Class, *Strom*, pp. 249–50; Schüler, pp. 105–6.

186 BA, ZSg 1, 263/4, Satzung des Reichs-Hammer-Bundes.
187 UB Freiburg, NL Schemann II D, Elfter Bericht über die GV, Freiburg 1911; ADB (1909), 394–5; ADB (1911), 61; Class, *Strom*, p. 50. Houston Stewart Chamberlain did not fall into this orbit until the war years, in large part because he and Schemann did not get along: cf. Peck, p. 92.
188 ADB (1902), 151; ADB (1912), 399; ADB (1913), 1.
189 Stark, pp. 120–1.
190 ZStAP, ADV 661, Stössel to Class, Potsdam, 16.12.08; cf. ADB (1907), 297–300; ADB (1912), 383. When in 1910 the League published an anthology of articles from the *Alldeutsche Blätter*, one of the principal rubrics under which these articles were grouped was '*Rassenfrage*': *Zwanzig Jahre*.
191 See ADB (1912), 341–3; Hasse, *Zukunft*, pp. 48–50; Bonhard, p. 182.
192 For instance: ZStAP, ADV 188, Geiser to Hasse, Berlin, 23.5.04; Hasse, *Zukunft*, pp. 56–7; ADB (1906), 98–9; ADB (1910), 211–12.
193 ADB (1909), 58.
194 ADB (1902), 124; ADB (1906), 37–9; ADB (1909), 333–5; ADB (1912), 389–91; Frymann/Class, *Kaiserbuch*, pp. 51–2; Hobohm and Rohrbach, pp. 141–2; cf. Pulzer, pp. 226–35.
195 ZStAP, ADV 95, GFA, Berlin, 4.7.14; ADB (1909), 351; ADB (1912), 219–20; Frymann/Class, *Kaiserbuch*, pp. 43, 191–2.
196 ADB (1913), 359–62; cf. Hasse, *Zukunft*, pp. 71–2; ADB (1913), 226.
197 Frymann/Class, *Kaiserbuch*, pp. 32–4, 37; ADB (1907), 384–6; ADB (1911), 58–9.
198 ADB (1913), 322–5; cf. ADB (1904), 425–6; ADB (1907), 419.
199 See ADB (1902), 187–8; ADB (1914), 61.
200 ADB (1912), 252–3; cf. ADB (1910), 5.
201 Einhart, p. 5; cf. ADB (1899), 364; ADB (1908), 216–17; Gerstenhauer, p. 9; Frymann/Class, *Kaiserbuch*, p. 30.
202 Hasse, *Zukunft*, p. 69; ADB (1907), 383–5; ADB (1913), 220–1.
203 ADB (1907), 104; ADB (1911), 57–8; ADB (1913), 220–1.
204 ZStAP, ADV 95, GFA, Berlin, 4.7.14.
205 ZStAP, ADV 355, Gebsattel, Gedanken ... October 1913; Lange, *Reines Deutschtum* (1904), pp. 246–7; Frymann/Class, *Kaiserbuch*, pp. 74–8; ADB (1910), 8.
206 ADB (1911), 187–9.
207 ZStAP, ADV 94, GFA, Stuttgart, 18.4.14; Hasse, *Zukunft*, p. 17; ADB (1906), 321–2; ADB (1911), 57–8, 352–3; ADB (1912), 382–3.
208 ADB (1909), 354.
209 Wintzer, p. 76; ADB (1906), 99; ADB (1911), 437–8; ADB (1912), 47.
210 ZStAP, ADV 43, GFA, Gotha, 9–10.4.04.
211 ADB (1906), 83; ADB (1911), 71.
212 Hasse, *Weltpolitik*, p. 67.
213 Frymann/Class, *Kaiserbuch*, pp. 136–88.
214 ZStAP, ADV 455, Schäfer to Class, Steglitz, 6.4.12; ADV 661, Stössel to Class, Potsdam, 16.12.08; cf. ADB (1907), 297–300; ADB (1912), 383; Lohalm, p. 38.
215 ZStAM, Rep. 195 Nr. 115, Schoultz, Reisebericht, Frankfurt a. M., 31.5.14; ADV 86, GFA, Erfurt, 6.9.12; ADV 196, Class to Gerstenhauer, Mainz, 21.10.12; Class, *Strom*, p. 130; Lohalm, pp. 45–6.
216 Hasse, *Besiedlung*, p. 3; Hasse, *Zukunft*, pp. 61–2, 67; ADB (1902), 95–6; ADB (1903) 77–8.
217 Ludwig Kuhlenbeck, *Rasse und Volkstum* (Munich, 1905); Bonhard, pp. 97–9.

11 The Fronde

Early in 1909, shortly before his fall from power, Bernhard von Bülow discussed the Pan-German League at some length during a meeting of the Prussian Cabinet. The League was, he complained, 'a cross for our foreign policy to bear'. It had accomplished 'nothing practical', but had instead 'managed to provoke all the other nations at the same time'. After speaking of his attempts to work through the men thought to be moderates in the organization – chief among them Liebert – Bülow urged the assembled ministers 'to do everything in their power to ensure that the Pan-German League not behave too irrationally in the future'.[1]

Bülow's lament was understandable in light of the attacks which he had suffered at the hands of the League and which had reached a new crescendo in the aftermath of the *Daily Telegraph* affair. Yet his futile attempts to bring moderation to the organization betrayed once again his misunderstanding of the dynamics that underlay the League's opposition to official policies. Bülow's ministers were not able to bring pressure on the League, nor were their successors. Indeed, as the League recovered from its financial and ideological crises, it became the spearhead of a national opposition far larger, more vocal, and more dangerous than anything Bülow had had to face. Although the challenge this opposition posed to the government's authority stopped short of open revolt, it was none the less profoundly disturbing to the men who governed the country; and it left its imprint on the policies they pursued in the years immediately prior to the war.

Prelude: the Crisis in the German Navy League

For most of the prewar period the Pan-German League was the principal proponent of a national opposition to the German government. For a brief period, however, this distinction passed to another patriotic society. Of all the patriotic societies, the German Navy League was at first glance the least likely to be at odds with the government, given the official support it enjoyed. Initially, this support had seemed to reward the expectations of the officials who were responsible for encouraging it. The Navy League had evolved into a huge, governmentalist organization *par excellence*, gearing its demands and activities to the suggestions passed down to it from the Imperial Naval Office.

Both the Navy League's enormous membership and its accessibility to official influence were critical to Tirpitz's plans, in which a plebiscitary element figured large from the start.[2] The building of warships was to be founded on a broad and stable majority in the Reichstag – a parliamentary constellation, Tirpitz was convinced, which depended for its durability on the participation of the Catholic Center Party. The role of the Navy League was to bring together a massive popular coalition, with Catholics in a central role, in order to reinforce the parliamentary majority and, if necessary, to exert pressure on deputies who wavered in their support of the naval estimates. At the same time, however, considerations of foreign as well as domestic policy demanded that the agitation of this popular coalition remain coordinated with Tirpitz's guidelines. These dictated the enlargement of the fleet by increments gradual enough both to preserve a parliamentary coalition in their support and to dampen British alarm over a growing German navy.

At first Tirpitz's calculations appeared vindicated by the fact, at least with respect to domestic politics. Not only did the Reichstag handily pass the two bills he submitted in 1898 and 1900, but the Navy League lived up to the role he had planned for it. Its membership of a quarter million in 1902 was imposing by any standard. While many of these members were doubtless drawn from other patriotic societies, the Navy League succeeded in invading social and confessional regions normally off limits to the others; not only did it attract a larger contingent of lower-middle-class members – subaltern officials, clerks, artisans, and other small businessmen – but it also drew in a large number of Catholics, particularly in Bavaria and the Rhineland.[3]

Paradoxically, the very success of the Navy League's recruitment posed problems for the Imperial Naval Office. The League's huge membership made the organization financially secure and, unlike the Colonial Society, unbeholden to official agencies for its income. The bonds that tied the Navy League to the government soon proved to be less durable than those that operated on the Colonial Society and involved money.[4] Because the Navy League was involved in agitation whose political undertones were difficult to ignore, the government officials who had initially fostered the expansion of the organization were reluctant to assume permanent roles of leadership, preferring to hand these over to private citizens. To be sure, *Landräte* and other officials continued to chair local chapters in many parts of the country, particularly in the rural north and east, where the 'naval movement', largely an urban phenomenon, remained weak. In the western and central regions of the country, though, the officials stepped aside or confined themselves to ornamental roles. Into this gap moved a group of independent activists, who had been prominent neither in the founding of the Navy League nor, as a rule, in other patriotic societies. To the Navy League they now devoted their energies and loyalties, as they took on the burdens of administration and agitation. The principal loci of their power were the League's provincial and state federations, which, after reforms adopted in 1902 and 1903, exerted a decisive influence on the policies and composition of the national leadership.[5] In part because they had not been present at the birth of the Navy League, the new activists who began to determine the tenor of agitation had little sympathy for the Naval Office's ideas about their organization's proper role. Unable to appreciate the tactical nuances of Tirpitz's plan, they proposed to use the Navy League to speed up construction of the fleet, disregarding both the sentiments of the British and the hesitations of the Catholic

Center, a party which they regarded as an obstacle rather than as a necessary ally in building warships.

The figure who emerged as their leader exemplified both the temperamental and ideological divergences between these new activists and the men in Tirpitz's office. The career of August Keim was characterized throughout by spirited resistance to attempts to restrain his enormous energies. He was born in 1845, the son of a middle-class officer in the Hessian army.[6] He followed his father into a military career, fighting against the Prussians in 1866 before his unit was amalgamated into the Prussian army. His career advanced thereafter rather conventionally, limited perhaps by his social background and non-Prussian origins. After serving in the 1880s with the General Staff, however, he began, unbeknownst to his superiors, to dabble in journalism, publicly criticizing the state of the army's field artillery. His reputation as a publicist convinced Caprivi to take him on as public-information officer during the struggle with the Reichstag over military appropriations in 1892–3.[7] In this capacity Keim orchestrated an effective propaganda campaign during elections to the Reichstag in 1893. Thereafter he remained in Berlin, where he became involved in political intrigues surrounding the War Minister, Walter Bronsart von Schellendorf, and where he continued to write articles critical of the army's preparedness for war. The fall of Bronsart in 1896 left Keim vulnerable to the many enemies he had made, and they succeeded first in farming him out to Aachen as a regimental commander and then in forcing his retirement in 1898 with the rank of major general.

Shortly after the turn of the century Keim became active in the Navy League, rising by 1903 to a position in the national leadership. Here patterns that had marked his earlier career came again to the fore. Keim not only found in the Navy League an opportunity to put his propagandistic skills to work again, but he soon courted trouble with his superiors. His superiors this time, in fact if not in name, were in the Imperial Naval Office, and their guidelines for naval building and propaganda became a growing source of frustration to Keim and many other activists.

The complicated story of the conflict between the Navy League and the Naval Office has already been recounted at length.[8] Here it is appropriate only to emphasize several aspects of the story. At issue initially were specific provisions of Tirpitz's plan, which did not, Keim and his allies argued, provide adequately for the country's naval defense nor approach the limits of what was politically possible. Soon, though, the issue broadened. Keim began to draw into question not only the wisdom of the plan's specific features, but the authority of the Naval Office to prescribe either the parameters of the Navy League's propaganda or the guidelines of naval construction. Under Keim the Navy League began, in other words, to challenge the government over custodianship of naval policy. Nor was it possible to pretend that anything less was at stake once the emperor himself castigated Keim, in May 1905, for having 'arrogated the right' to determine the formation of the fleet – a presumption the Kaiser found 'impertinent [*ungehörig*] and a direct invasion of the monarch's power of command'.[9] By 1905, however, Keim's supporters were entrenched enough in the Navy

League that he survived this censure. His position had proved popular. The organization's membership continued to grow, as Keim's views provided a sense of momentum and purpose to the activists' enthusiasm.

For the German government the challenge posed by the Navy League was more disturbing than any of the attacks from the Pan-German League. The Navy League was much larger, and the orchestration of popular support for naval policy remained a critical part of Tirpitz's plans. Yet for several reasons, officials found it difficult to bridle the organization. In the first place, the scenario envisaged by Tirpitz required preserving the fiction that the expression of popular support for the navy was independent of the government. Tirpitz could expect that any public attempt to muzzle Keim would destroy this fiction. Another obstacle was the fact that both Bülow and the emperor tended to share Keim's belief that the pace of naval construction was too slow, and these two men sent out just enough signals to enable Keim and his friends to argue that their agitation had the blessing of official authority.[10] In the face of this divergence of opinion, Tirpitz struggled to hold Keim and the other so-called radicals in check through the medium of the more moderate state and provincial federations, particularly the Bavarian, in which the presence of large numbers of Catholics made the League's leaders sympathetic to Tirpitz's ideas about the gradual construction of the fleet with the support of a broad political alliance.

After 1905 the fronts solidified. As Keim and his supporters established themselves more firmly in the national leadership, they became more outspoken in their challenge to the government's competence and authority to preside over the naval build-up. Within the organization itself, antagonism between the radicals and moderates grew to the point where it threatened to split the Navy League, as the radicals' position turned into a direct attack on the Catholic Center Party. Meanwhile, neither the emperor nor the chancellor appreciated the implications of the dispute, and their disagreements with Tirpitz over the prudence of the radicals' demands for more ships continued to exclude the possibility of determined intervention to bring peace to the organization.

The dispute in the Navy League reverberated throughout the German-national public. The issue of the navy was the main theme at 'German evenings' and in meetings of other patriotic societies. Predictably, most chapters of the Colonial Society took the side of Tirpitz, while the Pan-German League aligned with the radicals.[11] From the moment the mounting antagonism in the Navy League became public, the Pan-Germans followed it with great interest, for they well realized that the implications of the crisis bore directly on themselves. The similarities between the Pan-German League's position and that of the radicals in the Navy League extended well beyond specific demands for ships.[12] The Pan-Germans and the naval radicals shared a common mentality and approach to politics, as well as a common rhetoric. They were both more comfortable in driving political antagonisms to their conclusion than in trying to compromise them. Their view of world politics was founded on the inevitability of conflict with Great Britain, their view of domestic politics on the inescapability of a reckoning with political Catholicism.[13] Both groups were convinced too that reinforcing the structure of domestic authority required the rapid building of the navy, and they were prepared to superimpose their own independent authority over that of the government to ensure that the navy fulfill its role.[14]

Yet the growth of the radicals' strength in the Navy League was not an unmixed blessing to the Pan-German League. The two organizations underwent their crises simultaneously; and as the Pan-Germans moved closer to a position of systematic opposition to the government, they found this position already occupied, at least with respect to the most current national issue, by an organization much larger, better financed, and more in the public eye than their own. The dearth of membership lists makes it impossible to be certain, but the likelihood seems great that some of the Pan-German League's decline in membership at this time was due to the exodus of people who saw in the Navy League a more credible and effective vehicle for expressing criticism of the government's policies.

Pan-Germans played, in any event, only a minor role in the radicalization of the Navy League, the impetus for which came for the most part from men whose entry into the German-national public had been through the Navy League itself. The growing strength of the radicals behind Keim was the product of forces within the Navy League itself and not the influence of any 'organized ginger-group' of Pan-Germans.[15] A number of Keim's chief supporters were, to be sure, also active in the Pan-German League; the most important of them were Liebert, Ernst zu Reventlow, and Friedrich Hopf, the man who led the chapters of both organizations in Dresden.[16] On the whole, though, the Pan-Germans' influence did not exceed the confines of moral support and increased cooperation with chapters of the Navy League in areas where the strength of the naval radicals was concentrated.[17]

Cooperation between the Pan-German League and the Navy League – in fact, coordinated action among all the patriotic societies – culminated early in 1907, in a remarkable episode during which the German government appeared fully to have adopted the position of the Pan-Germans and the naval radicals.[18] Late in 1906 Bülow dissolved the Reichstag, ostensibly because a majority of that body, led by the Catholic Center Party, had refused to approve supplementary funds for a German expeditionary force to Southwest Africa, where natives were in rebellion. Bülow apparently concluded that Keim's assessment of German politics was more accurate than Tirpitz's, that a more stable and reliable Reichstag majority was available with the exclusion of the Center, and that national issues – the navy, the empire, and anti-socialism – could be exploited to produce such a majority. This venture would entail ostracizing the Center, along with the socialists, and rallying the other parties, from the Conservatives to the Progressives, around the symbols of patriotism.[19]

The campaign that began early in 1907 was one of the most bitter in the history of German parliamentarianism. Its novelty lay not in the wholesale intervention of public officials on behalf of parties blessed with the *imprimatur* of 'national reliability', but in the government's attempt systematically to mobilize the German-national public.[20] The government's electoral manifesto came in the form of a public letter from Bülow to

Liebert, in his capacity as head of the Imperial League against Social Democracy.[21] In this document Bülow showed that he knew well what the national symbols meant to this audience; he conjured up the spectre of 'socialist subversion of the concepts of authority [*Obrigkeit*], property, religion and Fatherland', and then he called out the forces to do 'battle for the honor and well-being of the nation against Social Democrats, Poles, Guelphs, and the Catholic Center'.

Bülow established headquarters for the campaign in his own chancellery, and he and the chancellery's chief, Friedrich Wilhelm von Loebell, personally supervised the mobilization of opinion. To finance the campaign they persuaded leading businessmen to contribute to a special fund.[22] The expenditure of a large share of this money they then entrusted directly to the patriotic societies – the Colonial Society, the Imperial League against Social Democracy, and especially the Navy League.[23] Keim became the principal advisor to Bülow on campaign strategy, drawing on his experience from the election of 1893. The two men consulted on the themes to be emphasized in pamphlets, the people who were to be sent out as lecturers, and the electoral districts in which agitation was to be concentrated.[24] Altogether the Navy League produced close to 20 million brochures and leaflets, while the Imperial League sent out more than 10 million of its own.[25]

Bülow hoped that the socialists would be the principal object of attack and that the patriotic agitation would treat the Center Party more gently, distinguishing between Catholicism and its political organ. The Colonial Society had enough Catholics among its members that the tenor of its propaganda remained moderate, in keeping with Bülow's preferences. So naturally did the agitation of the Bavarian chapters of the Navy League.[26] The dominant tone of the campaign, however, was much more strident. Keim set it. His antipathy for the Center Party knew no bounds, and he made no effort to conceal it. Although he was merely pursuing the logic of Bülow's own strategy, Keim's explicit attacks on the patriotism of the Center became a source of embarrassment, particularly after it came to light that he had been hounding Catholics out of the Navy League and even proposing electoral alliances with Social Democrats to defeat candidates of the Center Party in run-offs.[27]

The militance that Keim injected into the campaign was well suited to the Pan-Germans, whose fortunes underwent a brief resurgence during the elections. Although they were still smarting from the criticism that both the emperor and Bülow had directed at them late in 1906, they resolved, as Hasse telegrammed to the chancellor (with a direct allusion to Bülow's recent attack), that 'no resentment should or will prevent us Pan-Germans from decisively supporting, with a warm heart and a clear head, the national policy of the federal government, which you have proclaimed against the Center and Social Democrats'.[28] Chapters of the Pan-German League thereupon joined with chapters of the other patriotic societies, veterans' associations, and patriotic workers' groups in a frantic campaign to mobilize sentiment in the German-national public behind the 'national parties'.[29]

These efforts revealed the extent to which reliance on the symbols and rhetoric of patriotism could, in the proper circumstances, obscure factional disputes among the political parties. The most important of these circumstances was the patent alliance between the government and the radical nationalists. Although the full extent of the government's connivance with Keim was not public knowledge during the campaign, it was clear that the demands of the radicals in the Navy League enjoyed the support of official authority.

Both Bülow and the radical forces whose aid he had enlisted had reason to be pleased with the results of the alliance. Although their popular vote rose, the Social Democrats found the size of their Reichstag deputation cut almost in half, while the parties that now made up the so-called Bülow block – Conservatives, Free Conservatives, Antisemites, National Liberals, and Progressives – emerged with a sizable majority. This they owed in no small way to the patriotic societies, which had not only produced an increase in the non-socialist vote, but had smoothed the way for electoral coalitions among the non-socialist parties.

Well might the Pan-Germans have congratulated themselves in the aftermath, for the elections appeared to vindicate their policy of opposition. The dissolution and the elections had brought, in Samassa's view, 'the justification for the efforts and program of the Pan-German League': persistent criticism of official policy had 'contributed a good part to the awakening of political insight which the German people displayed in the elections'.[30] Liebert, who had been elected with Keim's help, as a Free Conservative, was even more optimistic: 'all Pan-German demands in questions of the army, navy, colonies, and world-policy made up, so to speak, the electoral slogans. In view of the government's position, the League can now stand cheerfully behind the chancellor, supporting him and pushing him forward.'[31]

The optimism was premature. Bülow did, to be sure, appease the patriotic sentiment to which he owed his majority by pushing through the Reichstag bills which raised the pace of naval construction to four capital ships a year and banned the use of foreign languages in public meetings; in the Prussian diet he also sponsored a bill that provided for the expropriation of Polish property in the eastern provinces. Other developments soon suggested, however, that the chancellor was retreating from the position he had assumed during the elections and that he was willing to abandon the radical nationalists rather than break completely with the Center Party.

The elections of 1907 only exacerbated the tension within the German Navy League. Keim's assault on the Center pushed the more moderate forces, particularly those in the Bavarian federation, to the point of resigning. Tirpitz, who, in spite of the recent elections, had not abandoned his vision of a coalition that included the Center, now feared, with good reason, for the very survival of the Navy League. His strategy was to encourage the moderates to remain in the organization while lobbying quietly for the resignation of Keim. The strategy remained frustrated, however, as long as Bülow and the emperor continued to indicate their confidence in Keim, who seemed to have been the engineer of the new parliamentary coalition.[32]

On the surface, the dispute in the Navy League revolved now about the issue of the organization's political character. The moderates argued that Keim's behavior during the elections had pulled the League into the realm of party politics – a charge that Keim's supporters denied in contending that national issues like the navy stood *ipso facto* above this realm. The belabored argument over the scope of the realm of politics was the mask for the real issue, which remained, now exacerbated, the question of custodianship over one of the principal national symbols. The position of Keim and his supporters was that the Navy League had entitlement to determine independently the guidelines of naval building and, if necessary, to compel the government to accept them. The moderates continued to advocate Tirpitz's view that ultimate custodial authority resided in the Naval Office, whose guidelines were to define the limits of the Navy League's agitation.

The Pan-German League was centrally involved, in spirit if not in fact, in the growing crisis. In the eyes of Tirpitz and his supporters, the League became itself the symbol of the evil forces that were animating the naval radicals.[33] The people who charged that the Pan-Germans were behind Keim would have been hard pressed to substantiate their claims with specific names, but in a broader sense they were right. In contesting the government's authority in national issues, the radicals in the Navy League had brought to a head an issue that had long been basic to the Pan-Germans' own program.

Because the chancellor shared Keim's assessment of Tirpitz's building program and because Keim's approach to politics had borne such fruit during the elections, Bülow's appreciation of the issues at stake remained clouded. But by the end of 1907 even he was persuaded that a large-scale secession and possibly the collapse of the Navy League were too high a price to pay for keeping Keim. Late in the year the protector of the Bavarian federation, Prince Rupprecht, resigned in protest over Keim's leadership. Bülow and the emperor now at last tried to force Keim to quit. To their consternation, Keim, who still enjoyed the confidence of most of the Navy League, refused.[34] Bülow and the emperor were then compelled to use a drastic weapon. In January 1908 they announced that Prince Heinrich, the national protector of the Navy League, would resign if Keim were to stay.[35] Even Keim's most avid supporters could harbor no illusions about the impact of such a spectacular display of official disfavor: every other protector, as well as most of the public officials active in the organization, would have little choice but to resign, to be joined no doubt by a major portion of the membership.

Although it did not yet fully resolve the crisis in the Navy League, Keim's departure under pressure meant that the organization had ceded custodial authority over the navy back to the government. The Navy League's activity would not again clash significantly with the program of the Naval Office. When the new leader of the organization, Admiral Hans von Koester, announced his determination to preserve its independence of official control, he did so as a rhetorical flourish for the benefit of Keim's former supporters; but he was unwilling to push independence to the point of another crisis, and in practice he was careful to remain in consultation with the Naval Office.[36]

The real question was not the docility of the Navy League after Keim's resignation, but rather how many people would remain in it. If the removal of Keim had made the League more attractive to the moderates, it also raised the possibility of the mass withdrawal of Keim's supporters, who were calculated to number as many as 150,000.[37] In the event, some 15,000 of them did leave, principally in the radical centers of Hessen and Saxony, but Koester's loud defense of the League's independence kept the secession within manageable bounds.[38]

Koester's success signalled the failure of a project on which Keim had embarked immediately after his resignation. He had hoped to mobilize his followers in an independent *Flottenbund*, which would be a massive new center of opposition to official navy policy.[39] When most of his supporters chose not to leave the Navy League, Keim was left with another obvious option. Within weeks of leaving the Navy League he joined the Pan-German League, where, as he explained to Class, he 'now knew he belonged'.[40] The failure of his *Flottenbund* raised the possibility that many of his former followers might also find their way into the Pan-German League. In fact, several of Keim's friends took seats on the Pan-German League's board of national directors. Hermann Gerhard, who had been one of Keim's closest associates in the Navy League, where he coordinated what one official in the Naval Office described as the 'vilest Keim-agitation', became executive secretary of the Pan-German League in October 1908.[41] Gerhard and the others attempted to exploit their contacts in the Navy League on behalf of the Pan-German League, but their hopes for a large-scale migration were disappointed. It is impossible to determine just how many people left the Navy League for the Pan-German League, for the modest increase in the latter organization's membership at the end of 1909 was due at least in part to the reverberations of the *Daily Telegraph* affair.[42] Only a few local chapters of the Navy League, such as those in Mülheim and Rudolstadt, came over to the Pan-German League *en bloc*, and the total number of defectors probably did not exceed a thousand.[43]

Despite this disappointment, the outcome of the Navy League's crisis had far-reaching repercussions within the German-national public realm. To the Pan-German League it brought a propagandist of great energy, experience, and skill. The crisis left, in addition, a legacy of bitterness among Keim's supporters, many of whom – even those who had not chosen to join the Pan-German League – could be mobilized in the future into a more broadly based national opposition to official policies. Finally, the fate of the radicals around Keim in the Navy League was peripherally related to a development that set the stage for the mobilization of such a national opposition. This development was the collapse of the parliamentary coalition which the government's exploitation of patriotism had produced in 1907.

Translating the patriotic enthusiasm of the elections into legislation carried an expensive price tag. In particular, raising the pace of naval construction pushed the federal treasury, already strained by the costs of the

Tirpitz plan, beyond its limits and made necessary the tapping of new sources of revenue. The government hoped once again, by enlisting the services of the patriotic societies, to drape its program of financial reform in the mantle of patriotic necessity.[44] Officials foresaw, however, neither the dispiritedness that had set into the German-national public in the aftermath of the Navy League's crisis, nor the limitations of patriotic slogans in overcoming sectional interests. Patriotic societies did devote meetings to the theme of financial reform, and they supported the government's proposal; but their enthusiasm did not begin to match the determination with which the Conservative Party resisted the government's attempt to enact an inheritance tax, which the party calculated would weigh disproportionally on its own constituency.[45]

The recriminations that followed the demise of the inheritance tax in the Reichstag revealed the inherent limitations of relying on patriotic slogans alone to generate a broad anti-socialist *Sammlung*.[46] The effort was doomed by the want of a consensus among the agrarian, commercial, and industrial sectors over the distribution of the financial burdens of the specific policies that patriotic slogans seemed to demand. Failing this consensus, and given the fact that the Center Party had exploited Bülow's parliamentary fiasco to move out of the opposition into which it had been ostracized, the government would find it difficult in the future to orchestrate another patriotic campaign like that of 1907.[47] The circumstances of the Bülow block's collapse thus increased the chances not only that the mobilization of patriotic sentiment might take place independently of the government, but that this mobilization would accommodate the demands of the Conservative agrarians. And within a short time developments elsewhere, at the level of foreign policy and within the Pan-German League, combined to catalyze just such a mobilization.

Morocco

The collapse of the Bülow block and the dismissal of the chancellor in the summer of 1909 occurred as the Pan-German League was beginning to emerge from the crisis which its assault on the government's authority had brought on. The Pan-Germans hoped that the new chancellor would prove more receptive to their advice and services than his predecessor had been. They had some cause to believe that despite all the antagonism, the German government still viewed their activities in a favorable light. Even during the hottest stages of the conflict in 1908, contacts between the League and high officials in the chancellery, the Foreign Office, and other agencies had not lapsed entirely.[48] In spite of Bülow's unpleasant experiences with both the Pan-Germans and the Navy League, his assumption was still widely shared that mobilizing public opinion in support of patriotic causes was a sound strategy, one worth the price of public criticism from the Pan-Germans, whose energy made them useful and who could, in any event, be isolated as whipping boys. As one official in the Foreign Office's press bureau explained it, the Pan-Germans were like a 'pike in a fish pond, and if a

Pan-German movement did not exist, we would have to invent one'.[49]

The Pan-German League's honeymoon with Bethmann Hollweg was none the less brief. In his salutations to the new chancellor, Class expressed the hope that the League could henceforth 'work in quiet collusion with the government' and serve as 'independent auxiliaries', whose role would be 'to prepare the way for the difficult work the government faces, so far as this can be done from below'.[50] Bethmann's response was cautious but encouraging, for he agreed to meet with Class and Klingemann, who was then deputy chairman. The chancellor assured Class that he followed the League's activities with 'active interest' and that he would be glad if the 'mobilization of the forces in the League were to prepare the way for those who are responsible for governing the state'.[51]

A careful reading of the chancellor's words would have disclosed that the Pan-Germans had misplaced their hopes and that Bethmann was no more inclined than Bülow to cooperate with the Pan-Germans on their own terms and to pursue the policies they prescribed. In the event, the meeting between Bethmann and the Pan-German leaders never took place. Within months a series of minor incidents, including a public condemnation by the German ambassador to the United States of the 'Pan-Germans' bold flights of fantasy', culminated in an open break.[52] Early in 1910 a group of leading Pan-Germans announced to Bethmann that it had 'lost all confidence in the Foreign Office'.[53] Bethmann's response, which was published in the *Norddeutsche Allgemeine Zeitung*, was that of annoyed parent, but it stung no less than Bülow's derision. 'It is irresponsible', he chided, ' . . . for an organization like the Pan-German League, which professes in its statutes to be patriotic, to hurl such unworthy and groundless charges at the authorities.'[54] When this episode was followed by the government's announcement of a draft constitution for Alsace-Lorraine (which the League branded a capitulation to the French element), the Pan-Germans closed the book on the new chancellor and prepared to resume their opposition.[55]

The sequence of events that now transpired can be explained only as testimony to the resilience of the Pan-Germans' hopes that the government would need to make use of their services, as well as to the persistence in official circles of misconceptions about the dynamism of radical nationalism. For all their temperamental differences, Alfred von Kiderlen-Wächter shared with Bernhard von Bülow a belief in the salutary domestic impact of foreign-policy splashes and in what he called 'letting all the dogs bark', the tactic of manipulating public opinion to create the impression that his foreign policies were but moderate responses to pressure from a militant populace.[56] Within weeks of his becoming Foreign Minister in the summer of 1910, Kiderlen established contacts with Class and a number of other leading Pan-Germans.[57] He also began to pass money from the Foreign Office directly to the League's *Wehrschatz*; and in view of the plans Kiderlen was then devising to use the League, these funds bore all the marks of bribery.[58]

In a series of discussions with Class early in 1911, the Foreign Minister proposed a strategy that could only gratify the League. Kiderlen suggested a 'division of labor between the Foreign Office and the patriotic societies';

these groups were to 'present demands in the press and in their organizations', so that Kiderlen could then say to other governments: 'I am certainly conciliatory, but I have to take public opinion into account.' Accordingly, he told Class, the Pan-Germans should 'Scold and mock me all you want! It is necessary, and I have a thick skin!'[59] That Kiderlen was not being altogether candid, that he was prepared to abandon this arrangement when it no longer suited his purposes, was lost on Class, whose gullibility matched his desire to be called upon to play a constructive role with the government.[60]

The occasion for activating this 'alliance' was to be the resolution of the Moroccan issue.[61] Here the League and the Foreign Office shared an interest, albeit for different reasons. The League had never dropped its demand that the western half of Morocco be seized as a settlement colony, and the organization's interest in Morocco grew after 1908. Against a backdrop of diplomatic tension stimulated by continuing disputes over the Algeciras treaty, the League began to champion the claims of the Mannesmann brothers (who were friends of several members of the League's executive committee) to mineral rights in the southern and western parts of the country.[62] Kiderlen, on the other hand, evidently wanted to use an apparent French violation of the treaty to resolve the whole issue in a fashion that would reflect well on the government during impending elections for a new Reichstag.

During his conversations with Class the Foreign Minister dwelt at length on the subject of Morocco. Whatever Kiderlen might have said about his plans, he left Class with the impression that he was about to undertake a dramatic initiative, the purpose of which was to be the seizure of at least a portion of Moroccan territory as a German colony.[63] Class, who was beginning to feel that the moment had arrived for his 'personal intervention in history', agreed to place the newspapers over which he had some influence into the service of Kiderlen's plans and to prepare a pamphlet justifying the German claims to Morocco.[64]

The fruits of this agreement appeared immediately in the curious new accents in the Pan-German press – a group of publications that included not only the *Alldeutsche Blätter*, *Die Post*, and Reismann-Grone's *Rheinisch Westfälische Zeitung*, but Lange's *Deutsche Zeitung* and Liman's *Leipziger Neueste Nachrichten*.[65] These papers, which had long excoriated German diplomats, now began to publish unusually optimistic assessments of the state of German foreign policy, adding that the moment was ripe for a great deed in Morocco.[66] By June 1911 editorials in these papers were expressing impatience with the Foreign Office, and it is not clear whether this new attitude was part of Kiderlen's strategy or if it reflected genuine apprehensions among the Pan-Germans.[67] In any event, the Pan-Germans did not have long to wait. On 1 July 1911 the German gunboat *Panther* arrived at the Moroccan port of Agadir. In the Pan-German League the mood was jubilant, and the machinery set in motion to mobilize the chapters in support of the government's action.[68]

The *Panthersprung*, which was to have marked the culmination of cooperation between the League and the German government, brought instead a parting of ways that had more far-reaching political consequences than any previous episode. The Foreign Office discovered anew that it had conjured up forces beyond its control, that, as Kiderlen complained, public opinion had become, with the Pan-Germans' encouragement, so 'increasingly excited' that he 'could no longer restrain it.'[69] At the very moment the gunboat arrived in Agadir, Class was in the Foreign Office, where Arthur Zimmermann, the undersecretary, hinted that the German government would not insist on retaining Moroccan territory, but would be content with compensations, perhaps in the Congo.[70] Shortly thereafter, the Foreign Office urged leaders of the League to curb their agitation, lest they jeopardize a peaceful compromise settlement with the French.[71]

A compromise was the last thing the Pan-Germans wanted. They had geared their propaganda to the demand (which they believed the Foreign Office would make) that Germany receive at least the Atlantic coast of Morocco and the adjacent hinterland. This demand they refused to drop, and they were happy to run the risk of war with France.[72] Kiderlen was not; so the Pan-Germans instead declared war on him. As the Moroccan crisis escalated alarmingly in the summer with the intervention of the British on the French side, and as the German Foreign Office made clear its desire for compromise, the mobilization of opinion within the Pan-German League turned with increasing ferocity against both Britain and the German government.[73]

Morocco provided the Pan-German League with the galvanizing issue for which it had been groping ever since the end of the Boer War. Class later recalled that the summer of 1911 was a 'splendid, active time of struggle', in which the mood the Pan-Germans found everywhere was 'magnificent'; another leader reported that the 'joy in struggle of old was there'.[74] Chapters everywhere, including many that had long been dormant, swung into action, hosting meetings as large as in the days of the Boer protests. The national office dispatched lecturers to orchestrate the campaign.[75] The themes for the meetings were drawn largely from Class's pamphlet, which appeared in the middle of July and soon sold more than 50,000 copies.[76] The Foreign Office, which had been privy to its contents, had urged Class not to publish it, but succeeded only in persuading him to eliminate some of the more extravagant passages, notably the one in which he called for German annexation of most of eastern France in the event of war.[77] The rest of the pamphlet was sufficiently blunt in demanding the Atlantic coast of Morocco that it became the basis of the indictment against the government's policy of seeking compensations in apparent response to the British intervention.

This indictment, rehearsed relentlessly in the chapter meetings, was couched in terms that suggested the emotions that the Moroccan crisis had brought into play. The British intervention the League's spokesmen characterized as a 'presumption', to which the appropriate response in Germany was hatred.[78] The German government's conciliatory policy was thus shameful, an insult to German pride and intelligence.[79] The treaty which eventually specified the extent of the compensations the Pan-Germans called 'an intolerable humiliation of our Fatherland', a 'shameful debasement of the international political prestige [*Geltung*] of the German Empire', a 'Jena without war', and a reminder of the Heligoland treaty of 1890.[80]

The rhetoric was not new, nor was the challenge to the government which it carried; but the League's message resonated now in a way it had not in 1905, 1908, or 1910. The reasons lay not only in the war scare that followed British intervention in the crisis, but in the continuing disarray of the political right in Germany, a condition which promised to benefit the Social Democrats in up-coming elections to the Reichstag. The government's policy was thus a source of great frustration for the many people who hoped that the Moroccan venture would provide the cement for a new anti-socialist electoral coalition.

This frustration was evident throughout the German-national public, and the Pan-German League was both its beneficiary and the principal vehicle of its expression. The reason why the League's protest rallies were so large was that the other patriotic societies participated in them, in many localities as co-sponsors.[81] Even the Navy League and Colonial Society abandoned their reserve. The Navy League mobilized its chapters in hopes that the excitement would create sufficient pressure to pass additional naval appropriations. Its agitation was aggressive in tone and resurrected the proposition, dormant since Keim's departure, that 'if the government does not for tactical reasons consider it appropriate to propose a new naval bill, the nation must demand one'.[82] In the Colonial Society observers found 'more unrest [*Erregung*] than ever before'.[83] Chapters of the society joined those of the Pan-German League in condemning the idea of compensations, and even the Colonial Society's national leadership came out for a time in favor of annexing Moroccan territory, until the influence of the Foreign Office prevailed; the leadership thereupon backed down and, to the disgust of many chapters, mildly announced only its regret over the final settlement.[84]

The opposition took on new dimensions in November 1911, in an atmosphere of general hostility within the right-wing and National Liberal parties to the idea of compensations. The Colonial Secretary, Friedrich von Lindequist, resigned in protest over the settlement. Then, when Kiderlen and Bethmann attempted to defend the settlement and their own policies in the Reichstag, they met with a stormy reception, highlighted by a bitter speech from the Conservative leader, Ernst von Heydebrand und der Lasa, which in its belligerence and hostility to England rivalled what the Pan-German League was generating at its rallies.[85]

Bethmann and Kiderlen could do little to tame their critics. The traditional tactic of discrediting opposition to the government's foreign policies by ridiculing the Pan-Germans no longer worked. Bethmann's characterization of the Pan-Germans' demand for Moroccan annexations as utopian and 'fantastic playing around' did nothing to quiet the general criticism.[86] Nor did Kiderlen's attempt to make a laughing-stock out of Class by revealing to the Reichstag's budget commission the contents of the suppressed passages of Class's pamphlet on Morocco.[87] These public statements only provoked the League still further into accusations that the men who guided German policy – including the emperor – were unfit and were leading the country toward the abyss.[88]

The credibility of this charge was only enhanced in the light of what took place in January 1912. The socialists' success in the Reichstag elections was not unanticipated, but its magnitude was alarming in the extreme.[89] The continued disagreements among the parties of the right and center over financial reform, as well as the general impression that the Moroccan crisis had resulted in German humiliation, made unthinkable the resurrection of an electoral coalition held together by patriotic slogans and directed against the socialists. As a result, the parties of the right sustained losses nearly as dramatic as the Social Democratic gains.

In the Pan-German League and the wider German-national public – a prime constituency for these parties – the mood was lugubrious. 'A demonstration of the most calamitous significance' was the League's verdict on the elections.[90] A few months later Class delivered a more extended analysis of what he referred to as the 'Jewish elections'. The results symptomized the 'end of confidence' in the German government, the 'loss of authority by the highest ranks of the bureaucracy,' and the spread of the 'ferment of decomposition'. Embittered and dispirited by still another humiliation visited upon them by the government's foreign policy, the 'reliable national circles' of education and property had, according to Class, demonstrated their unhappiness by withdrawing from public life, enabling the socialists and their allies to claim the field.[91]

Whatever the accuracy of Class's analysis, the elections of 1912 and the lingering effects of the Moroccan crisis created a situation in which the mobilization of the 'reliable national circles' became possible on a broader basis and under different terms than ever before. The Pan-German League was about to become a major force in German politics, the driving spirit behind two massive coalitions which turned the national opposition into a formidable phenomenon on the eve of the war.

The German Defense League

In the network of national symbols in whose name patriotic activism was channeled, the German army occupied an inconspicuous position during most of the prewar period. The salience of the navy and the campaign by the government to mobilize patriotic sentiments around this symbol were responsible for the relative neglect of the army as a national issue, as was the reluctance of the country's leading soldiers to make the army an issue. After 1893, when the Reichstag had passed major new military appropriations, the policies of a succession of War Ministers were guided by a deep-seated social conservativism, the fear that additional increases in the size of the army would result in the further dilution of the officer corps with candidates from non-noble backgrounds, as well as in greater reliance on conscripts from urban areas, whose political views were feared tainted with socialism.[92] Despite the fact that Tirpitz's political strategy had produced a strong rival for limited financial resources, the persistence of these fears made the army's leaders reluctant to resort to similar plebiscitary techniques.[93]

The Moroccan crisis of 1911 rendered the conservative policies of the War Ministry untenable, as it produced a broad reorientation in strategic thinking in Germany.[94] Two lessons seemed irrefutable. The first was that the crisis had made the likelihood of war much more imminent; the second was that the German navy was not yet prepared for combat, nor would it be in the near future, failing a building program so vast that it stood no chance of parliamentary approval.[95] With the navy of dubious value, the army reemerged not only as the principal object of strategic concern, but as the primary symbol of national power, integrity, and security. When the emperor told the army's commanding officers in January 1912 that 'the navy is going to relinquish the main part of available public funds to the army', he signalled a change in priorities that corresponded to a widespread shift in public attitudes.[96]

The Pan-German League anticipated this shift. For several years its publicists had drawn attention to the army's reluctance to draft all the men who were eligible.[97] The League's interest in the army was a reflection of the increasing influence wielded in the League's leadership by a new group of men whose backgrounds were military. The central figure in this group was Keim, whose career, for all its eccentricities, epitomized an important phenomenon in the military and political history of Wilhelmine Germany.[98] Keim was but one of a number of high-ranking officers, many of whom were not noble, to have made careers in the expanding army after 1870 only to encounter trouble. Their ambition and dedication blinded them to the limits which social conservatism placed on the army's capacity for reform; and in their advocacy of reform they clashed repeatedly with their superiors. After retiring, resigning, or being forced from active service, they turned to journalism as a vent for their frustration. Some of them, like Keim, found homes in the Pan-German League or other patriotic societies.

Eduard von Liebert joined the Pan-German League before Keim did, but his career displayed many of the same features.[99] Like Keim, he served on the General Staff before becoming involved in political disputes which led to his leaving the army. Long an advocate of colonial empire, he was military governor of German East Africa from 1897 to 1901, before charges of brutality and incompetence prompted the Foreign Office to press for his recall. Shortly thereafter he was eased out of the army, a bitter man, and he fell in with a number of the patriotic societies.[100] Liebert's friend, Johannes von Wrochem, followed much the same route. Serving as deputy military governor in East Africa under Liebert's predecessor, he too had difficulties with the Foreign Office and was forced to return home. He retired in 1908 and soon afterwards joined the Pan-German League.[101]

For these and several other high-ranking retired officers, the Pan-German League provided a more cordial forum than the army for expressing the view that the inevitability of international conflict made necessary the exploitation of all Germany's reserves of manpower and the modernization of all arms of the service. For Keim, though, the League offered more. He never accepted his defeat at the hands of the Naval Office in 1908 and regarded the Pan-German League as the core around which to build a genuinely independent mass organization to promote German military power. And once his efforts to create a rival navy league collapsed, his eye turned naturally to the army, both as the object of his criticism and the beneficiary of his labors.[102]

Keim pursued this goal with a drive that made Class and other leaders of the Pan-German League fear an attempt to transform the organization into a tool of his own ambitions.[103] Keim's criticism of the army found little echo, however, before the Moroccan crisis changed entirely the context in which military questions were discussed in Germany and created a new opportunity for the Pan-German League.[104] When the League congregated in Düsseldorf in September 1911 for its annual convention, the Moroccan crisis and its implications were the main items of business. Expansion and reform of the army were, by common agreement in the executive committee, now indispensable; and the alarm over the Moroccan crisis promised to make conditions ideal for the mobilization of the German-national public in the service of the army. The League's own profile was still so controversial, however, that the leadership decided to establish a new, nominally independent patriotic society to orchestrate the campaign to generate popular pressure on both the government and the Reichstag. Establishing a new organization had the additional advantage of providing an outlet for the enormous energies of Keim, who was the obvious man to lead. it.[105]

Keim needed no persuasion of the importance of founding an 'army league on the model of the *old* Navy League'.[106] Together with Liebert and Wrochem, he laid the foundations for the new organization during the fall of 1911. An impressive list of notables agreed to endorse the manifesto Keim prepared, and on 19 December 1911 Keim announced his intentions in the press. The events of the previous summer, he explained, had demonstrated glaring weaknesses in the German army, which had in recent years fallen victim to mismanagement, partisan politics, and governmental penuriousness. It was essential, Keim concluded, to 'create an organization which will have an impact on military policy, one which will enlighten the German people about the urgent necessity of accelerating the expansion of our army in various ways, in order to increase its inner strength and to bring its fighting capabilities [*Kriegsbrauchbarkeit*] up to the highest possible level'.[107] Keim then baptized the organization the German Defense League (*Deutscher Wehrverein*).[108]

The establishment of the Defense League took place just as the elections to the Reichstag were delivering another blow to the German-national public. At the end of January 1912 Keim officially founded his organization at a giant rally in Berlin, which was attended by more than a thousand business leaders, parliamentarians, professors, and soldiers.[109] It was a measure of the consternation in the German-national public that the Defense League grew rapidly during the next several weeks, as Keim, Wrochem, and Liebert toured the country to establish local chapters from among the large audiences they attracted. By the end of February membership in the new organization stood at 7,000; by June it had reached 33,000 individual and 100,000 corporate members in 250 chapters, and in January 1913, on the anniversary of its founding, the Defense League comprised 55,000 individual and 150,000 corporate members.[110] Keim's new group thus grew quickly to the point where it ranked second in size only to the Navy League.

The Defense League invited other comparisons with the Navy League as well. Keim's initial manifesto implied clearly that the Defense League aspired to play the same role with respect to the army and to military policy that the Navy League had claimed over the navy when Keim himself had controlled that organization. In the speeches they delivered across the country while founding chapters, Keim and the other leaders of the Defense League made explicit their claim to act as custodians of military policy, as they subjected the composition, organization, and technical quality of the army to outspoken and wide-ranging criticism. The conclusion that all the criticism invited was that the men and agencies responsible for Germany's security and military policy – and in the first instance Keim meant the chancellor and the War Ministry – had proved themselves negligent or incompetent. 'The pressure of public opinion' had accordingly 'in the final analysis to compel even the parties and the government to do their duty'.[111] Unlike the Navy League, however, the Defense League remained independent of the government, so officials discovered that they could do little to tone down the criticism to which the Defense League subjected them.

Much of the Defense League's criticism of the army was technical in character, touching upon the failure to draft the number of men who were eligible each year, the inferiority of the German system for training reserves, weaknesses in the organization of the cavalry and artillery, and inadequate utilization of machine guns and airplanes.[112] Many of these criticisms reflected long-standing professional concerns of Keim and the men around him, and, given the demands of the grandiose operational plans the German army intended to follow, many of them were apt.[113] They were all rooted, however, in a vision of politics which differed from that of the Pan-German League mainly in the technical idiom in which it was expressed. The premise of this vision was that Germany faced a world of enemies, the foremost manifestations of which were the Russian and especially the French armies – institutions which, in Keim's perspective at least, were superbly organized and equipped for combat, supported by nations themselves morally disciplined for war.[114] The concern for the stability of order and authority, which was so central to the ideology of the Pan-German League, was conspicuous too in the literature of the Defense League, but again in a characteristic accent. The perils the country faced, in the view of the Defense League's publicists, included familiar forces, such as the peace movement, feminism, socialism, and foreign mores; but their danger lay in the manner they subverted the values of discipline, vigilance, and hierarchical authority, which the army embodied and whose continued vitality in the civilian populace was essential to the survival of the country.[115]

The ideology of the German Defense League was thus similar in fundamental ways to that of the Pan-German League. It was modified by admixtures which betrayed the background of the men who articulated it and which made it more consistent with what sociologists are calling a 'professional military ethic'.[116] The premonitions in this vision of impending conflict were, however, not only a reflection of this ethic, but symptomatic of the alarm the Moroccan crisis had raised. The imperatives in the vision called for the immediate expansion and reform of the German army, according to guidelines which the Defense League itself claimed, as the custodian of this national symbol, the authority to determine.

The programmatic and ideological similarities between the Defense League and the Pan-German League, as well as the prominence of August Keim in both organizations, left little doubt about the source of the Defense League's inspiration. Yet the dramatic expansion of the new organization meant that it would be far more than the Pan-German League in a new guise. In fact, the Defense League was a vast coalition which comprised the patriotic societies and other 'national organizations', as well as some important new elements. The significance of this coalition was that it revealed the extent to which other sectors of the German-national public were now willing to consolidate behind a program that so clearly reflected the position of the Pan-German League on the question of national opposition.

The rallies convoked during the spring of 1912 to establish local chapters of the Defense League were attended in the main by people who had already distinguished themselves in the German-national public, as members of the Pan-German League and other patriotic societies. The chapters put together at the rallies typically consisted of a core of these patriots, who then brought their own societies in as corporate members. The situation in Hamburg, for which the most evidence survives, was probably typical. Of the 200 men who signed the public document announcing the founding of the chapter, ninety-seven were members of the Pan-German League, the School Association, Language Association, Colonial Society, or the Navy League.[117] In most localities, though, the men who were leaders in other patriotic societies, particularly those who had been conspicuous in the Pan-German League, chose to hand over the positions of leadership in the Defense League to other men, in order to emphasize the appearance that broad new forces were being mobilized. In Berlin, for example, of the forty-five men who were listed in the board of local officers, only two were familiar from the Pan-German League, while two others were prominent in the Colonial Society, and still another was from the Navy League. In Halle, although the board of officers included two men who had been active in the Pan-German League, the majority were new men.

Despite this appearance, the Defense League comprised an alliance in most localities among existing patriotic societies, which came together because the sudden prominence of a cherished national symbol provided them with a unifying issue. Because the alliance was held together by little more than the issue of the army, however, its durability was uncertain. Keim made every effort to give the new organization as broad an appeal as possible. The subject of racist antisemitism was banned, and dues were held low – so low, in fact (at only 1 Mark), that Keim was compelled to seek subsidies from the Pan-German League.[118] The Defense League accordingly lacked either a program that looked beyond a specific issue or the resources to maintain a permanent infrastructure of local groups. As a result, the chapters of the Defense League survived in most localities less as autonomous groups than as appurtenances to other organizations in the local leagues of patriotic organizations.[119]

The Defense League was the most dramatic symptom of the radicalization of the German-national public in the aftermath of the Moroccan crisis and the federal elections of 1912. The success of this new organization was also an index of the growing cordiality between the Pan-German League and the other patriotic societies, as these other organizations came to accept the proposition, long advocated by the Pan-Germans, that the German government was not competent to determine or defend the national interest. The new cordiality on both the local and national levels between the Pan-Germans and the Eastern Marches Society antedated the Moroccan crisis; it was the result of the two organizations' common opposition to policies announced by the Prussian government late in 1910, the effect of which would be to suspend the expropriation of Polish property in the eastern provinces.[120]

The Moroccan crisis produced a more remarkable rapprochement between the Pan-German League and the two organizations with which its relations had been the most troubled. In the Colonial Society outrage over the Moroccan settlement persisted in many chapters despite the attempt by the organization's leadership to stifle it. It surfaced in the enthusiasm of the society's chapters for the Defense League and in the frequency with which they invited Liebert and other leading Pan-Germans to speak to them.[121] Racism also served as a bridge between these two organizations, as they joined forces in protesting against the government's policy of permitting marriages between German settlers and black Africans in the colonies.[122]

The mood in many quarters of the Navy League was no less restive after the Moroccan crisis, but the reordering of fiscal priorities to the benefit of the army made it difficult for the Imperial Naval Office to mollify the discontent with a dramatic new navy law.[123] At the same time, the reemergence of Keim, even as champion of the army, awakened memories in the Navy League, suggesting that the radicalism he had embodied was not dead.[124] Despairing of vigorous leadership in their own organization or in the Naval Office, many chapters joined forces with the Pan-German League in demanding more warships or joined the Defense League out of sympathy for Keim.[125]

If the Defense League consisted at its core of an alliance among the Pan-German League and other newly radicalized patriotic societies, the new organization also attracted fresh elements. The breakdown of the Defense League's cadres reveals a social profile that is in most respects familiar (see Appendix, Tables 11.1, 11.2, 11.3). The men who led the Defense League tended, like the leaders of other patriotic societies, to be academically educated officials, teachers, and professionals. In several important respects, however, the Defense League's profile was different. In the first place, the proportion of military officers was higher (12 percent) than in any other patriotic society save the staid Colonial Society, although this statistic is inflated because it hides a large number of men who were not professional soldiers in any strict sense, but who were middle-class professionals whose social pretensions demanded they secure reserve commissions as company-grade officers (see Appendix, Table 11.4). The mean social status and mean public administrative position in the Defense League were lower than in the other patriotic societies. These statistics reflect a relatively large number of subaltern officials in the postal and customs services and in the railroads (see Appendix, Table 11.5). Although the evidence is lacking in specific cases, it is certain that many of these officials were former non-commissioned officers who had been placed in the civilian bureaucracies as *Militäranwärter*.[126]

With the establishment of the German Defense League, the German-national public saw the more conspicuous participation of men whose cultural role was to serve as custodians of national security. Soldiers in uniform, as well as retired officers in *Zivil*, were the most prominent and numerous group in many chapters of the Defense League. In some places – such as Braunsberg in East Prussia, Cottbus, Landsberg an der Warthe, or Hameln in Hanover – the Defense League's chapters consisted largely of the troops of the local garrison or depot, or the staff of the local *Bezirkskommando*. Officers began to appear in uniform at meetings of the Pan-German League as well.[127]

The participation of the soldiers helped turn the German-national public into a powerful political force, which mobilized in the name of military reforms to be forced, if necessary, upon the government. I have investigated elsewhere and in more detail the role of the Defense League in the passage of the army laws of 1912 and 1913.[128] Here I propose only to highlight the aspects of the story that pertain to the theme of national opposition. As on numerous earlier occasions, only now with much higher stakes, government officials hoped to exploit the popular forces that the patriotic societies had mobilized, only to discover that these forces were too powerful to control.

As on previous occasions too, interagency struggles encouraged the intervention of these popular forces. At the center again was Tirpitz, who hoped to exploit the crisis atmosphere in the fall of 1911 to raise the building tempo from two capital ships per year (to which it had fallen) back to three. Arrayed against him were the Treasury Secretary, Adolf Wermuth, who insisted that new funds first be raised, and the chancellor, whose efforts to repair the country's relations with Great Britian would not have survived the kind of naval increases Tirpitz proposed. In order to block the Naval Office, Bethmann Hollweg summoned a new force into the dispute late in 1911. He invited the War Minister, Josias von Heeringen, to propose rival claims for the expansion of the army. Heeringen's reaction to the invitation was ambivalent, for he himself was sensitive to the ministry's traditional apprehensions about the social and political consequences of a large-scale expansion of the army. In the General Staff, on the other hand, an agency in which considerations of fighting quality were paramount, Bethmann's invitation was eagerly seized. Prodded by the soldiers in the General Staff, as well as by the chancellor, the War Minister submitted a plan for the most significant expansion in the army's effective strength since 1893. The plan called, among other things, for the creation of two new corps and the induction of 24,000 additional recruits annually. Armed with this plan, Bethmann succeeded in reducing by half the number of new capital ships Tirpitz would be allowed to build, although Wermuth resigned rather than accept the chancellor's view that the proposed expansion of both the army and navy would require no major new sources of revenue.

The complicated negotiations that produced this compromise proceeded just as the German Defense League was taking shape. By his own testimony,

Keim had no knowledge of them, although it was perfectly clear which of the competing agencies stood most to gain from the Defense League's activity.[129] The precise nature of Keim's contacts with the General Staff during the controversies over military estimates during the next eighteen months is difficult to determine. The presence of high-ranking officers in the Defense League, as well as Keim's own contacts in the officer corps, speaks for the likelihood that the Defense League was at least privy to the broad outlines of the General Staff's proposals.[130] In any event, the role of the Defense League throughout was to add weight to the arguments of the General Staff and to increase enormously the pressure on the War Ministry, the chancellor, and the Reichstag.

Bethmann soon learned that he had miscalculated and that international tensions could not cool in the atmosphere of alarm in which discussion of the army and navy bills took place in the spring of 1912. He appeared to have recognized his miscalculation when he confessed in May to the Bavarian minister in Berlin that Keim's presence would mean 'tactless and ruthless agitation'.[131] In fact, the announcement, presentation, and eventual passage of the bills were played out against a backdrop of just such agitation. The Defense League subjected the army to 'devastating' criticism, charging grave inadequacies in all its branches and calling, in view of an 'undoubtedly imminent war', for improvements far more comprehensive than those proposed by the government.[132] These charges made the rounds in the German-national public, in articles by Keim and others in the press, in pamphlets, in petitions and appeals to the Reichstag, and in chapters of patriotic societies throughout the country, particularly those of the Defense League, which sprouted like mushrooms in the German political landscape during the first six months of 1912.

Bethmann and Heeringen were naturally uncomfortable with the criticism, which the War Minister characterized as 'way out of proportion'.[133] Yet they faced a dilemma. For all the damage it appeared to do to the government's own authority, the agitation effectively promoted the passage of the military bills in the Reichstag. The logic of Keim's charges was that however inadequate the government's proposals, to reject them was unthinkable. Bethmann found it difficult, in any event, to muzzle the Defense League. Public humiliation was out of the question, for Keim's position had the support of the soldiers, and the government had conceded the need for major arms increases. Another possibility for exerting leverage surfaced early in 1912, as officials debated whether to designate the Defense League a political organization under the provisions of the federal law of associations of 1908. The effect of this move would be to bar active officers from membership, and while it would not be fatal to Keim's organization, the departure of the officers would deprive the Defense League of one of its most prestigious and authoritative components.[134] In the end, Bethmann and Heeringen decided not to press this issue, chiefly because the logic of their action would compel them to move against the Navy League and other patriotic societies as well, and thus to risk antagonizing the entire German-national public just as the army and navy bills were coming before the Reichstag.

The Reichstag passed the bills with large majorities in May 1912, after debates that found the parties of the right and the National Liberals making free use of the charges which the Defense League had popularized. These debates were, however, merely the prelude to a second round of controversy over the state of the army, for the Defense League's criticism of the government's proposals had struck a chord in both the army and the German-national public. Within days of the Reichstag's final passage of the bills, the Defense League called for massive additional increases, to include the genuine introduction of the principle of universal military service (which Keim claimed would increase by 25 percent the size of the annual classes of conscripts) and extensive organizational reforms. These demands then became the theme of the Defense League's continuing agitation, which drew attention to the areas of the army's inadequacy, the growing likelihood of war, and, in what one French observer described as 'violent attacks,' to the malfeasance of the government in responding so fecklessly to the challenges the country faced.[135]

In the fall of 1912 this agitation converged once again with the plans of the General Staff. Pressure for renewed expansion of the army gathered momentum in this agency in the wake of the defeat of the German-trained Turkish armies in the Balkan War and after a personnel shift put an energetic and ruthless champion of army reform in the position of principal advisor to Helmuth von Moltke, the Chief of the General Staff. No evidence is available of direct contacts between Keim and Erich Ludendorff, but the two men certainly shared a common appreciation of the army's weaknesses, the need for comprehensive modernization, and the imminence of war. Ludendorff's arrival on the scene set off another interagency battle, this time among the General Staff, the War Ministry, and the chancellor, over the need for still further increases in troop strength. With Ludendorff's encouragement, Moltke became the advocate of 'really decisive' increases, while Heeringen and Bethmann Hollweg fought to limit their scope – the War Minister because of continuing fears about the social ramifications of the General Staff's demands, the chancellor for fear of their financial and diplomatic consequences.[136] On 21 December 1912 Moltke laid before them a startling memorandum, which called for increases on a scale likely to appease even Keim. The principle of universal military service was henceforth to be rigidly enforced, as an additional 150,000 conscripts were to be called up each year.

The real issue in the interagency battle now became the extent to which Bethmann and Heeringen would be able to pare down these staggering demands. It was an unequal battle. Despite the attempts of the War Ministry and chancellery to urge moderation on the Defense League, the champions of the massive increases enjoyed the support of a fully mobilized German-national public.[137] The interagency negotiations took place in the context of a public debate, inspired and orchestrated in the main by the Defense League, over just how deficient the German army really was – a debate in which the antagonists appeared to many observers to be the War Ministry and the General Staff.[138] Long before news of the impending new army bill leaked into the press in March 1913, the German-national public was geared for it. The year 1913 was rich in occasions for patriotic celebration in Germany – it was not only the centennial of the Wars of Liberation but the twenty-fifth anniversary of the emperor's reign. Patriotic observances ran almost continuously early in the year, and a principal theme in them was army reform. The Defense League entered a new phase of expansion, as between February and July 1913 200 new chapters were set up.

This was August Keim's finest hour. Although he pronounced the bill which the government announced in the spring as the 'minimum of what must be demanded', he did not object when the new increases became known as the '*lex* Keim'.[139] He had found revenge for his expulsion from the Navy League, for no government agency could restrain his new organization. Indeed, the fact that the War Ministry had no agency analogous to Tirpitz's *Nachrichtenbüro* left the Defense League as the primary source of public information on military affairs, and the information that Keim and his colleagues dispensed added great weight to the arguments being advanced at the highest levels of government by the soldiers.[140] In the end, the resistance of Heeringen and Bethmann crumbled under the combined pressure of the General Staff and an aroused public. 'I shall pass on the bill exactly as the soldiers are demanding, with no cuts', wrote the exhausted chancellor in March 1913, 'otherwise the fellows will be back next year, and Keim and his friends will scream for more.'[141]

As in the previous year, a large majority, in which the Catholic Center Party joined the parties that had once made up the Bülow block, passed the huge arms bill in the Reichstag in June 1913. This event brought to an end the period in which the Defense League exerted a dominant influence in German politics. Keim and other leaders of the organization announced immediately after the Reichstag's action that the army was still dangerously understrength and that yet another bill was needed. Military reforms undertaken late in 1913 in France and Russia, particularly the lengthening of the term of service in the French army, did nothing to change their minds, but despite some sympathy in the army for another bill, army reform had ceased, at least temporarily, to be an issue compelling enough to sustain the mobilization of the German-national public.

None the less, the success of the German Defense League marked a high point in the mobilization of popular patriotism in Wilhelmine Germany, and the country's leaders had good reason to be uncomfortable with the spectacle. While the War Minister was concerned about the 'unholy confusion' the Defense League was sowing in the army, the chancellor found his hands tied, as the army bill took shape in early 1913, by the popular preoccupation with 'war, screaming for war, and with eternal armaments'.[142] Moreover, both the substance and the tenor of the agitation over the arms bills drew into question the competence and hence the authority of the government in the sensitive area of military policy. The charges of negligence and malfeasance echoed far beyond the meeting halls in which Keim raised them; they appeared widely in the press and informed the arguments of politicians during the Reichstag debates.

The Pan-German League was pleased for the very reasons the government was uncomfortable. The success of the Defense League seemed to confirm the wisdom of its new strategy of quietly inspiring other, more broadly based organizations; and Keim's organization did more to lend legitimacy to the concept of national opposition than the Pan-German League itself had been able to accomplish alone. If there were any blemish in the situation, it was the fact that not even the powerful issues of national security and army reform could overcome factional differences among the so-called national parties. The problems that had brought the collapse of the Bülow block resurfaced in 1913, as the staggering costs of the army increases at last made the tapping of major new revenues inescapable.[143] The ensuing controversy produced a curious coalition, as the Pan-German League and Defense League found themselves allied with the Social Democrats against the Conservatives in advocating a federal tax on capital gains. This situation was as intolerable for the Pan-German League as it was for the isolated Conservatives; and it led on the eve of the war to one last attempt to find a durable bond among the parties of the right and their extra-parliamentary allies.

Consolidation of the Right

The growing strength of Social Democracy was not merely a spectre that haunted the Pan-Germans; it was the dominant and in many respects the motive force in the history of politics in Wilhelmine Germany. The seemingly inexorable increase in the parliamentary strength of the Social Democrats after 1890 called forth a series of attempts to consolidate heterogeneous and frequently antagonistic parties and interest groups into an anti-socialist electoral coalition and parliamentary block.[144] Constructing an anti-socialist *Sammlung* was an arduous process. It never succeeded more than temporarily before 1914, for the issues that divided agrarians, the mercantile sector, and industry light and heavy (to say nothing of Catholics) were fundamental: they had to do with the relative weight, priority, and even the survival of these sectors in the evolution of German society. These issues were also omnipresent and surfaced in recurrent debates over tariff policy, taxation, social policy, and electoral reform.[145]

The rhetoric and symbolism of patriotism figured vitally in the attempts to forge an anti-socialist block, both because the socialists themselves had ideologically repudiated the national symbols and because these symbols provided the primary common ground among the factions of the non-socialist camp. However, even patriotism had its limits as a cohesive force. To reduce the problem to schematic form, the symbols and slogans of patriotism – from the navy and colonial empire to ridding the country of ethnic minorities and the 'protection of national labor' – all implied specific positions in the debates among these factions. Indeed, they exacerbated the debates in so far as they raised difficult questions about the distribution of the social costs of pursuing 'national policies'. By the turn of the century, the principal danger was that the agrarians would be permanently alienated, for the battle fleet and overseas empire implied the future primacy of the industrial and mercantile sectors.

The history of the Bülow block revealed the limitations of patriotism as a bond among the non-socialist factions. The Conservatives' refusal to accept a larger share of financial burdens created largely by the navy not only caused the collapse of the block but left the agrarians isolated and made their relationship to the national symbols problematic. The events of 1911–12, however, reintroduced the possibility of *Sammlung* around national issues as an avenue for the Conservative agrarians to break out of their isolation. As Heydebrand's famous speech to the Reichstag in November 1911 made clear, the Conservatives were willing to join the chorus of those who held the resolution of the Moroccan crisis to be a humiliation for the country and a sign of the government's incompetence to defend the national interest.[146] The elections to the Reichstag soon afterwards dealt another blow to this party's fortunes, as they emphasized the socialist danger more dramatically than ever before. In these circumstances a new formula for the consolidation of the right began to take shape. In this formula the symbols of patriotism implied not only a renewed campaign against the Social Democrats, but an onslaught against the institution of the Reichstag itself and the government of Bethmann Hollweg. Consolidation of the right began, in other words, to crystallize around a program of national opposition. And in the complicated negotiations to achieve this consolidation, the Pan-German League played a critical part.

For the Pan-Germans a durable consensus among the 'national parties' was not only an ideal; it was essential to the internal harmony of the organization itself. Although the dominant political orientation in the League was National Liberal, supporters of the Conservative and Antisemitic parties were numerous enough in the rank and file that their sentiments could not be disregarded. The collapse of the Bülow block produced tensions in a number of local chapters, as did the formation of the anti-agrarian front, the *Hansabund*, in 1909.[147] The situation in the strong chapter in Cologne was the most serious. Resentments among the National Liberals in the chapter were so bitter over the Conservative Party's opposition to financial reform that the chairman, who was also the leading figure in the local Conservative *Verein*, nearly resigned.[148] The efforts of the League's national leaders to minimize the antagonism among the parties resulted only in angry charges that the leadership had fallen under the control of the Conservatives.[149] These problems, which arrived in the wake of the League's own financial crisis, moved Class to complain in 1910 of how 'endlessly difficult' his job was to bring his flock of Antisemites, National Liberals, and even a few Progressives 'under a single Pan-German hat'.[150]

The response of Class and the rest of the leadership to the tensions that grew out of the fragmentation of the non-socialist block in 1909 was to try to steer the Pan-German League to the right, gently enough not to drive out the National Liberals in the membership, but visibly enough to accommodate the Conservatives who belonged to the League and to suggest avenues for the entry of the Conservative Party into a new anti-socialist block. Several circumstances recommended this response. The most important was the effect of the industrial subsidy on the perceptions of the League's leaders. The men who after 1909 underwrote the Pan-German League occupied positions on the extreme right of the National Liberal Party and were among the main proponents of a condominium with the Conservatives based upon tariff protection for the products of both agriculture and heavy industry. Although they joined it as a tactical maneuver, the *Hansabund* was hardly less distasteful to them than to the Conservatives, for it was dominated by leaders of the exporting industries, who appeared intent upon revising downward the whole structure of tariffs when existing legislation expired in 1917. In 1911, their isolation in the *Hansabund* obvious, Kirdorf, Krupp, and other heavy industrialists abandoned the organization amidst recriminations about the general leftward drift of the National Liberal Party under the leadership of Ernst Bassermann.

In the Pan-German League these men found a vehicle to translate their specific concerns into a broader ideological vision of social and political degeneration, the contours of which the League's racism furnished. In this light, the perils besetting German society appeared as a generalized drift toward democracy and the breakdown of authority – perils which the government was unable to counteract and which the National Liberal Party abetted through its sympathy for tariff reform, redrawing federal electoral districts to the benefit of urban areas, reforming the Prussian suffrage, and its opposition to strike-breaking legislation.[151] Responding to the influence of their beneficiaries, as well as to their own inclinations, leaders of the Pan-German League began after 1910 to invoke the symbolism of patriotism to sanction resistance both to the government's foreign policy and to that set of specific domestic reforms – from tariff liberalization to suffrage reform – which were associated with the parties of the left, including the left wing of the National Liberals.[152] Class and the other leaders calculated that this posture would suggest a consensus of sufficient strength to bind together, under the ideological tutelage of the League itself, a national block of right-wing or 'Old' National Liberals, Antisemites, Free Conservatives, and Conservatives.

The debacles of Morocco and the federal elections of 1912 set the stage for testing this calculation. Class's ties to the right-wing National Liberals – particularly to the Hessian leaders of this group, Cornelius Heyl zu Herrnsheim and Jacob Becker – had long been good and now grew stronger.[153] So too did the League's connections to the Free Conservative Party, the party of *Sammlung par excellence*, two of whose leading figures, Liebert and Stössel, were in Class's inner circle. In 1912 *Die Post*, of which leaders of the League were principal owners and whose editor was Class's confidant, Heinrich Pohl, became the party's organ.[154] The effect of these ties was evident in programmatic statements issued in the fall of 1912 by the party's leader, Octavio von Zedlitz-Neukirch, who announced that Germany's problems demanded, as a matter of first priority, 'the strengthening and broadening of national consciousness' and that in this process the role of the 'national agitational societies, the navy leagues, defense leagues [and] Pan-Germans' was 'indispensable'.[155] Statements like this prompted Hans Delbrück to warn that the Free Conservative Party could 'turn into an appendage of the Pan-German League'.[156]

The key, however, to the fulfillment of the Pan-German League's calculations remained the Conservative Party. Here the difficulties were serious, owing to a long-standing aversion to the Pan-Germans on the part of the national leadership of both the Conservative Party and the party's main ally, the Agrarian League. The roots of the aversion lay partially in the Pan-German League's National Liberal complexion, partially in the fact that the Conservatives had tended to support the government in questions of foreign policy.[157] The chief problem, however, remained the Pan-German League's views on the question of landholding in the Prussian east and the relationship of landholding to ethnic conflict. The struggle between Poles and Germans in the eastern provinces was, in the League's analysis, rooted in patterns of landholding in which German owners of otherwise unrentable large estates cultivated their lands by importing cheap Polish labor. The key to resolving the ethnic conflict which this practice encouraged was to resettle the east with a German yeoman peasantry, whose vitality represented the 'last anchor of salvation' for Germans in the east, a 'solid dike' against the Polish 'flood tide'.[158] To foster resettlement, the Pan-Germans called for wholesale public limitation of property rights. Most controversially, they advocated expropriation of large estates (whether in Polish or German hands), the parcellization of these estates into rentable family plots, and making them available on favorable terms for colonization by German peasants.[159] The men who dominated the Conservative Party and the Agrarian League spoke for precisely the large landholders whom the Pan-German League proposed to dispossess; they not only found these proposals anathema, but were uncomfortable, in spite of the antisemitism which they themselves exploited, with a view of politics and society that so emphasized the primacy of ethnic conflict. For this reason, the relationship between the Agrarian League and the Eastern Marches Society was also consistently uneasy.[160]

Despite the presence of Conservatives in the Pan-German League (including several in the national leadership), relations between the Pan-Germans and the agrarian leaders remained hostile as late as 1911.[161] Early in that year Class and Stössel had interviews with Heydebrand, which did not go well. Heydebrand recommended to the Pan-German leaders that if they wished closer ties to his party they should concentrate on establishing local Conservative *Vereine* in western and central Germany.[162]

Events soon compelled the agrarian leaders to reconsider their relationship to the Pan-German League. The full extent of the Conservatives' isolation was documented not only in the party's losses in the federal elections of 1912, but in elections to the Prussian diet the next year and in the fact that Conservative opposition no longer sufficed in 1913, as it had in 1909, to prevent the passage in the Reichstag of a tax bill which the party's leaders found repugnant. As the Conservatives' concern and bitterness over their isolation deepened, the Pan-Germans' program appeared increasingly attractive. The attraction grew as resentment over the government's handling of both the Moroccan crisis and the tax bill of 1913 made opposition more palatable to the Conservatives and as the accents in the League's agitation shifted away from the navy and overseas imperialism to the army and continental expansion to the east – subjects traditionally more consistent with the agrarians' own concerns.[163] Indications of the conclusions the Conservative leaders were drawing appeared as early as the fall of 1912, when Georg von Bülow announced in the party's journal that 'Pan-German movement is what we need – the inspiration [*Erfüllung*] of all political parties with a national disposition [*Gesinnung*] and energetic will for the tangible deed'.[164] The leaders of the Agrarian League were thinking along similar lines. Early in 1913 they raised the possibility of tapping into the German-national public by founding a network of local associations 'to cultivate patriotic and monarchist sentiment'.[165]

Paradoxically, an accommodation between the agrarians and the Pan-German League only became possible once the Conservatives lost on the tax bill in June 1913 – a bill that had the full support of the League. Angry as it left them with the chancellor, the Conservatives' defeat removed, at least temporarily, the financial issue which had stood in the way of using patriotism as the cement in a *Sammlung* of the right. Almost immediately after the tax issue had been resolved in the Reichstag, leaders of the Agrarian League, who also occupied top positions in the Conservative Party, entered into negotiations with leaders of the Pan-German League.

That the agrarians should look to the Pan-Germans as a remedy for their isolation was impressive testimony to the standing the Pan-Germans had by now won as custodians of the national symbols. The participation of the agrarians in a national consolidation of the right required the adjustment of patriotic symbolism to accommodate the agrarian leaders' vital interests; and the agrarians acknowledged that the Pan-Germans were the people who could best arrange the accommodation. The arrangement was eased by the fact that Pan-Germans and agrarians shared ideological assumptions of racist antisemitism and an obsession with the threat that socialism posed to proper patterns of social precedence. The principal issue was whether the League would provide the sanction of patriotism for the continued domination of the east by the large landowners.[166]

In June 1913 Class met for the first time with Cornelius von Wangenheim, the leader of the Agrarian League, to discuss establishing 'contacts [*Anschluss*] to achieve practical results'. Class made a 'very good impression' and appeared to Wangenheim to be 'averse to all national extravagances' (Wangenheim's impressions revealed a lot about his own perspective on foreign affairs).[167] This meeting was the prelude to a series of conferences during the summer of 1913 between the leaders of the two organizations. They agreed about the desirability of cooperation (*ein gegenseitiges Sich-in-die-Händearbeiten*). The Pan-German League was henceforth to serve 'more or less as specialist' for the Agrarian League in questions of foreign policy and other national issues. Conversely, the Agrarian League was to 'advise' the League on questions of economic policy and other domestic affairs.[168] The two sides agreed then to consult on the lines to be followed in their respective press organs and to exchange speakers.

The implications of the agreement were obvious. The Agrarian League would join with the forces in the Pan-German League which were denouncing the German government for its weakness in foreign and defense policy.

In return, the Pan-German League's commentary on domestic affairs would now display 'greater understanding for the work and goals of the Agrarian League', a greater sensitivity for the dangerous 'struggle of democracy against agriculture'.[169] In practice these formulas meant that the Pan-German League would drop its criticism of the large estates and possibly (although this issue had yet to be confronted) later support the Agrarian League's demands for an upward revision of agricultural tariffs.

The agreement brought substantial advantages to both sides. For the Agrarian League it pointed the way out of isolation, as it promised to blunt a loud and influential critic of the agrarians' tenacious defense of their own sectional interests. To the Pan-German League the arrangement brought an opportunity to purvey its views to an enormously expanded audience, for it provided access to the public realm of rural Protestant Germany, from which the League had hitherto been excluded. The fruits of the accommodation soon blossomed. Demands that had long been associated with the Agrarian League – to limit the stock exchange and prohibit department stores, for example – appeared in the literature of the Pan-German League.[170] When, early in 1914, the Pan-German League's board of national directors convened in Stuttgart, the featured guest was Wangenheim, who addressed the meeting on the subject of colonizing the east. It was necessary, he explained to the Pan-Germans, to preserve the 'natural stratification of the people' from the threat of too much industrialization. This task demanded the colonization of the eastern countryside, but in such a way as to preserve a natural balance and variety of landholding, from the tiny plots of farmworkers to the great noble estates. Above all, Wangenheim insisted, colonization must not jeopardize the position of the true custodians of German agriculture, the great landowners, the 'leaders and teachers of the other agricultural classes [*Stände*]'.[171]

As the Pan-German League gave increasing exposure in its ranks to the views of the Agrarian League, it received its own rewards. The organization began to enjoy better treatment in the Conservative press. The organ of the Agrarian League, the *Deutsche Tageszeitung*, whose editor was now Ernst zu Reventlow, covered the Pan-Germans' activities more fully and cordially.[172] The *Kreuzzeitung*'s view of the Pan-Germans, which had previously been largely negative, also became benevolent, though more slowly, under the encouragement of Wangenheim and Franz Sontag, a Pan-German who in the summer of 1913 became editor of the paper after working for *Die Post*.[173] Perhaps of more significance was the entry into the German-national public of a social group that had been practically absent before, as a significant number of peasants and estate owners became leaders of chapters of the Defense League after June 1913.[174]

One final advantage the Pan-German League hoped to exploit was the ties of the Agrarian League to important interest groups in other sectors of German society. At the same time they were negotiating with the Pan-Germans, leaders of the Agrarian League were conferring with representatives of the *Centralverband deutscher Industrieller*, who were no less alarmed than the agrarians about the capital-gains tax the Reichstag had recently passed, and with leaders of the *Reichsdeutscher Mittelstandsver-*

band, a large cover-organization founded in 1911 (with the encouragement of the Agrarian League itself and the financial backing of heavy industry) to shore up the artisanal guilds, chiefly by fighting the socialist unions.[175] In August 1913 the three groups coalesced publicly to form the 'Cartel of Productive Estates' (*Kartell der schaffenden Stände*), whose purpose was to combine the forces of agriculture, industry, and the handicrafts in 'combatting Social Democracy and the socialists' false doctrines'.[176]

The significance of the Cartel was not immediately apparent, nor after heated debate is it entirely clear today.[177] On paper it was a formidable alliance of groups whose memberships numbered several million people. That the Pan-German League would somehow be tied to it was clear in the eyes of both Wangenheim and Class.[178] The program of the Cartel was to be bathed in the light of patriotism. Now, however, the scope of the specific proposals so legitimized had become far more ambitious, for not only did the Cartel envisage an aggressive foreign policy and the salutary effects of war as weapons in the fight against socialism, but it made no secret of its desire – in the name of patriotism – both to unseat the government of Bethmann Hollweg and to change the constitution in order to downgrade or eliminate the Reichstag.[179] To the Pan-Germans the idea of changing the constitution was no surprise, for on the eve of the war they were working on their own version of the same scheme.

Va banque

'One could earlier take comfort in the belief that the Pan-Germans were a small, almost comical sect with no significance. One can no longer say that.'[180] Hans Delbrück was one of the most perceptive observers of German politics, and the warning he issued about the Pan-Germans in December 1913 was in no sense exaggerated. By the time he was writing, the cumulative impact of diplomatic tension (which the war in the Balkans kept alive), alarm over the country's military security, and anxiety over the growth of Social Democracy had created a situation in which the Pan-German League was a potent force in German politics. Its leaders were among the most skilled and influential opinion-leaders in the country – men to be respected, despised, or feared, but certainly no longer to be ridiculed.[181]

The indices of the League's new importance and influence extended far beyond the increases in the number of its chapters and members.[182] To an unprecedented extent, the organization now enjoyed a 'good press'. The circle of newspapers that could be called Pan-German, by virtue of their views and the connections of their editors, publishers, or managers was an impressive phenomenon. In addition to the core of Reismann-Grone's, Pohl's, and Liman's papers, it comprised Heinrich Rippler's *Tägliche Rundschau* and the *Berliner Neueste Nachrichten*, one of whose leading share-holders was Stössel and which in 1913 incorporated Lange's *Deutsche Zeitung*.[183] The League found its activities well covered too in Conservative, Free Conservative, and National Liberal papers all over the country.[184] In 1913 even the *Vossische Zeitung* published a lead article expressing appreciation of the League's recent accomplishments.[184]

Nor did these accomplishments, particularly the mobilization of opinion during the debates on the army bills, fail to impress officials in a number of government agencies, who in 1913 started cultivating the Pan-German League.[186] After a lapse of two years, contacts between the League and the Foreign Office resumed in August 1913. Zimmermann and Kiderlen's successor, Gottlieb von Jagow, conferred with the League's leaders and began again to pass money to the *Wehrschatz*.[187] The purposes they hoped thereby to serve were no doubt of the same order as those of Wilhelm Solf, the Colonial Secretary, who in the spring of 1914 tried (in vain) to persuade Class to support a treaty regulating the disposition of Portugese colonies in Africa, which the government had negotiated with Britain and was preparing to announce.[188]

Most remarkable were the ties which now developed between the Pan-German League and the Imperial Naval Office. The years just prior to the war were not happy ones for Tirpitz, whose plans for the fleet suffered from the competition of the army and the opposition of the chancellor. Tirpitz appeared as well to have become disenchanted with the Navy League just as one of his former top officials in the Naval Office was entering the inner circle of the Pan-German League.[189] Alfred Breusing had been Chief of the Admiralty Staff and head of the shipyards section of the Naval Office before his retirement in 1910. Thereafter he joined the Pan-German League, quickly became its expert in naval affairs, and in the summer of 1913 succeeded Klingemann as vice-chairman. He remained in regular contact with the Naval Office, assuring his former colleagues of his willingness 'to march at all times with the Naval Office in questions of naval policy'.[190] These contacts, which undoubtedly had Class's approval, were the product of the realization in both the Naval Office and the Pan-German League that naval construction was not, for the time being, a matter of top priority. In Breusing the League acquired a leader who was respected in Berlin, a man to whom doors were open not only in the Naval Office, but in the Foreign Office and chancellery as well. For the Naval Office, conniving with the Pan-Germans assured that the need for naval building would be kept aggressively in the public eye. In the event, the League's position under Breusing's guidance was to push, in tones gently critical of the Naval Office's apparent docility, for resuming the pace of building three capital ships per year.[191]

The most telling indications of the Pan-Germans' new importance were their role in the evolving configuration of domestic politics on the eve of the war and the extent to which their views on the question of national opposition had become current in the German-national public. The block on the right might well have emerged anyway, but the Pan-German League encouraged it significantly, by articulating, defining, and popularizing the militant slogans of national opposition which provided common ground for at least a temporary *Sammlung* of the major interest groups and political parties that represented agriculture, heavy industry, and the handicrafts. A formidable constellation of economic and political power thus joined a broad associational network in appropriating the League's programmatic canons – that the defense of authority at home justified driving from office any government unable or unwilling to risk the pursuit of aggressive policies toward the country's enemies, both foreign and domestic. Class, in sum, was not boasting idly when he wrote early in 1914 that 'we have set up an abundance of ties to leading men in all sectors – in a word, the consolidation of forces, which is the precondition for a powerful intervention, is proceeding, and I hope that we shall soon be able to demonstrate that we are more than our opponents claim'.[192]

Despite the Pan-Germans' successes of 1913, they had reason to temper their optimism. Before it could be put to the test, the Cartel's durability was questionable, and early indications were that patriotic slogans could not long conceal fundamental conflicts of interest among the constituent groups.[193] One painful indication of the problem was the continuation in the Pan-German League of hostility to the Agrarian League. The Pan-German League's executive committee did not disclose the agreement between the two organizations to the rank and file. To do so would have invited a major rift in the Pan-German League, for as the storm of protest over Wangenheim's speech in Stuttgart made clear, many members were still unwilling to support a program of internal colonization that preserved the power of the large landholders.[194]

Even had the nationalist block on the right proved cohesive, the question of its potential impact remained open. Parliamentary mathematics were not favorable. The skepticism of Catholics and a large block of National Liberals made it unlikely that men with ties to the Cartel groups could find a majority in the Reichstag for the policies they advocated. The most the parliamentary route offered was probably a stalemate, in which the parties on the right could obstruct the passage of measures for electoral reform, broadened social legislation, liberalized trade aggreements, and other programs that the Cartel opposed.[195]

No one was more alive to the limitations of the parliamentary system than Heinrich Class, who in the last years of peace concluded that the cause of patriotism required the overthrow of this system and who became the main figure in a conspiracy to do it. Class made no secret of his goals. In 1912, in the shock of the federal elections, he composed his most systematic political treatise since his speech to the Plauen congress in 1903. This one was even more provocative. Bearing the title *If I Were Emperor*, it revealed the extent of his desperation, his commitment to racist antisemitism, and his willingness to countenance the most extravagant schemes.[196] The focus of Class's attention was now the domestic situation. The results of the recent elections to the Reichstag were, he claimed, a final warning of impending catastrophe. The socialists' victory was symptomatic of a deeper crisis, the erosion of a 'sense of order', of the 'respect for the power of the state'.[197] The real agents of subversion were the Jews, who had exploited discontents over Germany's continuing diplomatic failures to infiltrate and forge an alliance among the manifold enemies of the state – socialists, Progressives, left-wing National Liberals, Poles, the Catholic Center, Danes, French people in the *Reichsland*, Hanoverian autonomists, and even the patriots who followed Friedrich Naumann.

Class's indictments differed from those of other racists only in being unusually candid and specific. More original were the remedies for which he called. The object, according to Class, was to reconcile the *Volk* and the state by transforming the state 'to correspond to the essence of the *Volk*'.[198] The critical change was to be the reform of the federal suffrage into a plural system, in order to guarantee the election of a 'parliament in which education and property have the influence they deserve'.[199] Out of such a parliament of 'virtuous men of character', a select few would distinguish themselves as fit for the highest offices, the advisors to the emperor and the whole nation.[200] The first official acts of these men would be to stamp out domestic subversion in all its forms. Jews were to lose their civil rights; newspapers were to be censored (without, however, encroaching upon the 'national' press, which, Class noted, had 'manfully and bravely managed to preserve its independence'). A socialist law would be passed with no holes; all Social Democratic deputies, party officials, editors, publishers, journalists, and union leaders were to be expelled from the country.[201] To fill the void in workers' lives created by the destruction of Social Democracy, Class envisaged a 'large-scale system of national rallies', 'patriotic festivals for the people', in which the 'best of all classes and occupations would cooperate' in the great effort of reconciliation.[202]

The plans Class announced were not idle fantasies, but rather the candid deductions of a man who had spent most of his adult life agonizing over the problem of authority in Germany and concluded that supreme authority belonged in the hands of men just like himself. Class's reforms would have transformed Germany into the Pan-German League writ large. The 'parliament of the best', which he described as the product of his suffrage reform, bore an unmistakable resemblance to the League's board of national directors, while his model for the elite of imperial advisors was just as unmistakably the League's executive committee.[203] The task of government was to create in Germany a single German-national public realm, again modeled after the League itself, in which political life would be elevated, by means of national rallies and festivals, into a powerful national consensus which transcended parochial interests of all kinds.[204]

Fearing that his candor might present legal difficulties and compromise the Pan-German League, Class published his treatise pseudonymously, revealing his identity as the author only to a select circle of friends.[205] It would be no exaggeration, though, to regard the book as a manifesto of the League. Money from the *Wehrschatz* subsidized its publication; despite some misgivings about Class's attack on the National Liberals, the League's chapters served as the book's distributors.[206] Thanks to their efforts, the book was in its fifth edition and had sold more than 20,000 copies by the outbreak of the war.[207]

Gratifying as was the reception of Class's book in the German-national public, the treatise itself was a final confession of the failure of a conception which had long guided the League – that the symbols of patriotism were so inherently compelling that they would themselves, aided only by a dynamic foreign policy, produce a broad consensus among Germans of all classes and confessions. Class's proposals betrayed his conclusion that this consensus would have to be abetted by force. In his eyes the significance of the rightist Cartel was to provide a solid block of support for the 'vast reform' of the state, which, he believed, could come only from above, in a *Staatsstreich*.[208] And in the last year of peace, Class and a small group of his friends found a critically placed ally who shared their belief.

The mercurial Crown Prince William first attracted the attention of the Pan-Germans in 1910, when he made his highly publicized remarks about the contrast between 'our German-national *Volkstum*' and 'attempts at internationalization, which threaten to efface our healthy ethnic distinctiveness'.[209] His presence the next year in the Reichstag gallery during the debate over the Moroccan settlement and his conspicuous gestures of sympathy for the speakers who condemned the settlement confirmed the impression that the Pan-Germans had a friend very near the throne; so did the crown prince's penchant for sending telegrams of greeting, which were much more effusive than protocol demanded, to congresses of the League and other patriotic societies.[210] When in September 1913 he wrote, on his own initiative, to Liebert, whom he knew, and spoke of his approval of the Pan-German League's work, Class resolved to act.[211]

Class was strengthened in his resolve by another man with important connections who had wandered into his inner circle in 1913. Konstantin von Gebsattel had been inspector of cavalry in the Bavarian army before he retired to his Franconian estate in 1910. Reading Class's *Si j'étais roi* galvanized the murky ideas he had formed about politics, and he immediately offered his services to the League. By the fall of 1913 he and Class had become close, and with Class's encouragement, Gebsattel composed a memorandum on the reform of German politics for circulation among his own friends – a document which read like an abstract of Class's own treatise.[212]

Late in October Class sent a copy of Gebsattel's memorandum to the crown prince, who was captivated.[213] The crown prince then forwarded the document to his father and Bethmann Hollweg, both of whom were alarmed enough about Gebsattel's proposals for a *Staatsstreich*, plural suffrage, and exclusionary legislation against the Jews that they scolded the crown prince at length. For all his own impatience with parliamentary institutions, the emperor had the sense to see that Gebsattel was a 'fanatical odd-ball' (*seltsamer Schwärmer*) and that the Pan-Germans who made such proposals were 'dangerous people', 'more dangerous to the monarchy and its stability than the wildest Social Democrat'. Gebsattel's proposals for driving the Jews from public life the emperor declared 'down-right childish: they would cause Germany's departure from the ranks of the civilized nations [*Kulturnationen*]'.[214] The chancellor's commentary on the memorandum was more deferential to the crown prince, but no more favorable. The document as a whole was 'fantastic', Bethmann wrote; Gebsattel's ideas about the Jews were 'impossible to take seriously'. The memorandum, Bethmann warned, 'treats the *Staatsstreich* like a bagatelle and conjures up castles in the air for the future'.[215]

Bethmann had reason to be concerned about a *Staatsstreich*, for the Pan-Germans plainly hoped to use the crown prince to this end, and Bethmann's chancellorship would undoubtedly be the first casualty. Late in November the crown prince did in fact urge his father to dismiss

Bethmann.[216] For his efforts, though, the crown prince was transferred in January 1914 from Danzig to a military post in Berlin, where his contacts could be more closely watched.[217] He continued none the less, to the concern of the chancellor and the annoyance of the emperor, to communicate his enthusiasms to the Pan-Germans.[218]

Despite the opposition of the emperor to their scheme, Class and Gebsattel persisted in conspiratorial plans which became more bizarre as war approached. They provided the crown prince with more literature, including Class's *Kaiserbuch*, which the crown prince read and gave to his father.[219] They also cultivated contacts in the emperor's entourage, one of whom, the former adjutant Ferdinand von Grumme-Douglas, wrote to Class in April 1914 that his own ideas 'fully conform to your views about our domestic politics'.[220] Meanwhile, Class and Gebsattel speculated about a new government to oversee the reforms they planned; as possible chancellors they spoke of Tirpitz – and themselves.[221] Finally, in order to promote their project, they decided early in 1914 to form a secret society, to be called the 'League of the Last' (*Bund der Letzten*), which would comprise only racially pure 'pioneers of an aristocratic world-view', 'men of achievement and character', whose efforts to combat democratization were to be financed by heavy industry.[222]

Class later claimed that he never put much stock in this secret society – a fantastic undertaking which certainly reflected the conspiratorial extremes of Gebsattel's thinking but which at the time had Class's enthusiastic support.[223] In all events, the conspiratorial route to recasting the German political system through the crown prince presented at least as many obstacles as the parliamentary route, and Class's receptivity to Gebsattel's schemes might well have reflected his own frustration.

Class had one other hope. The subject of war had always loomed large in the Pan-Germans' discussion of politics. In a world-view as fraught as theirs was with enemies, a violent settling of accounts seemed not only inevitable but attractive, a great endeavor that would unite and regenerate the nation.[224] From 1911 on, the Moroccan crisis and then the Balkan Wars made the discussion of war more prominent in the League, while the subject was a central feature in the propaganda of the Defense League and in the attempt to define unifying themes for an anti-socialist *Sammlung*. The Pan-German League's publicists and speakers commented openly about the imminence and desirability of war, and about the specific territorial gains – in France, European Russia, Asia Minor, and Central Africa – that should fall to Germany after its victorious conclusion.[225] And in Class's eyes, the subject of war as a regenerative force took on a new dimension in 1912, as he concluded that the patriotic enthusiasm that would accompany a successful war would lead to the election of a Reichstag willing to pass the sweeping domestic reforms he proposed.[226]

That the Pan-German League contemplated enthusiastically a war of expansion in 1914 is beyond question. It is another matter to charge, as some historians have, that the chancellor secretly sympathized with the Pan-Germans and that his policies in July 1914 were calculated to realize their goals.[227] All the evidence that has so far come to light suggests that prior to the war Bethmann Hollweg was not only temperamentally far removed from the Pan-German League, but that he held no sympathy for the racism, alarmism, and arrogance which were integral parts of the organization's outlook, nor for the extravagance of its aspirations. Unlike his predecessor and many other high officials, he well recognized the danger of stirring up popular emotions around patriotic issues.[228] These remarks are neither to dispute Bethmann Hollweg's share of the responsibility for the outbreak of war, nor to deny that the Pan-German League probably played at least an indirect role in the outcome of the July crisis.

Although they have to be pieced together from disparate sources, indications are that Bethmann Hollweg suffered a great deal at the hands of the Pan-Germans in the years just before the war and that he came to fear them. When he complained early in 1914 of 'shameless, chronic persecution from all sides', which was ruining his nerves, the source of the problem was not difficult to trace.[229] The German Defense League had portrayed him as incompetent to judge the requirements of national security. The rightist block accepted this verdict and joined the Pan-Germans in demanding his removal. Pan-German leaders had themselves come, via the crown prince, uncomfortably close to the mark in their attempts to undermine his position in the eyes of the emperor.

Bethmann's response to this assault was curious. While he openly expressed his fears of a *Staatsstreich*, he seemed to agree with the Pan-Germans in warning of the dangers of democratization.[230] But Bethmann meant by democratization something quite different than they. Early in 1912, when he presented the government's military bill to the Reichstag, he observed, clearly with respect to the Defense League:

> I regret the alarming rumors, which are being disseminated, perhaps in a misunderstood patriotism, in emotional [*erregt*] newspaper articles here and elsewhere, in order purportedly to promote the necessary armament measures . . . Peoples are frequently driven into wars by noisy minorities working under fantasies. This danger still exists today, and perhaps in even greater degree than before, since publicity, public opinion, and agitation have increased in weight and importance. Woe to him whose armaments are then incomplete![231]

Whatever the confounded intricacies of the chancellor's logic in insisting that the expansion of the army was necessary because fanatical agitation – in favor of expanding the army – was making greater the threat of war, his apprehension over the power of public opinion aroused in the name of patriotism was manifest. A year later he returned to the same theme in remarks before the Bundesrat about yet another army bill. War was not inevitable, he emphasized, but one could 'not assume that the progressive democratization of states means the preservation of peace. On the contrary, the influence of those who agitate for war is becoming ever greater.'[232] The same theme appeared finally in the essay which Bethmann's confidant Kurt Riezler published shortly before the war about the principles of world politics. In a passage that surely reflected the thinking of the chancellor,

Riezler wrote that 'In our time the threat of war lies in the domestic politics of those countries in which a weak government confronts a strong nationalist movement'.[233]

If Bethmann Hollweg hoped that his own beleaguered government's confrontation with a strong nationalist movement would ease after the passage of the massive arms bill of 1913, he was disappointed. In the wake of the consolidation of the rightist opposition to his government, the Zabern affair raised new trouble. The Pan-German League resumed its attack in print and from the podium, contending that the events in Zabern demonstrated anew the government's folly in trying to appease the provinces with a constitution in 1911.[234] Wrote one of the League's commentators: 'Political responsibility rests with the weak and lifeless souls who are today permitted to make policy in the provinces and in the country at large. How much longer?'[235]

Bethmann's behavior during the July crisis must be seen against the backdrop of a long-standing, well-orchestrated attack on his competence, integrity, courage, and patriotism. The effect of the attack lay not so much in any of the specific fateful decisions Bethmann or other officials made during the crisis, as in the ambience it created. These men operated, as the Chief of the Naval Cabinet recalled, 'under the pressure of a large part of the German people, which had been whipped into a frenzy of chauvinism by Navy Leaguers and Pan-Germans'.[236] In weighing the consequences of policies they thought available to them, they could not, in sum, ignore the sentiment in the German-national public; and this calculation could only make more attractive the bold moves on which they ultimately decided.

Paradoxically, the Pan-German League itself was subdued during most of the July crisis, for the organization was embroiled in a crisis of its own. The prospect of fighting alongside Austria–Hungary drove to the breaking point a dispute that had long been brewing in the League. A faction, which had strongholds in the chapters in Cologne, Dortmund, and Essen, never abandoned the position defended by the Austrian Pan-Germans and, until 1903, by the League itself, that the salvation of Germans in Austria demanded the downfall of the Habsburg monarchy.[237] When, during the last week of July, the executive committee resolved after heated debate to support a war waged in alliance with the monarchy, this faction resigned from the League. The secession produced a final irony in the prewar history of the Pan-German League. The leaders of the secession included Reismann-Grone and Pohl, the proprietors of two of the most bellicose newspapers in the country, which were to be found during the last days before the war in the same camp with the socialist press in urging a peaceful settlement of the crisis.[238]

Most of the antagonism within the League dissolved, however, upon the outbreak of war. The Pan-Germans entered the conflict surpassed by no one in their elation, proclaiming before the guns had begun to fire the grandiose war aims that were to make a compromise peace impossible.[239] But perhaps the greatest sentiment in the organization was relief – in the venting of the frustration which had been building up for years among the custodians of culture and authority, the defenders of the national symbols. 'As we prepare ourselves', Class wrote on 3 August 1914, let us think of all the injustice, all the envy and hate, which we have had to endure; all the fury which has collected [in us] shall be discharged, all the energy which has built up in a quarter century of inaction is to be put to the test – a whole nation demands expiation from the foreign peoples which surround it.[240]

Never before or afterwards would Class be in a better position to speak for the whole nation, but the perceptions of injustice, envy, and hate of which he wrote were those of the custodians themselves, the men who had at last, for a moment at least, helped turn most of the country into a German-national public realm in the name of the 'ideas of 1914'. Class later recalled the exhilaration of early August, 'how people who did not know one another at all were profoundly moved as they shook hands, as if making a silent vow to stand together until the end'.[241] It was a heady experience, and it left a fateful legacy.

Notes

1   ZStAP, RK 1415, Sitzung des Saaatsministeriums, Berlin, 13.2.09.
2   Deist, *Flottenpolitik*, esp. pp. 147–71; Berghahn, *Tirpitz-Plan*, esp. pp. 108–72.
3   Eley, 'Navy League', pp. 120–41; Eley, *Reshaping*, pp. 122–8.
4   Chickering, 'Patriotic societies', pp. 485–7.
5   Eley, 'Navy League', pp. 101–3.
6   See, in addition to Keim's memoirs, Class, *Strom*, pp. 83–4, 157–9.
7   Keim, pp. 5–67; Hammann, pp. 72–3; Nichols, p. 111.
8   Eley, 'Navy League', pp. 179–253; Eley, *Reshaping*, pp. 239–79; Deist, *Flottenpolitik*, pp. 147–247; Deist, 'Reichsmarineamt', pp. 296–317; Schilling, pp. 217–370; Keim, pp. 97–145.
9   BAMA, RM 3/v Nr. 9914, William to Menges and Keim, Basel, 5.5.05; cf. Dieter Fricke, 'Deutscher Flottenverein und Regierung 1900–1906', ZfG, vol. 30 (1982), p. 147.
10 Deist, *Flottenpolitik*, pp. 184–5; Schilling, p. 78.
11 ZStAP, ADV 7, Vorstandssitzung, 16.16.05; cf. ADB (1906), 15.
12 ADB (1904), 129–31; ADB (1905), 160, 433–4; cf. Hussmann, esp. pp. 66–72.
13 ADB (1904), 96; ADB (1905), 229.
14 ADB (1905), 61–2, 185–6, 210.
15 Eley, *Reshaping*, pp. 281–2.
16 BAMA, RM 3/v Nr. 9742, *passim*; ZStAP, ADV 188, Liebert to Class, Charlottenburg, 17.10.04; ADB (1906), 231–3; Eley, *Reshaping*, p. 271.
17 ADB (1904), 58; ADB (1906), 25, 34, 154, 388, 422; cf. ADB (1905), 102.
18 On the elections see: Dieter Fricke, 'Der deutsche Imperialismus und die Reichstagswahlen von 1907', ZfG, vol. 9 (1961), pp. 538–76; George Dunlap Crothers, *The German Elections of 1907* (New York, 1941).
19 See Bülow, *Memoirs*, Vol. 2, p. 304.
20 ZStAP, Rep. 90a, B III 2b Nr. 6, Bd. 153, Sitzung des königlichen Staatsministeriums, 17.12.06; cf. O'Donnell, pp. 433, 453.
21 *Schulthess*, Vol. 47 (1906), pp. 232–4; KRgS, Nr. 2 (2.1.07).
22 Fricke, 'Reichstagswahlen', pp. 554–62.
23 ZStAP, RK 1807, Guenther DS, 31.12.06; Loebell to Keim, 1.2.07; Fricke, 'Reichstagswahlen', pp. 567–8; Kuczynski, p. 165, n. 3; cf. Crothers, pp. 145, 162.
24 ZStAP, RK 1807, Keim to Loebell, Berlin, 4.1.07; GStA Munich, Gesandtschaft Berlin Nr. 1158, *Bayerischer Kurier*, 12.2.07.
25 ZStAP, RK 1807, DS, Bis 15. Januar versandt; BA, ZSg 1, 130/1, Die Tätigkeit des RgS im Jahre 1907.
26 ZStAP, DKG 509, Johann Albrecht RS, Berlin, 21.13.06; Lehmann to Johann Albrecht, Munich, 22.12.06; Hartrek to Abt. Trier, 7.2.07; cf. StA Hamburg, DFV III B, Salm-Horstmar RS, Berlin, 19.12.06.

27 StA Hamburg, DFV III 49, Braun RS, Augsburg, March 1907; GStA Munich, MA 77693, *Bayerischer Kurier*, 8.2.07; Keim, pp. 118–19.

28 ZStAP, ADV 190, Hasse to Class, 18.12.06; Hasse RS, Leipzig, 15.12.06; cf. ADB (1907), 1–3, 10–11, 17–18.

29 e.g. ADB (1907), 23, 30, 123, 131–2; ADB (1908), 210.

30 ADB (1907), 30–5.

31 ADB (1907), 50–2.

32 BAMA, RM 3/v Nr. 9915, Salm-Horstmar to Tirpitz, Berlin, 2.2.07; Keim, p. 118; Eley, 'Navy League', pp. 273–90.

33 GStA Munich, MA 77693, Lerchenfeld to StMin, Berlin, 23.3.07; BAMA, RM 3/v Nr. 9918, Boy-Ed to Tirpitz, Berlin, 23.9.08; ADB (1908), 1–2; Eley, 'Navy League', p. 320.

34 ibid., p. 290; cf. Georg Alexander von Müller, *Der Kaiser ... Aufzeichnungen des Chefs des Marinekabinetts Admiral Georg Alexander von Müller über die Aera Wilhelms II*, ed. Walter Görlitz (Göttingen, 1965), p. 138.

35 Deist, *Flottenpolitik*, pp. 224–9.

36 BAMA, RM 3/v Nr. 9918, Boy-Ed to Tirpitz, Berlin, [11.]7.08; Deist, *Flottenpolitik*, pp. 243–7, 264; Eley, 'Navy League', p. 263.

37 BAMA, RM 3/v Nr. 9918, Boy-Ed to Tirpitz, Berlin, 17.9.08.

38 BAMA, RM 3/v Nr. 9910, Uebersicht über Mitgliederbestand und Organisation ... 31.12.09; Deist, *Flottenpolitik*, p. 247; Eley, 'Navy League', pp. 314–15.

39 BAMA, RM 3/v Nr. 9910, Boy-Ed to Würtzburg, Berlin, 17.9.08.

40 ZStAP, ADV 192, Class to Keim, Mainz, 17.2.08; Class, *Strom*, p. 157.

41 BAMA, RM 3/v Nr. 9918, Boy-Ed to Tirpitz, Berlin, [11.]7.08; ZStAP, ADV 192, Itzenplitz to Class, Mülheim, 27.10.08; Class, *Strom*, p. 157; Eley, *Reshaping*, p. 284.

42 ZStAP, ADV 192, Geiser to Class, Berlin, 21.7.08; cf. *Class*, Strom, p. 141.

43 ZStAP, ADV 192, Geiser to Class, Berlin, 21.7.08; Gerhard to Class, Berlin, 4.12.08; ADV 193, Gerhard to Class, Berlin, 2.2.09.

44 BAMA, RM 3/v Nr. 9918, Capelle to Boy-Ed, Berlin, 10.10.08; ZStAP, ADV 192, Class to Reventlow, Mainz, 26.9.08.

45 ADB (1908), 386, 396; ADB (1909), 71, 139. For details of the defeat of the financial reform see Peter-Christian Witt, *Die Finanzpolitik des Deutschen Reiches von 1903 bis 1913: Eine Studie zur Innenpolitik des Wilhelminischen Deutschlands* (Lübeck and Hamburg, 1970), pp. 199–289; Eschenburg, pp. 176–257.

46 Eley, *Reshaping*, p. 252.

47 Gustav Schmidt, 'Paramentarisierung oder "Präventive Konterrevolution"? Die deutsche Innenpolitik im Spannungsfeld konservativer Sammlungsbewegungen und latenter Reformbestrebungen 1907–1914', in Gerhard A. Ritter (ed.), *Gesellschaft, Parlament und Regierung: Zur Geschichte des Parlamentarismus in Deutschland* (Düsseldorf, 1974), p. 257.

48 BA, NL Hugenberg 10, Class to Hugenberg, 2.4.08; ZStAP, ADV 581, Reventlow to Class, Charlottenburg, 15.10.08; ADV 193, Stranz to Class, Berlin, 15.4.09; ADV 82, GFA, Lübeck, 9.12.11; Class, *Strom*, pp. 51, 100–2, 132, 144, 150, 212.

49 Bonhard, p. 223.

50 ZStAP, RK 1415, Class to Bethmann Hollweg, Mainz, 19.8.09.

51 ZStAP, ADV 585, Bethmann Hollweg to Class, Hohenfinow, 26.8.09.

52 ADB (1909), 389–90, 421–2, 430–1; Class, *Strom*, pp. 147–9.

53 PAAA, Deutschland 169, Bd. 3, Itzenplitz to Bethmann Hollweg, Mülheim, 21.1.10; cf. ADB (1910), 49–50; Class, *Strom*, pp. 152–5.

54 ADB (1910), 49–50.

55 ZStAP, ADV 78, Reismann-Grone to Class, Essen, 28.12.10; ADV 194, Class to Strantz, Mainz, 18.3.10; ADB (1910), 162.

56 See Gordon A. Craig, *From Bismarck to Adenauer: Aspects of German Statecraft* (New York, 1965), pp. 39–42; Ernst Jäckh, *Kiderlen-Wächter: Der Staatsmann und Mensch*, 2 vols (Berlin and Leipzig, 1925), esp. Vol. 2, pp. 79–198; Willibald Gutsche, *Aufstieg und Fall eines Kaiserlichen Reichskanzlers: Theobald von Bethmann Hollweg 1856–1921. Ein politisches Lebensbild* (Berlin, 1973), p. 86.

57 ZStAP, ADV 408, Kiderlen to Class, 18.8.10; Reventlow to Class, Charlottenburg,

21.8.10; Samassa to Class, Halensee, 6.2.11; Liebert to Class, Berlin, 11.2.11; ADV 195, Pohl to Class, Berlin, 31.3.11; cf. Class, *Strom*, pp. 177–9.

58 ZStAP, ADV 408, Reventlow to Class, Charlottenburg, 24.8.10; Class to Kiderlen, 12.1.11; Zimmermann to Class, Berlin, 5.7.11; cf. Class, *Strom*, p. 181.

59 ZStAP, ADV 408, Class DS, Unterredung im Pfälzer Hof zu Mannheim am 19.4.11.

60 Reventlow and Samassa were not as easily deceived as Class: ZStAP, ADV 408, Reventlow to Class, Charlottenburg, 21.8.10; Samassa to Class, Halensee, 8.3.11.

61 See Jean-Claude Allain, *Agadir 1911: Une crise impérialiste en Europe pour la conquête du Maroc* (Paris, 1976); Emily Oncken, *Panthersprung nach Agadir: Die deutsche Politik während der Zweiten Marokkokrise 1911* (Düsseldorf, 1981); Ina Christina Barlow, *The Agadir Crisis* (Chapel Hill, NC, 1940); Wehner, pp. 65–70.

62 ZStAP, ADV 408, Class to Pohl, 24.6.11; ADB (1908), 165–70, 173–7, 206; ADB (1910), 49–50, 53–4; Hartmut Pogge von Strandmann, 'Rathenau, die Gebrüder Mannesmann und die Vorgeschichte der zweiten Marokkokrise', in Geiss and Wendt, pp. 251–70.

63 ZStAP, ADV 408, Class DS, Unterredung ... 19.4.11; Class, *Strom*, pp. 182, 202–5.

64 ibid., p. 207; Jäckh, Vol. 2, p. 122.

65 See Paul Gruschinske, 'Kiderlen-Wächter und die deutschen Zeitungen in der Marokkokrisis des Jahres 1911' (Diss. phil., Cologne, 1931), esp. pp. 7, 54.

66 ADB (1911), 109, 144–5, 151.

67 ADB (1911), 177–8, 185–6, 193–4, 219.

68 ADB (1911), 225–6; Class, *Strom*, pp. 208–9.

69 Jäckh, Vol. 2, p. 138.

70 ZStAP, ADV 408, Class DS, Unterredung im AA am 1.7.11; Class, *Strom*, pp. 205–8.

71 ZStAP, ADV 408, Reismann-Grone to Class, Essen, 8.7.11; Class, *Strom*, pp. 208–9.

72 ZStAP, ADV 408, Hänsch DS, 2.7.11; Pohl to Class, Berlin, 5.7.11; Class, *Strom*, p. 207.

73 See Klaus Wernecke, *Der Wille zur Weltgeltung: Aussenpolitik und Oeffentlichkeit im Kaiserreich am Vorabend des Ersten Weltkrieges* (Düsseldorf, 1969), pp. 31–88.

74 ADB (1912), 19–21; Class, *Strom*, pp. 210–11.

75 ZStAP, ADV 195, Ilges to Class, Cologne, 17.8.11; Class RS, Mainz, 12.8.11; ADB (1911), 281–2, 286–7, 302, 416–18.

76 Class, *West-Marokko deutsch!* (Munich, 1911); ADB (1911), 330; Wernecke, pp. 49–52.

77 ZStAP, ADV 322, Class to Wrochem, Mainz, 13.7.11; ADV 408, Beanstandeter Teil der Marokkoschrift; Class, *Strom*, pp. 208–9.

78 ADB (1911), 257–8, 298–9.

79 ZStAP, ADV 7, Vorstandssitzung, Düsseldorf, 9.9.11; ADB (1911), 252.

80 ADB (1911), 257–8, 394, 403, 417–18.

81 ADB (1911), 318–19, 339, 382–3, 417; ADB (1912), 19–21.

82 BAMA, RM 3/v Nr. 9911, Material für die Ansprachen in den Versammlungen; DFV RS, Welche Bedeutung haben die Vorkommnisse der letzten Monate für den DFV?; Eisendecher to Bethmann Hollweg, Karlsruhe, 6.2.12; ADB (1911), 226–7; cf. Deist, *Flottenpolitik*, p. 269.

83 ZStAP, DKG 519, Ausschusssitzung vom 3–4.11.11; cf. DKZ (7.10.11).

84 ADB (1911), 417; ADB (1912), 148–9; Pierard, pp. 246–7, 343–9.

85 StBR (9.11.11), 7716–20; cf. Wernecke, pp. 114–30.

86 StBR (9.11.11), 7710, 7712.

87 ADB (1911), 57–8; ADB (1912), 406–7; Class, *Strom*, p. 209.

88 ADB (1911), 418, 437–8.

89 See Jürgen Bertram, *Die Wahlen zum Deutschen Reichstag vom Jahre 1912: Parteien und Verbände in der Innenpolitik des Wilhelminischen Reiches* (Düsseldorf, 1964).

90 ADB (1912), 17–18; cf. ZStAM, Rep. 92 AI Lit. L, Liebert to Bovenschen, Blankenburg, 24.7.12.

91 Frymann/Class, *Kaiserbuch*, pp. 2–3, 15, 38, 44; Class, *Strom*, p. 222.

92 See Bernd F. Schulte, *Die deutsche Armee 1900–1914: Zwischen Beharren und Verändern* (Düsseldorf, 1977); Wiegand Schmidt-Richberg, 'Die Regierungszeit Wilhelms II.', in Hans Meier-Welcker *et al.* (eds), *Handbuch zur deutschen*

Militärgeschichte 1648–1939, 6 vols (Frankfurt a. M., 1966–81), Vol. 5, pp. 49–58, 107–22; Gerhard Ritter, *Staatskunst und Kriegshandwerk: Das Problem des 'Militarismus' in Deutschland*, 4 vols (Munich, 1954–68), Vol. 2, pp. 268–81; Eckart Kehr, 'Klassenkämpfe und Rüstungspolitik im kaiserlichen Deutschland', in *Der Primat der Innenpolitik*, pp. 87–110.

93 See Karl von Einem, *Erinnerungen eines Soldaten 1853–1933* (Leipzig, 1933), pp. 61–2.

94 See Rüdiger vom Bruch, '"Deutschland und England: Heeres- oder Flottenverstärkung?" Politische Publizistik deutscher Hochschullehrer 1911/12', MGM, no. 1 (1981), pp. 7–35.

95 See Deist, *Flottenpolitik*, esp. p. 292.

96 Müller, *Der Kaiser*, p. 105.

97 ADB (1909), 284–6; ADB (1910), 150–2; ADB (1911), 133–5.

98 Ritter, *Staatskunst*, Vol. 2, p. 138; Martin Kitchen, *The German Officer Corps, 1890–1914* (Oxford, 1968), p. 135.

99 See, in addition to Liebert's memoirs, Ritter, *Staatskunst*, Vol. 2, pp. 137–8; Fricke, 'Reichsverband', pp. 246–8.

100 ZStAP, ADV 369, Liebert to Hasse, Brandenburg, 5.7.01.

101 Class, *Strom*, p. 160; ADB (1910), 39.

102 ZStAP, ADV 7, Vorstandssitzung, Hamburg, 3.4.10; ADB (1910), 25–6; Keim, p. 159.

103 ZStAP, ADV 194, Stolte to Class, Berlin, 18.2.10; ADV 309, Class to Breusing, 25.10.13.

104 ADB (1911), 23–4.

105 ZStAP, ADV 196, Eiffe to Class, Toelz, 4.1.12; Class, *Strom*, pp. 160, 220–1.

106 ZStAP, ADV 406, Keim to Class, 14.9.11.

107 Keim, 'Ein Wehrverein', *Die Post*, 19.12.11.

108 On the Defense League see my 'Wehrverein'; Kurt Stenkewitz, 'Deutscher Wehrverein (DWV) 1912–1935', in Fricke, *Handbuch*, Vol. 1, pp. 574–81; Kuczynski, pp. 74–81; Hallgarten, Vol. 2, pp. 262–87. The dissertation of Erich Schwinn is of little value: 'Die Arbeit des deutschen Wehrvereins und die Wehrlage Deutschlands vor dem Weltkriege' (Diss. phil., Heidelberg, 1940). Marilyn Coetzee is preparing a dissertation on the organization at the University of Chicago.

109 'Die Gründung des Deutschen Wehrvereins', *Hamburger Nachrichten*, 30.1.12. The Defense League's executive committee included, in addition to Keim, who was chairman, Karl Litzmann and Wigand von Gersdorff (two retired generals), Hermann Paasche and Hermann von Dewitz from the Reichstag, the publisher Georg Büxenstein, Heinrich Rippler, who edited the *Tägliche Rundschau* and had become close to the Pan-German League during the summer of 1911, and the historian Dietrich Schäfer, who was also a member of the Pan-German League. The name of Heinrich Class appeared on the list too, inconspicuously, near the bottom.

110 *Hamburger Nachrichten*, 20.2.12; *Die Wehr* (June 1912), 2; ibid. (January 1913), 1.

111 ADB (1912), 134–7.

112 Chickering, 'Wehrverein', pp. 11–12.

113 See Herzfeld, *Rüstungspolitik*; Edmund Buat, *Die deutsche Armee im Weltkriege: Ihre Grösse und ihr Verfall* (Munich, 1921), pp. 11–24; Manfred Lachmann, 'Probleme der Bewaffnung des kaiserlichen Heeres', *Zeitschrift für Militärgeschichte*, vol. 2 (1967), pp. 23–37; Edgar Graf von Matuschka, 'Organisationsgeschichte des Heeres 1890 bis 1918', in Meier-Welcker, *Hanbuch*, Vol. 5, pp. 157–282.

114 For example: *Die Wehr* (June 1912), 18–19; *Die Wehr* (August 1913), 1–4.

115 *Die Wehr* (October 1913), Beilage, pp. 1–4; *Die Wehr*, (September 1913), 3–8; Keim, pp. 79–80, 89, 153, 275.

116 See Samuel P. Huntington, *The Soldier and the State: The Theory and Politics of Civil–Military Relations* (New York, 1957); Morris Janowitz, *The Professional Soldier: A Social and Political Portrait* (New York, 1960), pp. 233–56.

117 *Hamburgische Korrespondent*, 18.3.12. The breakdown was: Pan-German League, 19; School Association, 7; Language Association, 24; Colonial Society, 43; Navy League, 25.

118 ZStAP, DKG 330, Karl A. Kuhn RS, Das Doppelspiel des Generals A. Keim, Charlottenburg, 27.2.14; ADV 91, GFA, Leipzig, 17.10.13; ADV 93, GFA, Berlin, 10.1.14.

119 ZStAP, ADV 89, GFA, Berlin, 3.7.13; ADV 196, Ilges to Class, 31.5.12; ADV 197, Hofmeister to Class, Cologne, 9.1.13; ADV 626, Jakobs to Vietinghoff-Scheel, Rastatt, 11.1.14; ADB (1912), 31, 110, 186, 430; ADB (1913), 31, 55, 214–15, 271; ADB (1914), 141–2.

120 ADB (1911), 37–8, 50–1, 62–3, 87, 153–4, 199; cf. Hagen, p. 275.

121 DKZ (1911), 131–2, 631; DKZ (1912), 144; DKZ (1913), 459.

122 ZStAP, DKG 141, Holleben to Bethmann Hollweg, Berlin, 28.6.12; DKZ (1913), 273, 287; ADB (1912), 341–3.

123 BAMA, RM 3/v Nr. 9911, Hollweg to Salmuth, Berlin, 24.2.12; cf. Deist, *Flottenpolitik*, p. 269; Volker R. Berghahn, *Germany and the Approach of War in 1914* (New York, 1973), p. 112.

124 BAMA, RM 3/v Nr. 9911, Hollweg to Tirpitz, Berlin, 9.6.12.

125 ZStAP, ADV 309, Breusing to Class, Berlin, 2.6.13; ADB (1911), 226–7, 309; ADB (1912), 110–11, 175; ADB (1913), 66, 77–8, 154, 206; ADB (1914), 14; Stegmann, *Erben*, p. 278, n. 137.

126 Ferdinand von Ledebur *et al.* (eds), *Die Geschichte des deutschen Unteroffiziers* (Berlin, 1939), pp. 934–82.

127 StA Munich, RA 57840, Hahn and Ulsenheimer to Kgl. Polizeidirektion, Munich, 17.8.11; ZStAP, ADV 92, GFA, Remscheid, 6.12.13; ADB (1911), 174; ADB (1913), 139; Class, *Strom*, p. 275.

128 Chickering, 'Wehrverein', pp. 17–33.

129 'Die Gründung des Deutschen Wehrvereins', *Hamburger Nachrichten*, 30.1.12.

130 ZStAP, NL Gebsattel 1, Class to Gebsattel, Mainz, 23.9.13; cf. Chickering, 'Wehrverein', p. 32, n. 102.

131 GStA Munich, Gesandtschaft Berlin Nr. 1158, Lerchenfeld to St Min, Berlin, 15.5.12.

132 'Begründung eines Deutschen Wehrvereins', *Norddeutsche Allgemeine Zeitung*, 30.1.12.

133 ZStAP, RK 2273, Heeringen to Bethmann Hollweg, Wiesbaden, 6.4.12.

134 ZStAM, 2.2.1 Nr. 15474, *passim*.; BAMA, RM 3/v Nr. 9912, Löhlau to Capelle, Berlin, 4.10.13; ZStAP, ADV 88, GFA, Munich, 19.4.13; cf. Chickering, 'Wehrverein', p. 19.

135 Serret to Millerand, Berlin, 5.12.12; *Documents diplomatiques français*, 3rd Series (Paris, 1933), vol. 5, pp 4–5.

136 KRRW, vol. 1, pp. 156–7.

137 Chickering, 'Wehrverein', p. 32, n. 103.

138 StBR (8.4.13), 4561–2.

139 *Die Wehr* (April 1913), 3; *Die Wehr* (July 1913), 1; ADB (1913), 106–7; Kuczynski, p. 75.

140 Deist, *Flottenpolitik*, p. 322.

141 PAAA, NL Eisendecher, Bethmann Hollweg to Eisendecher, 23.1.13.

142 ibid., Bethmann Hollweg to Eisendecher, 25.6.13; BAMA, RM 3/v Nr. 9912, Löhlau to Tirpitz, Berlin, 26.9.13.

143 See Witt, *Finanzpolitik*, pp. 337–76.

144 For a review and critical commentary on the large literature on *Sammlungspolitik* see Geoff Eley, 'Sammlungspolitik, social imperialism, and the navy law of 1898', MGM, no. 1 (1974), pp. 29–63.

145 See Kenneth D. Barkin, *The Controversy over German Industrialization, 1890–1902* (Chicago, 1970).

146 Hans-Günther Zmarzlik, *Bethmann Hollweg als Reichskanzler: Studien zu Möglichkeiten und Grenzen seiner innerpolitischen Machtstellung* (Düsseldorf, 1957), p. 80.

147 ZStAP, ADV 195, Ilges to Class, Cologne, 5.8.11; ADB (1910), 83; cf. Wenck, p. 28.

148 ZStAP, ADV 193, Klitzing to Normann, Cologne, 27.7.09; ADV 194, Klitzing to Class, Cologne, 19.11.10.

149 ibid., Ilges to Class, Cologne, 22.9.10; ADV 195, Dieckmann to Class, Osnabrück, 12.4.11; ADB (1909), 241–2, 322.

150 ZStAP, ADV 194, Class to Fick, Mainz, 17.12.10.

151 See Saul, *Staat*, pp. 413–69; Stegmann, *Erben*, pp. 267–7.

152 UB Freiburg, NL Schemann II D, Vietinghoff-Scheel to Schemann, Mainz, 16.3.14; ZStAP, ADV 194, Class to Wolf, Mainz, 3.3.10; ADB (1910), 231; Frymann/Class, *Kaiserbuch*, pp. 37–8, 126–8, 200–2.

153 ZStAP, ADV 197, Class to Pohl, Mainz, 23.5.13; cf. Stegmann, *Erben*, pp. 173, 195, 197, 223.
154 Guratzsch, pp. 257–60; Stegmann, *Erben*, pp. 317, 319.
155 ibid., p. 320; Eley, *Reshaping*, p. 325; ADB (1912), 362.
156 Stegmann, *Erben*, p. 320.
157 ADB (1908), 1–2; ADB (1910), 118.
158 ADB (1902), 25; ADB (1907), 277–8; cf. Petzet, p. 52.
159 ZStAP, ADV 18, GFA, Berlin, 24.3.00; ADV 33, GFA, Eisenach, 23–24.5.02; ADV 59, GFA, Berlin, 11–12.5.07; ADB (1899), 145–7, 301–3; ADB (1907), 267–9, 384–6; cf. Hugenberg, pp. 280–97.
160 See Puhle, *Interessenpolitik*, pp. 151–2; Gentzen, p. 507; Hagen, p. 175.
161 Among the leaders with Conservative ties or leanings were Mirbach-Sorquitten, Reventlow, and Samassa, the last of whom attempted in vain to moderate the League's criticism of the large estates: ZStAP, ADV 194, Class to Schriftleitung der Kreuzzeitung, 4.2.01; ADB (1902), 395–6.
162 BA, NL Hugenberg 10, Class to Hugenberg, Mainz, 18.3.11; ZStAP, ADV 195, Stössel to Class, Potsdam, 4.2.11; Class, *Strom*, pp. 267–9. Peck p. 76, makes nonsense of these meetings.
163 See Berghahn, *Approach*, p. 135; Stegmann, *Erben*, p. 280; Eley, *Reshaping*, p. 322; cf. Zmarzlik, *Bethmann Hollweg*, p. 82.
164 Quoted in Stegmann, *Erben*, p. 325.
165 ZStAP, NL Wangenheim 8, Roesicke to Wangenheim, Görsdorf, 22.2.13; Wangenheim to Roesicke, 27.5.13.
166 See Puhle, *Interessenpolitik*, pp. 132–3; Levy, p. 255.
167 ZStAP, NL Wangenheim 8, Wangenheim to Roesicke, Berlin, 27.6.13; cf. Class, *Strom*, pp. 270–2.
168 ZStAP, ADV 90, GFA, Breslau, 5.9.13; ADV 246, Class RS, Mainz, 20.8.13.
169 ZStAP, ADV 90, GFA, Breslau, 5.9.13; ADV 246, Neumann to Eiffe, 6.7.13.
170 ADB (1913), 433; Frymann/Class, *Kaiserbuch*, p. 63; cf. Stegmann, *Erben*, p. 343.
171 ADB (1914), 147–52.
172 ZStAP, ADV 197, Class to Klitzing, Mainz, 27.9.13; ADV 246, Class RS, Mainz, 20.8.13; Kuczynski, p. 30.
173 ZStAP, ADV 197, Klitzing to Class, Cologne, 18.9.13; ADV 246, Class to Klitzing, Mainz, 20.7.13; ADB (1913), 249–50.
174 The connection between this influx and the negotiations between the Pan-Germans and the Agrarian League is only tentative, for no evidence survives to substantiate it. Of the fifty men in the Defense League's cadres who identified themselves as peasants, settlers, or *Gutsbesitzer*, thirty-nine appeared for the first time after June 1913.
175 See Stegmann, *Erben*, pp. 249–56, 352, 408; Gellately, pp. 190–1.
176 Stegmann, *Erben*, p. 366.
177 See Heinrich August Winkler, *Mittelstand, Demokratie und Nationalsozialismus: Die politische Entwicklung von Handwerk und Kleinhandel in der Weimarer Republik* (Cologne and Berlin, 1973), p. 53; cf. Dirk Stegmann, 'Hugenberg contra Stresemann: Die Politik der Interessenverbände am Ende des Kaiserreiches', VZG, vol. 24 (1976), p. 349, n. 99.
178 ZStAP, NL Gebsattel 1, Class to Gebsattel, Mainz, 28.8.13; ADV 90, GFA, Breslau, 5.9.13; Stegmann, *Erben*, pp. 356, 361, 389–90, 396–7, 403.
179 ibid., p. 381; cf. Stegmann, 'Hugenberg contra Stresemann', pp. 349–50; Kurt Riezler, *Tagebücher, Aufsätze, Dokumente*, ed. Karl Dietrich Erdmann (Göttingen, 1972), p. 183.
180 Hans Delbrück, 'Die Alldeutschen', in *Vor und nach dem Weltkrieg*, pp. 397–403.
181 Friedrich Meinecke's political acumen was more open to question than Delbrück's, but he shared Delbrück's fears of the Pan-Germans, whom he accused of lacking all sense for the 'active, free idea of the nation': 'Nationalismus und nationale Idee', *Politische Schriften und Reden* (Darmstadt, 1958), pp. 83–93. Meinecke was in a position to judge the Pan-Germans' influence more closely than were most scholars. For years he was an officer in the School Association's chapter in Freiburg, and early in 1912 he lent his signature to one of the Defense League's initial manifestos: GStA Dahlem, NL Meinecke 49, Gross to Meinecke *et ux.*, Karlsruhe, 5.10.14; Keim, p. 175.

182 ADB (1913), 239; Hartwig, 'Zur Entwicklung', p. 279.
183 ZStAP, ADV 79, GFA, Berlin, 22.4.11; Stegmann, *Erben*, pp. 171, 297.
184 ADB (1910), 367–9; ADB (1913), 339–40.
185 ADB (1914), 1.
186 See Dehio, pp. 84–5.
187 ZStAP, ADV 309, Breusing to Class, Berlin, 4.8.13; ADV 408, Breusing to Class, Berlin, 1.8.13.
188 Class, *Strom*, p. 284.
189 Deist, *Flottenpolitik*, pp. 279–80, 319; Hallgarten, Vol. 2, p. 189.
190 BAMA, RM 3/v Nr. 9780, Humann DS, 16.9.13.
191 ADB (1912), 106–7, 137–8, 178–9; ADB (1913), 15, 49–50.
192 ZStAP, ADV 198, Class to Bernuth, 3.1.14.
193 See Schmidt, 'Blockbildungen', p. 18; cf, Lohalm, p. 45; Saul, *Staat*, pp. 340–69.
194 ZStAP, ADV 246, Stössel to Class, Potsdam, 9.8.13; ADV 408, Arning to Class, Hanover, 21.4.14; ADB (1914), 173–4; cf. Class, *Strom*, p. 288, where the episode is misrepresented.
195 Schmidt, 'Blockbildungen', pp. 3–32; Schmidt, 'Parlamentarisierung', pp. 249–78; Schmidt, 'Deutschland am Vorabend des Ersten Weltkrieges', in Stürmer, *Das kaiserliche Deutschland*, pp. 397–433.
196 Daniel Frymann [pseud. Heinrich Class], *Wenn ich der Kaiser wär': Politische Wahrheiten und Notwendigkeiten* (Leipzig, 1912).
197 ibid., pp. 65–8.
198 ibid., pp. 133–4. On Class's reform plans see also Kruck, pp. 59–65.
199 Frymann/Class, *Kaiserbuch*, pp. 46–49, 55–7.
200 ibid., pp. 134–5.
201 ibid., pp. 65–8, 71–4.
202 ibid., pp. 68–69.
203 See Class, *Strom*, pp. 89–90.
204 Frymann/Class, *Kaiserbuch*, pp. 50–1.
205 BA, NL Hugenberg 10, Class to Hugenberg, Mainz, 11.5.12; Class, *Strom*, pp. 232–6.
206 ZStAP, ADV 196, Stössel to Class, Essen, 31.10.12; ADB (1912), 179–80, 255–6, 374, 388–9; ADB (1913), 39; ADB (1914), 191–2; cf. Werner, p. 77.
207 ADB (1914), 144.
208 Frymann/Class, *Kaiserbuch*, pp. 52–5, 204, 216–20; cf. Stegmann, *Erben*, pp. 300–4, 381.
209 ADB (1910), 290–1. On the conspiracy and the role of the crown prince see Hartmut Pogge von Strandmann, 'Staatsstreichpläne, Alldeutsche und Bethmann Hollweg', in Pogge von Strandmann and Imanuel Geiss, *Die Erforderlichkeit des Unmöglichen: Deutschland am Vorabend des ersten Weltkrieges* (Frankfurt a. M., 1965), pp. 7–45; Paul Herre, *Kronprinz Wilhelm: Seine Rolle in der deutschen Politik* (Munich, 1954), pp. 20–40.
210 ZStAM, 2.2.1 Nr. 15375, Ausschnitt aus 'Post', 14.5.12; ADB (1911), 389–91; ADB (1913), 159; Pogge von Strandmann, 'Staatsstreichpläne', p. 31.
211 ZStAP, ADV 197, Itzenplitz to Class, Mülheim, 22.9.13; Class to Klitzing, Mainz, 27.9.13.
212 ZStAP, ADV 355, Gedanken über einen notwendigen Fortschritt der inneren Entwicklung Deutschlands von Konstantin von Gebsattel, Bamberg, October 1913.
213 ZStAP, ADV 246, Planitz to Class, 2.11.13; cf. ADV 91, GFA, Leipzig, 17.10.13. On his contacts with the crown prince Class was less than candid in his memoirs: Class, *Strom*, p. 280.
214 Pogge von Strandmann, 'Staatsstreichpläne', pp. 23–6, 37–9; cf. Lamar Cecil, 'Wilhelm II. und die Juden', in Mosse, *Juden*, p. 343; cf. Zmarzlik, *Bethmann Hollweg*, pp. 37–8.
215 Pogge von Strandmann, 'Staatsstreichpläne', pp. 19–23, 32–6.
216 ibid., p. 28.
217 ibid., p. 30; cf. Herre, p. 36.
218 Riezler, p. 190; Zmarzlik, *Bethmann Hollweg*, p. 36.
219 ZStAP, ADV 198, Stössel to Class, Potsdam, 6.4.14; cf. Stegmann, *Erben*, p. 430.
220 ZStAP, ADV 198, Grumme-Douglas to Class, Rehdorf, 20.4.14; NL Gebsattel 1,

Gebsattel to Oldenburg-Januschau, Bamberg, 10.1.14; cf. Kruck, pp. 47–9; Stegmann, *Erben*, pp. 429–30.
221 ZStAP, NL Gebsattel 1, Class to Gebsattel, Mainz, 29.10.13; Gebsattel to Class, Bamberg, 23.12.13; St Moritz, 16.7.14.
222 UB Freiburg, NL Schemann II D, Class to Schemann, Mainz, 29.1.14; BA, NL Hugenberg 10, Class to Kirdorf, Mainz, 2.6.14; ZStAP, NL Gebsattel 1, Class to Gebsattel, Mainz, 2.5.14; cf. ADB (1911), 412; ADB (1912), 304; Lohalm, p. 44; Bronder, p. 123.
223 Class, *Strom*, p. 236.
224 For example: ADB (1894), 7; ADB (1903), 401–3; ADB (1908), 439; ADB (1909), 139; ADB (1910), 330; Hasse, *Zukunft*, p. 132.
225 For example: ADB (1912), 167, 185, 401–4; ADB (1913), 71, 154, 298–9, 438–9; ADB (1914), 14, 43–5, 91, 93, 227; Frymann/Class, *Kaiserbuch*, pp. 136–88.
226 ibid., pp. 52–5.
227 See Fritz Fischer, *Krieg der Illusionen*; Gutsche, esp. p. 105; Konrad H. Jarausch, *The Enigmatic Chancellor: Bethmann Hollweg and the Hubris of Imperial Germany* (New Haven, Conn. and London, 1973), pp. 108–47.
228 Zmarzlik, *Bethmann Hollweg*, p. 48; Riezler, pp. 178, 188; Walter Rathenau, *Tagebuch 1907–1922*, ed. Hartmut Pogge von Strandmann (Düsseldorf, 1967), pp. 148–9.
229 Gutsche, p. 107; cf. Herre, p. 38.
230 See Berghahn, *Approach*, p. 163; Stegmann, *Erben*, p. 416; Hallgarten, Vol. 2, p. 162.
231 StBR (22.4.12), 1300.
232 ZStAP, RK 1252/1, Niederschrift über die Besprechung über die Wehrvorlage und die Deckung ihrer Kosten am 10. und 11.3.13 (Bundesrat).
233 Quoted in Andreas Hillgruber, 'Riezlers Theorie des kalkulierten Risikos und Bethmann Hollwegs politische Konzeption in der Julikrise 1914', HZ, vol. 202 (1966), p. 339; cf. Stegmann, *Erben*, p. 281.
234 ZStAM, Rep. 195 Nr. 80, Bericht über Stuttgart, 21.4.[14]; ADB (1913), 447–48; ADB (1914), 70–1.
235 ADB (1913), 401.
236 Müller, *Der Kaiser*, p. 140.
237 ZStAP, ADV 7, Vorstandssitzung, Braunschweig, 1.12.12; ADB (1913), 135, 159; Class, *Strom*, pp. 252–63; Schödl, pp. 65–82.
238 ADB (1914), 278–9; Reismann-Grone, pp. 67–9; Class, *Strom*, p. 298; Schmidt, 'Reismann-Grone', pp. 318–21.
239 ADB (3.8.14); ADB (1914), 286.
240 ibid.
241 Class, *Strom*, p. 300.

Conclusion

Millions of Germans joined Heinrich Class in the public exhilaration of the first days of August 1914. One of them, a young man in Munich, later recalled that he was 'overcome by stormy enthusiasm', that he fell on his knees and 'thanked Heaven from an overflowing heart' for having 'the good fortune of being permitted to live at this time'.[1] The rhetorical flourishes with which Adolf Hitler described his feelings in 1914 were but one sign of the continuities between the public aspirations of the Pan-German League during the imperial period and the achievements of the National Socialists a generation later. The history of these continuities lies well beyond the scope of this study. Here only a few of the central features of the story deserve brief mention.

The turmoil of war, revolution, and civil war expanded and altered radically the character of the German-national public realm. The older patriotic societies (or their successors) and other 'national organizations' of the imperial period found themselves in the early 1920s amidst a network of new groups – paramilitary formations, political parties, and radical antisemitic societies – all of which claimed to speak or act in the name of the nation and which did so on a scale and in a style which many of the older organizations found difficult to comprehend. The Pan-German League none the less reasserted its claims to primacy within the expanded nationalist movement. In the attempt to ensure its own ideological predominance, the League employed a number of tactics, including the quiet inspiration of other organizations, infiltration, and (until inflation made the tactic impossible) financial support for other groups.[2]

These tactics met with but limited success when the Pan-Germans attempted to deal with the NSDAP. Scores of people drifted, chiefly through the avenue of the *Deutschvölkischer Schutz- und Trutz-Bund*, between the orbit of the Pan-German League and that of the Nazis.[3] It is difficult, though, to document the extent to which these personal ties resulted in the adoption by the Nazis of specific ideological or programmatic tenets from the Pan-Germans. Hitler and Class met several times in the early 1920s, and several features of the NSDAP's program, the 'Twenty-Five Points', resembled demands that Class first made in 1912, in his *Kaiserbuch*.[4] But the Nazis needed little direct inspiration from Class or his friends, for a general consensus reigned within the milieu of these patriotic organizations about what the word 'national' now symbolized. In most respects, this consensus was consistent with views the Pan-Germans had been articulating for years. 'National' thus implied an aggressive foreign policy (immediately in the form of defiance of the Versailles settlement, eventually in the form of continental and overseas expansion), opposition in the name of patriotism to the democratic regime in power, its replacement with some kind of 'national dictatorship', and racist antisemitism. Whatever the forms of mediation, the Pan-German League had served as a chief provider of practically all the elements that went into the ideological turbidity of the Nazis' program and Hitler's *Weltanschauung*.[5]

The conflicts between the Pan-Germans and the Nazis revolved less around ideological matters than they did around questions of authority and style. The Pan-German League never abandoned the view that academic education, *Bildung* and direct access to German culture, entitled the men who had it to precedence and authority in the public realm. Hitler of course rejected this proposition, and his contempt for the men who subscribed to it was scarcely veiled. In *Mein Kampf* his views were evident in his remarks about the prewar Pan-German movement in Austria. It had, he charged, been 'very feeble and tame', achieved 'bourgeois respectability and a muffled radicalism', but it had failed to understand that winning power required appealing to the masses.[6] Hitler felt the same way about the Pan-German League, which had groomed this respectability much more faithfully than the Austrians; and his charges were apt.

The Pan-Germans in return regarded Hitler as a barbarian, a man who lacked the essential cultivation required of a political leader. They found *Mein Kampf* an embarrassing and alarming document, not so much because of the ideas the book contained as because of its disorganization and stylistic abominations. These charges too were apt, but the Pan-Germans did not understand that Hitler's very lack of cultivation was a source of his immense appeal, that it enabled him to pose, in a way the Pan-Germans could not (even had they wished to), as a man of the common people, one who better understood the anxieties and frustrations these people were experiencing.

The Pan-Germans also failed to appreciate the more basic problem, that the character of the German-national public realm had changed, that the circumstances that bred radical nationalism after the war were of a different order than those that had nurtured it in Imperial Germany. Before the war, radical nationalism grew principally out of tensions experienced in sectors of the German upper-middle class. To the extent that the term 'crisis' is appropriate for this situation, it was a crisis of authority, which in the first instance affected the men who embodied and represented political and cultural authority in the Empire but who saw their authority challenged on several fronts. After the war, the term 'crisis' became an understatement; much broader social strata were affected, and the threat was not to their claims to embody culture or authority, but rather to their very social existence. In these circumstances, Hitler's vision of a German-national public realm (which he called the *Volksgemeinschaft*) was far the more attractive representation of a social experience shared broadly in the German lower-middle class. In the prewar era, educated men had made up, so to speak, the officer corps in the German-national public realm. The postwar era witnessed the mutiny of the lower-middle-class strata which had previously – and in a multitude of cases literally – comprised the foot-soldiers of the realm.

These changes were reflected in the new style of public discourse, which was epitomized in the monster rallies that Hitler staged in Munich and elsewhere and in the political violence attendant upon these and many other events. Although the Pan-Germans dabbled in a number of conspiracies whose goal was the violent overthrow of the republic, the League's leaders remained uncomfortable in embracing tactics of violence, and they were constantly reminded of the uncontrollability of the military men on whom they had to rely. Their sense of bewilderment over the style of politics in the new era was well captured by Franz Sontag, who had been active enough in the prewar League to remember how that organization had operated. 'The national movement', he observed in 1930, had, in contrast to earlier times, taken on 'strange forms':

Gone are the days in which one passed resolutions in meetings of the membership or in similar fashion unleashed a little storm in a water glass. What does a resolution, a petition, or even a national congress mean any more when at the same moment the *Stahlhelm* or the National Socialists are demonstrating in the streets in the strength of five army corps! Here, too, mass has become trump; in these circumstances the power of arms and fists counts for more as a means of political expression and persuasion than the post pithy lecture ... All the old voluntary associations ... have become practically meaningless in the face of the field-grey army in wind-breakers or brown-shirts, which has assembled beneath the symbols of the *Stahlhelm* or the swastika of the National Socialists, and in whose political, economic, and especially in whose social views the spirit of a new, younger generation takes flight toward goals that are presently still distant and hazy.[7]

For all that it contributed ideologically to the emergence of National Socialism, the Pan-German League was overwhelmed in the milieu in which radical nationalism flourished in the postwar crises. The League remained tied to concepts and prejudices of the imperial era, the era in which the organization took root and reached the apex of its influence. It would thus be appropriate to conclude with a brief discussion of the significance of the Pan-German League in the German Empire before the war. It would be useful in this discussion to return to some questions that have dominated the historiography of the League. These questions can be grouped under three broad headings – the political, which relate to the role that the League played in the governing of the *Kaiserreich*; the social, which address the League's significance in maintaining a social system dominated by the aristocracy and industrial bourgeoisie; and the cultural, which concern the extent to which the Pan-German League articulated and represented broader popular attitudes and fears.

The problem of the League's political significance is the easiest to resolve, despite all the controversy in recent years about this topic. It is beyond doubt that the men who governed the country well recognized the dangers of domestic political fragmentation and that they attempted consciously to bring a measure of domestic unity, and thus to reinforce the domestic structure of power, by pursuing aggressive foreign policies. It is no less clear that they attempted to generate support for these policies by resorting to plebiscitary tactics, by manipulating public opinion, notably through the patriotic societies. The history of most of these organizations attests to the success of Germany's rulers in controlling the popular expression of patriotism: the Colonial Society, the Eastern Marches Society, the School Association, and the Language Association were all domesticated, and they geared their activities to guidelines consistent with official policies.

However, the history of the Pan-German League (and, for a brief period, the Navy League) revealed that these tactics could have dangerous and unintended consequences. In all the patriotic societies, the mobilization of patriotism at the grass roots exploited anxieties and aspirations that grew out of the social experience of the educated and propertied middle class. The forces so mobilized were dynamic and emotionally volatile; and unless they were kept within tight confines, as they were in most of these societies, they could burst forth with a momentum that threatened not only the policies the government hoped to promote, but the government's own competence and power to shape foreign policy. The crisis in the Navy League provided an early warning of the dynamics involved, but not until 1911 did the situation really become critical for the government. Diplomatic humiliation over Morocco and the disastrous outcome of federal elections combined to raise the anxieties in the German upper-middle class to a new pitch, and, under the guidance of the Pan-German League, the sorcerers' apprentices turned on their masters. The anxieties crystallized around the issue of army reform, whose principal champion in the public realm was the German Defense League, an organization inspired by the Pan-Germans but which represented a broad coalition among the other, previously more docile patriotic societies. By the eve of the war, Germany's policy-makers were in genuine fear of the power of patriotic opinion. What had once been a successful tactic of rule had evoked forces which the German government could clearly no longer control.

The official documents reveal that the country's leaders persistently misunderstood the dynamism inherent in the popular mobilization of patriotism and that they used it unsuspectingly as a weapon in inter-agency rivalries. The documents do not, however, substantiate the charges of contemporary critics that the Pan-German League was the inspiring force behind German foreign policy. Officials hoped to use the League to promote policies they themselves had chosen. Their tactic would, to be sure, have made no sense but for a degree of consonance between these policies and the League's program. None the less, essential features of this program – the primacy of ethnicity in politics, the conspiratorial obsessions, and (certainly not least) a ruthless coherence – appear to have been foreign to the thinking of most of the men who shaped German foreign policy. These men felt the pressure of popular patriotism, most fatefully in the final crisis of 1914, but the pressure served less to dictate specific policies than to restrict the room of German statesmen for maneuver.

The social implications of the mobilization of patriotism in Imperial Germany were not unambiguous. It has become commonplace in Marxist–Leninist historiography, as well as in the recent West German literature, to portray the patriotic societies, particularly the Pan-German League, as tools of the dominant social groups in the German Empire, foremost among them the Junker aristocracy and the heavy-industrial bourgeoisie. This claim rests in part upon the argument that the mobilization of patriotism contributed to domestic social and political stability by diverting conflict outward; the claim rests too on the demonstrable ties that developed after 1909 between the Pan-German League and leading interest groups in the agricultural and heavy-industrial sectors.

The picture is too simple. In the first place, it bears reiteration that the officials who hoped to promote domestic stability by encouraging the mobilization of patriotism soon had grounds for alarm over the results of their efforts. The immediate consequence of the massive increases in the army on the eve of the war – increases whose magnitude was due in no small part to the agitation of the patriotic societies – was a significant shift within the institutional balance of power at the federal level. The need to raise the necessary revenues led to passage of the first major program of direct federal taxation, and the program came out of the most democratic institution in the country. It took little imagination to see that vesting the Reichstag with increased powers to tax would have profound social as well as political ramifications, particularly in view of the growing strength of the Social Democrats within that institution.

Identifying the agricultural and industrial elites as the primary beneficiaries of the Pan-German League's agitation raises other problems as well. The condominium among the League and the agricultural and heavy-industrial pressure groups did not emerge until just before the war, and even then its negotiation entailed such a rupture with the League's traditions that the leadership never dared divulge the true extent of the agreements to the membership. The Pan-German League, like the other patriotic societies, was a phenomenon of Imperial Germany's 'dominant classes', but, to continue in the same idiom, it represented principally a specific fraction of these classes, the *Bildungsbürgertum*. Not only did the League articulate a vision which reflected the social experience of this fraction, but it propounded the claims of this group both to social precedence and political authority.

To speak of the attitudes fostered in the Pan-German League as 'illiberal' may have some merit as a value judgment or as testimony to the diversity of the liberal experience in the modern West; as a description of a historical phenomenon in Germany the term is misleading at best.[8] The Pan-German League was a child of German liberalism. It retained the pretension of the *Bildungsbürgertum* to speak in the name of the German nation, which it defined as the *Volk*, an ethnic community which transcended not only the Hohenzollern monarchy's frontiers, but its political authority. After the turn of the century the League became increasingly explicit in rejecting the monarchy's authority to preside over the national symbols. And, at least until 1913, the League was even more open in repudiating the authority of the Junker aristocracy to speak in the name of the nation.

The fact that the Pan-German League claimed to speak in the name of the nation gave it a cultural significance that transcended the narrow confines implied by the social complexion of its membership. A national opposition was in this respect a more troubling spectacle than the Social Democrats. Unlike the Social Democrats, the patriots in the League did not reject the hegemonic network of national symbols; for all of the tension it implied with the Borussian tradition, the *Volk* was no counter-symbol like the class struggle. The paradox – and the danger – of a national opposition in Imperial Germany lay precisely in the congruity between the official symbolism and the symbols in whose name the opposition mobilized. The integrity of these symbols was never in dispute; at issue was rather their interpretation, or the authority to interpret them. In the opposition's interpretation, the monarchy itself was to be reduced to the status of pure symbol; it was to be deprived of the power to shape foreign policy, and custodial power over the entire network of national symbols (including the monarchy) was to be vested in the German-national public. As diplomatic setbacks and social tension accumulated, the competence of those who exercised power could be credibly challenged in the name of patriotism – first within the urban, Protestant middle class (the *locus classicus* of the German-national public realm), but then too in the broader constituency of rural Protestant Germany. As this challenge mounted, so did the currency of other tenets of the Pan-German League's interpretation of the national symbolism – not only that patriotism justified opposition to the regime in power, but that it demanded a resolute stand on the 'Jewish question' and an aggressive foreign policy, to eventuate in war.

Those who embraced this interpretation of the national symbolism included many of the most culturally powerful people in Imperial Germany. It remains, none the less, difficult to judge the precise extent to which this interpretation was shared. It is safe to conclude that on the eve of the war the anxieties and aggressive attitudes inherent in the Pan-German League's view of the world were far more widely shared, particularly in the Protestant upper-middle class, than they had been a quarter of a century earlier, at the League's birth. The reasons for the change lay less in the League's own agitation than in the combined impact of domestic social tension, which was reflected in the steady growth of the Social Democratic labor movement, and a series of international crises. In all events, the availability even before the war of a national symbolism with these aggressive connotations certainly eased the transition to National Socialism after the war.

Notes

1   Adolf Hitler, *Mein Kampf* (Boston, Mass., 1943), p. 161.
2   See especially the dissertations of Krebs and Chamberlain.
3   Lohalm, esp. pp. 283–330.
4   Georg Franz-Willing, *Die Hitlerbewegung: Der Ursprung 1919–1922* (Hamburg and Berlin, 1962), p. 80; Werner Maser, *Die Frühgeschichte der NSDAP: Hitlers Weg bis 1924* (Frankfurt a. M. and Bonn, 1965), pp. 93–6; Kruck, pp. 191–5.
5   Eberhard Jäckel, *Hitler's World View: A Blueprint for Power* (Cambridge, Mass., 1981), p. 120, overestimates, in my opinion, the degree of originality in Hitler's 'attempted synthesis'. See also Ernst Nolte, *Three Faces of Fascism: Action française, Italian Fascism, National Socialism* (New York, 1966), esp. pp. 402–25.
6   Hitler, pp. 101–9.

7   Alter, p. 24; cf. Reismann-Grone, p. 4.
8   See Fritz Stern, 'Introduction,' in *Failure of Illiberalism*, pp. xi–xliv; Jarausch, 'Liberal education as illiberal socialization', pp. 609–30.

Statistical Appendix

The population on which I based most of my calculations comprised just under 2,700 men who held local office in the Pan-German League between 1891 and 1914. Most of them I identified in the reports submitted by the chapters for publication in the League's journal. These reports I supplemented with rosters of local leaders which appeared in the Pan-German League's handbooks for the years 1899, 1901, 1905, 1908, and 1915 (the last volume did not yet reflect the dislocation of the war).[1] From all this data I was able first to draw conclusions about the activity of these men in the organization – how long they were active and the offices they held in the chapters. More significantly, these reports and rosters provided information about the kinds of people who were active in the chapters, for the Pan-Germans diligently observed the common practice of listing themselves by occupational labels. From these labels I was able to make inferences about levels of their education. I could also estimate which of the local leaders were noble or retired.

The idea of using this kind of information is not new. Mildred Wertheimer was the first to do it, and her findings have informed the conclusions of most subsequent historians of the Pan-German League. I went beyond her work in two respects. In the first place, my population was many times the size of hers, for she did not use the reports from the chapters in compiling her data. In the second place, I broke this information down into different analytical categories. From Wertheimer's own categories I found it difficult to know precisely what she was trying to measure. Her categories included 'teaching profession', 'businessmen', 'lawyers', 'physicians', 'nobility', 'Reichstag deputies', and several others.[2] Some of these categories, such as 'lawyers', described reasonably coherent social groups, bound by common background, training, and professional experience. Others, such as 'teaching profession', which presumably comprehended everyone from *Volksschullehrer* to *Ordinarius,* were so broad that they obscured crucial differences in background, training, and professional experience.

The deficiencies in Wertheimer's categories pointed to an underlying problem, a failure to distinguish between categories that relate to economic position and function and those that relate to social status – between class structure and hierarchy of status and prestige.[3] The one set of categories describes objective roles within an economic system; the other describes a social and cultural system structured not only by economic function and position, but by birth, education, tradition, and by other conventions and perceptions for which objective grounding may be largely lacking.

I attempted to account for this distinction by constructing two separate sets of occupational classifications, one for economic position and function and another for social status. The first presented comparatively few problems. The categories I used were those of the contemporary German census (see Tables 5.2, 5.7).[4] I did encounter several difficulties, chiefly the notorious and conscious ambiguity of the census-taker's rubric '(3.) Independents, top-level officials and employees', a label which grouped peasants and master artisans together with the wealthiest and most powerful men in the country. I was also compelled to adjust some of the subcategories of economic function to fit my own needs. My rubric '(B 9.) Industry: other or unclear' included a large number of men who listed their occupations only as *'Fabrikant'*, *'Fabrikdirektor'*, or *'Industrieller'*. Into the category of '(F.) Others' I placed students and the men who described themselves as *'Rentier'*, *'Rentner'*, or *'Privatier'*, as well as the four women who turned up in the membership.

It was more difficult to construct a set of categories to describe and measure social status (see Table 5.8). Because status rests to such a large extent upon subjective perceptions and other factors not easily measured, the undertaking impressed me as risky, but the importance of status as an explanation for the Pan-German League's behavior convinced me that the risks had to be run, even if the conclusions that emerged were shaky. I searched widely for models I might use for a social-status scale. I found helpful schemes in the contemporary literature, for the patriots were themselves interested in ways to group their membership lists according to social position.[5] I examined models devised by historians and sociologists.[6] Finally, I consulted several of my colleagues whose judgment I value.

The product of these labors was a social-status scale which reflected the various sources I consulted but was ultimately my own. I settled on a four-tiered model, which could accommodate distinctions based not only upon occupation, but upon wealth, education, and *Stand*. The four tiers were:

(1) *Low-level status:* included peasants, artisans, low-level employees *(Angestellte)*, and manual workers.
(2) *Mid-level status:* included public employees and teachers without an academic education, mid-level *Angestellte*, and most people who described themselves as *Kaufmann*.
(3) *High-level status:* included public officials, teachers, and professionals with an academic education, military officers below the rank of colonel, and substantial businessmen and managers.
(4) *Top-level status:* included high military officers, top-ranking public officials, the commercial and industrial elite, high nobles, and *ordentliche* professors.

Assigning people to the tiers involved some compromises which struck me as arbitrary – as well as considerable guess-work. The main problems were the ambiguous designations *'Kaufmann'* and *'Fabrikant'*. Unless I had additional evidence that suggested otherwise (as I did in the cases of some of the Hamburg merchants), I consistently placed people who called themselves *Kaufmann* in the 'mid-level' tier and the *'Fabrikanten'* (some of whom were doubtless artisans) in the 'high-level' tier as 'substantial businessmen'.[7] It must remain only a hope that this consistency might have neutralized some of the anomalies.

For all its problems, the social-status scale did prove useful. By assigning a numerical value to each of the tiers, I could calculate a figure for 'mean social status' as an index of the relative weight of the tiers within the organization. This .index in turn enabled me to make comparisons between the Pan-German League and other organizations, as well as comparisons among sectors of the Pan-German League itself.

Because a large segment of my population was publicly employed, I constructed a scale similar to the social-status scale for public administrative position. Again I used a four-tiered model:

(1) Low-level officials (of which there were extremely few).
(2) Subaltern officials without an academic education.
(3) Officials with an academic education.
(4) Top-level officials.

I assigned people to these tiers with more confidence than I did in the social-status scale, because administrative titles were generally more precise and because the educational qualifications for administrative positions were generally more clear. Academic education was the criterion for distinguishing between the second and third tiers. The difference between the third and fourth tiers, between high- and top-level officials, was more difficult to define. I normally resorted to a scale of salaries and placed all the men in the top level whose offices carried salaries in excess of ten thousand Marks on the Prussian scale of 1897.[8] Assigning numerical values to each of the tiers then enabled me to calculate, again for purposes of comparison, an index of 'mean public administrative position'.

The initial sorts and calculations for the population resulted in Tables 5.1, 5.2, 5.3.

I found additional information on a subpopulation of Pan-Germans who held national office in the organization – in the executive committee, whose membership lists I compiled for the entire period 1891–1914, and in the much larger national board of directors, whose membership list I examined only for the year 1899. Biographical dictionaries and other sources produced information about the years of birth and experiences abroad of a substantial number of these people. This information appears in Tables 5.4 and 5.5.

In order to compare the social composition of the Pan-German League's local leadership with that of leaders of other patriotic societies, I selected twenty-five communities in which chapters of the League existed alongside chapters of one or more of the other organizations. I chose these communities in order to provide as broad as possible a variation in size, economic complexion, and geographical distribution. Most of the communities were necessarily large, however, for smaller towns normally did not play host to several patriotic societies. The selection was further limited by the paucity of chapters of the Pan-German League in the east and

Table 5.1 Characteristics of Local Leaders of the Pan-German League

N	Retired		Noble		Academic education		Doctorate		Public administration		Mean social status	Mean public administrative position
	n	%	n	%	n	%	n	%	n	%		
2,688	77	3·1	59	2·2	1,433[b]	65·6	638	23·7	1,298[c]	53·9	2·74	2·79
	(2,445)[a]		(2,688)		(2,186)		(2,688)		(2,407)			

[a] This is the figure on which the percentage is calculated. It is N−MV

[b] Judging from occupation, this figure is distributed in the following manner:

	n	Pct
University	1,094	87·4
Technische Hochschule	139	11·1
Agricultural or forestry academy	15	1·2
Artistic Academy	3	0·2
Other or unclear	182	—

[c] This figure includes parliamentarians and those people whose positions were 'beamtenähnlich': Kommerzienrat, Medizinal- or Sanitätsrat, Justizrat.

Table 5.2 *Economic Positions and Functions of Local Leaders of the Pan-German League*

	Agriculture		Industry		Commerce		Domestic		Service/ professional		Other		Totals	
	n	%	n	%	n	%	n	%	n	%	n	%	n	%
1. Apprentices, workers	1	0·1	6	0·2	13	0·5	—	—	8	0·3	—	—	28	1·2
2. Mid-level employees, trained personnel	15	0·6	176	7·4	143	6·0	1	0·0	953	39·9	20[a]	0·8	1,308	54·8
3. Independents, top-level officials and employees	27	1·1	292	12·2	347	14·5	—	—	351	14·7	33[b]	1·4	1,050	44·0
TOTALS	43	1·8	474	19·9	503	21·1	1	0·0	1,312	55·0	53	2·2	2,386	100·0
Association index[c]	0·06		0·53		1·84		0·01		9·47		0·20			

[a] Students

[b] Rentner, Rentier, Privatier

[c] This figure indicates the degree to which these economic functions were over- or under-represented in the Pan-German League. To calculate it, I divided the percentage of the Pan-German League's local leadership in each of the six economic functions by the percentage of all male *Erwerbstätige* in each of the functions in 1907. If the index exceeds 1·0 the function was over-represented: Kaiserliches Statistisches Amt, *Statistisches Jahrbuch für das Deutsche Reich 1913* (Berlin, 1913), pp. 16–17; cf. Kaelble, 'Chancenungleichheit', pp. 128–9.

Table 5.3 *Local Leaders of the Pan-German League in Public Administration*

	Military n	Military %	General n	General %	Justice n	Justice %	Finance/taxation n	Finance/taxation %	Education[a] n	Education[a] %	Religion n	Religion %	Post/telegraph n	Post/telegraph %	Railroads[b] n	Railroads[b] %
1. Low-level officials	1	0·1	1	0·1	—	—	3	0·2	1	0·1	—	—	3	0·2	3	0·2
2. Subaltern officials without academic training	2	0·2	22	1·9	11	0·9	30	2·5	87	7·4	1	0·1	69	5·8	11	0·9
3. Officials with academic training	54	4·6	29	2·4	88	7·5	5	0·4	448	38·0	63	5·3	18	1·5	4	0·3
4. Top-level officials	5	0·4	5	0·4	3	0·2	—	—	38	3·2	2	0·2	—	—	—	—
TOTALS	62	5·3	57	4·8	102	8·6	38	3·2	574	48·7	66	5·6	90	7·6	18	1·5

	Customs n	Customs %	Industrial regulation n	Industrial regulation %	Construction[c] n	Construction[c] %	Health n	Health %	Land/forestry n	Land/forestry %	Local n	Local %	Other n	Other %	Totals n	Totals %
1. Low-level officials	—	—	—	—	1	0·1	—	—	1	0·1	1	0·1	—	—	15	1·3
2. Subaltern officials without academic training	4	0·3	1	0·1	20	1·7	—	—	2	0·2	8	0·7	4	0·3	272	23·1
3. Officials with academic training	1	0·1	2	0·2	57	4·8	12	1·0	12	1·0	38	3·2	6	0·5	837	71·0
4. Top-level officials	—	—	—	—	1	0·1	—	—	—	—	1	0·1	—	—	55	4·6
TOTALS	5	0·4	3	0·3	79	6·7	12	1·0	15	1·3	48	4·1	10	0·8	1,179	100·0

[a] Includes libraries, museums, and archives
[b] Includes harbors
[c] Includes mines and canals

Table 5.4   *Years of Birth of National Leaders of the Pan-German League*

	n	%
Before 1840	13	18·6
1841–5	7	10·0
1846–50	7	10·0
1851–5	17	24·3
1856–60	9	12·9
1861–5	9	12·9
1866–70	7	10·0
After 1870	1	1·4
MV	11	

Table 5.5   *Foreign Experience of National Leaders of the Pan-German League*

	n	%
Birth	11	29·7
Education	4	10·8
Residence	7	18·9
Extended travel	11	29·7
Marriage	3	8·1
Other	1	2·7
MV	44	

the paucity of chapters of the Eastern Marches Society in the west. The statistics I compiled thus probably understated the weight of agricultural occupations in the patriotic societies, although the distortion was doubtless not extreme, for with the exception of the Eastern Marches Society, none of these organizations was strong in the rural eastern parts of Germany. The communities I selected for study were Barmen, Berlin, Breslau, Cologne, Darmstadt, Dresden, Düsseldorf, Erfurt, Eisleben, Eisenach, Essen, Gotha, Hamburg, Halle, Hanover, Heppenheim, Karlsruhe, Kassel, Leipzig, Munich, Moers, Plauen, Pirna, Potsdam, and Stuttgart. From the reports which the chapters published in their societies' journals or from handbooks, I gathered information about the local leaders of the Geman Colonial Society,[9] the German Navy League,[10] the General German School Association (for which the information was very sparse),[11] the Eastern Marches Society,[12] and the General German Language Association.[13] For the comparison I sorted out the figures on the local leadership of the Pan-German League in the same twenty-five communities. I also compared the figures for the patriotic societies with those of the German Peace Society.[14] Given the concentration of the Peace Society's chapters in the southwest, however, a comparison based only on the twenty-five communities was impossible. Accordingly, the figures on the Peace Society's local leadership represented all the names I could identify throughout the country. The comparisons among all these organizations are in Tables 5.6, 5.7, and 5.8.

Comparing the local leadership in the Pan-German League with the rank and file of the same organization was difficult, for few membership lists survived. I found three – for Stuttgart in 1913,[15] for the town of Königstein in Saxony in 1914,[16] and for Hamburg in 1901.[17] In addition, statistics that the League itself published in 1901 made possible a comparison at least by economic function between the cadres and the broader membership.[18] I also compared these groups to all the men in the League whom I could identify as 'long-term activists'. These were men whose activity I could trace for a period of at least five years. Details of all these comparisons are in Tables 5.9, 5.10, and 5.11.

I also compared patterns of public employment in the local leadership of several patriotic societies. As in the previous comparisons among patriotic societies, the figures in the Table 5.12 were drawn from the twenty-five select communities.

In a large number of cases I determined the specific offices held by leaders of the local chapters of the Pan-German League. The breakdown in Table 8.1 reveals that the higher offices usually were in the hands of men of higher status and that this pattern prevailed at the national level as well.

Determining patterns of cross-affiliation among different patriotic societies presented difficulties. Only in Hamburg did I find complete local membership lists for several of these organizations, but even these were not entirely comparable documents. I compared the membership list of the Hamburg chapter of the Pan-German League for 1901,[19] the local School Association's register for 1903,[20] the Language Association's membership list for 1912,[21] the records for payment of dues in the Navy League for 1909–13,[22] and the lists of local guests attending the annual convention of the Colonial Society, which met in Hamburg in 1912.[23] One problem was that these lists did not cover a uniform period of time; another was the difficulty of identifying the same person on more than one list – a difficulty caused by similarities of name, job changes, retirements, sibling relationships, and misprints. I attempted to match first names and initials and occupations wherever these were listed, but I encountered many instances – of names like 'F. Schmidt, *Kaufmann*' or merely 'Dr Müller' – in which I was compelled in the last resort to guess. Subject to these caveats, the results of the survey of patriotic societies in Hamburg are in Table 9.1.

The membership figures and the number of local chapters, which I have plotted in Figures 10.1 and 10.2, came mainly from the *Alldeutsche Blätter*. For the years after 1903, when the published statistics began to misrepresent the situation, I calculated approximate figures on the basis of membership dues reported in annual budgets.

Finally, I drew the statistics on the German Defense League from reports of local chapters which appeared in this organization's journal.[24] For purposes of comparison, I ran the figures on the Defense League's local leaders next to those of all the Pan-German League's cadres in Tables 11.1, 11.2, and 11.3. I also compiled a more detailed analysis of the men in the Defense League with military occupations. This information appears in

Table 5.6 *Characteristics of Local Leaders of Patriotic Societies (and the German Peace Society)*

	N	Retired n (N−MV)	Retired %	Noble n (N−MV)	Noble %	Academic education n (N−MV)	Academic education %	Doctorate n (N−MV)	Doctorate %	Public administration[a] n (N−MV)	Public administration[a] %	Mean social status	Mean public adm. pos.
Pan-German League	625	36 (573)	6·3	23 (625)	3·7	369 (537)	68·7	202 (625)	32·3	303 (559)	54·2	2·81	2·90
Colonial Society[b]	750	109 (690)	15·8	120 (750)	16·0	398 (588)	67·7	199 (750)	26·5	510 (672)	75·9	3·24	3·39
Navy League	250	24 (227)	10·6	41 (250)	16·4	101 (165)	61·2	49 (250)	19·6	159 (220)	72·3	3·12	3·07
School Association[c]	52	— (52)	—	3 (52)	5·8	43 (48)	89·6	32 (52)	61·5	40 (46)	87·0	3·00	3·04
Eastern Marches Society[d]	185	38 (163)	23·3	22 (185)	11·9	122 (164)	74·4	56 (185)	30·3	122 (162)	75·3	3·04	3·14
Language Association[e]	195	15 (182)	8·2	5 (195)	2·6	112 (183)	61·2	52 (195)	26·7	142 (183)	77·6	2·82	2·86
Composite	2,057	222 (1,887)	11·8	214 (2,057)	10·4	1,145 (1,685)	68·0	590 (2,057)	28·7	1,276 (1,842)	69·3	3·03	3·13
Peace Society	414	2 (278)	0·1	10 (414)	2·4	144 (320)	45·0	56 (414)	13·5	144 (330)	43·6	2·57	2·66

[a] Includes parliamentarians and those whose occupations were 'beamtenähnlich'.
[b] No chapters in Eisleben, Heppenheim, Moers.
[c] No chapters in Eisleben, Heppenheim, Minden, Moers.
[d] No chapters in Barmen, Darmstadt, Düsseldorf, Eisenach, Eisleben, Heppenheim, Minden, Moers, Pirna, Plauen.
[e] No chapter in Heppenheim.

Table 5.7 Economic Functions of Local Leaders of Patriotic Societies (and the German Peace Society)

	Pan-German League		Colonial Society		Navy League		School Association		Eastern Marches Society		Language Association		Peace Society	
	n	%	n	%	n	%	n	%	n	%	n	%	n	%
A. Agriculture/forestry	2	0.4	4	0.6	4	2.0	—	—	2	1.3	1	0.6	7	2.2
1. Agriculture	2	0.4	3	0.5	4	2.0	—	—	2	1.3	1	0.6	6	1.9
2. Forestry	—	—	1	0.2	—	—	—	—	—	—	—	—	1	0.3
B. Industry	87	15.9	69	10.7	33	16.6	2	4.5	18	11.6	6	3.3	45	14.0
1. Mining	4	0.7	11	1.7	4	2.0	—	—	3	1.9	—	—	—	—
2. Metal processing	2	0.4	—	—	2	1.0	—	—	—	—	—	—	4	1.2
3. Machines/instruments	2	0.4	1	0.2	2	1.0	—	—	—	—	—	—	6	1.9
4. Chemicals	8	1.4	7	1.1	2	1.0	1	2.3	4	2.6	—	—	1	0.3
5. Textiles	—	—	—	—	—	—	—	—	—	—	—	—	4	1.2
6. Construction	38	6.9	16	2.5	11	5.5	1	2.3	7	4.5	3	1.7	5	1.6
7. Polygraphic	6	1.1	2	0.3	3	1.5	—	—	1	0.6	1	0.6	3	0.9
8. Artistic	2	0.4	1	0.2	—	—	—	—	—	—	—	—	3	0.9
9. Other or unclear	25	4.6	31	4.8	9	4.5	—	—	3	1.9	2	1.1	19	5.9
C. Commerce	130	23.7	110	17.1	44	22.1	—	—	14	9.0	36	19.9	62	19.3
1. Commerce	110	20.1	90	13.9	30	15.1	—	—	10	6.4	29	16.0	54	16.8
2. Insurance	—	—	—	—	—	—	—	—	—	—	—	—	—	—
3. Transportation	18	3.3	20	3.1	14	7.0	—	—	4	2.6	7	3.9	8	2.5
4. Hotels/restaurants	1	0.2	—	—	—	—	—	—	—	—	—	—	—	—
5. Other	1	0.2	—	—	—	—	—	—	—	—	—	—	—	—
D. Domestic	—	—	—	—	—	—	—	—	—	—	—	—	1	0.3
E. Service and professions	314	57.3	457	70.9	117	58.8	42	95.4	116	74.8	132	72.9	152	47.2
1. Military	29	5.3	145	22.5	25	12.6	1	2.3	25	16.1	9	5.0	1	0.3
2. Public administration	72	13.1	171	26.5	60	30.2	8	18.2	45	29.0	31	17.1	44	13.7
3. Religion	16	2.9	8	1.2	—	—	2	4.5	2	1.3	3	1.7	20	6.2
4. Education	140	25.5	81	12.6	23	11.6	28	63.6	29	18.7	86	47.5	63	19.6
5. Health	37	6.8	35	5.4	3	1.5	3	6.8	8	5.2	1	0.6	11	3.4
6. Private scholarship, journalism	19	3.5	12	1.9	3	1.5	—	—	7	4.5	2	1.1	11	3.4
7. Stenography	—	—	—	—	—	—	—	—	—	—	—	—	—	—
8. Music, expositions	1	0.2	5	0.8	3	1.5	—	—	—	—	—	—	2	0.6
9. Other	—	—	—	—	—	—	—	—	—	—	—	—	—	—
F. Other	15	2.7	5	0.8	1	0.1	—	—	5	3.2	6	3.3	55	17.1
1. Rentner, Privatier, etc.	7	1.3	5	0.8	1	0.1	—	—	—	—	3	1.7	6	1.9
2. Women	—	—	—	—	—	—	—	—	—	—	—	—	49	15.2
3. Students	8	1.4	—	—	—	—	—	—	5	3.2	3	1.7	—	—
	N = 548		N = 645		N = 199		N = 44		N = 155		N = 181		N = 322	

Table 5.8 Social Status of Local Leaders of Patriotic Societies (and the German Peace Society)

	Pan-German League		Colonial Society		Navy League		School Association		Eastern Marches Society		Language Association		Peace Society	
	n	%	n	%	n	%	n	%	n	%	n	%	n	%
Top-level status	38	6·9	229	33·9	72	33·0	6	13·6	29	18·0	13	7·4	9	2·8
1. High military officers (general and colonel)	3	0·5	69	10·2	16	7·3	—	—	11	6·8	2	1·1	—	—
2. Top-level officials	6	1·1	73	10·8	22	10·1	—	—	11	6·8	4	2·3	2	0·6
3. Professors (*ordentlich*)	12	2·2	23	3·4	2	0·9	6	13·6	4	2·5	3	1·7	2	0·6
4. Business elite	13	2·4	50	7·4	24	11·0	—	—	1	0·6	3	1·7	3	0·9
5. *Rittergutsbesitzer*	2	0·4	6	0·9	1	0·5	—	—	—	—	—	—	—	—
6. High nobility	1	0·2	8	1·2	7	3·2	—	—	2	1·2	1	0·6	2	0·6
7. Other	1	0·2	—	—	—	—	—	—	—	—	—	—	—	—
High-level status	370	67·2	388	57·5	108	49·5	34	77·3	112	69·6	116	64·8	155	47·8
1. Other commissioned officers	20	3·6	65	9·6	7	3·2	1	2·3	15	9·3	7	3·9	1	0·3
2. Academically educated officials	78	14·2	127	18·8	33	15·1	8	18·2	41	25·5	27	15·1	35	10·8
3. Academically educated teachers	99	18·0	51	7·6	15	6·9	19	43·2	20	12·4	62	34·6	30	9·3
4. Academically educated professionals	87	15·8	75	11·1	18	8·3	5	11·4	27	16·8	10	5·6	45	13·9
5. Substantial businessmen/high management	78	14·2	64	9·5	31	14·2	1	2·3	9	5·6	7	3·9	37	11·4
6. *Rentner, Privatier*, etc.	6	1·1	5	0·7	1	0·5	—	—	—	—	3	1·7	6	1·9
7. *Gutsbesitzer*	—	—	—	—	2	0·9	—	—	—	—	—	—	1	0·3
8. Other	2	0·4	1	0·1	1	0·5	—	—	—	—	—	—	—	—
Mid-level status	137	24·9	56	8·3	33	15·1	2	4·5	19	11·8	50	27·9	138	42·6
1. Subaltern officials	31	5·6	12	1·8	15	6·9	2	4·5	9	5·6	8	4·5	11	3·4
2. Other teachers	15	2·7	3	0·4	3	1·4	—	—	—	—	20	11·2	33	10·2
3. Merchants	70	12·7	37	5·5	7	3·2	—	—	5	3·1	20	11·2	37	11·4
4. Mid-level *Angestellte*	9	1·6	4	0·6	8	3·7	—	—	—	—	2	1·1	8	2·5
5. Students	9	1·6	—	—	—	—	—	—	5	3·1	—	—	—	—
(6. Women)	—	—	—	—	—	—	—	—	—	—	—	—	(49)	(15·1)
7. Other	3	0·5	—	—	—	—	—	—	—	—	—	—	—	—
Low-level status	6	1·1	2	0·3	5	2·3	2	4·5	1	0·6	—	—	22	6·8
1. Lower officials	—	—	—	—	—	—	2	4·5	—	—	—	—	—	—
2. Low-level *Angestellte*	3	0·5	—	—	—	—	—	—	—	—	—	—	2	0·6
3. Artisans	3	0·5	2	0·3	4	1·8	—	—	1	0·6	—	—	17	5·2
4. Workers	—	—	—	—	1	0·5	—	—	—	—	—	—	—	—
5. Peasants	—	—	—	—	—	—	—	—	—	—	—	—	3	0·9
	N = 551		N = 675		N = 218		N = 44		N = 161		N = 179		N = 324	

Table 5.9 *Characteristics of All Local Leaders and Long-Term Activists in the Pan-German League and of Members in Three Chapters*

	N	Retired n (N−MV)	Retired %	Noble n (N−MV)	Noble %	Academic education n (N−MV)	Academic education %	Doctorate n (N−MV)	Doctorate %	Public administration[a] n (N−MV)	Public administration[a] %	Mean social status	Mean public adm. pos.
All local leaders	2,688	77 (2,445)	3·1	59 (2,688)	2·2	1,433 (2,186)	65·6	638 (2,688)	23·7	1,298 (2,407)	53·9	2·74	2·79
Long-term activists	495	14 (481)	2·9	14 (495)	2·8	318 (420)	75·7	169 (495)	34·1	272 (477)	57·0	2·86	2·86
Stuttgart chapter													
Leaders	36	3 (28)	10·7	— (36)	—	21 (26)	80·8	7 (36)	19·4	13 (26)	50·0	2·79	3·00
Members	139	3 (129)	2·3	3 (139)	2·2	70 (111)	63·1	25 (139)	18·0	60 (118)	50·8	2·75	2·87
Königstein chapter													
Leaders	3	— (3)	—	— (3)	—	1 (2)	50·0	1 (2)	50·0	2 (3)	66·7	2·67	2·50
Members	31	— (31)	—	1 (31)	3·2	11 (25)	44·0	5 (31)	16·1	14 (30)	46·7	2·62	2·46
Hamburg chapter													
Leaders	42	— (37)	—	3 (42)	7·1	17 (37)	45·9	12 (42)	28·6	13 (37)	35·1	2·85	3·00
Members	831	1 (764)	0·1	5 (831)	0·6	189 (635)	29·8	110 (831)	13·2	91 (752)	12·1	2·41	2·81

[a] Includes parliamentarians and those whose occupations were 'beamtenähnlich'.

Table 5.10 Economic Functions of All Local Leaders and Long-Term Activists in the Pan-German League and of Members in Three Chapters

	All local leaders n	%	All members, 1901 n	%	Members in Stuttgart, 1913 n	%	Members in Königstein, 1914 n	%	Members in Hamburg, 1901 n	%	Long-term activists n	%
A. Agriculture/forestry	43	1·8	416	2·3	3	2·6	1	3·2	—	—	5	1·0
1. Agriculture	30	1·3			2	1·7	1	3·2	—	—	3	0·6
2. Forestry	13	0·6			1	0·9	—	—	—	—	2	0·4
B. Industry	474	19·9	2,673	14·7	27	23·1	4	12·9	81	10·8	84	17·7
1. Mining	26	1·1			2	1·7	—	—	—	—	3	0·6
2. Metal processing	7	0·3			—	—	—	—	2	0·3	2	0·4
3. Machinery/instruments	6	0·2			1	0·9	1	3·2	6	0·8	4	0·8
4. Chemicals	66	2·8			3	2·6	—	—	12	1·6	10	2·1
5. Textiles	11	0·5			—	—	—	—	2	0·3	2	0·4
6. Construction	149	6·3			15	12·8	—	—	32	4·3	20	4·2
7. Polygraphic	42	1·8			1	0·9	—	—	6	0·8	9	1·9
8. Artistic	6	0·2			1	0·9	—	—	3	0·4	1	0·2
9. Other or unclear	161	6·7			4	3·4	3	9·7	18	2·4	33	7·0
C. Commerce	503	21·1	4,904	27·0	32	27·4	8	25·8	518	69·0	83	17·5
1. Commerce	383	16·1			27	23·1	4	12·9	488	65·0	72	15·2
2. Insurance	1	0·1			—	—	—	—	1	0·1	—	—
3. Transportation	108	4·5			4	3·4	1	3·2	24	3·2	10	2·1
4. Hotels/restaurants	9	0·4			1	0·9	3	9·7	5	0·7	—	—
5. Other	2	0·1			—	—	—	—	—	—	1	0·2
D. Domestic	1	0·0	—	—	—	—	—	—	—	—	—	—
E. Service and professions	1,312	55·0	9,099	50·0	51	43·6	17	54·8	145	19·3	298	62·9
1. Military	62	2·6			3	2·6	4	12·9	1	0·1	7	1·5
2. Public administration/law	375	15·7			21	18·0	1	3·2	47	6·3	82	17·3
3. Religion	66	2·8			1	0·9	7	22·6	7	0·9	15	3·2
4. Education	583	24·4			13	11·1	4	12·9	26	3·5	133	28·1
5. Health	160	6·7			10	8·6	1	3·2	57	7·6	48	10·1
6. Private scholarship, journalism	57	2·4			3	2·6	—	—	5	0·7	13	2·7
7. Stenography	1	0·1			—	—	—	—	—	—	—	—
8. Music, expositions	6	0·2			—	—	—	—	2	0·3	—	—
9. Other	2	0·1			—	—	—	—	—	—	—	—
F. Others	53	2·2	1,091	6·0	4	3·4	1	3·2	7	0·9	4	0·8
1. Rentner, Privatier, etc.	33	1·4			1	0·9	—	—	7	0·9	4	0·8
2. Students	20	0·8			—	—	—	—	—	—	—	—
3. Women	—	—			3	2·6	1	3·2	—	—	—	—
	N = 2,386		N = 18,183		N = 117		N = 31		N = 751		N = 474	

Table 5.11 Social Status of Local Leaders and Long-Term Activists in the Pan-German League and of Members in Three Chapters

	All local leaders		Long-term activists		Members in Stuttgart, 1913		Members in Königstein, 1914		Members in Hamburg, 1901	
	n	*%*	*n*	*%*	*n*	*%*	*n*	*%*	*n*	*%*
Top-level status	101	4.2	29	6.1	6	5.0	—	—	11	1.5
1. High military officers	5	0.2	3	0.6	—	—	—	—	—	—
2. Top-level officials	14	0.6	—	—	—	—	—	—	—	—
3. Professors (*ordentlich*)	37	1.5	9	1.9	3	2.5	—	—	1	0.1
4. Business elite	38	1.6	14	3.0	3	2.5	—	—	10	1.3
5. *Rittergutsbesitzer*	3	0.1	1	0.2	—	—	—	—	—	—
6. High nobility	2	0.1	1	0.2	—	—	—	—	—	—
7. Other	2	0.1	1	0.2	—	—	—	—	—	—
High-level status	1,606	67.1	346	73.3	75	63.0	18	60.0	302	40.1
1. Other commissioned officers	45	1.9	—	—	—	—	—	—	—	—
2. Academically educated officials	386	15.4	72	15.3	24	20.2	4	13.3	42	5.6
3. Academically educated teachers	430	18.0	99	21.0	15	12.6	2	6.7	20	2.6
4. Academically educated professionals	361	15.1	97	20.6	15	12.6	6	20.0	99	13.1
5. Substantial business/management	356	14.9	73	15.5	20	16.8	6	20.0	134	17.8
6. *Rentner, Privatier,* etc.	31	1.3	4	0.8	1	0.8	—	—	7	0.9
7. *Gutsbesitzer*	10	0.4	1	0.2	—	—	—	—	—	—
8. Other	5	0.2	—	—	—	—	—	—	—	—
Mid-level status	633	26.4	96	20.3	37	31.1	12	40.0	414	55.0
1. Subaltern officials	198	8.3	27	5.7	10	8.4	2	6.7	10	1.3
2. Other teachers	85	3.6	14	3.0	—	—	5	16.7	5	0.7
3. Merchants	278	11.6	49	10.4	21	17.6	4	13.3	389	51.7
4. Mid-level *Angestellte*	47	2.0	5	1.1	3	2.5	—	—	10	1.3
5. Students	22	1.0	—	—	—	—	—	—	—	—
(6.) Women	—	—	—	—	(3)	(2.5)	(1)	(3.3)	—	—
7. Other	3	0.1	1	0.2	1	0.8	—	—	—	—
Low-level status	55	2.3	1	0.2	—	—	—	—	26	3.5
1. Lower officials	1	0.0	—	—	—	—	—	—	—	—
2. Low-level *Angestellte*	14	0.6	—	—	1	0.8	—	—	—	—
3. Artisans	26	1.1	1	0.2	—	—	—	—	2	0.3
4. Workers	1	0.0	—	—	—	—	—	—	24	3.2
5. Peasants	13	0.5	—	—	—	—	—	—	—	—
	N = 2,395		*N* = 472		*N* = 119		*N* = 30		*N* = 753	

Table 5.12 Local Leaders of Patriotic Societies in the Public Service

	Military			General			Justice			Finance/taxation			Education		
	ADV[a]	DKG[b]	DFV[c]	ADV	DKG	DFV	ADV	DKG	DFV	ADV	DKG	DFV	ADV	DKG	DFV
1. Low-level officials	—	—	—	—	—	—	—	—	—	—	—	—	—	—	—
2. Subaltern officials without academic training	0·4[d]	0·5	—	2·2	0·2	4·3	0·4	—	0·8	4·1	1·0	4·3	5·2	0·7	3·4
3. Officials with academic training	10·1	16·7	8·6	1·1	6·9	12·0	4·8	6·0	0·8	0·4	0·2	0·8	42·2	13·1	13·7
4. Top-level officials	1·1	16·7	14·5	—	9·0	3·4	—	2·1	2·6	—	0·2	1·7	4·8	6·2	1·7
TOTALS	11·6	33·9	23·1	3·3	16·1	19·7	5·2	8·1	4·3	4·5	1·4	6·8	52·2	20·0	18·8

	Religion			Post/telegraph			Railroads			Customs			Industrial regulation		
	ADV	DKG	DFV	ADV	DKG	DFV	ADV	DKG	DFV	ADV	DKG	DFV	ADV	DKG	DFV
1. Low-level officials	—	—	—	—	—	—	—	—	3·4	—	—	—	—	—	—
2. Subaltern officials without academic training	—	—	—	2·6	0·2	1·7	1·5	0·5	0·8	—	—	—	—	—	—
3. Officials with academic training	4·8	1·4	—	1·9	1·4	—	0·4	—	0·8	0·4	—	—	—	—	—
4. Top-level officials	0·8	0·2	—	—	0·7	0·8	—	1·0	1·7	—	—	—	—	—	—
TOTALS	5·6	1·7	—	4·5	2·4	2·5	1·9	1·4	6·8	0·4	—	—	—	—	—

	Construction			Health			Land/forestry			Local			Other			Totals		
	ADV	DKG	DFV	ADV	DKG	DFV	ADV	DKG	DFV	ADV	DKG	DFV	ADV	DKG	DFV	ADV	DKG	DFV
1. Low-level officials	—	—	—	—	—	—	—	—	—	—	0·2	0·8	—	—	—	—	—	3·4
2. Subaltern officials without academic training	0·8	—	0·8	—	—	—	—	—	—	—	—	—	—	—	—	17·2	3·3	17·1
3. Officials with academic training	6·0	4·8	5·1	0·8	0·5	—	—	—	—	1·9	5·5	4·3	0·8	0·7	2·6	75·4	57·1	48·7
4. Top-level officials	0·4	1·0	—	—	—	—	—	0·2	—	0·4	1·9	3·4	—	0·2	0·8	7·5	39·5	30·8
TOTALS	7·1	5·7	6·0	0·8	0·5	—	—	0·2	—	2·2	7·6	8·6	0·8	1·0	3·4	100·1	99·9	100·0

[a] ADV: Pan-German League. n = 268
[b] DKG: German Colonial Society. N = 420
[c] DFV: German Navy League. N = 117
[d] All figures are percentages of N.

Table 8.1 *Hierarchy in the Local Chapters and National Offices of the Pan-German League*

	N	Retired n (N–MV)	Retired %	Noble n (N–MV)	Noble %	Academic education n (N–MV)	Academic education %	Doctorate n (N–MV)	Doctorate %	Public administration[c] n (N–MV)	Public administration[c] %	Mean social status	Mean public adm. pos.
Chairman or deputy chairman	846[b]	23 (810)	2·8	30 (846)	3·5	619 (730)	84·8	306 (846)	36·2	518 (795)	65·2	2·94	2·95
Secretary or Treasurer[a]	848[b]	14 (781)	1·8	5 (848)	0·6	338 (702)	48·1	119 (848)	14·0	343 (771)	44·5	2·54	2·49
All local officers	2,688	77 (2,445)	3·1	59 (2,688)	2·2	1,433 (2,186)	65·6	638 (2,688)	23·7	1,298 (2,407)	53·9	2·74	2·79
National Board of Directors (1899)	142	12 (141)	8·5	16 (142)	11·3	103 (142)	72·5	63 (142)	44·4	91 (138)	65·9	3·13	3·16
Executive committee	76	6 (74)	8·1	13 (76)	17·1	60 (76)	78·9	29 (76)	38·2	47 (75)	62·7	3·25	3·24

Includes deputy secretary or deputy treasurer.
The discrepancy between the sum of these two figures and the total number of local leaders is due to the fact that many local leaders were not listed by specific office or were listed simply as 'members of the board of officers' (*Vorstandsmitglieder* or *Beisitzender*).
Includes parliamentarians and those whose positions were '*beamtenähnlich*'.

Table 9.1 *Patterns of Cross-Affiliation among Patriotic Societies in Hamburg*

| | | *Also members of:* | | | |
	Pan-German League	Colonial Society	School Association	Language Association	Navy League
Members of:					
Pan-German League (N = 753)	—	47 (·07)[a]	61 (·31)	83 (·08)	141 (·04)
Colonial Society (N = 674)	47 (·06)	—	30 (·15)	66 (·07)	110 (·03)
School Association (N = 195)	61 (·08)	30 (·04)	—	35 (·04)	56 (·02)
Language Association (N = 980)	83 (·11)	66 (·10)	35 (·18)	—	111 (·04)
Navy League (N = 3,165)	141 (·19)	110 (·16)	56 (·29)	111 (·11)	—
TOTAL	332	253	182	295	418
Cross-affiliation index[b]	(·44)	(·38)	(·93)	(·30)	(·13)

[a] This figure is the percentage of the organization in the column (in this case the Colonial Society) made up of members of the organization in the row (in this case the Pan-German League).

[b] This figure indicates the proportion of the organization in the column that is made up of men with multiple memberships. It is not a straight percentage, owing to the fact that some men were members of more than two patriotic societies.

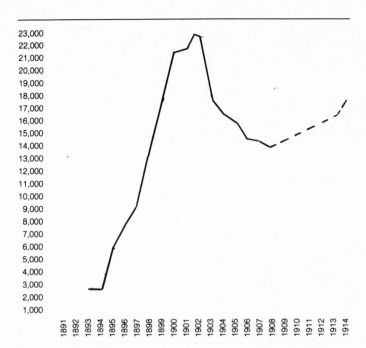

Figure 10.1 *Membership in the Pan-German League, 1891–1914*

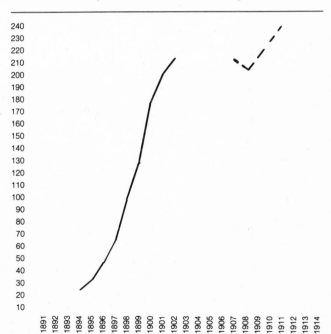

Figure 10.2 *Local chapters of the Pan-German League, 1891–1914*

Table 11.1 Characteristics of Local Leaders of the German Defense League

| | N | Retired | | Noble | | Academic education | | Doctorate | | Public administration[a] | | Mean social status | Mean public adm. pos. |
		n (N−MV)	%	n (N−MV)	%	n (N−MV)	%	n (N−MV)	%	n (N−MV)	%		
German Defense League	978	79 (882)	9·0	53 (978)	5·4	365 (813)	44·9	118 (978)	12·1	583 (863)	67·6	2·63	2·71
Pan-German League (all local leaders)	2,688	77 (2,445)	3·1	59 (2,688)	2·2	1,433 (2,186)	65·6	638 (2,688)	23·7	1,298 (2,407)	53·9	2·74	2·79

[a] Includes parliamentarians and those whose positions were 'beamtenähnlich'.

Table 11.2 *Economic Functions of Local Leaders of the German Defense League*

	German Defense League		Pan-German League	
	n	*%*	*n*	*%*
A. Agriculture/forestry	*67*	*7·9*	*43*	*1·8*
1. Agriculture	55	6·4	30	1·3
2. Forestry	12	1·4	13	0·6
B. Industry	*111*	*13·0*	*474*	*19·9*
1. Mining	6	0·7	26	1·1
2. Metal processing	2	0·2	7	0·3
3. Machinery/instruments	5	0·6	6	0·2
4. Chemicals	16	1·9	66	2·8
5. Textiles	—	—	12	0·5
6. Construction	40	4·7	149	6·3
7. Polygraphic	4	0·5	42	1·8
8. Artistic	—	—	6	0·2
9. Other	38	4·5	161	6·7
C. Commerce	*146*	*17·1*	*503*	*21·1*
1. Commerce	61	7·2	383	16·1
2. Insurance	—	—	1	0·1
3. Transportation	77	9·0	108	4·5
4. Hotels/restaurants	8	0·9	9	0·4
5. Other	—	—	2	0·1
D. Domestic	—	—	*1*	*0·0*
E. Service and professions	*500*	*58·7*	*1,312*	*55·0*
1. Military	114	13·4	62	2·6
2. Public administration/law	172	20·2	375	15·7
3. Religion	18	2·1	66	2·8
4. Education	157	18·4	583	24·4
5. Health	25	2·9	160	6·7
6. Private scholarship, journalism	14	1·6	57	2·4
7. Stenography	—	—	1	0·1
8. Music, expositions	—	—	6	0·2
9. Other	—	—	2	0·1
F. Others	*28*	*3·3*	*53*	*2·2*
1. *Rentner, Privatier,* etc.	5	0·6	33	1·4
2. Students	7	0·8	20	0·8
3. Women	16	1·9	—	—
	N = 852		N = 2,386	

Table 11.3 *Social Status of Local Leaders of the German Defense League*

	German Defense League		Pan-German League	
	n	%	*n*	%
Top-level status	*68*	*7·9*	*101*	*4·2*
1. High military officers	40	4·6	5	0·2
2. Top-level officials	6	0·7	14	0·6
3. Professors *(ordentlich)*	8	0·9	37	1·5
4. Business elite	7	0·8	38	1·6
5. *Rittergutsbesitzer*	5	0·6	3	0·1
6. High nobility	2	0·2	2	0·1
7. Other	—	—	2	0·1
High-level status	*443*	*51·2*	*1,606*	*67·1*
1. Other commissioned officers	64	7·4	45	1·9
2. Academically educated officials	140	16·2	368	15·4
3. Academically educated teachers	77	8·9	430	18·0
4. Academically educated professionals	82	9·5	361	15·1
5. Substantial business/management	70	8·1	356	14·9
6. *Rentner, Privatier*, etc.	5	0·6	31	1·3
7. *Gutsbesitzer*	5	0·6	10	0·4
8. Other	—	—	5	0·2
Mid-level status	*304*	*35·1*	*633*	*26·4*
1. Subaltern officials	131	15·1	198	8·3
2. Other teachers	65	7·5	85	3·6
3. Merchants	51	5·9	278	11·6
4. Mid-level *Angestellte*	34	3·9	47	2·0
5. Students	7	0·8	22	1·0
(6. Women)	(16)	(1·8)	—	—
7. Other	—	—	3	0·1
Low-level status	*50*	*5·8*	*55*	*2·3*
1. Lower officials	3	0·3	1	0·0
2. Low-level *Angestellte*	5	0·6	14	0·6
3. Artisans	14	1·6	26	1·1
4. Workers	2	0·2	1	0·0
5. Peasants	26	3·0	13	0·5
	N = 865		N = 2,395	

Table 11.4 *Army Officers in the German Defense League*

	Active		Reserve		Retired		Non-noble[b]		Totals
	n	%[a]	n	%	n	%	n	%	
All officers	35	27·1	24	18·6	72	55·8	99	76·7	129[c]
General	3	2·3	—	—	—	—	1	33·3	3
Generalleutnant	3	2·3	—	—	6	4·6	4	44·4	9
Generalmajor	2	1·6	—	—	9	7·0	9	81·8	11
Oberst	2	1·6	—	—	9	7·0	8	72·7	11
Oberstleutnant	2	1·6	—	—	15	11·6	10	58·8	17
Major	4	3·1	—	—	10	7·8	12	85·7	14
Hauptmann	10	7·8	13	10·1	8	6·2	29	93·5	31
Rittmeister	3	2·3	3	2·3	4	3·1	4	50·0	8[c]
Oberleutnant	3	2·3	5	3·9	5	3·9	13	100·0	13
Leutnant	1	0·8	3	2·3	6	4·6	8	80·0	10
Fähnrich	2	1·6	—	—	—	—	1	50·0	2

[a] Unless otherwise indicated, these figures are percentages of the total army officers (N = 129).
[b] These figures are percentages of the officers in each grade.
[c] The discrepancy between this figure and the sum of the first three columns is due to the fact that several of these officers were listed as both reserve and retired.

Table 11.4. Discrepancies between the figures in Table 11.4 and those in Tables 11.1, 11.2, and 11.3 were due to the fact that several of the officers in the Defense League held reserve commissions and listed both their rank in the reserves and their civilian occupation. In the first three tables I coded them by their civilian occupation; in Table 11.4 I used their military rank. In Table 11.5 I tabulated information about leaders of the Defense League in the public sector.

Table 11.5 *Local Leaders of the German Defense League in Public Administration*

	Military		General		Justice		Finance/ taxation		Education		Religion		Post/ telegraph		Railroads	
	n	%	n	%	n	%	n	%	n	%	n	%	n	%	n	%
1. Low-level officials	—	—	1	0·2	—	—	—	—	—	—	—	—	2	0·4	—	—
2. Subaltern officials without academic training	5	0·9	8	1·5	2	0·4	17	3·1	64	11·8	2	0·4	24	4·4	10	1·8
3. Officials with academic training	75	13·8	19	3·5	25	4·6	5	0·9	81	14·9	16	3·0	12	2·2	1	0·2
4. Top-level officials	40	7·4	1	0·2	2	0·4	1	0·2	8	1·5	—	—	1	0·2	—	—
TOTALS	120	22·1	29	5·4	29	5·4	23	4·2	153	28·2	18	3·3	39	7·2	11	2·0

	Customs		Industrial regulation		Construction		Health		Land/ forestry		Local		Other		Totals	
	n	%	n	%	n	%	n	%	n	%	n	%	n	%	n	%
1. Low-level officials	—	—	—	—	1	0·2	—	—	—	—	—	—	—	—	4	0·7
2. Subaltern officials without academic training	19	3·5	2	0·4	10	1·8	—	—	9	1·7	19	3·5	6	1·1	197	36·3
3. Officials with academic training	4	0·7	1	0·2	11	2·0	7	1·3	6	1·1	21	3·9	3	0·6	287	53·0
4. Top-level officials	—	—	—	—	—	—	—	—	—	—	1	0·2	—	—	54	10·0
TOTALS	23	4·2	3	0·6	22	4·1	7	1·3	15	2·8	41	7·6	9	1·7	542	100·0

Notes

1 *Alldeutsches Werbe- und Merkbüchlein* (Munich, 1899); *Der Alldeutsche Verband im Jahre 1901* (Berlin, 1902); *Handbuch des Alldeutschen Verbandes* (Munich, 1905); *Handbuch des Alldeutschen Verbandes* (Munich, 1908); *Handbuch des Alldeutschen Verbandes* (Munich, 1915).
2 Wertheimer, p. 66.
3 See William H. Hubbard and Konrad H. Jarausch, 'Occupation and social structure in modern Central Europe: some reflections on coding professions', *QUANTUM Information*, no. 11 (July 1979), pp. 10–19; cf. M. B. Katz, 'Occupational classification in history', *Journal of Interdisciplinary History*, vol. 3 (1973), pp. 63–99; Ringer, pp. 16–18.
4 See Kaiserliches Statistisches Amt, *Statistik des Deutschen Reiches*, Vol. 204 (Berlin, 1909), pp. 2–4.
5 ZStAP, DKG 735, Vorschläge zur Rubrizierung der ausserordentlichen Mitglieder nach Ständen, April 1911; cf. 'Hauptberuf und Berufsstellung der Väter der reichsangehörigen Studierenden in den bischöflichen Klerikalseminaren im Sommerhalbjahre 1902 und im Winterhalbjahre 1902/1903', Kaiserliches Preussisches Statistisches Landesamt, *Preussische Statistik*, Vol. 193, *Statistik der preussischen Landesuniversitäten 1902/03* (Berlin, 1905), pp. 196–7; Schmoller, pp. 29–31.
6 Hartmut Kaelble, 'Chancenungleichheit und akademische Ausbildung in Deutschland 1910–1960', GG, vol. 1 (1975), esp. p. 130, n. 10; Horst Handke, 'Einige Probleme der inneren Struktur der herrschenden Klassen in Deutschland', in Fritz Klein (ed.), *Studien zum deutschen Imperialismus vor 1914* (Berlin, 1976), pp. 10–19; Sheehan, *Liberalism*, p. 240; O'Donnell, p. 88; Urner, pp. 595–612. Despite the author's claims that prestige can be measured by a uniform scale in entirely discrete societies and historical epochs, I found too many cases in which Donald Treimann's 'standard occupational prestige scale' contradicted my own impressions (and those of my colleagues): Donald J. Treimann, *Occupational Prestige in a Comparative Perspective* (New York, 1976); Treimann, 'Problems of concept and measurement in the comparative study of occupational mobility', *Social Science Research*, vol. 4 (1975), pp. 183–230.
7 See Ringer, pp. 91–2.
8 See Lotz, pp. 604–5, 661–4.
9 DKZ (1891–1913).
10 StA Münster, Obpr. 3797, DFV, Verzeichnis des Präsidiums, des Vorstandes, der Geschäftsführenden Organe, der Vertrauensmänner, der Hauptauschüsse, Kreis- und Ortsausschüsse, sowie deren Geschäftsstellen nach dem Stande vom 1.1.00; StA Hamburg, Deutscher Flottenverein, II, 2, *Handbuch des Deutschen Flottenvereins (e.V.)* (Berlin, 1913).
11 BA, ZSg 1–142/3, VDA, Jahresbericht 1909; ZSg 1–142/5, VDA, Verzeichnis der Landesverbände und Ortsgruppen 1904; StA Bremen, Sentatsregistratur Nr. 72, VDA, Verzeichnis der Landesverbände und Ortsgruppen 1898.
12 OM (1896–1914).
13 ZASV (1894–1914).
14 *Die Friedens-Blätter* (1903–8); *Der Völker-Friede* (1910–14); Alfred H. Fried, *Handbuch der Friedensbewegung* (Vienna and Leipzig, 1905; 2d edn, 2 vols, Berlin and Leipzig, 1911–13).
15 ZStAP, ADV 626.
16 ibid.
17 StA Hamburg, A 440/27, Kapsel 1, Mitglieder-Verzeichnis und Satzungen der Ortsgruppe Hamburg des Alldeutschen Verbandes (1901). I have since learned that another list exists for the Lübeck chapter in the Staatsarchiv Lübeck.
18 *Der Alldeutsche Verband im Jahre 1901*, p. 10.
19 StA Hamburg, A 440/27, Kapsel 1, ADV Mitglieder-Verzeichnis (cf. n. 17).
20 StA Hamburg, Amtsgericht Hamburg B 1966–5, Allgemeiner Deutscher Schulverein, Ortsgruppe Hamburg, Mitgliederverzeichnis 1903.
21 StA Hamburg, Oberschulbehörde V Nr. 704, Allgemeiner Deutscher Sprachverein, Zweigverein Hamburg, Mitgliederverzeichnis vom 1.10.12.

22   StA Hamburg, Deutscher Flottenverein I, 1, Hamburger Landesverband des deutschen Flottenvereins, Mitgliederverzeichnis 1909–1913.
23   StA Hamburg, A 906/6, Kapsel 1, Teilnehmerverzeichnis für die Hamburger Tagung der Deutschen Kolonialgesellschaft, 3–7.6.12; Cl. VII Lit. Rf. Nr. 150h, vol. 1, Teilnehmerverzeichnis für die Hamburger Tagung der Deutschen Kolonialgesellschaft, 3–7.6.12, Erster Nachtrag, Zweiter Nachtrag.
24   *Die Wehr* (1912–14).

Bibliography

Archival Sources

Allgemeines Staatsarchiv, Munich (Bayerisches Hauptstaatsarchiv, Abteilung, I)
  MInn 73547, 73551 (Deutsche Flottenvereine); 73585 (Verein zur Verbreitung guter volksthümlicher Schriften)

Badisches Generallandesarchiv, Karlsruhe
  60/1711 (Deutscher Flottenverein)
  60/1722 (Gobineau-Vereinigung)
  60/1747 (Deutscher Ostmarkenverein)

Bergbauarchiv, Bochum
  55/8 7010 (Deutscher Ostmarkenverein, Alldeutscher Verband)
  55/8 7015 (Bismarck-Gesellschaft)
  55/8 7016 (Abwehrorganisation gegen die Sozialdemokratie)

Bundesarchiv, Coblenz
  Nachlass Alfred Hugenberg
  Zeitgeschichtliche Sammlung (ZSg 1), 2 (Alldeutscher Verband); 130 (Reichsverband gegen die Sozialdemokratie); 142 (Verein für das Deutschtum im Ausland); 195 (Deutscher Flottenverein); 211 (Deutscher Kolonialgesellschaft); 263 (Reichshammerbund); E/105 (Deutschbund)

Bundesarchiv-Militärarchiv, Freiburg i.B.
  RM 3/V (Reichsmarineamt) Nr. 28, 9907–19 (Deutscher Flottenverein); 88 (Flottenvereine 1895–1904); 89 (Allgemeiner Deutscher Sprachverein); 9942 (Reventlow); 9780 (Breusing); 9906 (Vereins-Satzungen); 9935 (Allgemeiner Deutscher Schulverein); 9937–8 (Flottenbund deutscher Frauen); 9940 (Deutsche Kolonialgesellschaft; 10407 (Lehmann)
  RM 5/V (Admiralstab) Nr. 1315, 5368 (Flottenvereine); 5351 (Deutscher Schulverein)

Geheimes Staasarchiv, Berlin-Dahlem
  Nachlass Friedrich Meinecke
  XII HA/IV Nr. 285 (Deutscher Ostmarkenverein); Nr. 286 (Reichsverband gegen die Sozialdemokratie)
  Rep. 6B Nr. 81 (Landratsamt Meseritz)
  Rep. 30 I, Präsidialabteilung Nr. 85 (Deutscher Ostmarkenverein)

Geheimes Staatsarchiv, Munich (Bayerisches Hauptstaatsarchiv, Abteilung II)
  MA 77693–4 (Deutscher Flottenverein)
  Bayerische Gesandtschaft, Berlin, Nr. 1156 (Vereine und Gesellschaften); Nr. 1158 (Deutscher Flottenverein)

Hauptstaatsarchiv Stuttgart
E 14, Bü Nr. 1344–5 (Deutscher Flottenverein); Nr. 1361 (Deutsche Kolonialgesellschaft); Nr. 1382 (Allgemeiner Deutscher Schulverein) J 46 I, Nr. 191 (Deutscher Wehrverein)

Historisches Archiv der Gute-Hoffnungs-Hütte, Oberhausen
300127 (Politsche und nationale Angelegenheiten) 30019326 (Nachlass Paul Reusch), 1, 16, 25

Landesarchiv Berlin
Rep. 42 Acc. I 743 Nr. 8950 (Deutscher Ostmarkenverein); Nr. 8952 (Deutscher Flottenverein); Nr. 8962 (Reichsverband gegen die Sozialdemokratie)

Landesarchiv Schleswig
Oberpräsidium Nr. 1626 (Deutscher Flottenverein) Landratsamt Oldenburg Nr. 608 (Reichsverband gegen die Sozialdemokratie)

Landeshauptarchiv Koblenz
Oberpräsidium der Rheinprovinz Nr. 7043–4 (Patriotische Feste); Nr. 7059 (Deutsche Vereinigung); Nr. 9529, 9661 (Deutscher Flottenverein)

Politisches Archiv des Auswärtigen Amtes, Bonn
Nachlass Karl von Eisendecher Deutschland 169 (Alldeutscher Verband)

Staatsarchiv Bremen
Senatsregistratur v. 2. Nr. 202 (Deutscher Flottenverein); Nr. 548 (Deutsche Kolonialgesellschaft); Nr. 824 (Deutscher Ostmarkenverein); U.1.A. Nr. 72 (Verein für das Deutschtum im Ausland)

Staatsarchiv Detmold
M2 Halle, Amt Versmold Nr. 867 (Deutscher Flottenverein)

Staatsarchiv Hamburg
A 906/6 (Deutsche Kolonialgesellschaft) Bestand Deutscher Flottenverein Amtsgericht Hamburg B 1966–5 (Allgemeiner Deutscher Schulverein) Oberschulbehörde V, Nr. 704 (Allgemeiner Deutscher Sprachverein) Cl. VII Lit. Rf. Nr. 150 (Deutsche Kolonialgesellschaft) Politische Polizei Nr. S1859 (Deutscher Wehrverein); S4669 (Deutschbund); S4887 (Deutscher Ostmarkenverein); S4930 (Deutsche Friedensgesellschaft); S6934 (Deutscher Flottenverein); S14980 (Hamburgischer Verband für die Bekämpfung der Sozialdemokratie); V452 (Alldeutscher Verband)

Staatsarchiv Hanover
Landratsamt Zellerfeld Nr. 950 (Reichsverband gegen die Sozialdemokratie)

Staatsarchiv Münster
Oberpräsidum Nr. 3797 (Deutscher Flottenverein); Nr. 5457 (Deutsche Vereinigung) Kreis Hattingen, Landratsamt Nr. 216 (Deutscher Flottenverein) Kreis Schwelm, Landratsamt Nr. 176

Stadtarchiv Coburg
A7504 (Förderung des Deutschen Schulvereins)

Stadtarchiv Hanover
Nr. 42 (Volksbund für das Deutschtum im Ausland)

Stadtarchiv Wuppertal
P III 79, 191, 237 (Deutscher Flottenverein); 186 (Deutsche Kolonialgesellschaft); 206 (Allgemeiner Deutscher Sprachverein); 208 (Allgemeiner Deutscher Schulverein)

Universitätsbibliothek, Freiburg i. B.
Nachlass Ludwig Schemann

Zentrales Staatsarchiv, Abteilung Merseburg
Rep. 2.2.1 (Geheimes Zivilkabinett) Nr. 15007–10 (Bestimmungen wegen Förderung der deutschen Sprache); 15265–6 (Sozialdemokratie und Anarchie); Nr. 15469–74 (Deutscher Flottenverein)
Rep. 77 (Preussisches Ministerium des Innern), Tit. 662 Nr. 91 (Deutschbund); Nr. 104 (Deutscher Flottenverein); Nr. 133 (Alldeutscher Verband); Nr. 144 (Deutscher Wehrverein); Tit. 871 Nr. 1 (Beförderung des Deutschtums und die polnische Agitation); Tit. 1053 Nr. 241 (Allgemeiner Deutscher Sprachverein)
Rep. 92 (Nachlass Albert Bovenschen)
Rep. 195 (Deutscher Ostmarkenverein)
Rep. 195a (Deutscher Frauenverein für die Ostmarken)

Zentrales Staatsarchiv, Abteilung Potsdam
Bestand Alldeutscher Verband
Bestand Deutsche Kolonialgesellschaft
Nachlass Konstantin von Gebsattel
Nachlass Cornelius von Wangenheim
Reichskanzlei Nr. 915 (Kolonialgesellschaften); Nr. 1415 (Die Alldeutschen); Nr. 1586–9 (Verbreitung guter Schriften); Nr. 1807 (Reichstagswahlen 1907); Nr. 2236 (Deutsche Schulen und Lehrer im Ausland); Nr. 2261–2 (Flottenvereine); Nr. 2273 (Deutscher Wehrverein)
Auswärtiges Amt, Rechtsabteilung Nr. 22668–80 (Vergrösserung der Kaiserlichen Marine); Nr. 38402–6 (Deutscher Schulverein/Verein für das Deutschtum im Ausland)

Published Documents

Documents diplomatiques français (1871–1914), First and Second and Third Series, 29 vols (Paris, 1929–1955).
Gooch, G. P., and Temperley, Harold (eds), *British Documents on the Origins of the War*, 11 vols (London, 1926–38).
Kaiserliches Preussisches Statistisches Landesamt, *Preussische Statistik*, Vol. 193, *Statistik der preussischen Landesuniversitäten 1902/03* (Berlin, 1905).
Kaiserliches Statistisches Amt, *Statistik des Deutschen Reiches*, Vol. 204 (Berlin, 1909).
Kaiserliches Statistisches Amt, *Statistisches Jahrbuch für das Deutsche Reich 1913* (Berlin, 1913).

Lepsius, Johannes, *et al.* (eds), *Die Grosse Politik der europäischen Kabinette 1871–1914: Sammlung der diplomatischen Akten des Auswärtigen Amtes*, 40 vols (Berlin, 1926–7).
Reichsarchiv, *Kriegsrüstung und Kriegswirtschaft*, 2 vols (Berlin, 1930).
Schulthess' Europäischer Geschichtskalender 1890–1914 (Munich, 1891–1915).
Stenographische Berichte über die Verhandlungen des Reichstages (Berlin, 1890–1914).
Thomas Mann—Heinrich Mann Briefwechsel 1900–1949 (Frankfurt a. M., 1969).

Journals

Alldeutsche Blätter, 1894–1914
Deutsche Kolonialzeitung, 1891–1913
Das Deutschtum im Ausland, 1909–14
Die Friedens-Blätter, 1903–8
Korrespondenz des Reichsverbandes gegen die Sozialdemokratie, 1907, 1909–14
Mitteilungen des Allgemeinen Deutschen Verbandes, 1891–3
Die Ostmark, 1896–1914
Der Völker-Friede, 1910–14
Die Wehr, 1912–14
Zeitschrift des Allgemeinen Deutschen Sprachvereins, 1894–1914

German Patriotic Literature

Alldeutscher Verband, Gau Ruhr und Lippe, *Die Polen im Rheinisch-westfälischen Kohlenbezirk* (Munich, 1898).
Der Alldeutsche Verband im Jahre 1901 (Berlin, 1902).
Alldeutsches Werbe- und Merkbüchlein (Munich, 1899).
Alter, Junius [Franz Sontag], *Nationalisten: Deutschlands nationales Führertum der Nachkriegszeit* (Leipzig, 1930).
Basler, Theodor, *Das Deutschtum in Russland* (Munich, 1911).
Bley, Fritz, *Die alldeutsche Bewegung und die Niederlande* (Munich, 1897).
Bley, Fritz, *Die Weltstellung des Deutschtums* (Munich, 1897).
Class, Heinrich, *Die Bilanz des neuen Kurses* (Munich, 1903).
Class, Heinrich, *Marokko verloren?* (Munich, 1904).
Class, Heinrich, *West-Marokko deutsch!* (Munich, 1911).
Deutscher Flottenverein, *Handbuch des Deutschen Flottenvereins* (Berlin, 1913).
Deutscher Wehrverein, *Deutscher Wehrkalender 1914* (Oldenburg and Berlin, 1913).
Dunger, Hermann, *Die deutsche Sprachbewegung und der allgemeine deutsche Sprachverein 1885–1910: Festschrift zur 25. Jahrfeier des allgemeinen deutschen Sprachvereins* (Berlin, 1910).
Einhart [Heinrich Class], *Deutsche Geschichte* (Leipzig, 1909).
Festschrift zum fünfundzwanzigjährigen Bestehen des Hammer (Leipzig, 1926).
Flugschriften des Alldeutschen Verbandes, 34 vols (Munich, 1894–1914).
Frymann, Daniel [Heinrich Class], *'Wenn ich der Kaiser wär': Politische Wahrheiten und Notwendigkeiten* (Leipzig, 1912).
25. Jahre ostmärkische Arbeit und Kämpfe: Zum 25. jährigen Bestehen des Deutschen Ostmarkenvereins (Berlin, 1919)
Geiser, Alfred (ed.), *Deutsches Reich und Volk: Ein nationales Handbuch*, 2 vols (Munich, 1910).

Goebel, Julius, *Das Deutschtum in den Vereinigten Staaten von Nord-Amerika* (Munich, 1904).
Handbuch des Alldeutschen Verbandes (Munich, 1905).
Handbuch des Alldeutschen Verbandes (Munich, 1908).
Handbuch des Alldeutschen Verbandes (Munich, 1915).
Hasse, Ernst, *Die Besiedlung des deutschen Volksbodens* (Munich, 1905).
Hasse, Ernst, *Deutsche Grenzpolitik* (Munich, 1905).
Hasse, Ernst, *Das Deutsche Reich als Nationalstaat* (Munich, 1905).
Hasse, Ernst, *Die Zukunft des deutschen Volkstums* (Munich, 1907).
Alldeutschen (Berlin, 1895).
Hasse, Ernst, *Weltpolitik, Imperialismus und Kolonialpolitik* (Munich, 1908).
Hasse, Ernst, *Die Zukunft des deutschen Volkstrums* (Munich, 1907).
Hasse als Politiker (Leipzig, 1898).
Hochwart [Hermann Müller-Brandenburg], *Die Anderen und wir* (Leipzig, 1912).
Hofmann von Wellenhof, P., *Steiermark, Kärnten, Krain und Küstenland* (Munich, 1899).
Hugenberg, Alfred, *Streiflichter aus Vergangenheit und Gegenwart* (Berlin, 1927).
Hunziker, Jakob, *Schweiz* (Munich, 1898).
Kuhlenbeck, Ludwig, *Das Evangelium der Rasse: Briefe über das Rassenproblem* (Prenzlau, 1905).
Kuhlenbeck, Ludwig, *Rasse und Volkstum* (Munich, 1905).
Lange, Friedrich, *Reines Deutschtum: Grundzüge einer nationalen Weltanschauung*, 4th edn (Berlin, 1904).
Luther, Paul, *Deutsche Volksabende: Ein Handbuch für Volksunterhaltungsabende. Für die Praxis zusammengestellt* (Berlin, 1898).
Moulin-Eckart, Richard Graf du, *Deutschland und Rom* (Munich, 1904).
Nabert, H., *Das Deutschtum in Tirol* (Munich, 1901).
Osten-Sacken und von Rhein, Ottomar Freiherr von der, *Heeresvorlage und allgemeine Wehrpflicht* (Berlin, 1912).
Peters, Carl, 'Alldeutschland (1886)', in *Gesammelte Schriften* ed. Walter Frank, 3 vols (Munich, 1943–4), Vol. 3, pp. 275–8.
Petersen, Julius, *Das Deutschtum in Elsass-Lothringen* (Munich, 1902).
Petzet, Christian, *Die preussischen Ostmarken* (Munich, 1898).
Prager, Erich, *Die Deutsche Kolonialgesellschaft 1882–1907* (Berlin, 1908).
Reichsverband gegen die Sozialdemokratie, *Handbuch für nichtsozialdemokratische Wähler* (Berlin, 1907).
Reventlow, Ernst Graf zu, *Deutschland in der Welt voran?* (Berlin, 1905).
Reventlow, Ernst Graf zu, *Kaiser Wilhelm II und die Byzantiner* (Munich, 1906).
Reventlow, Ernst Graf zu, *Was würde Bismarck sagen?* (Berlin, 1909).
Rolfs, Wilhelm, *Deutsche Nationalfeste: Auskunftsbüchlein für Jedermann, der sich darüber unterrichten will* (Munich and Leipzig, 1898).
Rüsten, Rudolf (ed.), *Was tut not? Ein Führer durch die gesamte Literatur der Deutschbewegung* (Leipzig, 1914).
Schemann, Ludwig, *Fünfundzwanzig Jahre Gobineau-Vereinigung 1894/1919: Ein Rückblick* (Strasburg and Berlin, 1919).
Schultheiss, Franz Guntram, *Deutschnationales Vereinswesen: Ein Beitrag zur Geschichte deutschen Nationalgefühls* (Munich, 1897).
Schultheiss, Franz Guntram, *Deutschtum und Magyarisierung in Ungarn und Siebenbürgen* (Munich, 1898).
Semrau, Hans, *Der Deutsche Ostmarkenverein und die völkische Erziehung der Ostmarkdeutschen* (Lissa, 1907).
Stauff, Philipp, *Das deutsche Wehrbuch* (Wittenberg, 1912).

Stuemer, Willibald von, and Duems, Erich, *Fünfzig Jahre Deutsche Kolonialgesellschaft 1882–1932* (Berlin, 1932).
Türk, Karl, *Böhmen, Mähren und Schlesien* (Munich, 1898).
Warum muss Deutschland sein Heer verstärken? (Berlin, 1912).
Wer die Wehr-Vorlage verwirft ist ein Volksfeind! (Berlin, 1913).
Weyer, Bruno, *Deutschlands Seegefahren: Der Verfall der deutschen Flotte und ihr geplanter Wiederaufbau* (Munich, 1898).
Wintzer, Wilhelm, *Die Deutschen im tropischen Amerika* (Munich, 1900).
Wolzogen, Hans von, 'Zur Gobineau-Bewegung', in *Aus deutscher Welt: Gesammelte Aufsätze über deutsche Art und Kultur* (Leipzig, 1910), pp. 102–11.
10. Jahre Reichsverband: Festgabe der Hauptstelle des 'Reichsverbands gegen die Sozialdemokratie' in Berlin zum 9. Mai 1914 (Berlin, 1914).
Zwanzig Jahre alldeutscher Arbeit und Kämpfe (Leipzig, 1910).

Other Contemporary Literature

Andler, Charles, *Collection de documents sur le pangermanisme* (Paris, 1915).
Bourdon, Georges, *L'énigme allemand: Une enquête chez les allemands ce qu'ils present – ce qu'ils veulent – ce qu'ils peuvent* (Paris, 1913).
Bülow, Bernhard von, *Deutsche Politik* (Berlin, 1916).
Chéradame, André. *Le Plan pangermaniste démasqué* (Paris, 1916).
Choisy, Gaston, *Chez nos ennemis à la veille de la guerre* (Paris, 1915).
Degener, Hermann A. L., *Wer Ist's?* (Leipzig, 1903–28).
Delbrück, Hans, 'Die Alldeutschen,' *Vor und nach dem Weltkriege: Politische und historische Aufsätze 1902–1925* (Berlin, 1926), pp. 397–403.
Fried, Alfred. H., *Handbuch der Friedensbewegung* (Vienna and Leipzig, 1905); 2nd edn, 2 vols (Berlin and Leipzig, 1911–13).
Gobineau, Arthur de, *Essai sur l'inégalité des races humaines*, 4 vols (Paris, 1853–5).
Hobohm, Martin, *Die alldeutsche Bewegung eine politische Schuld und Gefahr* (n.p., n.d.).
Hobohm, Martin, and Rohrbach, Paul, *Die Alldeutschen* (Berlin, 1919).
Kalkoff, H., *Organisationshandbuch der Nationalliberalen Partei des Deutschen Reiches 1912/13* (Berlin 1912).
Klein, Franz, *Das Organisationswesen der Gegenwart: Ein Grundriss* (Berlin, 1913).
Krysiak, Fritz, *Hinter den Kulissen des Ostmarkenvereins: Aus den Geheimakten der preussischen Nebenregierung für die Polenausrottung* (Posen, 1919).
Lederer Emil, *Die Privatangestellten in der modernen Wirtschaftsordnung* (Tübingen, 1912).
Meinecke, Friedrich, 'Nationalismus und nationale Idee', *Politische Schriften und Reden* (Darmstadt, 1958), pp. 83–93.
Organisations-Handbuch der Nationalliberalen Partei des Deutschen Reiches (Berlin, 1907).
Penzler, Johannes, *Fürst Bismarck nach seiner Entlassung*, 7 vols (Leipzig, 1897–8).
Reismann-Grone, Theodor, *Der Erdenkrieg und die Alldeutschen* (Mülheim, 1920).
Schemann, Ludwig, *Gobineaus Rassenwerk: Aktenstücke und Betrachtungen zur Geschichte und Kritik des Essai sur l'inégalité des races humaines* (Stuttgart, 1910).
Schmoller, Gustav, *Was verstehen wir unter dem Mittelstande? Hat er im 19. Jahrhundert zu- order abgenommen?* (Göttingen, 1897).
Usher, Roland G., *Pan-Germanism* (London, 1914).
Vergnet, Paul, *La France en danger: L'oeuvre des pangermanistes* (Paris, 1913).
Wenck, Martin, *Alldeutsche Taktik* (Jena, 1917).

Autobiography

Bernhardi, Friedrich von, *Denkwürdigkeiten aus meinem Leben* (Berlin, 1927).
Bethmann Hollweg, Theobald von, *Betrachtungen zum Weltkrieg*, 2 vols (Berlin, 1919).
Bülow, Bernhard von, *Memoirs of Prince von Bülow*, 4 vols (Boston, Mass., 1931–2).
Class, Heinrich, *Wider den Strom* (Leipzig, 1932).
Einem, Karl von, *Erinnerungen eines Soldaten 1853–1933* (Leipzig, 1933).
Gerstenhauer, Max Robert, *Der völkische Gedanke in Vergangenheit und Zukunft: Aus der Geschichte der völkischen Bewegung* (Leipzig, 1933).
Hammann, Otto, *Der neue Kurs: Erinnerungen* (Berlin, 1918).
Heuss, Theodor, *Vorspiele des Lebens: Jugenderinnerungen* (Tübingen, 1953).
Hitler, Adolf, *Mein Kampf* (Boston, Mass., 1943).
Keim, August, *Erlebtes und Erstrebtes: Lebenserinnerungen von Generalleutnant Keim* (Hanover, 1925).
Kuhlenbeck, Ludwig, *Lausanne: Ein Wort zur Berichtigung und Abwehr* (Munich, 1908).
Liebert, Eduard von, *Aus einem bewegten Leben: Erinnerungen* (Munich, 1925).
Litzmann, Karl, *Lebenserinnerungen*, 2 vols (Berlin, 1927-8).
Lubarsch, Otto, *Ein bewegtes Gelehrtenleben* (Berlin, 1931).
Ludendorff, Erich, *Mein militärischer Werdegang: Blätter der Erinnerung an unser stolzes Heer* (Munich, 1937).
Meinecke, Friedrich, *Erinnerungen 1901–1919* (Stuttgart, 1949).
Müller, Georg Alexander von, *Der Kaiser ... Aufzeichnungen des Chefs des Marinekabinetts Admiral Georg Alexander von Müller über die Aera Wilhelms II*, ed. Walter Görlitz (Göttingen, 1965).
Müller-Brandenburg, Hermann, *Von Schlieffen bis Ludendorff* (Leipzig, 1925).
Nicolson, Harold, *The Later Years, 1945–1962* (New York, 1968).
Rathenau, Walter, *Tagebuch 1907–1922*, ed. Hartmut Pogge von Strandmann (Düsseldorf, 1967).
Riezler, Kurt, *Tagebücher, Aufsätze, Dokumente*, ed. Karl Dietrich Erdmann (Göttingen, 1972).
Schäfer, Dietrich, *Mein Leben* (Berlin and Leipzig, 1926).
Schemann, Ludwig, *Lebensfahrten eines Deutschen* (Leipzig and Hartenstein, 1925).
Wermuth, Adolf, *Ein Beamtenleben* (Berlin, 1922).
Westarp, Kuno Graf, *Konservative Politik im letzten Jahrzehnt des Kaiserreichs*, 2 vols (Berlin, 1935).

Secondary Literature

Ackermann, Nathan W., and Jahoda, Marie, *Anti-Semitism and Emotional Disorder: A Psychoanalytic Interpretation* (New York, 1950).
Adorno, T. W., *et al.*, *The Authoritarian Personality* (New York, 1950).
Allain, Jean-Claude, *Agadir 1911: Une crise impérialiste en Europe pour la conquête du Maroc* (Paris, 1976).
Allen, William Sheridan, *The Nazi Seizure of Power: The Experience of a Single German Town, 1930–1935* (Chicago, 1965).
Allport, Gordon W., *The Nature of Prejudice* (Cambridge, Mass., 1954).
Anderson, Eugene N., *The First Moroccan Crisis, 1904–1906* (Chicago, 1930).

Anderson, Paula Relyea, *The Background of Anti-English Feeling in Germany, 1890–1902* (Washington, DC, 1939).

Arendt, Hannah, *The Origins of Totalitarianism* (Cleveland, Ohio, and New York, 1958).

Bade, Klaus J., *Friedrich Fabri und der Imperialismus in der Bismarckzeit: Revolution – Depression – Expansion* (Freiburg, 1975).

Baier, Roland, *Der deutsche Osten als soziale Frage* (Cologne and Vienna, 1979).

Bair, Henry, 'Carl Peters and German colonialism' (PhD Diss., Stanford University, 1968).

Baranger, Willy, 'The ego and the function of ideology', *International Journal of Psycho-Analysis*, vol. 39 (1958), pp. 191–5.

Barkin, Kenneth D., *The Controversy over German Industrialization, 1890–1902* (Chicago, 1970).

Barlow, Ina Christina, *The Agadir Crisis* (Chapel Hill, NC, 1940).

Barnes, Harry Elmer, *The Genesis of the World War* (New York, 1926).

Barta, Erwin, and Bell, Karl, *Geschichte der Schutzarbeit am deutschen Volkstum* (Dresden, 1930).

Barzun, Jacques, *Race: A Study in Superstition* (New York, 1937).

Bausinger, Hermann, 'Vereine als Gegenstand volkskundlicher Forschung', *Zeitschrift für Volkskunde*, vol. 55 (1959), pp. 98–104.

Bell, Karl, 'Geschichte des Vereins für das Deutschtum im Ausland', in Barta and Bell, pp. 101–201.

Berger, Peter, Berger, Brigitte, and Kellner, Hansfried, *The Homeless Mind: Modernization and Consciousness* (New York, 1974).

Berger, Peter, and Luckmann, Thomas, *The Social Construction of Reality* (New York, 1976).

Berghahn, Voker R., *Germany and the Approach of War in 1914* (New York, 1973).

Berghahn, Volker R., *Rüstung und Machtpolitik: Zur Anatomie des Kalten Krieges vor 1914* (Düsseldorf, 1973).

Berghahn, Volker R., *Der Tirpitz-Plan: Genesis und Verfall einer innenpolitischen Krisenstrategie unter Wilhelm II* (Düsseldorf, 1971).

Bergmann, Klaus, *Agrarromantik und Grossstadtfeindschaft* (Meisenheim, 1970).

Bergstraesser, Arnold, 'Max Webers Antrittsvorlesung in zeitgeschichtlicher Perspektive', *Vierteljahrshefte für Zeitgeschichte*, vol. 5 (1957), pp. 209–19.

Bertram, Jürgen, *Die Wahlen zum Deutschen Reichstag vom Jahre 1912: Parteien und Verbände in der Innenpolitik des Wilhelminischen Reiches* (Düsseldorf, 1964).

Bethge, Werner, 'Bund Jungdeutschland (BJD) 1911–1933 (1924–1933 Arbeitsgemeinschaft der vaterländischen Jugend)', in Fricke, *Handbuch*, Vol. 1, pp. 162–76.

Bettelheim, Bruno, and Janowitz, Morris, *Dynamics of Prejudice: A Psychological and Sociological Study of Veterans* (New York, 1950).

Biddis, Michael D., *Father of Racist Ideology: The Social and Political Thought of Count Gobineau* (London, 1970).

Blackbourn, David, 'The *Mittelstand* in German society and politics, 1871–1914', *Social History*, no. 4 (January 1977), pp. 409–34.

Blackbourn, David, *Class, Religion and Local Politics in Wilhelmine Germany: The Centre Party in Württemberg before 1914* (New Haven, Conn. and London, 1980).

Blaich, Fritz, *Staat und Verbände in Deutschland zwischen 1871 und 1945* (Wiesbaden, 1979).

Blasius, Dirk, 'Psychohistorie und Sozialgeschichte', *Archiv für Sozialgeschichte*, vol. 17 (1977), pp. 383–403.

Böhm, Ekkehard, *Ueberseehandel und Flottenbau: Hanseatische Kaufmannschaft und deutsche Seerüstung 1879–1902* (Düsseldorf, 1972).

Böhme, Helmut, *Deutschlands Weg zur Grossmacht: Studien zum Verhältnis von Wirtschaft und Staat während der Reichsgründungszeit 1848–1881* (Cologne, 1966).

Böhme, Helmut, 'Emil Kirdorf: Ueberlegungen zu einer Unternehmerbiographie', *Tradition*, vol. 15 (1968), pp. 282–300; vol. 16 (1969), pp. 21–49.

Boissevain, Jeremy, *Friends of My Friends: Networks, Manipulators and Coalitions* (Oxford, 1974).

Boissevain, Jeremy, and Mitchell, J. Clyde (eds), *Network Analysis: Studies in Human Interaction* (The Hague, 1973).

Bonhard, Otto, *Geschichte des Alldeutschen Verbandes* (Berlin, 1920).

Boog, Horst, 'Graf Ernst zu Reventlow (1869–1943): Eine Studie zur Krise der deutschen Geschichte seit dem Ende des 19. Jahrhunderts' (Diss. phil., Heidelberg, 1965).

Borch, Herbert von, *Obrigkeit und Widerstand: Zur politischen Soziologie des Beamtentums* (Tübingen, 1954).

Böttger, Siegwart, and Fritsch, Werner, 'Deutschnationaler Handlungsgehilfen-Verband (DHV) 1893–1934', in Fricke, *Handbuch*, Vol. 1, pp. 702–14.

Bourdieu, Pierre, *Outline of a Theory of Practice* (Cambridge, 1977).

Broszat, Martin, 'Die antisemitische Bewegung im Wilhelminischen Deutschland' (Diss. phil., Cologne, 1952).

Bruch, Rüdiger von, '"Deutschland und England: Heeres- oder Flottenverstärkung?" Politische Publizistik deutscher Hochschullehrer 1911/12', *Militärgeschichtliche Mitteilungen*, no. 1 (1981), pp. 7–35.

Brückner, Peter, *et al.*, 'Perspectives on the fascist public sphere', *New German Critique*, vol. 11 (1977), pp. 94–132.

Bruford, Walter Horace, *The German Tradition of Self-Cultivation: 'Bildung' from Humboldt to Thomas Mann* (Cambridge, 1975).

Buat, Edmund, *Die deutsche Armee im Weltkriege: Ihre Grösse und ihr Verfall* (Munich, 1921).

Burchardt, Lothar, 'Professionalisierung oder Berufskonstruktion? Das Beispiel des Chemikers im wilhelminischen Deutschland', *Geschichte und Gesellschaft*, vol. 6 (1980), pp. 326–48.

Butler, Rohan D'O., *The Roots of National Socialism, 1783–1933* (London, 1941).

Cameron, Norman A., 'Paranoid conditions and paranoia', in Silvano Arieti (ed.), *American Handbook of Psychiatry*, 3rd edn, 6 vols (New York, 1974–5), Vol. 3, pp. 676–94.

Cameron, Norman A., 'The paranoid pseudo-community', *American Journal of Sociology*, vol. 49 (1943), pp. 32–8.

Cameron, Norman A., 'The paranoid pseudo-community revisited', *American Journal of Sociology*, vol. 64 (1959), pp. 52–8.

Caplan, Jane, '"The imaginary universality of particular interests": the "tradition" of the civil service in German history', *Social History*, vol. 4 (1979), pp. 299–317.

Carsten, F. L., *Fascist Movements in Austria: From Schönerer to Hitler* (Beverly Hills, Calif., 1977).

Cecil, Lamar, 'Wilhelm II. und die Juden', in Mosse, *Juden,* pp. 313–48.

Chamberlain, Brewster S., 'The enemy on the right: the *Alldeutsche Verband* in the Weimar Republic, 1918–1926' (PhD Diss., University of Maryland, 1972).

Charmatz, Richard, *Oesterreichs innere Geschichte von 1848 bis 1907,* 2 vols (Leipzig, 1911–12).

Chickering, Roger, 'Der "Deutsche Wehrverein" und die Reform der deutschen Armee 1912–1914', *Militärgeschichtliche Mitteilungen*, no. 1 (1979), pp. 7–33.

Chickering, Roger, *Imperial Germany and a World without War: The Peace Movement and German Society, 1892–1914* (Princeton, NJ, 1975).

Chickering, Roger, 'Patriotic societies and German foreign policy, 1890–1914', *International History Review,* vol. 1 (1979), pp. 470–89.

Clarke, J., *et al.* (eds), *Working-Class Culture: Studies in History and Theory* (New York, 1979).

Cohen, Abner, *The Politics of Elite Culture: Explorations in the Dramaturgy of Power in a Modern African Society* (Berkeley, Calif. and Los Angeles, 1981).

Cohen, Abner, *Two-Dimensional Man: An Essay on the Anthropology of Power and Symbolism in Complex Society* (Berkeley, Calif. and Los Angeles, 1974).

Cole, Terence F., 'The *Daily Telegraph* affair and its aftermath: the Kaiser, Bülow and the Reichstag, 1908–1909', in John C. G. Röhl and Nicholaus Sombart (eds), *Kaiser Wilhelm II: New Interpretations* (Cambridge, 1982), pp. 249–68.

Conrad-Martius, Hedwig, *Utopien der Menschenzüchtung: Der Sozialdarwinismus und seine Folgen* (Munich, 1955).

Conze, Werner, 'Heinrich Class', *Neue deutsche Biographie,* Vol. 3, p. 263.

Craig, Gordon A., *From Bismarck to Adenauer: Aspects of German Statecraft* (New York, 1965).

Crew, David F., *Town in the Ruhr: A Social History of Bochum* (New York, 1979).

Crothers, George Dunlap, *The German Elections of 1907* (New York, 1941).

Cunningham, H., *The Volunteer Force* (London, 1975).

Dehio, Ludwig, 'Thoughts on Germany's mission, 1900–1918', *Germany and World Politics in the Twentieth Century* (London, 1965), pp. 72–108.

Deist, Wilhelm, *Flottenpolitik und Flottenpropaganda: Das Nachrichtenbüro des Reichsmarineamts 1897–1914* (Stuttgart, 1976).

Deist, Wilhelm, 'Reichsmarineamt und Flottenverein 1903–1906', in Schottelius and Deist, pp. 116–45.

Demeter, Karl, *Das deutsche Offizierkorps in Gesellschaft und Staat 1650–1945,* 4th edn (Frankfurt a. M., 1965).

Dreitzel, Hans P., *Elitebegriff und Sozialstruktur: Eine soziologische Begriffsanalyse* (Stuttgart, 1962).

Dukes, Jack Richard, 'Helgoland, Zanzibar, East Africa: colonialism in German politics, 1884–1890' (PhD Diss., University of Illinois, 1970).

Dülffer, Jost, 'Deutsche Kolonialherrschaft in Afrika', *Neue Politische Literatur,* vol. 26 (1981), pp. 458–73.

Eley, Geoff, 'The German Navy League in German politics, 1898–1909' (Diss. phil., Brighton, Sussex, 1974).

Eley, Geoff, 'Die "Kehrites" und das Kaiserreich: Bemerkungen zu einer aktuellen Kontroverse', *Geschichte und Gesellschaft,* vol. 4 (1978), pp. 91–107.

Eley, Geoff, *Reshaping the German Right: Radical Nationalism and Political Change after Bismarck* (New Haven, Conn. and London, 1980).

Eley, Geoff, 'Reshaping the right: radical nationalism and the German Navy League, 1898–1908', *The Historical Journal,* vol. 21 (1978), pp. 327–54.

Eley, Geoff, 'Sammlungspolitik, social imperialism, and the navy law of 1898', *Militärgeschichtliche Mitteilungen,* no. 1 (1974), pp. 29–63.

Endres, F. C., 'Soziologische Struktur und ihr entsprechende Ideologien des deutschen Offizierkorps vor dem Weltkriege', *Archiv für Sozial Wissenschaft und Sozial Politik,* vol. 58 (1927), pp. 483 ff.

Engelberg, Ernst, 'Zur Entstehung und historischen Stellung des preussisch-deutschen Bonapartismus', in Fritz Klein and Joachim Streisand (eds), *Beiträge zum neuen Geschichtsbild: Zum 60. Geburtstag von Alfred Meusel* (Berlin, 1956), pp. 236–51.

Epstein, Klaus, 'Erzberger and the German colonial scandals', *English Historical Review,* vol. 74 (1959), pp. 637–63.

Eschenburg, Theodor, *Das Kaiserreich am Scheideweg: Bassermann, Bülow und der Block* (Berlin, 1929).

Evans, Richard J., *The Feminist Movement in Germany, 1894–1933* (London, 1976).

Evans, Richard J., 'Introduction: Wilhelm II's Germany and the historians', in Evans (ed.), *Society and Politics in Wilhelmine Germany* (New York, 1978), pp. 11–39.

Fay, Sidney B., *The Origins of the World War*, 2 vols (New York, 1928–30).

Fehrenbach, Elisabeth, *Wandlungen des Kaisergedankens 1871–1918* (Munich and Vienna, 1969).

Fetscher, Iring (ed.), *Rechtsradikalismus* (Frankfurt a. M., 1967).

Fick, Heinz, *Der deutsche Militarismus der Vorkriegszeit: Ein Beitrag zur Soziologie des Militarismus* (Potsdam, 1932).

Field, Geoffrey G., *Evangelist of Race: The Germanic Vision of Houston Stewart Chamberlain* (New York, 1981).

Firth, Raymond, *Symbols: Public and Private* (Ithaca, NY, 1973).

Fischer, Fritz, *Griff nach der Weltmacht: Die Kriegszielpolitik des kaiserlichen Deutschland 1914/1918* (Düsseldorf, 1961).

Fischer, Fritz, *Krieg der Illusionen: Die deutsche Politik von 1911 bis 1914* (Düsseldorf, 1969).

Fischer, Wolfram, 'Staatsverwaltung und Interessenverbände im Deutschen Reich 1871–1914', in Heinz-Josef Varain (ed.), *Interessenverbände in Deutschland* (Cologne, 1973), pp. 139–61.

Fox-Genovese, Elizabeth, and Genovese, Eugene D., 'The political crisis of social history: a Marxian perspective', *Journal of Social History*, vol. 10 (1976), pp. 205–20.

Franz-Willing, Georg, *Die Hitlerbewegung: Der Ursprung 1919–1922* (Hamburg and Berlin, 1962).

Freeden, Michael, 'Eugenics and progressive thought: a study in ideological affinity', *The Historical Journal*, vol. 22 (1979), pp. 645–71.

Freisel, Ludwig, 'Das Bismarckbild der Alldeutschen: Bismarck im Bewusstsein des Alldeutschen Verbandes von 1890 bis 1933. Ein Beitrag zum Bismarckverständnis des deutschen Nationalismus' (Diss. phil., Würzburg, 1964).

Freudenthal, Herbert, *Vereine in Hamburg: Ein Beitrag zur Geschichte und Volkskunde der Geselligkeit* (Hamburg, 1968).

Fricke, Dieter, 'Der deutsche Imperialismus und die Reichstagswahlen von 1907', *Zeitschrift für Geschichtswissenschaft*, vol. 9 (1961), pp. 538–76.

Fricke, Dieter, 'Deutscher Flottenverein und Regierung 1900–1906', *Zeitschrift für Geschichtswissenschaft*, vol. 30 (1982), pp. 141–57.

Fricke, Dieter, 'Reichsverband gegen die Sozialdemokratie (RgS) 1904–1918', in Fricke, *Handbuch*, Vol. 2, pp. 620–30.

Fricke, Dieter, 'Der Reichsverband gegen die Sozialdemokratie von seiner Gründung bis zu den Reichstagswahlen von 1907', *Zeitschrift für Geschichtswissenschaft*, vol. 7 (1959), pp. 237–80.

Fricke, Dieter, *et al.* (eds), *Die bürgerlichen Parteien in Deutschland: Handbuch der Geschichte der bürgerlichen Parteien und anderer bürgerlicher Interessenorganisationen vom Vormärz bis zum Jahre 1945*, 2 vols (Berlin, 1968–70).

Galos, Adam, Gentzen, Felix-Heinrich, and Jakobczyk, Witold, *Die Hakatisten: Der Deutsche Ostmarken-Verein (1893–1934). Ein Beitrag zur Geschichte der Ostpolitik des deutschen Imperialismus* (Berlin, 1966).

Gann, L. H., and Duignan, Peter, *The Rulers of German Africa, 1884–1914* (Stanford, Calif., 1977).

Gay, Peter, *Art and Act: On Causes in History—Manet, Gropius, Mondrian* (New York, 1976).

Geertz, Clifford, 'Ideology as a cultural system', in *The Interpretation of Cultures: Selected Essays* (New York, 1973), pp. 193–233.

Geiss, Imanuel, and Wendt, Bernd Jürgen (eds), *Deutschland in der Weltpolitik des 19. und 20. Jahrhunderts: Fritz Fischer zum 65. Geburtstag* (Düsseldorf, 1974).

Gellately, Robert, *The Politics of Economic Despair: Shopkeepers and German Politics, 1890–1914* (Santa Barbara, Calif., 1974).

Gentzen, Felix-Heinrich, 'Deutscher Ostmarkenverein (DOV) 1894–1935', in Fricke, *Handbuch,* Vol. 1, pp. 502–12.

Gerth, Hans, and Mills, C. Wright, *Character and Social Structure: The Psychology of Social Institutions* (London, 1954).

Gilbert, Sandra M., and Gubar, Susan, *The Madwoman in the Attic: The Woman Writer and the Nineteenth-Century Literary Imagination* (New Haven, Conn., and London, 1979).

Glaser, Hermann, *Spiesserideologie: Von der Zerstörung des deutschen Geistes im 19. und 20. Jahrhundert* (Freiburg i. B., 1964).

Goffman, Erving, *Frame Analysis: An Essay on the Organization of Experience* (New York, 1974).

Goldhagen, Erich, 'Weltanschauung und Endlösung: Zum Antisemitismus der nationalsozialistischen Führungsschicht', *Vierteljahrshefte für Zeitgeschichte,* vol. 24 (1976), pp. 378–405.

Gollwitzer, Heinz, 'Der Cäsarismus Napoleons III. im Widerhall der öffentlichen Meinung Deutschlands', *Historische Zeitschrift,* vol. 173 (1952), pp. 23–75.

Gottwald, Herbert, 'Antiultramontaner Reichsverband (AUR) 1906–1920 (1916–1920 Deutscher Reichsverband für staatliche und kulturelle Unabhängigkeit)', in Fricke, *Handbuch,* Vol. 1, pp. 41–3.

Gottwald, Herbert, 'Deutsche Vereinigung (DV) 1908–1933', in Fricke, *Handbuch,* vol. 1, pp. 629–36.

Graham, Loren R., 'Science and values: the eugenics movement in Germany and Russia in the 1920s', *American Historical Review,* vol. 82 (1977), pp. 1133–64.

Greenblum, Joseph, and Pearlin, Leonard I., 'Vertical mobility and prejudice: a socio-psychological analysis', in Reinhard Bendix and Seymour Martin Lipset (eds), *Class, Status, and Power: A Reader in Social Stratification* (Glencoe, Ill., 1953), pp. 480–91.

Grieswelle, Detlef, 'Antisemitismus in deutschen Studentenverbindungen des 19. Jahrhunderts', in *Student und Hochschule im 19. Jahrhundert: Studien und Materialien* (Göttingen, 1975), pp. 366–79.

Groh, Dieter, 'Base-processes and the problem of organization: outline of a social history research project', *Social History,* vol. 4 (1979), pp. 265–83.

Groh, Dieter, 'Cäsarismus: Napoleonismus, Bonapartismus, Führer, Chef, Imperialismus', in Otto Brunner *et al.* (eds), *Geschichtliche Grundbegriffe: Historisches Lexikon zur politisch-sozialen Sprache in Deutschland* (Stuttgart, 1972–   ), Vol. 1, pp. 726–71.

Groh, Dieter, 'Je eher desto besser! Innenpolitische Faktoren für die Präventivkriegsbereitschaft des Deutschen Reiches 1913/1914', *Politische Vierteljahrsschrift,* vol. 3 (1972), pp. 501–21.

Gruschinske, Paul, 'Kiderlen-Wächter und die deutschen Zeitungen in der Marokkokrisis des Jahres 1911' (Diss. phil., Cologne, 1931).

Guratzsch, Dankwart, *Macht durch Organisation: Die Grundlegung des Hugenbergischen Presseimperiums* (Düsseldorf, 1974).

Gutsche, Willibald, *Aufstieg und Fall eines Kaiserlichen Reichskanzlers: Theobald von Bethmann Hollweg 1856–1921. Ein politisches Lebensbild* (Berlin, 1973).

Habermas, Jürgen, *Strukturwandel der Oeffentlichkeit: Untersuchung zu einer Kategorie der bürgerlichen Gesellschaft* (Neuwied and Berlin, 1962).

Hagen, William W., *Germans, Poles and Jews: The Nationality Conflict in the Prussian East, 1772–1914* (Chicago, 1980).

Hallgarten, George W. F., *Imperialismus vor 1914: Die soziologischen Grundlagen der Aussenpolitik europäischer Grossmächte vor dem ersten Weltkrieg,* 2nd edn, 2 vols (Munich, 1963).

Haltzel, Michael H., 'The Russification of the Baltic Germans: a dysfunctional aspect of imperial modernization', in Arvid Ziedonis, Jr, *et al.* (eds), *Baltic History* (Columbus, Ohio, 1974), pp. 143–52.

Hamel, Iris, *Völkischer Verband und nationale Gewerkschaft: Der Deutschnationale Handlungsgehilfen-Verband 1893–1933* (Frankfurt a. M., 1967).

Hampe, Peter, 'Sozioökonomische und psychische Hintergründe der bildungsbürgerlichen Imperialbegeisterung', in Vondung, *Bildungsbürgertum,* pp. 67–79.

Handke, Horst, 'Einige Probleme der inneren Struktur der herrschenden Klassen in Deutschland vom Ende des 19. Jahrhunderts bis zum ersten Weltkrieg', in Fritz Klein (ed.), *Studien zum deutschen Imperialismus vor 1914* (Berlin, 1976), pp. 85–114.

Hartwig, Edgar, 'Alldeutscher Verband (ADV) 1891–1939 (1891–1894 Allgemeiner Deutscher Verband)', in Fricke, *Handbuch,* Vol. 1, pp. 1–26.

Hartwig, Edgar, 'Zur Politik und Entwicklung des Alldeutschen Verbandes von seiner Gründung bis zum Beginn des Ersten Weltkrieges (1891–1914)' (Diss. phil., Jena, 1966).

Haude, Günter, and Possekel, Kurt, 'Verein für das Deutschtum im Ausland (VDA) 1881–1945 (1881–1908 Allgemeiner Deutscher Schulverein; 1933–1945 Volksbund für das Deutschtum im Ausland)', in Fricke, *Handbuch,* Vol. 2, pp. 716–29.

Hauk, Manfred, *Bismarck ohne Amt: Fürst Bismarck nach seiner Entlassung 1890–1898* (Munich, 1977).

Hauser, Oswald, 'Obrigkeitsstaat und demokratisches Prinzip im Nationalitätenkampf. Preussen in Nordschleswig', *Historische Zeitschrift,* vol. 192 (1962), pp. 318–61.

Heffter, Heinrich, *Die deutsche Selbstverwaltung im 19. Jahrhundert: Geschichte der Ideen und Institutionen* (Stuttgart, 1950).

Heidhorn, G., *Monopole—Presse—Krieg: Die Rolle der Presse bei der Vorbereitung des Ersten Weltkrieges* (Berlin, 1960).

Heintz, Peter, *Soziale Vorurteile: Ein Problem der Persönlichkeit, der Kultur und der Gesellschaft* (Cologne, 1957).

Heitzer, Horstwalter, *Der Volksverein für das katholische Deutschland 1890–1918* (Mainz, 1979).

Henning, Hansjoachim, 'Kriegervereine in den preussischen Westprovinzen: Ein Beitrag zur preussischen Innenpolitik zwischen 1860 und 1914', *Rheinische Vierteljahrsblätter,* vol. 32 (1968), pp. 430–75.

Henning, Hansjoachim, *Das westdeutsche Bürgertum in der Epoche der Hochindustrialisierung 1860–1914: Soziales Verhalten und soziale Strukturen. Das Bildungsbürgertum in den preussischen Westprovinzen* (Wiesbaden, 1972).

Herre, Paul, *Kronprinz Wilhelm: Seine Rolle in der deutschen Politik* (Munich, 1954).

Herwig, Holger, *'Luxury' Fleet: The Imperial German Navy, 1888–1918* (London, 1980).

Herzfeld, Hans, *Die deutsche Rüstungspolitik vor dem Weltkriege* (Bonn and Leipzig, 1923).

Hildebrand, Klaus, *Vom Reich zum Weltreich: Hitler, NSDAP und koloniale Frage 1919–1945* (Munich, 1969).

Hillgruber, Andreas, 'Riezlers Theorie des kalkulierten Risikos und Bethmann

Hollwegs politische Konzeption in der Julikrise 1914', *Historische Zeitschrift*, vol. 202 (1966), pp. 333–51.

Hintze, Otto, 'Der Beamtenstand', in *Soziologie und Geschichte: Gesammelte Abhandlungen zur Soziologie, Politik und Theorie der Geschichte*, ed. Gerhard Oestreich, 2nd edn (Göttingen, 1964), pp. 66–125.

Hofstadter, Richard, 'The paranoid style in American politics', in *The Paranoid Style in American Politics and Other Essays* (New York, 1967), pp. 3–40.

Holzbach, Heidrun, *Das 'System Hugenberg': Die Organisation bürgerlicher Sammlungspolitik vor dem Aufstieg der NSDAP* (Stuttgart, 1981).

Hortleder, Gerd, *Das Gesellschaftsbild des Ingenieurs: Zum politischen Verhalten der Technischen Intelligenz in Deutschland* (Frankfurt a. M., 1970).

Hubatsch, Walther, *Die Aera Tirpitz: Studien zur deutschen Marinepolitik 1890–1918* (Göttingen, 1955).

Hubbard, William, and Jarausch, Konrad H., 'Occupation and social structure in modern Central Europe: some reflections on coding professions', *QUANTUM Information*, no. 11 (July 1979), pp. 101–19.

Huerkamp, Claudia, 'Aerzte und Professionalisierung in Deutschland: Ueberlegungen zum Wandel des Arztberufs im 19. Jahrhundert', *Geschichte und Gesellschaft*, vol. 6 (1980), pp. 349–82.

Hunt, James Clark, *The Peoples' Party in Württemberg and Southern Germany, 1890–1914* (Stuttgart, 1975).

Huntington, Samuel P., *The Soldier and the State: The Theory and Politics of Civil–Military Relations* (New York, 1957).

Hussmann, Josefine, 'Die Alldeutschen und die Flottenfrage' (Diss. phil., Freiburg, 1945).

Inkeles, Alex, 'Some sociological observations on culture and personality studies', in Clyde Kluckholm and Henry A. Murray (eds), *Personality in Nature, Society, and Culture*, 2nd edn (New York, 1956), pp. 577–92.

Izenberg, Gerald, 'Psychohistory and intellectual history', *History and Theory*, vol. 14 (1975), pp. 139–55.

Jäckel, Eberhard, *Hitler's World View: A Blueprint for Power* (Cambridge, Mass., 1981).

Jäckh, Ernst, *Kiderlen-Wächter: Der Staatsmann und Mensch*, 2 vols (Berlin and Leipzig, 1925).

Jacobsen, Edith, *The Self and the Object World* (New York, 1964).

Jaeger, Hans, *Unternehmer in der deutschen Politik (1890–1918)* (Berne, 1967).

Janowitz, Morris, *The Professional Soldier: A Social and Political Portrait* (New York, 1960).

Jarausch, Konrad H., *Academic Illiberalism: Students, Society, and Politics in Imperial Germany* (Princeton, NJ, 1982).

Jarausch, Konrad H., 'Die Alldeutschen und die Regierung Bethmann Hollwegs: Eine Denkschrift Kурt Riezlers vom Herbst 1916', *Vierteljahrshefte für Zeitgeschichte*, vol. 21 (1973), pp. 435–68.

Jarausch, Konrad H., *The Enigmatic Chancellor: Bethmann Hollweg and the Hubris of Imperial Germany* (New Haven, Conn. and London, 1973).

Jarausch, Konrad H., 'Liberal education as illiberal socialization: the case of students in Imperial Germany', *Journal of Modern History*, vol. 50 (1978), pp. 609–30.

Jaszi, Oscar, *The Dissolution of the Habsburg Monarchy* (Chicago and London, 1929).

Jenks, William A., *Austria under the Iron Ring, 1879–1893* (Charlottesville, Va, 1965).

Jeran, Eberhard, 'Deutsche Turnerschaft (DT) 1868–1936', in Fricke, *Handbuch*, Vol. 1, pp. 605–19.

Jerussalimski, A. S., *Die Aussenpolitik und die Diplomatie des deutschen Imperialismus am Ende des 19. Jahrhunderts* (Berlin, 1954).

Jochmann, Werner, 'Struktur und Funktion des deutschen Antisemitismus', in Mosse, *Juden,* pp. 389–477.

Johnson, Richard, 'Culture and the historians', in Clarke, *Working-Class Culture,* pp. 41–71.

Johnson, Richard, 'Three problematics: elements of a theory of working-class culture', in Clarke, *Working-Class Culture,* pp. 201–37.

Judt, Tony, 'A clown in regal purple: social history and the historians', *History Workshop,* no. 7 (Spring 1979), pp. 69–94.

Jung, Dietrich, 'Der Alldeutsche Verband und die Marokkofrage' (Diss. phil., Bonn, 1934).

Kaelble, Hartmut, 'Chancenungleichheit und akademische Ausbildung in Deutschland 1910–1960', *Geschichte und Gesellschaft,* vol. 1 (1975), pp. 121–45.

Kaelble, Hartmut, *Industrielle Interessenpolitik in der Wilhelminischen Gesellschaft: Centralverband Deutscher Industrieller 1895–1914* (Berlin, 1967).

Kaelble, Hartmut, 'Social mobility in Germany, 1900–1960', *Journal of Modern History,* vol. 50 (1978), pp. 439–61.

Kann, Robert A., *The Multinational Empire: Nationalism and National Reform in the Habsburg Monarchy, 1848–1918,* 2 vols (New York, 1950).

Kardorff, Siegfried von, *Wilhelm von Kardorff: Ein nationaler Parlamentarier im Zeitalter Bismarcks und Wilhelms II. 1828–1907* (Berlin, 1936).

Kasl, Stanislav V., 'Status inconsistency: some conceptual and methodological considerations', in John P. Robinson *et al., Measures of Occupational Attitudes and Occupational Characteristics* (University of Michigan, Institute for Social Research, 1969), pp. 377–95.

Katz, M. B., 'Occupational classification in history', *Journal of Interdisciplinary History,* vol. 3 (1973), pp. 63–99.

Kehr, Eckart, 'Klassenkämpfe und Rüstungspolitik im kaiserlichen Deutschland', in *Der Primat der Innenpolitik,* pp. 87–110.

Kehr, Eckart, *Der Primat der Innenpolitik: Gesammelte Aufsätze zur preussisch-deutschen Sozialgeschichte im 19. und 20. Jahrhundert,* ed. Hans-Ulrich Wehler (Frankfurt a. M. and Berlin, 1965).

Kehr Eckart, *Schlachtflottenbau und Parteipolitik 1894–1901: Versuch eines Querschnitts durch die innenpolitischen, sozialen und ideologischen Vorausset-zungen des deutschen Imperialismus* (Berlin, 1930).

Kehr, Eckart, 'Soziale und finanzielle Grundlagen der Tirpitzschen Flotten-propaganda', in *Der Primat der Innenpolitik,* pp. 130–48.

Kelly, Alfred, *The Descent of Darwin: The Popularization of Darwinism in Germany, 1860–1914* (Chapel Hill, NC, 1981).

Kennedy, Paul M., *The Rise of the Anglo-German Antagonism, 1860–1914* (London, 1980).

Kennedy, Paul M., *The Samoan Tangle: A Study in Anglo-German Relations, 1878–1900* (New York, 1974).

Kennedy, Paul M., and Nicholls, Anthony J. (eds), *Nationalist and Racialist Movements in Britain and Germany before 1914* (London, 1980).

Ketelsen, Uwe-Karsten, *Völkisch-nationale und nationalsozialistische Literatur in Deutschland 1890–1945* (Stuttgart, 1976).

Kitchen, Martin, *The German Officer Corps, 1890–1914* (Oxford, 1968).

Klauss, Klaus, 'Die deutsche Kolonialgesellschaft und die deutsche Kolonialpolitik von den Anfängen bis 1895' (Diss. phil., Berlin, 1966).

Klein, Fritz, *et al., Deutschland im Ersten Weltkrieg,* 3 vols (Berlin, 1968–70).

Klessmann, Christoph, *Polnische Bergarbeiter im Ruhrgebiet 1870–1945: Soziale*

Integration und nationale Subkultur einer Minderheit in der deutschen Industriegesellschaft (Göttingen, 1978).

Knutson, Jeanne N., *The Human Basis of the Polity: A Psychological Study of Political Men* (Chicago and New York, 1972).

Koch, Hansjoachim W., *Der Sozialdarwinismus: Seine Genese und sein Einfluss auf das imperialistische Denken* (Munich, 1973).

Koch, Walter, *Volk und Staatsführung vor dem Weltkriege* (Stuttgart, 1935).

Kocka, Jürgen, 'The First World War and the "Mittelstand": German artisans and white-collar workers', *Journal of Contemporary History,* vol. 8 (January 1973), pp. 101–24.

Kocka, Jürgen, *Klassengesellschaft im Krieg 1914–1918* (Göttingen, 1973).

Kocka, Jürgen, 'Zur Problematik der deutschen Angestellten 1914–1933', in Hans Mommsen et al. (eds), *Industrielles System und politische Entwicklung in der Weimarer Republik* (Düsseldorf, 1974), pp. 792–811.

Kocka, Jürgen, 'Theory and social history: recent developments in West Germany', *Social Research,* vol. 47 (1980), pp. 426–57.

Kocka, Jürgen, *Unternehmerverwaltung und Angestelltenschaft am Beispiel Siemens 1847–1914: Zum Verhältnis von Kapitalismus und Bürokratie in der deutschen Industrialisierung* (Stuttgart, 1969).

Koshar, Rudy, 'Two "Nazisms": the social context of Nazi mobilization in Marburg and Tübingen', *Social History,* vol. 7 (1982), pp. 27–42.

Kratsch, Gerhart, *Kunstwart und Dürerbund: Ein Beitrag zur Geschichte der Gebildeten im Zeitalter des Imperialismus* (Göttingen, 1969).

Krebs, Willi, 'Der Alldeutsche Verband in den Jahren 1918 bis 1939: ein politisches Instrument des deutschen Imperialismus' (Diss. phil., Berlin, 1970).

Kriegbaum, Günther, *Die parlamentarische Tätigkeit des Freiherrn C. W. Heyl zu Herrnsheim* (Meisenheim, 1962).

Kröll, Ulrich, *Die internationale Buren-Agitation 1899–1902: Haltung der Oeffentlichkeit und Agitation zugunsten der Buren in Deutschland, Frankreich und den Niederlanden während des Burenkrieges* (Münster, 1973).

Kruck, Alfred, *Geschichte des alldeutschen Verbandes 1890–1939* (Wiesbaden, 1954).

Krutmann, Friedrich, 'Die Aussenpolitik in der Tageszeitung "Die Post" von 1890 bis 1914' (Diss. phil., Leipzig, 1933).

Kubie, Laurence S., 'The nature of the neurotic process', in Silvano Arieti (ed.), *American Handbook of Psychiatry,* 3rd edn, 6 vols (New York, 1974–5), Vol. 3, pp. 3–16.

Kuczynski, Jürgen, *Studien zur Geschichte des deutschen Imperialismus, Vol. 2, Propagandaorganisationen des Monopolkapitals* (Berlin, 1950).

Kuhl, Hermann von, *Der Generalstab in Vorbereitung und Durchführung des Weltkrieges,* 2nd edn (Berlin, 1920).

Kuhn, Harald E., *Soziologie der Apotheker: ein Beitrag zur Soziologie des Gesundheitswesens* (Stuttgart, 1963).

Kulka, O. Dov, 'Richard Wagner und die Anfänge des modernen Antisemitismus', *Bulletin des Leo Baeck Instituts,* vol. 4 (1961), pp. 281–300.

Lachmann, Manfred, 'Probleme der Bewaffnung des kaiserlichen deutschen Heeres', *Zeitschrift für Militärgeschichte,* vol. 6 (1967), pp. 23–37.

Learned, William Setchel, *The Oberlehrer: A Study of the Social and Professional Evolution of the German Schoolmaster* (Cambridge, Mass., 1914).

Ledebur, Freiherr Ferdinand von, et al. (eds), *Die Geschichte des deutschen Unteroffiziers* (Berlin, 1939).

Lederer, Emil, 'Die Angestellten im Wilhelminischen Reich', in *Kapitalismus,* pp. 51–82.

Lederer, Emil, *Kapitalismus, Klassenstruktur und Probleme der Demokratie in Deutschland 1910–1940,* ed. Jürgen Kocka (Göttingen, 1979).

Lederer, Emil, 'Klasseninteressen, Interessenverbände und Parlamentarismus', in *Kapitalismus,* pp. 33–50.

Leibenguth, Peter, 'Modernisierungskrisis des Kaiserreichs an der Schwelle zum wilhelminischen Imperialismus: politische Probleme der Aera Caprivi (1890–1894)' (Diss. phil., Cologne, 1975).

Lenk, Kurt, *'Volk und Staat': Strukturwandel politischer Ideologien im 19. und 20. Jahrhundert* (Stuttgart, 1971).

Lepenies, Wolf, 'Arbeiterkultur: Wissenschaftssoziologische Anmerkungen zur Konjunktur eines Begriffs', *Geschichte und Gesellschaft,* vol. 5 (1979), pp. 125–36.

Lepenies, Wolf, 'Probleme einer historischen Anthropologie', in Reinhard Rürup (ed.), *Historische Sozialwissenschaft: Beiträge zur Einführung in die Forschungspraxis* (Göttingen, 1977), pp. 126–59.

Lepsius, M. Rainer, 'Parteiensystem und Sozialstruktur: zum Problem der Demokratisierung der deutschen Gesellschaft', in *Wirtschaft, Geschichte und Wirtschaftsgeschichte: Festschrift zum 65. Geburtstag von Friedrich Lütge* (Stuttgart, 1966), pp. 371–93.

Levy, Richard S., *The Downfall of the Anti-Semitic Political Parties in Imperial Germany* (New Haven, Conn. and London, 1975).

Linnemann, A., 'Friedrich Lange und die Deutsche Zeitung' (Diss. phil., Berlin, 1938).

Lohalm, Uwe, *Völkischer Radikalismus: Die Geschichte des Deutschvölkischen Schutz- und Trutz-Bundes 1919–1923* (Hamburg, 1970).

Lotz, Albert, *Geschichte des deutschen Beamtentums* (Berlin, 1909).

Luckman, Thomas, and Berger, Peter L., 'Social mobility and personal identity', *Archives européennes de sociologie,* vol. 5 (1964), pp. 331–44.

Lynd, Helen Merrell, *On Shame and the Search for Identity* (New York, 1958).

McClelland, Charles E., *State, Society and University in Germany, 1700–1914* (Cambridge, 1980).

McGrath, William J., *Dionysian Art and Populist Politics in Austria* (New Haven, Conn. and London, 1974).

MacIntyre, Alasdair, 'Rationality and the explanation of action', *Against the Self-Images of the Age: Essays on Ideology and Philosophy* (New York, 1971), pp. 244–59.

Maser, Werner, *Die Frühgeschichte der NSDAP: Hitlers Weg bis 1924* (Frankfurt a. M. and Bonn, 1965).

Mason, T. W., 'Women in Nazi Germany', *History Workshop,* no. 2 (1977), pp. 74–113.

Massing, Paul W., *Rehearsal for Destruction: A Study of Political Anti-Semitism in Imperial Germany* (New York, 1949).

Mattheier, Klaus J., 'Drei Führungsorganisationen der wirtschaftsfriedlich-nationalen Arbeiterbewegung: Reichsverband gegen Sozialdemokratie, Förderungsausschuss und Deutsche Vereinigung in der Auseinandersetzung um die "Gelben Gewerkschaften" in Deutschland 1904 bis 1918', *Rheinische Vierteljahrsblätter,* vol. 37 (1973), pp. 244–75.

Mattheier, Klaus, *Die Gelben: Nationale Arbeiter zwischen Wirtschaftsfrieden und Streik* (Düsseldorf, 1973).

Matuschka, Edgar Graf von, 'Organisationsgeschichte des Heeres 1890 bis 1918', in Hans Meier-Welcker *et al.* (eds), *Handbuch zur deutschen Militärgeschichte 1648–1939,* 6 vols (Frankfurt a. M., 1966–81), vol. 5, pp. 157–282.

Mayer, Arno J., *Dynamics of Counterrevolution in Europe, 1870–1956: An Analytical Framework* (New York, 1971).

Mayer, Arno J., 'The lower middle class as a historical problem', *Journal of Modern History*, vol. 47 (1975), pp. 4–36.

Mayntz, Renate, *Soziale Schichtung und sozialer Wandel in einer Industriegemeinde: Eine soziologische Untersuchung der Stadt Euskirchen* (Stuttgart, 1958).

Meisner, Heinrich Otto, *Der Kriegsminister 1814–1914: Ein Beitrag zur militärischen Verfassungsgeschichte* (Berlin, 1940).

Merton, Robert K., 'Bureaucratic structure and personality', *Social Forces*, vol. 18 (1940), pp. 560–8.

Messerschmidt, Manfred, 'Militär und Schule in der wilhelminischen Zeit', *Militärgeschichtliche Mitteilungen*, no. 1 (1978), pp. 51–76.

Messerschmidt, Manfred, 'Reich und Nation im Bewusstsein der wilhelminischen Gesellschaft', in Schottelius and Deist, pp. 11–33.

Methfessel, Werner, 'Evangelischer Bund zur Wahrung der deutsch-protestantischer Interessen (EB) seit 1886', in Fricke, *Handbuch*, Vol. 1, pp. 787–91.

Meyer, Folkert, *Schule der Untertanen: Lehrer und Politik in Preussen 1848–1900* (Hamburg, 1976).

Meyer, Henry Cord, *Mitteleuropa in German Thought and Action, 1815–1945* (The Hague, 1955).

Meyer, Jürg, 'Die Propaganda der deutschen Flottenbewegung' (Diss. phil., Berne, 1967).

Meyer, Klaus, *Theodor Schiemann als politischer Publizist* (Frankfurt a. M. and Hamburg, 1956).

Mielke, Siegfried, *Der Hansa-Bund für Gewerbe, Handel und Industrie 1909–1914: Der gescheiterte Versuch einer antifeudalen Sammlungspolitik* (Göttingen, 1976).

Miller, C. W., 'The paranoid syndrome', *A.M.A. Archives of Neurology and Psychiatry*, vol. 45 (1941), pp. 953–63.

Mittmann, Ursula, *Fraktion und Partei: Ein Vergleich von Zentrum und Sozialdemokratie im Kaiserreich* (Düsseldorf, 1976).

Mock, Wolfang, '"Manipulation von oben" oder Selbstorganisation an der Basis? Einige neuere Ansätze in der englischen Historiographie zur Geschichte des deutschen Kaiserreiches', *Historische Zeitschrift*, vol. 232 (1981), pp. 358–75.

Moore, Harriett, and Kleinig, Gerhard, 'Das soziale Selbstbild der Gesellschaftsschichten in Deutschland', *Kölner Zeitschrift für Soziologie und Sozialwissenschaft*, vol. 12 (1960), pp. 86–119.

Morsey, Rudolf, 'Die deutschen Katholiken und der Nationalstaat zwischen Kulturkampf und Erstem Weltkrieg', *Historisches Jahrbuch*, vol. 90 (1970), pp. 31–64.

Mosse, George L., *The Crisis of German Ideology: Intellectual Origins of the Third Reich* (New York, 1964).

Mosse, George L., 'Friendship and nationhood: about the promise and failure of German nationalism', *Journal of Contemporary History*, vol. 17 (1982), pp. 351–67.

Mosse, George L., *The Nationalization of the Masses: Political Symbolism and Mass Movements in Germany from the Napoleonic Wars through the Third Reich* (New York, 1975).

Mosse, George L., *Toward the Final Solution: A History of European Racism* (New York, 1978).

Mosse, Werner E. (ed.), *Juden im Wilhelminischen Deutschland 1890–1914* (Tübingen, 1976).

Mühlen, Patrick von zur, *Rassenideologien: Geschichte und Hintergründe* (Berlin and Bonn-Bad Godesberg, 1977).

Müller, Fritz Ferdinand, *Deutschland—Zanzibar—Ostafrika: Geschichte einer deutschen Kolonialeroberung 1884–1890* (Berlin, 1959).

Müller, Helmut, and Fieber, Hans-Joachim, 'Deutsche Kolonialgesellschaft (DKG) 1882 (1887)–1933', in Fricke, *Handbuch*, Vol. 1, pp. 390–407.

Müller, Josef, *Die Entwicklung des Rassenantisemitismus in den letzten Jahrzehnten des 19. Jahrhunderts* (Berlin, 1940).

Murphy, Richard C., 'The Polish trade union in the Ruhr coal field: labor organization and ethnicity in Wilhelmian Germany', *Central European History*, vol. 11 (1978), pp. 335–47.

Negt, Oskar, and Kluge, Alexander, *Oeffentlichkeit und Erfahrung: Zur Organisationsanalyse von bürgerlicher und proletarischer Oeffentlichkeit* (Frankfurt a. M., 1972).

Nemiah, John C., 'Anxiety: signal, symptom, and syndrome', in Silvano Arieti (ed.), *American Handbook of Psychiatry*, 3rd edn, 6 vols (New York, 1974–5), Vol. 3, pp. 91–109.

Nichols, J. Alden, *Germany after Bismarck: The Caprivi Era, 1890–1894* (Cambridge, Mass., 1958).

Nipperdey, Thomas, 'Die anthropologische Dimension der Geschichtswissenschaft', *Gesellschaft, Kultur, Theorie*, pp. 33–58.

Nipperdey, Thomas, *Gesellschaft, Kultur, Theorie: Gesammelte Aufsätze zur neueren Geschichte* (Göttingen, 1976).

Nipperdey, Thomas, 'Interessenverbände und Parteien in Deutschland vor dem Ersten Weltkrieg', *Gesellschaft, Kultur, Theorie*, pp. 319–37.

Nipperdey, Thomas, 'Nationalidee und Nationaldenkmal in Deutschland im 19. Jahrhundert', *Gesellschaft, Kultur, Theorie*, pp. 133–73.

Nipperdey, Thomas, 'Die Organisation der bürgerlichen Parteien in Deutschland vor 1918', *Historische Zeitschrift*, vol. 185 (1958), pp. 550–602.

Nipperdey, Thomas, *Die Organisation der deutschen Parteien vor 1918* (Düsseldorf, 1961).

Nipperdey, Thomas, 'Verein als soziale Struktur in Deutschland im späten 18. Jahrhundert und frühen 19. Jahrhundert', in Hartmut Boockmann *et al.*, *Geschichtswissenschaft und Vereinswesen im 19. Jahrhundert: Beiträge zur Geschichte historischer Forschung in Deutschland* (Göttingen, 1972), pp. 1–44.

Nipperdey, Thomas, 'Wehlers "Kaiserreich": Eine kritische Auseinandersetzung', *Gesellschaft, Kultur, Theorie*, pp. 360–89.

Nolte, Ernst, *Three Faces of Fascism: Action française, Italian Fascism, National Socialism* (New York, 1966).

Nussbaum, Manfred, *Vom 'Kolonialenthusiasmus' zur Kolonialpolitik der Monopole: Zur deutschen Kolonialpolitik unter Bismarck, Caprivi und Hohenlohe* (Berlin, 1962).

Nydes, Jules, 'The paranoid-masochistic character', *Psychoanalytic Review*, vol. 50 (Summer 1963), pp. 55–91.

Obershall, Anthony, *Social Conflicts and Social Movements* (Englewood Cliffs, NJ, 1973).

O'Donnell, Anthony J., 'National Liberalism and the mass politics of the German right, 1890–1907' (PhD Diss., Princeton University, 1973).

Oncken, Dirk, 'Das Problem des Lebensraums in der deutschen Politik vor 1914' (Diss. phil., Freiburg, 1948).

Oncken, Emily, *Panthersprung nach Agadir: Die deutsche Politik während der zweiten Marokkokrise 1911* (Düsseldorf, 1981).

Opler, M. K., 'Cultural anthropology and social psychiatry', *Journal of Psychiatry*, vol. 113 (1956), pp. 304–9.

Pähler, Karl H., 'Verein und Sozialstruktur: Versuch einer soziologischen Analyse', *Archiv für Rechts- und Sozialphilosophie*, vol. 42 (1956), pp. 197–227.

Parsons, Talcott, 'Democracy and social structure in pre-Nazi Germany', in *Essays in Sociological Theory* (Glencoe, Ill., 1954), pp. 104–23.

Pascal, Roy, *From Naturalism to Expressionism: German Literature and Society 1880–1918* (London, 1973).

Peck, Abraham, *Radicals and Reactionaries: The Crisis of Conservatism in Wilhelmine Germany* (Washington, DC, 1978).

Pierard, Richard Victor, 'The German Colonial Society, 1882–1914' (PhD Diss., State University of Iowa, 1964).

Pierenkemper, Toni, *Die westfälischen Schwerindustriellen 1852–1913* (Göttingen, 1979).

Piers, G., and Singer, M. B., *Shame and Guilt: A Psychoanalytic and a Cultural Study* (Springfield, Ill., 1953).

Pogge von Strandmann, Hartmut, 'The Kolonialrat: its significance and influence on German politics from 1890 to 1906' (Diss. phil., Oxford, 1970).

Pogge von Strandmann, Hartmut, 'Nationale Verbände zwischen Weltpolitik und Kontinentalpolitik', in Schottelius and Deist, pp. 296–317.

Pogge von Strandmann, Hartmut, 'Rathenau, die Gebrüder Mannesmann und die Vorgeschichte der zweiten Marokkokrise', in Geiss and Wendt, pp. 251–70.

Pogge von Strandmann, Hartmut, 'Staatsstreichpläne, Alldeutsche und Bethmann Hollweg', in Pogge von Strandmann and Imanuel Geiss, *Die Erforderlichkeit des Unmöglichen: Deutschland am Vorabend des ersten Weltkrieges* (Frankfurt a. M., 1965), pp. 7–45.

Poliakov, Leon, *The Aryan Myth: A History of Racist and Nationalist Ideas in Europe* (New York, 1974).

Pöls, Werner, 'Bismarckverehrung und Bismarcklegende als innenpolitisches Problem der Wilhelminischen Zeit', *Jahrbuch für die Geschichte Mittel- und Ostdeutschlands*, vol. 20 (1971), pp. 183–201.

Poulantzas, Nicos, *Fascism and Dictatorship: The Third International and the Problem of Fascism* (London, 1974).

Prost, Antoine, *Les Anciens Combattants et la société française 1914–1939*, 3 vols (Paris, 1977).

Puhle, Hans-Jürgen, *Agrarische Interessenpolitik und preussischer Konservatismus im Wilhelminischen Reich (1893–1914): Ein Beitrag zur Analyse des Nationalismus in Deutschland am Beispiel des Bundes der Landwirte und der Deutsch-Konservativen Partei* (Hanover, 1967).

Puhle, Hans-Jürgen, 'Parlament, Parteien und Interessenverbände 1890–1914', in Stürmer, *Das kaiserliche Deutschland*, pp. 340–77.

Pulzer, Peter G. J., *The Rise of Political Anti-Semitism in Germany and Austria* (New York, 1964).

Rappaport, Armin, *The Navy League of the United States* (Detroit, Mich., 1962).

Reinhard, Wolfgang, '"Sozialimperialismus" oder "Entkolonisierung der Historie"? Kolonialkrise und "Hottentottenwahlen" 1904–1907', *Historisches Jahrbuch*, vol. 97/8 (1978), pp. 384–417.

Ringer, Fritz K., *Education and Society in Modern Europe* (Bloomington, Ind., 1979).

Ritter, Gerhard, *Staatskunst und Kriegshandwerk: Das Problem des 'Militarismus' in Deutschland*, 4 vols (Munich, 1954–68).

Röhl, J. C. G., 'The disintegration of the *Kartell* and Bismarck's fall from power, 1887–1890', *Historical Journal*, vol. 9 (1966), pp. 60–89.

Röhl, J. C. G., *Germany without Bismarck: The Crisis of Government in the Second Reich, 1890–1900* (Berkeley, Calif. and Los Angeles, 1967).

Rohter, Ira S., 'Social and psychological determinants of radical rightism', in Robert A. Schönberger (ed.), *The American Right Wing: Readings in Political Behavior* (New York, 1969), pp. 193–237.

Rokeach, Milton, *The Open and Closed Mind: Investigations into the Nature of Belief Systems and Personality Systems* (London, 1960).

Rosenberg, Hans, *Grosse Depression und Bismarckzeit: Wirtschaftsablauf, Gesellschaft und Politik in Mitteleuropa* (Berlin, 1967).

Ross, Ronald J., *Beleaguered Tower: The Dilemma of Political Catholicism in Wilhelmine Germany* (Notre Dame, 1976).

Roth, Guenther, *The Social Democrats in Imperial Germany: A Study in Working-Class Isolation and National Integration* (Totowa, NJ, 1963).

Rothe, Hans-Joachim, 'Deutscher Sängerbund (DSB) 1862–1945', in Fricke, *Handbuch,* Vol. 1, pp. 541–53.

Rürup, Reinhard, and Nipperdey, Thomas, 'Antisemitismus—Entstehung, Funktion und Geschichte eines Begriffs', in Rürup, *Emanzipation und Antisemitismus: Studien zur 'Judenfrage' der bürgerlichen Gesellschaft* (Göttingen, 1975), pp. 95–114.

Rüschemeyer, Dietrich, 'Modernisierung und die Gebildeten im Kaiserlichen Deutschland', *Kölner Zeitschrift für Soziologie und Sozialpsychologie,* vol. 16 (Sonderheft 1972), pp. 515–29.

Rüschemeyer, Dietrich, 'Professionalisierung: theoretische Probleme für die vergleichende Geschichtsforschung', *Geschichte und Gesellschaft,* vol. 6 (1980), pp. 311–25.

Saladino, Salvatore, 'Italy', in Hans Rogger and Eugen Weber (eds), *The European Right: A Historical Profile* (Berkeley, Calif. and Los Angeles, 1966), pp. 208–60.

Sartre, Jean-Paul, *Anti-Semite and Jew* (New York, 1965).

Sauer, Wolfgang, 'Das Problem des deutschen Nationalsaates', in Hans-Ulrich Wehler (ed.), *Moderne deutsche Sozialgeschichte* (Cologne and Berlin, 1966), pp. 407–36.

Saul, Klaus, 'Der "Deutsche Kriegerbund": Zur innenpolitischen Funktion eines "nationalen" Verbandes im kaiserlichen Deutschland', *Militärgeschichtliche Mitteilungen,* no. 2 (1969), pp. 95–159.

Saul, Klaus, 'Der Kampf um die Jugend zwischen Volksschule und Kaserne: Ein Beitrag zur "Jugendpflege" im Wilhelminischen Reich 1890–1914', *Militärgeschichtliche Mitteilungen,* no. 1 (1971), pp. 97–143.

Saul, Klaus, *Staat, Industrie, Arbeiterbewegung im Kaiserreich: Zur Innen- und Aussenpolitik des wilhelminischen Deutschlands 1903–1914* (Düsseldorf, 1974).

Scharff, Alexander, 'Deutsche Ordnungsgedanken zum völkischen Leben in Nordschleswig vor 1914', in *Schleswig-Holstein in der deutschen und nordeuropäischen Geschichte* (Stuttgart, 1969), pp. 9–42.

Schieder, Theodor, *Das Deutsche Reich von 1871 als Nationalstaat* (Cologne and Opladen, 1961).

Schiefel, Werner, *Bernhard Dernburg 1865–1937: Kilonialpolitiker und Bankier im wilhelminischen Deutschland* (Zurich, 1974).

Schilling, Konrad, 'Beiträge zu einer Geschichte des radikalen Nationalismus in der Wilhelminischen Aera 1890–1909: Die Entstehung des radikalen Nationalismus, seine Einflussnahme auf die innere und äussere Politik des Deutschen Reiches und die Stellung von Regierung und Reichstag zu seiner politischen und publizistischen Tätigkeit' (Diss. phil., Cologne, 1968).

Schmidt, Gustav, 'Deutschland am Vorabend des Ersten Weltkrieges', in Stürmer, *Das kaiserliche Deutschland,* pp. 397–433.

Schmidt, Gustav, 'Innenpolitische Blockbildungen am Vorabend des Ersten Weltkrieges', *Aus Politik und Zeitgeschichte* (Beilage zum *Parlament*), no. 20 (1972), pp. 3–32.

Schmidt, Gustav, 'Parlamentarisierung oder "Präventive Konterrevolution"? Die deutsche Innenpolitik im Spannungsfeld konservativer Sammlungsbewegungen und latenter Reformbestrebungen 1907–1914', in Gerhard A. Ritter (ed.), *Gesellschaft, Parlament und Regierung: Zur Geschichte des Parlamentarismus in Deutschland* (Düsseldorf, 1974), pp. 249–74.

Schmidt, Klaus Werner, 'Die "Rheinisch-Westfälische Zeitung" und ihr Verleger Reismann-Grone', *Beiträge zur Geschichte Dortmunds und der Grafschaft Mark*, vol. 69 (1974), pp. 241–382.

Schmidt-Richberg, Wiegand, 'Die Regierungszeit Wilhelms II.', in Hans Meier-Welcker *et al.* (eds), *Handbuch zur deutschen Militärgeschichte 1648–1939*, 6 vols (Frankfurt a. M., 1964–81), Vol. 5, pp. 9–155.

Schmitt, Heinz, *Das Vereinsleben der Stadt Weinheim an der Bergstrasse* (Weinheim, 1963).

Schödl, Günter, *Alldeutscher Verband und deutsche Minderheitenpolitik in Ungarn 1890–1914: Zur Geschichte des deutschen 'extremen Nationalismus'* (Frankfurt a. M., 1978).

Schottelius, Herbert, and Deist, Wilhelm (eds), *Marine und Marinepolitik im kaiserlichen Deutschland 1871–1914* (Düsseldorf, 1972).

Schüler, Winfried, *Der Bayreuther Kreis von seiner Entstehung bis zum Ausgang der Wilhelminischen Aera: Wagnerkult und Kulturreform im Geist völkischer Weltanschauung* (Münster, 1971).

Schulte, Bernd F., *Die deutsche Armee 1900–1914: Zwischen Beharren und Verändern* (Düsseldorf, 1977).

Schulz, Gerhard, 'Ueber Entstehung und Formen von Interessengruppen in Deutschland seit Beginn der Industrialisierung', *Politische Vierteljahrsschrift*, vol. 2 (1961), pp. 124–54.

Schulz, Gerhard, 'Imperialismus im 19. Jahrhundert', *Das Zeitalter der Gesellschaft: Aufsätze zur politischen Sozialgeschichte der Neuzeit* (Munich, 1969), pp. 112–72.

Schüssler, Wilhelm, *Die Daily-Telegraph-Affaire: Fürst Bülow, Kaiser Wilhelm und die Krise des zweiten Reiches 1908* (Göttingen, 1952).

Schwinn, Erich, 'Die Arbeit des deutschen Wehrvereins und die Wehrlage Deutschlands vor dem Weltkriege' (Diss. phil., Heidelberg, 1940).

Schwonder, Dietrich, *Bevor Hitler kam: Eine historische Studie* (Hanover, 1964).

Seggern, Christina von, 'The Alldeutscher Verband and the German Nationalstaat' (PhD Diss., University of Minnesota, 1974).

Sell, Manfred, 'Die deutsche öffentliche Meinung und das Helgolandabkommen im Jahre 1890' (Diss. phil., Cologne, 1926).

Sennett, Richard, *Authority* (New York, 1980).

Sewell, William H., Jr, *Work and Revolution in France: The Language of Labor from the Old Regime to 1848* (Cambridge, 1980).

Shafer, Roy, 'Ideals, the ego ideal, and the ideal self', in Robert R. Holt (ed.), *Motives and Thought: Psychoanalytic Essays in Honor of David Rappaport* (New York, 1967), pp. 131–74.

Shapiro, David, *Neurotic Styles* (New York, 1965).

Sheehan, James J., *German Liberalism in the Nineteenth Century* (Chicago, 1978).

Sheehan, James J., 'Liberalism and the city in nineteenth-century Germany', *Past and Present*, no. 51 (May 1971), pp. 116–37.

Sheehan, James J., 'What is German history? reflections on the role of the *nation* in German history and historiography', *Journal of Modern History*, vol. 53 (1981), pp. 1–23.

Silverman, Dan P., *Reluctant Union: Alsace-Lorraine and Imperial Germany, 1871–1918* (University Park and London, 1972).

Simmel, Georg, 'Die Geselligkeit (Beispiel der Reinen- oder Formalensoziologie)', in *Grundfragen der Soziologie: Individuum und Gesellschaft* (Berlin and Leipzig, 1917).

Simmel, Georg, 'Superordination and subordination', in *The Sociology of Georg Simmel*, ed. Kurt H. Wolff (New York and London, 1950), pp. 181–303.

Simon, Klaus, *Die württembergischen Demokraten: Ihre Stellung und Arbeit im Parteien- und Verfassungssystem in Württemberg und im Deutschen Reich* (Stuttgart, 1969).

Smith, Woodruff D., *The German Colonial Empire* (Chapel Hill, NC, 1978).

Smith, Woodruff D., 'The ideology of German colonialism, 1840–1906', *Journal of Modern History*, vol. 46 (1974), pp. 641–62.

Smith, Woodruff D., 'The ideology of German colonialism, 1840–1918' (PhD Diss., University of Chicago, 1972).

Stackelberg, Roderick, *Idealism Debased: From Volkish Ideology to National Socialism* (Kent, Ohio, 1981).

Stark, Gary D., *Entrepreneurs of Ideology: Neoconservative Publishers in Germany, 1890–1933* (Chapel Hill, NC, 1981).

Staudinger, Hans, *Individuum und Gemeinschaft in der Kulturorganisation des Vereins* (Jena, 1913).

Stegmann, Dirk, *Die Erben Bismarcks: Parteien und Verbände in der Spätphase des Wilhelminischen Deutschlands. Sammlungspolitik 1897–1918* (Cologne and Berlin, 1970).

Stegmann, Dirk, 'Hugenberg contra Stresemann: die Politik der Interessenverbände am Ende des Kaiserreiches', *Vierteljahrshefte für Zeitgeschichte*, vol. 24 (1976), pp. 329–78.

Stein, Leon, *The Racial Thinking of Richard Wagner* (New York, 1950).

Steinberg, Jonathan, *Yesterday's Deterrent: Tirpitz and the Birth of the German Battle Fleet* (New York, 1965).

Steinberg, Michael Stephen, *Sabres and Brown Shirts: The German Students' Path to National Socialism, 1918–1935* (Chicago, 1977).

Steinkühler, Manfred, 'Gobineau au jugement de ses contemporains d'Outre-Rhin' (Diss. phil., University of Paris, 1961).

Stenkewitz, Kurt, 'Deutscher Wehrverein (DWV) 1912–1935', in Fricke, *Handbuch,* Vol. 1, pp. 574–81.

Stenkewitz, Kurt, *Gegen Bajonett und Dividende: Die politische Krise in Deutschland am Vorabend des ersten Weltkrieges* (Berlin, 1960).

Stern, Fritz, 'The political consequences of the unpolitical German', *The Failure of Illiberalism: Essays on the Political Culture of Modern Germany* (New York, 1972), pp. 3–25.

Stern, Fritz, *The Politics of Cultural Despair: A Study in the Rise of Germanic Ideology* (Berkeley, Calif. and Los Angeles, 1961).

Stern, J. P., *Hitler: The Führer and the People* (Berkeley, Calif. and Los Angeles, 1975).

Stribrny, Wolfgang, *Bismarck und die deutsche Politik nach seiner Entlassung (1890–1898)* (Paderborn, 1976).

Stürmer, Michael, 'Bismarckstaat und Cäsarismus', *Staat* (Zeitschrift für öffentliches Recht und Verfassungsgeschichte), vol. 12 (1973), pp. 467–98.

Stürmer, Michael (ed.), *Das kaiserliche Deutschland: Politik und Gesellschaft* (Düsseldorf, 1970).

Stürmer, Michael, *Regierung und Reichstag im Bismarckstaat 1871–1880: Cäsarismus oder Parlamentarismus* (Düsseldorf, 1974).

Sullivan, H. S., 'The paranoid dynamism', in *Clinical Studies in Psychiatry* (New York, 1956), pp. 145–65.

Swanson, David W., *et al.*, *The Paranoid* (Boston, 1970).

Theweleit, Klaus, *Männerphantasien: Frauen, Fluten, Körper, Geschichte* (Frankfurt a. M., 1977).

Thomas, Donald E., Jr, 'Idealism, romanticism, and race: the "Weltanschauung" of Houston Stewart Chamberlain' (PhD Diss., University of Chicago, 1971).

Thompson, E. P., *The Making of the English Working Class* (New York, 1963).

Thompson, E. P., *The Poverty of Theory and Other Essays* (New York and London, 1978).

Tims, Richard W., *Germanizing Prussian Poland: The H.K.T. Society and the Struggle for the Eastern Marches in the German Empire, 1894–1919* (New York, 1941).

Tipton, Frank B., Jr, *Regional Variations in the Economic Development of Germany in the Nineteenth Century* (Middletown, Conn., 1976).

Tirrell, S. R., *German Agrarian Politics after Bismarck's Fall* (New York, 1951).

Titze, Hartmut, 'Die soziale und geistige Umbildung des preussischen Oberlehrerstandes von 1870 bis 1914', *Zeitschrift für Pädagogik*, 14 Beilage (1977), pp. 107–28.

Toth, Hans, *The Social Psychology of Social Movements* (Indianapolis, Ind., 1965).

Townsend, Mary Evelyn, *The Rise and Fall of Germany's Colonial Empire, 1884–1918* (New York, 1930).

Treimann, Donald J., *Occupational Prestige in a Comparative Perspective* (New York, 1976).

Treimann, Donald J., 'Problems of concept and measurement in the comparative study of occupational mobility', *Social Science Research*, vol. 4 (1975), pp. 183–230.

Ullmann, Hermann, *Pioniere Europas: Die volksdeutsche Bewegung und ihre Lehren* (Munich, 1956).

Urner, Klaus, *Die Deutschen in der Schweiz: Von den Anfängen des Kolonienbildung bis zum Ausbruch des Ersten Weltkrieges* (Frauenfeld and Stuttgart, 1976).

Voigt, Gerd, *Otto Hoetzsch 1876–1946: Wissenschaft und Politik im Leben eines deutschen Historikers* (Berlin, 1978).

Volkov, Shulamit, *The Rise of Popular Antimodernism in Germany: The Urban Master Artisans, 1873–1896* (Princeton, NJ, 1976).

Vondung, Klaus, *Magie und Manipulation: Ideologischer Kult und politische Religion des Nationalsozialismus* (Göttingen, 1971).

Vondung, Klaus, 'Probleme einer Sozialgeschichte der Ideen', in Vondung, *Bildungsbürgertum*, pp. 5–19.

Vondung, Klaus (ed.), *Das wilhelminische Bildungsbürgertum: Zur Sozialgeschichte seiner Ideen* (Göttingen, 1976).

Vondung, Klaus, 'Zur Lage der Gebildeten in der Wilhelminischen Zeit', in Vondung, *Bildungsbürgertum*, pp. 20–33.

Wächter, Emil, *Der Prestigegedanke in der deutschen Politik von 1890–1914* (Arau, 1941).

Walker, Mack, *Germany and the Emigration, 1816–1885* (Cambridge, Mass., 1964).

Weber, Christoph, *Der 'Fall Spahn' (1901): Ein Beitrag zur Wissenschafts- und Kulturdiskussion im ausgehenden 19. Jahrhundert* (Rome, 1980).

Weber, Eugen, *Action française: Royalism and Reaction in Twentieth Century France* (Stanford, Calif., 1962).

Weber, Max, 'Bureaucracy', in *From Max Weber: Essays in Sociology*, ed. H. H. Gerth and C. Wright Mills (New York, 1946), pp. 196–244.

Weber, Max, 'Politics as a vocation', in *From Max Weber*, pp. 77–128.

Wehler, Hans-Ulrich, *Bismarck und der Imperialismus* (Cologne and Berlin, 1969).

Wehler, Hans-Ulrich, *Das Deutsche Kaiserreich 1871–1918* (Göttingen, 1973).

Wehler, Hans-Ulrich, 'Zur Funktion und Struktur der nationalen Kampfverbände im Kaiserreich', in Werner Conze, *et al.* (eds), *Modernisierung und nationale Gesellschaft im ausgehenden 18. und 19. Jahrhundert* (Berlin, 1979), pp. 113–23.

Wehler, Hans-Ulrich, 'Geschichtswissenschaft und "Psychohistorie"', *Innsbrucker Historische Studien*, vol. 1 (1978), pp. 201–13.

Wehler, Hans-Ulrich, 'Die Polen im Ruhrgebiet bis 1918', *Vierteljahrsschrift für Sozial- und Wirtschaftsgeschichte*, vol. 48 (1961), pp. 203–35.

Wehler, Hans-Ulrich, 'Die Polenpolitik im Deutschen Kaiserreich', in Kurt Kluxen and W. L. Mommsen (eds), *Politische Ideologien und nationalstaatliche Ordnung* (Munich, 1968), pp. 297–316.

Wehler, Hans-Ulrich, 'Psychoanalysis and history', *Social Research,* vol. 47 (1980), pp. 519–36.

Wehler, Hans-Ulrich, 'Sozialdarwinismus im expandierenden Industriestaat', in Geiss and Wendt, pp. 132–43.

Wehler, Hans-Ulrich, 'Zum Verhältnis von Geschichtswissenschaft und Psychoanalyse', *Historische Zeitschrift*, vol. 209 (1969), pp. 529–54.

Wehner, Siegfried, 'Der Alldeutsche Verband und die deutsche Kolonialpolitik der Vorkriegszeit' (Diss. phil., Greifswald, 1935).

Weidenfeller, Gerhard, *VDA: Verein für das Deutschtum im Ausland. Allgemeiner Deutscher Schulverein (1881–1918). Ein Beitrag zur Geschichte des deutschen Nationalismus und Imperialismus im Kaiserreich* (Berne and Frankfurt a. M., 1976).

Weinstein, Fred, and Platt, Gerald M., *Psychoanalytic Sociology: An Essay on the Interpretation of Historical Data and the Phenomena of Collective Behavior* (Baltimore, Md and London, 1973).

Wernecke, Klaus, *Der Wille zur Weltgeltung: Aussenpolitik und Oeffentlichkeit im Kaiserreich am Vorabend des Ersten Weltkrieges* (Düsseldorf, 1969).

Werner, Lothar, *Der Alldeutsche Verband 1890–1918* (Berlin, 1935).

Wertheimer, Mildred S., *The Pan-German League, 1890–1914* (New York, 1924).

White, Dan S., *The Splintered Party: National Liberalism in Hessen and the Reich, 1867–1918* (Cambridge, Mass., 1976).

Whiteside, Andrew G., *The Socialism of Fools: Georg Ritter von Schönerer and Austrian Pan-Germanism* (Berkeley, Calif. and Los Angeles, 1975).

Williams, Raymond, *Culture and Society, 1780–1950* (New York, 1958).

Williams, Raymond, *Marxism and Literature* (Oxford, 1977).

Winkel, Hans, 'Kyffhäuserverband der Vereine deutscher Studenten (KVDS) 1881–1919', in Fricke, *Handbuch*, Vol. 2, pp. 313–19.

Winkler, Heinrich August, *Mittelstand, Demokratie und Nationalsozialismus: Die politische Entwicklung von Handwerk und Kleinhandel in der Weimarer Republik* (Cologne and Berlin, 1973).

Winzen, Peter, *Bülows Weltmachtkonzept: Untersuchungen zur Frühphase seiner Aussenpolitik 1897–1901* (Boppard a. R., 1977).

Winzen, Peter, 'Prince Bülow's Weltmachtpolitik', *Australian Journal of Politics and History*, vol. 22 (1976), pp. 227–42.

Witt, Peter-Christian, *Die Finanzpolitik des Deutschen Reiches von 1903 bis 1913: Eine Studie zur Innenpolitik des Wilhelminischen Deutschlands* (Lübeck and Hamburg, 1970).

Witt, Peter-Christian, 'Innenpolitik und Imperialsmus in der Vorgeschichte des 1. Weltkrieges', in Karl Holl and Günther List (eds), *Liberalismus und imperialistischer Staat: Der Imperialismus als Problem liberaler Parteien in Deutschland 1890–1914* (Göttingen, 1975), pp. 7–34.

Wolff, Kurt H. (ed.), *The Sociology of Georg Simmel* (New York and London, 1950).

Wulf, Amandus, 'Deutscher Flottenverein (DFV) 1898–1934 (1919–1931 Deutscher Seeverein)', in Fricke, *Handbuch*, Vol. 1, pp. 432–49.

Zmarzlik, Hans-Günther, *Bethmann Hollweg als Reichskanzler: Studien zu Möglichkeiten und Grenzen seiner innerpolitischen Machtstellung* (Düsseldorf, 1957).

Zmarzlik, Hans-Günther, 'Ernst Hasse', *Neue Deutsche Biographie,* vol. 8, pp. 39–40.

Zmarzlik, Hans-Günther, 'Das Kaiserreich als Einbahnstrasse?', in Karl Holl and Günther List (eds), *Liberalismus und imperialistischer Staat: Der Imperialismus als Problem liberaler Parteien in Deutschland 1890–1914* (Göttingen, 1975), pp. 62–71.

Zmarzlik, Hans-Günther, 'Der Sozialdrawinismus in Deutschland als geschichtliches Problem', *Vierteljahrshefte für Zeitgeschichte,* vol. 11 (1963), pp. 246–73.

Zunkel, Friedrich, *Der rheinisch-westfälische Unternehmer* (Cologne, 1962).

Index

Action française 23
Adler, Viktor 32
Agadir 6, 264
Agrarian League (*Bund der Landwirte*) 47, 184, 198
  and antisemitism 233
  and Pan-German League 138, 214, 280–2, 284, 296n
  and *Sammlung* 279–82
Algeciras 219, 263
Alldeutsche Blätter 4, 18, 54, 76, 93, 105, 122, 153, 156–7, 163, 168, 170, 175, 222, 224, 240, 251n, 263, 306, 313
Alldeutsche Kegelvereinigung 163
Alldeutscher Verband, *see* Pan-German League
Alldeutsches Liederbuch 162
Allgemeine-Unfalls-Versicherungs-Bank (Leipzig) 53
Allgemeiner Deutscher Schulverein, see German School Association
Allgemeiner Deutscher Sprachverein, see German Language Association
Allgemeiner Deutscher Verband zur Vertretung Deutsch-Nationaler Interessen, see General German League for Representation of German-National Interests
Allgemeiner Deutscher Verein, *see* General German Association
Allgemeiner Plattdeutsch-Verband (Essen) 198
Alsace-Lorraine 28, 93, 122, 285, 289
  constitution for 228, 262
  German Colonial Society and 150n
  in ideology of Pan-German League 79
  Pan-German League in 138, 141
American Defense Society 4
Ammon, Otto 239, 241
Anderson, Pauline 10–12
antisemitic organizations 185, 198, 241 299
antisemitic political parties 144, 203, 233, 236, 241, 259, 277–8
antisemitism 1, 75, 102, 200, 214, 232–4, 271, 279–80, 285, 300
Antiultramontaner Reichsverband 139
Antivivisection *Verein* 164
Arendt, Otto 46
Army Bill, of 1893 273

  of 1912 6, 272, 288
  of 1913 6, 272, 283, 289
Arnim-Muskau, Hermann Graf von 50, 66
aryans 234, 236–7, 239–40, 242
Association for Commercial Geography and Colonial Policy (Leipzig) 31, 53
Associations of German Students (*Vereine deutscher Studenten*) 44, 147–8, 233
Austria-Hungary, see Habsburg monarchy

Bachem, Karl 139
Badeni, Casimir 64, 79, 231
Balkan Wars 274, 282, 287
Barnes, Harry Elmer 4
Bartels, Adolf 239
Barthelmess, Professor 195
Basler, Theodor 105
Bassermann, Ernst 134, 220–1, 278
Baumann, Max 110
Bechly, Hans 200
Becker, Jacob 279
Bedarf Deutschland Kolonien? 30
Below, Georg von 280
Bennecke, Paul 168
Bergbau-Verein 227
Berger, Peter 75
Berliner Neueste Nachrichten 67, 283
Bethmann Hollweg, Theobald von 8, 256–6, 272–7, 280, 282–3, 286–7
  and Moroccan crisis 265–6
  and Pan-German League 262, 288–9
Biddiss, Michael 237
Bismarck collection (*Bismarck-Sammlung*) 119n
Bismarck, Otto von 8, 24, 25–7, 67, 104, 184, 203, 215
  colonial policy 34–5, 38–9
  in ideology of Pan-German League 81, 95–6, 100n
  and national symbolism 40, 44–5, 195
  in opposition 46–7, 51, 52, 56, 62,
  and patriotic societies 38, 46
  in rituals of Pan-German League 152, 158, 165, 168
Bismarck towers 158, 168, 195
Bley, Fritz 98n, 162, 214
Boeckel, Otto 214
Boeckh, Richard 33
Boer collection (*Burensammlung*) 65

Boer War 14, 64, 78, 170, 185, 195, 222
  Pan-German League and 92, 134, 138,
    162, 174, 178n, 213, 226, 230, 264
Boers 74, 208n, 220
Bohemia 27, 31, 53, 65, 82–3, 144–5, 163,
  167, 186
Bohemian String Quartet 122
Bonhard, Otto 4–7, 11, 98n
Bonhard, Philipp 180n, 217
Borussian tradition 145, 304
Bovenschen, Albert 202
Braun, Lily 170
Breusing, Alfred 128, 283–4
Bülow, Bernhard von 72n, 221–2
  and Hasse 53, 174, 213
  and Navy League 256–60, 262
  and Pan-German League 63–4, 65–9, 167,
    220–1, 215, 253 262, 281
Bülow block, 259, 261, 275–6, 277–8
Bürgervereine 194, 199
Bund für Heimatschutz 241
Bund der Landwirten, see Agrarian League
Bund der Letzten (League of the Last) 287
Bundesgeschichte 8–9
Bundesrat 289
Burschenschaften 147–8
Büxenstein, Georg 294n

Calmbach, Christian 110, 141
Calmbach, Heinrich 110, 141, 180n, 217
Caplan, Jane 116
Caprivi, Leo von 46–8, 51, 55–6, 62, 215, 255
Cartel of Productive Estates 282, 284, 286
Catholic church, in France 24
Catholic Center Party 139, 198, 203, 259,
  275, 285
  and crisis in Navy League 254–6
  and elections of 1907 257–9
Catholicism 139–9, 148, 199, 201
  and Pan-German League 85, 102, 123,
    138–40, 175, 217, 256
Catholics 14, 24–5, 46–7, 63–4, 128, 144,
  198, 206, 276
  in patriotic societies 188, 203, 205, 256,
    258
Central Association for Commercial
  Geography and German Interests
  Abroad 31–3
Central Association of German Industrialists
  60, 121n, 229, 282
Central Association of German Navy
  Leagues Abroad 61
Centralverband deutscher Industrieller, see
  Central Association of German
  Industrialists
Chamberlain, Houston Stewart 239, 245,
  251n
chambers of commerce 31

choral societies 24, 28, 44, 184
Christianity 81, 85, 215, 234–5
Class, Heinrich 5, 8, 86, 104–5, 129, 156,
  165, 170, 173, 176, 180n, 198, 221,
  227–9, 241, 248n, 260, 262–6, 268,
  278–84, 288, 290, 292n, 294n, 299
  and antisemitism 236, 240, 244–5, 266
  career of 69, 128, 132n, 214–15, 223,
    226–9, 278
  and crown prince 286–7
  and Hasse 214–15, 217
  as ideologist 76, 95, 130, 215–17, 284–6,
    288
  memoirs 6–7, 9, 11, 248n, 296n
  and Moroccan crisis of 1911 264–6
  and radicalization of Pan-German League
    217–23
  and Sammlung 278–82
Clauss, professor 195
Coetzee, Marilyn 293n
Cohen, Abner 102
Cohn, Norman 22n
colonial movement 33–40, 44, 46, 48–9, 53,
  58
Columbia University 3
Communists 9
Conservative Party, 47, 50, 52, 201, 203, 257,
  259, 261, 276–7, 278–82
  and Pan-German League 66, 277–83, 295n
constitution of 1871 24, 27, 77
constitutional crisis (Prussian) 58
Crowe memorandum 19n
Czechs 27, 31, 36, 144–5, 167
  in ideology of Pan-German League 82–3,
    85–6, 123, 234

Dahn, Felix 100n
Daily Telegraph affair 63, 222–3, 226, 232,
  253, 261
Danes 28, 78, 82, 208n, 285
Darwin, Charles 80, 239, 242
Dehio, Ludwig 3
Dehn, Paul 119n
Delbrück, Hans 4, 279, 282
Deutsch, Karl 21n
Deutschbund 235–5, 241
Deutsche Burschenschaft 147–8
Deutsche Geschichte (Class) 76
Deutsche Gesellschaft für Rassenhygene 242
Deutsche Gesellschaft für Vorgeschichte
  241–2
Deutsche Kolonialgesellschaft, see German
  Colonial Society
Deutsche Politik 76
Deutsche Tageszeitung 281
Deutscher Kolonialverein, see German
  Colonial Association
Deutscher Verein fuer das nördliche

Schleswig, see German Association for North Schleswig
Deutsche Vereinigung 139
Deutsche Zeitung 250n, 235–6, 263, 283
Deutscher Bund für Regeneration 185
Deutscher Flottenverein, see German Navy League
Deutscher Schillerbund (Ulm) 198
Deutscher Schulverein (Austria), *see* German School Association (Austria)
Deutscher Wehrverein, see German Defense League
Deutsches Wochenblatt 46
Deutsches Zentralarchiv 11
Deutschnationaler Handlungsgehilfen-Verband, see German-National Commercial Employees Union
Deutsch-österreichscher Alpenverband 199
Deutschvölkischer Schutz- und Trutz-Bund 299
Dewitz, Hermann von 294n
Deye, Richard 162
Die Post 279, 282–3
Doebel, Hermann 110
Dreadnought 220
Driessmann, Heinrich 239
Dühring, Eugen 234
Dvořák, Antonin 122

Eastern Marches Society 59, 109, 119n, 144, 179n, 189–90, 198, 201–3, 206, 240, 249n, 279, 302, 312, 314–16
  and other patriotic societies 185–7, 189–90, 193–4, 196
  and Pan-German League 55–6, 138, 190–2, 196, 271
Edward VII 123
elections (Austrian) of 1879 31
elections, of 1878 24
  of 1893, 255, 258
  of 1903 82, 145, 202, 214, 221, 230, 245n
  of 1907 257–60
  of 1912 12, 263, 265–6, 268–9, 271, 277–8, 280, 285, 302
Eley, Geoff 14–16
Eliot, T. S. 160
emigration, German 91, 29–31, 34, 36
Engel, Ernst 533
Engels, Friedrich 76
Ennereccus, Ludwig 50
Erikson, Erik 126
Essay on the Inequality of Human Races 236–41
eugenics movement 239
Evangelischer Bund 44, 64, 139, 199
Evangelical trade unions 201
Ewich, Hans 109

Eycken, Hans von 50, 53
Eynern, Ernst von 50

Fabri, Friedrich 30, 34, 39, 50
fascism 17
Fay, Sidney 4
Federal Republic of Germany, historians in 7–9, 12–14, 17, 302
feminists 171
Fick, Adolf 49–50, 105, 122, 140, 167, 233
Fick, Friedrich 140
Findeisen, Adolf 110
Fischer, Fritz 12–13
Flottenbund 260
Förster, Paul 233
Foundations of the Nineteenth Century 239
France 24, 58, 111, 180n, 263–4, 269, 275
  in ideology of Pan-German League 1, 78, 85, 265
Franco-Prussian War 53
Frauengabe Berlin-Elberfeld 57
Free Conservative party 50, 203, 229, 259, 278–9, 283
Free Corps 17
Freud, Sigmund 16, 85, 126
Friedjung, Heinrich 32
Fritsch, Theodor 241

Gebsattel, Konstantin von 248n, 286–7
Geertz, Clifford 109
Geiser, Alfred 105, 133, 141, 148, 190, 193
General German Association 54
General German League 44–54
General German League for Representation of German-National Interests 44–5
General German Language Association, *see* German Language Association
General Staff 255, 267, 273–5
geographical societies 31
Geographical Society (Greifswald) 194
German Association for North Schleswig 47, 144, 208n
German Colonial Association 34–6, 44–5
German Colonial Society 9, 53, 48–9, 66, 77, 150n, 185, 198, 202, 214, 218, 223–5, 258, 265
  early history 36–40, 44–6
  and government 66, 189–90, 217, 254, 302
  membership 106–7, 115, 194, 199, 272, 312–16, 320, 322
  and naval agitation 57–9, 61–2
  and other patriotic societies 61, 185, 187, 189–90, 195–6, 256, 270, 294n
  and Pan-German League 50–1, 55, 68, 134, 190–2, 196–7, 208n, 271
German Democratic Republic, historians in and Pan-German League 10–12, 13
German Defense League ix–x, 9, 268–76,

German Defence League – *contd.*
    282, 288, 296n, 312–13, 324–28
German East Africa 35–6, 44, 48, 50, 267–8
German East Africa Company 35–6, 39, 50
German evenings (*Deutsche Abende*) 196,
    200, 256
German Language Association 36–8, 40, 50,
    194, 302, 312–16, 322
  and other patriotic societies 185–7,
    189–90, 196, 270, 294n
  and Pan-German League 190
German Navy League 9, 14, 60–2, 179n,
    224–5, 258, 265, 274–5, 289
  crisis 220, 253–61, 302
  founding, 60–2
  and government 66, 109, 189–90, 206,
    217, 262, 302
  membership 106–7, 115, 188, 194, 203,
    205, 312–16, 320, 322
  and other patriotic societies 60–2, 185–90,
    193–6, 269–70, 294n
  and Pan-German League 190–2, 197, 271
German Peace Society, 106–7, 312, 314–16
German People's party 140–1
German School Association 32–3, 36–8, 40,
    44–5, 53, 194, 208n, 224, 249n, 296n,
    302, 312–16, 322
  and other patriotic societies 185–7,
    189–90, 193, 196, 270, 294n
  and Pan-German League 50–1, 55, 190
German School Association (Austria) 32
German-National Commercial Employees
    Union 47, 200, 205, 233, 241
Germanization 28, 38, 55, 79, 138, 234
Gerhard, Hermann 119n, 260
Gersdorff, Wigand von 294n
Gesellschaft für Deutsche Kolonisation, *see*
    Society for German Colonialization
Gestapo 6
Gobineau, Arthur de 236–40, 242–3, 245
Gobineau Society 238, 240–1
Gobineau-Vereinigung, *see* Gobineau Society
Goethe 155
Goffman, Erving 155–6, 165
Gothic script 175–6
Great Britain 3, 24, 64–9, 180n
  German diplomatic relations with 35, 39,
    48, 58, 63, 264–5, 273, 283
  and German navy 56, 60, 254
  in ideology of Pan-German League 74, 77,
    79, 85
Great Depression 29–31
Grossdeutsch political tradition 26, 80, 138,
    147, 201
Grumme-Douglas, Ferdinand von 287
Guaranty Fund 54, 225
Guelphs, *see* Hanoverian separatism
Gutberlet, Heinrich 162

Habermas, Jürgen 156, 177
Habsburg monarchy 37, 63, 98n, 139
  ethnic conflict in 27–8, 32–3, 51, 64–66,
    134, 217
  in ideology of Pan-German League 74,
    78–80, 82–3, 231, 234, 289–90
  in program of Pan-German League 289–90
Haeckel, Ernst 146
Hallgarten, George 10
Hamburger Nachrichten 143
Hamlet 94
Hammer 241
Hanoverian separatism 161, 174, 258, 285
Hansabund 228, 277–8
Hansemann, Ferdinand von 55
Harden, Maximilian 96
Hartwig, Edgar 11–12, 18, 119n
Hasse, Ernst 31, 46, 50, 53, 54, 58, 101,
    104, 144, 148, 183, 214, 249n
  and antisemitism 236, 245, 249n
  and Bülow 63, 67–8, 174, 213, 221, 258
  as chairman of Pan-German League 54–5,
    173, 175, 225–6
  and Class 69, 214–15, 217, 219
  death of 165, 223, 225, 228
  as ideologist 76–7, 91, 94, 130, 159
*Hauptverband Deutscher Flottenvereine im
    Auslande*, *see* Central Association of
    German Navy League Abroad
Hayes, Carlton 3–4
Heeringen, August von 58, 61
Heeringen, Josias von 272–6
Heinrich, Prince of Prussia 61, 260
Heligoland Treaty 48, 51, 265
Hellwig, Karl 241
Hentschel, Willibald 240
Herder, J. G. 33, 98n
Herero uprising 178n
Hering, Johannes 240
Heydebrand und der Lasa, Ernst von 266,
    277, 279–80
Heydt, Karl von der 46, 50, 52–3, 225, 240
Heyl zu Herrnsheim, Cornelius 193, 278–9
Hirsch, Wilhelm 227
Hitler, Adolf 6, 22n, 184, 299, 301
Hoensbroech, Paul von 139
Hoetzsch, Otto 146
Hohenlohe-Schillingfuerst, Prince Chlodwig
    zu 215
Hollmann, Friedrich 57, 59
Honoratioren 14, 111–18, 128
Hopf, Friedrich 195, 257
Hübbe-Schleiden, Wilhelm 30, 50
Hugenberg, Alfred 49–52, 57, 70n, 105, 191,
    227–9

Ibsen, Heinrik 168
Ideas of 1914 290
ideology 74–5, 109–10, 125–6

If I Were Emperor (Wenn ich der Kaiser wär) 76, 285–7, 299
Imperial Naval Office 57–60, 66, 185, 219, 271–2
  Nachrichtenbüro 58–9, 61, 275
  and Navy League 60, 219, 253–5, 268
  and Pan-German League 174, 219–20, 283–4
Imperial League against Social Democracy 201–2, 222, 228, 257–8
Iron Ring 31, 64
Itzenplitz, Karl 180n, 217, 227

Jagow, Gottlieb von 283
Jameson raid 56
Jannasch, Robert 31
Jarausch, Konrad 146–7, 150n
Jesuits 123, 138, 139
Jews 1, 6, 144, 233, 235, 239, 251n, 285, 286–7, 304
  in ideology of Pan-German League 234, 242–4
  in Pan-German League 52, 160, 249n
July crisis 288–90
Jungliberalen 204

Kampf um das Deutschtum 76
Kann, Robert 27
Kardorff, Wilhelm von 50
Kartell der schaffenden Stände, see Cartel of Productive Estates
Kaufmännische Vereine 199
Kehr, Eckart 9–13, 197
Keim, August 182n, 268
  career of 128, 150n, 255, 267
  and elections of 1907 258–9
  and German Defense League 268–71, 273–6
  and German Navy League 255, 261, 265, 268
Kennemann, Hermann 55
Kiderlen-Wächter, Alfred von 263–6, 283
Kirdorf, Emil 9, 11, 50, 227–9, 247n, 278
Klingemann, Karl 119n, 180n, 214, 217, 227, 228, 283
Klitzing, Max von 119n
Kluge, Alexander 177
Koch, Max 160, 249n
Kölnische Volkszeitung 139
Kölnische Zeitung 48, 67
Koester, Hans von 260
Kollmann, Wilhelm 95, 201, 225
Kolonialrat 39
Kosinna, Gustav 239
Krause, Ernst 239
Krause, Robert 105
Kreuzzeitung 282

Kriegervereine, see veterans' associations
Kruck, Alfred 8, 11, 70n
Kruger, Paul 64, 67, 162, 219, 222
Krupp family 227
Krupp firm 227–9, 278
Krupp, Friedrich 50, 60
Kuczynski, Juergen 10–11
Kuhlenbeck, Ludwig 128, 138–9, 213, 245,
Kulturkampf 138–9
Kyffhäuserverband der Vereine deutscher Studenten 147–8

labor movement 25, 46, 128, 183, 198–9, 304
Lagarde, Paul de 80, 234–5, 240
Lamprecht, Karl 146
Landtag (Prussia) 38, 40
Langbehn, Julius 80, 234
Lange, Friedrich 234–6, 241, 250n, 263, 283
Langhans, Paul 241
Lass, Hermann 109
Lattmann, Wilhelm 233
leagues of patriotic associations 196, 200, 203, 271
Lebensraum 37
Lederer, Emil 116
left-liberals 34, 140, 214
Lehmann, Julius 59, 61, 139, 151n, 242
Lehr, Adolf 50, 53–4, 58, 61, 68–9, 105, 133, 215, 236
Leibenguth, Peter 47
Leipziger Neueste Nachrichten 144, 264, 283
Lenbach, Franz von 168
Lenzmann, Julius 130
Lessing, Gotthold Ephraim 181n
Levetzow, Albert von 54
Liebenfels, Adolf Lanz von 240
Liebermann von Sonnenberg, Max 233
Leibert Eduard von 174, 182n, 221, 243, 253, 257, 259, 269, 279, 286
  career of 128, 267–8
  as head of Imperial League against Social Democracy 202, 222, 257
Liman, Paul 144, 263, 283
Lindequist, Friedrich von 265
List, Friedrich 80
Litzmann, Karl 294n
London Library 160
London *Times* 2
Los-von-Rom movement 64, 139
Louis Napoleon 24
Lubarsch, Otto 233
Lucas, Alexander 50
Luckmann, Thomas 75
Ludendorff, Erich 274
Lueger, Karl 32
Luxemburg, Rosa 170

Machtergreifung 184
Mahan, Alfred Thayer 57

Mann, Heinrich 166
Mann, Thomas 166
Mannesmann brothers 263
Marcinkowsky Association 28
Marschall von Bieberstein, Alfred 55
Marx, Karl 12–13, 76, 177
Marxism 76
Marxist-Leninist historiography 13, 109, 223, 229, 302
Mason, Tim 126
Mein Kampf 300
Meinecke, Friedrich 296n
Mirbach-Sorquitten, Julius Graf von 46, 50, 295n
Mitteleuropa 78
Mittelstand 89–92, 107, 119n, 199, 235
Möller, Fritz 109
Moltke, Helmuth von 274
Mommsen, Theodor 3
Morocco 2
    crisis of 1905–6 218–20, 230
    crisis of 1911 263–8, 267–8, 270–1, 277–8, 280, 286–7, 302
Mosel-Dampfschifffahrts-AG 71n
Mosse, George 178n
Moulin-Eckart, Richard Graf du 182n, 214
Münchner Allgemeine Zeitung 67

Nachrichtenbüro, see Imperial Naval Office
Nahmer, Adolf von der 227
National Liberal party 14–15, 34, 50, 52–4, 80, 143–5, 188, 214, 228, 233, 259, 265, 274, 278, 284
    and patriotic societies 203–5, 229, 277–9, 283, 285–6
National Security League 4
National Socialism 1–2, 6–9, 80, 185, 299–301, 304
Nationale Zeitung 214
Nationalpartei 52
Naumann, Friedrich 285
naval agitation 7, 9–10, 57–62, 64, 81, 91, 138, 198
naval bills 59–60
    of 1898 58, 254
    of 1900 60–1, 254
    of 1905 220, 230
Naval Cabinet 57
Navy League of the United States 23
Negt, Oskar 177
Neuhaus, Gustav 109
New Course 46–7, 52
Nicolson, Harold 160
Nicmann, Wilhelm 227
Nietzsche, Friedrich 80, 98n
Nipperdey, Thomas 25, 113
Norddeutsche Allgemeine Zeitung 262
North Schleswig 28, 47, 78–9, 82, 91

Oehlerking, Otto 109
Olmütz 48
Oncken, Dirk 80
Operating and Agitational Fund 225

Paasche, Hermann 294n
Pan-German family bulletin board
    (*Alldeutsche Familientafel*) 168
Pan-German League x, 1–15, 17–18, 23, 62, 64–9, 79, 198, 200–2, 228, 258–9, 263–6, 267–8, 276–82, 285–90, 299–300
    activities of 65, 152–72, 223–5
    and Agrarian League 138, 196n, 214, 280–2, 284, 296n
    and antisemitism 233–45
    archive 11, 18
    and Catholicism 138–40
    crisis in 213–45, 253, 262
    early history 18, 53–62, 65, 68, 74
    and Eastern Marches Society 55, 138, 196
    executive committee (*geschäftsführender Ausschuss*) 172–5, 182n, 214–19, 225, 227, 243–5, 248n, 263, 268, 285, 260–308
    finances 223–30, 244–5, 253, 278
    founding, 60–2
    and German Colonial Society 134, 197
    and German Defense League 269–71, 294n
    and German Navy League 61, 197, 256–7, 259–61
    and government 66, 109, 189–90, 206, 217, 262, 302
    historiography of x, 4–15, 23, 303, 306, 321
    ideology of 2, 12, 16–18, 67, 69, 75–97, 102, 108, 114, 116–18, 122–30, 131n, 133, 139, 152, 155, 159, 161–4, 169, 170, 176, 213, 223–4, 226, 229–30, 253, 269–70, 287, 304
    influence 148, 205–7, 282–4, 304
    literature of 16–18, 76, 81–2, 94, 97n, 105, 127, 129, 131n, 234, 244, 281
    membership 11, 17, 37, 102–11, 114–18, 122, 127, 134–5, 199, 205, 213, 223, 225–6, 228–9, 257, 272, 303, 306–26
    national board of directors (*Vorstand*) 172–4, 217, 227, 249n, 260, 281, 285, 308, 321
    and navy 56–62, 66, 219–20
    opposition to government 15, 18, 62–9, 84, 117–18, 125–6, 158, 177–8, 188, 197, 207, 213–23, 230–32, 253, 259, 262, 265, 270, 302
    organization and structure 3, 59 133–48, 158–61, 172–6, 179n, 228–9
    and other patriotic societies 18, 185–97, 205, 208n, 217, 245, 271

Plauen congress 214–17, 285
praesidium (*Hauptleitung*) 172
program of 2, 64, 74–81, 108, 134, 140,
    161–2, 217, 230–1, 236, 243, 302
radicalization of 68–9, 217–23
Pan-Germanism 4, 7, 78
Pan-Germans (Austria) 64, 75, 79, 139, 153,
    185, 231, 233, 289, 300
Pan-Slavism 4
Panther 264
Parsons, Talcott 126
Pascal, Roy 81
patriotic Societies 9–11, 14–15, 23–6, 28, 46,
    57–62, 198–205, 223, 235, 253–4, 256,
    258, 261, 265, 271, 273, 286, 299, 303
    and antisemitism 233, 240
    early history 18, 31–40, 44, 76, 188
    membership 37, 106, 185, 187–8, 206,
        272, 308, 314–16, 320
    relations among 15, 18, 45, 49–50, 53, 136,
        178, 185–97
    rivalry with government 80, 133, 178,
        188–90, 263, 272, 302
peace movement ix–x, 124, 146, 242, 269
Pernerstorfer, Engelbert 32
Peters, Carl 35–6, 39, 44–6, 48–50, 233–4
Petzoldt, Gustav 217
Platt, Gerald 126
Plötz, Alfred 239, 242
Pohl, Heinrich 180n, 283, 290, 279
Poles 27–8, 91, 138, 144, 259, 271, 279, 285
    Pan-German League and 82, 85, 123, 124,
        134, 191–2, 227, 230, 234
political parties 2, 12, 14–15, 34, 25, 47, 52,
    80, 202–3, 265–6, 274
Politisch-Anthropologische Revue 242
Possehl, Ludwig 95, 143
Primrose League 23
Progressive party 130, 143, 145, 203, 257,
    259, 285
Protestantism 85, 138–40, 142–3, 145, 148,
    184, 188, 198–9, 206, 281, 304

racism (see also antisemitism) 1, 6, 233–45,
    278, 280, 285, 288, 300
Recklinghausen, Wilhelm von 193, 195
Rehbein, Arthur 162
Reichsarchiv 11
Reichsdeutscher Mittelstandsverband 282
Reichstag (see also elections) 13, 24–5, 34,
    47, 54, 130, 134, 203, 220–1, 255, 257,
    261, 265–6, 268, 273–5, 277, 280, 284,
    286, 288, 294n, 303
    Bülow and 63, 167
    and navy 58, 60–2, 253, 259
    Pan-German League criticism of 62, 140,
        215, 222, 282

Pan-Germans in 53–5, 67–8, 174, 213–14,
    221, 245n
patriotic Societies and 38–9,
Reichstagswahlverein von 1884 (Hamburg)
    204
Reichsverband gegen die Sozialdemokratie,
    see Imperial League against Social
    Democracy
Reines Deutschtum 235
Reinsurance treaty 51
Reismann-Grone, Theodor 50–1, 66, 119n,
    180n, 217, 227, 263, 283, 290
Reusch, Paul 248n
Reuter, Fritz 110
révanchisme 4
Reventlow, Ernst Graf zu 128, 150n, 170,
    180n, 182n, 257, 281, 292n, 295n
Rheinisch-Westfälische Zeitung 227, 263,
    283
Rhyn, Atz von 162
Riegel, Hermann 36
Riezler, Kurt 289
Rippler, Heinrich 283, 294n
Ritter, Albert 241
Röttger, Max 121n
Rohmeder, Wilhelm 162
Rohrbach, Paul 4
Rosenberg, Hans 23, 29
Royal Evangelical Gymnasium, Ratibor 134
Rupprecht, Prince of Bavaria 260
Russia 27–8, 51, 58, 105, 269, 275
    in ideology of Pan-German League 11,
        77–8, 83, 85, 89, 96, 123

Samassa, Paul 69, 76, 105, 208n, 217, 219,
    230–1, 240, 259, 292n, 295n
Sammlung 203, 229, 261, 265, 276–82, 284,
    288–9
Samoa 58, 66
Sartre, Jean-Paul 75
Saxon Statistical Bureau 53
Schäfer, Dietrich 146, 294n
Scheffel, Josef Viktor von 95, 100n
Schellendorf, Walter Bronsart von 255
Schemann, Ludwig 237–41, 251n
Schieder, Theodor 26
Schiemann, Theodor 146
Schmidt-Gibichenfels, Otto 242
Schmoller, Gustav 107
Schönerer, Georg von 32, 64, 185
Schroeder-Poggelow, Wilhelm 50, 52, 248
Schutzvereine 28–9
Schweinburg, Viktor 60
Scupin, Hans 110
Sedantag 195
Senden-Bibran, Gustav von 57
Shafer, Roy 127
shooting clubs 24

Simons, Paul 50, 180n, 217, 225, 227
Slavs 77, 82, 242
Slovenes 27, 82, 122
Societa Nazionale Dante Alighieri 23
Society for German Colonization 35–6, 44–5, 47–8
Society for the Eastern Marches, see Eastern Marches Society
Social Democratic party (Social Democracy) 2, 9, 12, 25, 47, 67, 128, 140, 142–5, 152, 161, 175, 206, 214–15, 232, 257–9, 265–6, 276, 280, 282, 285, 303
  in ideology of Pan-German League 79, 85, 92–3, 123, 139, 217, 242, 244
  and patriotic Societies 188, 200–5
social imperialism 30, 56
Solf, Wilhelm 283
Sontag, Franz 5, 197, 282, 301
South Africa 2, 56, 58, 64–9, 74, 152, 215
Southwest Africa 171, 257
sport clubs 199, 206
Stahlhelm 301
Stern, J. P. 75
Stinnes, Hugo 227–8
Stössel, Georg Freiherr von 217, 241, 250n, 279, 283
Stolberg-Wernigerode, Graf Udo von 66
Strindberg, August 168–9
student corporations 24, 146–8, 159, 185, 205, 233, 241
Stürmer, Michael 24
Südwestafrikanische Siedlungsgesellschaft 208n
Suk, Josef 122
Suttner, Bertha von 170
Switzerland 37, 78

Taafe, Eduard von 31–2, 36, 64
Tägliche Rundschau 234–5, 283, 294n
Theweleit, Klaus 17
Third Reich 1, 6–7
Thirty Years' War 81
Thompson, E. P. 75
Tiedemann-Seeheim, Heinrich von 55, 191
Tille, Alexander 239
Tirpitz, Alfred von 9, 57, 63, 220, 267, 272–3, 287
  and German Navy League 60–1, 253–7, 259–60, 283
  and Pan-German League 58, 60–1, 283
Titze, Hartmut 115
Tolstoy, Leo 168
Tory party 24
trade unions 201, 229, 282
Treaty of Versailles 3, 299
Treitschke, Heinrich von 80, 98n, 214, 233
Tschaikowsky, Peter Illich 122
Twenty-Five Points 299

ultramontanism 123, 138, 242
United States 23, 26, 37, 78, 218
  historians in, and Pan-German League 3–4, 10, 23
  in ideology of Pan-German League 77, 79, 85, 88, 91
Untertan, Der 166

Verbände vaterländischer Vereine, see leagues of patriotic associations
Verein für Handelsgeographie und Kolonialpolitik 31
Vereine deutscher Studenten, see Associations of German Students veterans' associations 185, 200, 205–6, 258
Vietinghoff-Scheel, Leopold von 119n, 241
Volksverein für das katholische Deutschland 198, 203
Vossische Zeitung 283

Wagner, Richard 162, 237–40, 249n
Wangenheim, Cornelius von 280–82, 284
Wars of Liberation 275
Weber, Ernst von 30
Weber, Max 12, 112
Wehler, Hans-Ulrich 12–14, 21n, 29
Wehrschatz 225–6, 228, 248n, 263, 283, 286
Weimar Republic 3, 5
Weinstein, Fred 126
Wenn ich der Kaiser wär', see If I Were Emperor
Wermuth, Adolf 272–3
Werner, Anton von 154, 168
Werner, Lothar 6–7, 252n
Werner, Ludwig 233
Wertheimer, Mildred 3–10, 23, 103, 306
West Africa 34
West German Association for Colonization and Export 34
Weyer, Bruno 71n
White, Dan 143
Whiteside, Andrew 75
Wildenbruch, Ernst von 100n
William II 46, 64, 56–7, 184, 218–19, 267, 275, 286–7, 288
  and crisis in Navy League 255–6, 258–60
  and Pan-German League 158, 168, 221–3, 231–2, 266
William, Crown Prince 286–8
Wilser, Ludwig 239, 241
Wilson, Woodrow 4
Winter, Paul 195
Winterstein, Franz 110, 122, 195
Winzen, Peter 63
Wislicenus, Johannes 49–50, 105
Wislicenus, Paul 50
Wolf, Karl-Hermann 64, 153
Woltmann, Ludwig 239, 242

workers' organizations, patriotic 185, 201–2,
    205, 228, 258
World War I 2–4, 8, 12, 23, 46, 304
    war aims controversy 3, 290
World War II 7–8, 10
Wrochem, Johannes von 268–9
*Württembergischer Verein für
    Handelsgeographie* 193

youth groups 185, 206

Zedlitz-Neukirch, Octavio von 279
Zetkin, Clara 170
Zimmermann, Arthur 264, 283
Zimmermann, Oswald 233
Zmarzlik, Hans-Günther 1
Zollverein 79